TOWN AND COUNTRY PUBLIC LIBRARY DISTRICT
3 2990 00038 4564

D0982992

THE D-DAY ATLAS

Barfleur
über St. Pierre
O.T. BESTANDSLAGER
H.V.P.
Mar.Laz.
Arge. PFALZ
LATSCHA
Z
O.T-EINHEIT
MICHEELS
COLLIGNON
RAEBEL-WERKE
Mia.
Arge. PFALZ

Charles Messenger

THE D-DAY ATLAS

Anatomy of the Normandy Campaign

With 178 illustrations, including
71 full-color maps

Frontispiece: US infantrymen pause under German unit signs during the advance on Cherbourg.

First published in hardcover in the United States of America in 2004 by Thames & Hudson Inc., 500 Fifth Avenue, New York, New York 10110

thamesandhudsonusa.com

Library of Congress Catalog Card Number 2003112847

ISBN 0-500-25123-1

Printed and bound in Slovenia by Mladinska Knjiga Tiskarna

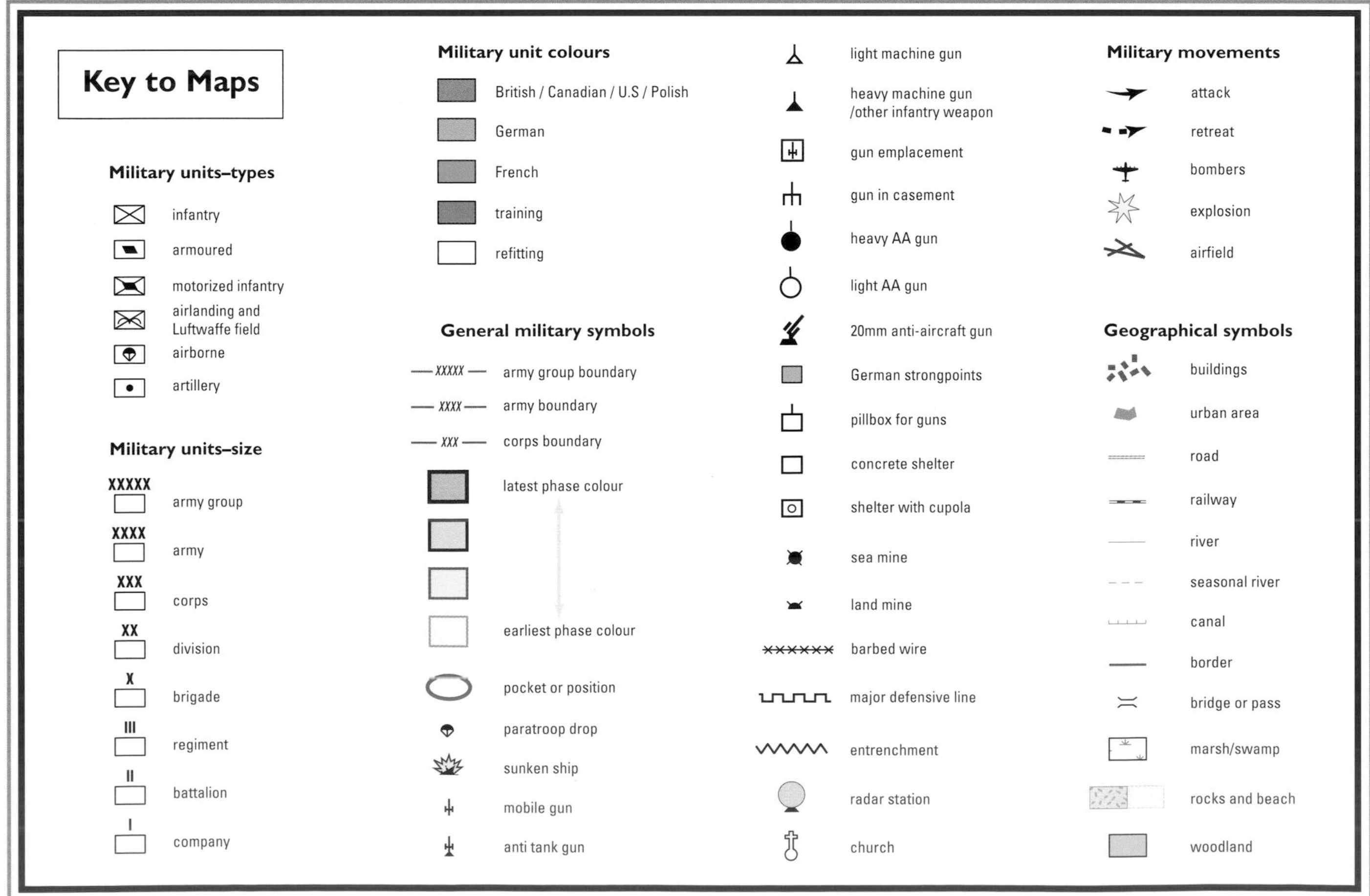

CONTENTS

PREFACE

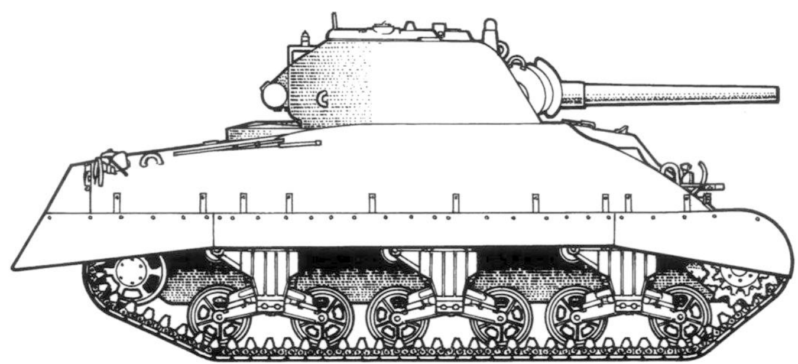

M4 Sherman, the main Allied tank in Normandy. It mounted a 75mm gun and had a crew of five.

The 60th anniversary of one of the most momentous undertakings of World War 2, at least as far as the Western Allies were concerned, is a good reason to revisit Normandy 1944 once more. In today's 21st-century world, where events seem to follow one another with increasing rapidity, it is all too easy to think of 1939–1945 as mere history with no relevance to today. Yet, even though they are now in their eighties and nineties, there are still a sizeable number of people who participated in the Normandy campaign. In addition, many of the problems with which commanders, planners and those who fought at the sharp end grappled are just as pertinent today. Coalition warfare, with the likelihood of friction among allies, and the conduct of amphibious operations against hostile shores, as well as the intelligent handling of land, sea and air assets are factors which worry military men and women today to exactly the same degree as they did all those years ago.

British soldiers training for D-Day.

This book makes no pretence at being a detailed in-depth study. Rather, it is a straightforward account of how the two sides perceived what was going on and what actually took place. Many previous works on the subject have tended to imply that the planning and preparation for Overlord only really began with the appointment of the Chief of Staff to the Supreme Allied Commander (COSSAC) in the spring of 1943.

DC-3 Dakota transports being prepared for the D-Day airborne assault.

This is far from the case and I have taken trouble to stress that planning for a return to the Continent of Europe began almost as soon as the last Allied soldier left the beaches of Dunkirk in May 1940. A parallel theme is the development of an amphibious capability, without which D-Day could never have taken place. This could only come through experience and it is for this reason that I have briefly reviewed all amphibious landings in the European and Mediterranean from Norway 1940 to Anzio 1944. By the same token, the continuous Anglo-US strategic debate is an essential backdrop.

Once the Allies were ashore in Normandy, they knew that they would face no walkover. Yet they were surprised by the extent of the German resistance, handicapped as it was by Hitler's meddling and their many low-grade divisions, as will be seen from the Divisions appendix. In spite of their overwhelming matériel supremacy, something that Rommel, at least, acknowledged from the start, the Allied soldiers had to learn to adapt the hard way in the claustrophobic Normandy *bocage*. After a lengthy phase of attrition, German Army Group B did eventually crumble. While Falaise marks the end of the Normandy campaign, it is important to describe what happened next, when the Allies became victims of their own success.

In terms of terminology, it is important to point out that in American and German parlance of the day 'Regiment' meant a brigade-size force, while the British and Canadians referred to armoured, engineer, and artillery battalions by this term. To avoid confusion, I have referred to British and Canadian units as battalions. Likewise reference to a German 'battle group' or *Kampfgruppe* refers to an all-arms group based on a battalion or brigade-sized force.

Finally, I hope that I have treated both Allies and Germans with equal fairness. Both sides generally fought bravely and honourably, although there were exceptions, which have been detailed in other books. Apart from one case, I have felt that to discuss these incidents in this book would be inappropriate. It remains to thank one or two people for their help. I much appreciate the encouragement, advice, and support given by the staff of Thames & Hudson. The same goes to Bill Jackson and Peter Phillips of Cartographica and particular tribute goes to Malcolm Swanston and his team also of Cartographica. Without their superb maps, this book would not have seen the light of day. As many as possible are based on those of the time. This is important, since sixty years of house-and-road building have altered much of Normandy as it was in 1944 and can give a very misleading impression.

Charles Messenger
London
November 2003

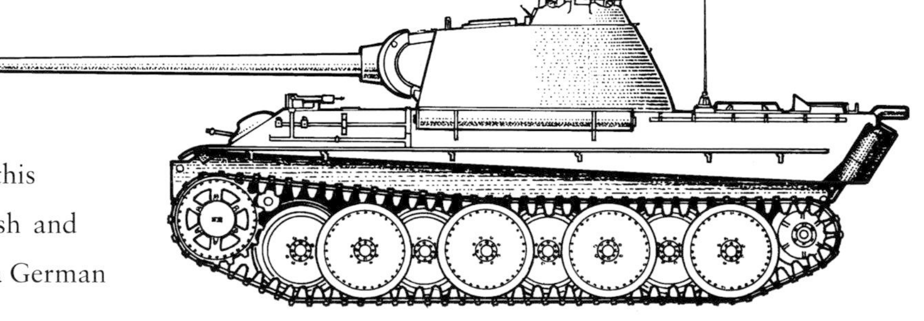

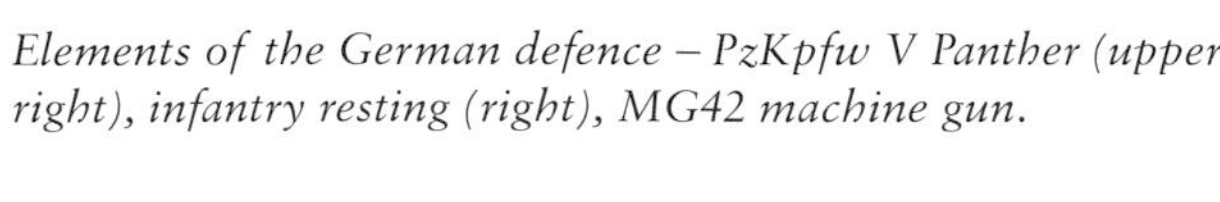

Elements of the German defence – PzKpfw V Panther (upper right), infantry resting (right), MG42 machine gun.

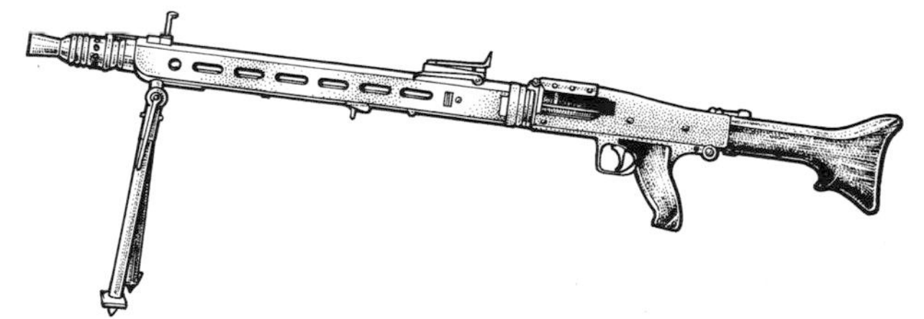

Chapter One

Planning and Preparation

On the morning of 4 June 1940, German troops entered the French port of Dunkirk. In the knowledge that during the previous week the Royal Navy had managed to rescue nearly 340,000 Allied troops from the trap that the Germans had set around the port, Prime Minister Winston Churchill made his famous speech of defiance: 'We shall fight on the beaches, we shall fight in the fields .... We shall never surrender.' The following day, the victorious German armies turned south to overrun the remainder of France. On 9 June, the French sought an armistice. Three days later, they signed an armistice with the Germans and then did the same with Italy, which had attacked the south of France on 20 June. The whole of Continental Western Europe was now under Hitler's thrall.

Few external commentators gave Britain much chance of holding out for long. The Army had left most of its heavy weapons in France and the RAF, whose strength was slender compared to that of the Luftwaffe, had also suffered during the Dunkirk evacuation. Only the Royal Navy remained relatively intact, but Luftwaffe attacks on shipping in the English Channel during July, the first phase of what was to become the Battle of Britain, forced the Admiralty to lay down that no warship larger than a destroyer would be allowed in these waters. Across the Channel, Hitler had, on 2 July, ordered preparations to be made for an invasion of Britain and the Army produced a plan just over two weeks later. Yet, as he stated in a triumphant speech in the Reichstag on 19 July, he

The final German plan called for a considerably narrower landing frontage than the original. Even so, it was wider than that used in the cross-Channel invasion four years later. The German invasion fleet aimed to hug the coast as long as possible before crossing the Channel at its nearest point. Once ashore, the main aim was to encircle London, rather than attempt to take the capital by storm.

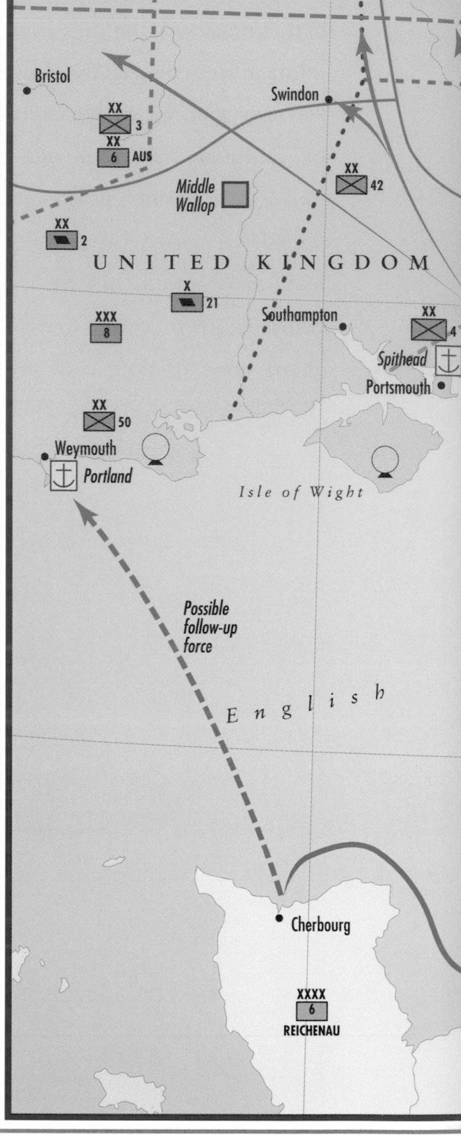

British troops withdraw through the battered City of Dunkirk.

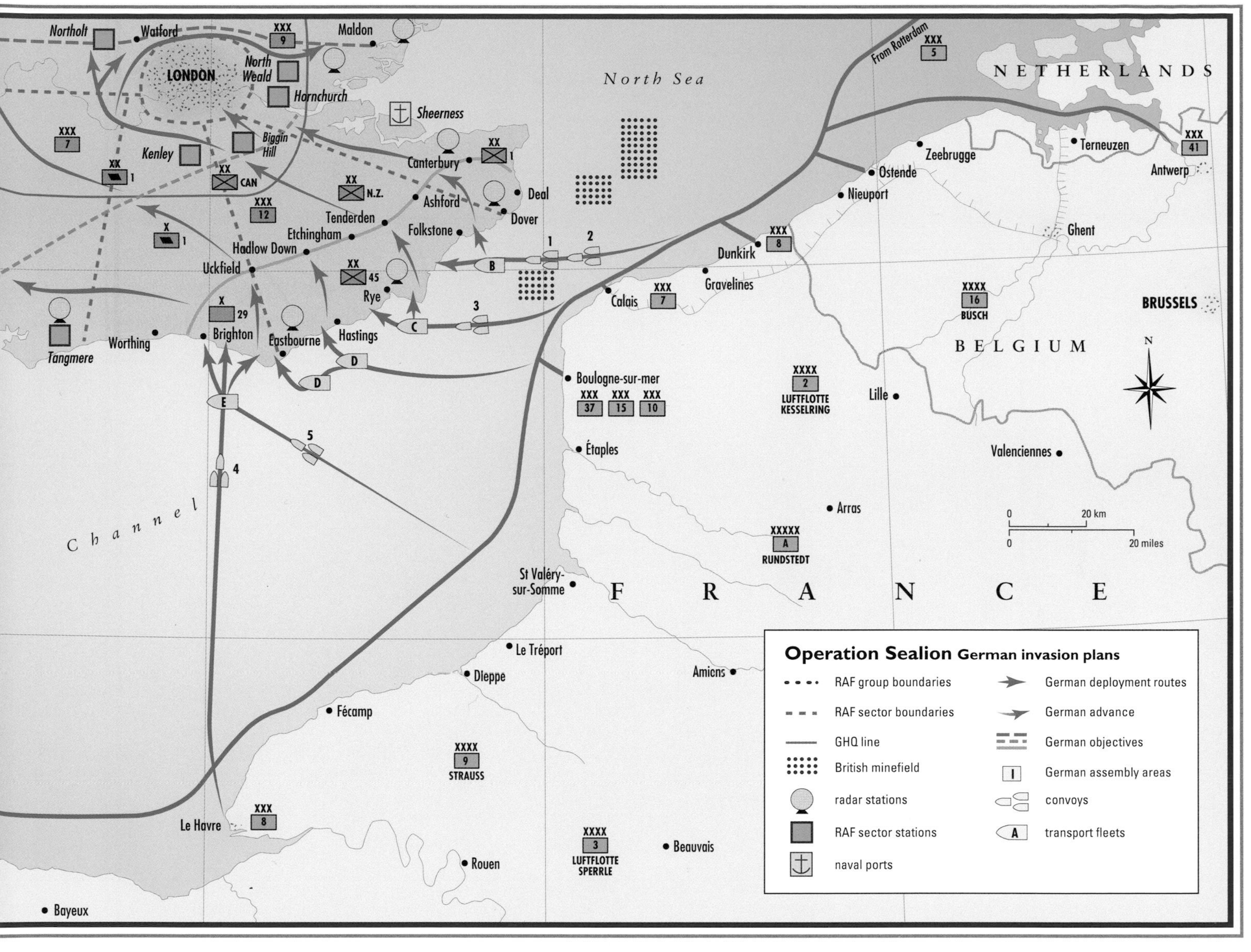

still hoped that Britain would make peace, a notion that was immediately rejected by Churchill.

Consequently, the German preparations for invasion continued. But there were serious differences between the Army and the Navy. The former regarded the operation as merely a river crossing, and wanted to land on as broad a front as possible so as to prevent the British being able to concentrate their reserves against the beachhead. The German Navy, conscious of the unpredictable nature of the Channel and the powerful threat presented by the Royal Navy, argued for a narrow front. Besides which, Germany possessed no amphibious capability for such a large undertaking. Instead, the authorities were forced to scour the inland waterways of Europe for barges, which then had to be converted so that they could be used as landing craft. In view of this, Hitler accepted that the invasion could not take place before mid-September. But by then the window of opportunity would be narrow, since the waters in the Channel would be influenced by the vagaries of the autumn weather. He therefore had a mind to postpone Operation Sealion, as it was codenamed, until May 1941, but ordered preparations to continue for a September assault. To the fury of the German Navy, Hitler accepted the Army's plan for landings on a frontage of some 200 miles, although he did later compromise. He realised, however, as did both the Army and the Navy, that air supremacy over the Channel and the landing area was essential to the success of Sealion. The burden was thus shifted onto the shoulders of Hermann Goering's Luftwaffe. During August and the first half of September 1940, the German Air Force struggled in vain to sweep the RAF from the skies over

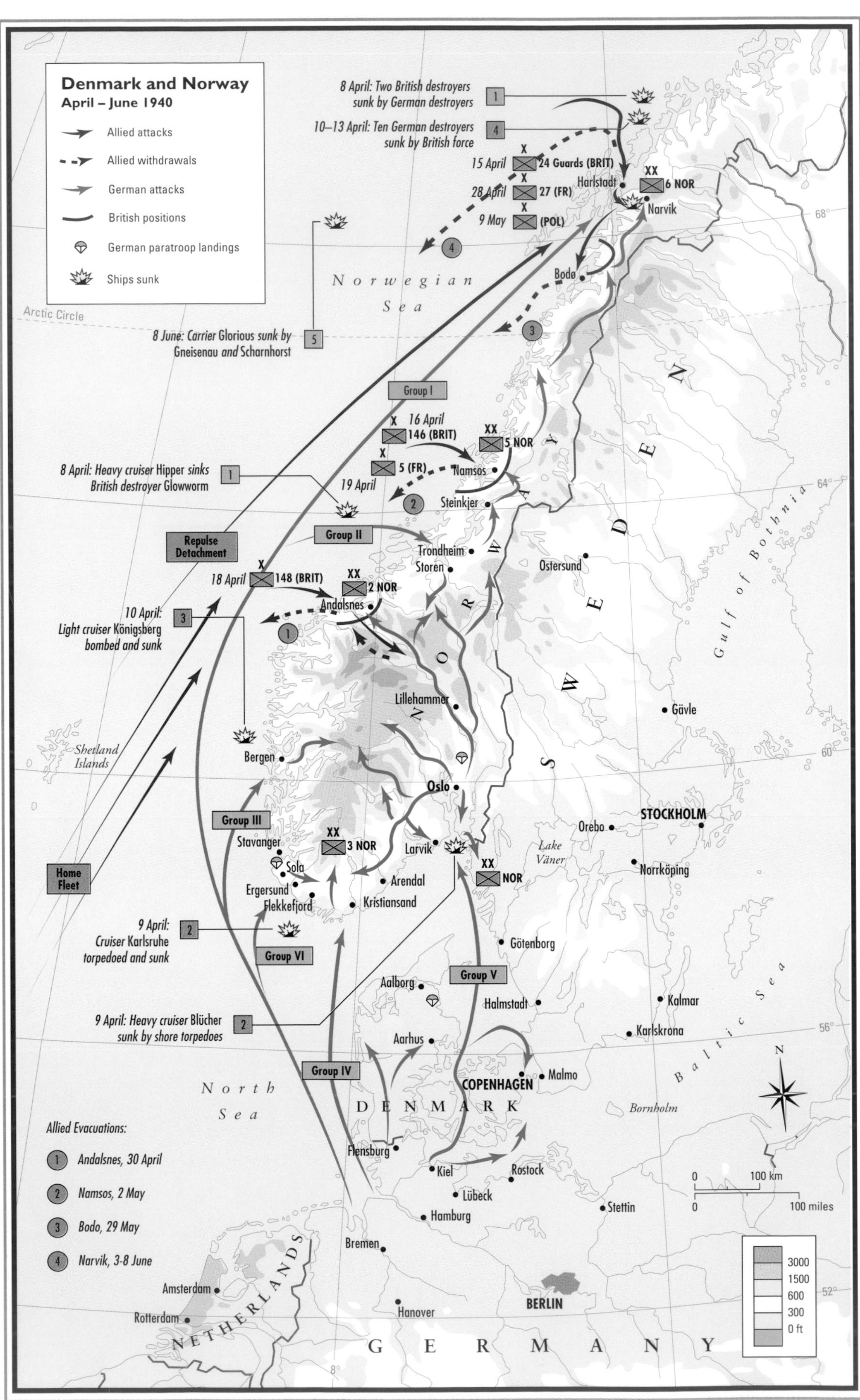

The initial German landings in Denmark and Norway took the defenders, who were ill equipped, by surprise. The use of airborne troops to seize Norwegian airfields was a critical factor in the German success. The Allied landings were poorly co-ordinated and, although they enjoyed naval superiority, they lacked the same in the air. Only at Narvik did the Allies enjoy a degree of success, but it proved too isolated for a force to be maintained there.

southern England. The climax came on 15 September, when 58 German aircraft were shot down for the loss of 26 British. Two days later, Hitler postponed Sealion indefinitely and turned his eyes eastwards to the Soviet Union. Britain would now be subjected to a winter and spring of prolonged air bombardment, the Blitz, designed to wear down the morale of the British people.

Yet, if Britain seemed to be wholly on the defensive during the summer and autumn of 1940, underneath the surface the first stirrings of offensive action were being felt. As early as 3 June, Churchill had circulated a memorandum to his Chiefs of Staff calling for offensive action through the formation of raiding forces. This was the genesis of the Commandos, who mounted their first operation, an abortive raid on the French coast, on the night 24/25 June. Simultaneously, Churchill sought to fan the flames of resistance to the Nazis in Occupied Europe through the setting up of the Special Operations Executive.

He also looked to RAF Bomber Command to mount a sustained air offensive against Germany, but it would be some time before it possessed sufficient suitable aircraft to make such a campaign effective. Churchill also ordered his staff to draw up plans for more ambitious projects. These included operations against the Azores and Canaries in the event of a German threat to them and one to destroy the Finnish port of Petsamo, through which nickel and iron-ore, vital to Germany's war industry, passed. Finally, on 5 October 1940, Churchill ordered a plan to be prepared for major ground operations on the European mainland with a view to advancing to Germany's major industrial region in the west, the Ruhr. It was this directive which provided the starting point for the D-Day landings.

All these plans assumed a significant amphibious capability, something which Britain did not possess in 1940. Between the wars, little thought had been given to developing such a weapon, largely because memories of the carnage surrounding the Gallipoli landings in 1915 had convinced most that such operations were not practicable. Indeed, in 1930 there were precisely three landing craft in Britain. True, in May 1938 the Inter-Services Training and Development Centre (ISTDC) was established at Portsmouth to develop amphibious techniques and this did result in orders for a few more landing craft, but at the outbreak of war it was temporarily all but disbanded, although it was resurrected at the end of 1939. The first British attempt at amphibious warfare was the landings in Norway in April 1940. These were initially unopposed by the Germans, but, not least because the Germans quickly achieved air supremacy, they could not be sustained and one after another of the landing forces had to be evacuated. Some of the precious stock of landing craft were lost, as well as others at Dunkirk. The net result was that in summer 1940 amphibious resources and expertise were still woefully lacking. This was borne out by the fiasco at Dakar in September 1940.

This was de Gaulle's attempt to establish a Free French foothold in French North-West Africa with considerable

An early British landing craft. It was designated the Landing Craft Mechanized (LCM). Much of the construction of the amphibious fleet for D-Day was, however, carried out in the United States.

British Commandos carry out a practice landing in Scotland. For much of the early part of the war they were one of the few means the British had of directly attacking the Germans in occupied western Europe. They also helped to develop amphibious warfare. The US Rangers were later modelled on the Commandos.

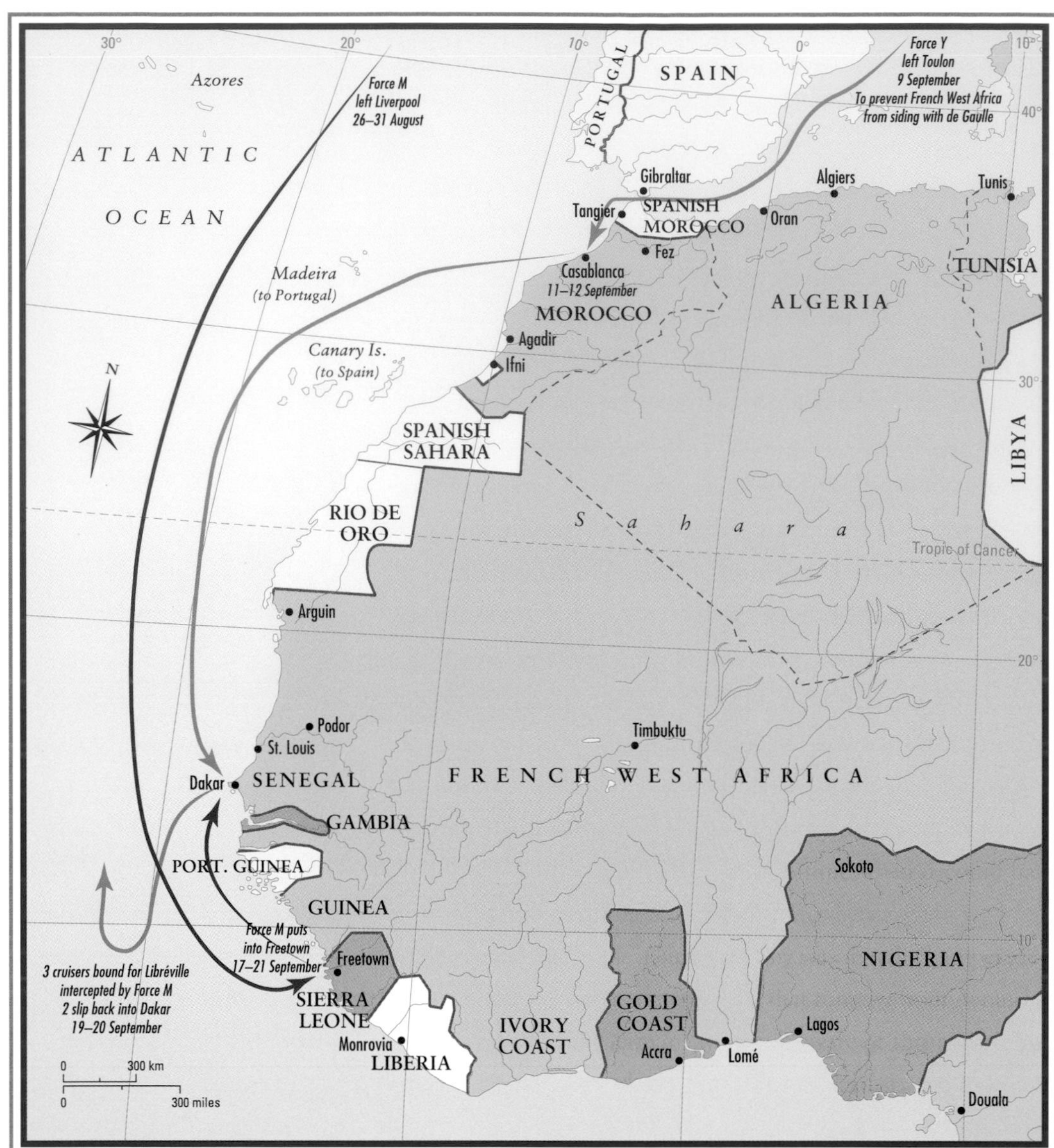

The interception of the three French cruisers on 19-20 September alerted the French in Dakar. The defences were much stronger than the planners of Operation Menace realized and they did inflict embarrassing damage on Force M when it attempted to carry out a landing during 23-24 September. The lessons learnt from this fiasco were taken to heart for subsequent Allied amphibious landings.

British naval and some military support. Intelligence on the Vichy French military strength at the port and the will to resist was poor. The landing troops, both British Royal Marines and Free French, had no training for the operation, which had been hastily mounted, and liaison between the British commanders and de Gaulle was poor. When the force appeared off Dakar, it was surprised by the intensity of the fire from the shore. Air attacks mounted from the carrier *Ark Royal* were also repulsed and, after the battleship HMS *Resolution* had been torpedoed by a Vichy French submarine, the force made an ignominious withdrawal. Dakar reinforced the need to build up an effective amphibious capability and, to this end, a Combined Training Centre was opened at Inverary in Scotland in January 1941 to teach and develop landing techniques. Admiral Sir Roger Keyes, who had planned and executed the famous Zeebrugge Raid of St George's Day 1918, was appointed Director of Combined Operations. The first fruits of these efforts came in March 1941 with a highly successful Commando raid on the Lofoten Islands off northern Norway.

In spite of the planning and efforts by the British to develop the tools needed for re-entering the Continent of Europe, Churchill realized from the outset that, while Britain could defend itself, it lacked the resources to defeat Hitler and Mussolini on its own. Only the United States of America

(Right) Most operations were carried out by very small groups and were designed to test the Germans defences and, if possible, seize prisoners. Those in Norway played their part in tying down German troops. A further series of reconnaissance operations to check beach obstacles was carried out by the Commandos in mid-May 1944.

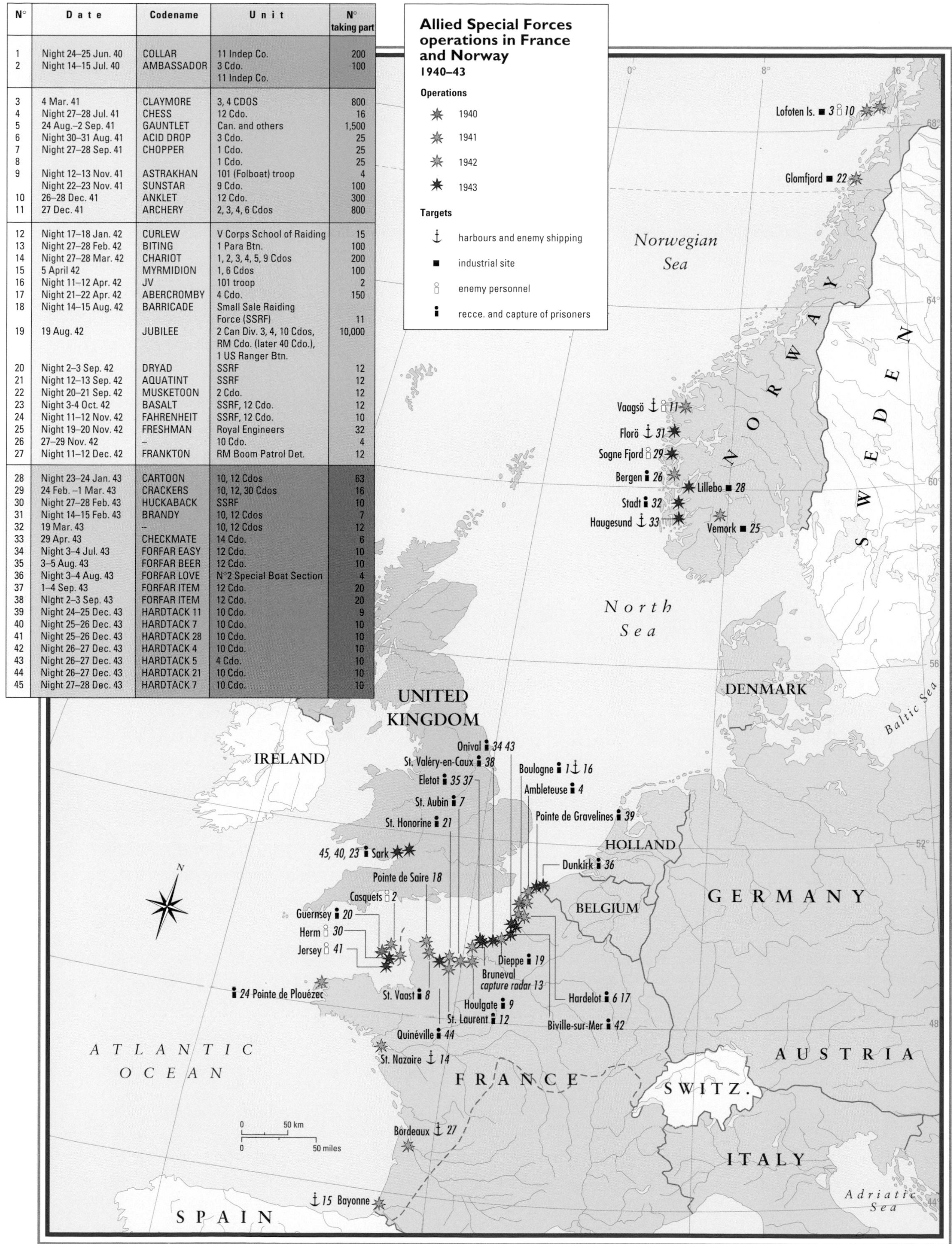

N°	Date	Codename	Unit	N° taking part
1	Night 24–25 Jun. 40	COLLAR	11 Indep Co.	200
2	Night 14–15 Jul. 40	AMBASSADOR	3 Cdo. 11 Indep Co.	100
3	4 Mar. 41	CLAYMORE	3, 4 CDOS	800
4	Night 27–28 Jul. 41	CHESS	12 Cdo.	16
5	24 Aug.–2 Sep. 41	GAUNTLET	Can. and others	1,500
6	Night 30–31 Aug. 41	ACID DROP	3 Cdo.	25
7	Night 27–28 Sep. 41	CHOPPER	1 Cdo.	25
8			1 Cdo.	25
9	Night 12–13 Nov. 41	ASTRAKHAN	101 (Folboat) troop	4
	Night 22–23 Nov. 41	SUNSTAR	9 Cdo.	100
10	26–28 Dec. 41	ANKLET	12 Cdo.	300
11	27 Dec. 41	ARCHERY	2, 3, 4, 6 Cdos	800
12	Night 17–18 Jan. 42	CURLEW	V Corps School of Raiding	15
13	Night 27–28 Feb. 42	BITING	1 Para Btn.	100
14	Night 27–28 Mar. 42	CHARIOT	1, 2, 3, 4, 5, 9 Cdos	200
15	5 April 42	MYRMIDION	1, 6 Cdos	100
16	Night 11–12 Apr. 42	JV	101 troop	2
17	Night 21–22 Apr. 42	ABERCROMBY	4 Cdo.	150
18	Night 14–15 Aug. 42	BARRICADE	Small Sale Raiding Force (SSRF)	11
19	19 Aug. 42	JUBILEE	2 Can Div. 3, 4, 10 Cdos, RM Cdo. (later 40 Cdo.), 1 US Ranger Btn.	10,000
20	Night 2–3 Sep. 42	DRYAD	SSRF	12
21	Night 12–13 Sep. 42	AQUATINT	SSRF	12
22	Night 20–21 Sep. 42	MUSKETOON	2 Cdo.	12
23	Night 3-4 Oct. 42	BASALT	SSRF, 12 Cdo.	12
24	Night 11–12 Nov. 42	FAHRENHEIT	SSRF, 12 Cdo.	10
25	Night 19–20 Nov. 42	FRESHMAN	Royal Engineers	32
26	27–29 Nov. 42	–	10 Cdo.	4
27	Night 11–12 Dec. 42	FRANKTON	RM Boom Patrol Det.	12
28	Night 23–24 Jan. 43	CARTOON	10, 12 Cdos	63
29	24 Feb. –1 Mar. 43	CRACKERS	10, 12, 30 Cdos	16
30	Night 27–28 Feb. 43	HUCKABACK	SSRF	10
31	Night 14–15 Feb. 43	BRANDY	10, 12 Cdos	7
32	19 Mar. 43	–	10, 12 Cdos	12
33	29 Apr. 43	CHECKMATE	14 Cdo.	6
34	Night 3–4 Jul. 43	FORFAR EASY	12 Cdo.	10
35	3–5 Aug. 43	FORFAR BEER	12 Cdo.	10
36	Night 3–4 Aug. 43	FORFAR LOVE	N°2 Special Boat Section	4
37	1–4 Sep. 43	FORFAR ITEM	12 Cdo.	20
38	Night 2–3 Sep. 43	FORFAR ITEM	12 Cdo.	20
39	Night 24–25 Dec. 43	HARDTACK 11	10 Cdo.	9
40	Night 25–26 Dec. 43	HARDTACK 7	10 Cdo.	10
41	Night 25–26 Dec. 43	HARDTACK 28	10 Cdo.	10
42	Night 26–27 Dec. 43	HARDTACK 4	10 Cdo.	10
43	Night 26–27 Dec. 43	HARDTACK 5	4 Cdo.	10
44	Night 26–27 Dec. 43	HARDTACK 21	10 Cdo.	10
45	Night 27–28 Dec. 43	HARDTACK 7	10 Cdo.	10

could provide these and so Churchill embarked on a campaign to persuade President Franklin D. Roosevelt to bring his country into the war on the British side. It was to be a difficult struggle. While Roosevelt had every sympathy with the British cause, he was very conscious that the majority of his countrymen continued to support the isolationism that had kept America out of the League of Nations. They had no wish to become embroiled in another European war. Even so, Roosevelt did what he could to help the British. In August 1940, he supplied fifty elderly destroyers to the Royal Navy in exchange for the lease of British naval bases in the Caribbean. He also sent a team of military observers across to Britain and, in preparation for what he saw as America's eventual inevitable entry into the war, set up a programme for increased shipbuilding and implemented limited conscription. Roosevelt's position became more secure after the November 1940 presidential election and one of the first steps of his second presidency was to introduce his Lend-Lease Bill to Congress. This would enable the USA to supply Britain and China, embroiled in a desperate struggle against the Japanese, with war matérial, which could be repaid in kind after the war. This became law in early March 1941. Simultaneously, he agreed to joint talks between the British and US military staffs.

President Franklin D. Roosevelt and Prime Minister Winston Churchill meet on board the battleship HMS Prince of Wales *in Placentia Bay, Newfoundland, in August 1941. While Churchill failed to persuade the President to enter the war, the Atlantic Charter that they drew up provided a vision for a new post-war world and was the blueprint for the United Nations.*

Even though the USA's foreign policy was strictly isolationist, the US military still needed strategic scenarios on which to base planning and armed forces structure. Prior to the outbreak of World War 2 these were very hypothetical and considered war against single countries. These included Germany and Japan, but also even Canada and Britain. As war clouds gathered in Europe during summer 1939, there was a rethink and a new series of plans was drawn up. These were based on the premise of the probability of war against more than one enemy and in more than one theatre. While the earlier plans had single colour names (Red, Orange, Blue, etc), the new set came out under the title of Rainbow. Rainbow-1 and -2 were concerned with defence of the US and its trade, as well as protecting democratic powers, notably the Philippines, in the Pacific. Rainbow-3 covered the Western Pacific and was aimed at Japan, while Rainbow-4 dealt with the South America option. Rainbow-5, however, not only acted as a blanket cover for the first four, but also provided for the sending of forces to Europe or Africa to help the British and French defeat Germany and Italy. It was with this background that the US staff entered what were called the ABC (America, Britain, Canada) talks. They were held in Canada and at the end of March 1941 firm agreement was reached. Priority, once America entered the war, would be the defeat of Germany and Italy and the main US military effort would be in the European theatre. A strategic defence would be conducted against Japan, with the US Navy giving priority to the Pacific. The talks provided a firm basis for planning, even though the agreements made were not binding on either country.

Potential US operations in both Europe and the Pacific would inevitably contain an amphibious element, but the US

(Right) Many of these plans reflected Churchill's rstless determination to strike back at the Germans. In particular, he favoured a landing in Norway, although his military staff were very much against this because of the difficulties of supporting a force at such a range from Britain. The Americans were dedicated to Round-Up from the outset, but were eventually persuaded to postpone it in favour of invading French North-West Africa.

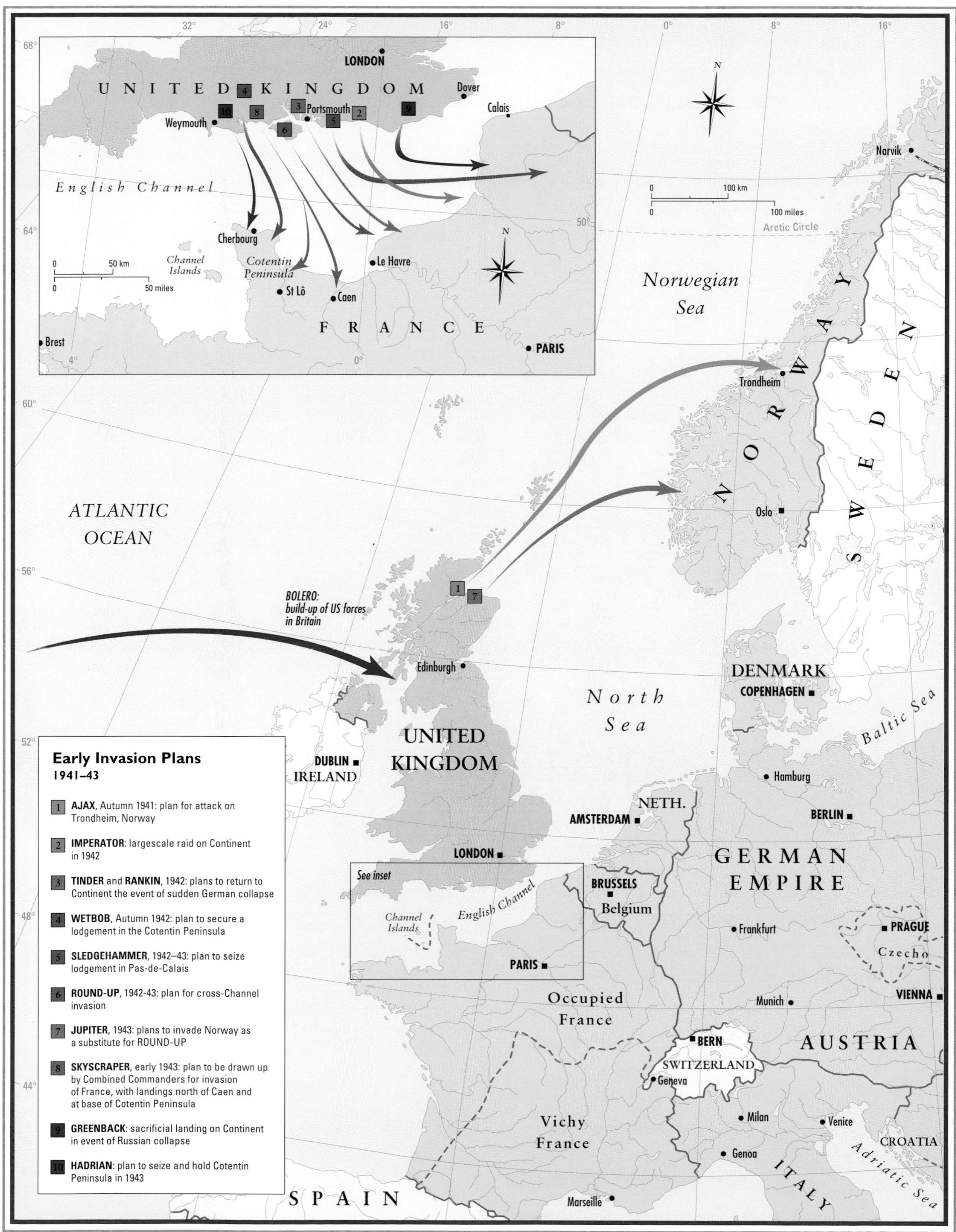

Early Invasion Plans
1941–43
1 AJAX, Autumn 1941: plan for attack on Trondheim, Norway
2 IMPERATOR: largescale raid on Continent in 1942
3 TINDER and RANKIN, 1942: plans to return to Continent the event of sudden German collapse
4 WETBOB, Autumn 1942: plan to secure a lodgement in the Cotentin Peninsula
5 SLEDGEHAMMER, 1942–43: plan to seize lodgement in Pas-de-Calais
6 ROUND-UP, 1942-43: plan for cross-Channel invasion
7 JUPITER, 1943: plans to invade Norway as a substitute for ROUND-UP
8 SKYSCRAPER, early 1943: plan to be drawn up by Combined Commanders for invasion of France, with landings north of Caen and at base of Cotentin Peninsula
9 GREENBACK: sacrificial landing on Continent in event of Russian collapse
10 HADRIAN: plan to seize and hold Cotentin Peninsula in 1943
LONDON
UNITED KINGDOM
Dover
Calais
Portsmouth
Weymouth
English Channel
Cherbourg
Channel Islands
Cotentin Peninsula
Le Havre
St Lô
Caen
FRANCE
Brest
PARIS
50 km
50 miles
100 km
100 miles
Arctic Circle
Narvik
Norwegian Sea
Trondheim
NORWAY
SWEDEN
Oslo
ATLANTIC OCEAN
BOLERO: build-up of US forces in Britain
Edinburgh
DENMARK
COPENHAGEN
North Sea
Baltic Sea
UNITED KINGDOM
DUBLIN
IRELAND
Hamburg
NETH.
AMSTERDAM
BERLIN
LONDON
GERMAN EMPIRE
See inset
BRUSSELS
Belgium
English Channel
Channel Islands
Frankfurt
PRAGUE
Czecho
PARIS
Occupied France
Munich
VIENNA
BERN
AUSTRIA
SWITZERLAND
Geneva
Vichy France
Milan
Venice
CROATIA
Genoa
ITALY
Adriatic Sea
SPAIN
Marseille

capability in this field was limited, although considerably ahead of that of the British in 1939. This was thanks to the US Marine Corps, which worked hard during the 1920s and 1930s to develop amphibious doctrine for what became the Fleet Marine Force, whose primary role was establishing forward bases in the Pacific in the event of war against Japan. They even developed an amphibious armoured vehicle, the Landing Vehicle Tracked (LVT), which became a crucial element of the successful island-hopping operations in the Pacific. Where the Marine Corps was frustrated, however, was in the lack of suitable amphibious shipping. Furthermore, it was not until 1940 that the US Army began to display any interest in amphibious warfare.

On 22 June 1941, The Germans invaded the Soviet Union, putting a very different complexion on the war. For Britain it meant a significant reduction in pressure, but as the Germans drove deeper into Russia, clamour grew within Britain and from Moscow for the immediate opening of a Second Front to draw off German divisions. This was beyond the British capability since there was still only sufficient shipping to carry 6,000 men at one time. Even so, Churchill did order his military staff to draw up plans for a large-scale raid on northern France, mentioning specifically the Cherbourg peninsula, but the concept was rejected as impracticable. Meanwhile, Roosevelt was slowly extending his assistance to the British. In April he extended the zone in the western Atlantic in which US warships would protect their own merchant vessels almost to Iceland, simultaneously deploying troops to Greenland. In July 1941, US troops also relieved the British garrison in Iceland. Then, in August 1941 came the historic meeting between Roosevelt and Churchill off Newfoundland. Nothing concrete came out of it, however. The British Chiefs of Staff were disappointed that their American opposite numbers appeared to have a very defensive view of the western hemisphere and had little clear-cut strategy for the defeat of Germany. The Americans, on the other hand, thought that the British focus on the Mediterranean was an irrelevancy and the likely effect on Germany of strategic bombing over-emphasized. They also criticized the British lack of focus on planning a major campaign in Europe.

HMS Campbeltown wedged into the lock gates at St Nazaire moments before exploding, vapourizing the large group of German soldiers inspecting the wreck.

British dreams of the USA finally entering the war were at last realized in December 1941. As a result of the Japanese air attack on the US Pacific Fleet base at Pearl Harbor, Hawaii on the 7th, Roosevelt declared war against Japan. He hesitated to declare war on Germany, but Hitler solved the problem by declaring war on the USA. Churchill immediately set sail in the battleship HMS *Duke of York* to meet Roosevelt in Washington DC in what was to be the first of many Allied strategic conferences. Even though American interests were more directly threatened by Japan, Roosevelt did agree to uphold the decisions made at the ABC talks earlier in the year. The priority would remain on first defeating Germany. Strategy would be directed by Churchill and Roosevelt through the Combined Chiefs of Staff (CCS), which comprised the US Chiefs of Staff and the British Military Mission to the USA. As for the way ahead, the Washington Conference had four major plans to consider. Sledgehammer was a major operation somewhere in Western Europe to be mounted in 1942 to relieve pressure on the Russians. Round- Up, the preferred US option, was a cross-Channel invasion in 1943. The British, on the other hand, pushed for Gymnast, which was an invasion of French North-West Africa. At the time, the British forces in Libya had just mounted a successful counter-offensive and Gymnast was seen as a way of threatening the rear of the Axis forces and securing the whole of North Africa. The one plan on which both sides agreed was Bolero, a build-up of US forces in Britain. Indeed, the first US troops arrived before the end of January 1942.

The focus of the debate which would occupy the Allies for much of 1942 was Round-Up versus Gymnast. The

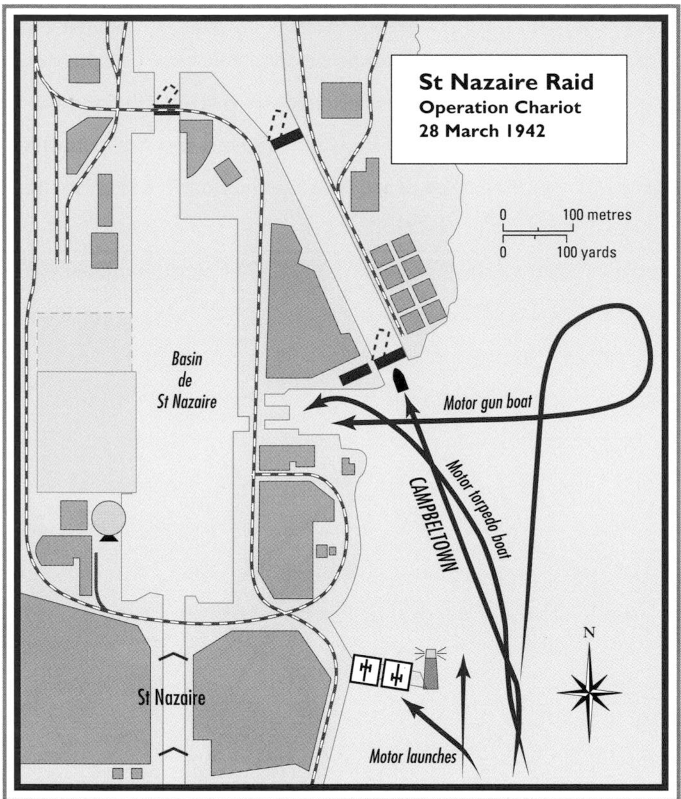

This was one of the most spectacular and successful of the cross-Channel raids. The Commandos provided demolition teams and were responsible for neutralizing the dock defences. Motor launches were used instead of landing craft and HMS Campbeltown, packed with explosives, was to literally ram the lock gates. She was disguised as a German torpedo boat. Casualties were heavy, however, with over 350 killed or captured.

British were lukewarm over the former, believing that there would not be enough amphibious shipping to ensure success. This itself was measured in terms of the Landing Ship Tank (LST), which was ocean-going and with draught sufficiently shallow to be capable of delivering tanks direct to the landing beach. The British view was that at least fifty LSTs would be needed for Round-Up, but, because the development of an effective type had been slow, they doubted whether sufficient would be available in time. Both sides blew hot and cold over Gymnast, the British especially so after Rommel mounted a successful counter-offensive in Libya in January 1942. But Sledgehammer, too, caused much heart-searching. While the Russians had succeeded in rebuffing the Germans in front of Moscow in December 1941 and had mounted limited counter-offensives, there were grave doubts whether they could stand up to an inevitable renewed German offensive in spring 1942. The British planners therefore began to examine in detail how Sledgehammer could be mounted. Admiral Lord Louis Mountbatten, who was now Chief of Combined Operations, favoured the Cherbourg peninsula, but this was rejected because the distance from Britain meant that insufficient air cover could be provided. On the other hand, he rejected a raid on the Pas-de-Calais on the grounds that re-embarkation would be very difficult in the light of the expected German reaction. The US view was summed up by General George C. Marshall, Chairman of the Joint Chiefs of Staff, namely that Sledgehammer should only be mounted if the situation on the Eastern Front became desperate, or if there was a fatal weakening of the German forces in the West. One good thing, however, did come out of these discussions. This was the realization that it was essential that the ports on Britain's south coast, which had been allowed to decay since summer 1940, were made fully functional once more and, indeed, improved, since it was from them that any major cross-Channel assault would be mounted.

In the meantime, during winter 1941-2 two large-scale and successful Commando raids had been carried out. The first, on 27 December 1941 was against the Norwegian port of Vaagso. It was followed, on the night of 27/28 March 1942, by an operation to deny the Germans the use of the dry dock at the French Atlantic port of St Nazaire. This was done by ramming an elderly destroyer filled with explosives against the dock gates. There were also, as there had been in 1941, a series of small-scale Commando raids on the French Atlantic coast with the object of testing the German defences. All these helped to develop amphibious techniques. At the same time, because British shipyards were filled to capacity building other types of ship, increasing orders for amphibious shipping were placed with the Americans. Thus, during 1942 the Allied amphibious capability began to grow.

In April 1942, the Japanese onrush in the South West Pacific began to threaten Australia. The Americans felt forced to divert two divisions earmarked for Bolero and were forced to admit that they would have less than three divisions in Britain by mid-September. This was another nail in the coffin for Sledgehammer and the British Chiefs of Staff decided that a major cross-Channel raid should be mounted instead, although planning for Sledgehammer would continue. But Roosevelt, conscious of both the sacrifices that the

Russians were making and that if US troops were not in action in Europe soon, US public opinion might well start to agitate for priority to be switched to the Pacific, was still keen that Sledgehammer should go ahead in some form. Pressure, too, came from the Russians themselves, with foreign minister Vyacheslav Molotov flying to London and then Washington to plead the Russian case. While the British would make no immediate commitment, Roosevelt did reassure Molotov that a Second Front would be opened before the end of 1942, although he was careful not to say where.

The British became more and more convinced that Sledgehammer was merely a sacrificial operation which would gain little. In this context, Churchill had been pressuring Roosevelt to reconsider Gymnast as an alternative. General George Marshall remained totally opposed to this and even proposed a Pacific option to the President, which, of course, ran totally counter to the Germany First agreement. Indeed, Roosevelt rejected it, likening the proposal to 'taking up your dishes and going away', and by mid-July was coming round to Gymnast. Simultaneously, the British Joint Planning Staff were telling the Chiefs of Staff that it would not be possible to mount Round-Up within twelve months of Gymnast. Roosevelt now sent Marshall to London to resolve the dilemma. Supported by General Dwight D. Eisenhower, the recently appointed Commanding General European Theatre of Operations (ETOUSA), Marshall proposed gaining a lodgement in the Cotentin peninsula in autumn 1942 and holding it until Round Up was mounted. The British pointed out the difficulties with the weather at that time of year. They were supported by the US Navy representatives in Britain and on this Sledgehammer foundered. It was, in Eisenhower's eyes, 'the blackest day in history'.

The Dieppe Raid was essentially a frontal assault against a well defended position, with insufficient fire support (naval) to deal with the numerous coastal batteries. The only successes were by No.4 Commando in silencing the Hess Battery and No.3 Commando, which successfully distracted the Goebbels Battery. Valuable lessons were learnt for the D-Day landings, but at a high cost.

Throughout this debate, however, the British, had been preparing a major cross-Channel raid. It was Mountbatten's HQ which decided on the port of Dieppe as a target, believing it to be lightly defended. The original plan, approved by the British Chiefs of Staff in May 1942, envisaged a frontal assault by 2nd Canadian Division, with airborne forces being used to neutralize the coastal batteries on the flanks. The assault would be preceded by an attack by RAF Bomber Command and there would be extensive fighter support, which it was hoped would draw the Luftwaffe into the air and inflict heavy casualties upon it. General Bernard Montgomery, then in charge of South-East Army, was in overall charge. He held two rehearsals in June and decided that the raid should go ahead on 4 July or the first fine day after that. Unfortunately, there was a spell of bad weather in early July, which forced a postponement. Montgomery

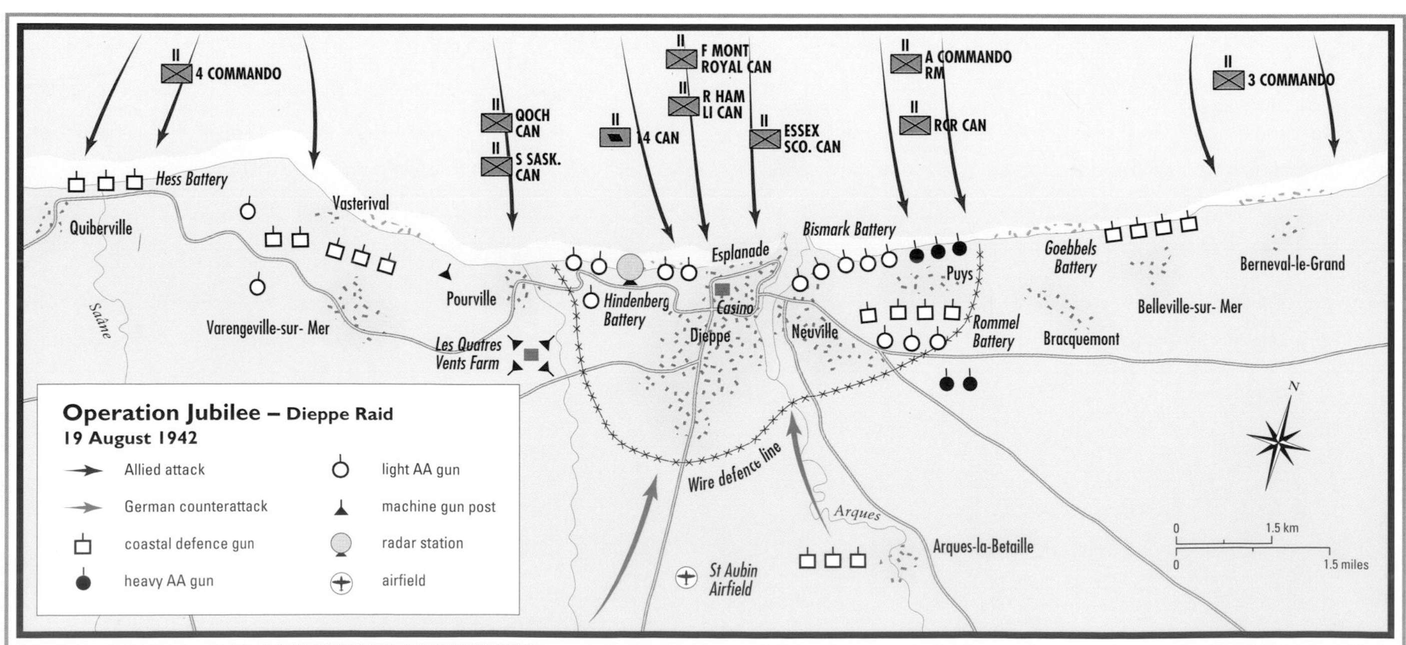

Germans inspect the beach at Dieppe after the disastrous raid in August 1942. Many of the tanks could not get off the beach because the shingle jammed their tracks. It was as a result of this that the British developed specialized armoured vehicles to facilitate the landing of tanks and enable them to get off the beach.

believed that it should be cancelled, fearing that the raid had been compromised, but Mountbatten insisted that it go ahead. It was rescheduled for August, but changes were now made. The preliminary air bombardment was cancelled through fears of inflicting French civilian casualties and the airborne element was also withdrawn because of weather uncertainties. In its place, Commandos were detailed to deal with the coastal batteries. Another problem was that the Navy maintained its policy of no warship larger than a destroyer being allowed in the Channel, which severely limited the fire support for the landings.

After a 24-hour postponement because of the weather, the raiding force sailed from four South Coast ports on the evening of 18 August. They arrived off Dieppe before dawn and the raid began. It was a disaster, with only the Commandos on the flanks enjoying any success. The Germans had been expecting something and were ready. The Canadians were subjected to heavy fire as they approached the beaches and the 4.7-inch guns of the supporting destroyers proved ineffective. Many of those who got ashore were shot down before they could get off the beach. A battalion of hastily converted Churchill tanks found the shingle too much for their tracks to cope with and were all knocked out. The landing force commander, who was on board one of the destroyers, had little idea of what was happening and sent in follow-up waves, which also suffered. In the skies above, the battle did not go as the British expected. They lost 106 aircraft, while the Luftwaffe had only forty-eight shot down. General Roberts, the Force Commander, realized at 9am that withdrawal was the only answer, but it took another four hours to complete. Some four thousand men, mainly Canadians, were left behind dead or prisoners of war.

For the Germans, Dieppe was a major propaganda coup. Many Canadians regarded it, and still do today, as a needless slaughter. Indeed, it remains one of the major controversies of World War 2. Yet valuable lessons for subsequent amphibious assaults were learnt. First, security had to be very much tighter. Naval gunfire support needed to be very much heavier. Air supremacy had to be established before the landings took place. The landing force commander needed a dedicated command ship with good communications to the shore, the air, and the naval element. Armoured Fighting Vehicles (AFV) had to be developed which could get ashore and cope with the inevitable obstacles that would be found on the landing beach and beyond. Finally, to land at a defended port was to court failure. When the cross-Channel invasion did come, it would have to be over open beaches,

U.S. troops land in North Africa as part of the Allied Operation Torch.

but without the facilities of a port how was the force ashore to be supplied and reinforced so that it could push inlan

Dieppe did give an indication of what might have happened if Sledgehammer had taken place, but, in any event, it was now history. On 30 July 1942 the Allies confirmed that Gymnast, now renamed Torch, would take place on 7 October. The original plan was for US-only landings at Oran and Casablanca, but, on British insistence, landings were also to take place at Algiers with British participation. This would put the Allies considerably closer to Tunis, which was the final objective. Since this meant assembling more shipping, Torch was postponed until the end of October. Because the operation was largely American, Eisenhower was put in charge, which was personal consolation for the cancellation of Sledgehammer. There were, however, serious implications for Round-Up. While the landings at Casablanca were to be mounted from the USA, the forces for the other two landings would sail from Britain. This meant drawing on the Bolero forces and would put a brake on the build-up for Round-Up. Furthermore, a significant proportion of the US Eighth Air Force in Britain, which was just beginning to join the RAF in the air offensive against Germany, was also sidetracked to Torch. Furthermore, Stalin would have to be told that there would be no Second Front in Europe in 1942. To this end, Churchill and Roosevelt's personal representative, Averell Harriman, flew to Moscow in mid-August. Stalin grudgingly accepted Churchill's explanation that 'it was as well to strike at the belly as the snout' of a crocodile.

The Torch landings themselves duly took place on 8 November 1942, just as Bernard Montgomery, who had taken charge of the British Eighth Army in Egypt in August, was beginning to pursue Rommel into Libya after his decisive breakthrough attack at El Alamein. The Vichy French put up little more than token resistance and sought an armistice after three days. The lessons of Dakar and Dieppe had been learnt in terms of command and control at Oran and Algiers in that the landing force commander for each did have a dedicated command ship. At Casablanca, however, General George S. Patton did not, which he found frustrating, especially since he was not able to get ashore until long after he wanted to. Poor navigation and confusion on the landing beaches pointed to inexperience, and the loading of the ships left much to be desired, since many of the items that the force required as soon as it landed were not immediately accessible.

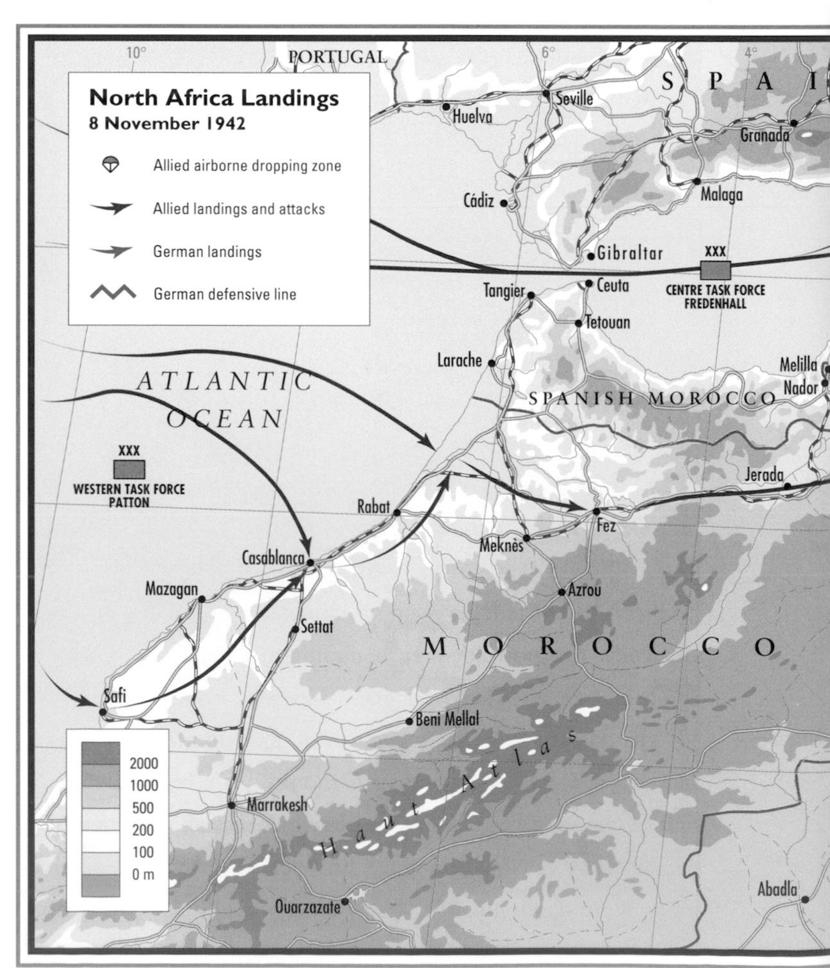

With Morocco and Algeria secured, the Allies quickly moved into Tunisia. The initial landings had taken the Axis powers by surprise, but they reacted quickly and were soon flying troops into Tunisia. As the Allies advanced into the country, a series of engagements took place. Even so, the Allies managed to reach 20 miles from Tunis before they were finally halted. German counter-attacks and an adverse air situation forced the Allies to halt and, by the end of 1942, stalemate ensued.

It was in this climate that Roosevelt and Churchill met once more, this time at Casablanca, Morocco in mid-January 1943. Prior to the Conference, Churchill's own view had been that Tunisia could be secured in January 1943. The Allies would then go on to capture Sardinia, to neutralize Italy by the end of March, and then begin preparing for Round-Up, which could be mounted in August or September 1943. His Chiefs of Staff did not agree, however. They argued that it would simply take the pressure off the Germans while Round-Up was being prepared and that there was not the shipping available, especially to make good the shortfall in Bolero brought about by Torch. Rather, they said, it would be better to concentrate on the Mediterranean during 1943 and knock Italy out of the war. To this Churchill agreed. In Washington, however, the general feeling was that Round-Up must be the priority for 1943. The US Army planners were, however, pessimistic. They feared that logistics might mean that it could not be mounted before mid-1944 and were concerned over the heavy casualties suffered at Dieppe. Hence, unlike the British, the Americans arrived at Casablanca with no clear-cut strategy on the way ahead. This was to be to their grave disadvantage.

The Casablanca Conference itself did reach a number of significant decisions. The better-prepared British team got

Torch represented the first major Anglo-US operation in the European theatre. The landings took the Axis by surprise and the only significant, albeit brief, opposition was at Algiers. It was also the first time that the Allies used airborne forces on a large scale, primarily to secure airfields. Unfortunately, once they advanced into Tunisia, they found themselves with very long lines of communication. This and the semi-mountainous terrain meant that the campaign lasted very much longer than planned.

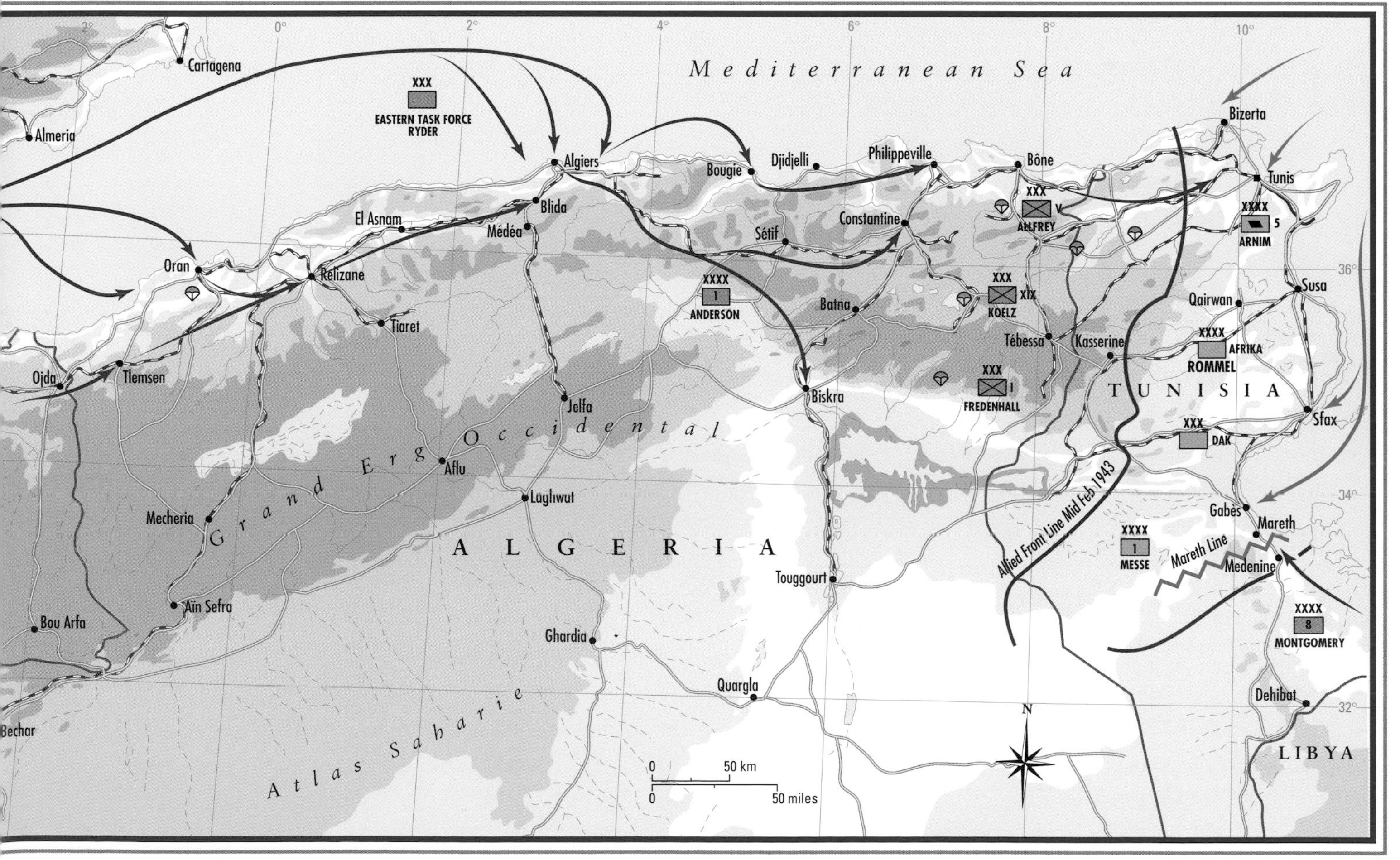

General George S. Patton commanded the 7th Army during the invasion of Sicily.

before his appointment was confirmed by the Combined Chiefs of Staff and he could gather a planning team, but this did give him time to study the work that had been done by another British body which had been considering the problem for some time.

The Combined Commanders committee had been established on a part-time basis before the end of 1941 to consid-

Apart from the airborne element, which was widely scattered, the initial landings went well. The Americans then cleared the western half of the island, while the British advanced up the east coast. While the Italian will to fight was fading, the German forces on Sicily conducted a skilful withdrawal and managed to escape across the Strait of Messina.

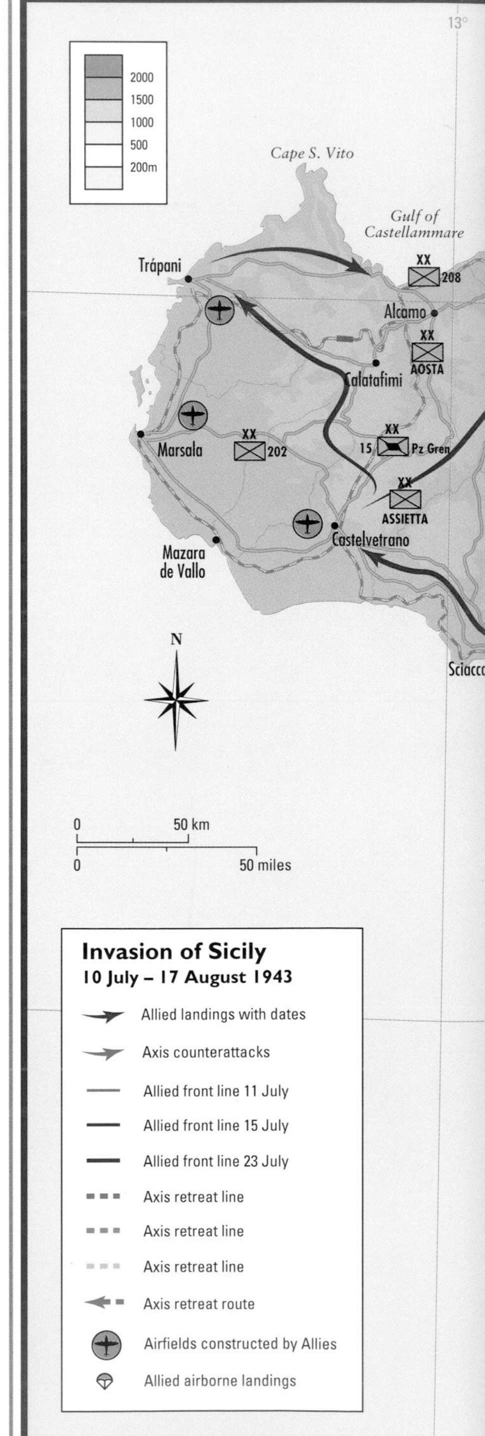

its way over priority for the Mediterranean in 1943, with Sicily being the next objective after North Africa had been cleared of the Axis presence. The Americans, however, were not prepared to agree to further operations in the Mediterranean after Sicily. Bolero was to continue, with a target of 384,000 US troops in Britain by 1 August 1943 and well over 900,000 by the end of the year. While a full-scale cross-Channel invasion was out of the question in 1943, it was agreed that a combined planning staff for it should be set up in Britain under a British officer. On the other hand, more limited operations might be feasible, including, if a favourable situation developed, establishing a lodgement. These, however, were mere contingencies to which the British agreed to placate the Americans. In the wider context, both sides agreed that winning the Battle of the Atlantic was a priority because of the U-boat threat to the supply lines from North America. Finally, the USAAF and RAF were to mount a combined bomber offensive, codenamed Pointblank. The aim was to pave the way for invasion by fatally weakening the German war industry and the morale of the people.

The Tunisian campaign continued, with Montgomery forcing Rommel back across the border with Libya and entering the country himself. Thereafter it was a question of gradually squeezing the Axis forces from the south and from the west. Not, however, until early May did they finally surrender. In the midst of this, on 12 March 1943, Lieutenant-General Frederick Morgan was appointed Chief of Staff to the Supreme Allied Commander (COSSAC) and tasked with producing a coherent plan for Round Up in line with the decision made at Casablanca. It would be a month er the problems of a cross-Channel invasion. It consisted of a senior sailor, a soldier, and an airman and produced a number of papers for the British Chiefs of Staff. One of the final tasks of the Combined Commanders was to consider possible landing areas. They considered these in terms of air cover, enemy airfields, the German naval threat, enemy fixed defences, the ability of the Germans to use flooding as a defensive weapon and to deploy reserves, the presence of ports, and landing beaches. Their conclusions were that fighter cover was needed over the beaches and that airfields must be captured early so as to maintain air support once the force advanced inland. The rate of build-up of the force must be at least equal to the deployment of German reserves, and the beaches themselves needed to be sheltered

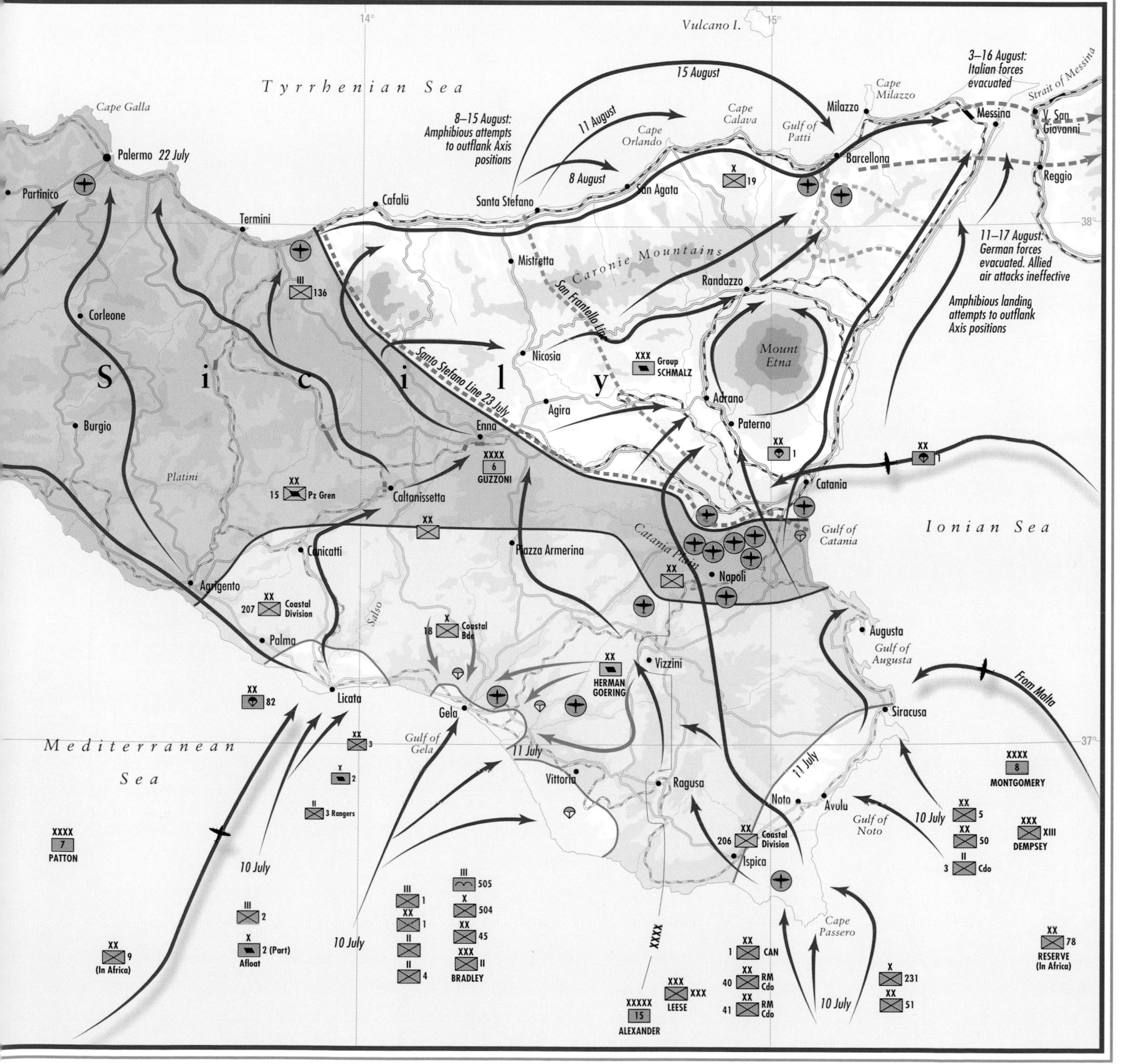

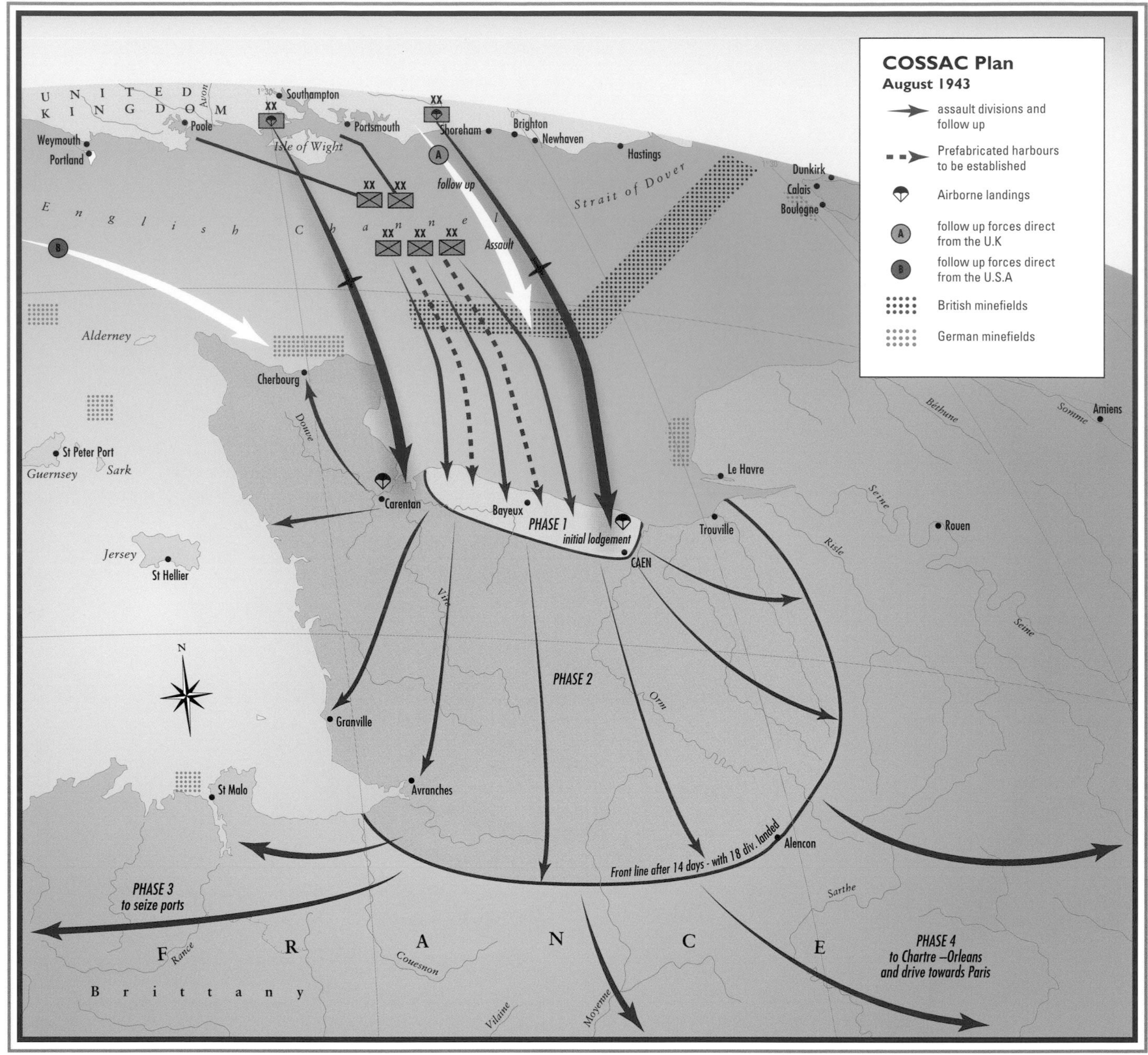

The initial assault would be made by US First Army, with one US, one British, and one Canadian divisions. One airborne division was to be used on each flank, with that in the east tasked with capturing Caen. On D+7 the Canadian First Army would be formed, with responsibility for the eastern half of the lodgement, while HQ 21st Army Group took over command from US First Army.

from the weather. They stressed the need to capture a sizeable port early. They dismissed the Dutch coast as being beyond adequate fighter cover and also because the country was too prone to inundation. Belgian beaches were too exposed and of limited capacity. The Combined Commanders also did not consider the Pas-de-Calais as suitable, even though it was closest to the English coast and thus maximum air cover could be provided. The defences were too strong, most beaches were exposed and all were dominated by cliffs. The sector could, however, be used for a feint attack. The coast around the mouth of the River Seine suffered much the same problems. In addition, the beaches were too small. Moving to Normandy, the coast north of Caen was much more promising. The Seine provided a natural flank for the landing forces, the beaches were of reasonable size and sheltered, and there were good airfields in the Caen area. The defences were also weaker than to the east. The only major drawback was the lack of a suitable port. The Cotentin peninsula, on the other hand, did have the port of Cherbourg, but the beaches were more limited and the base of the peninsula could cause a bottleneck, which would make a break-out difficult. But the Commanders did conclude that if the Caen sector was selected, there would have to be a subsidiary operation against the eastern side of the Cotentin peninsula so as to secure Cherbourg. In this lay the foundations of the eventual Overlord plan. As for Brittany and the Bay of Biscay, these were beyond the range of fighter cover and only suitable for subsidiary operations to capture further ports once the main assault had been mounted.

This appreciation provided COSSAC with a most useful basis for his planning. He was also aware that the British GHQ Home Forces had for a long time been gathering intelligence in support of Round-Up planning. It came from several sources. Continuous photographic air reconnaissance missions were being flown; there was information obtained from radio intercepts, including Ultra material from decryptions of Enigma traffic. Further information was provided by the various Resistance movements. Commando raids also brought back valuable intelligence on the German defences. There had even been a drive to collect people's holiday postcards and photographs of coastal areas. A further source of intelligence was pigeons. Since the spring of 1941, they had been dropped by parachute over Occupied Europe. Each had a questionnaire, which the finder was invited to complete. In all, over 16,500 pigeons were despatched and nearly 2,000 did return to their lofts.

COSSAC arranged his staff so that each of the planning branches – Navy, Army, Air, Administrative – had two principal staff officers, one British and one American. The only exception was Intelligence, which had just a Briton in charge. To gain a better understanding of the planning of amphibious operations, he sent one of his senior officers to monitor the planning of Husky, as the invasion of Sicily was codenamed. In May there was another Allied conference, Trident, which was held in Washington DC. This confirmed that Round-Up, while not possible in 1943, would be mounted by 1 May 1944. It was envisaged that nine divisions, including two airborne, would be available for the actual assault, with twenty earmarked as follow-up divisions. Four US and three British divisions would be sent back to Britain from the Mediterranean after 1 November. With regard to future operations in this theatre, Trident confirmed that there should be subsequent assaults to Husky, with the aim of knocking Italy out of the war. The Americans opted for Sardinia, while the British wanted to invade the Italian mainland, but no decision was made.

It was clearly helpful that COSSAC knew the forces that would be at his disposal, but the critical factor was the amount of amphibious shipping which would be available. The production of landing craft, in particular, in the USA was low throughout 1943, and there were the demands from the Pacific to be met. It did not appear that there would be anything like enough to transport the seven assault divisions across the Channel. Consequently, the COSSAC planners decided that the initial assault could be undertaken by only three divisions. He accepted the Combined Commanders' conclusion that the Caen sector was the only suitable area for the assault and intended to use the airborne divisions to secure the flanks of the beachhead. Once ashore, the invasion force would advance into the Cotentin peninsula to secure Cherbourg, and then move south and west into Brittany and across the Seine. Simultaneously, COSSAC had to develop two further plans. The first, Cockade, was a series of deception operations designed to keep the German forces pinned down in the West. It had three elements. Starkey was aimed at an early reduction in strength of the Luftwaffe in northern France and the Low Countries through a feint assault on the Pas De Calais. This was mounted on 8 September 1943, with British forces carrying out an embarkation exercise on the Kent coast. However, the Germans failed to react and so it was a failure. Wadham was aimed at Brittany and was an American responsibility. It consisted of air attacks on U-boat bases, air reconnaissance, the mobilization of certain divisions in the USA, and the leakage of false information. The final element, Tindall, was designed to tie down German forces in Norway through air reconnaissance and the display of dummy aircraft and gliders on Scottish airfields. The other area that COSSAC

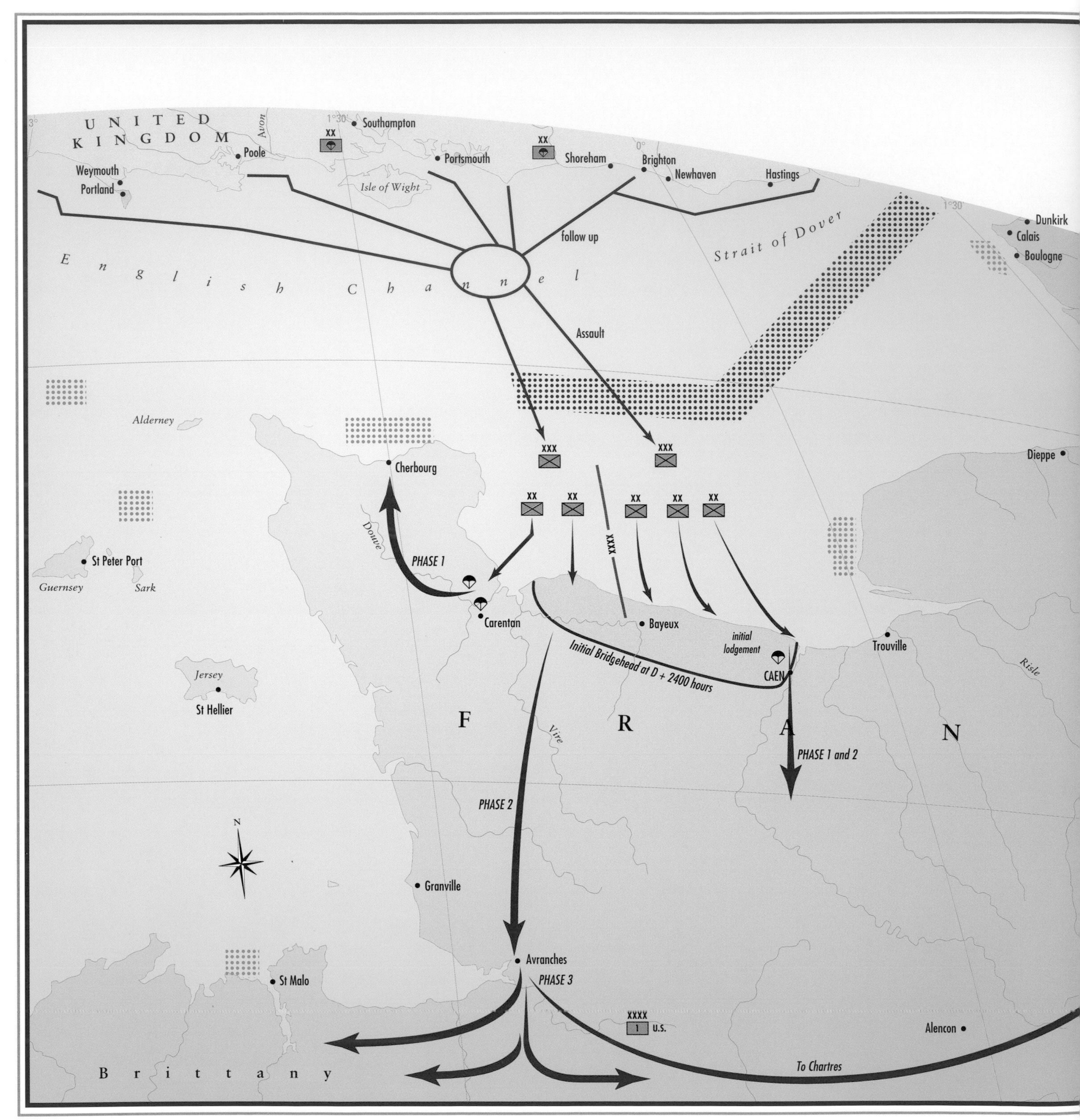

Apart from extending to initial assault westwards and increasing the force to five divisions, with separate sectors for the American and British/Canadian formations, the main difference from the COSSAC plan was the decision that the Americans carry out the break-out from the west rather than the British and Canadians across the Seine. Instead, they would shield the break-out and draw the maximum German forces away from the Americans.

had to consider was what to do in the event of a weakening of the German defences in the West. He drew up plans under the codename Rankin to deal with three eventualities. Rankin A was based on the premise that the Germans thinned out their coastal defences, but did not abandon any

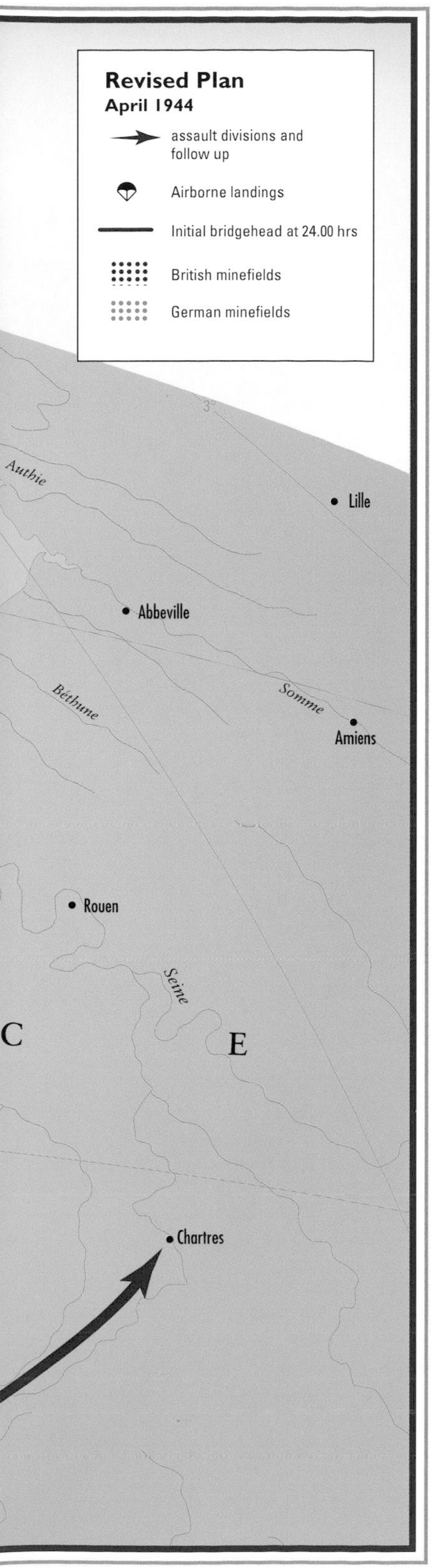

territory. Rankin B dealt with evacuation of a portion or portions of the defences, while Rankin C was in response to a sudden German collapse and did forecast what eventually came to pass, namely the occupation of Berlin by the Allies and the division of Germany into zones of occupation.

COSSAC's plan for the cross-Channel invasion was presented at the Allied conference held at Quebec (Quadrant) in August 1943. The Sicily landings had taken place on 10 July. The coast defences were comparatively weak and what counter-attacks there were against the beachheads were hesitant. Only the airborne element did not go well. Poor navigation and high winds resulted in scattered drops mainly in the wrong place. Apart from this, in the view of the COSSAC staff there was little relevant to Overlord, which Round-Up had now been renamed. The Americans now had a change of heart over the next objective and agreed that, with Italy near to collapse, landings should take place on the mainland. This meant, however, that landing craft due to be returned to Britain and others which were to be redeployed to Burma would now be retained in the Mediterranean. These measures were approved at Quadrant, as was the COSSAC Overlord plan. It was recognized, however, that the size of the German forces in France was a very significant factor in mounting Overlord and that the initial assault force should, if possible, be increased by 25 per cent. This, however, was dependent on more amphibious shipping becoming available than was forecast. Quadrant also took on an American proposal for landings in the south of France. These were seen both as a diversion and an adjunct to Overlord. But if the German strength grew so strong as to put Overlord in doubt, a new plan, Imperator, was to be drawn up for an invasion of Norway. This reflected a near obsession on the part of the British prime minister, who had throughout the past three years constantly prodded his staff to consider an attack on this country.

COSSAC was now instructed to proceed with the detailed planning and preparation for Overlord. Ground forces, in the shape of the British 21st Army Group and US 1st Army Group, were already being allocated to him, although the latter was as yet a paper organization. Two commanders had been appointed. The Overlord air commander was to be Sir Trafford Leigh-Mallory, whose Allied Expeditionary Air Force (AEAF) of fighters and day bombers of the US Ninth Air Force and British 2nd Tactical Air Force, together with transport aircraft, was already in being. The naval commander was to have been the Commander-in-Chief Portsmouth, Admiral Sir Charles Little, but Churchill

Eisenhower and Montgomery attend a U.S. exercise in early 1944. Both men made a great effort to be seen by their troops.

objected to this on the grounds that he lacked the necessary capacity to deal with such a major undertaking. Instead, he proposed Sir Bertram Ramsay, the man who had masterminded the evacuation from Dunkirk, and had then been the deputy naval commander for Torch and in charge of the naval forces supporting the British landings on Sicily. He had also served as a member of the Combined Commanders. This was accepted by the Combined Chiefs of Staff, although Ramsay himself would not return to Britain until December 1943. A land commander had yet to be chosen, as had the Supreme Commander, although the US media had concluded that Marshall was the front-runner. This left COSSAC himself in an awkward position, since he had no executive powers. His charter therefore had to be hastily amended by the Combined Chiefs of Staff.

The Italian landings duly went ahead. The British made virtually unopposed landings in the toe of Italy on 3 September. In Lisbon, Portugal, on the same day, an Italian representative signed an armistice agreement with the Allies. It was agreed that this would be kept secret until the second landing. This took place at Salerno on 8 September in the face of fierce and unexpected German opposition. There was also a serious flaw in the planning in that the beachhead was too wide for the available amphibious lift, making it difficult to defend. Even so, the Germans did eventually withdraw, enabling the Allies to break out. But hopes that Rome might be quickly secured were soon dashed. The Germans reacted quickly, pouring in reinforcements through northern Italy and taking advantage of the hilly and mountainous terrain. The autumn rains slowed the Allied progress still further and by the end of the year they were held up by the formidable Gustav Line in the mountains south of Rome. This was to have a bearing on Overlord.

Allied relations in the Mediterranean became strained in autumn 1943. In the immediate aftermath of the Italian surrender, Churchill gave orders for the Dodecanese islands in the Aegean to be occupied. It was part of his desire to bring Turkey into the war on the Allied side and develop a campaign in the Balkans. The problem was that the British garrisons on the islands lacked air support and the Americans were not prepared to divert any from Italy. The German forces in Greece took advantage of this and overran the garrison on Cos at the beginning of October. Churchill ignored advice to withdraw the remaining garrisons and they, too, were forced to surrender. It was another salutary lesson that air-power rather than sea power was often the decisive factor.

Battle-hardened US and British divisions were sent back from Italy to Britain in line with the decision made at Trident. The question over who would be the overall commander for Overlord was also finally resolved. It had been agreed that it should be an American, while his subordinate single-service commanders were to be British. Roosevelt wanted to appoint Marshall, as much as anything to reward him for his outstanding service as Chairman of the Joint Chiefs of Staff. Marshall himself was more than willing. But others close to the President advised him that Marshall was more valuable where he was and, indeed, would be very difficult to replace. The only other option was Eisenhower, who now had over a year's experience as a coalition commander and certainly had the diplomatic skills to bind the Allies together, even if he had no combat experience alower level. As for the ground commander, Montgomery was the obvious choice. In spite of his bumptious character, which did at times irritate Americans, he had clarity of mind and drive, and had proved himself the most successful British general of the war so far. Thus, at the end of 1943, both handed over their commands, with Eisenhower being replaced by General Sir Henry Wilson.

At the beginning of January, Montgomery arrived back in Britain, while Eisenhower flew back to the States for a short break. But they left a skeleton in the Italian cupboard. As early as October 1943, with the Allied advance slowing, thought began to be given to making an outflanking attack from the sea. By the end of November this had crystallized into a landing at Anzio, just over thirty miles south of Rome, once the Allied forces had reached a point fourty miles to the south of the Italian capital. Going back to the basic measure of amphibious shipping, the LST, there were 105 in theatre at the time. Fifty-six of these should have been sent back to Britain for Overlord by mid-December. But, in view of the stalemate on the Gustav Line, General Mark Clark, who had originated the Anzio plan and was commanding the US Fifth Army, now proposed that it be mounted as soon as possible. Churchill and Roosevelt agreed that the LSTs could be retained. The Anzio landings duly went ahead on 22 January 1944. They achieved initial surprise, but instead of exploiting this and advancing inland, the landing force concentrated on consolidating the beachhead. The Germans soon reacted and the Allies found themselves fighting desperately to retain their foothold. As for the main force, it continued to butt its head in vain against the Gustav Line. The upshot was that the majority of the LSTs earmarked for Overlord had to be retained to support the Anzio beachhead. This would influence the timing of Overlord.

Eisenhower had already seen a copy of the COSSAC plan for Overlord at the end of October 1943, well before he was given overall command of it, and commented that there was insufficient punch in the initial attack. Montgomery had his first sight of it when he was shown a copy by Churchill during a stopover at Marrakesh on his way back to Britain. He agreed with Eisenhower's view and also stated that the landing front was too narrow and would inevitably lead to congestion on the beaches as follow-up forces were landed. He wanted each corps to have its dedicated group of beaches so that its follow-up divisions could land on them, and stressed that the British and American beaches must be kept separate. On 3 January he convened the first of many meetings at St Paul's School, London. The COSSAC staff presented their plan, which Montgomery immediately tore to shreds. Four days later, he produced his own plan. The landing frontage was greatly extended and now stretched from the east coast of the Cotentin peninsula to the west bank of the River Orne. Five divisions would now make the initial assault, two from the US First Army in the west and three from the British Second Army in the east. The task of the Americans would be to seize Cherbourg and then advance south and west into Brittany and east towards Paris, while the British provided a shield for them. It was, in many ways, remarkably similar to the Combined Commanders' appreciation of February 1943.

But COSSAC had been constrained by likely amphibious shipping availability and doubts remained whether there would be sufficient to support a five-division landing.

Eisenhower arrived in Britain on 12 January. Two days later General Morgan held his last weekly staff meeting, and on 17 January Eisenhower took over, the headquarters now becoming Supreme Headquarters, Allied Expeditionary Force (SHAEF). He had brought his own chief of staff, Walter Bedell Smith, and so Morgan stepped into the background, although he remained on the SHAEF staff. At the same time, a Deputy Supreme Allied Commander was appointed, the British airman Arthur Tedder, with whom Eisenhower had worked closely in the Mediterranean. On 21 January, Eisenhower held his first conference and approved Montgomery's plan. He was, however, very conscious of the shipping problem. In order to ensure that there was enough for the revised Overlord, he asked the Combined Chiefs of Staff if the invasion could be postponed until June. They eventually agreed, albeit grudgingly, stipulating that D-Day must now be 31 May or a few days either side. There was also the question of the simultaneous landings in the south of France, codenamed Anvil. The British, who had never really been in favour of them, pointed out that this operation merely served to aggravate the shipping problems and pressed for its cancellation. The Americans were resistant to this and the debate continued.

In spite of this, the detailed planning of Overlord could now get underway. There was, however, another debate over how the airborne forces should be used. Eisenhower wanted two airborne divisions in the initial phase, with a third as an immediate follow-up. The British were concerned over the lack of transport aircraft, but were won round when they were assured that these would become available. General Marshall saw them as a spearhead, however. He wanted to use all four airborne divisions in Britain and drop them well inland so as to act as a blocking force against the German mobile reserves moving to counter the landings. Eisenhower resisted this on the grounds that lightly armed paratroops would be no match for tanks. Consequently, the two US airborne divisions would be used to help secure Utah Beach, while the British Division secured the left flank.

Detailed beach reconnaissance was carried out by specialist teams. There was particular concern over the types of obstacle that the Germans were placing on them. Beaches also had to be found in Britain which were similar to those that would be used in Normandy so that the assaulting troops could train on them. The US assault divisions were the 1st Infantry Division, veterans of Tunisia and Sicily, and the unblooded 4th Infantry Division, which arrived in Britain in January 1944. The British contribution was much the same in terms of experience. The 50th (Northumbrian) Division had fought in North Africa from 1941 onwards,

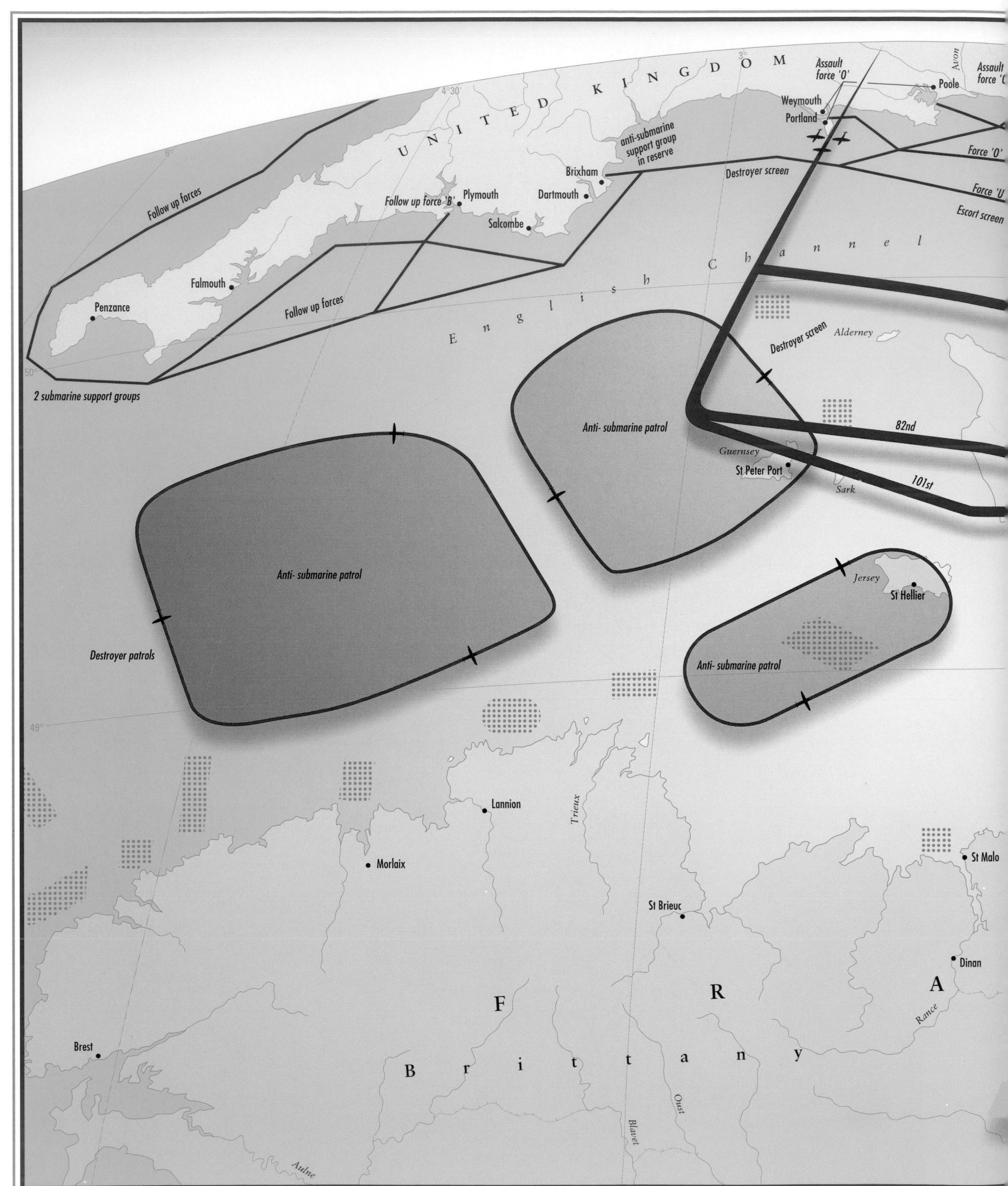

U N I T E D K I N G D O M
Assault force 'O'
Poole
Assault force 'U'
Weymouth
Portland
anti-submarine support group in reserve
Force 'O'
Brixham
Destroyer screen
Force 'U'
Follow up forces
Follow up force 'B'
Plymouth
Dartmouth
Escort screen
Salcombe
E n g l i s h C h a n n e l
Falmouth
Penzance
Follow up forces
Destroyer screen
Alderney
2 submarine support groups
Anti- submarine patrol
82nd
Guernsey
St Peter Port
101st
Sark
Anti- submarine patrol
Jersey
St Hellier
Destroyer patrols
Anti- submarine patrol
Lannion
Trieux
Morlaix
St Malo
St Brieuc
Dinan
F R A
Rance
Brest
B r i t t a n y
Oust
Blavet
Aulne

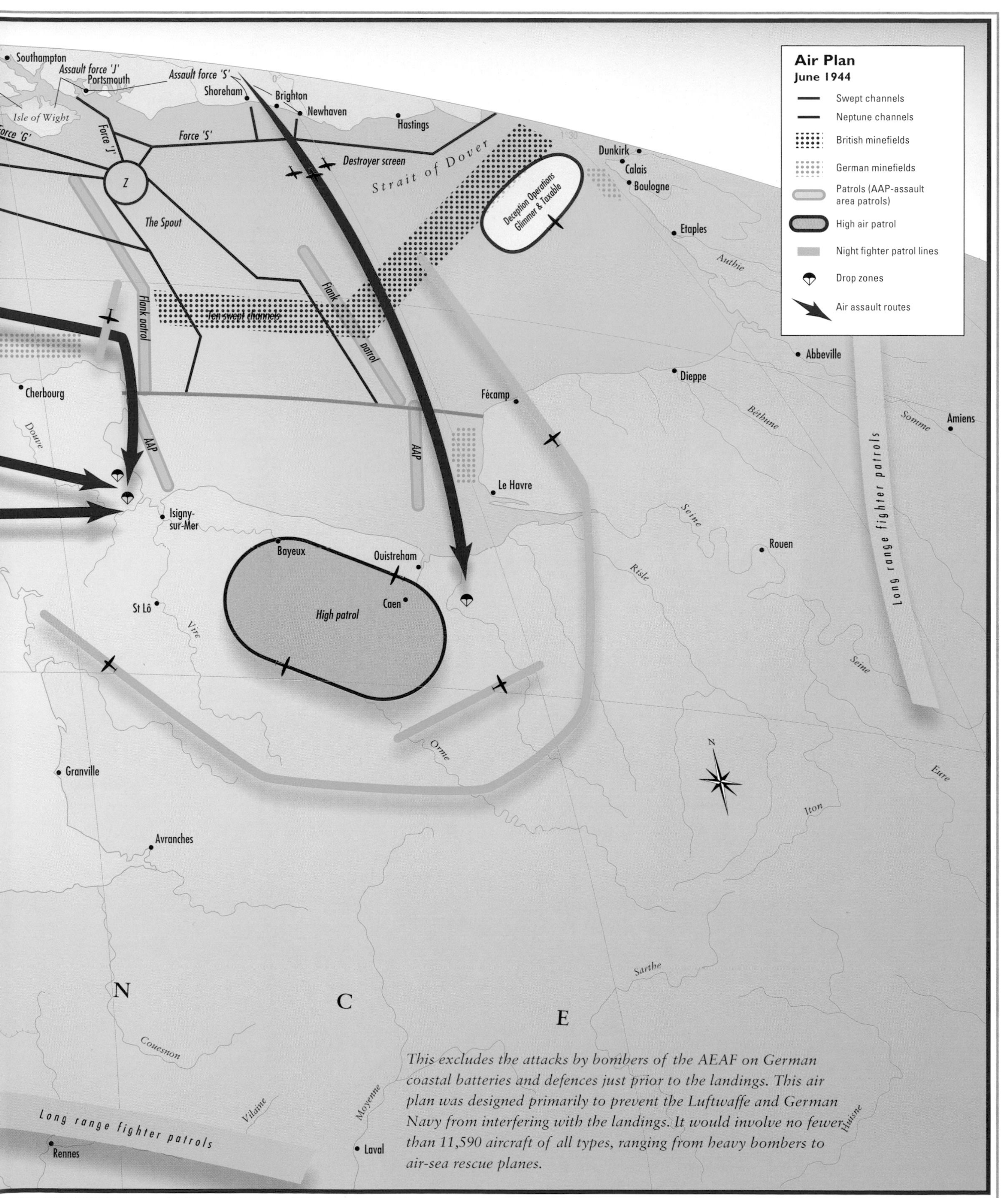

This excludes the attacks by bombers of the AEAF on German coastal batteries and defences just prior to the landings. This air plan was designed primarily to prevent the Luftwaffe and German Navy from interfering with the landings. It would involve no fewer than 11,590 aircraft of all types, ranging from heavy bombers to air-sea rescue planes.

U.S. troops embark in landing craft for one of the early D-Day rehearsals. Later they would progress to cross-decking from transport vessels to landing craft.

while the 3rd Infantry Division had not seen combat since France in 1940. The 3rd Canadian Division had been in Britain since arriving from Canada in July 1941. Of the airborne divisions, the US 82nd had served in North Africa and Sicily, but the 101st was without combat experience, as was the British 6th Airborne Division. Those divisions which had not seen recent combat did, however, have some veterans posted in. Now, while the ground forces intensified their training, other elements of the Overlord plan were already being put into effect.

The Allies knew full well that the Germans were expecting them to launch a cross-Channel assault at some time and that the options of where it would strike were limited. It was also impossible to hide the growing activity in ports along the English South Coast as the shipping required for Overlord was gathered. What the Allies could do, however, was to deceive the Germans. Under the codename of Bodyguard an elaborate deception plan had been drawn up. It had two aims. The first was to present threats elsewhere to dissuade the Germans from bringing in reinforcements from other theatres of war. The other was to make the Germans believe that the main assault would be in the Pas-de-Calais. There were three essential elements to Bodyguard. Fortitude North aimed to tie down the sizeable German forces in Norway through presenting the threat of a diversionary attack, which would be followed by an assault on the Pas-de-Calais in July 1944. One of the key elements was the establishment of a fictional British Fourth Army in Scotland, with its own radio communications. Fortitude South was implemented somewhat later and concentrated on the Pas-de-Calais. It was based on the mythical 1st US Army Group (FUSAG) based in south-east England. The flamboyant General George S. Patton, who was already regarded as one of the most thrusting Allied commanders, was placed in charge in the hope that the Germans would be sure that he would be involved in any major assault. Once the Normandy landings had taken place, Fortitude South would be maintained to convince the Germans that they were a diversion and that the main landing was still to come. Finally, there was Zeppelin, which aimed to tie down German troops in the Balkans. To aid the deception, much use was made of German agents, whom the British had captured and turned. Under what was called the Double Cross system, they transmitted false information back to Germany.

In the event, while the Germans did not reinforce from Norway or the Balkans, they only really believed Fortitude South.

The other part of Overlord which was initiated early was the air campaign. The first task of the AEAF was to fatally weaken the Luftwaffe in France and the Low Countries. On 20 February 1944, the Allied air forces began a systematic assault on the Luftwaffe. The heavy bombers of the Eighth Air Force in Britain and the Fifteenth Air Force in Italy launched massive attacks on German aircraft factories in southern Germany, while the AEAF concentrated on airfields. Big Week, as it became known, struck a crippling blow from which the Luftwaffe never really recovered. However, what the Allied air forces should do next was the subject of a fierce debate. Eisenhower supported a plan conceived by a British scientist, Solly Zuckerman. Based on experience in Italy, he proposed a campaign against communications, with the idea of destroying road and railway communications leading into Normandy so that the Germans could not deploy their reserves. For this to be effective, Eisenhower needed the services of the Eighth Air Force and RAF Bomber Command, which were not part of the AEAF or under his command. They were still pursuing the Pointblank strategy agreed at Casablanca and had very different ideas on how to proceed. The American view, as postulated by General Carl Spaatz, commanding the US Strategic Air Forces (USSAF), was that oil should be the prime target in that this would totally cripple the German war effort. Indeed, he began to concentrate on this target immediately on the conclusion of Big Week. Air Chief Marshal Sir Arthur ('Bomber') Harris, who was in charge of RAF Bomber Command, was convinced that morale held the key. If that of the German people could be broken by a continuation of the 'round the clock bombing' to which they were being subjected, there would be no need for an invasion. The Bomber Barons also resented the prospect of being

The Allied High Command for D-Day – Standing (left to right) General Omar Bradley (First U.S.Army), Admiral Sir Bertram Ramsay (Naval Commander), Air Chief Marshal Sir Trafford Leigh-Mallory (Air Commander), General Walter Bedell Smith (Chief-of-Staff). Sitting (left to right) Air Chief Marshal Sir Arthur Tedder (Deputy Supreme Commander), General Dwight Eisenhower (Supreme Allied Commander), General Sir Bernard Montgomery (21st Army Group).

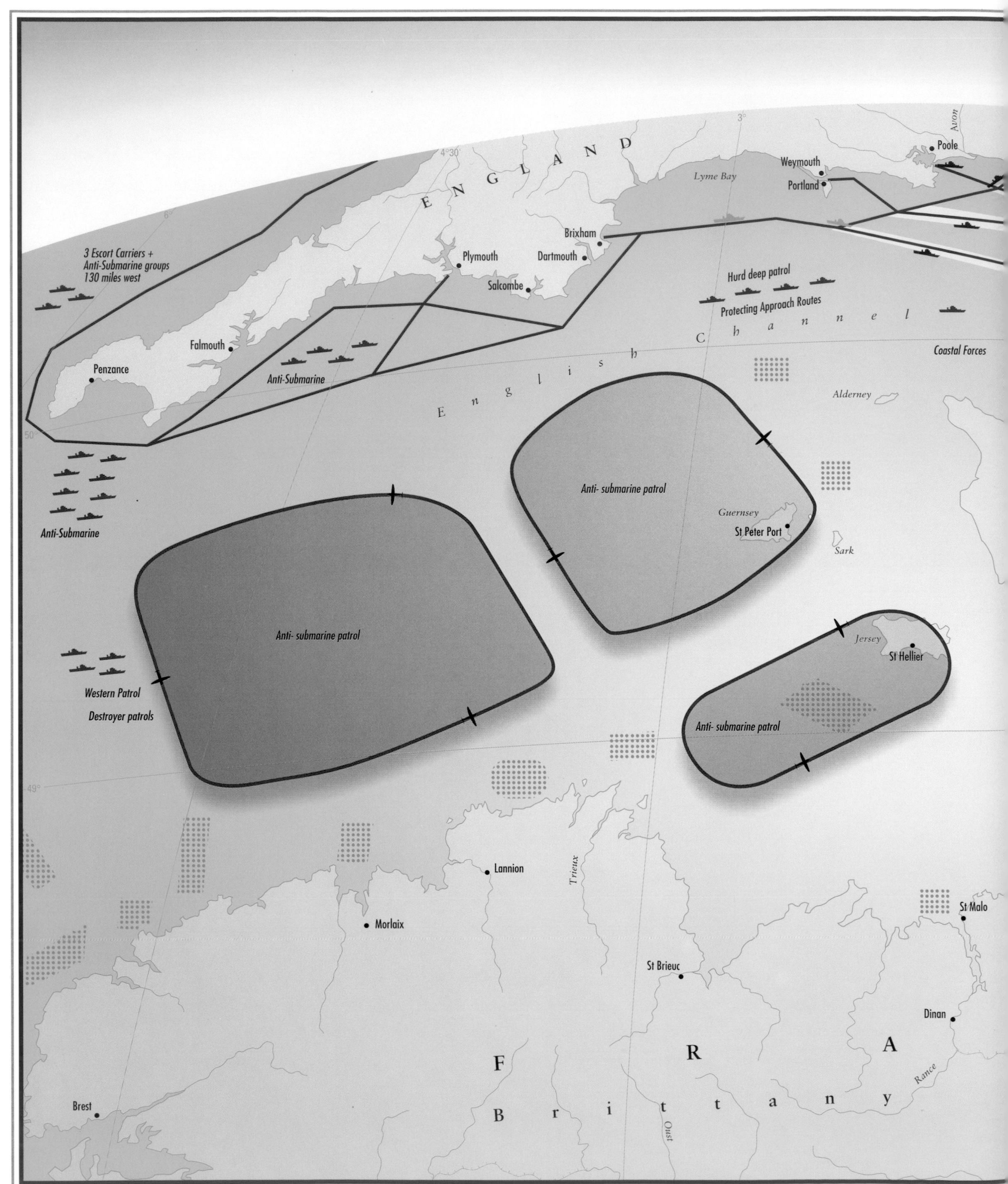

ENGLAND
Poole
Weymouth
Portland
Lyme Bay
Brixham
Dartmouth
Plymouth
Salcombe
Falmouth
Penzance
3 Escort Carriers + Anti-Submarine groups 130 miles west
Anti-Submarine
Hurd deep patrol
Protecting Approach Routes
English Channel
Coastal Forces
Alderney
Anti- submarine patrol
Guernsey
St Peter Port
Sark
Jersey
St Hellier
Western Patrol
Destroyer patrols
Lannion
Trieux
Morlaix
St Brieuc
St Malo
Dinan
Rance
Brest
Oust
FRANCE
Brittany

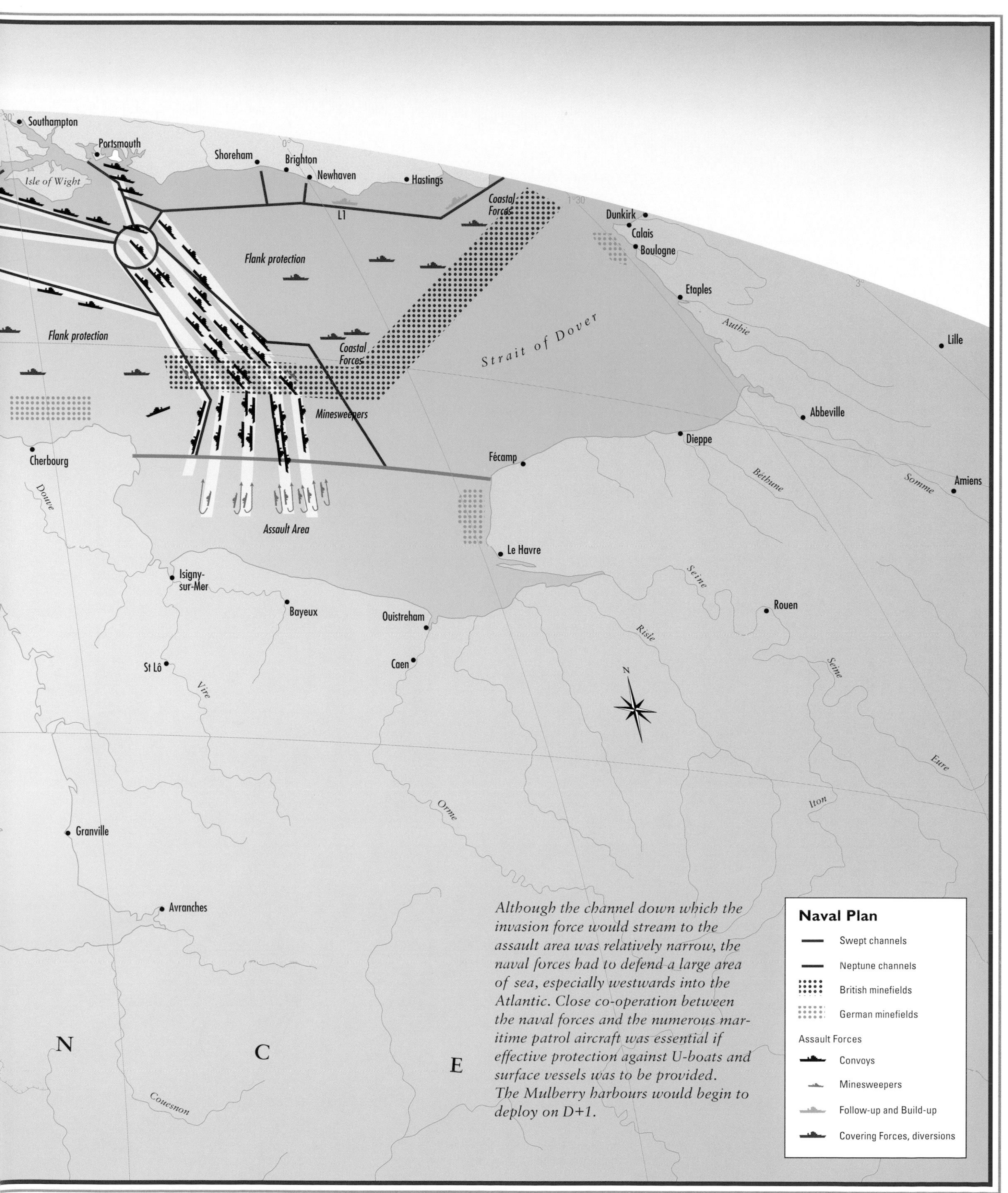

Although the channel down which the invasion force would stream to the assault area was relatively narrow, the naval forces had to defend a large area of sea, especially westwards into the Atlantic. Close co-operation between the naval forces and the numerous maritime patrol aircraft was essential if effective protection against U-boats and surface vessels was to be provided. The Mulberry harbours would begin to deploy on D+1.

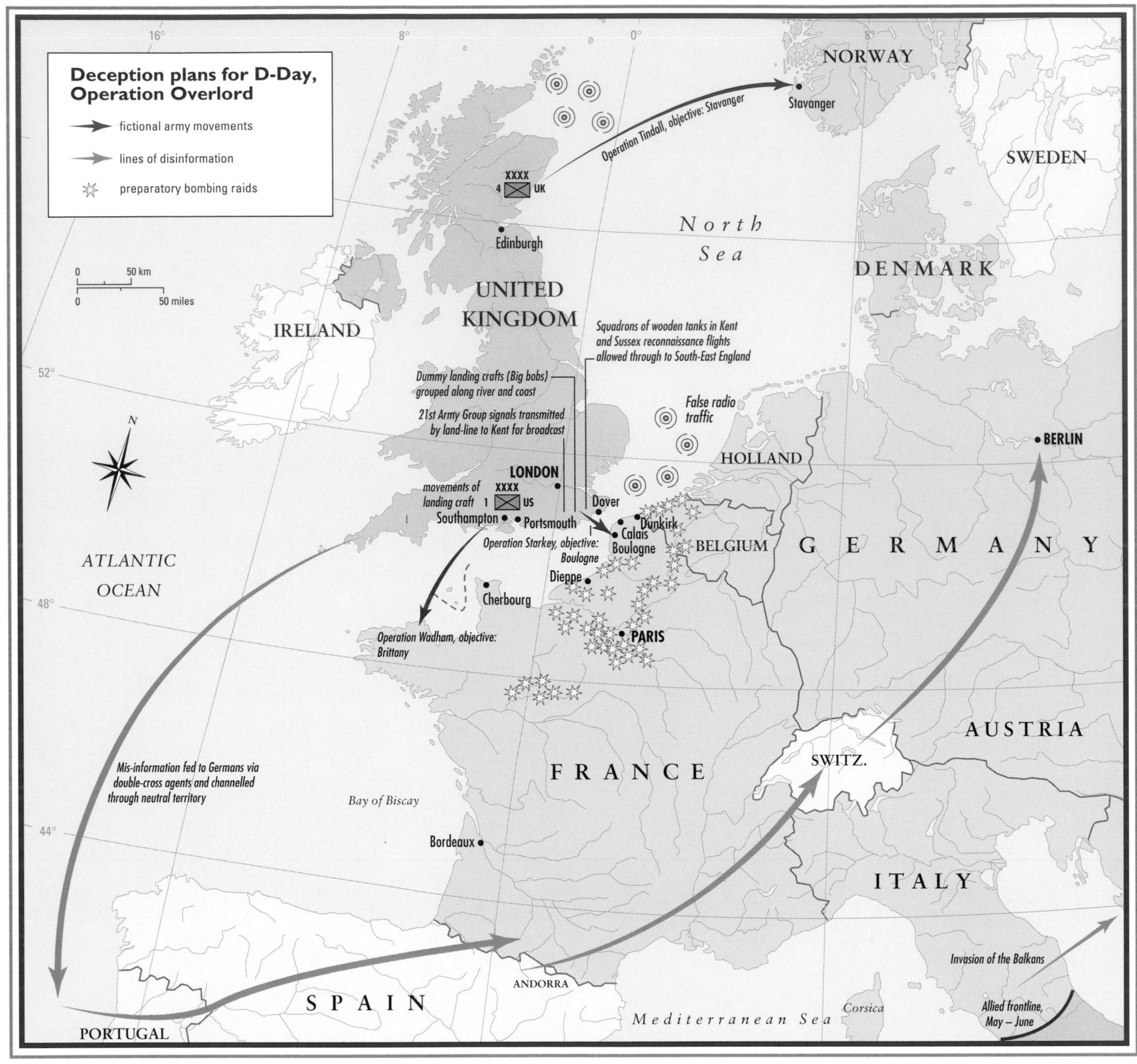

Operation Bodyguard was multi-faceted and very elaborate. The key elements were the dummy US 1st Army Group and British Fourth Army. The part played by the preparatory air campaign, which dropped the major part of its bomb tonnage on areas outside Normandy, should also not be ignored. The double-cross agents, whom the British had turned, were also very valuable.

put under the control of Leigh-Mallory.

Eisenhower believed that campaigns against oil and morale would take too long to achieve a significant effect and his Deputy, Tedder, supported him. The command problem was overcome by Tedder personally conducting the Air Plan, but Spaatz and Harris were still resistant to the Transportation plan. Eisenhower became so frustrated that he threatened to resign. The crunch came at a meeting held on 25 March. Eisenhower stuck to his guns and won the day. The strategic air forces were placed under his control from 14 April and the Transportation plan was put into effect. In support of Fortitude, for every bomb that was dropped in the Normandy area, and this included attacks on coastal batteries and airfields, two were dropped outside it.

While the air debate continued, the question of obtaining sufficient amphibious lift for Overlord remained a problem. The stalemate at Anzio continued and Anvil remained in being. Eisenhower realized that Anvil could not be mounted simultaneously with Overlord and that it should be postponed. This was especially since Wilson, whose forces were still unable to break through the Gustav Line in Italy, warned that a break-out from Anzio was unlikely before mid-May and he wanted to keep his LSTs. Eventually, the Combined Chiefs of Staff agreed to the postponement of Anvil and that LSTs be sent back to Britain from the Mediterranean. They would, however, be replaced by new LSTs from the United States, where production had significantly increased during the winter. This would enable Wilson to capture Rome by the time D-Day took place. Even so, some of the LSTs did not return to Britain until just three weeks before the Normandy landings.

Another race against time involved technology. The post-Dieppe decision that the landings would have to be on open beaches led to the need to develop some form of artificial port to enable reinforcements, supplies, and heavy equipment to be landed.

Work began in Britain in 1943 to develop such a floating harbour. The concept for what eventually became known as the Mulberries was agreed at the Quebec Conference. Two were to be constructed. Mulberry A would support the US beaches and have a capacity of unloading 5,000 tons per day, while Mulberry B, with a 7,000-ton capacity, would operate in the British sector. In essence, they consisted of breakwaters, with piers within them. Construction did not begin until December 1943. Massive amounts of concrete and steel were required, as well as a very large work force. The operation involved firms all over Britain. The various elements were then towed to South Coast ports, where they were sunk to conceal them from German air reconnaissance. Getting them positioned in time was one of Admiral Ramsay's greatest concerns, but it was done. Another means of keeping the Allies supplied once they were ashore was to be the laying of an oil pipeline in the English Channel. Development work on PLUTO (PipeLine Under The Ocean) had been initiated by the British Combined Operations in 1942. A pumping station was established on the Isle of Wight and trawlers towing huge drums of the flexible piping would then lay it

Constructing one of the many massive concrete caissons which provided the foundations for the Mulberry harbours.

German soldiers preparing beach obstacles run for cover as low-flying Allied photograph reconnaissance aircraft passes over. The obstacles shown were designed to impale landing craft and would be hidden at high tide. Some had explosive devices attached.

between here and Cherbourg, once that port had been captured.

The spectre of the beached and knocked-out Churchill tanks at Dieppe prompted the development of specialized types of armoured vehicle. At the forefront of these was the Duplex Drive (DD) swimming tank. This came in the form of a kit consisting of a collapsible canvas screen to give the tank buoyancy and a propeller system, which was driven off the tank's gearbox. It enabled the vehicle to swim at four knots and all the tanks in the initial assault would use this means of getting onto the beaches rather than being landed directly from landing craft. The British also developed other types – flail tanks for clearing mines, bridge-laying tanks, flamethrower tanks, tanks mounting a spigot mortar for attacking concrete blockhouses, and others which would lay track over boggy ground. Known affectionately as the Funnies, they were concentrated in the British 79th Armoured Division.

To give the troops fire support as they were closing into the beaches, the Landing Craft Support (LCS) had been developed. A few, but by no means enough, were used at Dieppe. There were Landing Craft Guns (LCG) each armed with two 4.7-inch guns and LCT (R), which fired salvoes of 5-inch rockets, and, to provide protection against air attack, the Landing Craft Flak (LCF). These would escort the landing waves into the shore, while the warships remained offshore. Each of the five main landing beaches had its own dedicated naval task force, which included a command ship. The warships involved ranged from battleships down to gunboats. Minesweepers, too, played a vital part. First, they had to sweep the approaches to the beaches and then the lanes in which the naval bombardment forces would operate. It was important, too, to protect the flanks of landings, especially against the U-boat threat. To this end, they were covered by anti-submarine vessels and aircraft. All in all, just under 6,500 vessels of all types would be involved.

As April 1944 progressed, operations orders, some running into hundreds of pages, were issued. Nothing could be left to chance and every detail had to be covered. But, for security reasons, the assaulting forces were not informed of their precise objectives. Indeed, security was a constant worry and there were a number of breaches. One scare, which proved to be mere coincidence, was the appearance of many of the Overlord codewords as answers to a *Daily Telegraph* crossword puzzle. There were briefcases with secret documents left unattended, and individuals in the know who let slip indiscreet remarks in public. The biggest scare of all came on the night 27/28 April, when German E-boats got among the amphibious shipping carrying elements of the US 4th Infantry Division during a landing exercise at Slapton Sands on the South Devon coast. Three LSTs were sunk and other vessels damaged, and some 640 soldiers and sailors lost their lives. Ten of them were officers who were cleared to highest security level, Bigot, and there were fears, until their bodies were found, that some might have been captured. As it was, a veil of secrecy was drawn over the incident and it was not until well after the war that the next-of-kin of those who perished learned what had happened. The three torpedoed LSTs represented the only reserve available for Overlord and replacements had to be hurriedly sent from the Mediterranean, such was still the pressure on amphibious shipping.

Another security aspect concerned what to tell the Governments-in-Exile in Britain, in particular de Gaulle and his Free French. His HQ was notoriously insecure and there were fears that the cat would be out of the bag if he was told too early. It was therefore decided to tell de Gaulle only on the very eve of launching Overlord.

Towards the end of April, Montgomery and Ramsay moved to their HQ for Overlord at Southwick House, Portsmouth, while Eisenhower remained at SHAEF, which was located, since March, at Bushey Park close to the Thames on the western outskirts of London. During 3–8 May Ramsay conducted Exercise Fabius, the final invasion exercise, with all five naval task forces being involved. A week later, on 15 May, Eisenhower held a final conference at St Paul's School, London. Both King George VI and Churchill were present and each commander presented his final plan. Montgomery, in particular, spoke with great confidence. He spoke of getting well inland on the first day and would then 'crack about and force the battle to swing our way'. Churchill, who had been pessimistic over the chances of success, and he was by no means alone, was filled with a sense of optimism. Indeed, he wanted to set sail with the invasion force and watch the naval bombardment. It was only by enlisting the help of the King that he was eventually persuaded against this. The only key item not revealed at the conference was the actual date for D-Day, for Eisenhower had still to decide on this and would not do so for another week.

In the meantime, there were a number of further scares. On the night 17/18 May a beach reconnaissance team was captured by the Germans. Luckily, it was in the Pas-de-Calais and so helped further Fortitude South. There were difficulties in bringing the Mulberry parts back to the surface because of pumping equipment inadequacies. A US naval officer mentioned the place and rough date of the invasion and was promptly sent Stateside. Twelve copies of a SHAEF advance communiqué announcing the invasion blew out of a window in the War Office. Eleven were quickly located and the twelfth was handed over to a sentry on Horse Guards Parade by a civilian who was apparently wearing thick glasses. These incidents, and others like them, were wearing on the nerves of those at the very top of the Overlord tree.

As for D-Day itself, it had to fit in with a number of requirements, all weather-related. The air forces wanted a moonlit night so that they could be confident of landing the paratroops and gliders in the right place. The navies wanted to cross the Channel under cover of darkness and to open the bombardment in daylight so that target identification would be easier. The armies wanted to land at low tide and have a full day to consolidate the beachheads. There were just two periods in June in which these conditions were present, one beginning on the 4th and the other later in the month. Eisenhower opted for the night 4/5 June for the mounting of Overlord so as to give himself the maximum possible leeway and informed his subordinate commanders on 23 May that D-Day itself, when the Allies set foot on French soil, would be 5 June.

Now began the move of the ground assault forces to their ports of embarkation. The roads of southern England were clogged with military convoys, all travelling to carefully planned march schedules. The troops moved into staging camps, which were sealed from the outside world. Here they went about their final preparations and briefings in which they were finally told their objectives. In the skies above, the final phase of the preliminary air campaign began. On 31 May, the assembly of the naval task forces started and vessels began to be loaded. That night, ten sonic underwater buoys were laid at the entrances to the lanes which the naval task forces would use to cross the Channel. This was to guide the minesweepers. The BBC

Sherman tanks being loaded on board an LST. They were reversed into the ship so that they would arrive on the beach with their thicker frontal armour to the fore.

began to send coded messages to alert the French Resistance. All seemed to be going generally to plan, but one crucial factor remained a concern.

From 29 May onwards, Eisenhower ordered his chief meteorologist, Group Captain J. M. Stagg, to hold a daily weather briefing for himself and his senior commanders. At the time, there was a hot spell over England, but there were growing doubts that it would hold up. Stagg himself had daily conferences with three agencies, the Admiralty in London, the British Central Forecasting Office at Dunstable in Bedfordshire, and the USAAF weather centre at Teddington on the Thames west of London. From 1 June they were anxiously watching a ridge of high pressure over the Atlantic, which they hoped would reach the British Isles. Signs grew that it was beginning to slip south. Dunstable was gloomy, while Widewing put a more optimistic gloss on its forecasts. The Admiralty took a middle position, but on 3 June began to support the Dunstable view that a depression was about to arrive over the English Channel. Stagg also took the Dunstable view and at 4.15am on 4 June passed this to Eisenhower, who had established himself at Portsmouth two days earlier. At the time, though, the weather was still bright and clear and the assault troops were embarking. At 9.30pm that evening Stagg gave out another forecast. This time he was certain that 5 June would be stormy, with a low cloud base, the very worst conditions. Eisenhower decided to sleep on it, but did go so far as to warn the US Navy carrying the troops to Utah and Omaha, since they had the furthest to go. Eisenhower and his subordinates had another session with Stagg at 4.30am the following morning. By this time the weather was beginning to deteriorate. Stagg said that sea conditions were slightly better, but the cloud base would remain low. Eisenhower turned to his subordinates. Montgomery was all for continuing, Tedder and Leigh-Mallory argued for a postponement, while Ramsay would not commit himself. Eisenhower, conscious that he had only one chance to launch Overlord, decided on a 24-hour postponement and the message was sent out. The US naval task forces and other vessels already at sea returned to port. The only vessels which could not were two British midget submarines deployed off the British landing beaches to act as navigational beacons. They were forced to continue to remain submerged in a sea that grew ever more unruly.

The question that now haunted Eisenhower and, indeed, everyone else involved, was would the weather improve. If it did not, he could not keep the troops cooped up in their ships until the next favourable day, which was 19 June, and to disembark them would have a serious effect on morale. There was also the fear that a delay might compromise the whole operation. On the evening of 4 June, Eisenhower and his commanders met Stagg again at Southwick House. He reported that there would be a 36-hour break in the weather. The rain would stop, the winds would moderate, but cloud would still be present. Montgomery was again for proceeding, Leigh-Mallory and Tedder thought that air operations would be hampered, and Ramsay told Eisenhower that he must tell the US naval task forces one way or the other within the next half hour. If they sailed again and were recalled, it would take them 48 hours to turn round, which would take the invasion outside the window for the right conditions. The ultimate decision rested with Eisenhower. At 9.45 pm he said: 'I am quite positive that the order must be given.' D-Day was on for 6 June and the ships began to sail.

US Paratroopers prepare to board their aircraft on the evening of 5 June.

The assault divisions moved into their concentration areas close to the South Coast in the weeks before D-Day. Apart from the US 29th Division, which was the follow-up division for Omaha, the remainder were deployed from west to east in accordance with the position of their beaches. This avoided the danger of congestion and confusion caused by the various naval forces having to cross one another's paths. Reinforcing formations would move into these concentration areas once they had been vacated by the assault divisions.

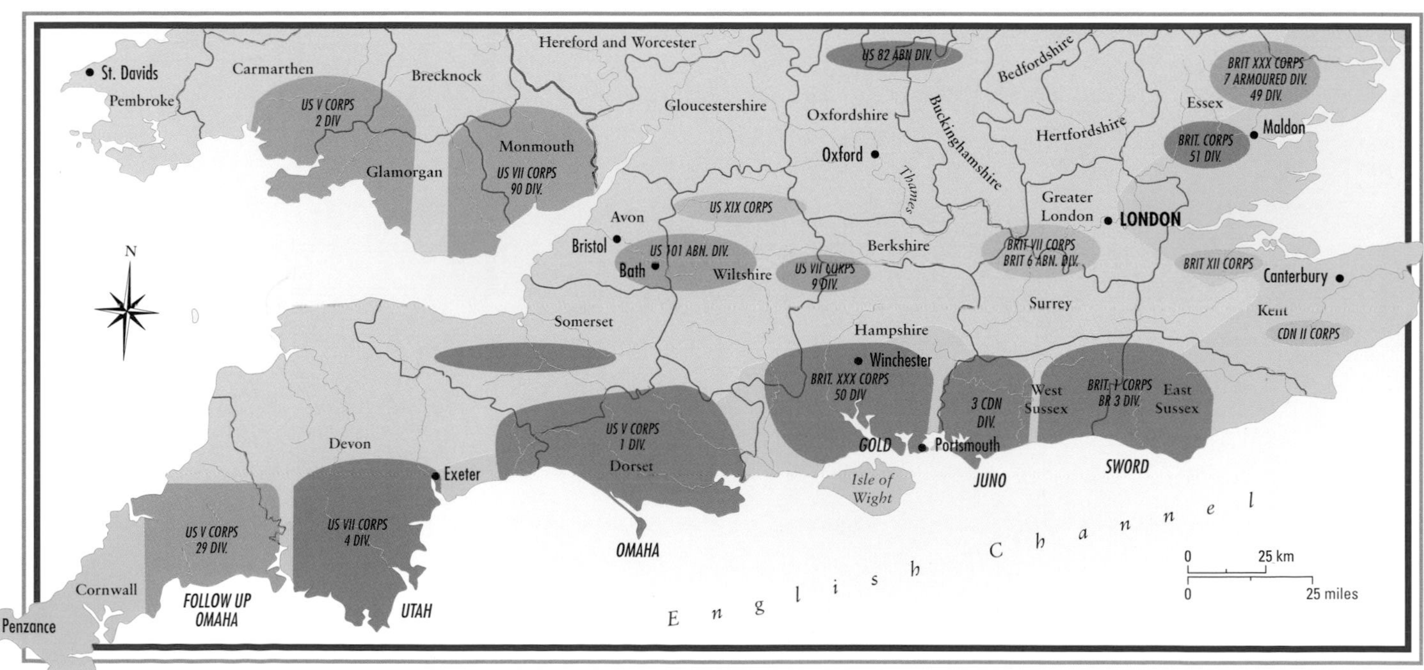

Chapter Two

Fortress Europe

When, in autumn 1940, Hitler decided to abandon the idea of invading Britain and turn on Stalin's Russia, he went over to the defensive in the West. France itself had been split into two as a result of the June 1940 Armistice. The northern half came under German military government. The south was allowed a degree of autonomy under the government of Marshal Philippe Pétain, although the coastal regions remained under Italian (the Mediterranean coast) or German control. The Luftwaffe presence in France remained strong so as to pursue its bombing campaign against Britain, while the Kriegsmarine now deployed to France, notably a significant part of its U-boat arm, which took advantage of the French Atlantic ports. In contrast, the bulk of the ground forces which had taken part in the victorious summer 1940 campaign were redeployed to prepare for the attack on Russia. The rump that remained was formed into Army Group D under the elderly Field Marshal Erwin von Witzleben, who was also made Commander-in-Chief West. His divisions were generally low grade and were seen as little more than a police force.

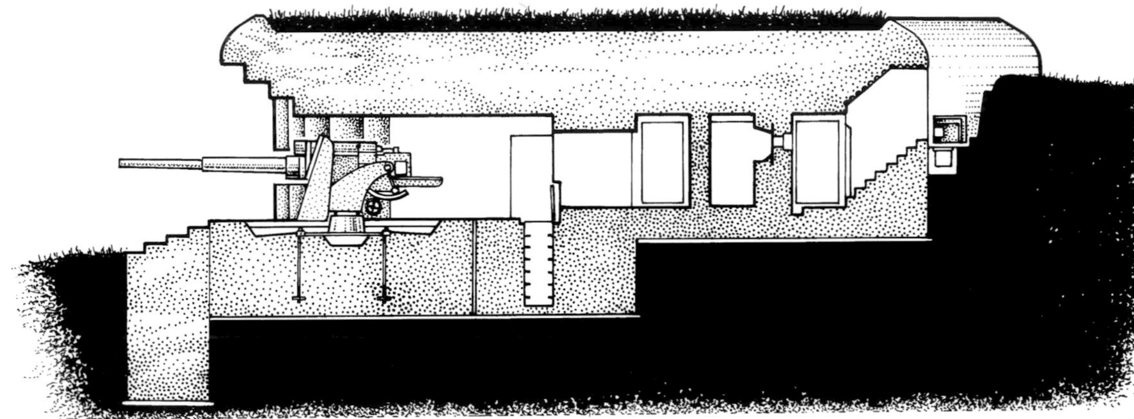

A cross-section of a typical gun emplacement on the Atlantic Wall, which gives an indication of the large amount of concrete used. The gun in this case is a 50mm coastal gun.

Along the coasts work gradually began to emplace coastal batteries. These had initially been deployed to protect Axis shipping in the English Channel during what was to have been Operation Sealion and to bombard the English coast. Fixed concrete emplacements began to be constructed in September 1940, but priority was given to Norway, reflecting Hitler's desire to secure his northern flank for the invasion of Russia. The cross-Channel Commando raids showed how vulnerable the French coast was and the St-Nazaire operation, in particular, concerned Hitler. Priority was therefore given to the protection of ports and to the construction of concrete pens to protect the U-boats from air attack.

Not until 1942 did the creation of what became known as the Atlantic Wall begin in earnest. Many of the ports were personally designated Festungen, or fortresses, by Hitler in the belief that if and when invasion came it would have to be close to a port. He amplified his vision in a directive issued in August 1942, which called for the establishment of a network of concrete strongpoints. These would each be manned by up to seventy men armed with machine guns and anti-tank weapons. In all, there were to be 15,000 of these strongpoints, although Fritz Todt, in charge of the Reich labour organization, doubted whether he could complete more than 6,000 by spring 1943. As 1943 wore on further problems arose. Todt had to

(Right) This map shows the position before Hitler's Directive No. 51 of 3 November 1943 took effect. Prior to this, the biggest weakness that von Rundstedt was suffering was a shortage of mobile formations, with only 21st Panzer Division permanently assigned to him. Many of his other divisions were also low grade.

German machine gun post on the Atlantic Wall.

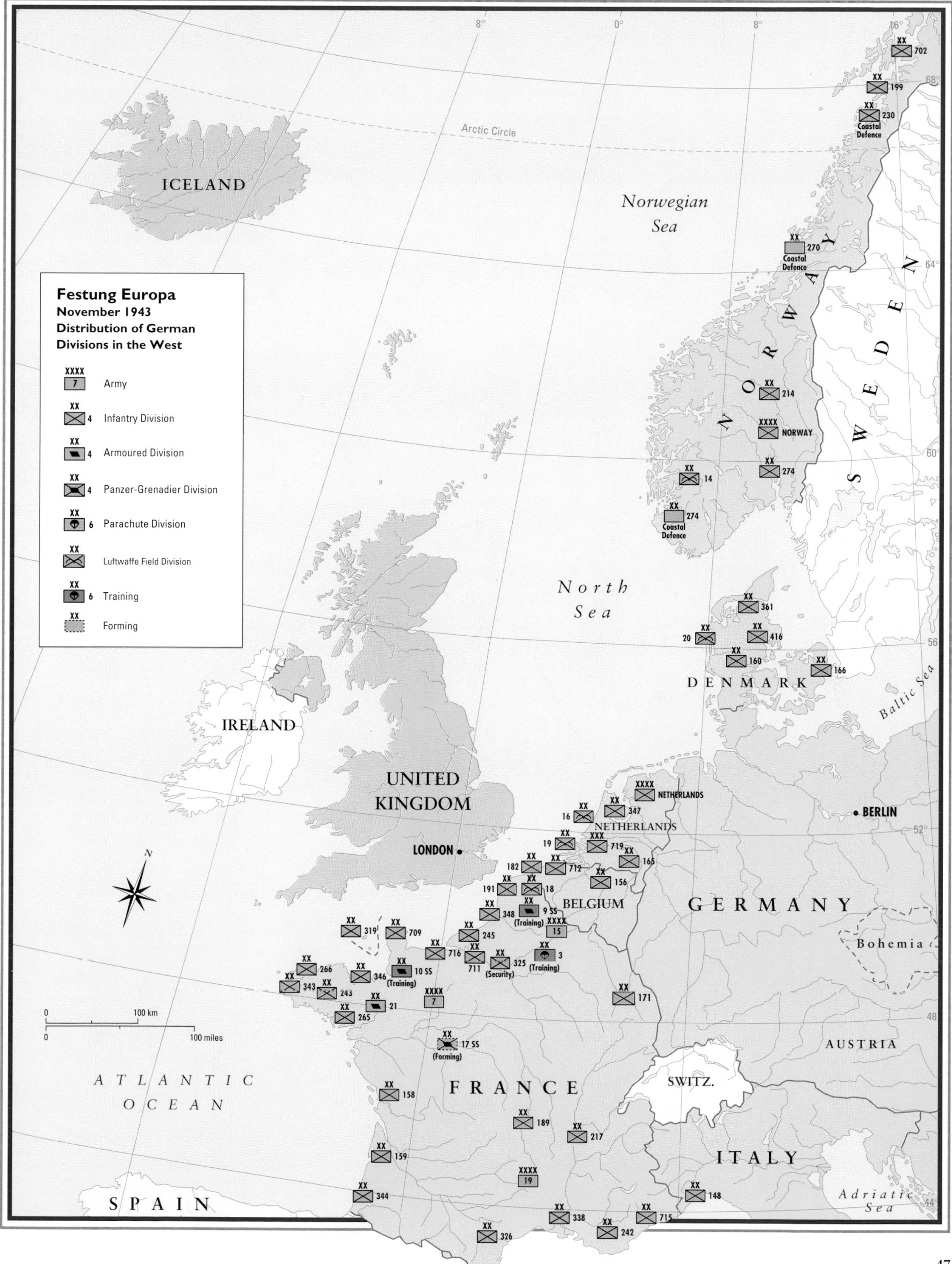
Festung Europa
November 1943
Distribution of German Divisions in the West
Army
Infantry Division
Armoured Division
Panzer-Grenadier Division
Parachute Division
Luftwaffe Field Division
Training
Forming
ICELAND
Arctic Circle
Norwegian Sea
NORWAY
SWEDEN
North Sea
DENMARK
Baltic Sea
IRELAND
UNITED KINGDOM
LONDON
NETHERLANDS
BELGIUM
GERMANY
BERLIN
Bohemia
AUSTRIA
SWITZ.
FRANCE
ITALY
Adriatic Sea
SPAIN
ATLANTIC OCEAN
Coastal Defence
(Training)
(Security)
(Forming)
100 km
100 miles

A sentry guarding a 105mm coastal gun. The armament used in the Atlantic Wall ranged from 25mm anti-tank weapons to massive 305mm guns.

divert some of the labour working on the Atlantic Wall to repair bomb damage in Germany and the decision to begin fortifying the Mediterranean coast after the Allied invasion of Sicily further dissipated the effort.

In March 1942, von Witzleben fell sick and was replaced by Gerd von Rundstedt, the doyen of the Prussian officer corps. By this time, his forces had been increased from a low of eighteen divisions during the winter 1940–41 to twenty-five, which were organized in three armies. First Army covered the coastal region of south-west France, while the north-west, from the River Loire to Caen, came under Seventh Army. Finally, Fifteenth Army was responsible for the coast from Caen to the Belgian port of Zeebrugge. The Dutch coast, which also came under von Rundstedt, was the responsibility of the military commander in the Netherlands, a Luftwaffe general. The chain of command, however, was by no means clear-cut. Von Rundstedt may have been the theatre commander, but he was actually only responsible for coast defence and the Navy and Luftwaffe were only answerable to him in this respect. Internal security came under the military governors of France and Belgium and Luftwaffe General Christiansen in the Netherlands and they answered directly to Hitler's supreme headquarters, the Oberkommando der Wehrmacht (OKW). There was also a separate chain of command for the SS police. Consequently, in many ways von Rundstedt had his hands tied.

Von Rundstedt's forces became more stretched in November 1942. In response to the French scuttling their fleet at Toulon, Hitler ordered the military occupation of Vichy France. But what concerned von Rundstedt most was a lack of mobile reserves. He became convinced that the only way to defeat an amphibious assault was on the beaches themselves. Reserves which could be quickly deployed were essential. During the last half of 1942 and in 1943 he did receive Panzer and Panzer Grenadier divisions, but these were either newly formed or mere skeletons from the Eastern Front. The former needed training, while the latter, once they had been brought back up to strength, were redeployed to other theatres of war. Indeed, by autumn 1943 von Rundstedt was left with just three Panzer Grenadier divisions as a mobile reserve, one of

The most significant improvement since November 1943, apart from strengthening the physical defences of the Atlantic Wall, was the dramatic increase in the number of panzer divisions. Hitler's decision to place four of them under direct control as OKW reserve would prove a costly error. The Static divisions were designated such, because they had very limited transport and were not capable of quick redeployment.

Festung Europa, German Defences in the West
June 1944

Armoured Reserves: in OKW Reserve
Army boundaries
Army Group boundaries
Rear boundary of the OB West
XX Field Infantry Division
XX Panzer Division
XX Parachute Division
XX Static Division
XX Refitting
XX Training
XX Luftwaffe Infantry Division

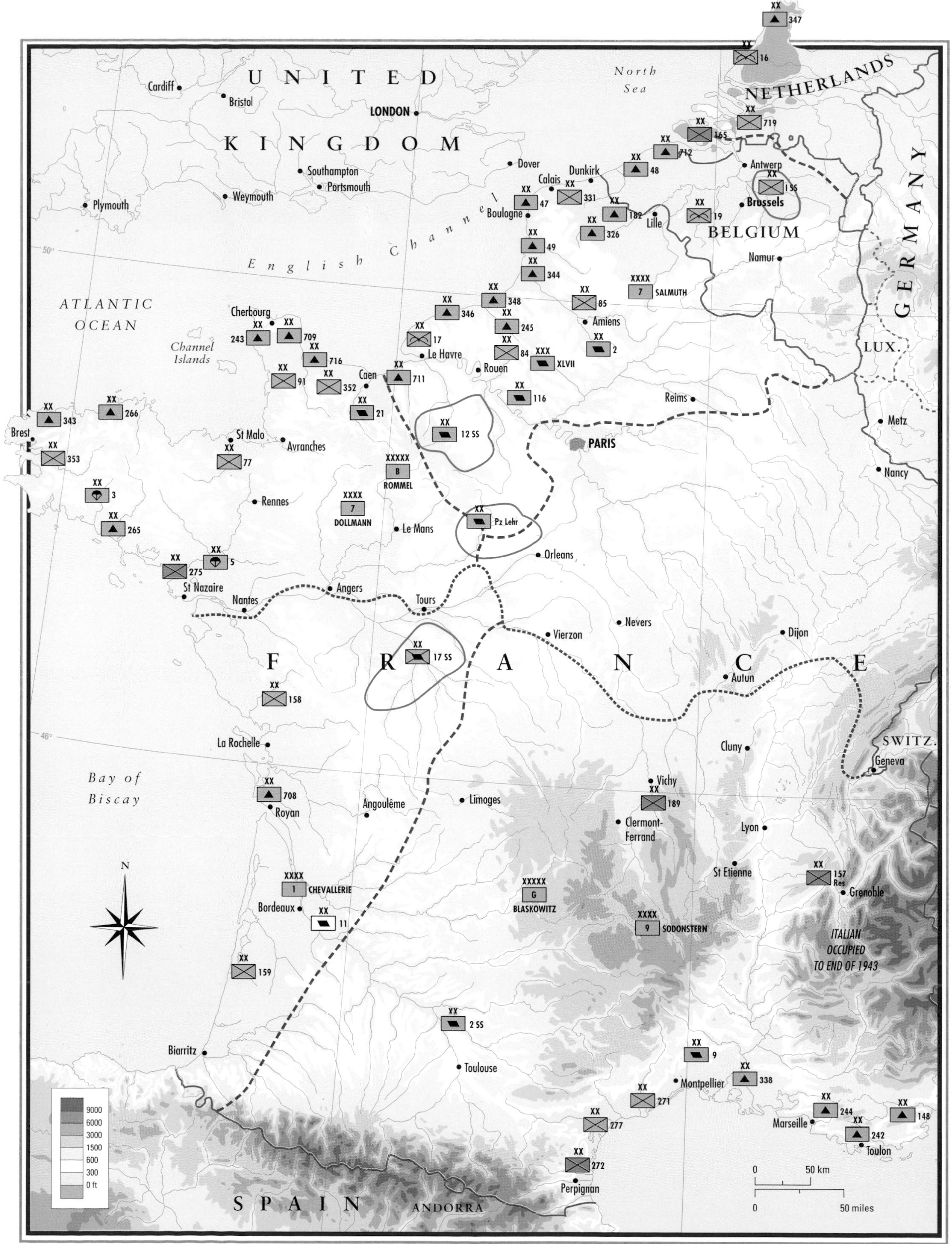
UNITED KINGDOM
Cardiff
Bristol
LONDON
Southampton
Portsmouth
Weymouth
Plymouth
Dover
North Sea
NETHERLANDS
GERMANY
BELGIUM
LUX.
SWITZ.
SPAIN
ANDORRA
ATLANTIC OCEAN
Channel Islands
English Channel
Bay of Biscay
FRANCE
ITALIAN OCCUPIED TO END OF 1943
Calais
Dunkirk
Boulogne
Lille
Antwerp
Brussels
Namur
Amiens
Le Havre
Rouen
Caen
Cherbourg
Reims
Metz
Nancy
PARIS
St Malo
Avranches
Brest
Rennes
Le Mans
Orleans
Angers
Tours
Nantes
St Nazaire
Vierzon
Nevers
Dijon
Autun
Cluny
Geneva
La Rochelle
Vichy
Clermont-Ferrand
Lyon
St Etienne
Grenoble
Royan
Angoulême
Limoges
Bordeaux
Biarritz
Toulouse
Montpellier
Marseille
Toulon
Perpignan
XX 347
XX 16
XX 719
XX 165
XX 712
XX 48
XX 155
XX 331
XX 47
XX 182
XX 19
XX 326
XX 49
XX 344
XXXX 7 SALMUTH
XX 85
XX 348
XX 346
XX 245
XX 17
XX 84
XXX XLVII
XX 2
XX 243
XX 709
XX 716
XX 91
XX 352
XX 711
XX 21
XX 116
XX 12 SS
XX 343
XX 266
XX 353
XX 77
XXXXX B ROMMEL
XX 3
XXXX 7 DOLLMANN
XX 265
XX Pz Lehr
XX 275
XX 5
XX 17 SS
XX 158
XX 708
XX 189
XX 157 Res
XXXXX G BLASKOWITZ
XXXX 1 CHEVALLERIE
XX 11
XXXX 9 SODONSTERN
XX 159
XX 2 SS
XX 9
XX 338
XX 271
XX 277
XX 272
XX 244
XX 242
XX 148
N
9000
6000
3000
1500
600
300
0 ft
0 50 km
0 50 miles
50°
46°

which was entirely untrained.

Von Runstedt's growing concern, set against the backdrop of a now inevitable Allied invasion of Western Europe, prompted him to present a survey on the defences in his theatre to Hitler. He pointed out that he had some 1,600 miles of coast to defend and there was no way in which a solid barrier could be created. As it was, he could provide little more than a screen of troops to cover the Atlantic coast, that is if he was to develop any form of effective defence on the more vulnerable Channel coast. While the Atlantic Wall was "indispensable and valuable for battle as well as propaganda", an invasion could only be defeated through the use of "a mobile and armoured reserve", which he did not have. Von Rundstedt's report had the desired effect. On 3 November 1943, less than a week after he submitted it, Hitler issued Directive No 51.

Sowing 'dragon's teeth'. These concrete obstacles were used to prevent tanks from getting off the beach.

It accepted that everywhere German forces were now on the defensive: "The danger in the East remains, but a greater danger now appears in the West; an Anglo-Saxon landing!" To this end, the West would be reinforced, especially with mobile forces, anti-tank weapons, and artillery. Two days later, he ordered Field Marshal Erwin Rommel to carry out an inspection tour of the defences.

In British and, to a lesser degree, American eyes, Rommel was an outstanding general who had demonstrated a flair in North Africa, which had earned him the name 'the Desert Fox'. He had latterly been given command of Army Group B, with responsibility for the defence of northern Italy. However, Albert von Kesselring, the German theatre commander had decided that he would defend the whole of Italy and not just the north and so Rommel found himself with a headquarters, but with no role to play. Now he went racing round the coasts of France and the Low Countries, while von Rundstedt wondered whether he had been sent to replace him as commander-in-chief. His own view of Rommel reflected that of many other senior German officers, namely that he had won his spurs in a mere sideshow and had not experienced the 'real war' on the Eastern Front. Von Rundstedt respected Rommel's bravery and considered him a good operational commander, but not fitted for the higher levels of command. Indeed, he called Rommel 'Field Marshal Cub'. But the Desert Fox had experienced the growing matériel power of the Anglo-US alliance at first hand and had developed a healthy respect for it.

Von Rundstedt did not actually meet Rommel until 19 December 1943, at the conclusion of Rommel's tour of inspection. Von Rundstedt stressed his lack of a decent reserve and Rommel appears to have agreed that the situation appeared grim. Eight days later, Rommel presented his report to C-in-C West. He believed that the most likely landings areas were the Pas-de-Calais and the area between Boulogne and the River Somme. He foresaw the Allies enjoying air superiority, which meant that it would be difficult to deploy the reserves if they were too far inland. Furthermore, the Atlantic Wall, as it stood, would not stand up to the might of the Allied air and sea bombardment and, once the Allies had secured beachheads, it would be very difficult to drive them back into the sea.

They must therefore be defeated on the beaches, which was in line with von Rundstedt's thinking. Rommel appeared to be reasonably satisfied with the Pas-de-Calais sector and wanted to concentrate on strengthening the Boulogne-Somme coast, especially through laying extensive minefields and beach obstacles. He also wanted to deploy two of the reserve divisions in this sector. Rommel's report was generally accepted by Hitler and he was placed in charge of the coast from the Netherlands to the mouth of the River Loire, but under von Rundstedt's overall command. He now set in train a high-pressure programme to strengthen the defences, which soon began to show results.

By March 1944 von Rundstedt had eight Panzer and two Panzer Grenadier divisions under his command. These were formed into Panzer Group West under the command of Geyr von Schweppenburg. At the same time, OKW was looking again at the likely Allied landing areas. They concluded that Normandy was also a possibility and that there could be feints, both on the Atlantic and Mediterranean coasts. Von Schweppenburg saw this estimate as a strong reason for keeping the armour concentrated so that it could strike in any direction. Rommel, however, was still insistent that it be deployed close to the coasts, which, of course, meant dissipating it. Von Rundstedt tried to calm the troubled waters with a compromise. He allocated three divisions to Army Group B and the same number to Army Group G, which covered the Atlantic coast south of the Loire and the Mediterranean. The remaining four would be retained by Panzer Group West. This did not really satisfy either and at the end of April Hitler decided that Panzer Group West was not to be deployed without his permission. Thus, von Rundstedt had lost all control of his mobile divisions. This would have a significant bearing on what actually happened on D-Day.

On 8 May 1944, von Rundstedt made another appreciation of the situation. He was well aware of the growing intensity of the Allied air campaign and intelligence reports suggested that the invasion might well take place during the first half of May and that it could fall anywhere between the Scheldt and the tip of Brittany. He noted that the main Allied concentrations were in the Southampton-Portsmouth area and that their preparations were complete, which was still far from the case. He believed, however, that the most likely landing area would be along the Boulogne-Normandy coast. Once the danger period passed with no move from the enemy, von Rundstedt breathed a sigh of relief.

A growing distraction for von Rundstedt was the French Resistance, which was gathering strength. It had always been a major target for SOE, but, as in the other countries of Occupied Europe, it took time to create an effective network. One of the main problems was the number of Resistance organisations involved. Indeed, no fewer than six SOE sections were involved with France, ranging from F Section, perhaps the best known, which worked with the independents, RF Section, responsible for the Gaullists, who also had their own co-ordinating section in de Gaulle's headquarters in Britain, and the small EU/P Section, which handled Polish agents. There were also Socialist Resistance movements and, after Hitler's invasion of Russia, a Communist organization. However, it was F Section which took the lead as far as the British were concerned. Its first task was to establish Resistance networks, or 'circuits'. SOE agents usually operated in teams of three – an organizer, a radio operator and a courier. Many of the last-named were women, since they tended to attract less suspicion. In the early years, SOE found that it was easier to operate in Vichy France, rather than in the German-occupied north. Even so, the south had its dangers, notably from the paramilitary police force, the Milice. While F Section concentrated on those groups with no significant political affiliations, it also made efforts to co-ordinate with other networks, with varying success. One of the important aspects of SOE's job was to arrange for supplies of weapons, explosives and ammunition to be delivered to the Resistance. These were usually dropped by parachute.

Initially, the Resistance concentrated on making life difficult for the Germans through sabotage of French industry working for them, ambushes of vehicles and assassinations. It also published underground newspapers. But only a very small percentage of the French people were involved. Most understandably tried to get on with their lives as best they could. While some of Right Wing persuasion actively collaborated with the occupiers and were responsible for the betrayal of Resistance members, the majority had little option but to offer passive collaboration, especially when German troops were billeted in their homes. Yet, the fact that most people attempted to lead a normal life acted as a vital camouflage, without which the Resistance would have found it very much more difficult to operate.

In 1942, the Germans instituted compulsory labour service in Germany for young Frenchmen. To avoid this, many fled to the forested and hilly hinterland of southern France. This came to the attention of the SOE and its US counterpart, the Office of Strategic Services (OSS), and arms supplies were arranged for the Maquis, as these groups were known, from the Corsican brushwood which had traditionally hidden resisters. It was clear, however, that much closer co-operation was needed for the Resistance to become truly effective. De Gaulle had sent his own emissary, Jean Moulin, to France at the beginning of 1942 to effect this, but it took him nearly eighteen months to form the Conseil National de la Resistance (CNR). This had representatives of all the main Resistance groups and was directed by de Gaulle from London. Shortly afterwards, Moulin was betrayed by a fellow agent under torture by the Gestapo and was executed.

The establishment of the CNR was, however, timely. The COSSAC plan for the invasion of France envisaged a preliminary phase designed to wear the Germans down. Besides air and sea action, propaganda, political and economic pressure, and sabotage were to be employed. The French Resistance had a valuable part to play in this and in autumn 1943 COSSAC began to take over SOE and OSS operations. The emphasis was on sending back information on German deployments, but the pattern of sabotage and ambushes continued, as did assassinations. Indeed, von Rundstedt himself noted that by the end of 1943 there was a serious problem with communications between northern and southern France, because of ambushes, and that at times HQ Army Group G at Toulouse was virtually cut off. In the north of the country, especially near the coastal areas, life for the Resistance was much more difficult. The coasts themselves were barred to civilians without special permits and there was also a preponderance of German troops. Furthermore, the Gestapo was steadily penetrating many of the networks and arresting key personnel. So serious did this become that on 18 February 1944 the RAF mounted a daring and very skilful low-level Mosquito raid on the prison at Amiens, which held a number of Resistance members, enabling a number of them to escape.

February 1944 also saw the formation by de Gaulle of the Force Françaises d'Intérieur (FFI) under General Marie Pierre Koenig, hero of the Free French stand against Rommel at Bir Hacheim in June 1942. This embraced all the Resistance movements, although some Communist groups remained outside it. Initially, it consisted of just 30,000 men, including the Maquis, but was to rise to over 200,000 by D-Day. The FFI was to play a significant part in the Transportation Plan, but the Allies did not want it to strike early, but to wait until D-Day, when it could really hinder the deployment of the German mobile reserves. SOE and OSS agents briefed them on their targets, many of which were railway cuttings. To co-ordinate the efforts of the FFI and ensure that their operations tied in with the main campaign plan Jedburgh teams were formed. Each consisted of an American, a Briton, and a Frenchman, with a radio. They were to parachute into France from D-Day onwards and work with local Resistance units. Under the codename Cooney, the French Special Air Service (SAS) in Britain was to drop similar three-man teams into Brittany to operate with FFI elements, their initial object the destruction of railway lines into Normandy to prevent the deployment of reserves. There were also two-man intelligence-gathering teams known as Sussex. They were recruited from members of the French Army in North Africa and trained by MI6 and began to deploy in February 1944. Unlike the Jedburgh and Cooney teams, they did not wear uniform.

By the beginning of June 1944 all was ready as far as the French Resistance was concerned. All they needed to know was when D-Day would happen. On the evening of 1 June the BBC transmitted a series of coded messages, which told the Resistance that D-Day was imminent. On the German side, the picture was somewhat different. Von Rundstedt informed Hitler on 30 May that he did not think that invasion was likely in the very immediate future. OKW was not so sure and, on 2 June, asked von Rundstedt why he had not increased the alert state. He replied that this would only affect the French railways, whose rolling stock would be commandeered for moving reinforcements and matériel. This would merely aggravate discontent among the French. The storm that blew up in the Channel further convinced von Rundstedt that the threat was low, but German weather forecasting was unable to look far into the Atlantic and so did not detect the break in the weather which would allow D-Day to take place on 6 June. Consequently, C-in-C West allowed Rommel to depart on a short leave to Germany on 5 June, during which the Desert Fox intended to call on Hitler to demand further reinforcements. Von Rundstedt himself planned a four day inspection trip of part of the Cotentin peninsula. He would set out on 6 June.

Rommel left General Friedrich Dollmann in charge of Army Group B. He commanded the German Seventh Army, which was responsible for Normandy and Brittany. In terms of the quality of its troops, it was significantly worse off than its eastern neighbour, Hans von Salmuth's Fifteenth Army, which covered the coast from east of Caen to Zeebrugge, since the High Command still believed that the Pas-de-Calais or the Boulogne-Somme sector were the most likely landing areas. Many of Dollmann's troops were either Ostruppen, Russians who had enlisted in the German Army to fight Communism, or Volksdeutsche, ethnic Germans from the enlarged Reich, and their fighting power was inferior to that of the ordinary German soldier. The only quality formation he had was the II Parachute Corps, which was Army Reserve. Three divisions held the portion of the coast on which the Allies would actually land. The 716th Division covered that north of Caen and had a frontage of 21 miles, far too wide, especially for a formation which consisted in general of older soldiers from Rhineland and Westphalia and most of whom had not experienced combat. General Wilhelm Richter, the commander, had constructed a series of strongpoints, but they were too far apart from one another and he lacked the troops to provide any depth to the defence. Facing Omaha Beach was the 352nd Division.

This had only been formed in November 1943, but most of its men had seen combat. It was not deployed to the coast until March 1944, however, and found itself working desperately to improve the defences along some 35 miles of coast. Finally, there was the 709th Division, which was very similar in character to the 716th and covered the coast from Utah up to Cherbourg. The one mobile division available was 21st Panzer Division. This was scattered on both sides of the River Orne, with its artillery on the coast, not a particularly satisfactory position. Its commander, General Edgar Feuchtinger, was a Nazi favourite, but an inefficient soldier, whom Rommel had been unable to sack because of his powerful political connections. Dollmann, like his masters, did not think that the invasion was about to be mounted and decided to hold a map exercise for many of his subordinate commanders at Rennes, which lies at the base of the Brittany peninsula. It was to begin on 6 June and most commanders travelled there the day before. As for Feuchtinger, he decided to spend the night 5/6 June with his mistress in Paris.

A 155mm coastal defence gun in its massively built concrete emplacement. When firing out to sea these guns came under the command of Admiral Kranke but when engaging targets on the beaches they came under Army Command. This complication proved a serious weakness in German defensive operations.

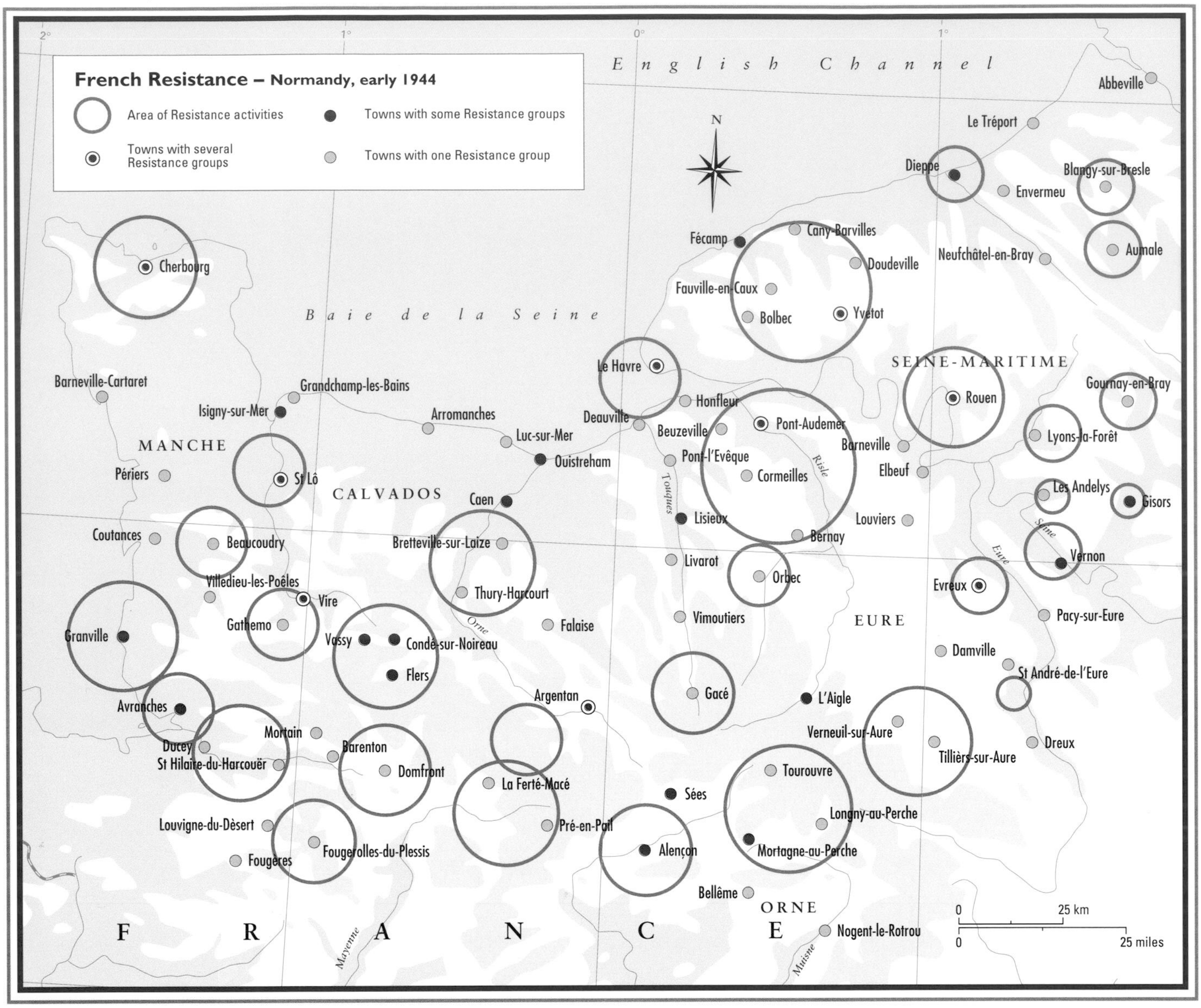
French Resistance – Normandy, early 1944
Area of Resistance activities
Towns with some Resistance groups
Towns with several Resistance groups
Towns with one Resistance group
English Channel
Baie de la Seine
MANCHE
CALVADOS
SEINE-MARITIME
EURE
ORNE
FRANCE
N
Abbeville
Le Tréport
Dieppe
Envermeu
Blangy-sur-Bresle
Aumale
Neufchâtel-en-Bray
Fécamp
Cany-Barvilles
Doudeville
Fauville-en-Caux
Bolbec
Yvetot
Cherbourg
Le Havre
Honfleur
Deauville
Beuzeville
Pont-Audemer
Pont-l'Evêque
Cormeilles
Barneville
Elbeuf
Rouen
Gournay-en-Bray
Lyons-la-Forêt
Les Andelys
Gisors
Vernon
Louviers
Bernay
Lisieux
Livarot
Orbec
Vimoutiers
Evreux
Pacy-sur-Eure
Damville
St André-de-l'Eure
Barneville-Cartaret
Grandchamp-les-Bains
Isigny-sur-Mer
Arromanches
Luc-sur-Mer
Ouistreham
Périers
St Lô
Caen
Coutances
Beaucoudry
Bretteville-sur-Laize
Thury-Harcourt
Villedieu-les-Poêles
Vire
Gathemo
Vassy
Condé-sur-Noireau
Falaise
Flers
Granville
Avranches
Argentan
Gacé
L'Aigle
Mortain
Ducey
St Hilaire-du-Harcouët
Barenton
Domfront
La Ferté-Macé
Verneuil-sur-Aure
Tillières-sur-Aure
Dreux
Tourouvre
Sées
Longny-au-Perche
Mortagne-au-Perche
Louvigne-du-Dèsert
Fougerolles-du-Plessis
Fougères
Pré-en-Pail
Alençon
Bellême
Nogent-le-Rotrou
Touques
Risle
Orne
Seine
Eure
Mayenne
Huisne
0 25 km
0 25 miles
2°
1°
0°
1°

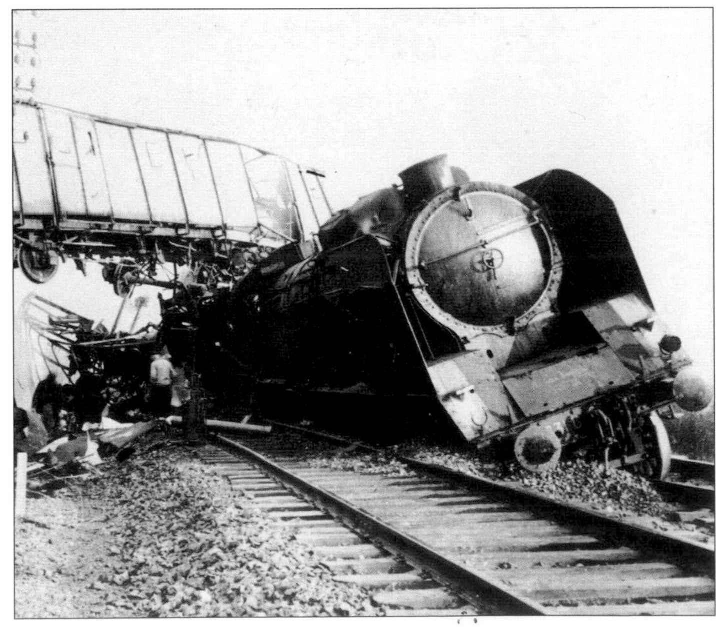

The Resistance in the Normandy area had much more difficulty in operating than that in the hinterland of central and southern France. Apart from the larger presence of German troops, there was very restricted access to the coastal areas. During the months before D-Day, the Resistance was more concerned with intelligence gathering and preparing to play its part in the attacks on road and rail communications leading into Normandy.

The results of a French Resistance sabotage attack. The Resistance proved an increasing irritation for the Germans but it needed to be held in check in the weeks before D-Day so that its operations against communications could be tied into the overall allied plan.

One of the major activities of the Resistance was the sabotage of French industry being used by the Germans to assist their war effort. From small beginnings in 1942, it intensified in 1943, once the Resistance began to become better organized. Much of it was very subtle and went unnoticed by the Germans. The Resistance also began to make direct attacks on German troops and communications, although these often resulted in dire reprisals against the local population.

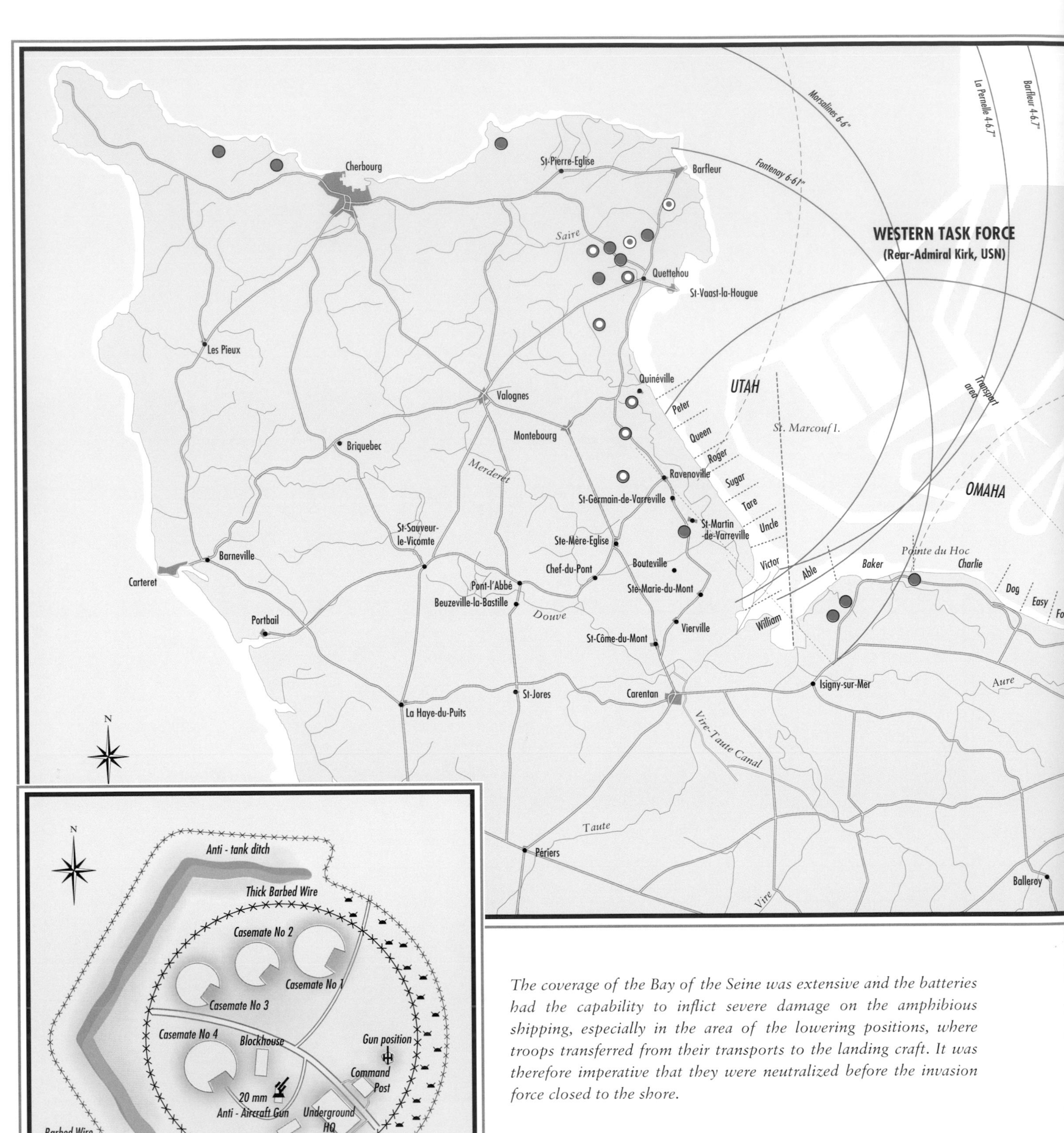

The coverage of the Bay of the Seine was extensive and the batteries had the capability to inflict severe damage on the amphibious shipping, especially in the area of the lowering positions, where troops transferred from their transports to the landing craft. It was therefore imperative that they were neutralized before the invasion force closed to the shore.

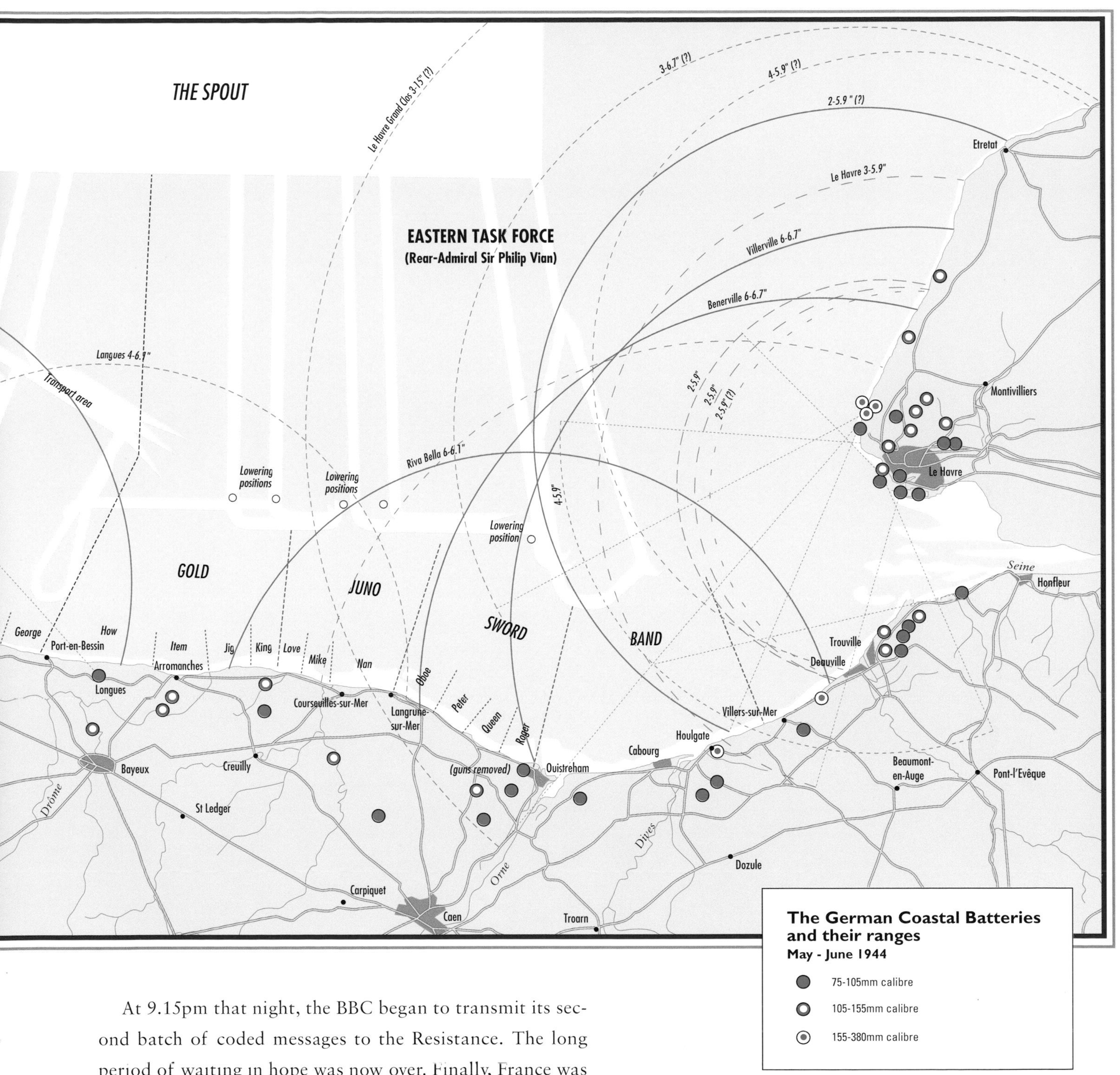

At 9.15pm that night, the BBC began to transmit its second batch of coded messages to the Resistance. The long period of waiting in hope was now over. Finally, France was about to be liberated and there was work to be done to help the Allies ashore. The German military intelligence, the Abwehr, noted that the broadcast went on considerably longer than the usual five to ten minutes and became suspicious. They alerted von Rundstedt's headquarters and he ordered a heightened state of alertness. He also warned that there might well be an increased level of sabotage. Sentries and gun crews on the coast stared out to sea through the gloom of the cloudy night, but all seemed quiet. Then came the sound of aircraft engines, but this was nothing different to what had happened over many past nights. At 1.30am von Rundstedt's headquarters received reports of parachute landings on the east side of the Cotentin peninsula. The state of alert was raised still further. But was it a mere raid or the beginning of the invasion?

Chapter Three

D-Day

The first D-Day actions by the Allies were a series of airborne deception operations mounted by the RAF. Almost as soon as dusk had fallen on 5 June, Lancaster bombers of 617 Squadron, the Dambusters, were overflying the Strait of Dover in a precise elliptical course, dropping strips of aluminium foil known as Window. Below them sixteen small ships towed balloons fitted with reflectors. The idea was to present to the German coastal radars a picture of a convoy crossing towards the Pas-de-Calais. Stirlings of 218 Squadron were carrying out a similar exercise off Boulogne, while other Stirlings and Halifaxes dropped dummy parachutes and various devices to represent rifle fire in order to simulate airborne landings well to the south of the drop zones of the two US airborne divisions. These had a vital task, blocking the approaches to Utah beach.

A week before D-Day many of the Drop Zones (DZ) for the two US airborne divisions had to be changed because air reconnaissance had revealed that the Germans had placed obstacles on the original selections. Trafford Leigh-Mallory, the overall Allied air commander, was also very concerned

Apart from the landings on Juno and Sword, which were conducted by one corps, each of the other major landing beaches was the responsibility of a single corps. Utah and Omaha were under the overall direction of Bradley's US First Army, while the remainder came under Dempsey's Second British Army. Unlike the original COSSAC plan, this meant that there would be no major organizational changes once the Allies advanced inland.

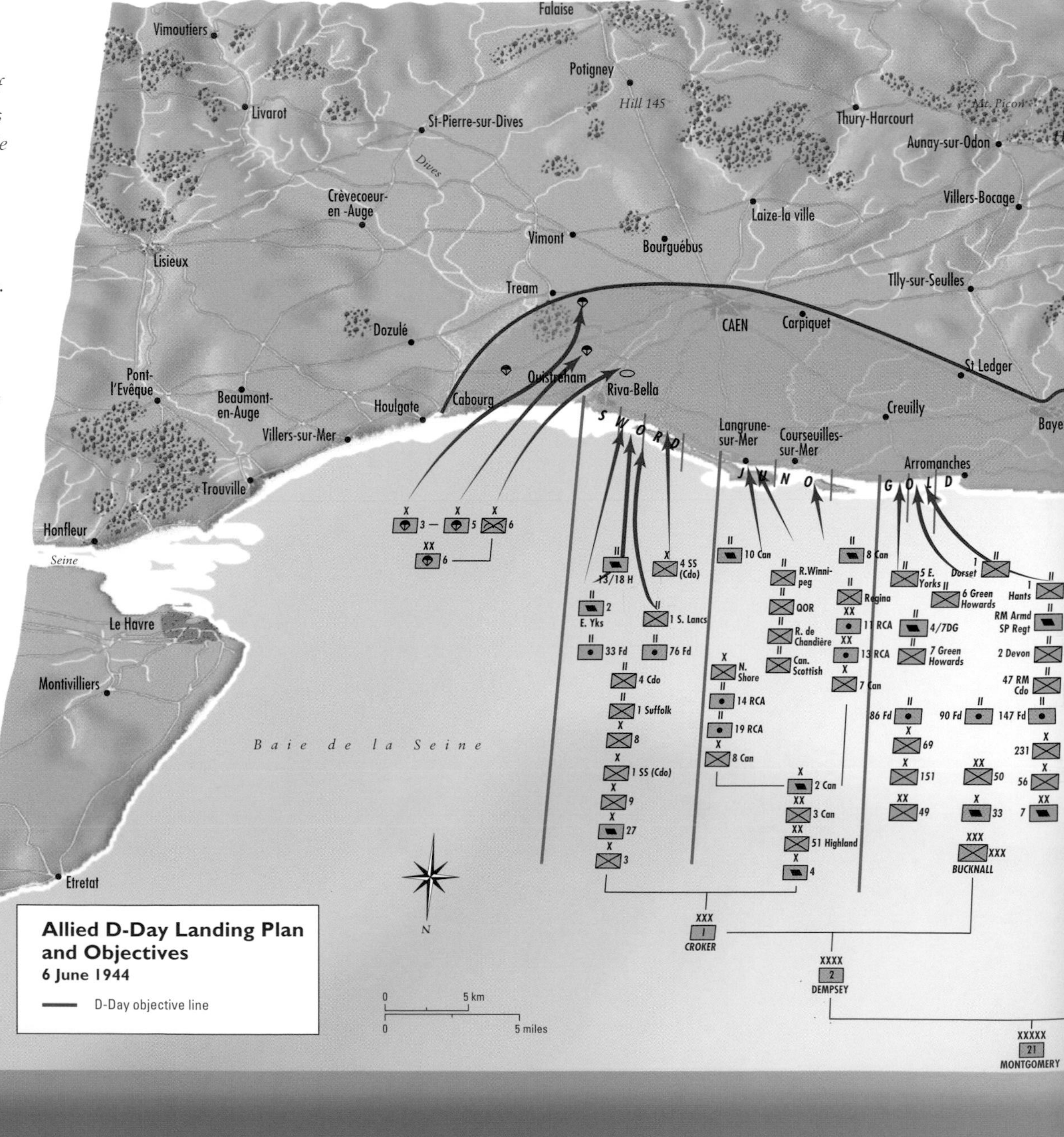

that adverse weather conditions might precipitate a disaster. A further problem was that there were insufficient aircraft to transport the two divisions in one lift, something which applied to the British 6th Airborne Division as well. The 82nd and 101st Airborne Divisions were preceded by pathfinder groups whose task was to drop thirty minutes before the main landings to mark the DZs with beacons. The aircraft would not fly direct to the DZs, but would execute a dog-leg over the Cotentin peninsula so that the approach would be from the south-east in order to assist surprise. This created problems for the navigators. High winds did not help, and neither did the fact that many of the marking beacons did not function. Pilots also dropped the paratroops at far too great a height, partly because of the anti-aircraft fire from the ground. In consequence, the landings were very scattered. Apart from the 709th Division on the coast, there were two other German formations in the area. Opposing the airborne drops in the north was the 91st Airlanding Division, a recently raised formation, which had been deployed to the Cotentin peninsula just two weeks earlier. It was responsible for the defence of

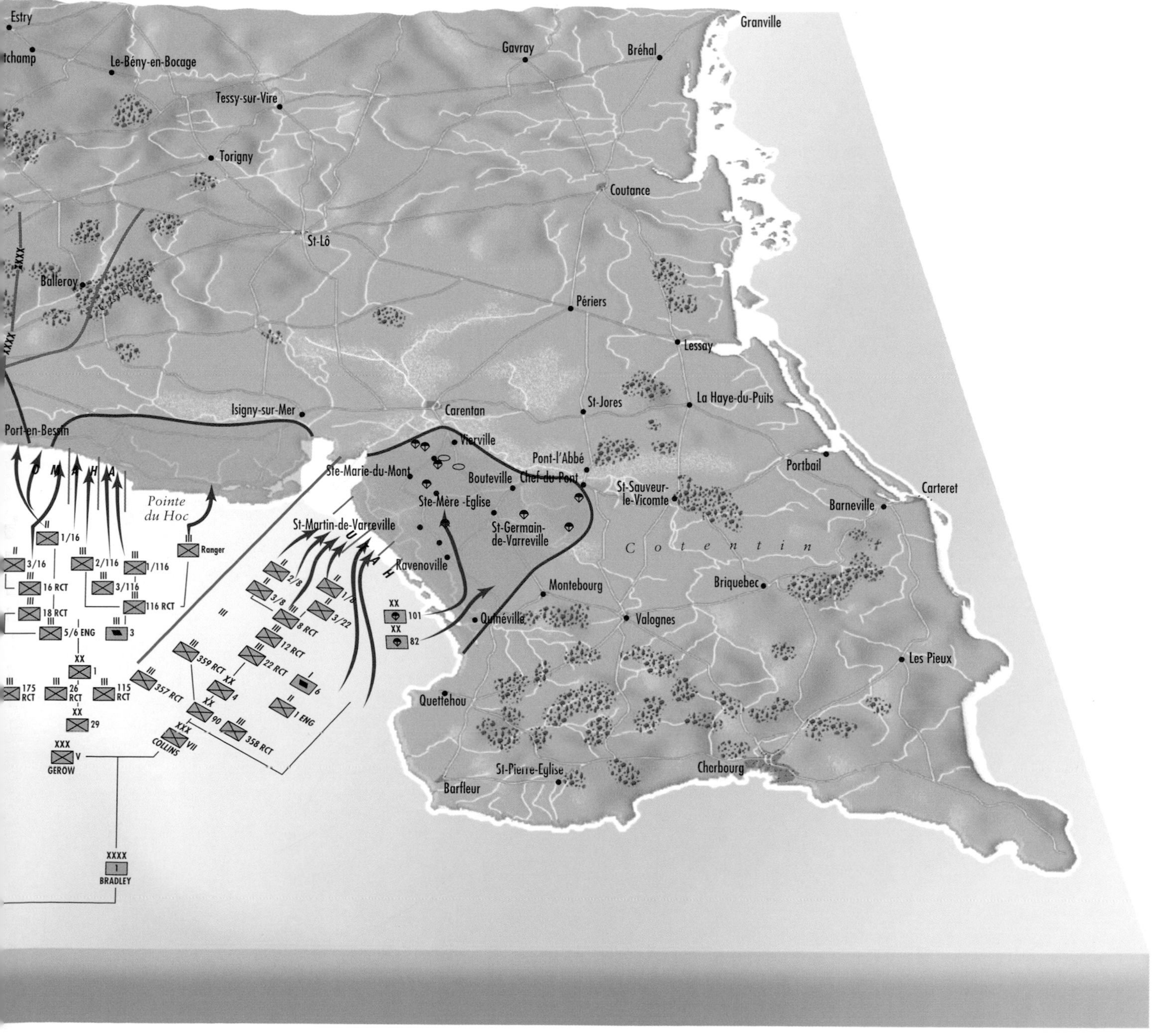

the southern part of the peninsula, from the west coast to the River Merderet. It had, however, carried out some training in anti-airborne operations. In the south, and based at Carentan was Colonel Freiherr Friedrich-August von der Heydte's 6th Parachute Regiment. This was part of 2nd Parachute Division, which was refitting in the Cologne area of Germany prior to moving to France.

The first to land, at 1.30am on 6 June, was Major-General Maxwell Taylor's 101st Airborne Division, the Screaming Eagles. Its task was to drop two miles behind Utah beach and secure the causeways leading to it. The landings were very scattered, with some sticks being dropped as much as ten miles from their DZ. It naturally took time for small groups of men to orientate themselves in the darkness. To help them identify one another, each man had been issued with a small metal object, which when pressed made a noise like a cricket. Inevitably, some of these fell into German hands and were used to trap the US paratroops. The 502nd Parachute Regiment was more fortunate than the other regiments in that it was able to gather sufficient men together to quickly secure St-Martin-de-Varreville and then move to the coast, where they discovered an unmanned coastal battery whose guns had been removed. After this, they established themselves astride the causeway at Audouville-la-Hubert. One small group attacked the village of Le Mézieres, in which men of the neighbouring St-Martin coastal battery were billeted. Entering one house after another, they killed or captured some 150 German soldiers. Other elements established road-blocks around Foucarville. One battalion of the Regiment dropped in the 82nd Airborne Division's sector near St-Mère-Église. The battalion commander managed to gather some 250 men together and began to move eastwards towards Utah.

General Taylor himself dropped with the 501st Regiment whose DZ was just west of St-Marie-du-Mont. Luckily, the regimental commander landed roughly in the right place. His key objective was the lock on the Douve River at La Barquette, since it was feared that the Germans might use it to flood the surrounding area. The 501st's other objectives were to blow bridges on the road running from St-Côme-du-Mont south to Carentan, capturing the former village if possible, and destroy the railway bridge over the Douve to its west. Colonel Howard R. Johnson, the regimental commander, collected some 150 men and secured the lock at La Barquette against minimum opposition. But, when other parts of the regiment tried to advance to the Douve bridges they faced increasing resistance from von der Heydte's German paratroops. The American paratroopers did not know at the time that German engineers had demolished the bridges. The commander of the third regiment of the Screaming Eagles, the 506th, which Eisenhower had visited just before they boarded their planes, had the worst time. The drop was scattered, but within two hours of landing Colonel Robert F. Sink was able to gather ninety men of his own HQ and fifty from his 1st Battalion and establish himself at Culoville. He was principally tasked with securing the southern exits from Utah Beach. His 3rd Battalion, which would drop with the 506th south of Vierville, was to capture bridges over the Douve at Le Port. The 2nd Battalion, or at least the 200 men who could be collected, were advancing towards the exits at Hodienville and Pouppeville well before dawn, but soon ran into German machine guns, which brought them to a halt. Sink had no communication with the Battalion and so decided to send the fifty men of the 1st Battalion that he had with him to tackle the Pouppeville beach exit. They, too, were considerably slowed by German opposition. Sink, however, had little contact with this group once it set out and also little with Divisional HQ, which Maxwell Taylor had established at Hiesville. Worse, Sink's HQ was in the midst of a German artillery battalion and he was continually faced with attempts to infiltrate his position. His poor communications with Maxwell Taylor caused the latter to send the divisional reserve, the 3rd Battalion of the 501st to Pouppeville, which it reached at 8am.

Major-General Matthew Ridgway's 82nd Airborne Division suffered much the same confusion. His DZs were to the west of those of 101st Airborne and his overall task was to clear from the River Merderet east to the coast and to establish a bridgehead on the west bank of the river. A major problem was that this sector was close to the assembly area of the 91st Airlanding Division. Initially, matters went well. The 505th Regiment's DZ was just west of St-Mère-Église. It

(Right) Although its drop was just as scattered as that of the 82nd Airborne Division, 101st Airborne had a slightly easier task in that it was closer to Utah beach and so could expect to link up earlier with the troops landing here. It was able to distract German troops defending Utah and also secured routes inland for the US VII Corps.

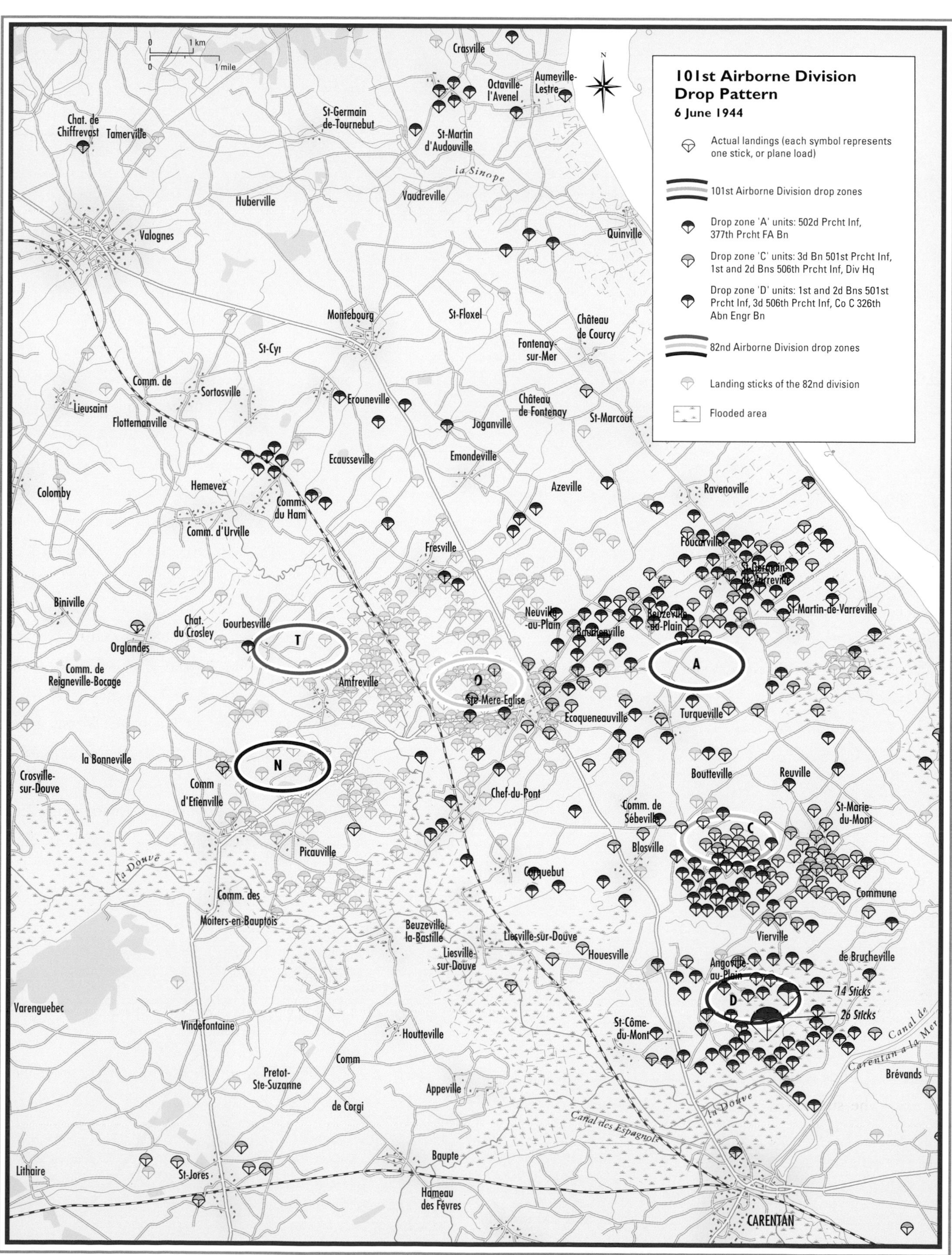

101st Airborne Division
Drop Pattern
6 June 1944
Actual landings (each symbol represents one stick, or plane load)
101st Airborne Division drop zones
Drop zone 'A' units: 502d Prcht Inf, 377th Prcht FA Bn
Drop zone 'C' units: 3d Bn 501st Prcht Inf, 1st and 2d Bns 506th Prcht Inf, Div Hq
Drop zone 'D' units: 1st and 2d Bns 501st Prcht Inf, 3d 506th Prcht Inf, Co C 326th Abn Engr Bn
82nd Airborne Division drop zones
Landing sticks of the 82nd division
Flooded area
0 1 km
0 1 mile
N
Crasville
Octaville-l'Avenel
Aumeville-Lestre
St-Germain de-Tournebut
St-Martin d'Audouville
Chat. de Chiffrevast
Tamerville
la Sinope
Huberville
Vaudreville
Valognes
Quinville
Montebourg
St-Floxel
Château de Courcy
St-Cyr
Fontenay-sur-Mer
Comm. de Sortosville
Lieusaint
Flottemanville
Erouneville
Château de Fontenay
Joganville
St-Marcouf
Emondeville
Ecausseville
Hemevez
Colomby
Comm. du Ham
Azeville
Ravenoville
Comm. d'Urville
Fresville
Foucarville
St-Germain-de-Varreville
Biniville
St-Martin-de-Varreville
Chat. du Crosley
Gourbesville
Neuville-au-Plain
Beuzeville-au-Plain
Bouteville
Orglandes
T
A
Comm. de Reigneville-Bocage
Amfreville
O
Ste-Mere-Eglise
Ecoqueneauville
Turqueville
la Bonneville
N
Boutteville
Reuville
Crosville-sur-Douve
Comm d'Etienville
Chef-du-Pont
Comm. de Sébeville
St-Marie-du-Mont
C
Blosville
Picauville
la Douve
Carquebut
Comm. des Moiters-en-Bauptois
Commune
Beuzeville-la-Bastille
Liesville-sur-Douve
Vierville
Liesville-sur-Douve
Houesville
de Brucheville
Angoville-au-Plain
14 Sticks
D
26 Sticks
Varenguebec
Vindefontaine
St-Côme-du-Mont
Canal de Carentan a la Mer
Houtteville
Comm
Brévands
Pretot-Ste-Suzanne
Appeville
de Corgi
la Douve
Canal des Espagnols
Baupte
Lithaire
St-Jores
Hameau des Fèvres
CARENTAN

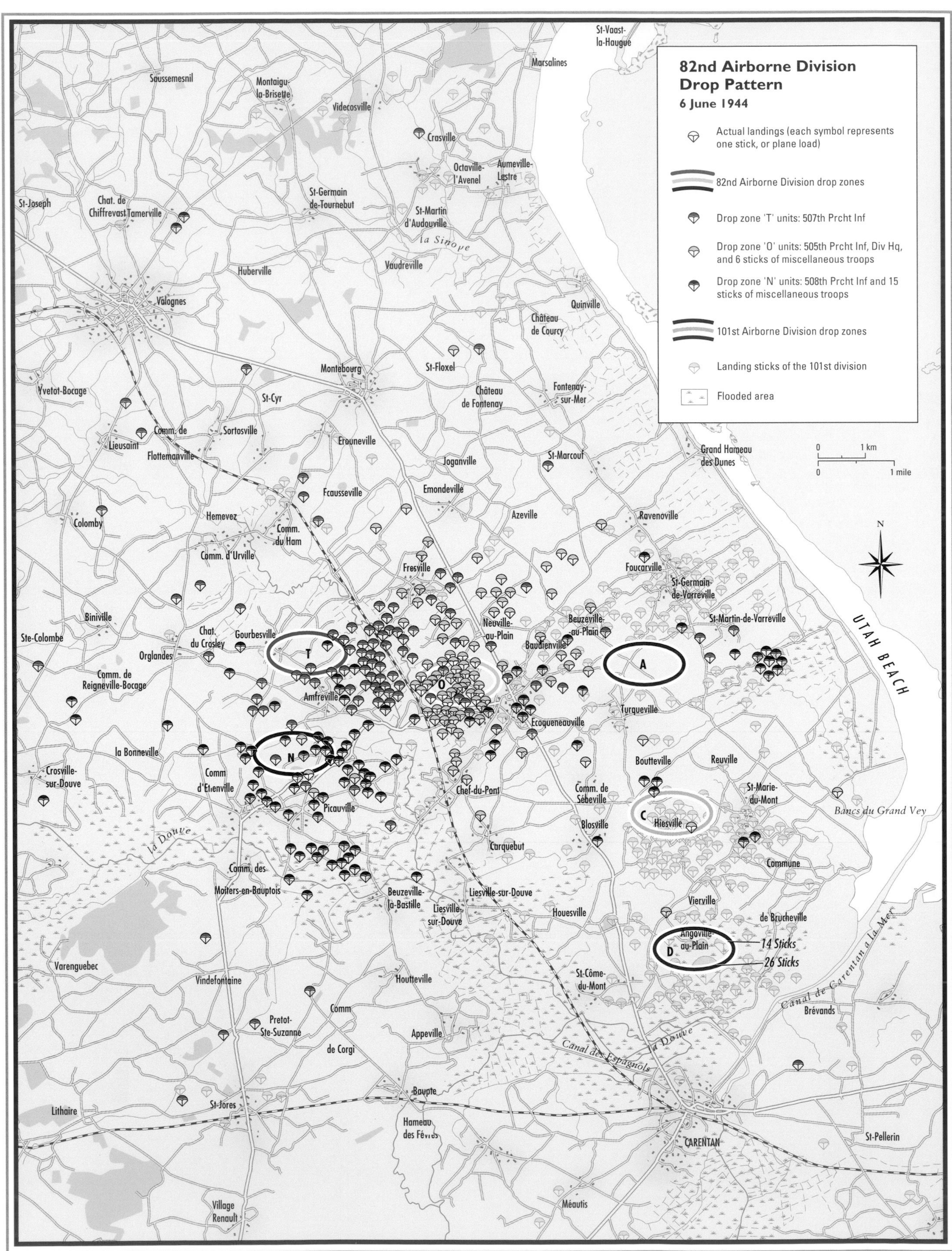

82nd Airborne Division Drop Pattern
6 June 1944
Actual landings (each symbol represents one stick, or plane load)
82nd Airborne Division drop zones
Drop zone 'T' units: 507th Prcht Inf
Drop zone 'O' units: 505th Prcht Inf, Div Hq, and 6 sticks of miscellaneous troops
Drop zone 'N' units: 508th Prcht Inf and 15 sticks of miscellaneous troops
101st Airborne Division drop zones
Landing sticks of the 101st division
Flooded area
0 1 km
0 1 mile
N
UTAH BEACH
St-Vaast-la-Hougue
Marsalines
Saussemesnil
Montaigu-la-Brisette
Videcosville
Crasville
Octaville-l'Avenel
Aumeville-Lestre
St-Joseph
Chat. de Chiffrevast
Tamerville
St-Germain de-Tournebut
St-Martin d'Audouville
la Sinope
Vaudreville
Huberville
Valognes
Quinville
Château de Courcy
Montebourg
St-Floxel
Yvetot-Bocage
St-Cyr
Château de Fontenay
Fontenay-sur-Mer
Lieusaint
Comm. de Flottemanville
Sortosville
Erouneville
Joganville
St-Marcouf
Grand Hameau des Dunes
Fcausseville
Emondeville
Colomby
Hemevez
Comm. du Ham
Azeville
Ravenoville
Comm. d'Urville
Fresville
Foucarville
St-Germain-de-Varreville
Biniville
Ste-Colombe
Chat. du Crosley
Gourbesville
Orglandes
Neuville-au-Plain
Beuzeville-au-Plain
Baudienville
St-Martin-de-Varreville
T
O
A
Comm. de Reigneville-Bocage
Amfreville
Turqueville
Ecoqueneauville
la Bonneville
N
Boutteville
Reuville
Crosville-sur-Douve
Comm d'Etienville
Chef-du-Pont
Comm. de Sébeville
St-Marie-du-Mont
Picauville
C
Hiesville
Blosville
Bancs du Grand Vey
la Douve
Carquebut
Commune
Comm. des Moitiers-en-Bauptois
Beuzeville-la-Bastille
Liesville-sur-Douve
Houesville
Vierville
de Brucheville
Angoville-au-Plain
D
14 Sticks
26 Sticks
Canal de Carentan à la Mer
Varenguebec
Vindefontaine
Houtteville
St-Côme-du-Mont
Comm
Brévands
Pretot-Ste-Suzanne
Appeville
de Corgi
la Douve
Canal des Espagnols
Baupte
Lithaire
St-Jores
Hameau des Fèvres
CARENTAN
St-Pellerin
Village Renault
Méautis

was to seize the town, secure crossings over the Merderet in the La Fiere and Chef-du-Pont area and establish a defensive line. The pathfinders had managed to clearly mark the DZ and, although the 505th's planes were scattered, they were able to turn back and drop the paratroops in a fairly concentrated pattern, although a few did actually land in the town itself. Furthermore, there were no Germans in the vicinity. The Regiment's 3rd Battalion was to capture St-Mère-Église and moved swiftly. It entered the town and used just knives, bayonets, and grenades to secure it well before dawn, killing ten Germans and capturing thirty others. It quickly established a perimeter defence and cut the communications cable running up to Cherbourg. The other two battalions had further to go in establishing a defence line and seizing the crossings over the Merderet. The 2nd Battalion, responsible for the former task, would, however, be ordered back to St-Mère-Église well after daylight as German pressure on the town increased. The success of the 1st Battalion in securing the crossings would be dependent on the other two regiments which landed west of the river.

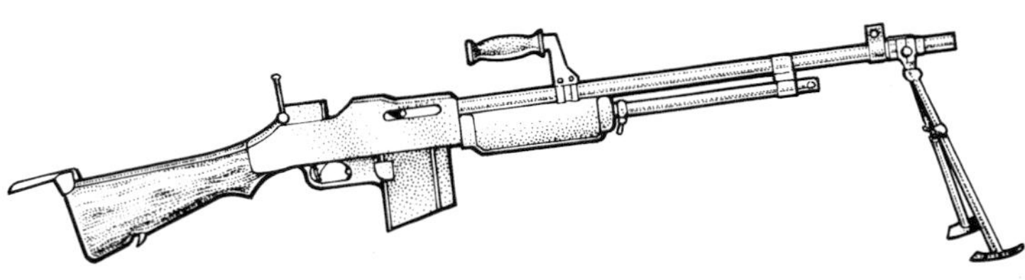

Browning Automatic rifle (BAR). Originally developed in 1917, it was used as a support weapon by US infantry squads.

The 507th and 508th Parachute Infantry Regiments were to drop between the Rivers Douve and Merderet and secure the west bank of the latter. This would then become the perimeter for the Utah beachhead. Because 91st Airlanding Division was already present in the drop area, the pathfinders were unable to mark the DZs. Consequently, the aircraft crews were unable to identify them and overshot. The result was a very scattered drop, with many of the paratroopers landing in the marshy ground bordering the Merderet. The one recognisable feature was the embankment which carried the railway running from Carentan to Cherbourg and it was to this that the men headed and began to gather. One group, under Brigadier-General James A. Gavin, the Assistant Divisional Commander, did try to move down along the edge of the marshes, but were unable to make any progress before dawn, because of the time it took to locate and extricate heavy equipment. As for those on the embankment, which numbered some 600 men from a variety of units, they began to move south towards the crossing at La Fiere. Many others found themselves fighting for their survival and were unable to progress to their objectives. The initial drops had caught the Germans by surprise, but they soon began to recover, although General Wilhelm Falley, commanding 91st Airlanding Division, was killed. He had been on his way to the map exercise at Rennes when the intensity of air activity caused him to turn back. Shortly before reaching his HQ, he heard machine gun fire and got out of his staff car to investigate. A few moments later he was shot dead by a paratrooper of the 508th. At 4am the first wave of US glider-borne troops came in to land. These were vital, since they had the heavier weapons which the paratroopers would need to hold the perimeter. However, the now thoroughly alert Flak defences opened up a heavy fire and a number of the tug aircraft were shot down. Some three-quarters of the gliders did manage to reach the landing zones, but many of them crashed into the marshes or ran up against thick hedgerows and stone walls. Casualties in personnel were surprisingly

US paratroops moving towards their RV in Normandy. They had numerous minor clashes with Germans on D-Day. Hence the anxious expression of the man covering the rear.

(Left) The 82nd Airborne Division's principal task was to secure crossings over the River Merderet, but the scattered nature of its drop made it initially impossible to achieve. Luckily a reasonable number of men did land in or around the DZ near St-Mére-Église, making it the first French village to be liberated on D-Day. Thereafter it became the cornerstone of the paratroop's defence.

British 6th Airborne Division 6 June 1944

- Intended landing zones
- Actual landing zones
- Bridge captured
- Bridge destroyed
- Battery destroyed
- German strong points
- German resistance points

The Division's overall task was to secure the area between the Rivers Dives and Orne, so that this could become the left flank of the Allied beachhead. It was therefore crucial to seize the bridges over the Dives to prevent counter-attack by elements of Fifteenth Army. Once 9th Parachute Bn had destroyed the Merville battery, it was sent to help hold the southern line defences. The Division remained in France until the end of August 1944.

light, although the Assistant Commander of the 101st Airborne was among the killed. Many of the jeeps and artillery guns were, however, lost. Now, with the coming of daylight and the American landings at Utah soon to take place, the German Seventh Army began to organize operations to seal the American lodgement and eradicate it. The 709th Division, with a regiment of the 91st under its command, was ordered to clear the area to the east of the Merderet, while the remainder of the 91st attacked in the

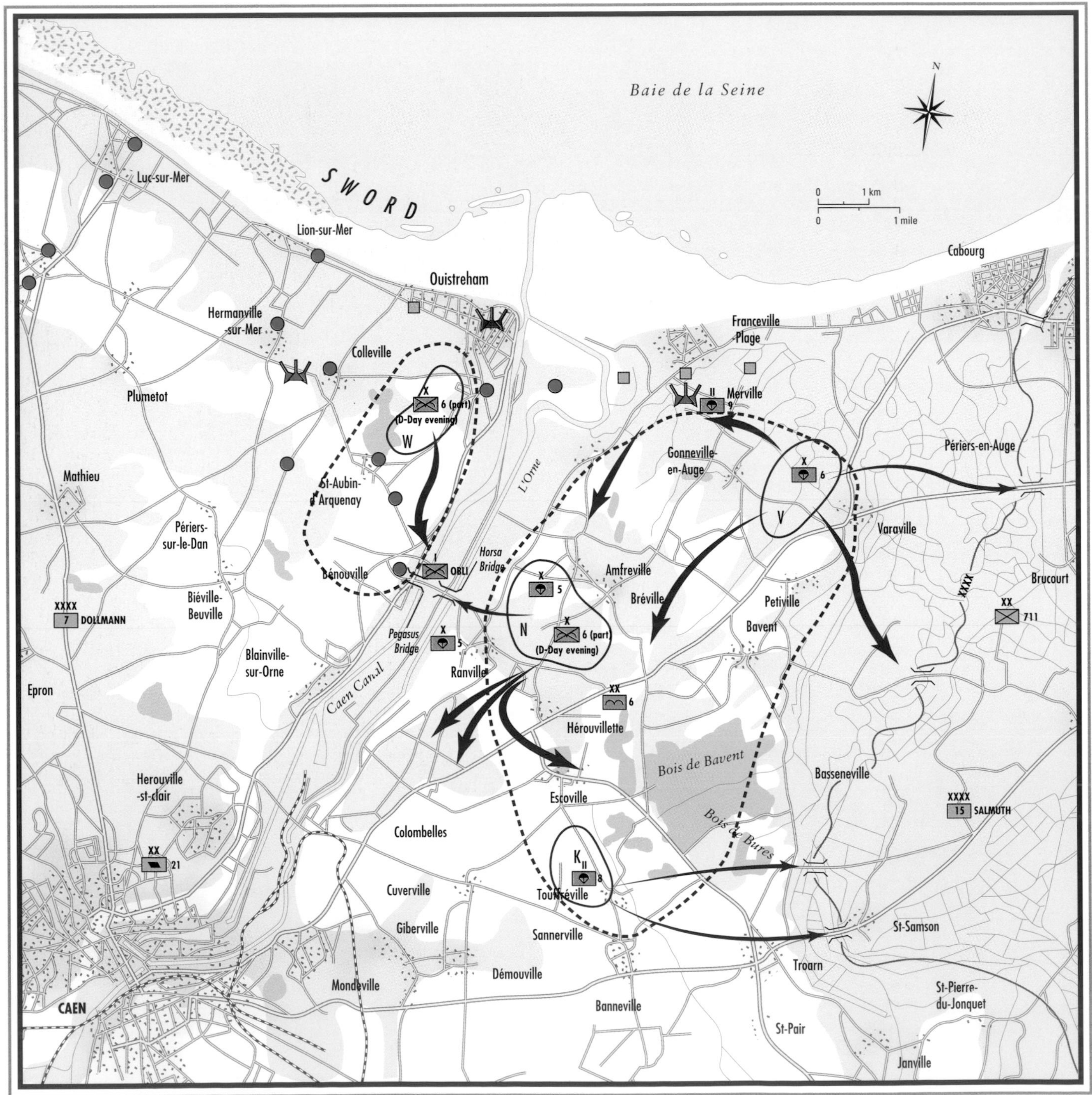

west. Von der Heydte's 6th Parachute Regiment was placed under command of the 91st and would attack from the south. The question now was whether the US paratroopers in their largely disorganized state could fend off these attacks and link up with the troops of the 4th Infantry Division on Utah.

Far to the east, at the other end of the Allied landing beaches, the British 6th Airborne Division had experienced similar problems to the Americans. General Richard ('Windy') Gale had the mission of landing between the Rivers Dives and Orne, securing bridges over both and providing a shoulder for the landings on Sword Beach so that German reserves approaching from the east and south-east could be blocked. He also had to capture and destroy a coastal battery at Merville, which could fire into the flank of the Sword landing. Pathfinders from the 22nd Independent Parachute Company landed between twenty and thirty minutes after midnight. High winds caused dispersal and, once on the ground, they found that many of their Eureka beacons did not function. One of those that did was set up in the wrong place.

The next phase was a daring glider operation. A company of the 2nd Oxfordshire and Buckinghamshire Light Infantry under the command of Major John Howard took off in six gliders, their objective the bridges over the River Orne and Caen Canal at Bénouville. Three gliders were allocated to each bridge and all would land on the narrow strip between the two waterways. They were 'to finish their landing run as close to the bridges as is consistent with avoiding injury to the gliderborne troops', as the operational order laid down. The pilots themselves carried out extensive flying practice by night. They also had a detailed model of the area and a film made from air photographs, which simulated the approach to the target. The three gliders bound for the canal bridge landed within yards of it and, after a brief fire fight, seized it. Two out of the other three landed by the river bridge, which again was quickly captured. The third was released at the wrong cast-off point and came to rest by a bridge over the River Dives, seven miles away from the correct bridge. The troops on board secured this and then made there way to their original objective. It was, as Trafford Leigh-Mallory stated, 'one of the most outstanding flying operations of the war'.

The tasks of the 5th Parachute Brigade were to send one battalion to reinforce Howard's men on the Canal and Orne bridges, while the other two captured Ranville and the adjacent high ground just east of the Orne. Many of its men were blown off course, and only some 200 could be gathered to help Howard, although more trickled in during the night. The other two battalions managed to capture Ranville, although, as at Sainte-Mère-Eglise, a number landed in the town and were killed or captured, and by daylight were also dug in around La Bas de Ranville. Many men of the 3rd Parachute Brigade landed in the flooded area bordering the

Gliders after landing. It was necessary to remove the tail section to extract vehicles and heavy weapons.

River Dives, four of whose bridges they had to demolish. Nevertheless, they succeeded and then dug in around Le Mesnil and Bois Bavent. One battalion, Lieutenant-Colonel Terence Otway's 9th, had a more challenging job, the destruction of the Merville Battery. This was well protected by concrete and earth, minefields and barbed wire and was defended by 130 Germans, armed with machine guns and 20mm cannon. Otway and his men carried out numerous

The real achievement was landing the gliders so close to the bridges and it was this that enabled Major John Howard's men to achieve complete surprise. Howard himself led the capture of Pegasus Bridge and was later relieved by Commandos, while the Ranville Bridge group was relieved by 7th Parachute Battalion.

rehearsals on a 1:1 scale model. The plan was that they should drop out of sight of the battery, which would have been pounded by some 100 Lancaster and Halifax bombers to destroy the barded wire and at least some of the mines. Gliders carrying engineers with their heavy equipment would land and clear lanes through the minefield, after which the 9th Parachute Battalion would make its attack. Three gliders were simultaneously to crash-land on top of the battery.

Like the other drops, that of the Battalion was scattered and Otway was only able to assemble one quarter of his 600 men. Worse, the bombing had been inaccurate and the barbed wire and minefield were largely intact and the gliders carrying the engineers had landed well away from their proper Landing Zone. Of the three gliders due to land on the battery itself, one's tow rope broke and it was forced to return to England, while the second was hit by flak and landed 200 yards away and those inside found themselves engaging a German patrol, which prevented them from taking part in the assault. The third managed to land within 50 yards. In spite of all this, Otway was determined to carry on. Sappers with him cleared lanes by digging for mines with their bayo-

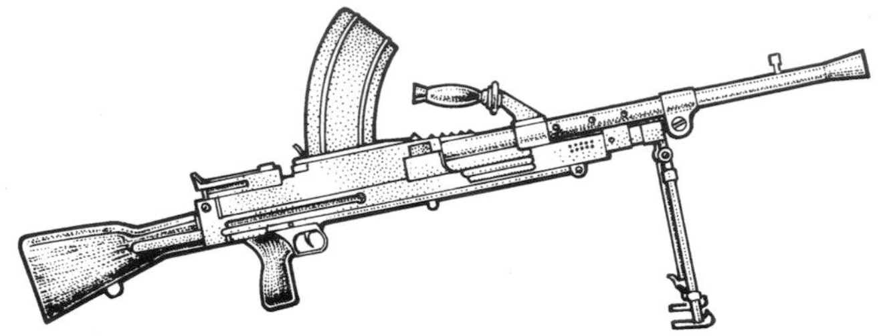

The British Bren light machine gun. It was much lighter and easier to handle than the US BAR.

nets and, after silencing six of the ten machine guns defending the battery, Otway's men passed through and reached its entrance. After a short but grim hand-to-hand battle, the guns were in their possession. Instead of being of 150mm calibre, as expected, they turned out to be small-calibre Czech guns of 1914–18 origin. The paratroops destroyed them with plastic explosive and withdrew to the area north of Bréville and dug in. While the stragglers of the Division attempted to join up with their units, the remainder, like their US counterparts, prepared for the inevitable German counter-attack and hoped that they would be reinforced by troops from Sword Beach before it came.

There were other necessary preliminaries to the actual beach landings. First, bombers of RAF Bomber Command attacked the coastal batteries, dropping almost 5,000 tons of bombs, which included those used against the Merville Battery, mostly through cloud. The bombers overcame this to a degree through the use of Oboe, a radar system fitted to Mosquitoes, which would mark the target for the bombers. With the coming of daylight, the US Eighth and Ninth Air Forces would join in, together with medium bombers, fighter-bombers and fighters of 2 ATAF. The results of the campaign over the past few months to destroy the Luftwaffe in northern France and the Low Countries were now to be revealed. During D-Day the Allies flew nearly 15,000 sorties, while the Germans were able to manage only 319.

It was now the turn of the Allied navies. Each of the five task forces was preceded by minesweepers. Such was the success of their operations in clearing mines in the Channel that only two vessels were sunk in it on D-Day, a destroyer and an LST. By 2 am on 6 June the minesweepers were off the beaches. They had two tasks, to clear the approaches of mines and also the lanes which the bombarding ships would use. They faced a problem in that the Germans had laid several delayed-action mines, which remained on the sea bottom until activated. Consequently, continual sweeping was required and no stretch of water could be guaranteed to be totally free of mines. Indeed, this was the major cause of loss of Allied ships off Normandy.

Commandos dig in by the gliders used to transport John Howard and his men to the bridges over the Caen Canal and River Orne.

The bombarding ships task was to silence the German coastal batteries and they were organized in three groups. The heavier vessels in each task force – battleships, monitors, cruisers – were positioned some 11,000 yards from the coast and operated in lanes parallel to the shoreline, in which they could manoeuvre. The destroyers, on the other hand, had to approach within 5,500 yards and then anchor. Although this made them more vulnerable to German fire, they would be less prone to falling victim to the delayed-action mines. The final group was the support landing craft, with their miscellany of weapons, which would go in with the assaulting troops. To provide some protection for the bombarding ships and for the landing craft as they neared the shore, Bostons of the RAF's No. 2 Group laid a smokescreen. As for the targets, every battery within range of the landing force was to be engaged, from Villerville, near to the mouth of the Seine, in the east to Barfleur in the west. Fighter aircraft were to be used to spot for the ships' guns and control their fire.

There was a debate between the British and Americans on how long the opening bombardment should be. The British favoured opening fire two hours before the leading landing craft hit the shore to ensure that the batteries were silenced, while the Americans opted for forty minutes in hope of achieving some surprise. H-hour on the two US beaches was to be 6.30am and so the US-commanded Western Task Force would open fire at 5.50am. On the British beaches, fire would open at 5.30am, once it was light enough for the spotter aircraft to see their targets. H-hour here would be 7.15am for Sword and Gold, 7.20am for the right sector of Juno, and 7.30am for the left. In total, five battleships, two monitors, nineteen cruisers, and fifty-eight destroyers and gunboats would take part in the bombardment, with each of the larger ships designated a particular battery as its target.

As it happened, it was the Germans who opened fire first. With the coming of dawn, they began to spot ships through the murk. At 5.05am a battery opened fire on the destroyers USS *Fitch* and *Corry* off Utah. Twenty minutes later, the German guns engaged minesweepers operating off the same beach and the British cruiser HMS *Black Prince* returned fire. A duel now developed, and at 5.36am Admiral Morton L. Deyo, commanding Force U's bombardment group, decided to begin his bombardment. At 6.10am, the aircraft began to lay a smokescreen, but the plane which was to cover *Corry*

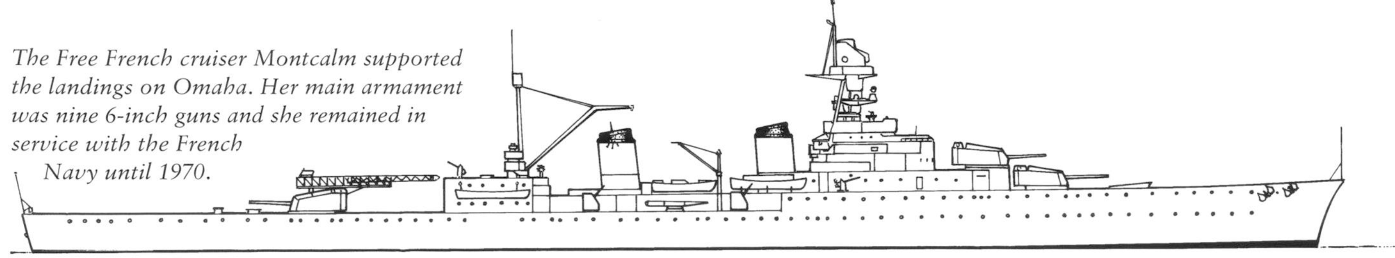

The Free French cruiser Montcalm supported the landings on Omaha. Her main armament was nine 6-inch guns and she remained in service with the French Navy until 1970.

was shot down, leaving her as the only vessel exposed to the shore. The full weight of the local German batteries turned on the destroyer. While manoeuvring to avoid their fire, she was struck by a mine, which broke her back. Two other destroyers quickly moved in and rescued her crew, who suffered forty-six casualties. By now the ships of all five naval forces were engaging the batteries, while the destroyers off the American beaches moved in to suppress strongpoints just

Launched in 1911, the USS Arkansas was the oldest US battleship to serve in World War 2. Her primary armament was twelve 12 -inch guns and she supported the Omaha landings and the assault on Cherbourg.

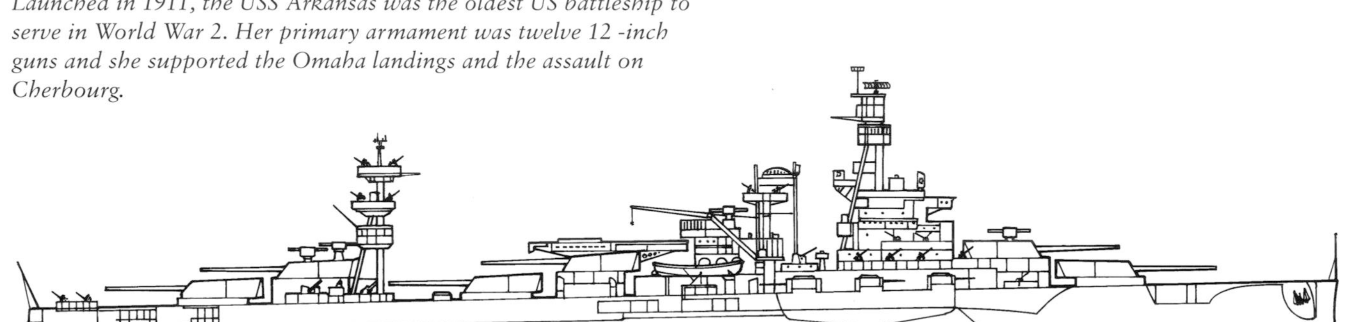

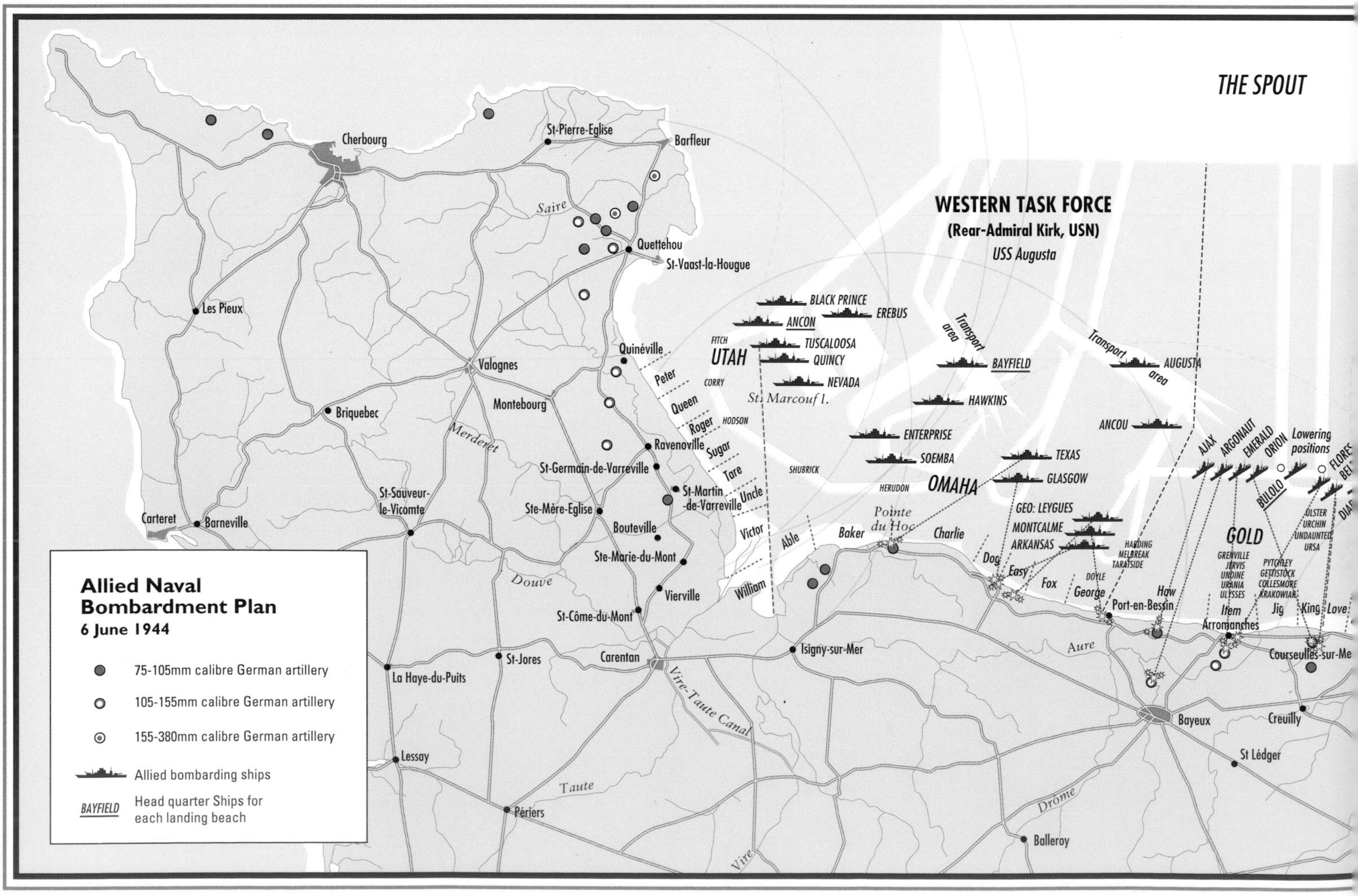

Allied Naval Bombardment Plan
6 June 1944

- 75-105mm calibre German artillery
- 105-155mm calibre German artillery
- 155-380mm calibre German artillery
- Allied bombarding ships
- BAYFIELD — Head quarter Ships for each landing beach

WESTERN TASK FORCE
(Rear-Admiral Kirk, USN)
USS Augusta

THE SPOUT

beyond the beaches. Meanwhile, as H-hour approached, bombers launched more attacks.

For the assaulting troops, conditions during the Channel crossing had been uncomfortable and a number suffered from seasickness. All, though, were relieved that the time of waiting was finally over. Once dawn broke, the convoys were under constant fighter air cover, while on the flanks roamed maritime patrol aircraft watching for any signs of U-boats or German surface vessels. At sea, too, flotillas of anti-submarine vessels also kept constant watch.

Utah Beach was the responsibility of General J. Lawton Collins's US VII Corps. He was a veteran of the Pacific campaigns on Guadalcanal and New Georgia and was known as 'Lightning Joe' from the divisional patch of the 25th Division, which he had commanded against the Japanese. He was tasked with cutting off the Cotentin peninsula and securing Cherbourg. Utah itself was less than a mile and a half long and was characterized by gently sloping sand backed by a sea wall, between four and twelve feet high. Behind the beach there was some flooding, which made the causeways leading inland from the beach vital. Because the beach was relatively narrow, Collins decided that the initial landing would be made by just one reinforced Regimental Combat Team (RCT) of the 4th Infantry Division. This was to advance off the beach to the River Merderet and link up with the airborne troops. Eighty-five minutes after H-hour, a second RCT would land and move north to secure the high ground around Quinéville. The 4th Division's final RCT would land at H+4 hours, advance north-west and seize a crossing over the Merderet. Finally, a reserve RCT, from 90th Division, would also land. Sherman DD tanks would also swim ashore to support the first waves ashore. Collins himself, together with General Raymond O. Barton, commander of the 4th Division, were on board the HQ ship USS *Bayfield*.

Eleven miles from the shore, the troops trans-shipped to their landing craft, not an easy task given the sea state, but one in which they had received much training. The run to the

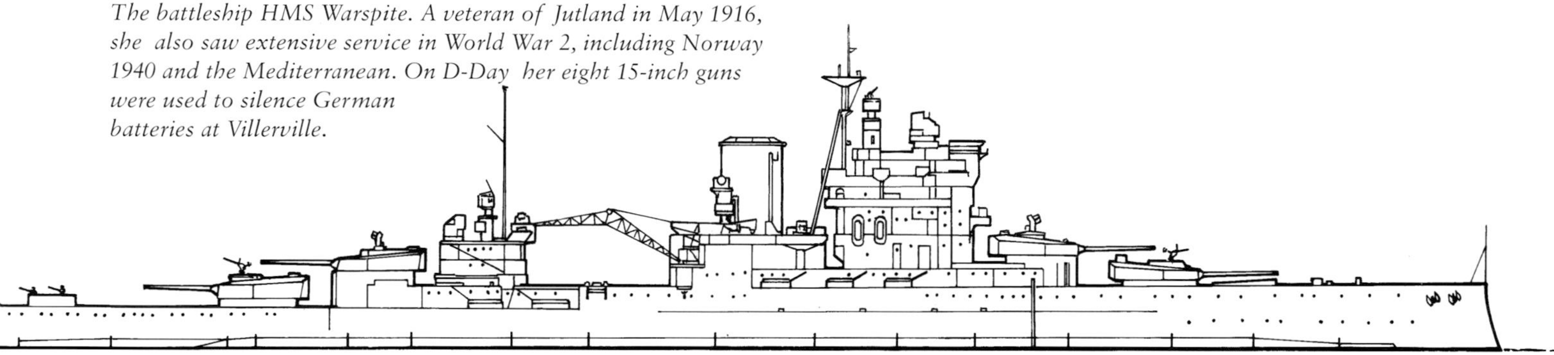

The battleship HMS Warspite. A veteran of Jutland in May 1916, she also saw extensive service in World War 2, including Norway 1940 and the Mediterranean. On D-Day her eight 15-inch guns were used to silence German batteries at Villerville.

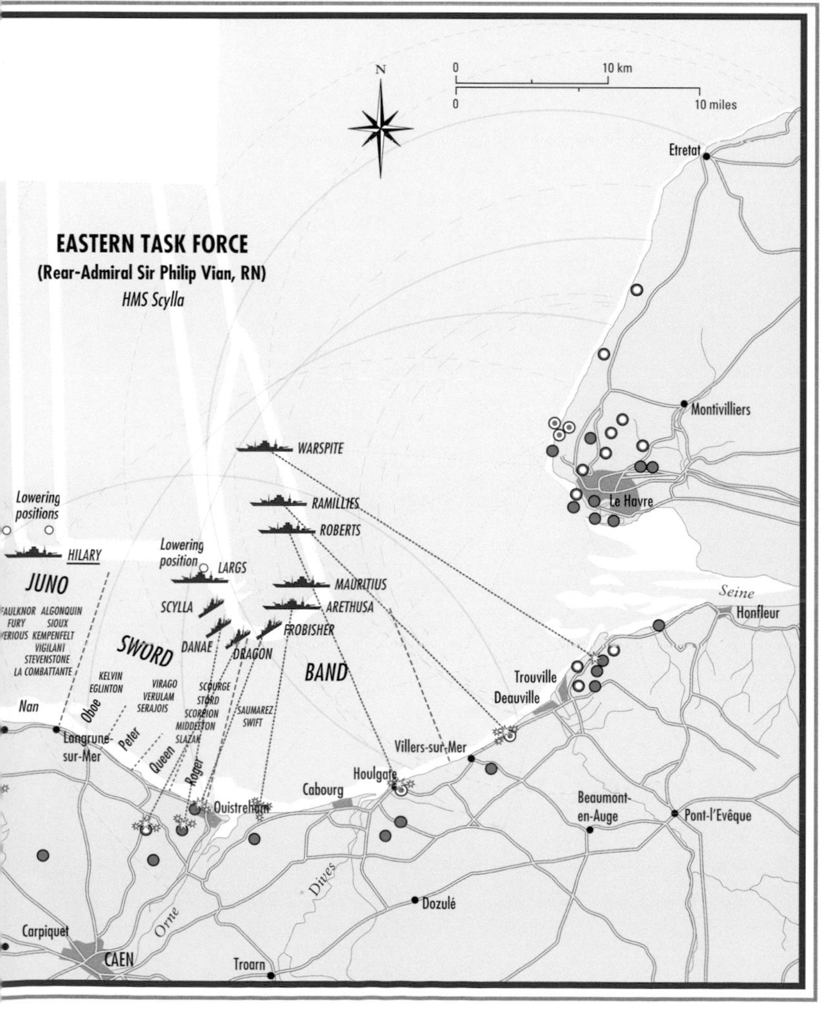

The underlined ships' names represent HQ ships, one for each main landing beach. They had elaborate radio communications and had the naval and landing force commanders on board. The channels had been swept of mines and the larger warships anchored offshore, each given a particular coastal battery to engage. Destroyers (indicated on the map just by their names) engaged the shore defences and helped to shoot the landing craft into the shore.

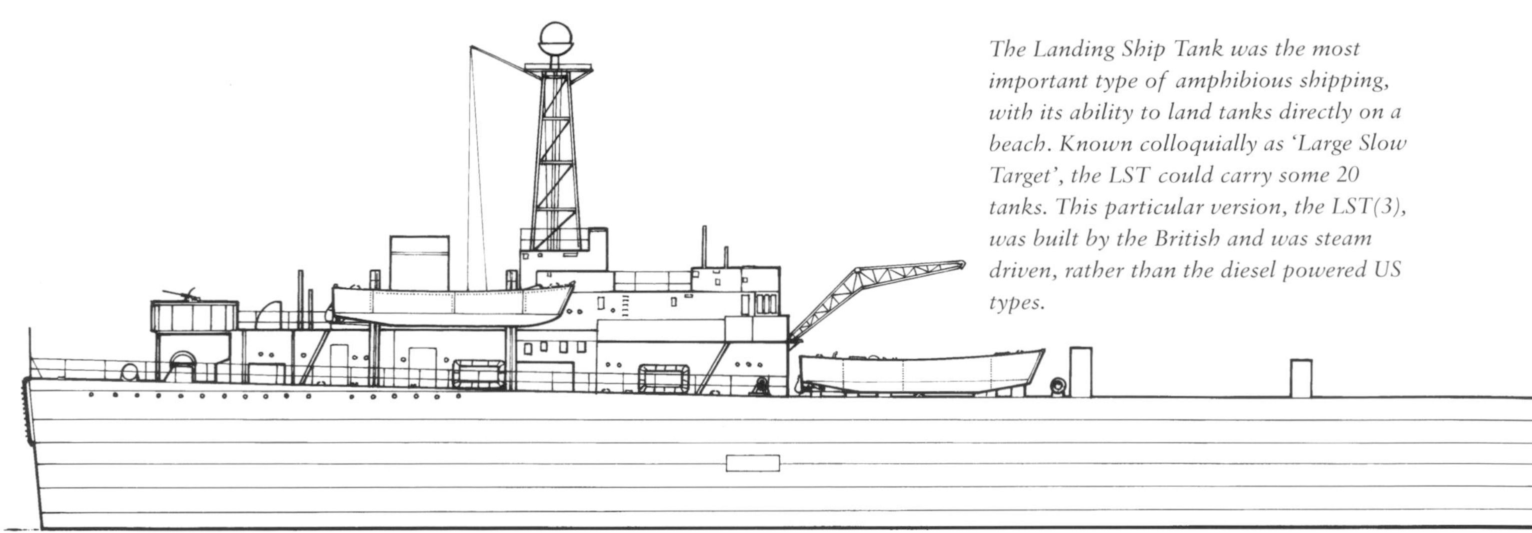

The Landing Ship Tank was the most important type of amphibious shipping, with its ability to land tanks directly on a beach. Known colloquially as 'Large Slow Target', the LST could carry some 20 tanks. This particular version, the LST(3), was built by the British and was steam driven, rather than the diesel powered US types.

Landing Craft Tank (Rocket). This was a variant of the LCT, with the tank deck occupied by a battery of either 792 or 1,080 5-inch rockets. These were fired electrically in salvoes and were designed to pulverize beach defences.

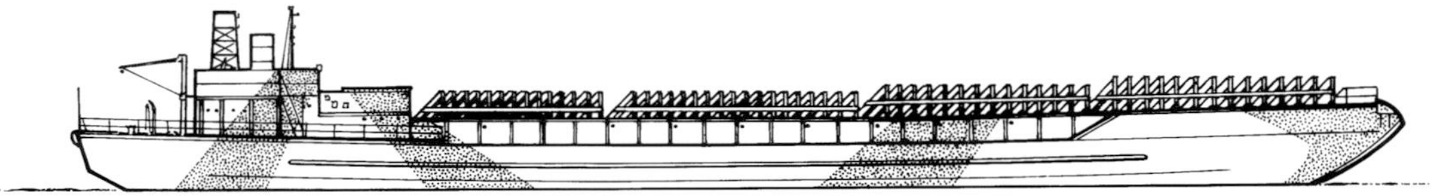

shore was long and uncomfortable in the rough sea. Not until they were halfway there could those on board the landing craft see the French coast, but they were guided by craft equipped with radars and radios. The intention was to release the tanks into the water from their Landing Craft Tank (LCT) five miles from the shore, but progress through the water was slow. En route, one of the patrol craft responsible for guiding them to the beach was sunk, as was an LCT, both victims of mines. With time being lost, it was decided not to launch the tanks until they were one mile from the shore. The naval and air bombardment, together with the smokescreen, reduced visibility. As the leading waves of landing craft closed to the shore two pairs of Landing Craft Gun, armed with 4.7-inch guns, deployed to the flanks to provide supporting fire. Then, there was a hail of rockets from the seventeen LCT(R) supporting the assault.

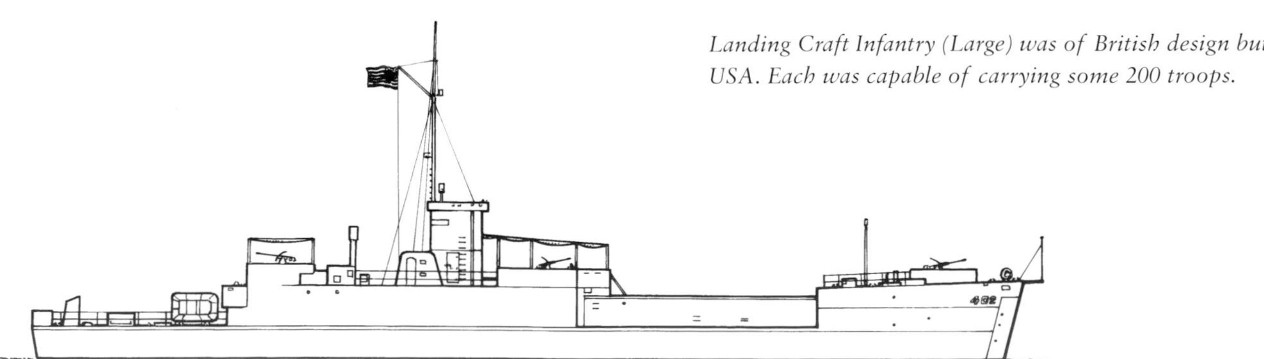

Landing Craft Infantry (Large) was of British design but built in the USA. Each was capable of carrying some 200 troops.

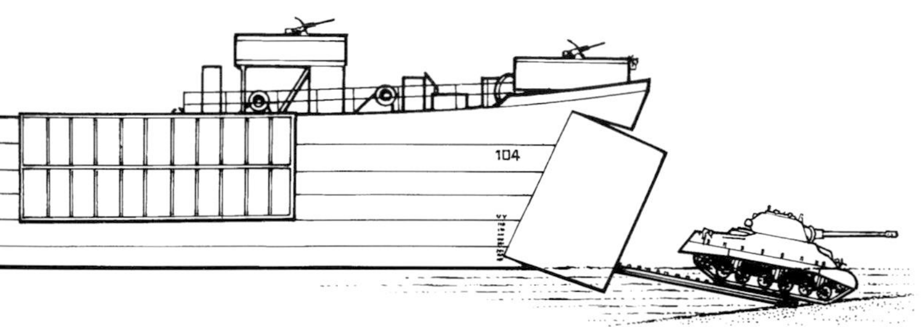

US troops crossdeck to their landing craft prior to landing.

On shore, one battalion of the 709th Division was responsible for Utah, with another in depth behind it. Its defences were still incomplete. Indeed, only one of the Division's thirty-four planned strongpoints had been finished. The beaches were not mined and had few obstacles, with those below the waterline not having any explosives attached. The defenders on Utah were also dazed from the bombing and naval bombardment, which had cut their communications. Indeed, it would not be until the afternoon that the German higher command became aware of the Utah landings. This was as well for the attackers, since they found themselves having to wade ashore through some 100 yards of water. Landing with them was the Assistant Divisional Commander of the 4th Division, Brigadier-General Theodore Roosevelt Jr, son of the President and a veteran of not only North Africa and Sicily, but World War 1 as well, during which he had been twice wounded. He and others quickly realized that none of the features of the beach were recognizable. Because of the obscuration and a strong current, they had landed 2,000 yards south of where they should have been. Roosevelt reacted quickly to the changed circumstances, which were helped by the fact that the defences on this beach were much weaker than on the correct one. He adjusted the attack plans and diverted the follow-up waves. The surviving DD tanks, twenty-eight in all, got ashore ten minutes after H-hour.

Roosevelt saw that there were two priorities, pushing

Barrage balloons were used to protect these LSTs en route to Normandy against low-level air attack.

inland and securing the correct beach. The latter proved a problem, mainly because the German gun line on a ridge overlooking the beach could not be overrun. Even so, the beach was secured, although the troops were not able to advance much towards Quinéville to the north. Better progress was made with the advance inland. One causeway proved to be both undefended and mine-free. Four others were already in the hands of 101st Airborne. The troops were therefore able to advance, with the DD tanks protecting their flanks, and link up with the paratroopers. Much of the 101st's effort had been directed on capturing Pouppeville, which fell at midday. The Germans here retreated towards the beaches and were caught by the advancing elements of 4th Division. The remainder of the 101st were holding a line on the River Douve north of Carentan. Luckily, the Germans did not put in any form of concerted counter-attack, partly because the Carentan canal was the boundary between 709th and 352nd Divisions and there appear to have been co-ordination problems. The 82nd Airborne was in a very much more parlous state. Scattered groups were still west of the Merderet and under increasing pressure from the Germans. The bridge at La Fiere was taken, but the Americans were forced away from it by a determined German counter-attack. General Ridgway himself decided to anchor his defence on St-Mère-Église and established blocking positions on the roads leading into it. This enabled him to restore some cohesion, but, as night fell on D-Day, the 82nd was still isolated.

On the evening of 6 June, the second wave of gliders arrived carrying elements of the airborne divisions' Glider Infantry regiments with much needed heavy weapons. This time, the landings went better, largely because the gliders landed away from the fighting and had fighter cover, which was able to suppress much of the flak. Even so, over 60 per cent of the gliders were write-offs and some 200 men were killed, although this time most the jeeps and guns were saved. The salient result of the day, however, was that the troops who had landed at Utah were firmly ashore and had achieved this with less than 200 casualties. Teddy Roosevelt, whose quick and clear thinking and calm courage had single-handedly restored order from what might have become total chaos, was awarded the Congressional Medal of Honor. Sadly, he was to die of a heart attack five weeks later just as he was about to be given command of a division.

If Utah was reasonably successful, even though the D-Day objectives were only partially achieved, Omaha came close to disaster. It was six miles long and the only possible landing

Part of the invasion fleet at sea. In all nearly 6500 vessels, ranging from battleships to tugs, took part.

beach between the Carentan estuary and Arromanches, which represented the western end of the British beaches. It was in the shape of a gentle crescent bounded at each end by cliffs. At low water there was a stretch of some 200–300 yards of sand littered with obstacles, but at high tide this was reduced to a few yards of shingle backed by a sea wall up to twelve feet in height. Behind this there was a shelf some 200 yards wide, on which, in the eastern half, ran a coast road. An anti-tank ditch had been constructed here. Beyond the shelf were cliffs some 150 feet high on which were situated numerous strongpoints. Two German regiments from 352nd Division held this sector, which was the most heavily defended of all the Allied beaches.

Clarence R. Huebner's 1st Infantry Division, 'the Big Red One', was to carry out the landings. His overall mission after landing was to advance in step with the British south towards St Lô. For this he would come under the orders of General Leonard T. Gerow's V Corps, which was responsible for the Omaha plan. The intention was to land two RCTs abreast, the 16th on the left and the 116th, which had been detached from 29th Division, on the right. The 18th Regimental Combat Team would be the follow-up. Omaha was more exposed to the weather than Utah. Even so, trans-shipping to the landing craft would take place at the same distance from the shore, ie, eleven miles. Likewise, the DD tanks, which were to land first, together with armoured bulldozers and demolition engineers, would be released 5,500 yards from the coast. All this was because of the threat of the coastal batteries. It was, however, hoped that the air and naval bombardment would neutralise them sufficiently to enable the troops to get over the cliffs and secure the four entrances to the beach that ran through them. The nearest battery was at Pointe du Hoc, three miles east of Omaha, and, it was believed, consisted of five or six 155mm guns. This was of particular concern because it could shoot into the flank of the landing flotilla. While it was to be the target of the battleship USS *Texas*, it was decided to make doubly sure that it could not influence events, by landing two Ranger battalions to destroy the guns.

One blessing for Force O, the ships off Omaha, was that the Germans had laid no delayed-action mines in the area. They were in position by 2.20am and the transports carrying the assault troops were ready to begin trans-shipping them half an hour later. The sea, with a strong north-west wind blowing, was much rougher than off Utah and caused much discomfort to the troops once they were in their landing craft, but by 4.30am they were en route for the shore. At 5.30am a battery at Port-en-Bessin opened up on the battleship USS *Arkansas*. It was joined by other batteries, which engaged the destroyers, but that at Pointe du Hoc remained strangely silent. It was light enough for a spotter plane to be present and it was able to ensure that the batteries were neutralized just as the main bombardment opened at 5.50am.

The dominant bluff, defences and beach obstacles all helped to make Omaha the most problematic of the D-Day beaches.

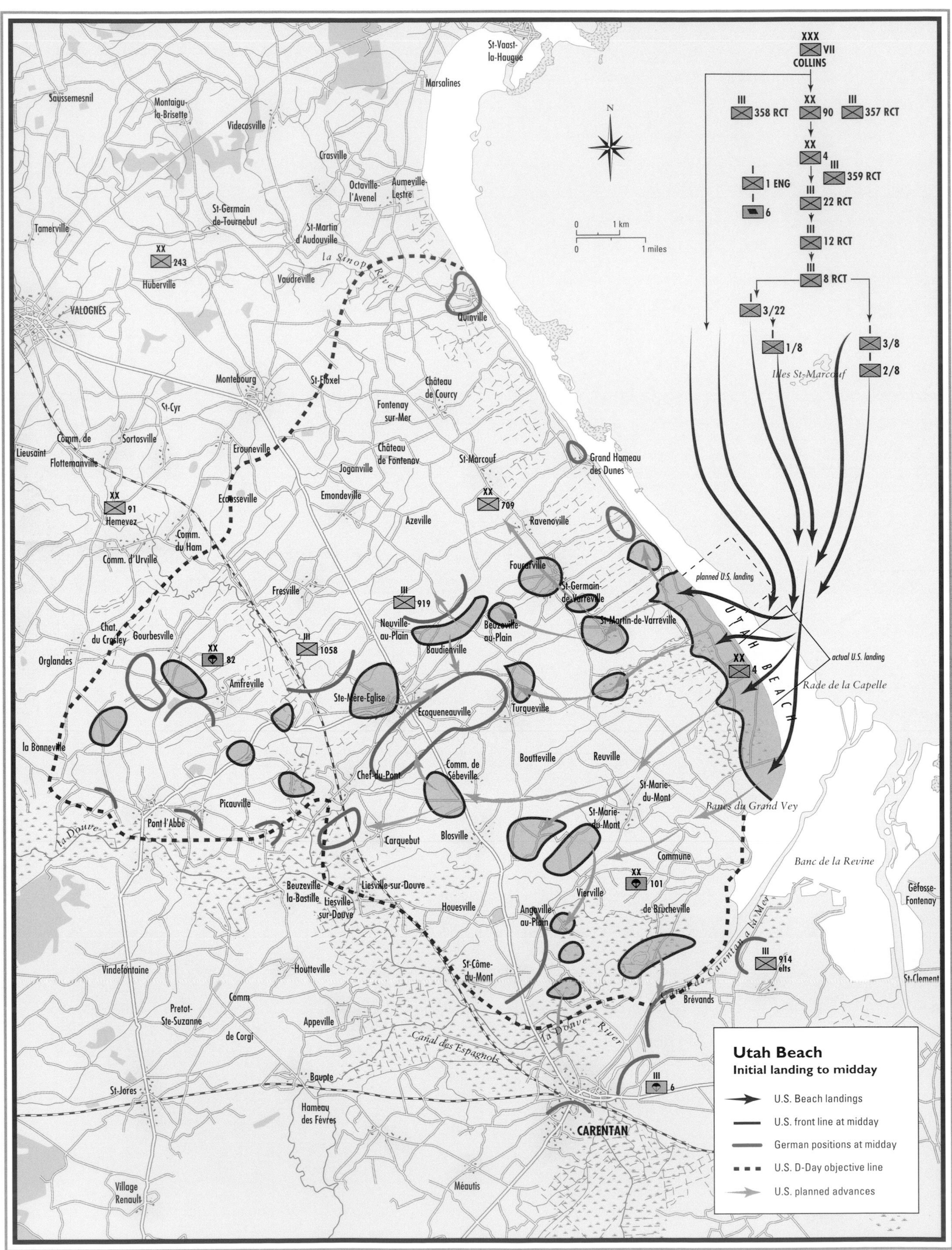
Utah Beach
Initial landing to midday
U.S. Beach landings
U.S. front line at midday
German positions at midday
U.S. D-Day objective line
U.S. planned advances
XXX VII COLLINS
358 RCT
90
357 RCT
4
359 RCT
1 ENG
6
22 RCT
12 RCT
8 RCT
3/22
1/8
3/8
2/8
243
91
709
919
1058
82
101
914 elts
6
St-Vaast-la-Haugue
Marsalines
Saussemesnil
Montaigu-la-Brisette
Videcosville
Crasville
Octaville-l'Avenel
Aumeville-Lestre
St-Germain-de-Tournebut
St-Martin d'Audouville
Tamerville
la Sinope River
Vaudreville
Huberville
VALOGNES
Quinville
Montebourg
St-Floxel
Château de Courcy
St-Cyr
Fontenay sur-Mer
Comm. de Flottemanville
Sortosville
Lieusaint
Erouneville
Château de Fontenay
Joganville
St-Marcouf
Grand Hameau des Dunes
Ecausseville
Emondeville
Hemevez
Azeville
Ravenoville
Comm. du Ham
Comm. d'Urville
Foucarville
Fresville
St-Germain-de-Varreville
planned U.S. landing
St-Martin-de-Varreville
UTAH BEACH
actual U.S. landing
Neuville-au-Plain
Beuzeville-au-Plain
Baudienville
Chat. du Castey
Gourbesville
Orglandes
Amfreville
Ste-Mère-Eglise
Ecoqueneauville
Turqueville
Rade de la Capelle
la Bonneville
Boutteville
Reuville
Comm. de Sébeville
Chef-du-Pont
St-Marie-du-Mont
Picauville
Pont l'Abbé
la Douve
Carquebut
Blosville
Bancs du Grand Vey
Commune
Banc de la Revine
Beuzeville-la-Bastille
Liesville-sur-Douve
Vierville
Houesville
Angoville-au-Plain
de Brucheville
Géfosse-Fontenay
Vindefontaine
Houtteville
St-Côme-du-Mont
Canal de Carentan à la Mer
St-Clement
Pretot-Ste-Suzanne
Comm
de Corgi
Appeville
Brévands
la Douve River
Canal des Espagnols
Baupte
St-Jores
Hameau des Fèvres
CARENTAN
Village Renault
Méautis
0 1 km
0 1 miles
N

(Left) The 4th Infantry Division landed on the wrong beach, but quickly adjusted to this. The key early success was securing the causeways leading inland from the beach. This enabled it to link up with elements of 101st Airborne, but much of this and 82nd Division were still very scattered and the Germans were setting about dealing with isolated pockets. The 4th Division's efforts to advance northwards were also being frustrated by heavy fire.

Ten minutes later, 480 B-24 Liberators flew over and dropped their bombs. As on Utah, there was a thirtysecond delay before bomb release to avoid hitting the landing craft and none of the coastal defences were touched. Meanwhile, the DD tanks supporting 116 RCT were launched. Almost immediately, some began to founder in the rough sea and only five out of thirty-two eventually reached the shore. Three of them survived only thanks to the LCT commander pulling up his ramp when the first of the tanks he was carrying drowned. Those carrying the tanks to support the other RCT also ran into the shore and landed them one minute before H-hour. Some of the landing craft in the leading waves were swamped during the run-in and as a result almost all their supporting field artillery was lost. Obscuration and the current played its part, as on Utah, with troops landing in the wrong place and being disorientated. Many landed shoulder-deep in water and struggled to get ashore with all the equipment they were carrying. Under intense German fire, many fell. Those who did make it onto dry land sought shelter under the sea wall or among the beach obstacles, but found that many of their radios did not work. Officers running between groups to try to restore cohesion were shot down and confusion reigned. Out at sea in their HQ ship, Gerow and Huebner had little idea of what was happening.

The Rangers, who were under command of 116 RCT, also had their problems. The idea was that Lieutenant- Colonel James E. Rudder's 2nd Ranger Battalion would make the initial attack on Pointe du Hoc, a small triangular cape some 120 feet high with almost vertical cliffs. The shingle beach below was covered by numerous machine guns and it appeared a suicidal mission. Rudder devised an ingenious way of surmounting the cliffs, using landing-craft-mounted rocket launchers, which would fire ropes and rope ladders with grapnels attached to the end to anchor the ropes and ladders to the top of the cliffs. His men also had extension ladders, some borrowed from the London Fire Brigade. The landing craft became so swamped during the run-in that the Rangers had to use their helmets as bailers. Two even sank, including the one carrying their stores. The navigating launch then mistook another feature for the Pointe du Hoc. Rudder realized the error just in time, but the little flotilla then had to beat its way up the coast in the face of a head wind. It was also being engaged by machine gun fire from the shore. A British and then a US destroyer laid down suppressive fire and the Rangers finally reached their objective at 7.08am, when they should have landed at 6.30am. With the destroyer USS *Satterlee* and the navigating launch providing covering fire, the rope grapnels were fired. Many held and 150 Rangers quickly began to scale the cliffs. Once on top, they fanned out over the point, discovering that the guns they had come to spike were mere telegraph poles put there until the battery casemates could be completed.

US troops start to move off the beach at Utah.

The plan was for the captors of Pointe du Hoc to now be reinforced by the balance of the 2nd Rangers and the whole of the 5th Rangers, but Colonel Max Schneider, commanding the group, was not told of their success. Hence, he adopted the secondary plan, which was to land with 116 RCT on the westernmost Omaha beach. On Pointe du Hoc itself, Rudder's men continued mopping up operations and also patrolled as far as the Grandcamp–Vierville road. One of these patrols discovered four of the Pointe du Hoc guns camouflaged in a field and rendered them inoperable with thermite bombs. The Germans were, however, well aware what had happened and launched a series of counter-attacks, the third of which forced the Rangers back onto the point. By the end of D-Day, Rudder was in a critical situation, with a third of his men casualties and ammunition running low.

Back on Omaha, at 7am the follow-up waves had begun to land, but the incoming tide was now up to the shingle below the sea wall. This caused growing congestion and at 8.30am the beachmaster was forced to order that no more vehicles be landed. As it was, he had had to divert some equipment carrying landing craft to less congested beaches, which added to the confusion. Even so, by this time the COs of the two leading RCTs had landed, as well as the Assistant Divisional Commander of 29th Division, and some semblance of order began to be established. Men began to infiltrate the gaps in the cliffs behind the beach and knock out the strongpoints on them. At noon elements of 116 RCT, including the Rangers, had secured Vierville and in the late afternoon the balance of 29th Division began to land. Before nightfall the headquarters of V Corps had been established, but the situation was still serious. The Americans held a beachhead some 4,000 yards long and 1,000 yards deep. A concerted counterattack could still drive them back into the sea.

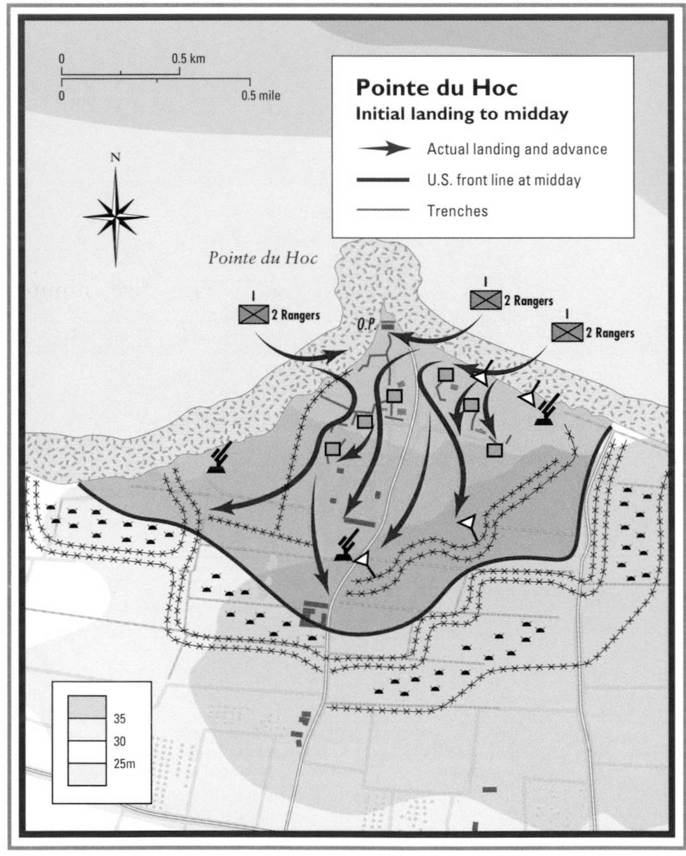

Rudder's Rangers' approach from the sea took the battery by surprise and circumvented most of its defences. They successfully secured the position by midday, but discovered that the actual guns had been removed. Their intention now was to exploit inland, but, because of the setbacks on Omaha, they were to find themselves isolated.

Liberators overfly the invasion fleet. Their target was coastal batteries but cloud hampered them.

There was better fortune on the British beaches, although there was still frustration. Some six miles east of Omaha was the westernmost of these beaches, Gold. The terrain here was somewhat different to Omaha. The beach was fringed merely by low sand dunes and behind it lay somewhat boggy ground intersected by dykes. One problem was that much of the foreshore was made up of blue clay, which made it difficult for vehicles to traverse. Gold lay in the eastern part of 352nd Division's sector and was covered by two battalions, supported by the Division's mobile reserve, which consisted of a further three battalions. The beaches had both underwater and exposed obstacles, which included mines attached to posts. There were also plenty of strongpoints overlooking the beach and the villages were well fortified. The area behind the beach was also littered with anti-tank obstacles.

The 50th (Northumbrian) Division, also known as the

Tyne and Tees, contained men largely from the north-east of England. For D-Day, however, it had been given an additional infantry brigade, 231, which was made of battalions from the south-west of England, 8th Armoured Brigade, a battalion of flail tanks for mine clearance, some flamethrower tanks, and 47 Royal Marine Commando. There were also Centaur tanks mounting a 95mm howitzer from the Royal Marines Support Group. Major-General Douglas Graham, the divisional commander, had already taken part in the Salerno landings, during which he had been wounded. His plan was to land with two brigades up, 231 in the west and 69 Brigade in the east, and then to use his other two brigades as follow-up. The Royal Marine Commando was given a special task of landing on the extreme right flank of 231 Brigade and then advancing west to seize Port-en-Bessin and link up with the Americans on Omaha. Once ashore, the Division's main objective was to secure the high ground south of Bayeux by the end of D-Day.

US naval demolition teams dealing with beach obstacles, many of which had explosives attached to them. Drawing by American artist Mitchell Jamieson (1915-76).

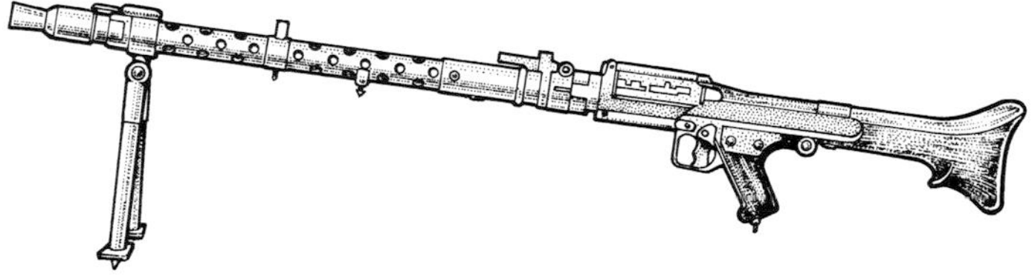

German MG42 machine gun. At 1200 rounds per minute it had a significantly faster rate of fire than Allied types.

The air and naval bombardments followed much the same pattern as on the other beaches, although, of course, the naval bombardment was to last for two hours. Force G, however, had no battleships and was built around four British cruisers. They opened fire at 5.30am and the cruiser HMS *Ajax* found itself engaged in a duel with the coastal battery at Longues, which was not subdued until 8.45am. Otherwise, there was very little response from the shore. Because of the rough seas it was decided not to swim the DD tanks of 8th Armoured Brigade ashore. They would be landed instead, together with the Centaurs. The first waves landed at 7.25am, five minutes before H-Hour. On Jig beach, the right-hand lead battalion of 231 Brigade, the 1st Hampshires, had a grim time. Because of the decision not to swim them, they arrived on the beach with no Sherman DDs. Only five out of the ten Centaurs allocated to it were landed, the others having been sunk, and these five were quickly knocked out on the beach. A number of the flail tanks fell victim to the blue clay. The Hampshires' primary task was to capture Le Hamel, but the preliminary bombardment had left it virtually unscathed. The defenders were full of fight and the Hampshires suffered heavy casual-

Troops struggle ashore on Omaha Beach after their landing craft has sunk. The weather conditions did not help in an already difficult situation.

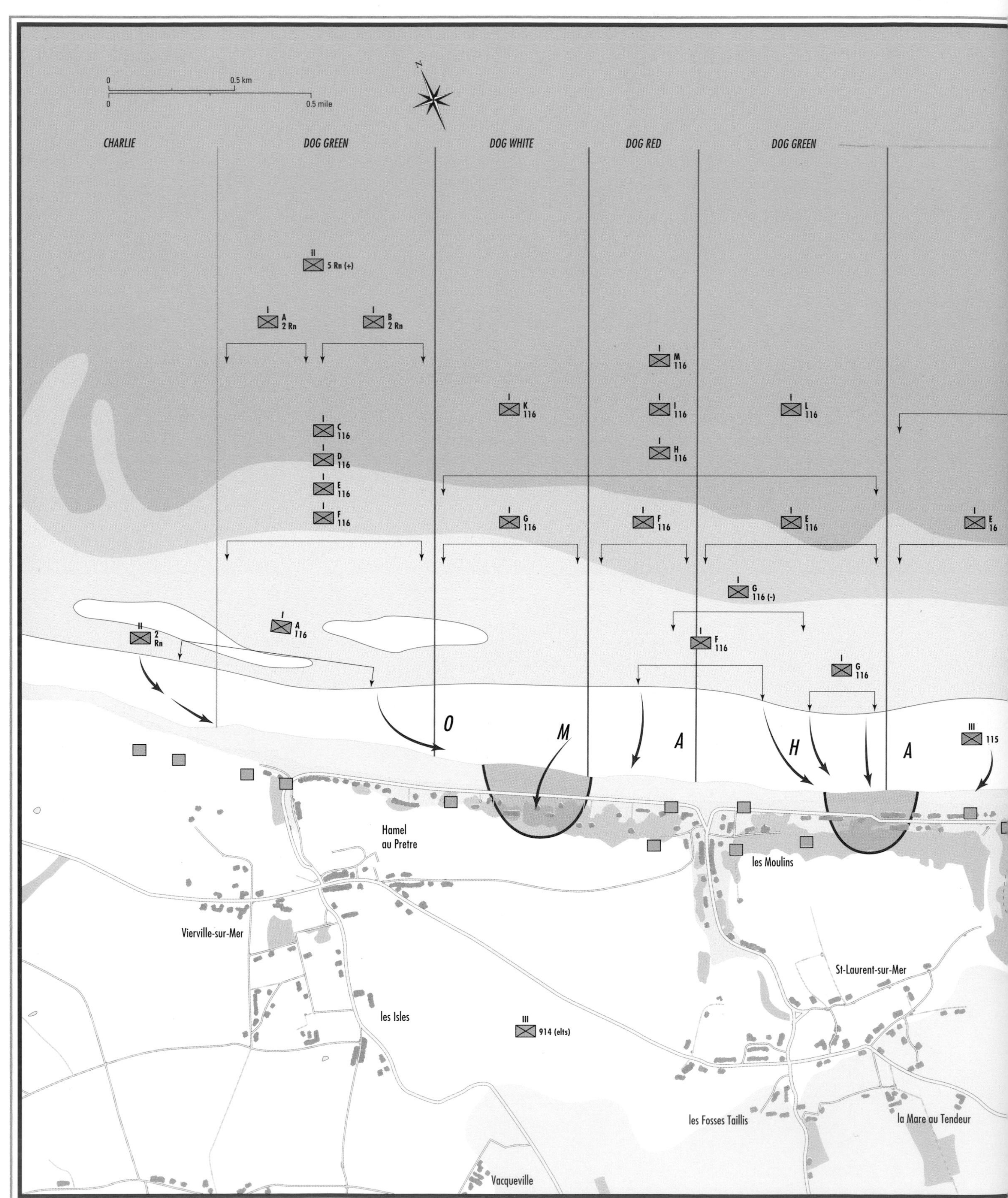

0
0.5 km
0
0.5 mile
N
CHARLIE
DOG GREEN
DOG WHITE
DOG RED
DOG GREEN
II 5 Rn (+)
I A 2 Rn
I B 2 Rn
I M 116
I K 116
I I 116
I L 116
I C 116
I D 116
I H 116
I E 116
I F 116
I G 116
I F 116
I E 116
I E 16
I G 116 (-)
I A 116
II 2 Rn
I F 116
I G 116
O
M
A
H
A
III 115
Hamel au Pretre
les Moulins
Vierville-sur-Mer
St-Laurent-sur-Mer
les Isles
III 914 (elts)
les Fosses Taillis
la Mare au Tendeur
Vacqueville

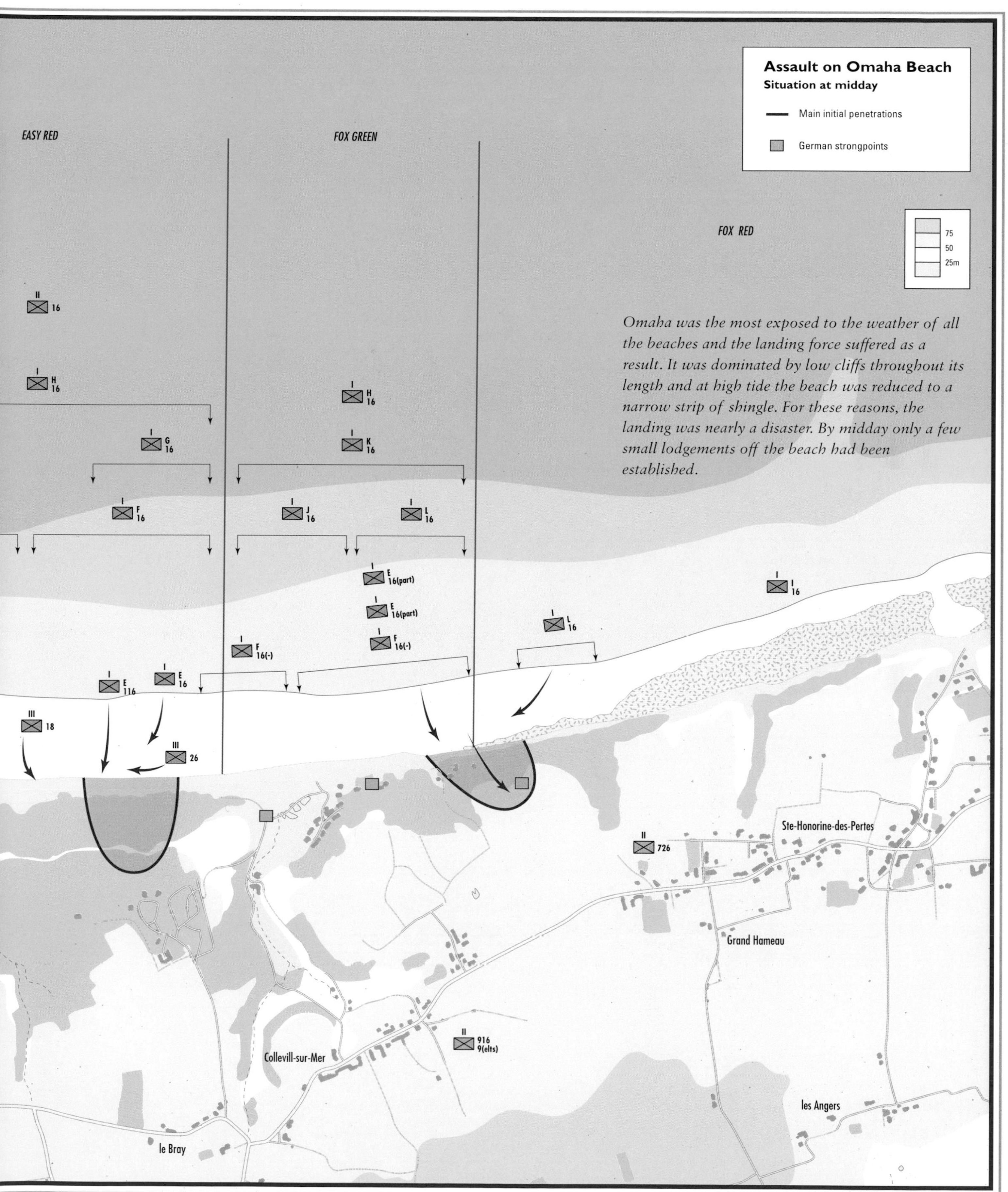

Omaha was the most exposed to the weather of all the beaches and the landing force suffered as a result. It was dominated by low cliffs throughout its length and at high tide the beach was reduced to a narrow strip of shingle. For these reasons, the landing was nearly a disaster. By midday only a few small lodgements off the beach had been established.

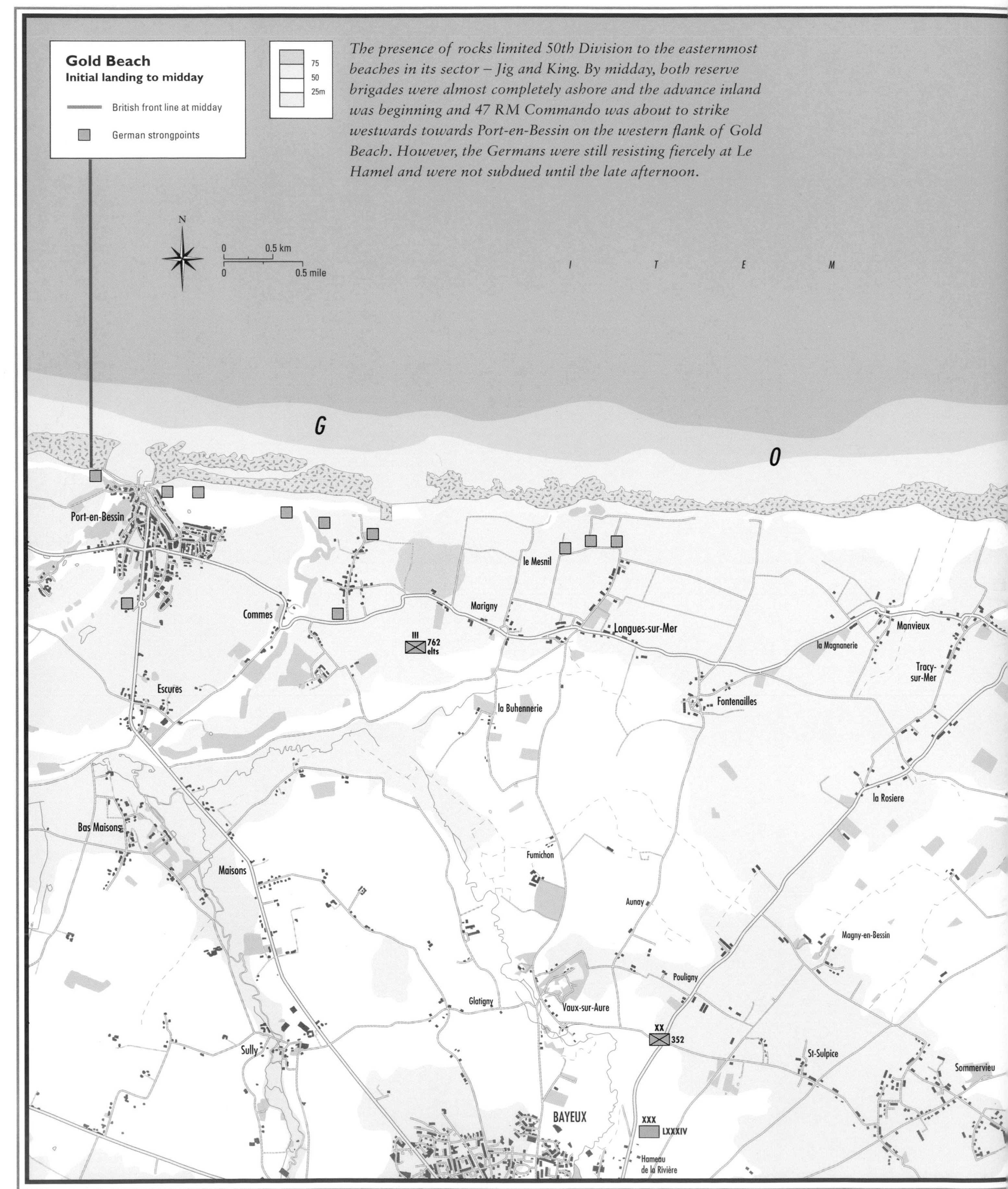

The presence of rocks limited 50th Division to the easternmost beaches in its sector – Jig and King. By midday, both reserve brigades were almost completely ashore and the advance inland was beginning and 47 RM Commando was about to strike westwards towards Port-en-Bessin on the western flank of Gold Beach. However, the Germans were still resisting fiercely at Le Hamel and were not subdued until the late afternoon.

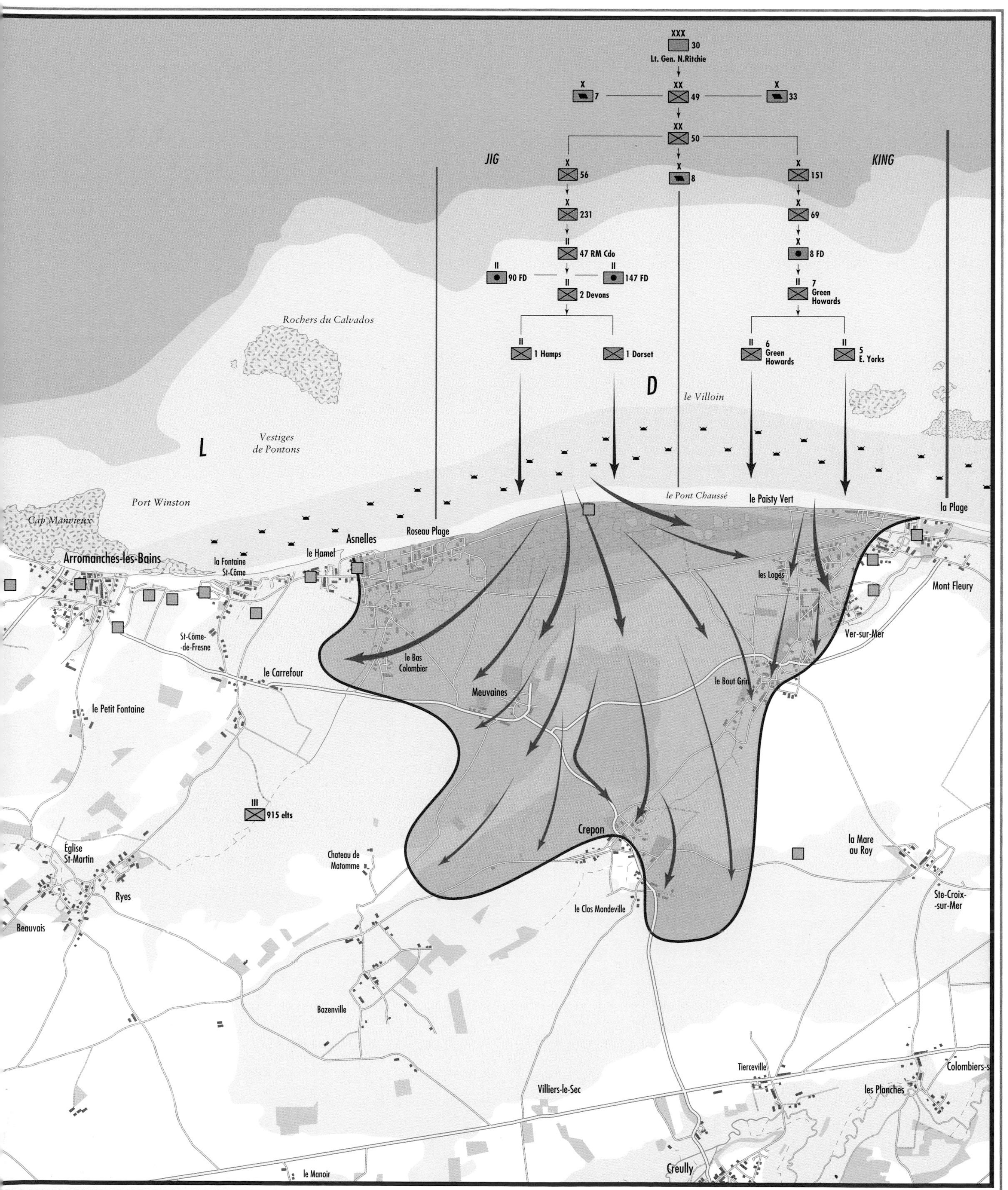

XXX
30
Lt. Gen. N.Ritchie
X
7
XX
49
X
33
XX
50
JIG
KING
X
56
X
8
X
151
X
231
X
69
II
47 RM Cdo
X
8 FD
II
90 FD
II
147 FD
II
2 Devons
II
7 Green Howards
Rochers du Calvados
II
1 Hamps
1 Dorset
II
6 Green Howards
II
5 E. Yorks
D
le Villoin
L
Vestiges de Pontons
Port Winston
le Pont Chaussé
le Paisty Vert
la Plage
Cap Manvieux
Roseau Plage
Asnelles
Arromanches-les-Bains
la Fontaine St-Côme
le Hamel
les Loges
Mont Fleury
St-Côme-de-Fresne
le Bas Colombier
Ver-sur-Mer
le Carrefour
Meuvaines
le Bout Grin
le Petit Fontaine
III
915 elts
Crepon
la Mare au Roy
Église St-Martin
Chateau de Matomme
Ryes
Ste-Croix-sur-Mer
Beauvais
le Clos Mondeville
Bazenville
Tierceville
Colombiers-s
Villiers-le-Sec
les Planches
le Manoir
Creully

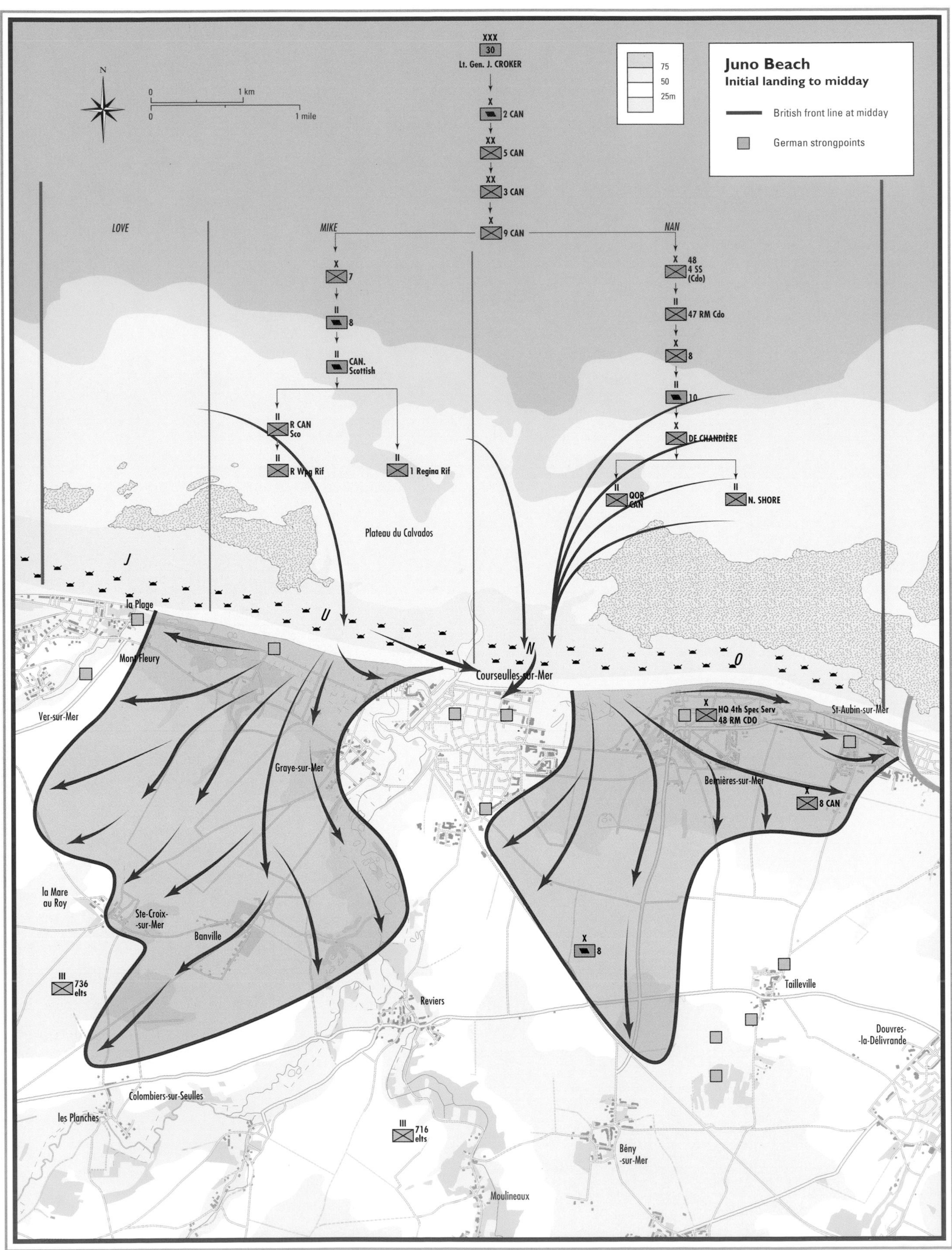
Juno Beach
Initial landing to midday
British front line at midday
German strongpoints
75
50
25m
0
1 km
0
1 mile
N
XXX
30
Lt. Gen. J. CROKER
2 CAN
5 CAN
3 CAN
9 CAN
LOVE
MIKE
NAN
7
8
CAN. Scottish
R CAN Sco
R Wpg Rif
1 Regina Rif
48 4 SS (Cdo)
47 RM Cdo
8
10
DE CHANDIÈRE
QOR CAN
N. SHORE
Plateau du Calvados
J
U
N
O
la Plage
Mont Fleury
Ver-sur-Mer
Courseulles-sur-Mer
HQ 4th Spec Serv 48 RM CDO
St-Aubin-sur-Mer
Graye-sur-Mer
Bernières-sur-Mer
8 CAN
la Mare au Roy
Ste-Croix--sur-Mer
Banville
736 elts
Reviers
Tailleville
Douvres--la-Délivrande
Colombiers-sur-Seulles
les Planches
716 elts
Bény -sur-Mer
Moulineaux

(Left) As with Gold Beach, offshore rocks resulted in a narrow landing area. This did cause increasing congestion once the reserve brigade began to land at 11.40 am. The two assault brigades, even though they landed behind schedule, were quickly off the beaches. Only the strongpoints in and around Courseulles-sur-Mer presented any significant problems.

ties, including both the CO and Second-in-Command killed. The 1st Dorsets experienced fewer problems on the left part of Jig Beach. Flail tanks and Armoured Vehicles Royal Engineers (AVREs) landed with the leading waves, providing immediate armoured support. They quickly cleared the beach obstacles and were soon advancing inland, skirting round east of Le Hamel. On King Beach the story was much the same as for the Dorsets, although the left -hand battalion of 69 Brigade was pinned down for a while under the sea wall and had to call in naval fire support to extricate itself.

At 8.15am the follow-up battalion of 231 Brigade landed and incurred casualties from Le Hamel. It sent one company to assist the Hampshire, while the remainder began to advance south-west. Immediately afterwards, the Royal Marine Commandos came ashore, but not before three out of their five landing craft had been holed by underwater obstacles. The survivors had to swim ashore, but No 47 quickly reorganised and was soon advancing to Port-en-Bessin. They fought a sharp action for the village of La Rosière and reached a piece of high ground just south of Port-en-Bessin and dug in for the night. Meanwhile the follow-up battalion of 69 Brigade had also landed and this was followed by the other two brigades in the Division, although 56 Brigade had to be allocated a different beach because of the threat from Le Hamel. Both these brigades were completely on shore by midday. The 50th Division now began to advance inland, forcing the Germans back with heavy casualties. Le Hamel was eventually secured and by nightfall the Division had penetrated over three miles inland, although it was stopped short of Bayeux.

Sherman Duplex Drive (DD). The turret and upper part of the hull were protected by a canvas screen, with the propellor providing propulsion. Once on shore, the screen and duplex could be removed.

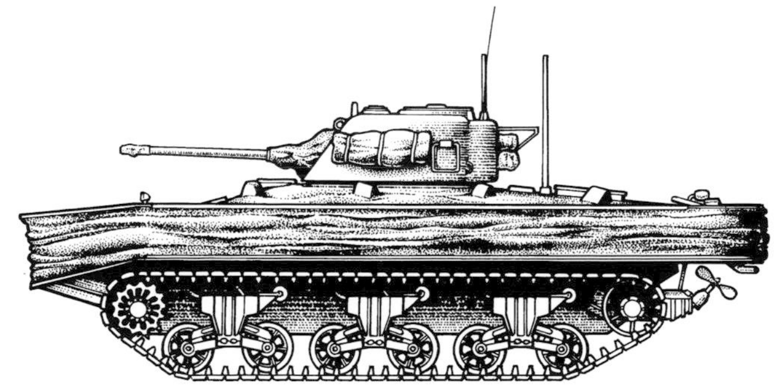

Canadian troops come ashore on Juno Beach. They are clearly one of the follow-up waves but they are still under fire. Hence the tension in the men's faces.

Juno Beach was a Canadian affair and was to be assaulted by Major-General Rod Keller's 3rd Canadian Division. The main problem with the beach itself was offshore reefs, which restricted the entrances to it, to just one for Mike and one for Nan beaches. Indeed, while H-hour for Mike was 7.35am, that for Nan was ten minutes later to allow time for the tide to cover rocks off it, although these in the end proved to be just seaweed. Behind the beaches, the ground generally rose inland. The sector was part of that of the German 716th Division. One battalion covered the beaches themselves, with an 'East' battalion of doubtful quality in support. The further battalions provided depth to the defence and there was a mobile reserve in the shape of a Panzer Grenadier battalion of 21st Panzer Division. There

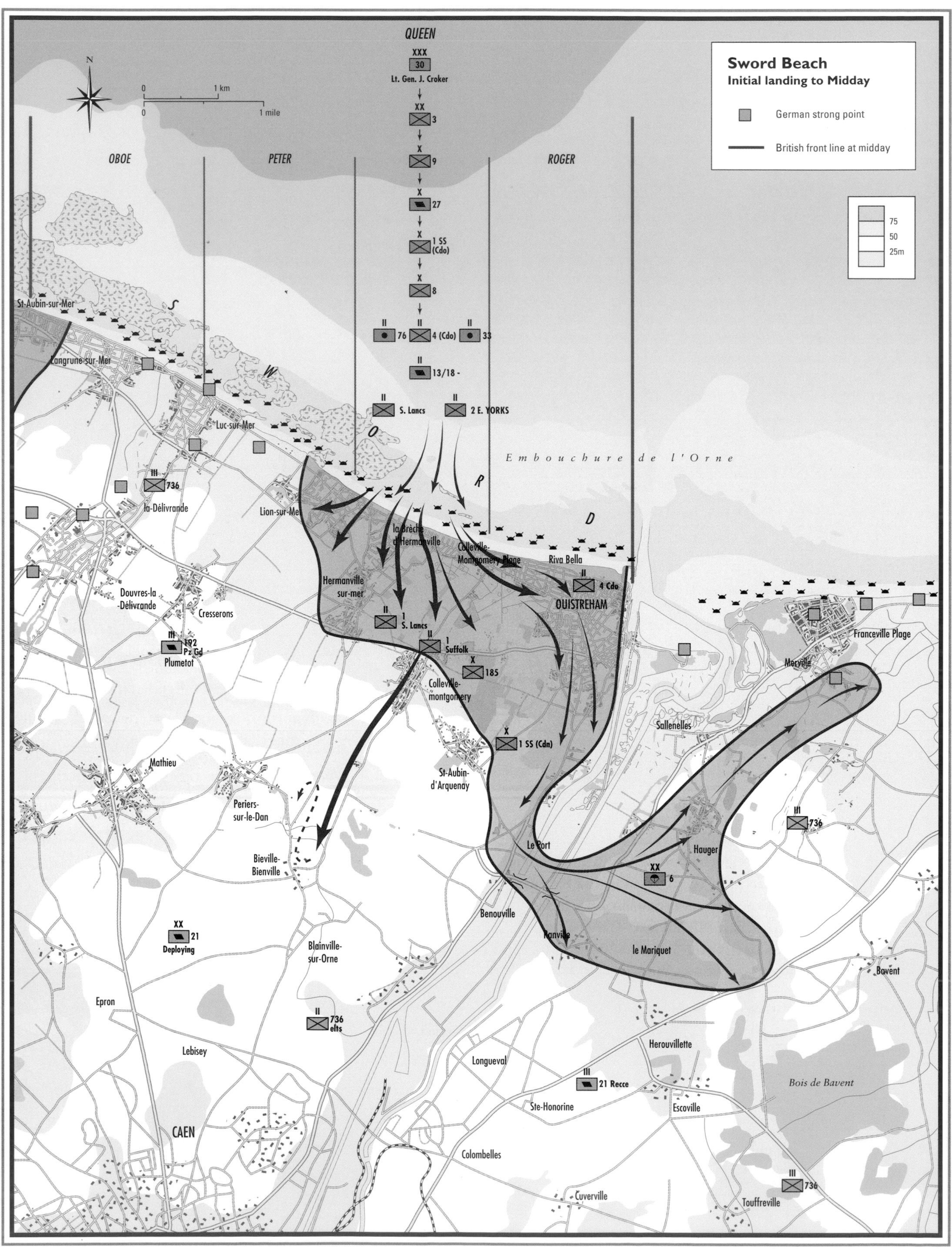
Sword Beach
Initial landing to Midday
German strong point
British front line at midday
75
50
25m
N
0
1 km
1 mile
QUEEN
XXX
30
Lt. Gen. J. Croker
XX
3
X
9
27
1 SS (Cdo)
8
76
4 (Cdo)
33
13/18 -
S. Lancs
2 E. YORKS
OBOE
PETER
ROGER
S
W
O
R
D
Embouchure de l'Orne
St-Aubin-sur-Mer
Langrune-sur-Mer
Luc-sur-Mer
Lion-sur-Mer
736
la-Délivrande
Douvres-la -Délivrande
Cresserons
192 Pz Gd
Plumetot
Hermanville sur-mer
la Brèche d'Hermanville
Colleville-Montgomery Plage
Riva Bella
4 Cdo
OUISTREHAM
1 S. Lancs
1 Suffolk
185
Colleville-montgomery
1 SS (Cdn)
Franceville Plage
Merville
Sallenelles
Mathieu
Periers-sur-le-Dan
St-Aubin-d'Arquenay
Bieville-Bienville
Le Port
Hauger
6
Benouville
Ranville
le Mariquet
21
Deploying
Blainville-sur-Orne
Bavent
Epron
736 elts
Lebisey
Herouvillette
Longueval
21 Recce
Bois de Bavent
Ste-Honorine
Escoville
CAEN
Colombelles
Cuverville
Touffreville

(Left) By midday, the British 3rd Division was firmly ashore. 185 Brigade was poised to advance on Caen, but was still awaiting its supporting tanks, which were held up on the exits of the beach. The Commandos of 1 Special Service Brigade were racing to relieve Howard's men on Pegasus Bridge. On the German side, 21st Panzer Division was beginning to deploy for a counter-attack, but was reacting to events much too slowly.

was also an anti-tank battalion deployed on the high ground south of Creully. As on the other beaches, the coast was protected by a number of strongpoints.

Keller's D-Day task was to secure the high ground west of Caen inclusive of the Caen–Bayeux road. In particular, he was to capture Carpiquet airfield. He planned to land with two brigades abreast, with the third landing on whichever beach had shown the most progress. This would then advance to the railway line running just south of the Caen Bayeux road and prepare to meet the expected German counter-attack. Keller was also given No. 48 Royal Marine Commando. This was to land on the extreme left flank, capture Langrune-sur-Mer, and link up with Sword Beach. There was also a Canadian armoured brigade, one battalion of which would land with each of the leading brigades, with two tank companies swimming ashore and the other being landed dryshod. The third tank battalion would support the follow-up brigade. Twenty-eight AVREs were also available for beach obstacle clearance. The Canadians had the smallest of the naval bombardment forces, with just two cruisers and eleven destroyers.

An initial problem occurred on the approach of Force J to the swept channels, with four of its groups straying into the wrong channels. Consequently, H-hour was postponed by ten minutes, but the naval bombardment opened on time. The swell and current also slowed the run-in to the shore. The two DD tank companies supporting 7 Brigade on the right were to be launched in the water 7,000 yards from the shore, but it was decided to reduce this to 4,000 yards. Twenty-two out of thirty-eight got onto the beach ahead of the infantry. They immediately began engaging strongpoints, but a number became trapped by the incoming tide and were immobilized. The infantry landed at 8.10am, twenty-five minutes after the amended H-hour, because of the sea conditions and the fact that a number of landing craft were lost to underwater obstacles. They then had a fierce battle on their hands to clear the strongpoints around Courseulles. The 8 Brigade DD tanks

Commandos, with bicycles to improve their mobility, come ashore on Sword Beach.

were released even closer in and found themselves merely having to wade ashore, but they arrived after the infantry, who themselves were just over fifteen minutes late. They, too, had a tussle to reduce the strongpoints on their beach. As on Gold, it was noted that the naval bombardment had a disappointing effect on these defences. The reserve battalions in each brigade arrived and were ashore by 9.30am, but the beaches, especially Mike, were beginning to suffer from congestion because of the limited exits from them. It was for this reason that 9 Brigade began to land on Nan at 11.30am, but its arrival immediately compounded the congestion.

No. 48 Commando landed at St-Aubin just before 8.45am. Two out of its six landing craft were caught on obstacles and some who tried to swim ashore were drowned. The other four beached at an angle, which meant that the men found themselves waist-deep in the sea. While organizing his men, the CO was wounded by mortar fragments, but continued in command. The Commandos then began to clear the houses on the beach and set up a base 1,000 yards inland from which they could attack Langrune. They managed to seize a strongpoint and houses in Luc-sur-Mer, just to the south, but Langrune itself held out and at dusk the Commandos were ordered to take up a defensive position. Thus, they were unable to make contact with the 3rd British Division on Sword. As for the main 3rd Canadian Division thrust inland, 9 Brigade was not able to begin doing this until 4pm, because of the beach congestion. It advanced towards Carpiquet airfield, but was held up by stiff resistance in the villages of Villons-les-Buissances and Ainsy. In the east, 7 Brigade made good contact with 50th (Northumbrian) Division and then also pressed southwards. Time, however, was against them and just before dusk they dug in for the night, although one troop of tanks did get to within one and a half miles of the final objective before being recalled. As it was, 3rd Canadian Division was roughly on the line of its intermediate D-day phase line. It could, however, take comfort from the fact that it had destroyed a good part of the German 716th Division.

It is at this point that tribute must be paid to the two British midget submarines (X-craft), positioned as navigation beacons off Juno and Sword. As a result of the postponement of D-Day, they were forced to spend no less than sixty-four hours submerged off the beaches. Yet, at 5am on 6 June they were still in their correct positions and began flashing their green lights to guide in the Canadian and British assault forces. It was, as Admiral Sir Bertram Ramsay commented, a feat of 'great skill and endurance'.

Sword itself presented many of the same problems as Juno when it came to suitable landing points. It was divided into four sub-sectors – Oboe, Peter, Queen and Roger. Rocks prevented access to Oboe, Peter, and the western end of Queen. Roger, too, was beset by shoals. Thus, Queen was the only possible landing beach and it meant that only one brigade could be landed at a time. Behind the beaches the ground was generally low-lying, apart from on the east flank, where high ground ran south to Caen. A ridge from this projected into the Sword sector and covered the direct routes leading from the coast to Caen. Sword was defended by the right half of 716th Division. This had three German and one 'East' battalions. The bulk of 21st Panzer Division provided the reserve, although it also had the secondary task of combating airborne landings. There was the usual pattern of underwater and beach obstacles, as well as strongpoints.

Major-General Tom Rennie, a Scotsman, who had fought with distinction in France 1940, where he was captured but escaped, North Africa and Sicily, commanded 3rd British Division. His D-Day task was to secure the high ground above Caen and, if possible, capture the city itself. First, his 8 Brigade would land with two battalions up, and supported by a battalion of DD tanks. The brigade was to secure Hermanville and St Aubin. Then, Lord Lovat's 1st Special Service Brigade of three Army and one Royal Marine Commando, together with two troops of French Commandos, would land, charged with relieving the airborne troops and John Howard's men on the bridges over the Caen Canal and River Orne. The second brigade of the Division, 185, would now come ashore and make the thrust to Caen, supported by a tank battalion from 27 Armoured Brigade. Finally, 9 Brigade would fill the two and a half-mile gap that had been created between 3rd Division and the Canadians and then advance in step with 185 Brigade. H-hour was to be 6.45am.

Force S had a powerful bombardment element, with two

battleships, a monitor, five cruisers and thirteen destroyers. The battleships and monitor were to neutralize the coastal batteries east of Sword, while the cruisers took on those covering Sword itself. The destroyers and support landing craft, which included 3rd Division's artillery, would engage the beach defences until the first landing craft touched down and then switch their fire to the flanks. Fire opened some five minutes earlier than scheduled and there was little response from the shore. Almost at the same time, the Germans enjoyed their one naval success of the day. Three E-boats had set out from Le Havre. They fired two torpedoes at the battleships *Warspite* and *Ramillies*, but missed. A third struck the Norwegian destroyer *Svenner*, sinking her, although her crew were rescued. *Warspite* then blew one E-boat out of the water and the others withdrew under a smokescreen. A similar attempt to disrupt the American landings was thwarted by bad weather. In the meantime, the LCTs carrying the DD tanks had reached the lowering position, but because of the sea condition, it was decided to release them 5,200 yards from the shore. At 7.30am the first tanks reached the shore, with thirty-one out of forty actually making the beach. AVREs and Centaurs also arrived.

The first infantry now landed and the Germans opened a heavy fire on the beach, killing, among others, the CO and two company commanders of the 1st South Lancashires. Even so, within forty minutes of landing the first clear lane up the beach had been opened and at 8.30am, the lead battalions began to move inland, securing Hermanville by 9am. Lovat's Commandos had begun to land and also took casualties. They cleared Ouistreham and then set off for the bridges, spurred on by messages that the paratroops were still holding them. They had to advance over four miles in three hours through territory held by now-thoroughly alert Germans. Remarkably, they reached the bridges just two minutes behind schedule. Back on the beaches themselves, six out of the eight planned lanes were open by 9.45am and 185 Brigade began to land. It was on shore within twenty-five minutes, but it took time to organize the troops in their assembly area prior to advancing on Caen and the vehicles were held up at the exits from the beach. General Rennie himself landed at 10.30am and soon afterwards the bulk of his division's artillery was ashore. By 2.45pm the reserve brigade was also complete. Meanwhile, 185 Brigade had been awaiting its supporting tanks, which had been delayed by the congestion on the beaches. At noon, the brigade commander decided to press on towards Caen. Meanwhile one of the battalions of 8 Brigade faced a difficult task in subduing a strongpoint codenamed Hillman, which was the HQ of the german 736th Regiment. It incurred heavy casualties and did not eventually overcome the position until the evening. This caused some delay in fully deploying the troops off the beaches. Warned that German tanks were advancing north from Caen, 185 Brigade continued its advance. At 4pm, after finally being joined by the tanks, its lead battalion secured Bieville, just two and a half miles north of Caen. Thirty minutes later, the Germans counter-attacked.

One of the significant features of D-Day was the German failure to launch a timely armoured counter-attack against at least one of the beaches. By 1.45am, as a result of the airborne landings, both the German Seventh and Fifteen Armies had been placed on maximum alert. At 4.25am von Rundstedt's headquarters requested that OKW release the Panzer reserves, but General Alfred Jodl, the Chief of Staff OKW, stated that Hitler was in bed, after taking a sleeping draught, and could not be woken. Even so, von Rundstedt agreed that the 12th SS Panzer Division could be placed under the control of Army Group B and it began to concentrate at Lisieux, thirty miles east of Caen.

The Norwegian destroyer Svenner (formerly HMS Shark) was one of the few warship victims on D-Day. She was hit amidships by an E-boat torpedo off Sword Beach and immediately broke in two.

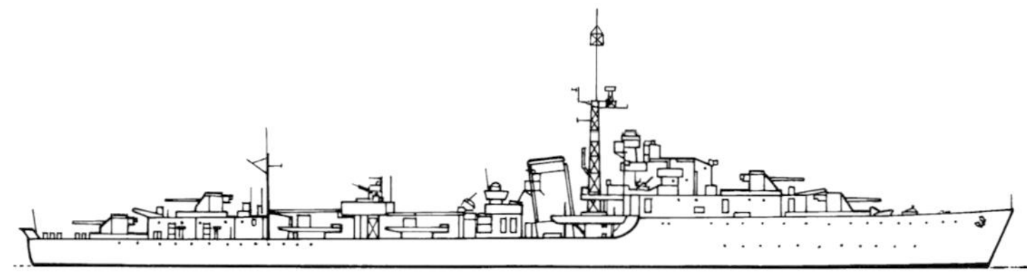

A German S-boat (Schnellboot 'fast boat'), known by the Allies as an E-boat (Eilboot 'boat in a hurry'). This particular model was armed with two torpedo tubes and two 20mm cannon. They were capable of speeds of up to 40 knots.

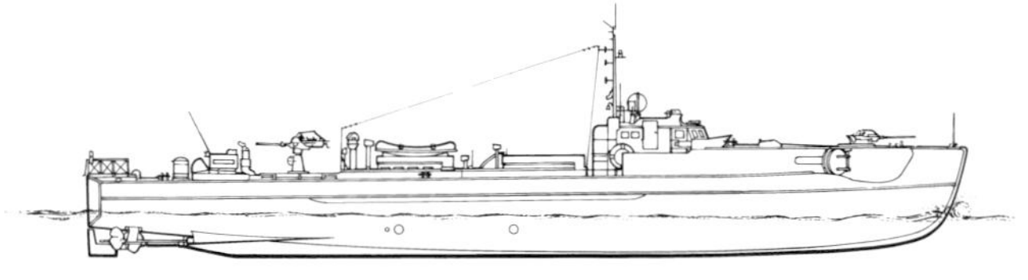

Rommel, too, had left orders that the two Panzer divisions in Fifteenth Army's area were not to be moved, since landings in Seventh Army's sector were likely to be a diversion from the main landings in the Pas-de-Calais. This left 21st Panzer Division, whose subordinate units were scattered. As early as 1.20am on D-Day, General Wilhelm Richter, commanding 716th Division, ordered 21st Panzer to carry out its secondary role of tackling the paratroops dropping east of the River Orne. With Feuchtinger, its commander, still away, indecision seems to have gripped his staff and it was not until 6.30am that the orders were given, and it was a further ninety minutes before units began to deploy. By now Feuchtinger had returned, but before his troops could really make contact with 6th Airborne Division he was

German PzKw IV. The Panzer divisions in Normandy were largely equipped with this tank. It was armed with a 75mm gun, but, unlike the heavier Panther and Tiger, it was matched by Allied tanks.

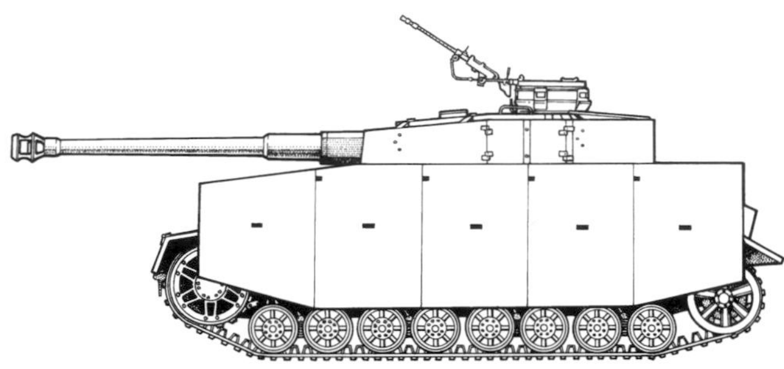

Because of the delays in Hitler's agreeing to the release of the reserve Panzer divisions, the only mobile formation in the landing area was 21st Panzer Division, which was deployed on both sides of the River Orne. At 8 am it began to attack the British 6th Airborne Division, but was then ordered to counter-attack Sword and Juno. The first attack, at about 4 pm, was hampered by Allied aircraft and beaten off by 185 Brigade. However, that evening 192 Panzer Grenadier Regiment did advance up the gap between the two beachheads before withdrawing, fearing it would be cut off.

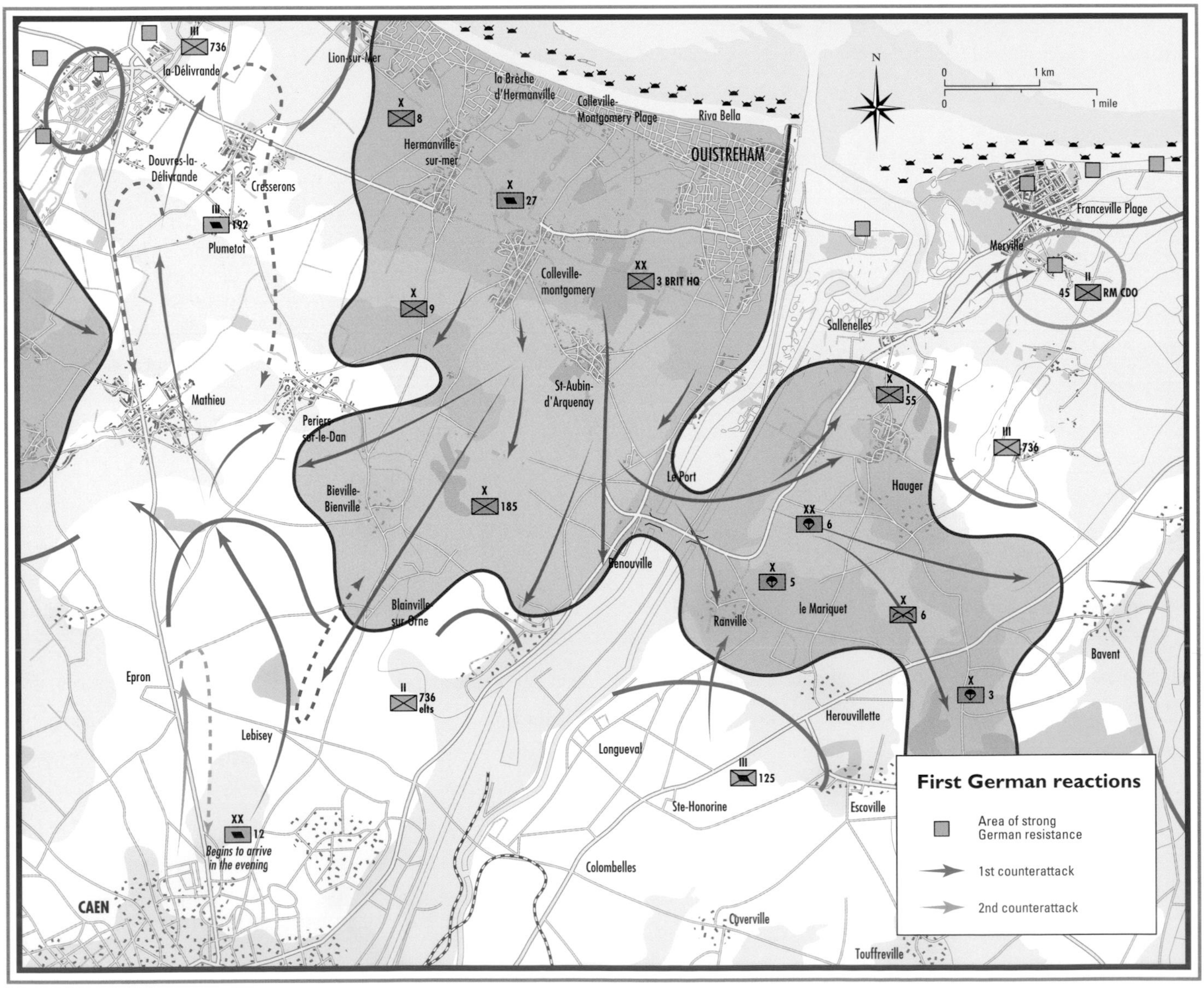

given fresh orders. These came from General Erich Marcks, commander of LXXIV Corps, who had lost a leg in the opening days of the invasion of Russia in June 1941 and was now facing the landings on the British beaches. Army Group B had placed 21st Panzer Division under his command and at midday he ordered Feuchtinger to counterattack the forces coming ashore on Sword and Juno. Feuchtinger left a Panzer Grenadier Regiment to deal with the airborne threat and began to redeploy the remainder, which, given the overwhelming Allied presence in the skies above, proved to be no easy task.

Von Rundstedt's HQ continued to badger OKW for an answer on the Panzer reserves and eventually received an answer at 2.30pm. The 12th SS Panzer Division was released to him, together with the Panzer Lehr, an elite formation made up of staffs from the various armour schools and based in the Le Mans area, and 17th SS Panzer Grenadier Division. The last-named had only been formed in October 1943 and was still very deficient in equipment. It was carrying out its final collective training near Poitiers, south of the River Loire. Sepp Dietrich's HQ I SS Panzer Corps was to co-ordinate this attack and would come under Seventh Army's command. Given the distance that they had to travel, the adverse air situation, and the disruption to the roads and railways caused by the Allied bombing and French Resistance, which carried out demolitions on nearly one thousand cuttings during D-Day, it would take time for these divisions to come into action.

Feuchtinger eventually launched his attack at 4.30pm. It was not a success. The 1st Suffolks at Bieville, supported by tanks and anti-tank guns, repulsed the main attack, quickly knocking out some twelve PzKw IVs. One Panzer Grenadier battalion did, however, manage to find the gap between the British 3rd and Canadian 3rd Divisions and at 8pm actually reached the coast. Soon after this the Airlanding Brigade of 6th Airborne Division began to arrive by glider. Some of the gliders landed south of where the Panzer Grenadier battalion was positioned and, fearing that it might be cut off, Feuchtinger ordered it to withdraw. Meanwhile, although harassed by Allied aircraft en route, 12th SS Panzer Division began to concentrate near Noyers, south-west of Caen. Sepp Dietrich had established his HQ near Falaise. He and his chief of staff then went forward to HQ 21st Panzer Division, which had also been placed under his command, to assess the situation. To his fury, Feuchtinger had gone off to see General Richter of 716th Division, but had failed to take a radio with him. Thus, the German efforts to immediately drive the Allies back into the sea on D-Day had proved a damp squib.

While they had failed to secure many of their D-Day objectives, the Allies could feel reasonably content. They had succeeded in landing some 150,000 men in Normandy at a cost of 9,000 casualties, considerably less than many had feared. The experience gained during the previous four years of amphibious operations had proved invaluable. But much still needed to be done. The five beachheads had to be linked up and expanded. Follow-up forces needed to be landed quickly so that the initial success could be exploited. At the same time, while a major German counter-attack had not materialized on D-Day itself, it was certain to come soon. As for the Germans, the day had been a bewildering one, catching many initially by surprise. Yet they were still unconvinced that Normandy was the invasion area. An assault elsewhere was still possible. They were cheered to learn that, having driven back from Germany, Rommel had returned to his headquarters on the evening of D-Day. With a significant armoured force now gathering, there was still time to defeat the Allies.

British Commandos move inland from Sword Beach to relieve the Airborne troops on the bridges over the Caen Canal and River Orne.

Chapter Four

The Beachhead Battles

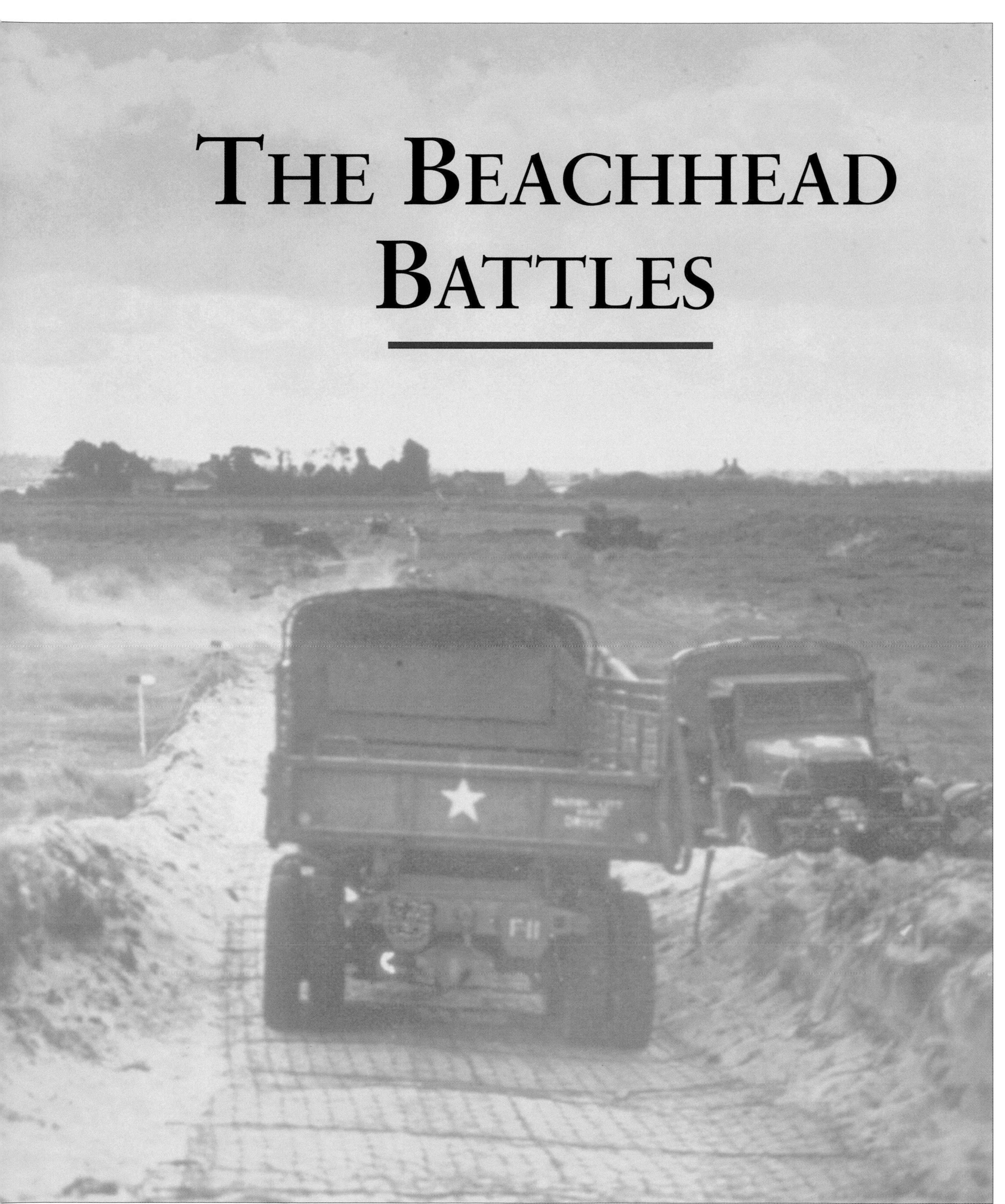

Erwin Rommel bids farewell to Field Marshal Gerd von Rundstedt and his Chief of Staff, General Günther Blumentritt, after a visit to his HQ at La Roche Guyon.

On the night of D-Day General Bernard Montgomery set sail from Portsmouth in the destroyer HMS *Faulknor*. Next morning, after the destroyer had missed its way and found itself off Cherbourg, he arrived off the invasion beaches. The main concern was Omaha, one that General Omar Bradley, commanding the US First Army, shared. Apart from the fact that its beachhead was the shallowest of the five, there was a yawning gap between it and the British Second Army which could be easily exploited by Rommel. Montgomery therefore decided that he would have to postpone US VII Corps's advance to Cherbourg from Utah. Instead, it was to link up with Omaha. To keep the Germans distracted, the British and Canadians were to continue to advance inland. To Rommel, sitting in his headquarters at the La Roche Guyon château on a loop in the Seine near Bonnières, Caen and Cherbourg were the two principal areas of interest. As long as both were held, the Allies would have neither a firm left flank nor a port. To do this, he would have to launch counter-attacks, although these could only be limited because his resources were already stretched. His main hopes rested on the armoured attack being prepared against the British and Canadians. Kurt ('Panzermeyer') Meyer and his 25th SS Panzer Grenadier Regiment had already deployed to block the Canadian advance on Carpiquet airfield and before dawn on 7 June a plan had been worked out for 21st Panzer and 12th SS Panzer Divisions to attack side by side to drive the Allies back into the sea. H-hour was planned for noon, but delays in the arrival of 12th SS Panzer Division's tanks meant that it had to be put back until 4pm.

On the Allied side, the Canadians had resumed their advance at 6.15am, with orders from General Keller to achieve

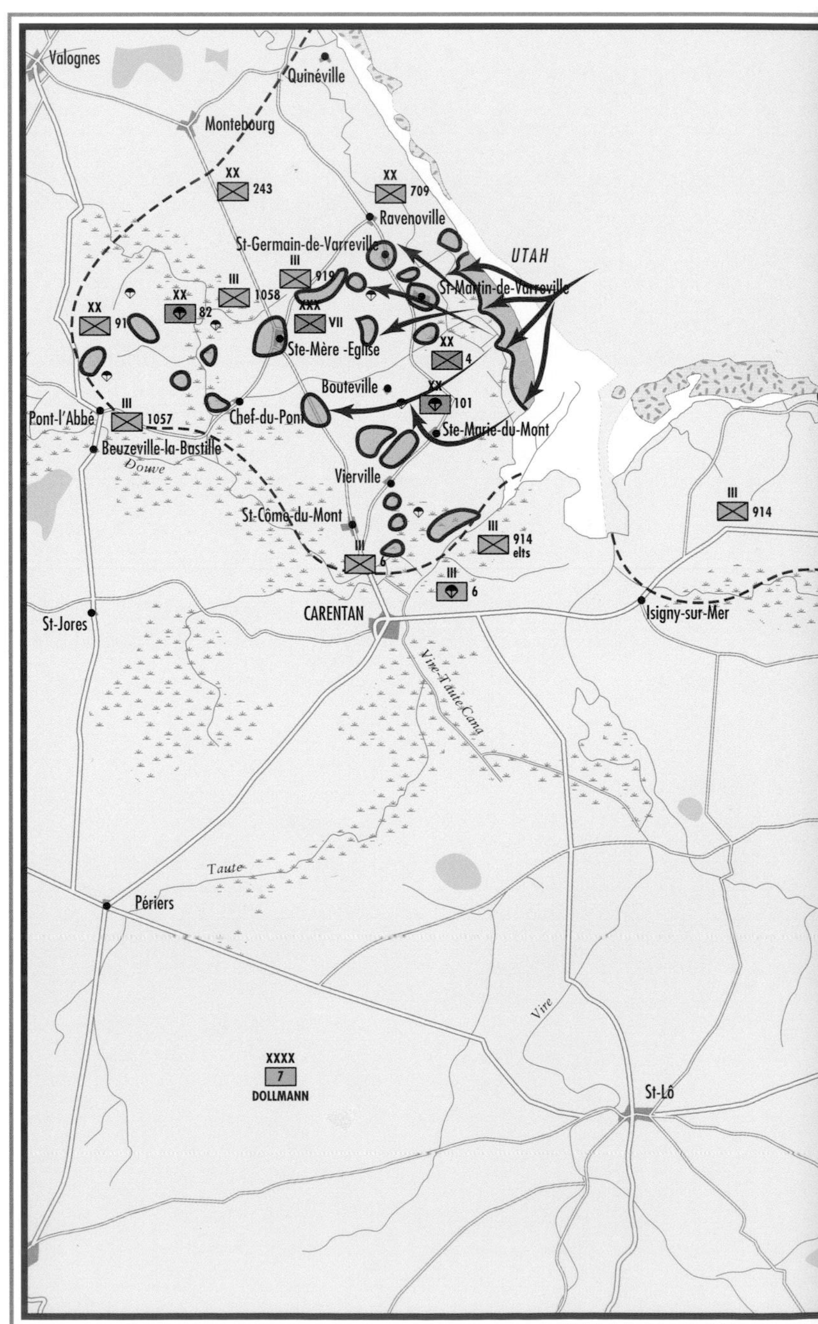

their D-Day objectives. Opposition was initially slight and, on the right, 7 Brigade advanced swiftly and secured the villages of Putot, Bretteville-l'Orgueilleuse and Norrey shortly after midday. Their objectives achieved, the Brigade dug in, ignoring a perfect opportunity to outflank Meyer's men covering Carpiquet airfield. On the left, 9 Brigade resumed its advance somewhat later. Again, the initial progress was promising. The Canadians entered Buron shortly before midday and just over an hour later they were in St-Authie, only two-and-a-half miles north of the airfield. They were now out of range of their own artillery. Worse, Meyer had spotted them. He decided to allow the Canadians to advance a little further, to Franqueville, where their flanks would be even more exposed, and then strike. His men caught the lead Canadian battalion and its supporting tanks totally off balance. They quickly recaptured St-Authie and by late afternoon had forced the Canadians out of Buron.

Although they had not achieved any of their ultimate D-Day objectives, the Allies could be well pleased with progress. Only Omaha had been a cause of real concern. The main tasks now were to link up the beachheads, unite US VII Corps with 82nd and 101st Airborne Divisions, and continue to advance inland. On the German side, the focus was on gathering sufficient armoured strength in the Caen area for an early and effective counter-attack.

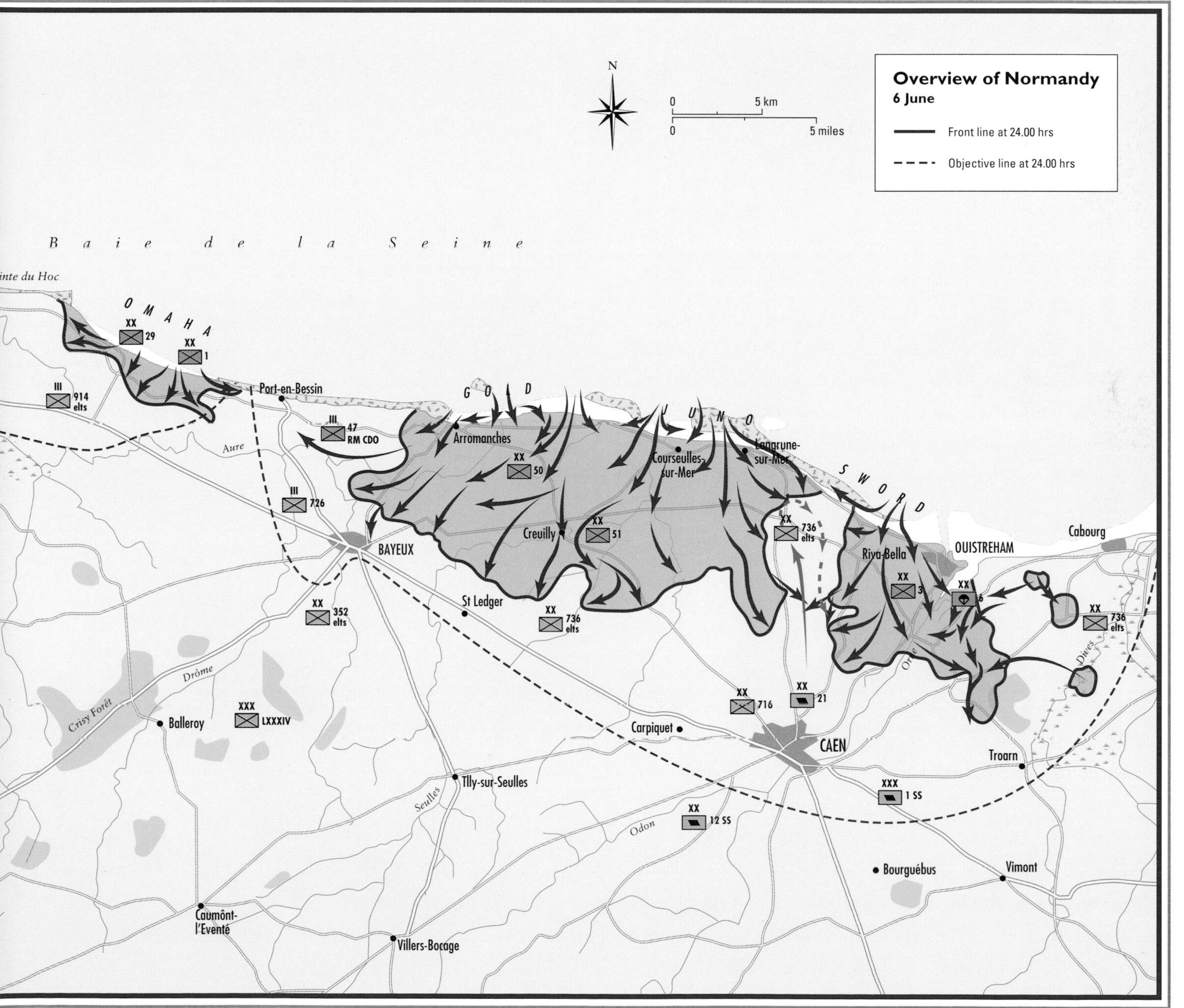

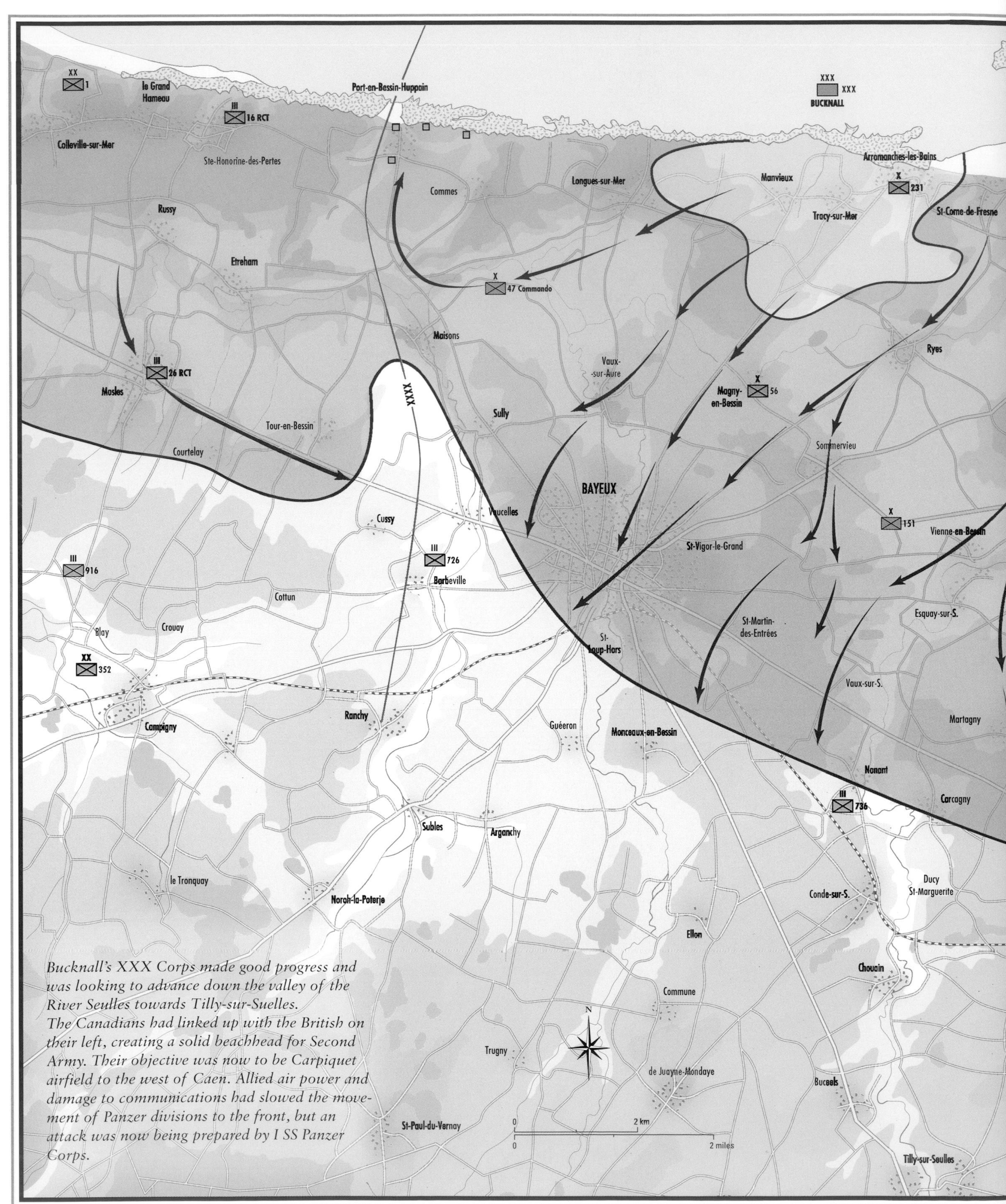

Bucknall's XXX Corps made good progress and was looking to advance down the valley of the River Seulles towards Tilly-sur-Suelles. The Canadians had linked up with the British on their left, creating a solid beachhead for Second Army. Their objective was now to be Carpiquet airfield to the west of Caen. Allied air power and damage to communications had slowed the movement of Panzer divisions to the front, but an attack was now being prepared by I SS Panzer Corps.

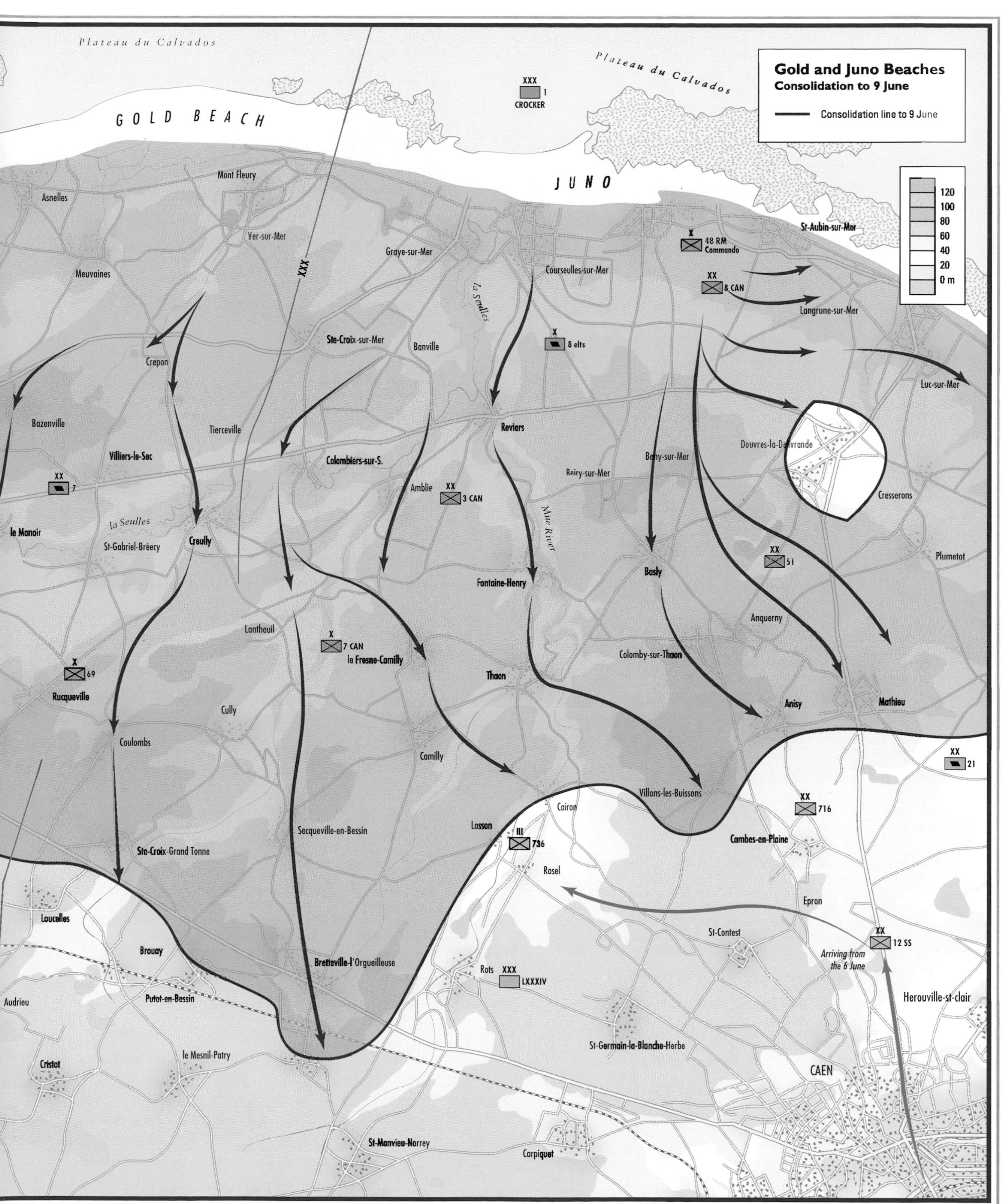
Gold and Juno Beaches
Consolidation to 9 June
Consolidation line to 9 June
120
100
80
60
40
20
0 m
Plateau du Calvados
GOLD BEACH
JUNO
XXX 1 CROCKER
Asnelles
Mont Fleury
Ver-sur-Mer
Meuvaines
Graye-sur-Mer
Courseulles-sur-Mer
X 48 RM Commando
XX 8 CAN
St-Aubin-sur-Mer
Langrune-sur-Mer
Luc-sur-Mer
Ste-Croix-sur-Mer
Banville
X 8 elts
Crepon
Bazenville
Tierceville
Reviers
Villiers-le-Sec
Colombiers-sur-S.
Douvres-la-Delivrande
Beny-sur-Mer
Beiry-sur-Mer
XX 7
Amblie
XX 3 CAN
Cresserons
le Manoir
la Seulles
St-Gabriel-Brécy
Creully
Mue River
Basly
XX 51
Plumetot
Fontaine-Henry
Lantheuil
Anquerny
X 7 CAN
le Fresne-Camilly
X 69
Rucqueville
Thaon
Colomby-sur-Thaon
Anisy
Mathieu
Cully
Coulombs
Camilly
XX 21
Villons-les-Buissons
Cairon
XX 716
Lasson
Secqueville-en-Bessin
III 736
Cambes-en-Plaine
Ste-Croix-Grand Tonne
Rosel
Epron
Loucelles
St-Contest
XX 12 SS
Arriving from the 6 June
Brouay
Bretteville-l'Orgueilleuse
Rots
XXX LXXXIV
Herouville-st-clair
Audrieu
Putot-en-Bessin
Cristot
le Mesnil-Patry
St-Germain-la-Blanche-Herbe
CAEN
St-Manvieu-Norrey
Carpiquet

These troops then withdrew to Les Buissons, around which the remainder of 9 Brigade were digging in.

The fighting also spilled over into the British 3rd Division's sector, halting the advance on Caen. But, in spite of Meyer's success in halting the advance, the planned counterstroke with 21st Panzer Division had proved abortive. Feuchtinger's division was under too much pressure to go over to the offensive. Furthermore, the Panzer Lehr was experiencing great difficulty in its move to the coast. Destroyed bridges necessitated diversions and during the daylight hours Allied air attacks were frequent. It was clear to Sepp Dietrich, commanding I SS Panzer Corps, that no concerted armoured counterattack would be possible until 8 June.

On Gold Beach, 50th Division enjoyed a better day than that of the other two British beaches. On the left, 69 Brigade managed to get across the Caen–Bayeux road and linked up with the Canadians. Tanks from 8 Armoured Brigade then passed through and began to advance on Villers-Bocage, but became embroiled in the Canadians' fight with Panzermeyer's SS men. In the west, Bayeux was captured and the high ground to its south-east secured, but the German defences on the River Drôme, which runs west of Caen, could not be forced. No. 47 Commando RM spent the day attempting without success to secure Port-en-Bessin, which would enable a link-up to be made with the Americans on Omaha. Here the remainder of 29th Infantry Division got ashore during the day, while the 1st Division managed to secure two bridgeheads over the River Aure, but could not reach Port-en-Bessin. Efforts to relieve Rudder's hard-pressed Rangers on Pointe du Hoc also failed. Even so, the German 352nd Division was beginning to buckle under the pressure, in spite of being reinforced by a brigade of cyclist troops during the day.Utah, too, faced problems. True, on the night 6/7 June a patrol from the beleaguered 82nd Airborne Division in Ste-Mère-Église managed to make contact with the US 4th Infantry Division, enabling some co-ordination. This was just as well, since the Germans had been gathering reinforcements, including a Panzer battalion, for an attack against the lightly armed paratroopers. When it did come, a US tank battalion was quickly deployed and played a major part in breaking up the assaults. But these attacks prevented 82nd Airborne from achieving its D-Day objective, securing crossings over the Merderet. The 101st Airborne also faced counter-attacks, which succeeded in isolating those groups which had reached the north bank of the Douve. As for the 4th Infantry Division, it continued to experience great difficulty in exploiting to the north. Nevertheless, the Allied beachheads were very much more secure than they had been the previous day and, with reinforcements being landed, the chances of the Germans being able to drive the Allies back into the sea were receding by the hour.

Canadian troops entering a village D+1.

During the night of 7/8 June, at HQ I SS Panzer Corps Sepp Dietrich was doing his best to try to cobble together another attack. He was aware that 21st Panzer Division remained under pressure and was still in no position to take part. Likewise, only the leading elements of the Panzer Lehr had arrived in the area of Fontenay-le-Pesnel and Tilly-sur-Seulles and the Division was thus in no position to strike. This left only 12th SS Panzer Division, but this was also incomplete. Fritz Witt, the divisional commander, realized that to have any chance good jump-off positions needed to be secured and as early as 3am his men began to attack the Canadians once more. They enjoyed mixed success. While they failed to drive the Canadians out of Norrey, one battalion did capture Putot, although it was forced out again that night. Elements of the Panzer Lehr did become embroiled, but suffered severely from artillery and more notably naval gunfire. Indeed, during the early days of the campaign, the Germans came to respect the power of the guns of the capital ships even more than Allied supremacy in the air. But while the attack achieved no significant gains, it did halt the Canadian advance and the thrust towards Villers-Bocage.

D-Day +2 also saw the link-up between Gold and Omaha beaches as a result of Port-en-Bessin being secured. The Rangers on Pointe du Hoc were finally relieved and the 29th Division advanced south and secured Isigny by nightfall, leaving the left flank of the German 352nd Division in the air. 101st Airborne Division was given the task of capturing Carentan, but the flooded area around the River Douve and the Carentan Canal restricted its operations. Furthermore, Von der Heydte's 6th Parachute Regiment, reinforced by elements of 77th Division,

The last German position close to the beaches to fall was the radar station at Douvres, which the British decided to leave to soak rather than attack it. The thrust by the British 3rd Division towards Caen was frustrated by stiff German resistance.

which had moved from Brittany on D-Day itself, was not prepared to give the town up without a fight and it did not fall until 12 June. Finally, on the following day VII Corps on Utah linked up with V Corps on Omaha, providing the Allies with one solid continuous beachhead across the whole front. Meanwhile, on 10 June, 90th Division, which had begun to land on Utah towards the end of D-Day, began to attack through 82nd Airborne with the aim of cutting off the base of the Cotentin peninsula, which Montgomery and Bradley had agreed was the best alternative to striking directly for Cherbourg.

The 90th Division, which had only arrived in Britain in April and was now experiencing its first combat, was soon in difficulties. Not least was a problem that all the Allied ground troops were facing – the unique nature of the terrain in Normandy. Although there were areas of open countryside, notably in the east, much of the region was dominated by the *bocage*, small fields bounded by banks topped with hedges. It provided a claustrophobic atmosphere and one that favoured the defence. Infantry were highly vulnerable to concealed machine guns and snipers, while armour advancing down the narrow and twisting lanes was easy prey for tank and anti-tank guns. When the tanks did try to get off the road and into the fields they were still liable to fall victim, especially when mounting the banks enclosing the fields. Many found it a bewildering experience which had not been covered in their training, whose emphasis had been on getting ashore rather than dealing with what the troops could expect once they advanced inland off the beaches. The 90th also suffered from poor leadership, which General Lawton Collins, the corps commander, recognized. Within a few days he sacked the divisional and two regimental commanders, but not before the Division had suffered nearly 3,000 casualties.

Over in the east, Rommel was still striving to concentrate his armour, while organizing local counter-attacks at the same time. I SS Panzer Corps had now been placed under Panzer Group

LSTs on one of the US Normandy beaches. Until the Mulberry harbours had been established, all reinforcements and supplies had to be landed directly onto the beaches.

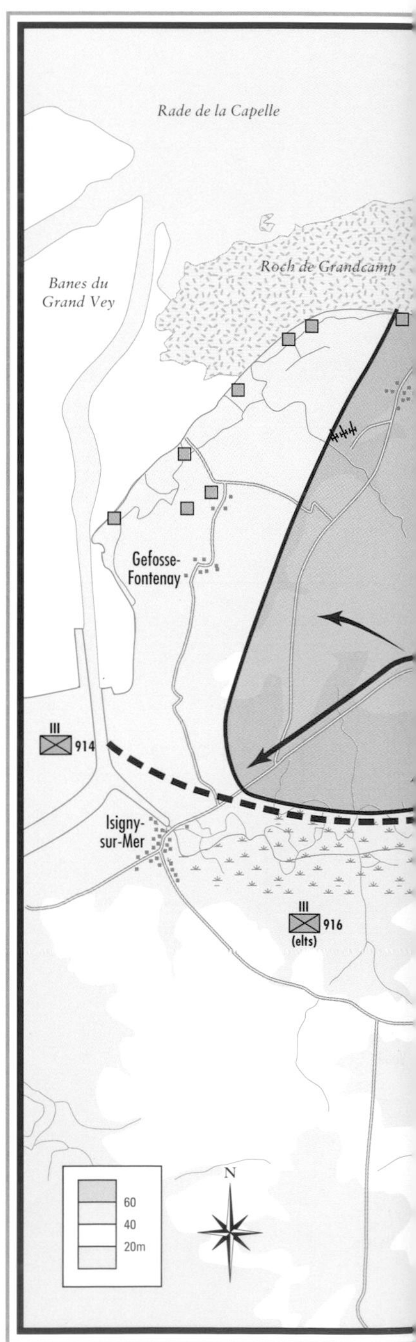

After its D-Day difficulties, V Corps began its advance inland and reached its 6 June objectives on the 8th. On the same day, 47 RM Commando finally entered Port-en-Bessin, thus achieving a link-up between Omaha and Gold beaches. The priority now was to achieve a similar link-up with VII Corps to the west.

West and Rommel visited Geyr von Schweppenburg on 10 June. Movement during daylight hours was now becoming nigh on impossible because of the air threat. This especially affected replenishment, with supply convoys often having to travel over 100 miles because of the destruction of forward dumps and bridges. In the afternoon of the 10th, shortly after Rommel had departed, the Panzer Group West HQ was hit by an air attack after being pinpointed by Ultra. Most of Geyr's staff were killed, and planning for a major counter-offensive came to a halt. Even so, Rommel continued to move armour into Normandy. The 2nd Panzer Division came from the Pas-de- Calais, leaving 116th Panzer to deal with any Allied assault north of the Seine, which the Germans had still not totally discounted. Furthermore, Hitler's favourite formation, the 1st SS Leibstandarte Panzer Division, which provided his own household troops, was en route from Belgium. This enabled Rommel to create another Panzer Corps, von Funck's XLVII, which deployed west of I SS Panzer Corps. He accepted, however, that there was little that he could do about the Cotentin peninsula except fight a delaying action to keep the Americans away from Cherbourg for as long as possible. Rather, he concentrated on thwarting the British Second Army.

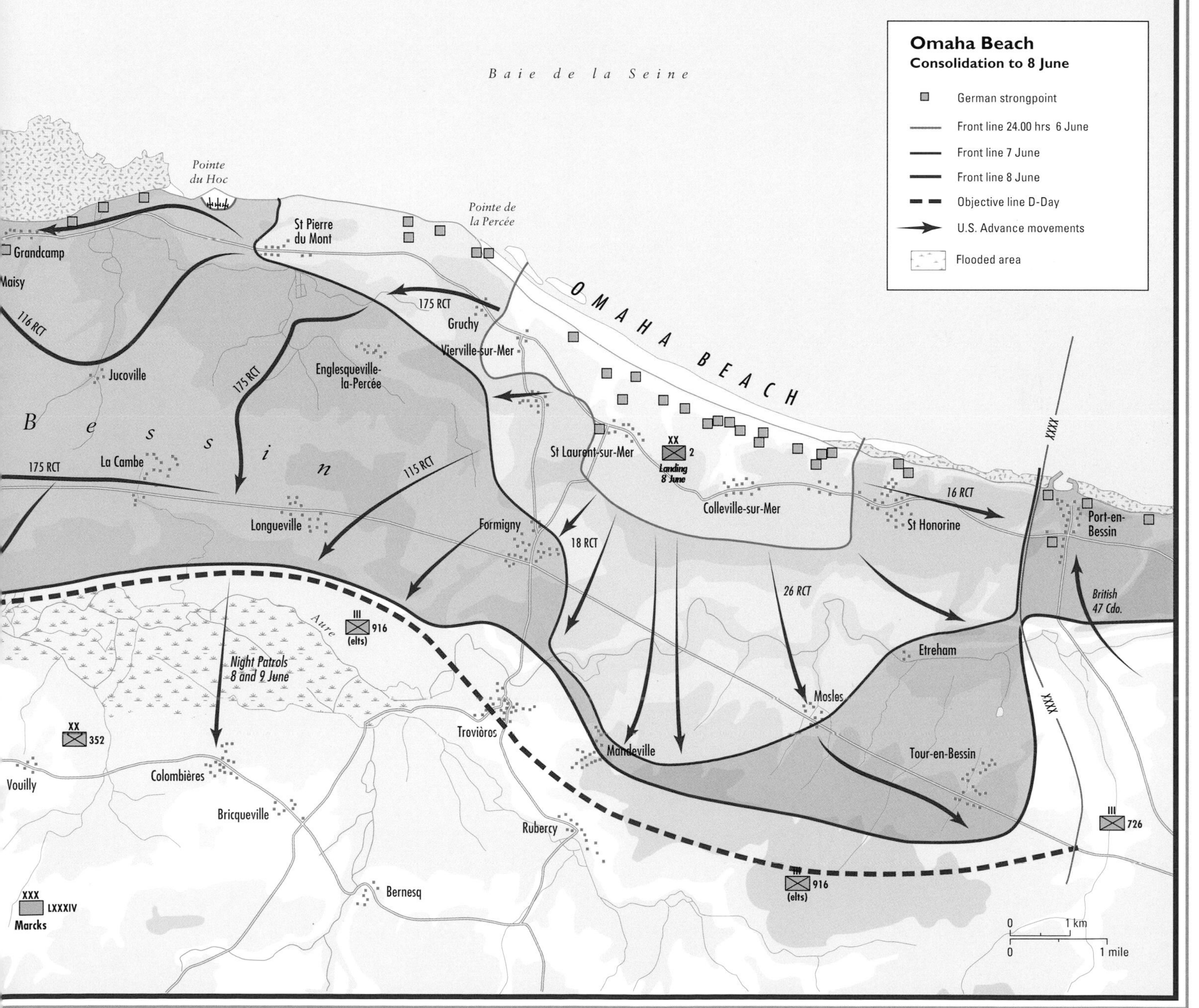

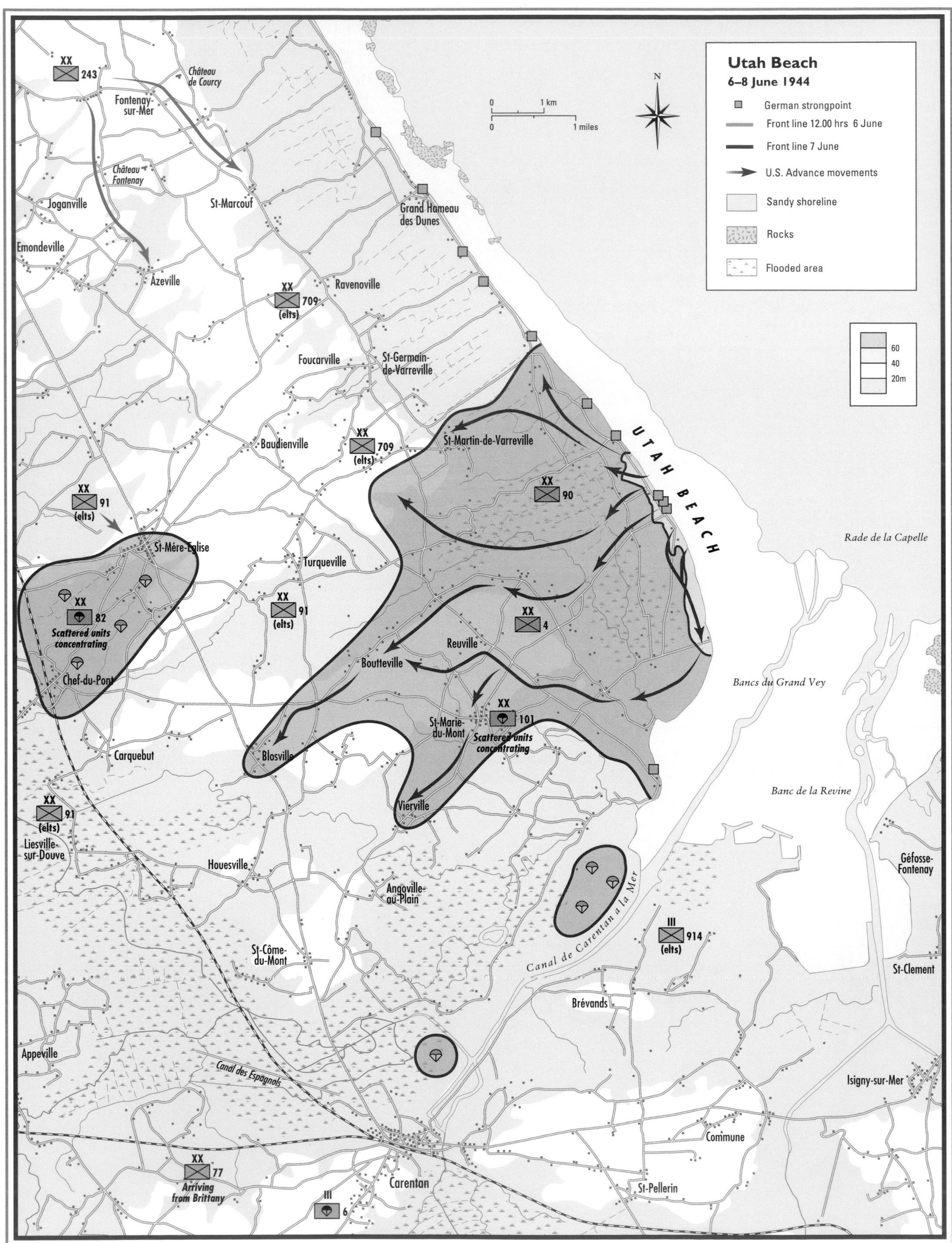
Utah Beach
6–8 June 1944
German strongpoint
Front line 12.00 hrs 6 June
Front line 7 June
U.S. Advance movements
Sandy shoreline
Rocks
Flooded area
60
40
20m
0 1 km
0 1 miles
N
UTAH BEACH
Rade de la Capelle
Bancs du Grand Vey
Banc de la Revine
Canal de Carentan a la Mer
Canal des Espagnols
Château de Courcy
Fontenay-sur-Mer
Château Fontenay
Joganville
St-Marcouf
Emondeville
Azeville
Grand Hameau des Dunes
Ravenoville
Foucarville
St-Germain-de-Varreville
St-Martin-de-Varreville
Baudienville
St-Mére-Eglise
Turqueville
Reuville
Boutteville
Chef-du-Pont
St-Marie-du-Mont
Blosville
Carquebut
Vierville
Liesville-sur-Douve
Houesville
Angoville-au-Plain
St-Côme-du-Mont
Géfosse-Fontenay
St-Clement
Brévands
Appeville
Isigny-sur-Mer
Commune
Carentan
St-Pellerin
XX 243
XX 709 (elts)
XX 709 (elts)
XX 91 (elts)
XX 90
XX 82 Scattered units concentrating
XX 91 (elts)
XX 4
XX 101 Scattered units concentrating
XX 91 (elts)
III 914 (elts)
XX 77 Arriving from Brittany
III 6

The first significant British threat came on 13 June, from the veteran 7th Armoured Division, the Desert Rats. The previous day its tanks reached Caumont and General George Erskine saw an opportunity to swing east and cut off the Panzer Lehr by securing Villers-Bocage. His leading tanks and mounted infantry occupied the village without resistance the following morning and then began to advance along the road to Caen. Unbeknown to them, a company from the 101st Heavy SS Tank Battalion had recently arrived in the area and was lying up in woods overlooking the road. Michael Wittmann, the company commander had four Tigers and one PzKpfw IV under his command. He was also a renowned tankman, with a high score of 'kills' from the Eastern Front. Rather than pick off the British advance guard, Wittmann decided on the bold approach of driving into Villers-Bocage itself. En route, he destroyed four

Recently relieved US paratroopers with a trophy.

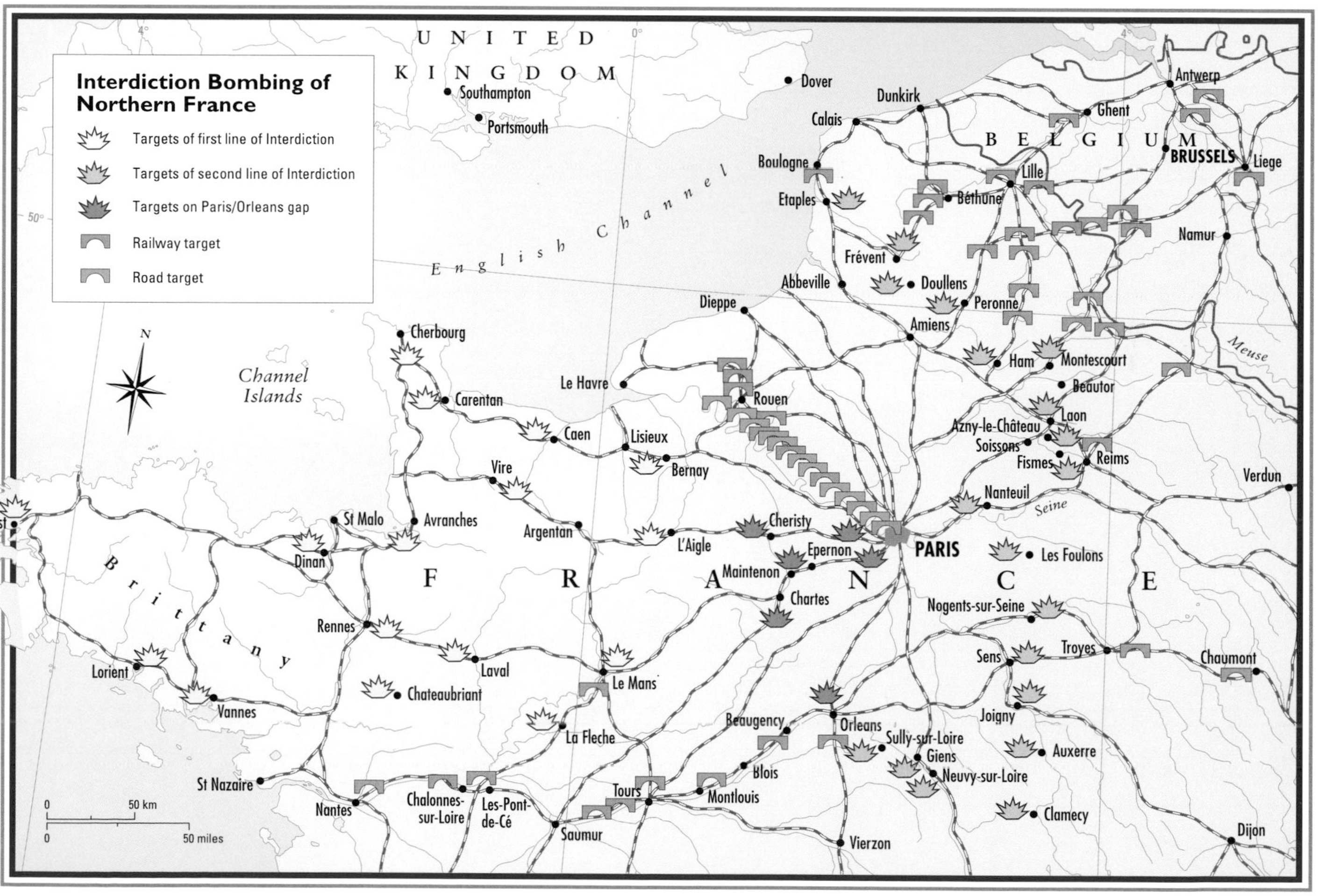

Interdiction Bombing of Northern France

Targets of first line of Interdiction
Targets of second line of Interdiction
Targets on Paris/Orleans gap
Railway target
Road target

(Left) While VII Corps completed its link-up with 101st Airborne Division, 82nd Airborne was still virtually isolated and under pressure. 90th Infantry Division was now ashore and 101st was ordered to capture Carentan. Because of the marshy terrain and fierce resistance from the German 6th Parachute Regiment, now being reinforced by elements of 77th Division, this proved a difficult operation.

(Above) It was once the Allies were ashore in Normandy that the effectiveness of the air campaign against communications, which had begun in earnest in April 1944, became critical. Aided by the French Resistance, the aim was to seal off Normandy itself and also develop an outer 'cordon' to hinder the movement of German reinforcements from Fifteenth Army to the east and from southern France.

Cromwell tanks and then, after charging through the village, shot up a column of tanks and other armoured vehicles, causing chaos and confusion. The British recovered and four Cromwells deployed in the village to prepare for Wittmann's return. When he did they ambushed him, knocking out his own Tiger, another one and his PzKpfw IV. Wittmann, however, managed to escape on foot to fight another day. What he had done was to single-handedly block a yawning gap, which, if properly exploited, could have unpinned the whole German defence. As it was, 2nd Panzer Division now began to deploy to fill the void and 7th Armoured Division, feeling dangerously exposed, pulled back.

The affair at Villers-Bocage caused Montgomery to rethink his strategy. He decided to abandon attempts to envelop Caen from the east and west. Instead he would go over to the defensive on the eastern flank and concentrate his efforts on the Villers-Bocage and Caumont sector. What concerned him was the arrival of 2nd Panzer Division and the danger that it might be employed against the Americans. Indeed, elements of it had clashed with the US V Corps in the Caumont area. Montgomery therefore decided that the British must maintain pressure here in order to tie down the German armour. Likewise, the concern expressed by General Leonard T. Gerow, commanding US V Corps, at the appearance of German tanks in his sector put paid to the concept of launching a break-out simultaneously with clearing the Cotentin peninsula and seizing Cherbourg. The American effort must be dedicated to the latter, Montgomery decided.

On the peninsula, the ill-fated US 90th Division was relieved by 82nd Airborne and 9th Infantry Divisions. In spite of the *bocage*, they pressed forward and reached the west coast on 18 June, thus isolating the German forces in the northern part of the peninsula. The capture of Cherbourg was now a mere matter of time, but the Allied supply problem had already begun to be eased by the deployment of the Mulberry harbours. The first Mulberry convoys had set sail on D-Day itself and work began on the construction of the breakwaters on the following day. The American Mulberry A was open for business on the afternoon of 16 June, but that at Arromanches (Mulberry B) took longer to put in place and work on it was interrupted by a three-day storm which blew up on 19 June. Worse, this almost destroyed the US Mulberry and resulted in the loss of some 600 vessels of all types. The storm drastically

Landing at a forward airstrip in Normandy. These were quickly established to ensure that the ground troops had the most effective tactical air support. The conditions show how unseasonably wet Normandy was in June 1944.

reduced the rate of supply and reinforcement of the beachhead, but, thanks to superhuman efforts, the Arromanches harbour was functioning on 29 June. The damage to Mulberry A had, however, been so severe that, apart from re-establishing the breakwater off Omaha, it was not rebuilt and parts of it were used in the completion of Mulberry B. At much the same time, PLUTO also came on stream and was soon delivering 8,000 tons of fuel per day into the beachhead.

The storm proved very much more effective than the German Navy in hampering the Allies. True, torpedo boats based at Cherbourg did have a few successes against the Americans before Admiral Theodor Krancke, commanding the German naval forces in the West, ordered the evacuation of the port after the Cotentin peninsula had been cut off. Great numbers of these vessels were based in the French Channel ports and presented a threat to shipping off the British beaches. This was largely nullified by air-power. RAF Coastal Command shadowed the ports, while RAF Bomber Command mounted a series of attacks on them. These were so successful that Krancke noted in despair at the end of June: 'The naval situation in the Bay of the Seine has completely deteriorated. It will be impossible to start the planned operations with the forces that have survived.' Air-power, too, played a significant role in removing the U-boat threat. Initially, the Germans deployed sixteen U-boats in the English Channel and a further nineteen in the Bay of Biscay to guard against an Allied landing on the French Atlantic coast. During the first two nights after the landings Allied aircraft sank four of the latter and damaged five others. As for those in the Channel, after three U-boats were sunk during the first three days of the landings Krancke laid down that only those equipped with *schnorkels*, enabling them to remain submerged for longer, should be used. This radically cut down the numbers of U-boats which could be employed. They did, however, have a few successes, sinking a British frigate and a destroyer on 15 June, while U-984 sank four American LSTs on 29 June. These, however, were merely pinpricks and, given the massive Allied maritime and air supremacy, there was little that the German Navy could do.

In Normandy itself, von Rundstedt and Rommel faced a real dilemma. They realized that the only way that they could defeat the Allies was by launching a major armoured counterstroke, but so stretched were the defences that all the available Panzer divisions were in the line and they lacked the infantry reserves to replace them so that they could be concentrated for the attack. They pleaded with Hitler to come and see for himself, which he did, holding a meeting with the two Field Marshals on 17 June in a bunker complex which had been constructed at Margival near Soissons for Hitler to oversee the invasion of Britain. Hitler first declared that Cherbourg must be held at all costs and ordered its garrison to be reinforced. Von Rundstedt then made some introductory remarks and handed the floor over to Rommel. He gave a detailed account of the situation and pointed out that the fall of Cherbourg was inevitable. He told Hitler that he believed that the Allied intention was to break out in the Caen–Bayeux area and advance to Paris, with a subsidiary operation to clear Brittany. To counter this, Rommel proposed to withdraw the Panzer divisions and strike the Allied thrust in the flanks. As a precursor to this it was essential to withdraw the German line so that it was out of range of naval gunfire. He then went on to plead for reinforcements and, with von Rundstedt's support, demanded freedom of action in the West without interference from Hitler's headquarters. Hitler appeared to ignore what Rommel told him and launched into a monologue on the V-1 flying-bomb offensive against England which had opened four days earlier. Rommel asked him if the V-1s could be used to attack the Allied beachheads and the English South Coast ports from which supplies and reinforcements were flowing to Normandy. Again, Hitler ignored him, launching another tirade which culminated with the boast that V-1s and jet aircraft would devastate Britain.

But while von Rundstedt was depressed by what had transpired, Rommel appeared uplifted. General Alfred Jodl, Chief of Operations at OKW, had told him that Paul Hausser's II SS Panzer Corps was en route from Russia and other reinforcements were also being sent to France. Hitler had also agreed to visit Rommel at his HQ the following day. This never took place, however. On the evening of the conference a rogue V-1 exploded close to Margival. It was too much for Hitler. He left immediately for Germany without informing von Rundstedt or Rommel. Two days later, Hitler ordered von Rundstedt to prepare a major armoured counter-attack in the Caumont area with the object of splitting the British from the Americans, but the time it was taking for reinforcements to arrive at the front meant that such an operation could not be

A British Vickers machine-gunner.

mounted immediately. Allied air-power and the French Resistance were imposing considerable delays on movement.

Take, for example, the case of the 2nd SS Panzer Division Das Reich. It had received its marching orders on 8 June to deploy to Normandy from the Toulouse area. It took ten days for the Division to reach its assembly area near St-Lô, but its heavy PzKpfw V Panther tanks were held up south of Angers and did not join the Division until the end of the month. So frustrated did the men of the Division become that they took their revenge on the inhabitants of the village of Oradour-sur-Glane near Limoges, herding them into the church and various barns, to which they then set light. Six hundred and forty-two men, women, and children perished and the village was totally burnt. Likewise, the communications leading out of Brittany were virtually severed, making it very difficult to redeploy formations from there. In consequence of this, von Rundstedt warned Hitler that the attack could not take place before 5 July.

The Cromwell tank was the most recent member of the British tank family.

Villers-Bocage

11–14 June 1944

- Front line 24.00 hrs 11 June
- Front line 24.00 hrs 14 June
- Advance of 7th Armoured Division 12 June to 24.00 hrs
- Advance of 7th Armoured Division 13 June
- German counter-attacks 13 June
- Retreat of 7th Armoured Division 13 June
- German counter-attacks 14 June
- Retreat of 7th Armoured Division 14 June
- British withdraw from salient 12 June

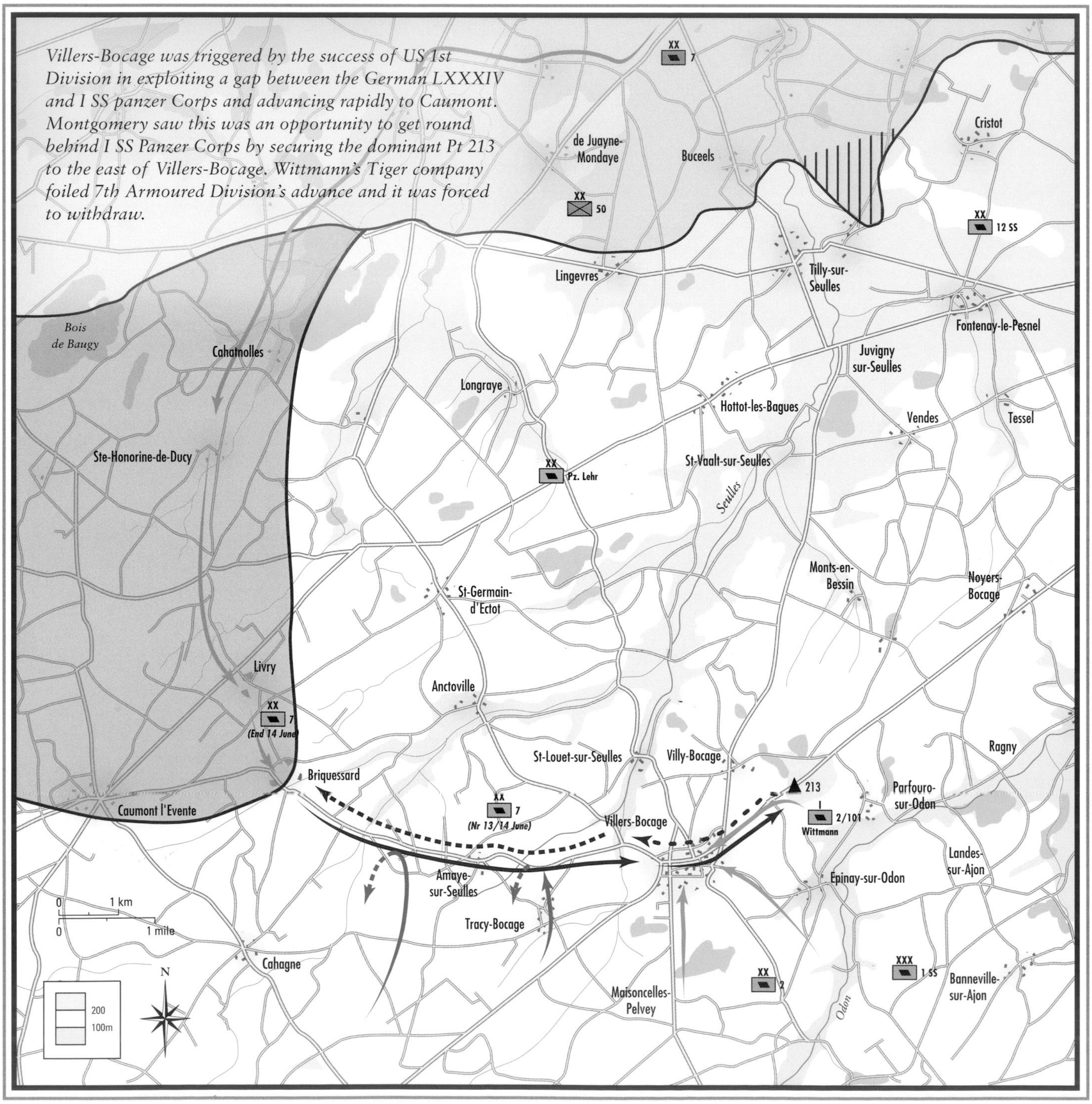

Villers-Bocage was triggered by the success of US 1st Division in exploiting a gap between the German LXXXIV and I SS panzer Corps and advancing rapidly to Caumont. Montgomery saw this was an opportunity to get round behind I SS Panzer Corps by securing the dominant Pt 213 to the east of Villers-Bocage. Wittmann's Tiger company foiled 7th Armoured Division's advance and it was forced to withdraw.

XX 7
de Juayne-Mondaye
Buceels
Cristot
XX 50
XX 12 SS
Lingevres
Tilly-sur-Seulles
Fontenay-le-Pesnel
Bois de Baugy
Cahatnolles
Juvigny sur-Seulles
Longraye
Hottot-les-Bagues
Vendes
Tessel
Ste-Honorine-de-Ducy
XX Pz. Lehr
St-Vaalt-sur-Seulles
Seulles
Monts-en-Bessin
Noyers-Bocage
St-Germain-d'Ectot
Livry
Anctoville
XX 7 (End 14 June)
Ragny
St-Louet-sur-Seulles
Villy-Bocage
Briquessard
213
Parfouro-sur-Odon
Caumont l'Evente
XX 7 (Nr 13/14 June)
Villers-Bocage
I 2/101 Wittmann
Landes-sur-Ajon
Amaye-sur-Seulles
Epinay-sur-Odon
0 1 km
0 1 mile
Tracy-Bocage
Cahagne
XX 2
XXX 1 SS
Banneville-sur-Ajon
N
200
100m
Maisoncelles-Pelvey
Odon

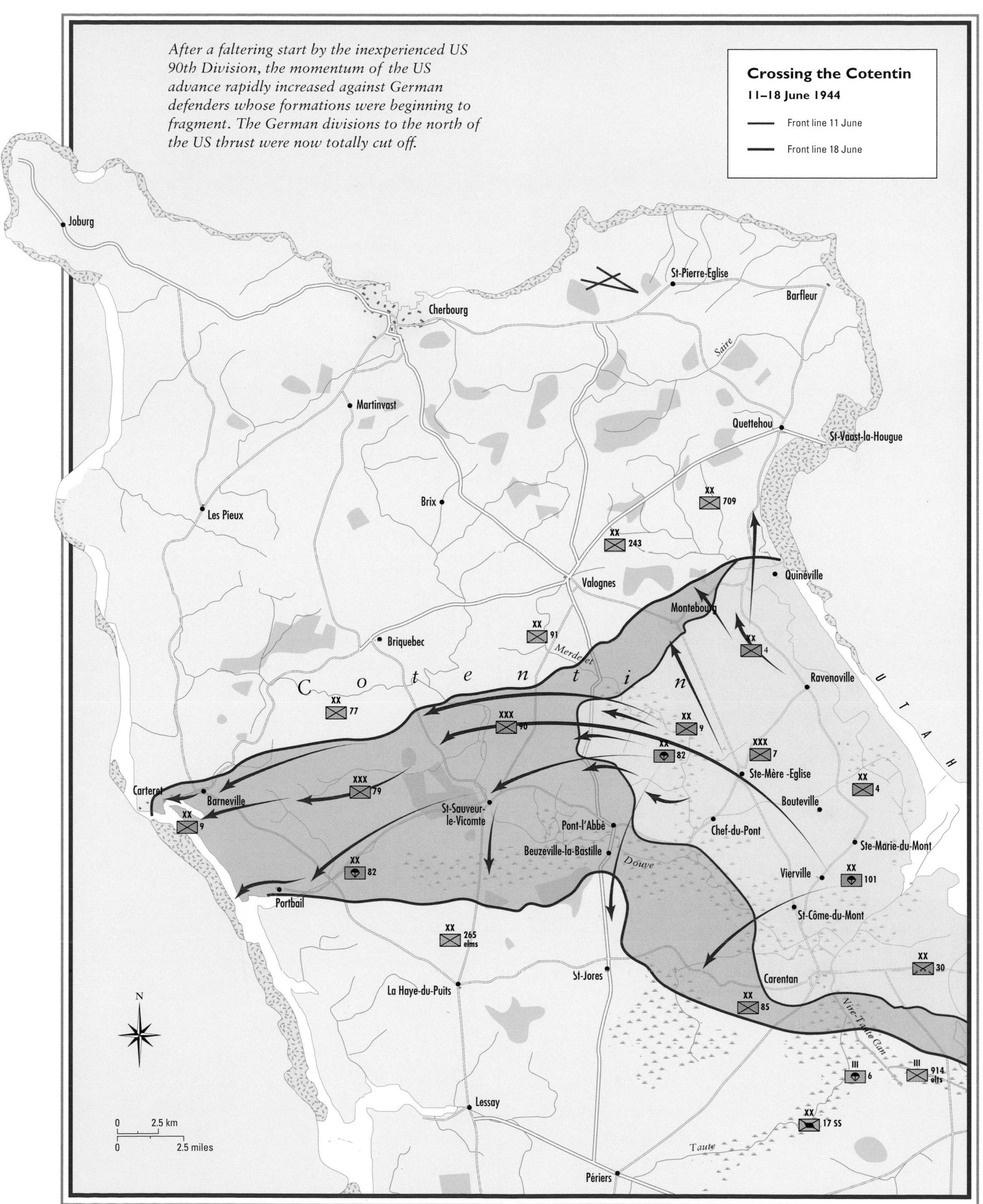
After a faltering start by the inexperienced US 90th Division, the momentum of the US advance rapidly increased against German defenders whose formations were beginning to fragment. The German divisions to the north of the US thrust were now totally cut off.
Crossing the Cotentin
11–18 June 1944
Front line 11 June
Front line 18 June
Joburg
Cherbourg
St-Pierre-Eglise
Barfleur
Saire
Martinvast
Quettehou
St-Vaast-la-Hougue
Brix
Les Pieux
709
243
Valognes
Quinéville
Montebourg
Briquebec
91
Merderet
4
C o t e n t i n
Ravenoville
UTAH
77
90
9
82
7
Ste-Mère -Eglise
Carteret
Barneville
79
St-Sauveur-le-Vicomte
Bouteville
Pont-l'Abbé
Chef-du-Pont
Beuzeville-la-Bastille
Ste-Marie-du-Mont
Douve
Vierville
101
Portbail
St-Côme-du-Mont
265 elms
30
St-Jores
Carentan
La Haye-du-Puits
85
Vire-Taute Can
N
6
914 elts
Lessay
17 SS
0 2.5 km
0 2.5 miles
Taute
Périers

US infantrymen fight their way through a French village.

On 24 June, the same day that the Commander-in-Chief West gave Hitler the unwelcome news about the armoured counter-attack, Hitler demanded another counter-attack be launched, this time against the Americans closing on Cherbourg. Von Rundstedt replied that this was impossible, but Hitler kept pressing. As it was, the port was protected by three defence lines, each based on a ridge and with 40,000 defenders, although some were East battalions of doubtful quality, and morale was, overall, low. The US VII Corps began to close on Cherbourg on 22 June, while Hitler exhorted the garrison to 'defend the last bunker and leave to the enemy not a harbour but a field of ruins'. Three days later, the assault proper began, supported by the guns of three battleships, four cruisers, and eleven destroyers. By the end of the day, the defences on the left and right wings had collapsed. Next day, having located the commander of Cherbourg, General Karl-Wilhelm von Schlieben, in a tunnel on the southern outskirts, the Americans demanded that he surrender. Von Schlieben refused, but rounds fired by tank destroyers into two of the entrances to the tunnel soon brought him, and the naval commander at Cherbourg, out, but he continued to refuse to surrender the whole of the city and port. But, as word got about that he had personally surrendered, other Germans began to put their hands up. The port capitulated on 28 June and German resistance on the peninsula ceased on 1 July. So the Allies now had their port, but much of its infrastructure had been destroyed by the Germans and it would take two months of repair work to make it fully operational.

German prisoners of war from Normandy are marched through the port of Dover on arrival in England.

While the battle for Cherbourg continued, Montgomery had been preparing a new attack designed to pave the way for

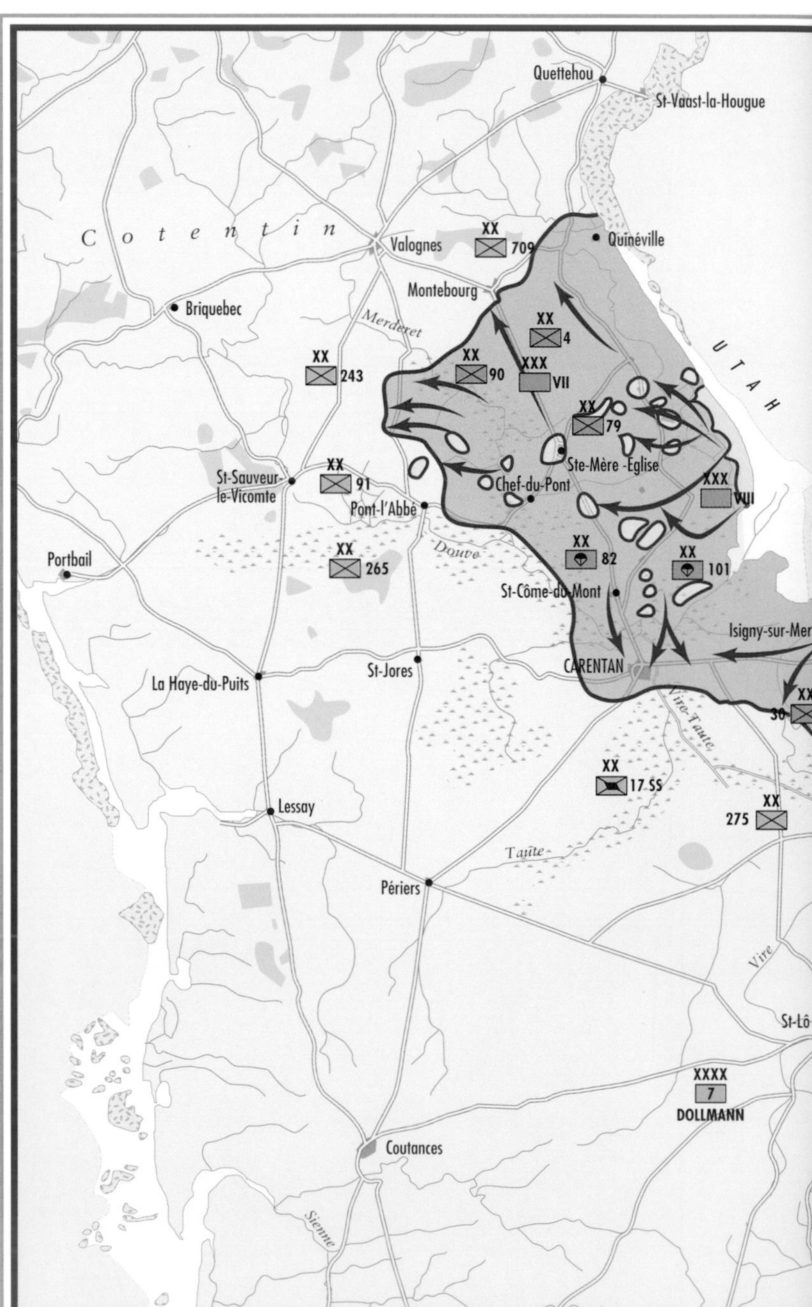

the American break-out. Again, it was to the west of Caen and the idea was to advance south and then east to seize the high ground south of the city. Montgomery's original intention was to launch the assault on 22 June, but the great storm which so damaged the Mulberries forced a postponement and it was not until 25 June that Operation Epsom got underway. The three days' grace that it gave Rommel was invaluable, enabling him to shore up his defences. The recently arrived 49th West Riding Division made the initial assault, which aimed to secure the right flank of the British VIII Corps and was partially successful. On the following day, the main attack stepped off, with 15th Scottish Division in the lead. Its task was to advance five miles to the River Odon, secure bridges over it and then allow 11th Armoured Division to pass through. The weather, however, was still poor and meant that little tactical air support could be provided because of the cloud cover. Resistance was fierce, notably from the now-battle-hardened young soldiers of the 12th SS Panzer Division, many of them ex-Hitler Youth members. Indeed, the Division's subsidiary title was the Hitlerjugend Division. Just after midday, General Dick O'Connor, commanding VIII Corps, released 11th Armoured Division in an effort to speed up momentum. It, too, was unable

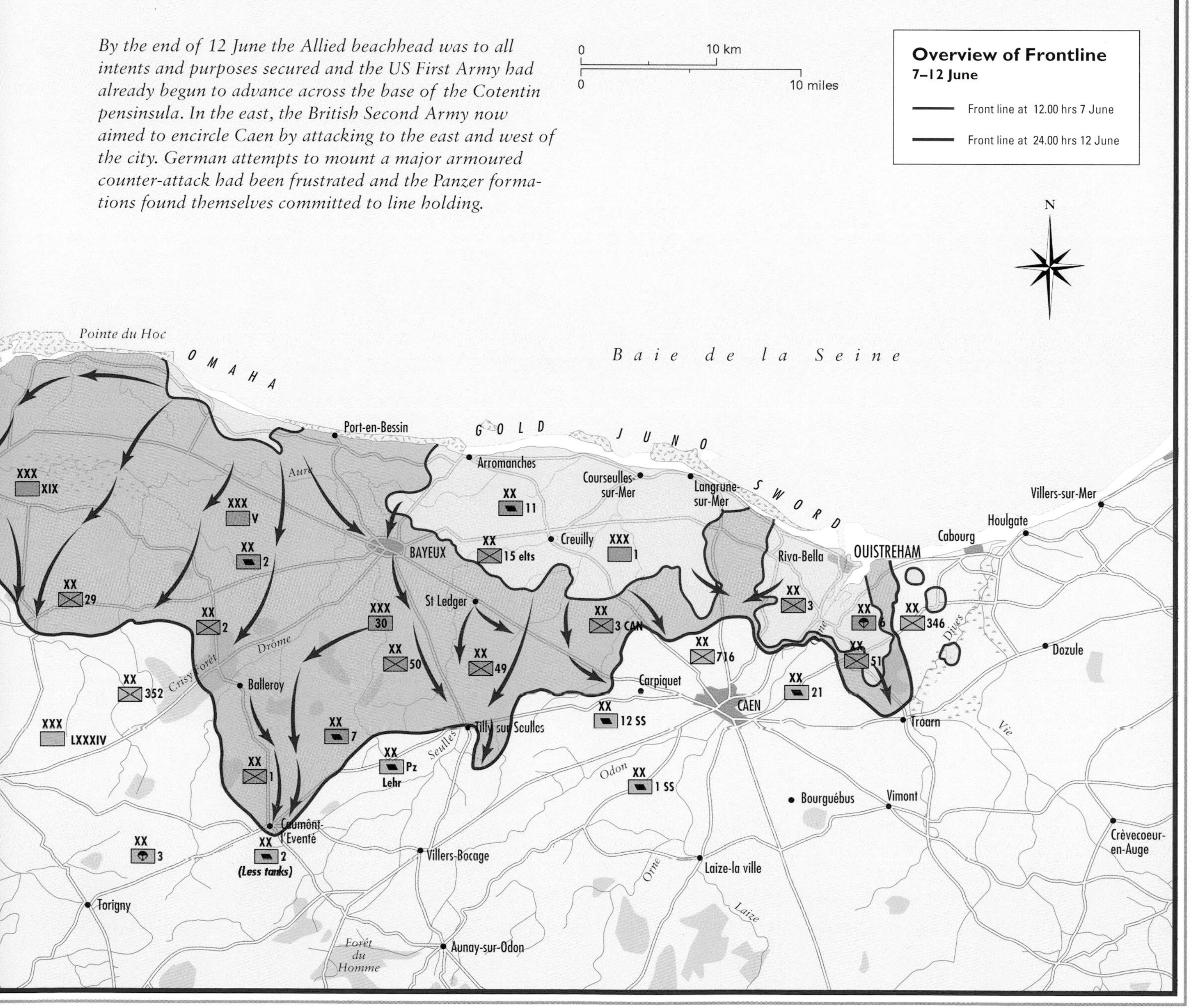

By the end of 12 June the Allied beachhead was to all intents and purposes secured and the US First Army had already begun to advance across the base of the Cotentin pensinsula. In the east, the British Second Army now aimed to encircle Caen by attacking to the east and west of the city. German attempts to mount a major armoured counter-attack had been frustrated and the Panzer formations found themselves committed to line holding.

Mulberry Harbour A
at St Laurant-sur-Mer largely destroyed in the storm of 19-21 June 1944

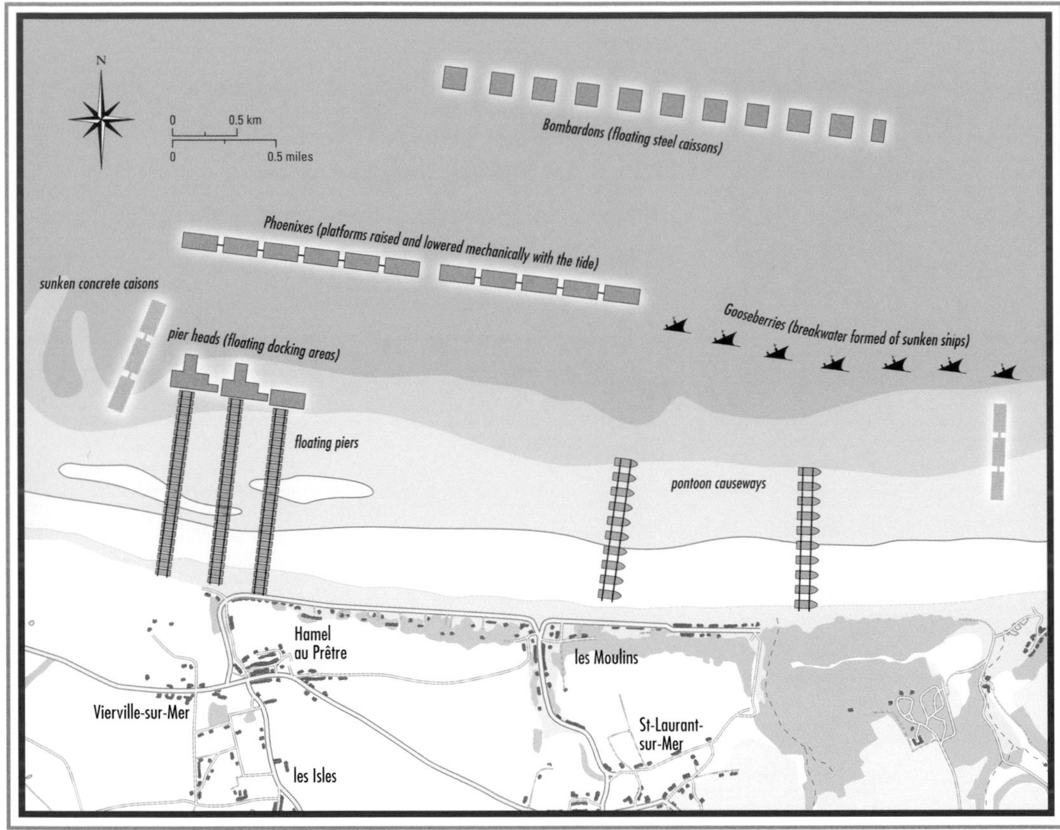

The US Mulberry appeared well protected, with its system of artificial breakwaters. On 18 June, the day that it opened for business, the weather was perfect. That evening the barometer began to fall and next day the waves and the wind began to increase. By 20 June it was blowing Force 6, and the Bombardons were only designed to resist winds up to this strength, while the Gooseberries could resist even less. Consequently, Mulberry A and the incomplete British Mulberry B began to break up.

to make much progress and at 6pm 15th Scottish once more took up the baton. Nightfall found its men struggling to gain the ridge north of the Odon. It was not the 'blitz' attack that Montgomery had envisaged, but it was keeping the German armour tied down.

During the night, 43rd Wessex Division was brought up to relieve 15th Scottish so that it could press on again next day. The weather was still poor, but, in spite of several German counter-attacks, the Division did succeed in capturing one intact bridge over the Odon. In the early evening 11th Armoured started to pass over it. By the time darkness fell it had secured the northern part of Hill 112, two miles south of the river. O'Connor was conscious, however, that several villages north of the Odon were still in German hands. Even so, on 28 June 11th Armoured struggled to secure the remainder of Hill 112, but with little further success. O'Connor then ordered it to halt, while the rear was tidied up. On 29 June, II SS Panzer Corps mounted a furious counter-attack from Villers-Bocage. The attack was repulsed, but marked the end of Epsom. The final element of it was to withdraw 11th Armoured Division from its exposed position on Hill 112.

Thus the German defence still proved firm and Montgomery was aware that fresh Panzer divisions were beginning to appear. Hopes that Omar Bradley might be able to begin his break-out had also been dashed by the great storm which had delayed the arrival of the US VIII Corps, whose participation was crucial to the operation. Undeterred, on 30 June Montgomery expounded his concept of the break-out to his subordinate commanders. While the British Second Army tied down the Germans between Caen and Villers-Bocage, the Americans would advance southwards and eastwards in a wide sweep so as to cut off the withdrawal of the German forces south of Paris. In the meantime, the pressure had to be kept up and Montgomery focussed again on Caen. He wanted to capture it by attacking on both sides to create a double envelopment.

On the German side, von Rundstedt and Rommel were becoming increasingly frustrated over Hitler's interference in the conduct of the campaign, in particular with his refusal to allow them to withdraw their forces out of range of the Allied naval guns. On the evening of 27 June both received a summons to Hitler's Bavarian mountain retreat at Berchtesgaden. They were not allowed to fly or go by train and had to face a 600-mile journey by car. Hitler once more harangued them, boasting of his 'miracle weapons', which would turn the tide in the West. All that von Rundstedt and Rommel needed to do was to halt the Allied advance and clear up their beachhead. The naval gunfire problem could be eradicated by the use of glider-bombs, which the Germans had already begun to employ against ships, and maximum employment of the German surface and sub-surface naval forces. Ground reinforcements were hardly mentioned, and for a very good reason. On 22 June the Russians had launched a major offensive on the Eastern Front, Operation Bagration. It had already thrown Army Group Centre into disarray and there was a very real danger that the Russians would tear an enormous hole in the German defences. In the face of this growing catastrophe, little could be spared for the West. Hitler had also instituted a witch hunt over the fall of Cherbourg and it seemed as though he blamed General Eugen Dollmann, the commander of Seventh Army. On the day that the two Field Marshals arrived at Berchtesgaden, Dollmann died of a heart

How a Mulberry harbour was laid out in theory. The key was the artificial breakwaters, which provided shelter for the vessels unloading at the piers.

What a Mulberry looked like in practice.

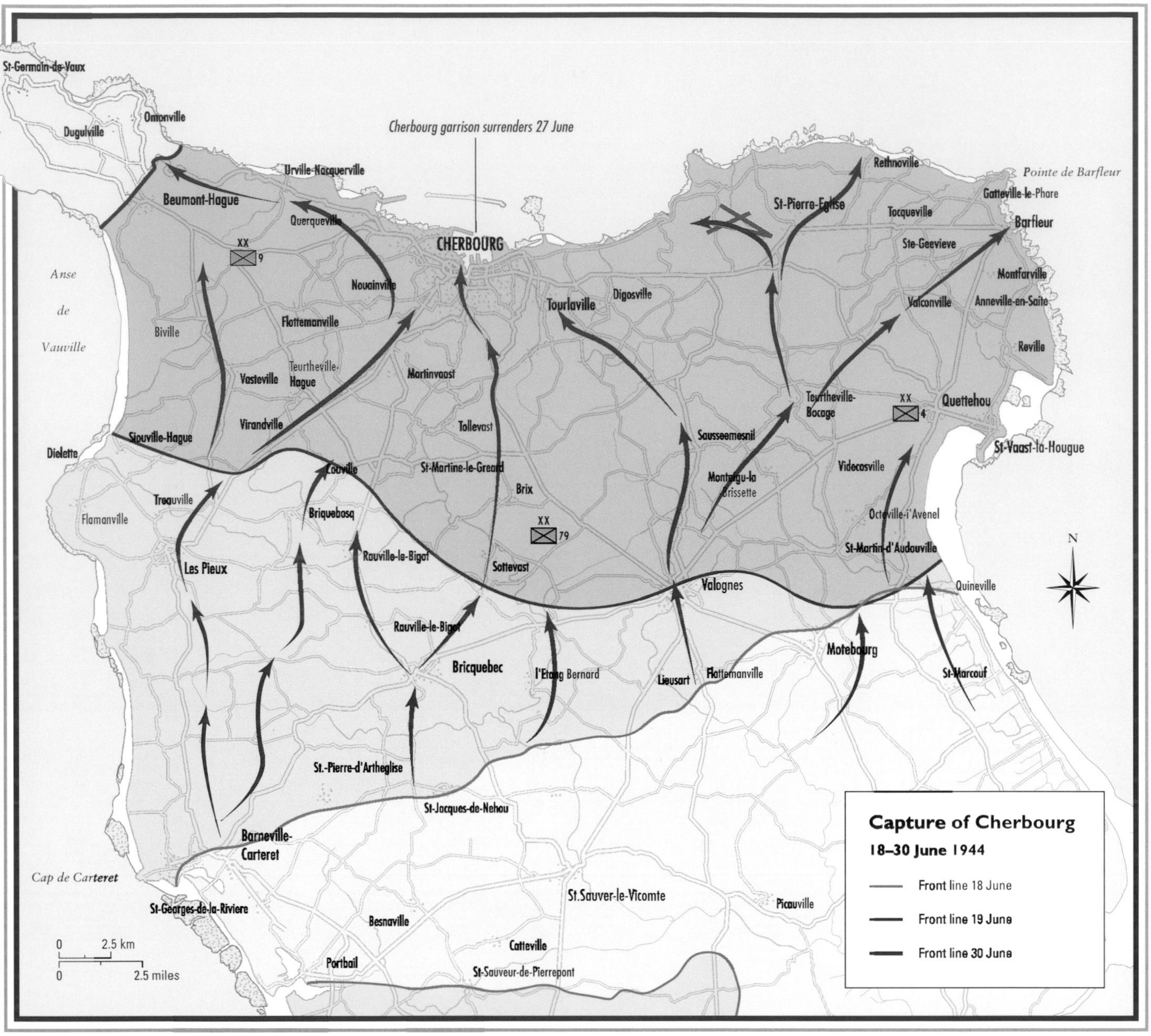

Capture of Cherbourg
18–30 June 1944
Front line 18 June
Front line 19 June
Front line 30 June
Cherbourg garrison surrenders 27 June
CHERBOURG
St-Germain-de-Vaux
Omonville
Dugulville
Beumont-Hague
Urville-Nacqueville
Querqueville
Nouainville
Flottemanville
Biville
Vasteville
Teurtheville-Hague
Virandville
Siouville-Hague
Dielette
Treauville
Flamanville
Les Pieux
Couville
Briquebosq
Rauville-le-Bigot
Martinvaast
Tollevast
St-Martine-le-Greard
Brix
Sottevast
Bricquebec
l'Etang Bernard
St.-Pierre-d'Artheglise
St-Jacques-de-Nehou
Barneville-Carteret
Cap de Carteret
St-Georges-de-la-Riviere
Besnaville
Portbail
Catteville
St-Sauveur-de-Pierrepont
St.Sauver-le-Vicomte
Picauville
Tourlaville
Digosville
Sausseemesnil
Montaigu-la Brissette
Valognes
Lieusart
Flottemanville
Motebourg
St-Marcouf
Quineville
St-Martin-d'Audouville
Octeville-l'Avenel
Videcosville
Teurtheville-Bocage
Quettehou
St-Vaast-la-Hougue
Reville
Anneville-en-Saire
Valconville
Montfarville
Ste-Geevieve
Barfleur
Gatteville-le-Phare
Pointe de Barfleur
Tocqueville
Rethnoville
St-Pierre-Eglise
Anse de Vauville
XX 9
XX 79
XX 4
N
0 2.5 km
0 2.5 miles

Bombardment of Cherbourg
25 June 1944
Approach channel N°1
Approach channel N°2
Approach channel N°3
Approach channel N°4
Fire support area N°1
Fire support areas N°3
Fire support areas N°4
USS Quincy
USS Tuscaloosa
USS Nevada
HMS Enterprise
HMS Glasgow
USS Arkansas
USS Texas
Battery 346
Battery 308
Battery N°2
Cherbourg
50°

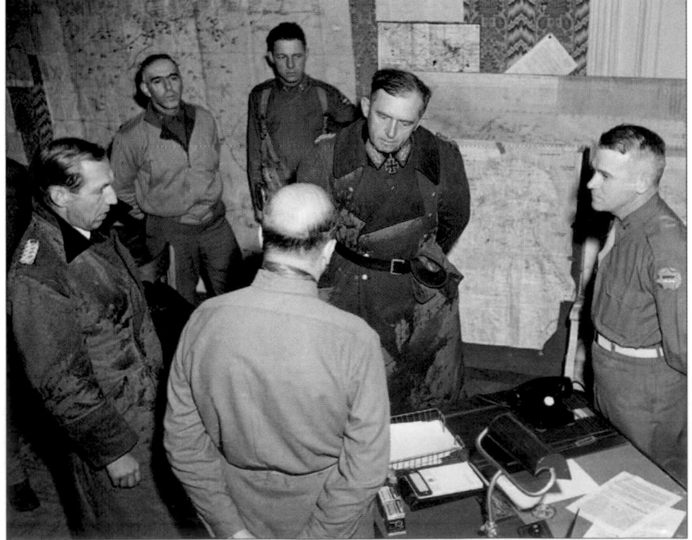

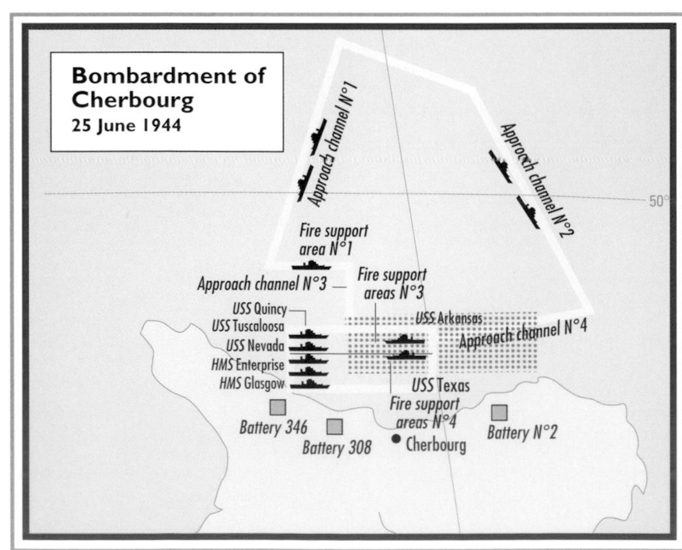

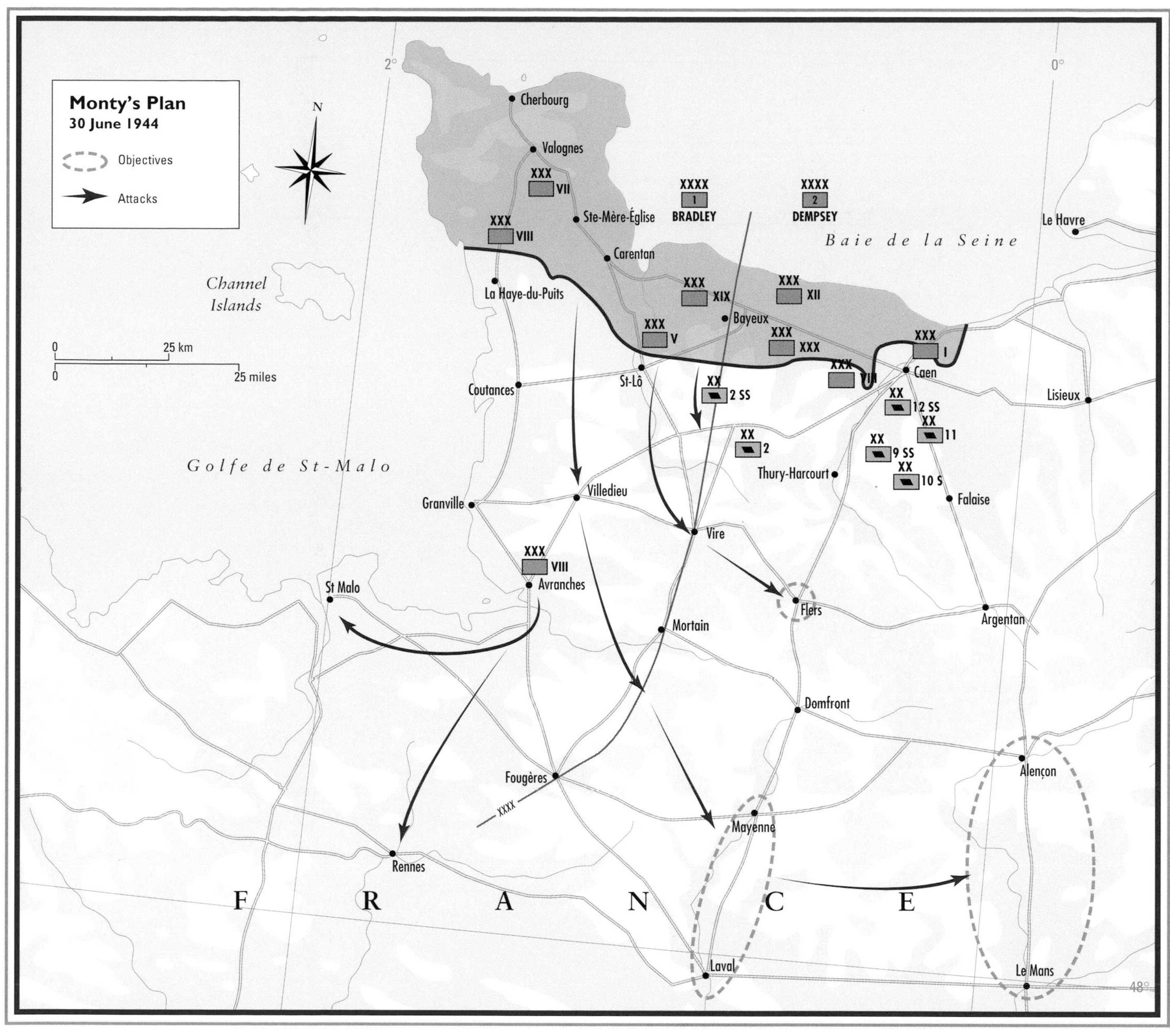

(Left) Although Hitler ordered Cherbourg to be defended to the last man, the shattered German divisions defending it offered only half-hearted resistance. The naval bombardment of the coastal batteries marked the end of Operation Neptune (see lower map), since the Allied ground forces in Normandy were now almost out of range of naval gunfire. The extreme north-west corner of the Cotentin peninsula was liberated on 1 July.

General Karl-Wilhelm von Schlieben, commanding Cherbourg, surrenders in the tunnel that was his HQ.

(Above) While the British Second Army kept as many Panzer divisions pinned down in the east, Bradley was to break out southwards and then send one corps to clear Brittany and secure its ports, while the remainder swung eastwards in a deep outflanking move designed to cut off the German withdrawal routes south of Paris.

attack. Von Rundstedt and Rommel demanded that the investigation be halted so that no slur would be attached to Dollmann's memory.

Further orders from Hitler awaited them when they arrived back at their respective headquarters late on 30 June. The salient over the Orne must be eradicated at once and on no account was Seventh Army to be driven out of the *bocage*. Simultaneously came a request from Geyr von Schweppenburg and SS General Paul Hausser, who had taken over Seventh Army, to be allowed to withdraw out of range of naval gunfire. Von Rundstedt immediately informed OKW and told Rommel to put in train preparations for this to happen. The answer came back from OKW that there was to be no withdrawal. It was the last straw for von Rundstedt. He immediately phoned Field

Marshal Wilhelm Keitel, Hitler's obsequious Chief of Staff at OKW, and told him that the only option was to make peace and that he himself had had enough. Hitler immediately relieved him and he was succeeded by Hans von Kluge, recently recovered from serious injuries received in a car crash on the Eastern Front.

Meanwhile, the Allies continued to grind on. West of Caen, the Canadians attacked on 3 July, their objective Carpiquet airfield. They managed to secure the village of the same name, but their old adversary 12th SS Panzer Division denied them the airfield. This, however, was a mere preliminary to the main assault on Caen. General Miles Dempsey, commanding the British Second Army, decided that maximum fire-power was the key that would unlock the door. Not only did he concentrate all the artillery that he could bring to bear, but he also intended to use naval gunfire and RAF Bomber Command to clear the way. Caen was in the sector controlled by Panzer Group West, now commanded by General Heinrich Eberbach, since Geyr von Schweppenburg had been sacked at the same time as von Rundstedt. North and west of the city was held by his dependable SS Panzer troops, while the east was defended by a Luftwaffe field division of more doubtful quality, but supported by elements of 21st Panzer Division. In the late afternoon of 7 July the battleship HMS *Rodney* engaged a hill just north of the city, which was considered a key point in the defences. That night 450 heavy bombers blasted the northern outskirts. At 11pm the artillery opened fire, pounding the German positions. At 4.20am on the 8th, ninety minutes before sunrise, the D-Day veterans of 3rd Infantry Division and the newly arrived 59th Division attacked. Numbed by the ferocity of the preparatory bombardment, the Germans in the forward defences succumbed quickly. The 3rd Canadian Division now began to attack from the west. By the end of the day it and 3rd British division had advanced two and a half miles, but 59th Division's progress was not as good, resulting in a two-mile gap between the former two formations. But the pressure on 12th SS Panzer Division had become almost unbearable and that night Eberbach agreed that all German forces around and in the city could withdraw to the south bank of the Odon. The British advance resumed at 3am on the following day, but the rubble in Caen, combined with a skilful rearguard action by the one remaining SS battalion north of the river meant that it took all day to reach the Odon bridges. By that time all had been blown and heavy fire from the south bank meant that no further progress could be made.

A recently captured officer briefs Americans on German dispositions. Prisoners were often willing to give information if interrogated soon after capture, when they would still be suffering from shock.

The Americans, too, had begun to press south. Montgomery's concept was for them to now swing south and east from Caumont and then attack into Brittany as well as breaking out eastwards. To Bradley the crucial first objective to enable all this to happen was the road communications centre at St-Lô. With his fourteen divisions now in place, outnumbering the Germans opposite First Army by at least three to one, it appeared straightforward. The terrain, however, was against him. Along the fifty miles of American front there were no open areas where he could deploy armour en masse. In the east the deep valley of the River Vire and the tenacious German hold on St-Lô itself gave him few

(Right) The Americans called it 'the battle of the hedgerows'. Advancing through some of the worst of the bocage and against desperate German resistance, the advance was slow compared to the recent operation in the Cotentin peninsula. Not until 18 July was St-Lô actually entered.

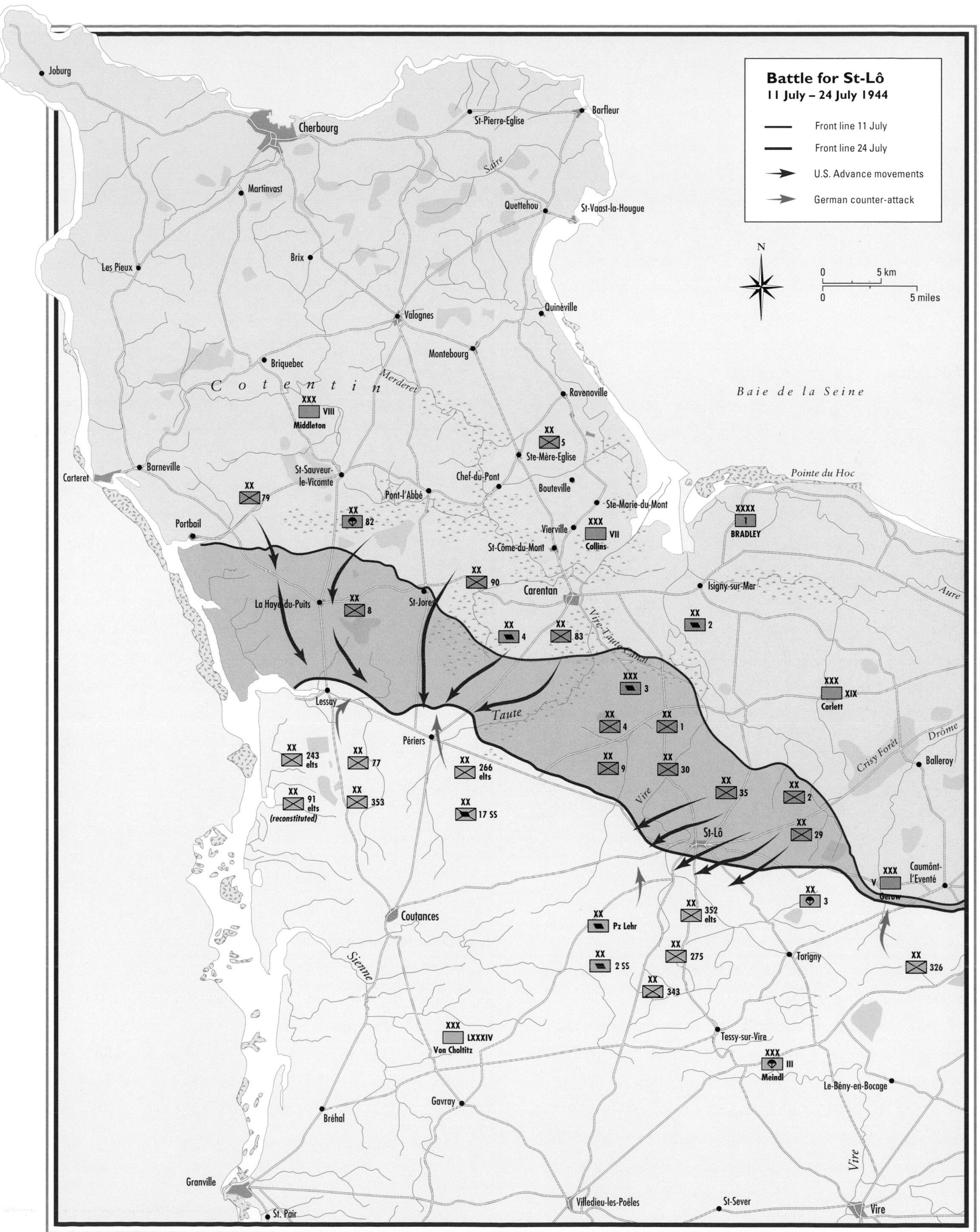
Battle for St-Lô
11 July – 24 July 1944
Front line 11 July
Front line 24 July
U.S. Advance movements
German counter-attack
0 5 km
0 5 miles
N
Joburg
Cherbourg
St-Pierre-Eglise
Barfleur
Saire
Martinvast
Quettehou
St-Vaast-la-Hougue
Brix
Les Pieux
Valognes
Quinéville
Montebourg
Briquebec
Cotentin
Merderet
Ravenoville
Baie de la Seine
XXX VIII Middleton
XX 5
Ste-Mère-Eglise
Barneville
Carteret
St-Sauveur-le-Vicomte
Chef-du-Pont
Bouteville
Pointe du Hoc
XX 79
Pont-l'Abbé
Ste-Marie-du-Mont
XXXX 1 BRADLEY
Portbail
XX 82
Vierville
XXX VII Collins
St-Côme-du-Mont
XX 90
Carentan
Isigny-sur-Mer
Aure
La Haye-du-Puits
XX 8
St-Jores
Vire-Taute Canal
XX 2
XX 4
XX 83
XXX 3
XXX XIX Corlett
Lessay
Taute
XX 4
XX 1
Périers
Drôme
XX 243 elts
XX 77
XX 266 elts
XX 9
XX 30
Cerisy Forêt
Balleroy
XX 91 elts (reconstituted)
XX 353
XX 17 SS
Vire
XX 35
XX 2
St-Lô
XX 29
XXX V Gerow
Caumônt-l'Eventé
XX 3
Coutances
XX Pz Lehr
XX 352 elts
Sienne
XX 275
Torigny
XX 2 SS
XX 343
XX 326
XXX LXXXIV Von Choltitz
Tessy-sur-Vire
XXX II Meindl
Le-Bény-en-Bocage
Gavray
Bréhal
Granville
Villedieu-les-Poêles
St-Sever
Vire
St. Pair

options. The centre of the sector was dominated by flooding with just one decent road, that running from Carentan to Périers, while the west was covered with thickly wooded hills and ridges. Nevertheless, to Bradley the right flank seemed to offer the best prospects, and it was here that the US VIII Corps kicked off the offensive on 3 July. Its opponent was the German LXXXIV Corps, formerly commanded one by one-legged General Erich Marcks, who had been killed by a US fighter-bomber on 12 June, and now under General Dietrich von Choltitz. He took maximum advantage of the terrain to make the American advance slow and costly. The US XIX and VII Corps experienced much the same frustration and by 10 July

An ammunitions truck takes a direct hit during the Canadian advance to Falaise.

Bradley was forced to call a halt, with St- Lô still firmly in German hands. But the attrition was having its effect. LXXXVIII Corps warned: 'The struggle cannot be maintained with the present forces for any length of time.'

Von Kluge had taken up his post as Commander-in-Chief West after a pep talk from Hitler which had fired him with the

Operation Epsom
24–30 June 1944

Front line 24 June
Front line 25 June
Front line 26 June
Front line 30 June
Allied advance
German counter-attacks
German retreat

Audrieu
Putot-en-Bessin
Cristot
Tilly-sur-Seulles
Fontenay-le-Pesnel
Juvigny-sur-Seulles
Tessel
Rauray
Vendes
Missy
Noyers-Bocage
Pz Lehr
9SS
11 SS

(Right) Epsom was in pursuit of Montgomery's plan to envelop Caen. The key objective was Hill 112, which was part of a ridge which dominated the area and which General Paul Hausser, commanding II SS Panzer Corps at the time, called 'the key to the back-door of Caen'. In the event, the British found themselves being attacked in the flanks of their narrow salient and, apart from a narrow bridgehead, were forced to withdraw north of the River Odon.

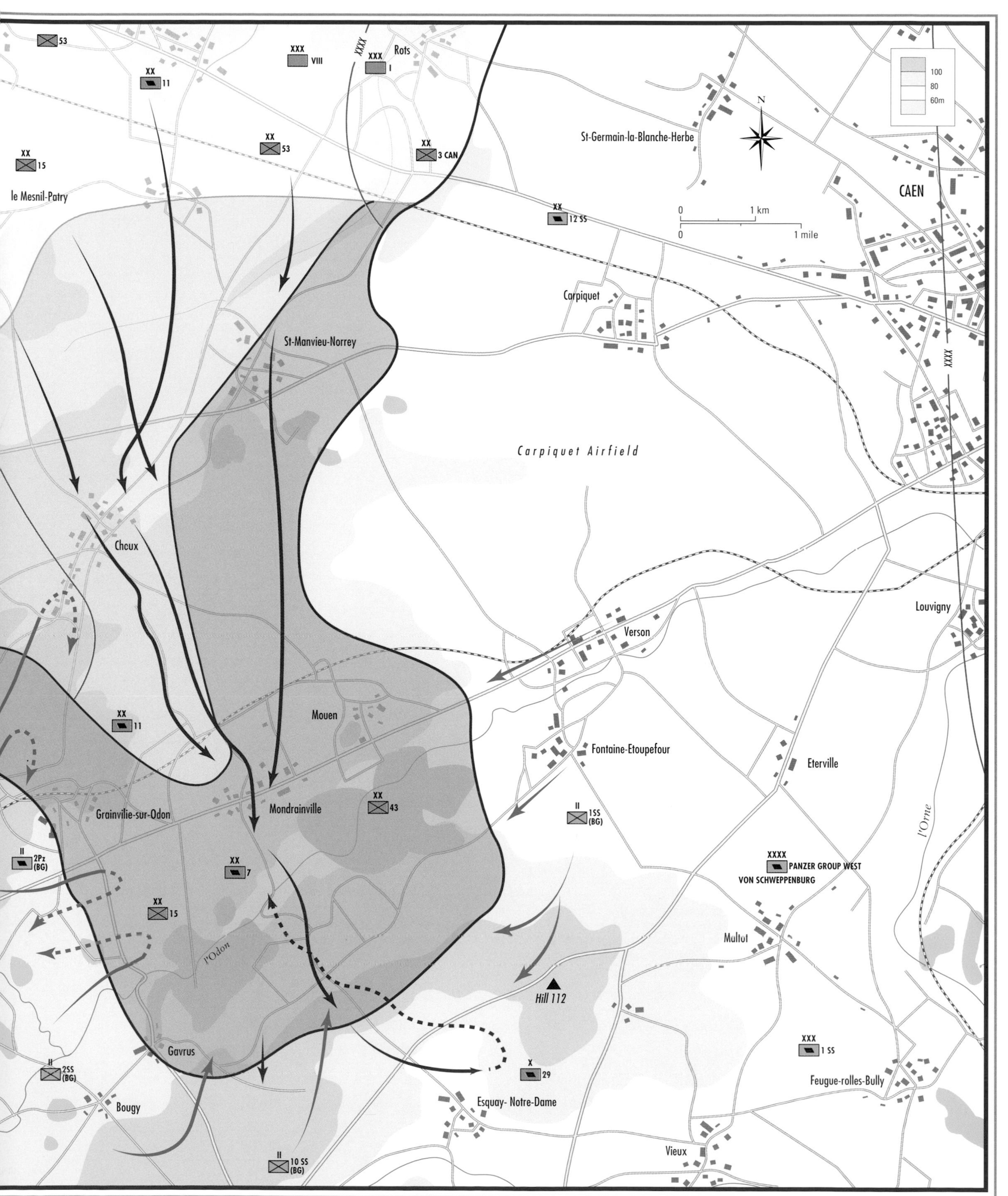

100
80
60m
N
53
XXX VIII
XXXX
XXX I
Rots
XX 11
XX 53
XX 3 CAN
XX 15
St-Germain-la-Blanche-Herbe
CAEN
le Mesnil-Patry
XX 12 SS
0 1 km
0 1 mile
Carpiquet
St-Manvieu-Norrey
Carpiquet Airfield
Cheux
Louvigny
Verson
Mouen
XX 11
Fontaine-Etoupefour
Eterville
Grainville-sur-Odon
Mondrainville
XX 43
II 1SS (BG)
l'Orne
II 2Pz (BG)
XX 7
XXXX PANZER GROUP WEST
VON SCHWEPPENBURG
XX 15
Maltot
l'Odon
Hill 112
XXX 1 SS
Gavrus
II 2SS (BG)
X 29
Feugue-rolles-Bully
Bougy
Esquay- Notre-Dame
Vieux
II 10 SS (BG)

belief that the problems that von Rundstedt and Rommel had described had been overemphasized. Consequently, his first meeting with Rommel at La Roche-Guyon on 3 July had served merely to get the latter's back up, especially when von Kluge told him that he was to obey his orders to the letter. It did not take long for the scales to be lifted from von Kluge's eyes. He began to appreciate how the sheer mass of Allied fire-power was wearing the defence down and came round to Rommel's viewpoint, especially after several further discussions with him. Encouraged by this, Rommel submitted a memorandum to his superior on 16 July. He pointed out that there had been 117,000 German casualties since D-Day, but that only 10,000 replacements had been sent. Army Group B was close to breaking point. Von Kluge passed this on to OKW, but it made little difference.

Caen at the end of Operation Charnwood. There was little left of it by the end of the campaign and it had to be totally rebuilt.

If there was frustration in the German high command in France, the Allies were also experiencing it. In spite of the pressure which they had been applying, Caen was still partially in German hands and St-Lô remained just outside the American grasp. There appeared to be stalemate. Certainly, Eisenhower thought this and began to query Montgomery's strategy, pointing out that the terrain in the west made it almost impossible for the Americans to break out. Rather, he suggested, Montgomery should consider a break-out in the east. Churchill, too, was becoming increasingly impatient. At the lower levels, morale was flagging and such was the growing belief that the German weapons systems were superior that Montgomery forbade mention of the matter in after-action reports. The troops, at least those who had been in Normandy from the beginning, were becoming very tired and casualties were increasing. Those among the British infantry were of particular concern, since there was a growing shortage of replacements in Britain.

Yet Montgomery remained self-confident. He reiterated his concept of the British keeping the German armour tied down while the Americans broke out. Bradley agreed to continue preparing for this, but expressed his concerns over the terrain in First Army's sector. Dempsey, who was present at this conference, held on 10 July, proposed that instead of an American attack, Second Army should take advantage of the good tank country around Caen and launch an all-out offensive there. Montgomery was initially undecided, but then agreed to allow Dempsey his head. He informed Eisenhower, who was delighted that Montgomery appeared to have listened to his advice, and offered all possible air support for Goodwood, as the operation was codenamed. But, while Eisenhower and Dempsey saw it as the Allied break-out, Montgomery took a more cautious approach. If it worked, well and good, but it was essential, in his eyes, that the eastern part of the beachhead be maintained as a 'bastion' on which the American operations could be anchored. Dempsey laid down his aim of establishing an armoured division in each of the Bretteville-sur-Laize, Vimont-Argentan and Falaise areas, but Montgomery deleted Argentan and Falaise, since he feared that this would over-extend Second Army and make it vulnerable to counter-attack. He saw Goodwood as being much more about wearing down the maximum German forces so as to facilitate the American break-out. In other words, he remained true to his original strategy.

The Goodwood attack was to take place just east of Caen. It would involve all three British armoured divisions – 7th, 11th and Guards. Their primary objective was the dominant Bourguébus Ridge, which ran north-west to south-east to the south-east of Caen. Once this had been secured, the armour would then advance towards Falaise. Simultaneously, 3rd Infantry Division would attack south-east and capture Troarn,

Charnwood's aim was finally to secure Caen. It marked the first significant use of allied 'carpet bombing'. While this did numb the defenders, it reduced much of the northern part of Caen to rubble, which made it difficult for the attackers. By the end of the operation, the Germans were still holding the area of the city to the south of the River Odon.

Operation Charnwood
7–9 July 1944

Front line 7 July (eve)
'3 map squares' bombing target area
Lancasters and Halifax bombers

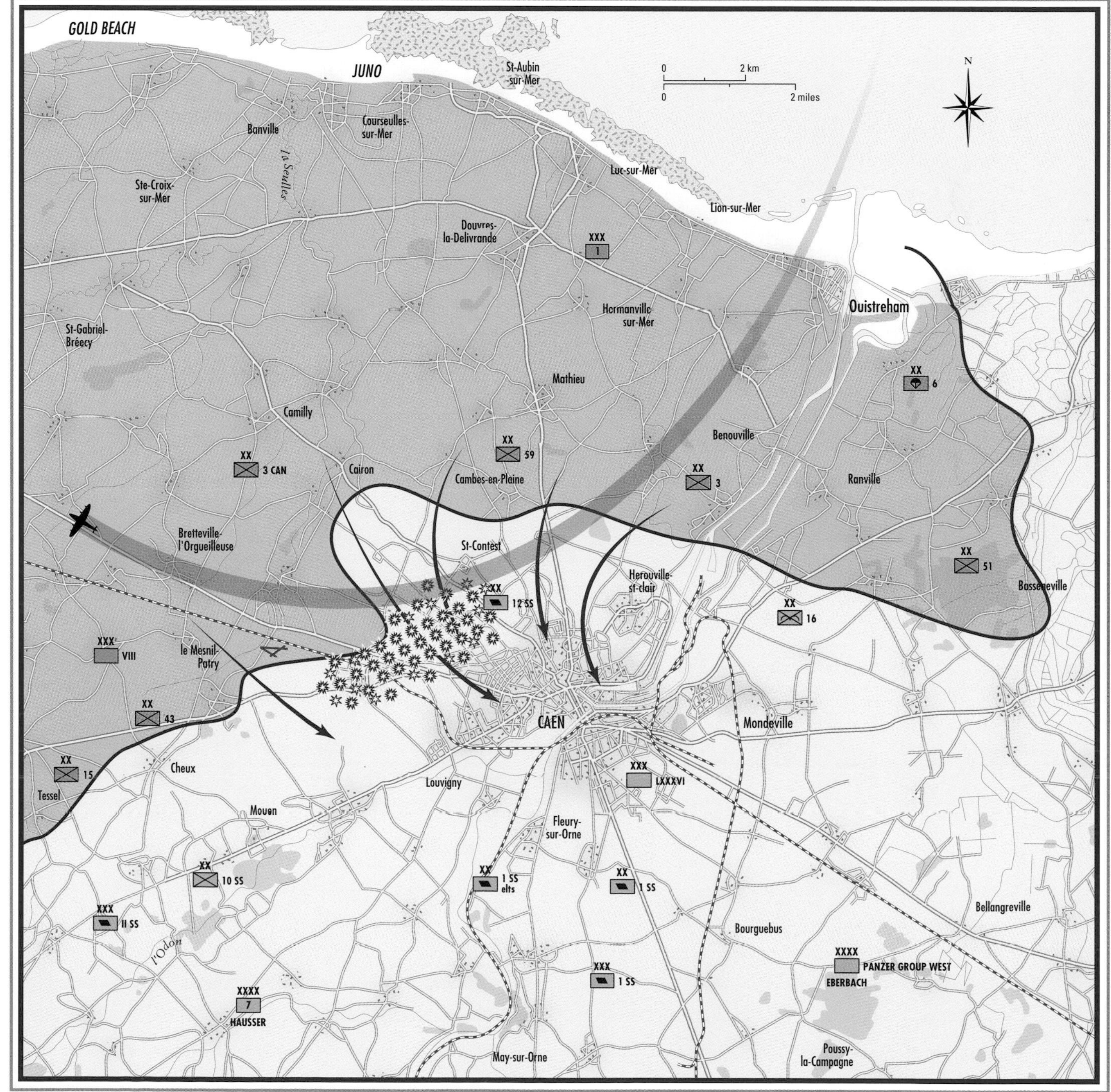

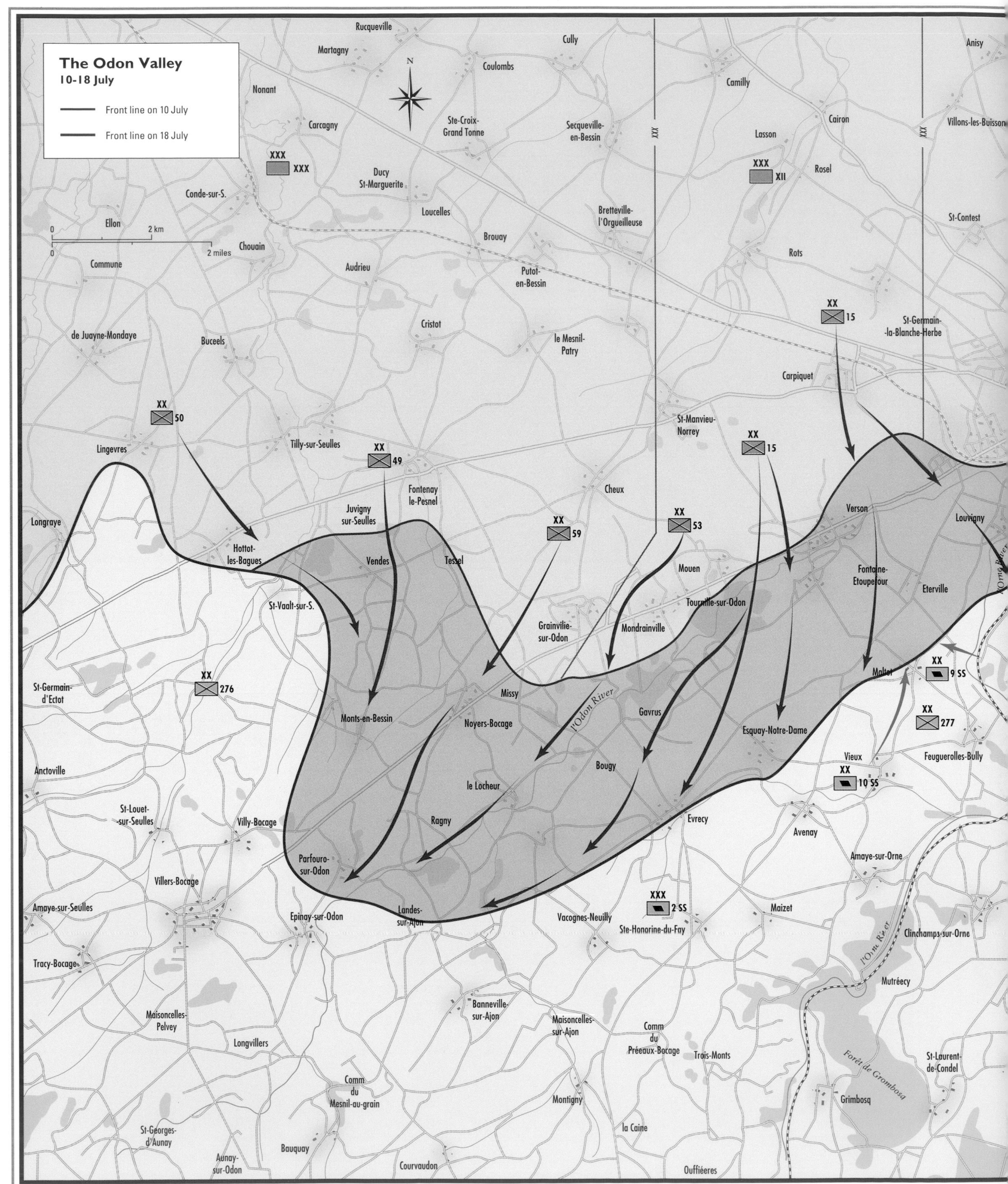
The Odon Valley
10-18 July
Front line on 10 July
Front line on 18 July
0 2 km
0 2 miles
N
Rucqueville
Martagny
Cully
Coulombs
Anisy
Nonant
Camilly
Carcagny
Ste-Croix-Grand Tonne
Secqueville-en-Bessin
Lasson
Cairon
Villons-les-Buissons
XXX XXX
XXX XII
Ducy St-Marguerite
Rosel
Conde-sur-S.
Loucelles
Bretteville-l'Orgueilleuse
St-Contest
Ellon
Brouay
Chouain
Commune
Audrieu
Putot-en-Bessin
Rots
XX 15
Cristot
St-Germain-la-Blanche-Herbe
de Juayne-Mondaye
Buceels
le Mesnil-Patry
Carpiquet
XX 50
St-Manvieu-Norrey
Lingevres
Tilly-sur-Seulles
XX 49
XX 15
Fontenay le-Pesnel
Cheux
Longraye
Juvigny sur-Seulles
XX 59
XX 53
Verson
Louvigny
Hottot-les-Bagues
Vendes
Tessel
Mouen
Fontaine-Etoupefour
Eterville
l'Orne River
St-Vaalt-sur-S.
Tourville-sur-Odon
Grainville-sur-Odon
Mondrainville
XX 276
Maltot
XX 9 SS
St-Germain-d'Ectot
Missy
l'Odon River
Gavrus
XX 277
Monts-en-Bessin
Noyers-Bocage
Esquay-Notre-Dame
Vieux
Feuguerolles-Bully
Bougy
XX 10 SS
Anctoville
le Locheur
St-Louet-sur-Seulles
Ragny
Evrecy
Villy-Bocage
Avenay
Parfouro-sur-Odon
Amaye-sur-Orne
Villers-Bocage
XXX 2 SS
Landes-sur-Ajon
Maizet
Amaye-sur-Seulles
Epinay-sur-Odon
Vacognes-Neuilly
Ste-Honorine-du-Fay
Clinchamps-sur-Orne
Tracy-Bocage
l'Orne River
Mutréecy
Banneville-sur-Ajon
Maisoncelles-sur-Ajon
Maisoncelles-Pelvey
Comm du Préeaux-Bocage
Longvillers
Trois-Monts
Forêt de Grombosq
St-Laurent-de-Condel
Comm du Mesnil-au-grain
Montigny
Grimbosq
St-Georges-d'Aunay
la Caine
Aunay-sur-Odon
Bauquay
Courvaudon
Ouffiéeres

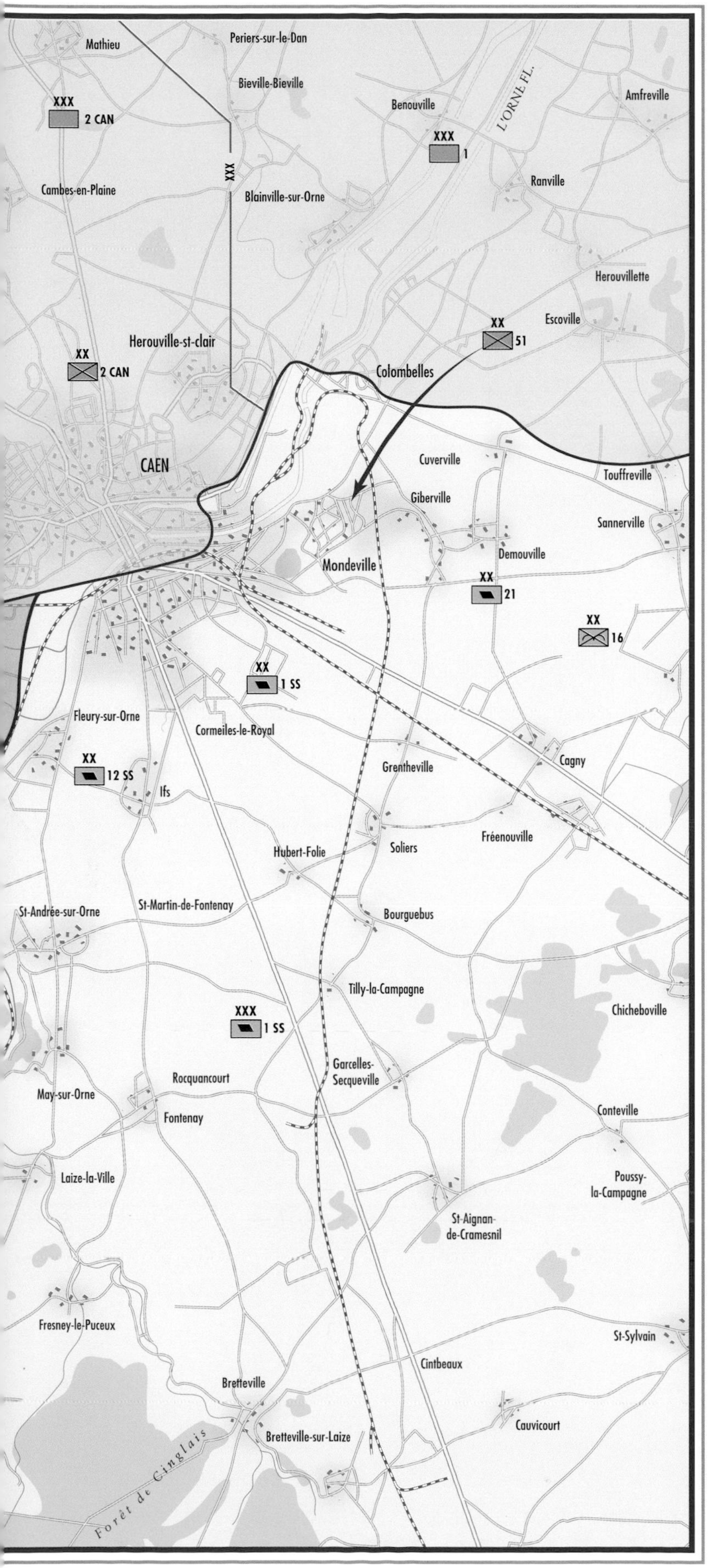

so as to secure the left flank of the armoured thrust, and the Canadian Corps would overrun the remainder of Caen and seize crossings over the River Orne to the south to enable the armour to advance towards Falaise. As to the area west of Caen, the remainder of the British Second Army had been continuing to maintain pressure and by 18 July, when Goodwood was mounted, had almost reached Villers-Bocage. Thus, Panzer Group West had been allowed little respite.

Rommel had read his opponent's mind well. The continuing attacks to the west of Caen were a good indicator, as well as the build-up of British armour in the sector. On 15 July he warned

(Left) No sooner had Charnwood ended, than the British Second Army renewed its attacks to the west of Caen. They were designed to maintain pressure on the Panzer divisions, while Bradley prepared his break-out operation.

Germans forming up for a local counter-attack.

the commander of 346th Division, which was east of Caen, of this, and did the same the following day to Panzer Group West and LXXXIV Corps. On 17 July he visited II SS Panzer Corps, which had recently suffered heavy casualties in the operations west of Caen, and then Sepp Dietrich's I SS Corps, which was east of the city. At about 4pm he left Dietrich's headquarters to return to his own, taking minor roads wherever possible to avoid the attentions of the ever-present Allied aircraft.

US troops make a local attack during the advance to St-Lô. The prone man in the foreground is about to fire a rifle grenade. The soldier on the extreme right is carrying an M1 anti-tank rocket launcher, commonly known as a Bazooka.

Unfortunately, he was forced to take the main road for part of the way and it was on a stretch of this that his car was attacked by an Allied fighter-bomber. Rommel's driver lost control and the car ended up in a ditch, with the Field Marshal unconscious from a severe fracture of the skull. It was to be the end of his active soldiering and, with the battle for Normandy about to enter its crucial phase, his presence would be sorely missed. As it was, he was not replaced and von Kluge took over command of Army Group B, while continuing to act as Commander-in-Chief West.

During the days before Goodwood the British armour had been deploying. Shortage of routes and the narrowness of the assembly area for the attack meant that the initial assault could only be carried out by one division. This was 11th Armoured commanded by General Pip Roberts, the youngest of the British divisional commanders and one who had fought throughout the North African campaign. The Guards Armoured Division would follow and come up on 11th Armoured's left, while 7th Armoured would move behind them and be prepared to lend its weight to either of the two lead divisions. Between 5.30am and 8.30am on 18 July, RAF Bomber Command, operating in clear conditions, with little flak and no German aircraft present, dropped no less than 5,000 tons of bombs on the villages east of Caen. Meanwhile, at 7.45am 11th Armoured Division began to advance under a rolling artillery barrage. So numbed were the defenders from 16th Luftwaffe Field Division and 21st Panzer Division, that there was initially little resistance. Indeed, not until the leading tanks reached Cagny, three-and-a-half miles from the start line, did the defence start to come alive. Sixteen tanks were quickly knocked out and the remainder veered away to the south-west, their

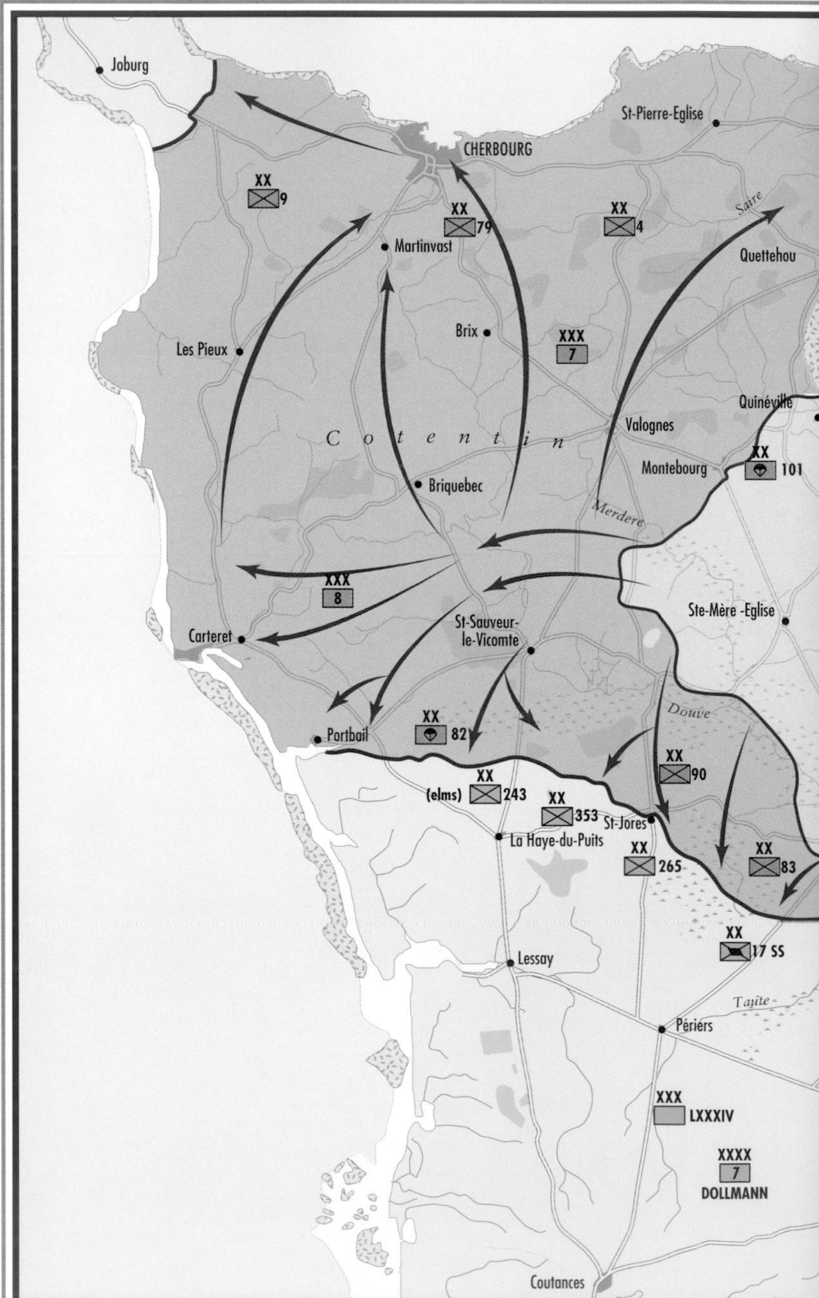

objective the dominant Bourguébus Ridge. The Division's infantry were, however, still trying to clear villages to the rear and the move of Guards and 7th Armoured Divisions had been delayed by traffic congestion on the few routes forward.

By now the Germans were recovering fast. Sepp Dietrich ordered 1st SS Panzer Division to move its tanks onto the Bourguébus Ridge and the Panthers of 501 SS Heavy Tank Battalion to the village of Frenouville on the eastern flank. As 11th Armoured Division's tanks crossed the Caen–Vimont railway line, they found themselves under heavy fire from the ridge to their front and from Frenouville on their flank. In addition, some of the villages to the rear had come alive again and were engaging both 11th Armoured and the two other divisions with anti-tank fire. Chaos began to reign and the advance ground to a halt. The British armour tried again on the following day, but made little progress. Indeed, Dietrich had now also brought 12th SS Panzer Division onto the ridge. Thunderstorms on 20 July were the last straw and the attack was halted.

The British breakthrough, if it was meant to be so, had failed at a cost of some 400 tanks. But there were consolations. The Canadians had succeeded in capturing the remainder of Caen,

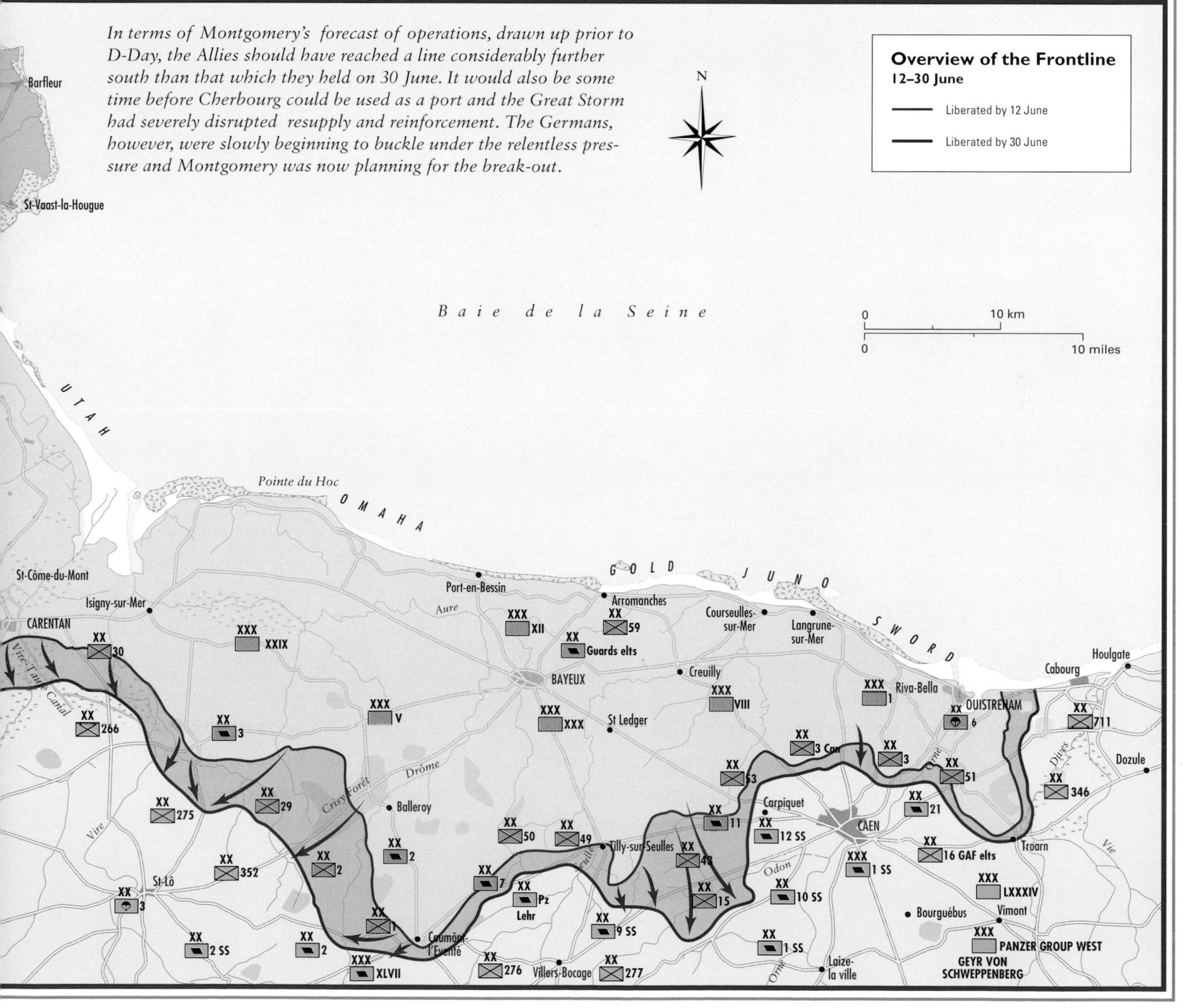

In terms of Montgomery's forecast of operations, drawn up prior to D-Day, the Allies should have reached a line considerably further south than that which they held on 30 June. It would also be some time before Cherbourg could be used as a port and the Great Storm had severely disrupted resupply and reinforcement. The Germans, however, were slowly beginning to buckle under the relentless pressure and Montgomery was now planning for the break-out.

American troops finally enter St-Lô, a knocked out Panther in their path.

although they then faced fierce counter-attacks. Bridgeheads over the Orne and Odon had been secured and six Panzer divisions had been kept tied down in the British sector. But Bradley's break-out operation, codenamed Cobra, had been scheduled for 20 July, which would have ensured that none of the Panzer divisions could be deployed to his sector in time. He was, as Dempsey had been for Goodwood, reliant on bombers paving the way for the initial assault, and the bad weather meant that they could not be used. Consequently, Cobra was postponed until 24 July. This meant an awkward pause, which could give the Germans time to recover.

Montgomery himself had been over-optimistic in his initial public utterances on the progress of Goodwood. Eisenhower and other senior officers at SHAEF were even more convinced that he had intended to break through. Now that he had failed, they were angry, especially at his protestations that the object of the exercise had been to tie down the German armour so as to facilitate Bradley's attack. Eisenhower felt that Montgomery had misled him and there were calls for him to be removed from command of 21st Army Group. On 20 July Churchill came over to France to see Montgomery, and some of his staff thought that it was to sack him. As it was, Montgomery took him into his Operations caravan and Churchill came out beaming with pleasure. Montgomery's position was still safe.

Churchill retired to spend the night on board the cruiser HMS *Enterprise*. The following morning he returned to 21st Army Group HQ, to be greeted with some astounding news.

Greetings to the liberators.

(Right) The debate over whether Montgomery intended Goodwood to be a break-out operation has continued to this day. The main problems with it were that the approach routes for the three armoured divisions were too narrow and that Sepp Dietrich, commanding I SS Panzer Corps, reacted quickly, occupying the dominant Bourguebus Ridge before the British tanks could reach it.

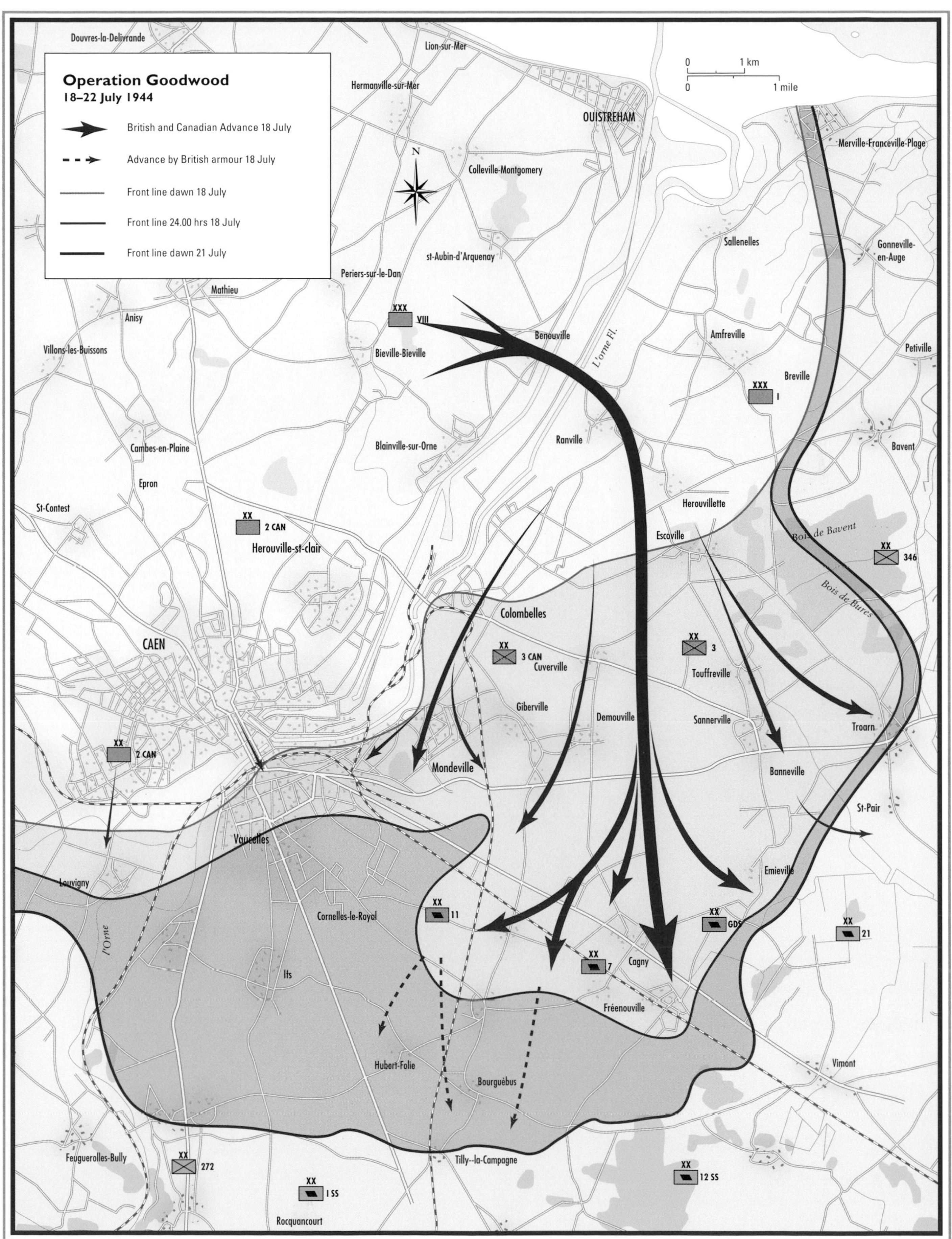

Operation Goodwood
18–22 July 1944
British and Canadian Advance 18 July
Advance by British armour 18 July
Front line dawn 18 July
Front line 24.00 hrs 18 July
Front line dawn 21 July
0 1 km
0 1 mile
N
Douvres-la-Delivrande
Lion-sur-Mer
Hermanville-sur-Mer
OUISTREHAM
Merville-Franceville-Plage
Colleville-Montgomery
Sallenelles
Gonneville-en-Auge
st-Aubin-d'Arquenay
Periers-sur-le-Dan
Mathieu
Anisy
XXX VIII
Benouville
L'orne Fl.
Amfreville
Petiville
Villons-les-Buissons
Bieville-Bieville
Breville
XXX I
Ranville
Bavent
Blainville-sur-Orne
Cambes-en-Plaine
Epron
Herouvillette
St-Contest
XX 2 CAN
Escoville
Bois de Bavent
XX 346
Herouville-st-clair
Bois de Bures
Colombelles
CAEN
XX 3 CAN
Cuverville
XX 3
Touffreville
Giberville
Demouville
Sannerville
Troarn
XX 2 CAN
Mondeville
Banneville
St-Pair
Vaucelles
Louvigny
Emieville
l'Orne
Cornelles-le-Royal
XX 11
XX GDS
XX 21
Ifs
XX 7
Cagny
Fréenouville
Vimont
Hubert-Folie
Bourguébus
Feugerolles-Bully
XX 272
Tilly-la-Campagne
XX 12 SS
XX 1 SS
Rocquancourt

An M5 Stuart (known by the British as a Honey) passes the victims of an earlier tank clash, a Sherman and a Panther.

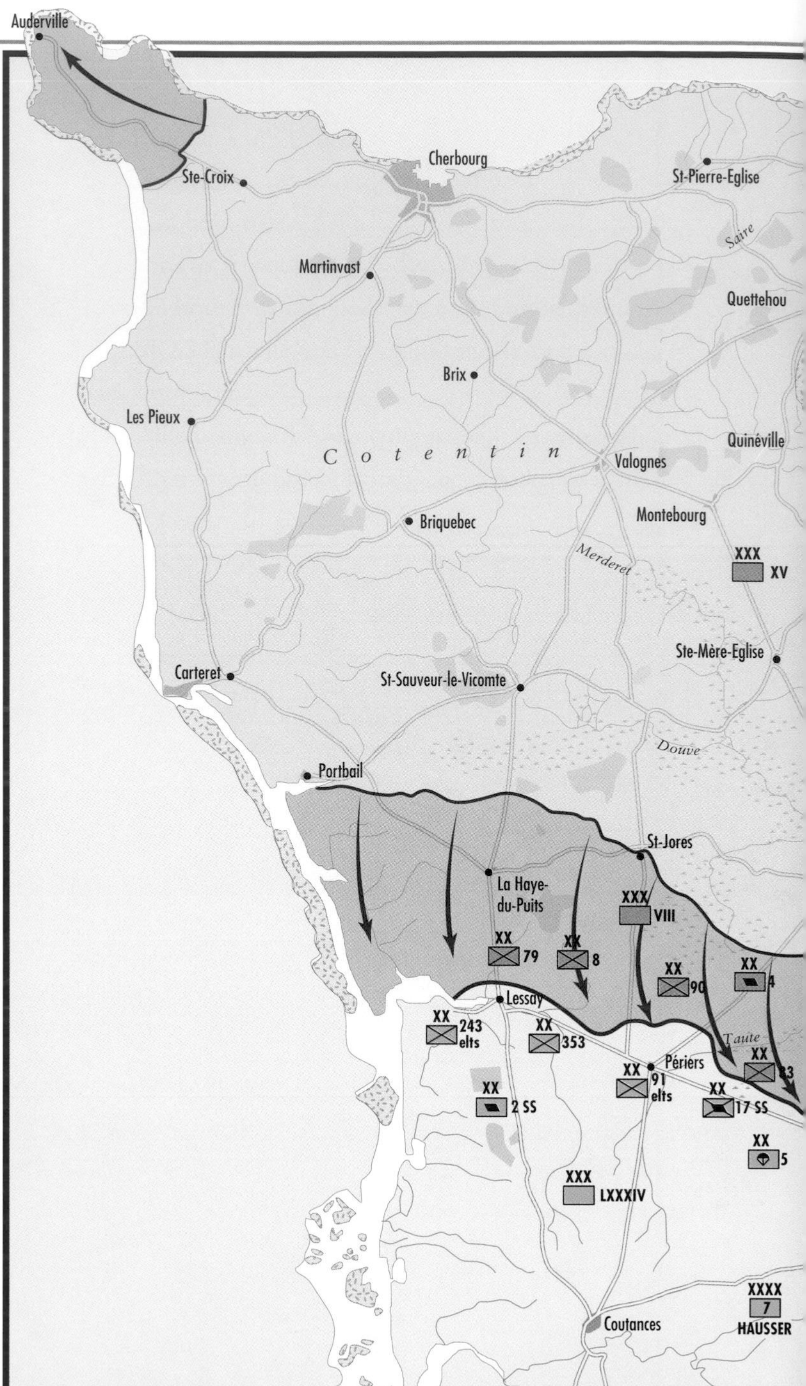

Ultra intercepts had revealed that there had been a coup against Hitler the previous day. What had actually happened was that Colonel Claus von Stauffenburg, a staff officer from the headquarters of the German Reserve Army, had visited Hitler's headquarters at Rastenberg in East Prussia, the so-called Wolf's Lair, for a conference. He carried a briefcase with a bomb concealed in it, which he placed under the conference table. He then excused himself, saying that he had to make a telephone call. The bomb duly exploded, killing some and wounding others present, but Hitler, apart from being very shaken, escaped the blast. Von Stauffenburg did not know this and telephoned his fellow conspirators in Berlin to say that the Führer was dead. They hesitated to organize the occupation of key buildings in Berlin until they had confirmation that this was so. They did spread the news of the bomb, including to the military governor of Paris, General Karl Heinrich von Stülpnagel, who was also in the plot. While the plotters in Berlin waited, von Stülpnagel immediately arrested Gestapo and SS members in the French capital. Word reached von Kluge of what had happened but, like the Berlin conspirators, he wanted confirmation and was not prepared to commit himself until he had it.

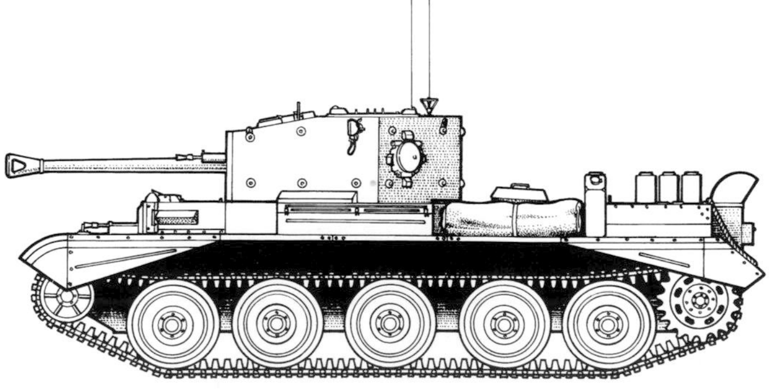

The British Cromwell tank, which had recently come into service with 11th Armoured Division. It had a 75mm gun, but its main drawback was its box-like armour, whose vertical faces made it easier to penetrate than sloped armour.

In Berlin, doubts still reigned. Keitel phoned the Commander of the Reserve Army in the mid-afternoon to assure him that Hitler was still alive. Even so, at 4pm the conspirators decided to

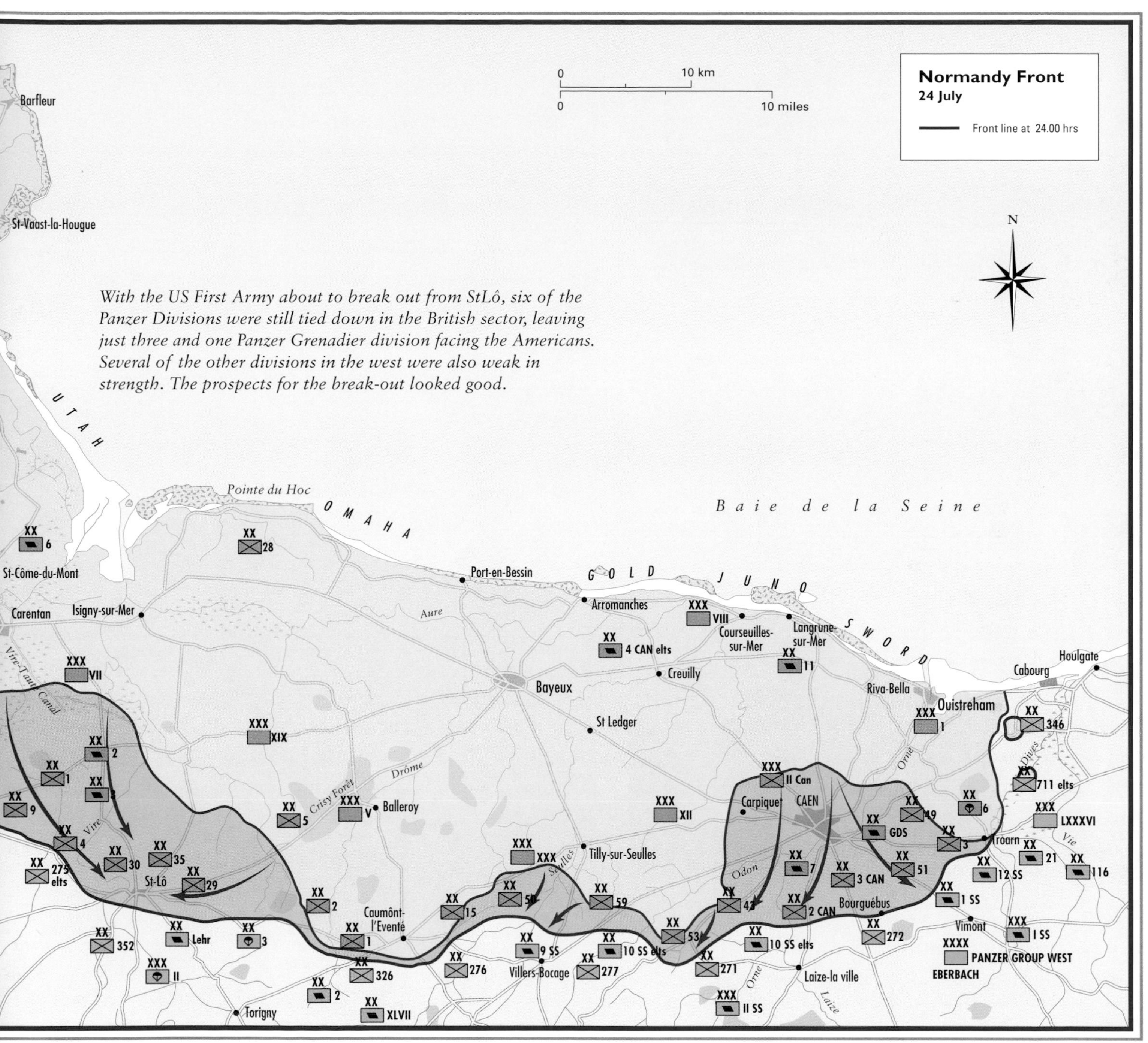

With the US First Army about to break out from StLô, six of the Panzer Divisions were still tied down in the British sector, leaving just three and one Panzer Grenadier division facing the Americans. Several of the other divisions in the west were also weak in strength. The prospects for the break-out looked good.

act. The commander of the Grossdeutschland Guard Battalion, Major Otto-Ernst Remer, was ordered to secure the official quarter of the city, which contained all the important government buildings. Unfortunately, one of propaganda minister Josef Goebbels' staff had been lecturing Remer's men that day and he suggested to Remer that confirmation be sought from Goebbels. In the meantime, Remer did as he had been told and deployed a cordon around the government buildings. He then received an order summoning him to Goebbels' office, where he was handed the telephone. Hitler was on the other end and ordered Remer to arrest the plotters. It was the end of the coup. Von Stülpnagel was forced to release his prisoners, and von Kluge, realizing that it had failed, openly condemned the plot.

To Churchill and Montgomery, the putsch, even though it had proved abortive, was a sign that cracks were appearing in the Nazi regime. Montgomery immediately issued a new directive. It was largely a repeat of previous directives, with the emphasis on the Americans gaining the Brittany peninsula and also swinging south-east towards Paris. But now that the British had the whole of Caen in their possession, Second Army was in

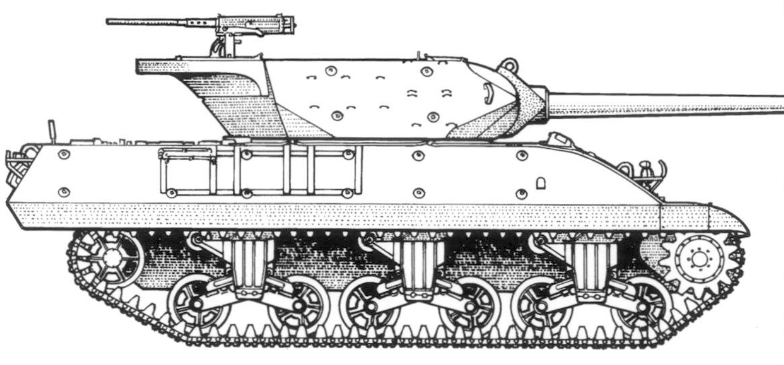

The US M10 Tank Destroyer. This mounted a 3-inch gun and had an open topped turret. The concept was to provide a highly mobile anti-armour force.

a good position to exploit any sudden development, including a regime collapse. In view of the delay imposed on mounting Cobra, it was essential that Dempsey kept the German armour tied down on his front. To this end, the newly created Canadian First Army was to take over the extreme eastern part of the front and drive the Germans back east of the River Dives, while the British Second Army was to push southwards from Caen towards Argentan and Falaise. In reply to a cable letter sent by Eisenhower on 21 July, which demanded that the British put the same effort into the offensive as the Americans were about to do, Montgomery assured him that 'there is not and never has been any intention of stopping offensive operations on the eastern flank'. For the time being, the ructions in the Allied camp had abated. All now looked to 24 July and for what they hoped would be the decisive battle which would bring the exhausting Normandy campaign to an end and even complete the destruction of the German forces in the West.

The PaK 40 75mm was the most widely used of the German anti-tank guns. While not having the same range as the '88', it was more manoeuvrable and easier to conceal.

A Sherman engages a water tower. Northern France was and still is littered with these, and they made very good observation posts.

The infamous 'Eighty-Eight'. It could destroy any Allied tank up to 2,000 yards and beyond, although this length of range was seldom achieved in the close country of Normandy.

British infantry skirmish through the remains of a French farmhouse.

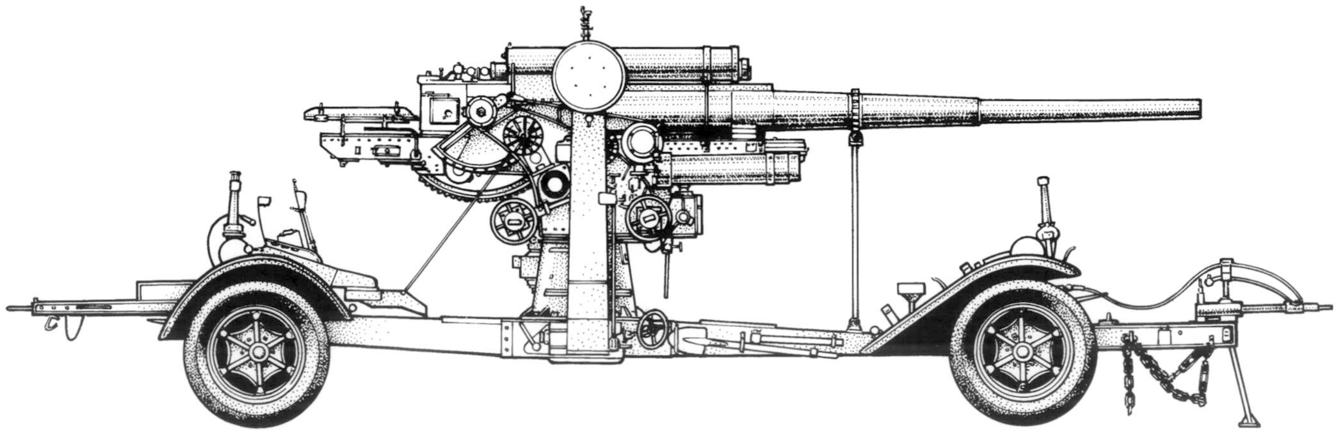

Chapter Five

Break-out

Bradley's plan for the break-out from Normandy was to attack on a 7,000-yard frontage just to the west of St-Lô. The task was given to Lawton Collins's VII Corps, which was swollen to four infantry and two armoured divisions. Three infantry divisions would carry out the initial break-in. Once they had achieved this, the remaining infantry division and the armour would thrust south-south-west towards Coutances with a view to trapping the bulk of the German Seventh Army with its back to the French Atlantic coast. It would then be the turn of General George S. Patton's US Third Army, which was assembling in the rear, to complete the break-out.

Crucial to the success of the initial phase of Cobra was the employment of 'carpet bombing' to numb the defenders, as it had done, at least temporarily, at the opening of Goodwood. Bradley himself was very keen that his troops should take maximum advantage of this and wanted them to withdraw no more than 800 yards from where the bombs would fall on the German defences. He also wanted the bombers to fly along the St-Lô–Périers road, which represented the start line for the attack. For safety reasons, the airmen wanted the forward troops to be no closer than 3,000 yards from the target and were unhappy about attacking with a lateral approach to the front since they feared that this would caused congestion in the air. Rather, they proposed that they should fly in from the north so that the danger from flak and the Luftwaffe could be minimized. After some debate both sides agreed that the safety margin should be 1,200 yards for fighter-bombers and 1,450 yards for the heavy bombers. Eighty minutes before H-hour, 350 fighter-bombers would attack the 250-yard strip just south of the road. After twenty minutes of this nearly 1,600 B-17s and B-24s would plaster the area to a depth of 2,500 yards from the road. This would bring the time up to H-hour and, as the attacking troops crossed the start line, more fighter-bombers would appear, followed by medium bombers, which would concentrate on the southern part of the target area. It represented a massive weight of bombs, which was just as well. While Collins had some 1,000 guns available to support his attack, ammunition was short, and only definitely identified strongpoints would initially be engaged.

St-Lô after its capture.

A B-24 Liberator during the carpet bombing which preceded Operation Cobra, the American break-out.

Although the weather forecast for 24 July was doubtful, there were indications that it would improve. Trafford Leigh-Mallory, the Allied air commander, therefore set the Cobra H-hour for 1pm and flew across to France to observe the air assault at first hand. On arrival, he saw no signs of the skies clearing and therefore

(Right) After the delay in mounting the attack, because of bombing problems, it quickly gained momentum. The Germans did attempt armoured counterstrokes against its flank, but these were too weak to have any effect. With the critical communications centre at Avranches secured by 31 July, Patton's newly established Third Army was ready to exploit.

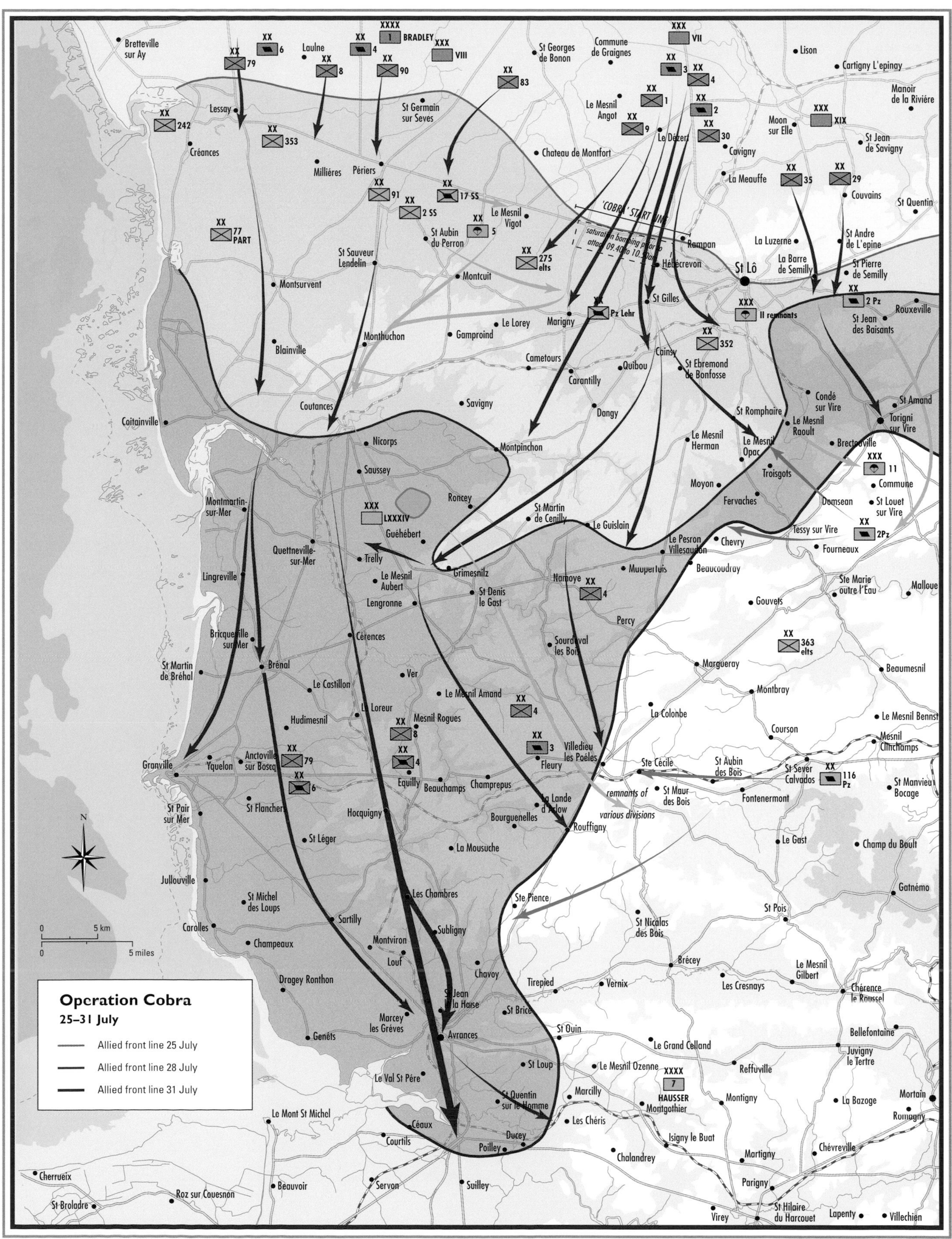
Operation Cobra
25–31 July
Allied front line 25 July
Allied front line 28 July
Allied front line 31 July
0 5 km
0 5 miles
N
XXXX
1
BRADLEY
XXX
VIII
XXX
VII
XXX
XIX
XXX
LXXXIV
XXX
II remnants
XXX
11
XXXX
7
HAUSSER
'COBRA' START LINE
saturation bombing prior to attack 09.40 to 10.30am
remnants of various divisions
Pz Lehr
17 SS
2 SS
2 Pz
2Pz
116 Pz
275 elts
363 elts
77 PART
Bretteville sur Ay
Laulne
St Georges de Bonon
Commune de Graignes
Lison
Cartigny L'epinay
Manoir de la Rivière
Lessay
Créances
St Germain sur Seves
Le Mesnil Angot
Moon sur Elle
St Jean de Savigny
Millières
Périers
Chateau de Montfort
Le Dézert
Cavigny
La Meauffe
Couvains
St Quentin
Le Mesnil Vigot
St Aubin du Perron
Rampan
La Luzerne
St Andre de L'epine
St Sauveur Lendelin
Montcuit
Hébécrevon
St Lô
La Barre de Semilly
St Pierre de Semilly
Montsurvent
St Gilles
Rouxeville
Le Lorey
Marigny
St Jean des Baisants
Blainville
Monthuchon
Gamproind
Cametours
Quibou
Cainsy
St Ebremond de Bonfosse
Carantilly
Savigny
Dangy
Condé sur Vire
St Amand
Coitainville
Coutances
St Romphaire
Le Mesnil Raoult
Torigni sur Vire
Nicorps
Montpinchon
Le Mesnil Herman
Le Mesnil Opac
Brectouville
Saussey
Troisgots
Commune
Moyon
Fervaches
Domsean
St Louet sur Vire
Roncey
Montmartin-sur-Mer
St Martin de Cenilly
Le Guislain
Tessy sur Vire
Guéhébert
Le Pesron Villesaudon
Chevry
Fourneaux
Quettneville-sur-Mer
Trelly
Grimesnilz
Maupertuis
Beaucoudray
Lingreville
Le Mesnil Aubert
Namoye
St Denis le Gast
Ste Marie outre l'Eau
Malloue
Lengronne
Gouvets
Percy
Bricqueville sur Mer
Cérences
Sourdeval les Bois
St Martin de Bréhal
Bréhal
Marguerav
Beaumesnil
Ver
Le Castillon
Le Mesnil Amand
Montbray
La Colonbe
Le Loreur
Hudimesnil
Mesnil Rogues
Le Mesnil Bennst
Courson
Villedieu les Poêles
Mesnil Clinchamps
Granville
Yquelon
Anctoville sur Bosq
Fleury
Ste Cécile
St Aubin des Bois
St Sever Calvados
Equilly
Beauchamps
Champrepus
St Manvieu Bocage
St Pair sur Mer
St Flanchers
Hocquigny
La Lande d'Airou
St Maur des Bois
Fontenermont
Bourguenelles
Rouffigny
St Léger
Le Gast
Champ du Boult
La Mousuche
Jullouville
Les Chambres
Gatnémo
St Michel des Loups
Ste Pience
St Pois
Carolles
Sartilly
Sublignv
St Nicalas des Bois
Champeaux
Montviron
Louf
Brécey
Le Mesnil Gilbert
Dragey Ronthon
Chavoy
Tirepied
Vernix
Les Cresnays
Chérence le Roussel
St Jean de la Haise
St Brice
Marcey les Grèves
Avranches
St Ouin
Genêts
Le Grand Celland
Bellefontaine
Juvigny le Tertre
St Loup
Le Mesnil Ozenne
Reffuville
Le Val St Père
Marcilly
Montigny
Mortain
St Quentin sur le Homme
La Bazoge
Romagny
Le Mont St Michel
Les Chéris
Montgothier
Céaux
Ducey
Isigny le Buat
Courtils
Poilley
Chalandrey
Martigny
Chévreville
Cherrueix
Beauvoir
Servon
Suilley
Parigny
Roz sur Couesnon
St Broladre
St Hilaire du Harcouet
Lapenty
Virey
Villechien

Planning a counterstroke into the American flank. A PzKw V Panther waits in the background.

decided to postpone the attack. By then, the bulk of the US Eighth and Ninth Air Forces had taken off and were en route to the target, intending to approach from the north. Some of the fighter-bombers received the turn-back order, but others did not and carried out their attacks. There was no direct radio communication with the heavies, but the early groups, seeing the dense cloud, aborted on their own initiative. Unfortunately, many of the final group, consisting of some 300 bombers, saw some breaks in the cloud and pressed on. Worse, one of the lead bombardiers was having trouble with his bomb-release mechanism and dropped his bombs prematurely. Others followed his example and the result was that it was the forward positions of the 30th US Infantry Division which suffered, with nearly 160 casualties inflicted on its men. It was not a good start for the long-awaited break-out, with Bradley especially angered that the airmen had ignored his request to approach from the west.

Cobra, however, had to go ahead and Bradley, encouraged by

(Right) Codenamed Operation Lüttich, such Panzer divisions which were ready for such a hastily prepared attack did make some progress under the cover of darkness and then mist, once dawn came. They were thwarted by 30th Infantry Division, which resolutely held its ground, and Allied air power, which wrought havoc once the mist cleared. It was the last significant German offensive action of the Normandy campaign.

a better weather forecast, was determined that it be launched on the following day. The airmen were, however, insistent that it was too late to recast their plans for a lateral approach to the target. Indeed, the air plan was to be exactly the same as on the 24th, except that the fighter-bombers would begin their attacks at 9.38am. Then came the B-17s and B-29s, 1,500 of them. At first all went well, with the lead groups dropping their bombs on target, but, as the bombing continued, they began to fall closer to the Americans' positions and then on top of them. Both the 4th and the luckless 30th Divisions were hit; this time the casualties were considerably heavier than the previous day, some 600 in all. Even so, the attack went ahead.

In some cases, the Germans had occupied the safety area from which the Americans had withdrawn and they had to fight to reclaim it. Even though the bombing had dazed the defenders, they put up some stiff resistance, especially the Panzer Lehr, which bore the brunt of the attack. As a result, the Americans were restricted to an advance of less than two miles on the first day. The 2nd SS Panzer and 17th SS Panzer Grenadier Divisions were also beginning to threaten on the right flank, but Lawton Collins was determined to press on. The following morning, after further carpet bombing, he released his second wave. On the right, 1st Infantry Division, supported by part of 3rd

Fighting their way out of the bocage. A US patrol tries to locate a German sniper.

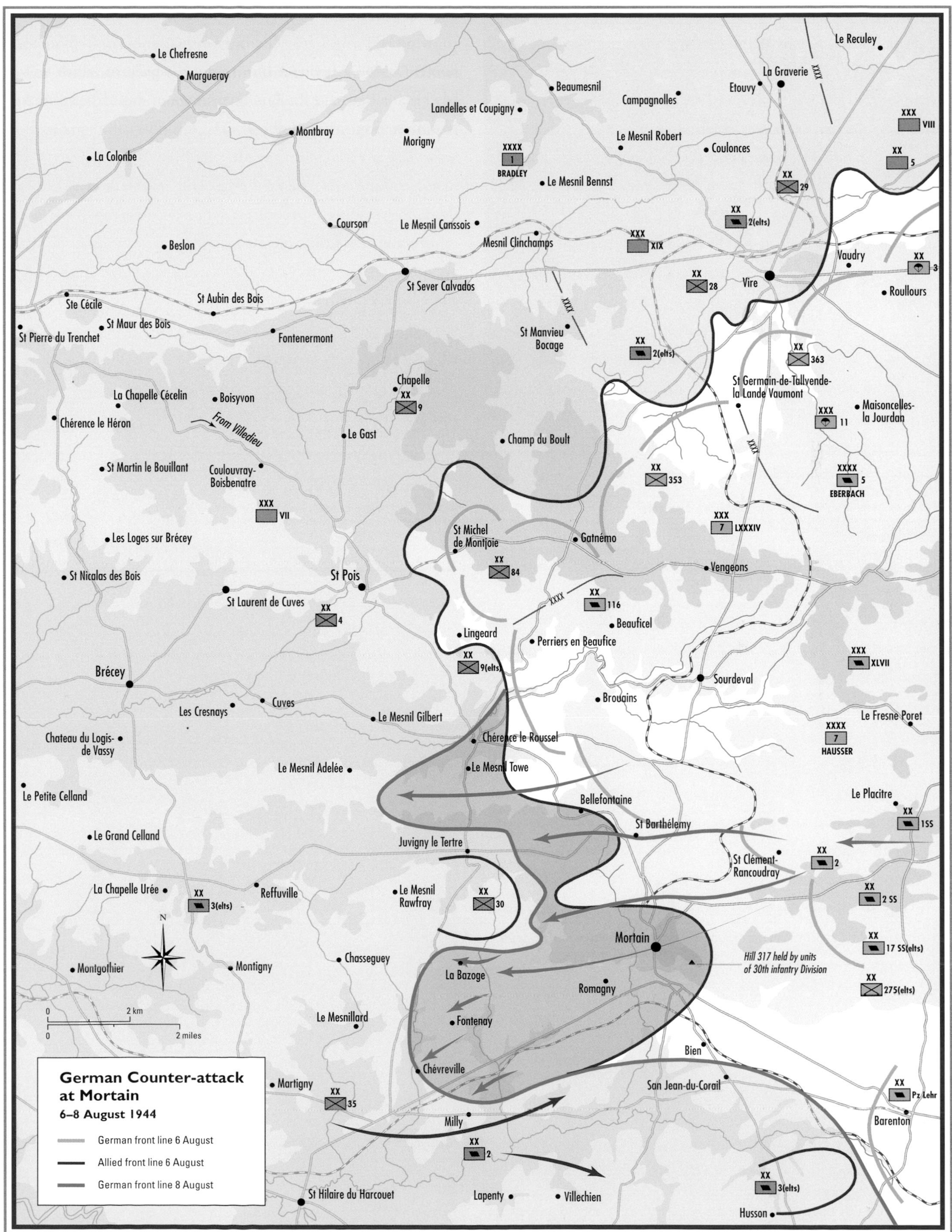
German Counter-attack at Mortain
6–8 August 1944
German front line 6 August
Allied front line 6 August
German front line 8 August
Hill 317 held by units of 30th Infantry Division
Mortain
Vire
St Pois
Brécey
Sourdeval
St Sever Calvados
St Hilaire du Harcouet
Barenton
From Villedieu
BRADLEY
EBERBACH
HAUSSER
0 2 km
0 2 miles

Armored Division, found it a struggle because of resistance from the two SS divisions and the cratering caused by the bombing, but 2nd Armored Division was able to punch through the remains of the Panzer Lehr and reached the St-Lô – Coutances railway by nightfall. By this time the Panzer Lehr itself had been reduced to a mere fourteen tanks. It was now noticeable that the Americans had learnt much from the previous weeks of *bocage* fighting. Co-operation between infantry and armour was very much closer than it had been. The tanks, too, were better able to cope with the terrain through the attachment of steel prongs to the front of them, an invention of a sergeant in a reconnaissance squadron. These were fitted to some sixty per cent of the US Shermans, which became known as Sherman Rhinos, and enabled them to cut their way through hedgerows and other obstacles. Another element was effective close air support. The AEAF fighter-bombers were now operating what was called the 'cab rank' system. It proved remarkably responsive, with aircraft constantly circling overhead until directed onto a target by a ground controller.

Von Kluge still believed that the main effort would be from the British sector. This was reinforced by a spoiling attack by the Canadians against the Bourguébus Ridge. Although it was unsuccessful, it dissuaded him from transferring Panzer divisions westwards during the first two critical days of Cobra. Not until the night of the 26/27, after the Canadians had called off their attack, did von Kluge order 2nd Panzer Division from the Orne sector and 116th Panzer Division from north of the Seine to move and strike at the eastern flank of the Americans, while 2nd SS Panzer and 17th SS Panzer Grenadier Divisions attacked from the west. It was too late.

Given the nature of the terrain and its restricted routes, 43rd Division was given an over-ambitious objective in the Bois du Homme. As it was, it left 15th Division with a very exposed flank by the end of the day. 11th Armoured Division's progress was initially slow, but on 31 July it would accelerate as it infiltrated its way through the thinly held German defences.

On 27 July the US VIII Corps struck towards Coutances, threatening to annihilate the infantry divisions of LXXXIV Corps. The two SS mobile divisions had to turn to meet this new threat, while 2nd and 116th Panzer Divisions struggled in the face of constant air attack to deploy to the area of the break-out. The following day saw VII Corps capture Coutances and the remnants of LXXXIV Corps in danger of being trapped to the south-east of the town. Bradley had originally intended to pause and regroup at this stage, but such was the growing momentum of the advance that he ordered it to continue, handing over control of VII Corps to Patton, who now began to swing south-east, leaving VIII Corps to advance towards Avranches. The 2nd and 116th Panzer Divisions did their best to try to slow the American advance by attacking VII Corps in the flank, but to little effect. Avranches fell to VIII Corps late on 30 July and a despairing von Kluge announced that his complete left flank was now in a state of collapse. The only way that he could prevent the complete disintegration of the front was to attack into the eastern flank of the American penetration, but his two Panzer divisions already in this area were too deeply embroiled. He would have to transfer additional divisions from the eastern part of the front, but Montgomery now set in a motion an operation to prevent this from happening.

A British Churchill VII infantry support tank. Heavily armoured and relatively slow moving, three Tank as opposed to Armoured brigades of these fought in Normandy.

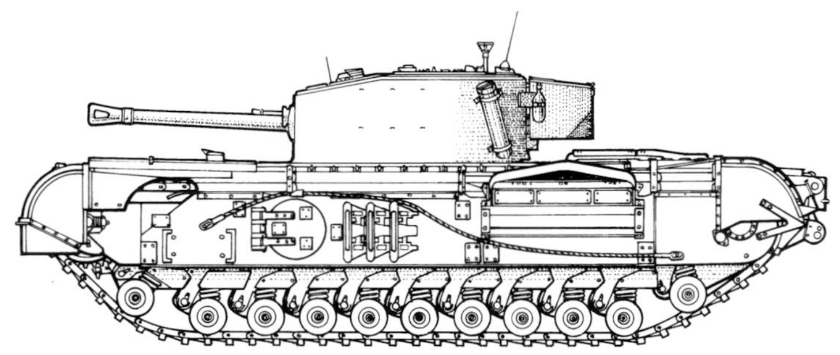

Apart from the Canadian attack east of Caen on the opening day of Cobra, Montgomery had planned further assaults to keep the German armour tied down. The British XII Corps was to attack west of Caen on 28 July towards Evrecy, followed two days later by a mainly armoured thrust by VIII Corps east of

The PzKw VI Tiger, with its 88mm gun, was the most formidable tank in the German armoury. They fought in Heavy Tank battalions.

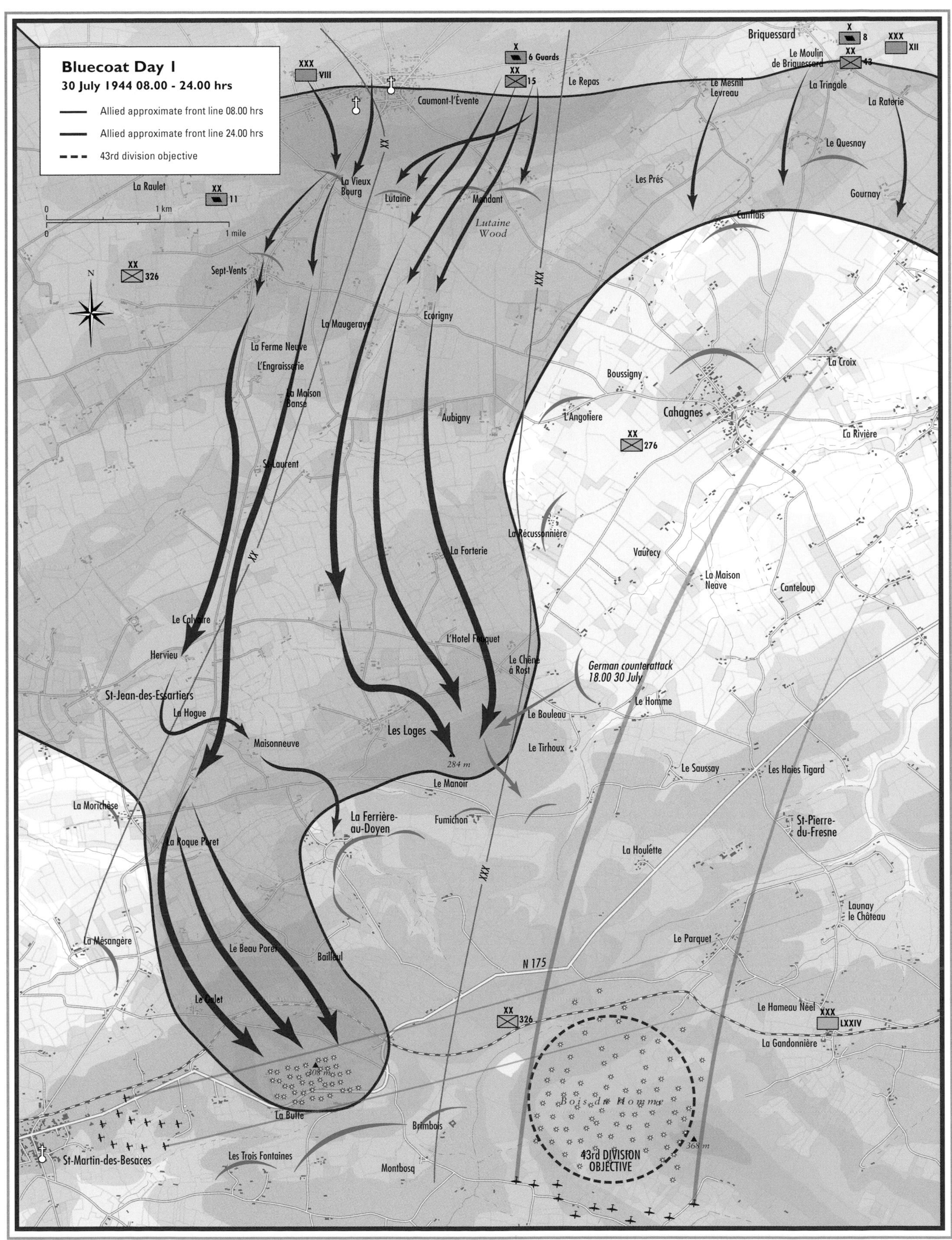
Bluecoat Day 1
30 July 1944 08.00 - 24.00 hrs
Allied approximate front line 08.00 hrs
Allied approximate front line 24.00 hrs
43rd division objective
German counterattack 18.00 30 July
43rd DIVISION OBJECTIVE
Caumont-l'Évente
Cahagnes
St-Jean-des-Essartiers
Les Loges
La Ferrière-au-Doyen
St-Pierre-du-Fresne
St-Martin-des-Besaces
Bois du Homme
Lutaine Wood
N 175

the River Orne and directed on Falaise. On the evening of 27 July, with Cobra progressing well and conscious that the Canadians had suffered heavily during their attack east of Caen, Montgomery changed his plans. Instead of continuing to attack the German strength in the east, he decided that British Second Army would mount a major assault through the bocage south of Caumont and on the boundary between the US and British forces. There were no significant German formations in this sector and he envisaged the attack as operating like a door swinging eastwards so as to ensure that Panzer Group West could not interfere with the American advance. Montgomery's intention was to mount Operation Bluecoat no later than 2 August, but there was a growing feeling, especially in the US media, that the British were leaving the fighting to the Americans. Consequently, he brought Bluecoat forward to 30 July.

At the time, the Caumont sector was held by the British XXX Corps, with just two infantry divisions. General Miles Dempsey's plan was to strengthen XXX Corps with 7th Armoured Division and to deploy VIII Corps with two armoured and one infantry divisions. Gerard Bucknall, the commander of XXX Corps, objected to the concept of a two-corps attack, pointing out that the shortage of routes in the Caumont area would create congestion and arguing that a single-corps headquarters was better able to react quickly to a sudden German collapse. Dempsey overruled him and laid down that the main attack would be made by Bucknall, with O'Connor's VIII Corps providing flank protection on his right. Bucknall would begin his attack with just his two infantry divisions – 43rd Wessex and 50th Northumbrian supported by an armoured brigade – with 7th Armoured Division being held in a concentration area north of Caumont until the initial objectives had been seized. Given the closeness of the country, these were ambitious, with 43rd Division being expected to advance over six miles in the first ten hours. Once they had been achieved, 7th Armoured was to pass through and exploit south-east to Mont Pinçon. VIII Corps would attack with 15th Division on the left and 11th Armoured on the right, with the Guards Armoured Division being initially held in reserve. Apart from guarding XXX Corps's left flank it was also to exploit to Pont Aunay, although Montgomery saw Vire as the key objective.

Bluecoat opened at 6am on 30 July, with 50th Division beginning its attack. Two and a half hours later, 43rd Division joined in. Their opponent was the inexperienced 276th Infantry Division, but it had taken advantage of the terrain to create a series of machine-gun nests and had also laid mines on the banks of the numerous streams in the area. These steps were very effective and 43rd Division, hampered by the fact that it was forced to attack on a very narrow frontage, which meant that only one brigade could be used at a time, was soon falling behind schedule.

Tigers lying up in a wood to conceal themselves from Allied aircraft.

VIII Corps fared better. The 15th Scottish Division, supported by tanks of the 6th Guards Tank Brigade, whose first action this was, penetrated to a depth of nearly six miles by the end of the day, in constrast to 43rd Division's bare mile and a half. The 11th Armoured Division, once it had broken through the forward German defences, made similar good progress and it seemed as though a break-through was possible.

During the night, 11th Armoured Division became entangled with elements of the US V Corps on its right, the reason being that the inter-Allied boundary had not been clearly defined. Even so, it pressed on at first light, with reconnaissance elements securing an intact bridge over the River Souleuvre. In contrast, the 15th Scottish Division was unable to advance further because

(Right) At one point it looked as though 11th Armoured Division had got into the rear of the German defences and was poised to seize the key communications centre of Vire. This, however, was determined to be in the American sector. Also VIII Corps was veering away from XXX Corps which had the main task of closing the door on the movement of Panzer divisions from the east to combat the US break-out.

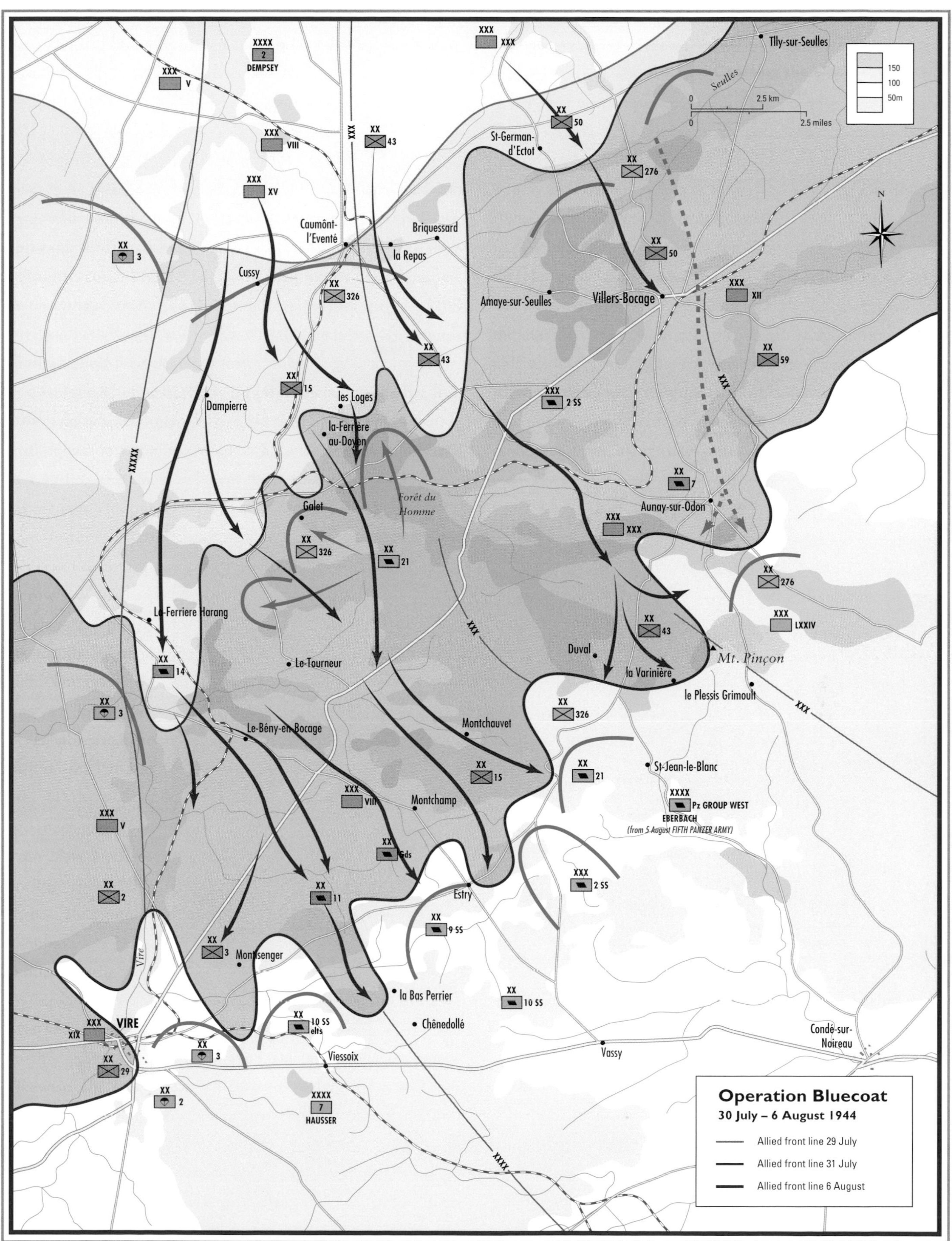
Operation Bluecoat
30 July – 6 August 1944
Allied front line 29 July
Allied front line 31 July
Allied front line 6 August
DEMPSEY
HAUSSER
Pz GROUP WEST
EBERBACH
(from 5 August FIFTH PANZER ARMY)
Tlly-sur-Seulles
St-German-d'Ectot
Caumônt-l'Eventé
Briquessard
la Repas
Cussy
Amaye-sur-Seulles
Villers-Bocage
les Loges
la-Ferrière au-Doyen
Dampierre
Forêt du Homme
Galet
Aunay-sur-Odon
Le-Ferriere Harang
Le-Tourneur
Duval
la Varinière
Mt. Pinçon
le Plessis Grimoult
Le-Bény-en-Bocage
Montchauvet
St-Jean-le-Blanc
Montchamp
Estry
Montisenger
la Bas Perrier
Chênedollé
VIRE
Viessoix
Vassy
Condé-sur-Noireau
Vire
Seulles
150
100
50m
2.5 km
2.5 miles

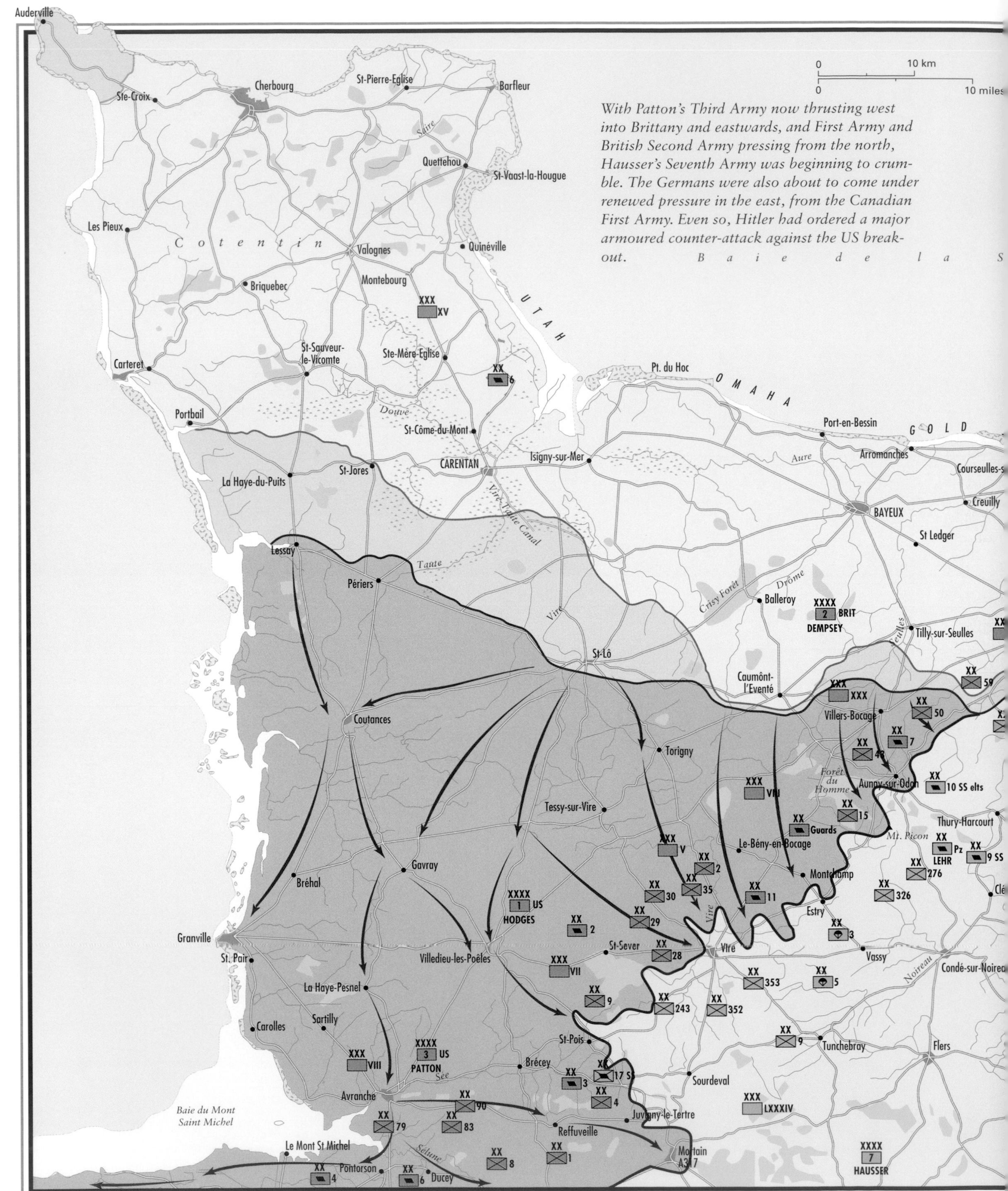

With Patton's Third Army now thrusting west into Brittany and eastwards, and First Army and British Second Army pressing from the north, Hausser's Seventh Army was beginning to crumble. The Germans were also about to come under renewed pressure in the east, from the Canadian First Army. Even so, Hitler had ordered a major armoured counter-attack against the US break-out.

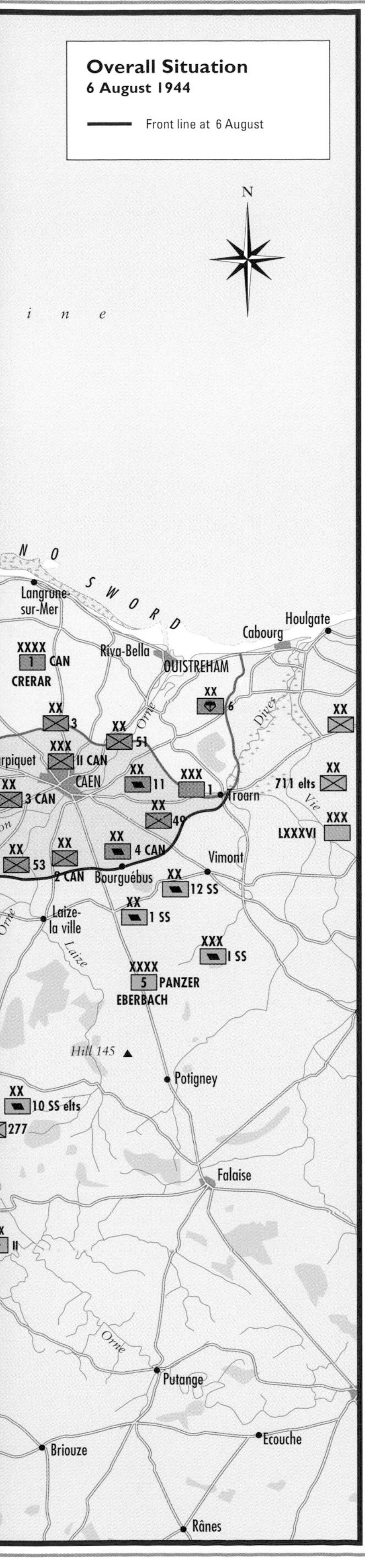

the slow progress of XXX Corps had left it with an open left flank. The Guards Armoured Division was also deployed, but traffic congestion in the Caumont area slowed its progress and not until late afternoon was it able to pass through 15th Scottish Division and then almost immediately ran into resistance. In the XXX Corps sector, 43rd Division made slightly better progress, but 50th Division continued to be held up, leaving the former still with an exposed left flank. Bucknall remained keen to deploy 7th Armoured Division and during the night it moved from north of Caumont to a forward assembly area south-east of the town. Congestion was bad and became even worse the following morning when it began to advance through the area captured by 43rd Division. There was only one road running south in this sector, that from Caumont to Breuil via Cahagnes. Worse, because of the open flank, it was under German artillery fire from the east. The congestion was aggravated because a brigade of 50th Division was also using the road with a view to launching an attack eastwards into the German salient facing 50th Division. Consequently, by nightfall on 1 August 7th Armoured's head was some three and a half miles south of Cahagnes while its tail was still north of Caumont.

Two of the leading lights of 12th SS Panzer Division. Fritz Witt (left) commanded the division until killed on 14 June, while Max Wünsche commanded its Panzer regiment. He was captured on 24 August.

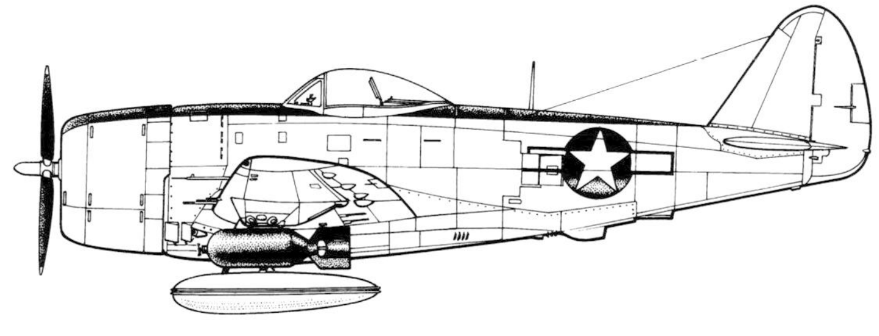

The American Republic P-47 Thunderbolt fighter-bomber, which could carry up to 2,500lbs of bombs or ten rockets.

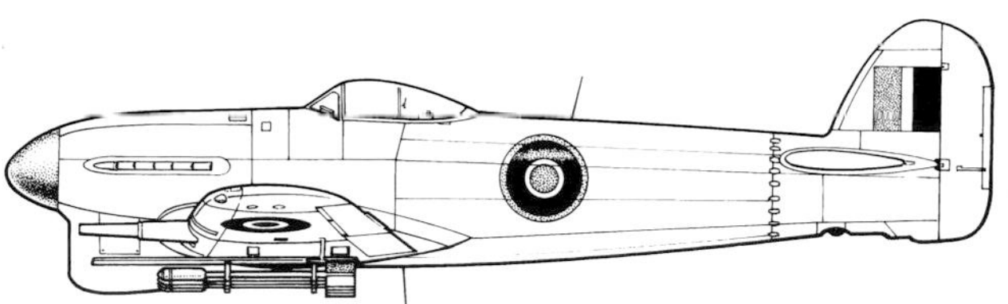

The British equivalent was the Hawker Typhoon, which made a particular contribution to frustrating the German counter-attack at Mortain.

These delays enabled Panzer Group West to deploy blocking forces. First to make an appearance was 21st Panzer Division, which was able to slow the progress of the Guards Armoured Division, although 11th Armoured continued to move south towards Vire, with only poor roads acting as a brake on progress. Then, II SS Panzer Corps began to arrive. The leading battle group of 10th SS Panzer Division had considerable difficulty in negotiating its way through Aunay-sur-Odon because of bomb damage, but by first light on 2 August the Division was in position covering the approaches to Aunay and Ondefontaine, which were now XXX Corps's next objectives.

If Bluecoat was not going to plan, at least as far as XXX Corps was concerned, it was preventing Panzer Group West from deploying armour to halt the American break-out. On 1 August, Patton's Third Army, which was to carry out the exploitation phase, officially came into being and Bradley was now an army group commander, command of the US First Army being given to Courtney H. Hodges, who had been Bradley's deputy. Eisenhower, who had never appointed Montgomery as the Allied land commander, decided that, although Bradley, as commander 12th US Army Group, was now equal in status to Montgomery and his 21st Army Group, he hesitated to take direct control of the land battle himself and was content to allow Montgomery to continue to have de facto control of the ground campaign. However, he never made this clear publicly and this was to cause further rifts.

As it was, Bradley's attention was now focussed on clearing Brittany and this was to be Patton's first priority. Troy H. Middleton's VIII Corps was given the task. Within the peninsula itself was the equivalent of some four German divisions, but their movements were hampered by the presence of some 50,000 members of the FFI, whose operations were co-ordinated by the Jedburgh teams which the Allies had inserted. On the afternoon of 1 August, General John S. Wood's 4th Armored Division passed through Pontaubault and entered Brittany, closing on its principal city, Rennes, before the end of the day. Wood himself was in favour of advancing south to Angers, where he would be in a position to turn the entire German left flank, but Middleton ordered him to stick to the original plan. Bypassing Rennes, which was left to 8th Infantry Division to occupy, Wood made for the port of Lorient on the Brittany south coast, while 6th Armored Division cleared the northern part of Brittany and reached Brest. Hitler declared both ports Festungen and hopes that the Allies could quickly turn them to their own use were dashed. Brest did not fall until 19 September, while Lorient, together with St-Nazaire further south on the Atlantic coast, held out until the end of the war. John S. Wood himself remained bitter at what he viewed as an unnecessary diversion, which had tied up one third of Patton's army at a time when it could have been employed much more decisively elsewhere.

The remainder of the Third US Army was initially hampered by the fact it was reliant on a single road, that running from Avranches to Pontaubault. The Germans were well aware of this and mounted a number of air attacks on the critical bridge carrying it over the River Sée at Avranches, albeit without damaging it. Thanks, however, to Patton's own determination and drive, he succeeded in passing no fewer than seven divisions down the road in just seventy-two hours, after which they began to fan out eastwards.

Meanwhile, in the British sector Bluecoat continued. Late at night on 1 August 11th Armoured Division was ordered to continue its advance south, with Vire and Tinchebray as its objectives, while the Guards Armoured advanced to Vassy and 15th Scottish protected the Guards' left flank. By the end of the day, 11th Armoured had reached the Vire–Vassy road, with its reconnaissance elements actually being engaged by German troops in Vire itself. The Guards Armoured, on the other hand, was blocked by elements of II SS Panzer Corps at Estry. Vire could

A US M8 105mm self-propelled howitzer mounted on a Sherman tank chassis, known as Priest by the British. Some had their guns removed to convert them to armoured personnel carriers.

(Right) Unlike previous major attacks in the east, Totalize was launched at night, aided by carpet bombing. Initial progress was good, but momentum slowed because of the inexperience of the armoured divisions, which had recently arrived in Normandy, and the bitter resistance offered by 12th SS Panzer Division.

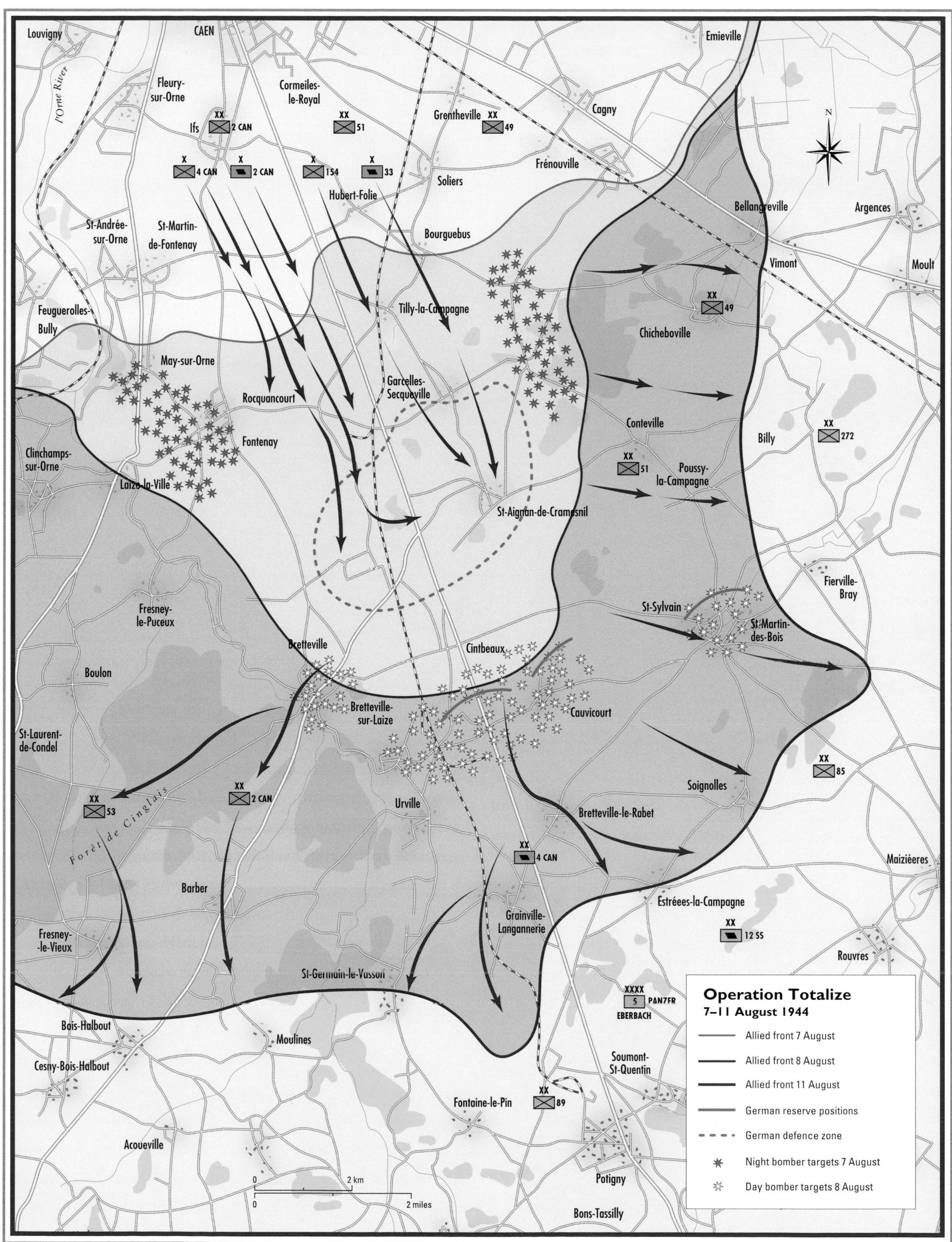
Operation Totalize
7–11 August 1944
Allied front 7 August
Allied front 8 August
Allied front 11 August
German reserve positions
German defence zone
Night bomber targets 7 August
Day bomber targets 8 August
Louvigny
CAEN
l'Orne River
Fleury-sur-Orne
Ifs
Cormeiles-le-Royal
Grentheville
Cagny
Emieville
Frénouville
Soliers
Hubert-Folie
Bourguebus
Bellangreville
Argences
Vimont
Moult
St-André-sur-Orne
St-Martin-de-Fontenay
Feuguerolles-Bully
May-sur-Orne
Tilly-la-Campagne
Chicheboville
Rocquancourt
Garcelles-Secqueville
Fontenay
Conteville
Billy
Clinchamps-sur-Orne
Laize-la-Ville
Poussy-la-Campagne
St-Aignan-de-Cramesnil
Fierville-Bray
St-Sylvain
St-Martin-des-Bois
Fresney-le-Puceux
Bretteville
Cintbeaux
Boulon
Bretteville-sur-Laize
Cauvicourt
St-Laurent-de-Condel
Soignolles
Urville
Bretteville-le-Rabet
Forêt de Cinglais
Barber
Maizièeres
Estrées-la-Campagne
Grainville-Langannerie
Fresney-le-Vieux
Rouvres
St-Germain-le-Vasson
Bois-Halbout
Moulines
Cesny-Bois-Halbout
Soumont-St-Quentin
Fontaine-le-Pin
Acoueville
Potigny
Bons-Tassilly
2 CAN
51
49
4 CAN
154
33
272
85
53
12 SS
5 PANZER
EBERBACH
89
2 km
2 miles

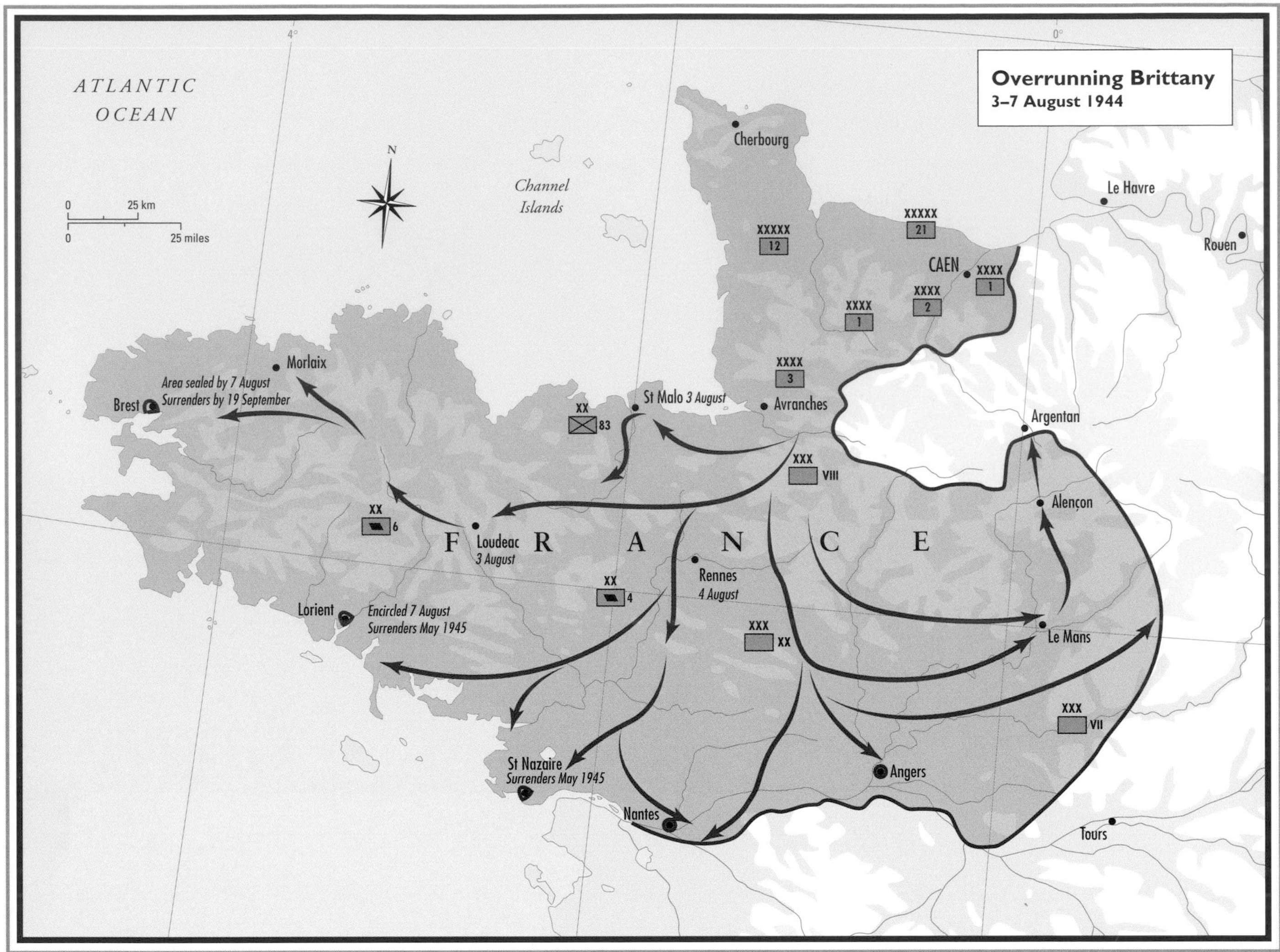

The remnants of the German forces in Brittany were soon overrun, thanks to a lightning advance by the US 4th Armored Division, followed by 6th Armored. But they could not achieve the garrisons of Brest and St Nazaire, which were under Hitler's orders not to submit. When Brest did finally fall, giving the Allies another port, it was too late to affect the supply crisis which had by then brought their thrust eastwards to a virtual halt.

still be taken, but on the evening of the 2nd Pip Roberts, commanding 11th Armoured, was ordered to halt. There were two reasons for this. First, it was decided that Vire was in the American sector, but also the direction of advance of the British VIII Corps was beginning to diverge from that of XXX Corps. This itself was still making little progress. The 10th SS Panzer Division was able to use infiltration tactics to block 43rd Division's advance on Ondefontaine and that of 7th Armoured on Aunay. Indeed, so frustrated did the army commander, Miles Dempsey become, that he sacked Bucknall, the corps commander, and the Desert Rats commander, Erskine, for lack of drive. He also ordered VIII Corps to turn to the south-east to conform with XXX Corps.

On the German side, an emissary from Hitler arrived at von Kluge's headquarters late on 2 August. He brought instructions that the front was to be restored at all costs. Von Kluge protested, stating that now the Americans had entered Mortain and the British were containing II SS Panzer Corps, there was no way of dealing with the yawning gap in the Avranches area. Rather, he argued, the only sensible course was to withdraw to the River Seine, using the Panzer divisions to delay the Americans while this happened. On 4 August Hitler rejected this out of hand. Von Kluge was to use all his armour to slice the break-out in the neck between Mortain and Avranches. It was not an order that the C-in-C West felt that he could disobey and, aware that Patton's armour was already approaching Le Mans, he decided that he must strike as soon as possible if Hausser's Seventh Army was not to be totally cut off. He therefore agreed with Hausser that the attack was to be mounted on the night of 6/7 August. But instead of the eight Panzer divisions that Hitler expected him to use, von Kluge was only able to deploy four – 1st SS, 2nd SS, 2nd and 116th. The British pressure made it impossible to release any others.

Allied air reconnaissance and Ultra gave indicators of what was afoot and Bradley was able to take precautions. He deployed five infantry divisions, supported by tanks, to cover the sector from Vire to Mortain and held back three of Patton's divisions west of Mortain. In addition, he attacked Vire itself. Recognizing its importance as a communications centre, the Germans used part of the force earmarked for the armoured counterstroke to counter-attack at Vire, but it was no avail and the town was in US hands by the end of 6 August. Worse for the Germans was that much of the armoured force was not in a position to cross the start line for the attack at the scheduled time, which was just after midnight. Von Kluge insisted there be no delay and those divisions which were ready did attack on time. The 2nd Panzer Division used the cover of darkness to advance seven miles towards Avranches, while the SS to their south regained Mortain. Early-morning fog was another welcome ally, but when it lifted the picture changed dramatically. US P-47 Thunderbolt and RAF Typhoon fighter-bombers were quickly in action, launching unceasing attacks on the German armour. Hitler had promised the support of 1,000 planes, but none were to be seen in the air, such was the continuing Allied mastery of it, and the attack quickly ground to a halt, with many crews simply abandoning their tanks, fearful of being struck by the rocket-firing Typhoons. Simultaneously, Bradley began to apply pressure to the flanks of the German penetration, threatening to cut it off.

A rough and ready means of cleaning the barrel of a British 25pdr gun after intense firing.

This marked the last significant clash between the Canadians and their now long-time adversary 12th SS Panzer Division, which held on to the ridge to the north of Falaise until the threat from 2nd Canadian Division from the west forced it to withdraw. Meanwhile, the Americans were advancing from the south, threatening to create a huge pocket to trap the bulk of the German forces in Normandy.

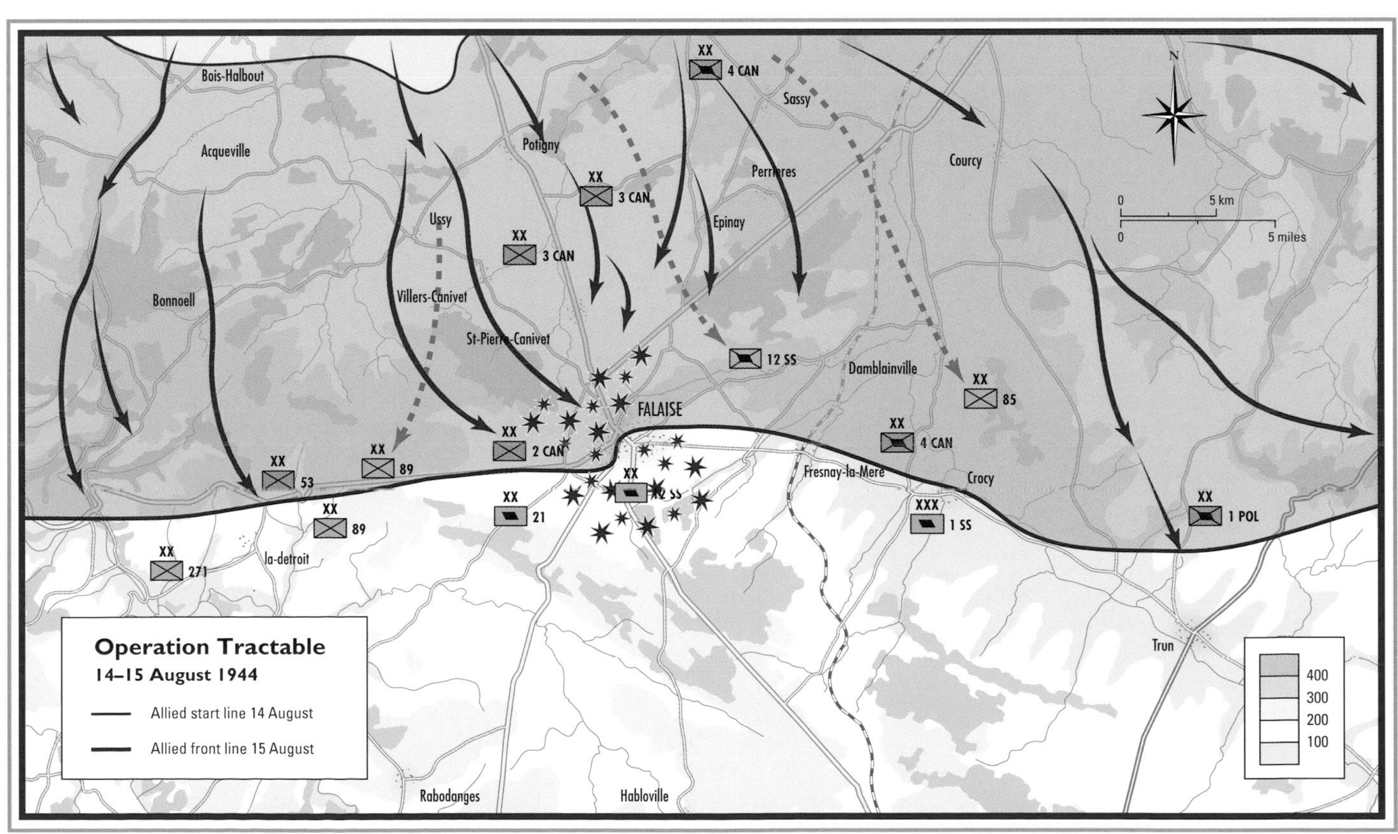

On the 21st Army Group front, the British had not been idle. XXX Corps maintained its pressure and by 6 August Aunay-sur-Odon was finally in its hands. The 43rd Division was also now tackling Mont Pinçon, which, after a grim battle, it secured on the same day. Further to the east, the Canadians launched Operation Totalize on the night of 7/8 August. The object was to break through the defences south and south-east of Caen and advance towards Falaise so as to block the retreat of the forces facing Second Army. At 11pm on the 7th, over 1,000 RAF heavy bombers attacked the defences on the flanks of the attack. 2nd Canadian and 51st Highland Divisions, each supported by an armoured brigade, then advanced. They quickly broke through, but some villages held out, which began to slow the advance. The Canadians' old opponents, 12th SS Panzer Division, then began to counter-attack. Nevertheless, General Guy Simonds, commanding Canadian II Corps, was determined to press on. The next phase was the release of his armoured divisions – 4th Canadian and 1st Polish, both in action for the first time. As they moved forward, 680 B-17s of the US Eighth Air Force attacked the villages to their front. Unfortunately, some of the bombs fell short, inflicting some 150 casualties on the Allied troops. Even so, the armour advanced and made progress. Simonds wanted to push on, but it halted for

With the Canadians temporarily halted short of Falaise, Patton's Third Army was beginning to advance north from the Argentan area to trap the German Seventh Army and much of Fifth Panzer Army. The Germans, however, managed to occupy Argentan and for the time being deny it to the newly arrived French 2nd Armoured Division.

the night, allowing the Germans a breathing space. They began to construct a new defence line on the River Laison and gradually fell back on this, covered by the Hitler Youth Division, which continued to fight tenaciously. As a result, the Canadian attack lost momentum and eventually came to a halt, short of the Laison, on 11 August.

What Totalize did achieve, however, was to dispel any further thoughts that von Kluge had of transferring divisions from 5th Panzer Army, as Panzer Group West had become on 5 August. This was in spite of further demands to do so from Hitler so that

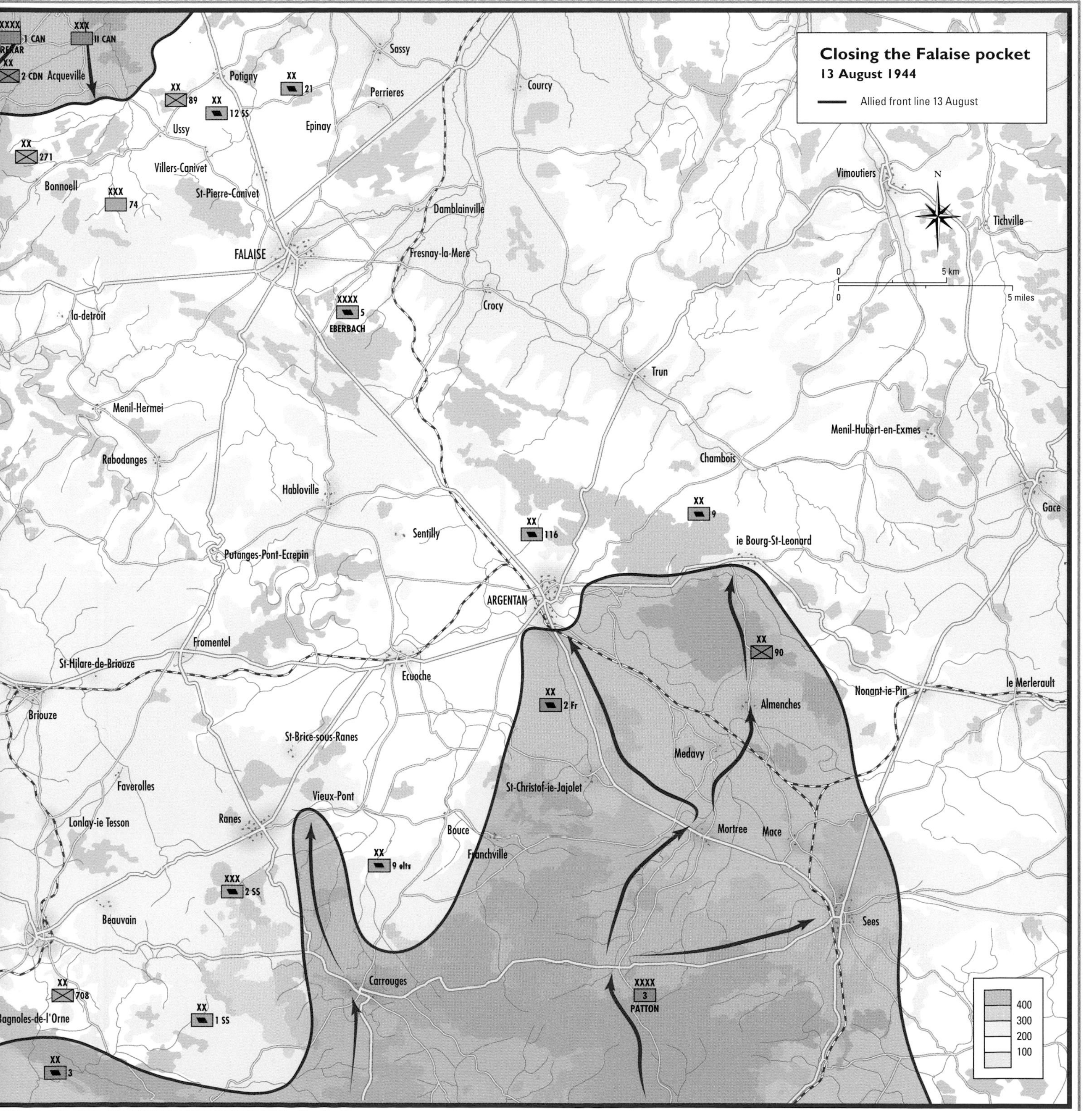

the American break-out could be halted. Von Kluge, though, was still fearful of disobeying the Führer, especially since there was a witch hunt on to arrest anyone that could have been involved in the 20 July attempt on his life. His only other available Panzer Division was the 9th, which had recently arrived from southern France and had been deployed to block Patton's deep thrust, which had reached the River Loire and turned east. In spite of Hausser's objections that this would enable the Allies to envelop both Seventh and Fifth Panzer Armies, von Kluge ordered it to move from Le Mans to Avranches. Hitler kept up his demands for

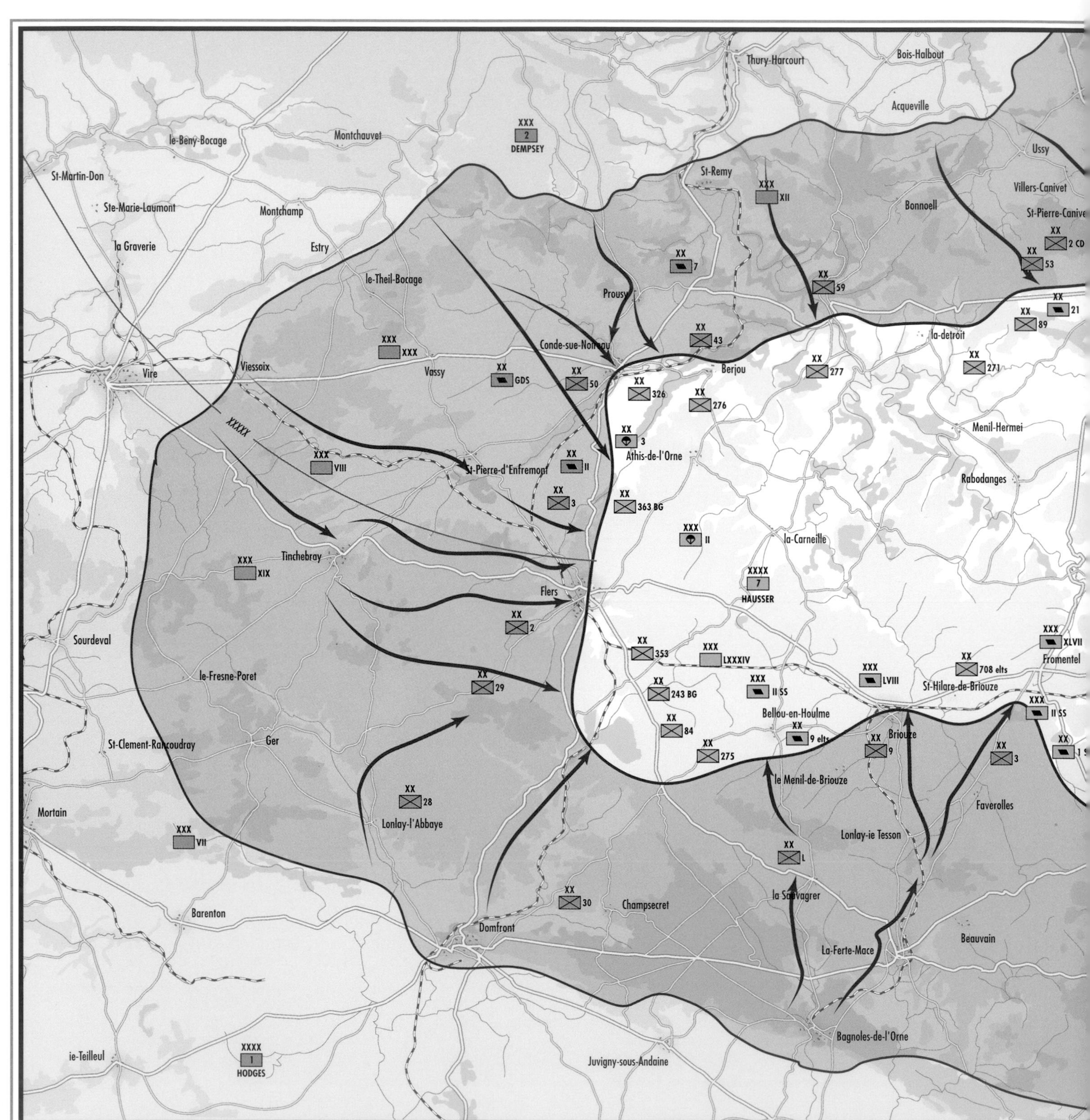

another attack westwards into the American flank, laying down that six Panzer divisions were to be used and that Fifth Panzer Army's commander, Heinrich Eberbach, was to command it. He reported to von Kluge on 9 August, but just after he arrived a report came through that Patton's armour was striking north from Le Mans and threatening Alençon, the main supply base for Seventh Army, and there were few troops available to defend it. Von Kluge knew that if Alençon fell, Seventh Army's fate would be sealed. He asked Hitler's permission to transfer Eberbach's armour to deal with this new threat, but received no positive answer, apart from a stream of signals questioning his motives. This prevarication played further into the hands of the Allies.

As the picture unfolded, Montgomery began to realize that there was an opportunity to trap and destroy the German armies west of the Seine rather than follow his original plan of advancing eastwards, north and south of Paris. This was reinforced by an Ultra intercept revealing the German intention to strike again, south of Mortain. He therefore issued fresh orders on 11 August. The Canadians were to press on to Falaise and then Argentan, while the British advanced to the Flers–Argentan road. Simultaneously, the Americans were to pass through Alençon and take up a line running from Carrouges east to Sées, which lies to the south-east of Argentan. This would trap the

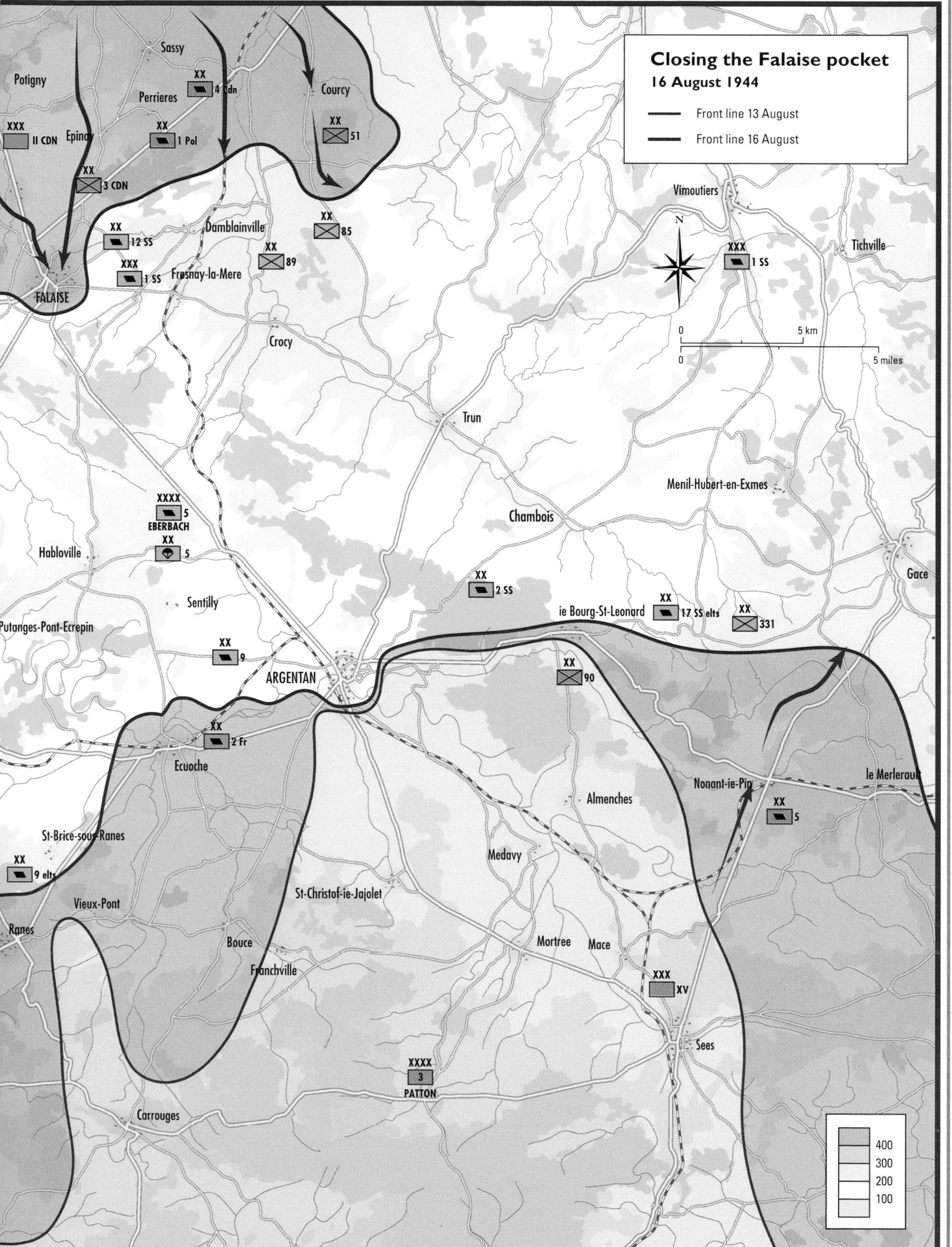

Bradley had decided that Patton should move no further north from Argentan for fear of clashing with the Canadians, who had now entered Falaise and would advance south to close the pocket. On the German side, Hitler had still not given permission for Hausser's Seventh Army, now being pounded from the air, to withdraw from the pocket.

German Seventh Army and the bulk of Fifth Panzer in a pocket, with no roads to provide escape routes to the east. But in case the Germans did manage to extricate sizeable forces from the pocket, Montgomery instructed Bradley to continue to plan for an airborne operation in the Chartres area, which he had previously ordered him to do to accelerate the advance towards Paris. Bradley was also to hold three divisions in the Le Mans area to link up with the airborne element at Chartres. In this way Montgomery hoped to prevent the Germans from creating a fresh defence line on the River Seine.

The Allied airborne forces themselves had experienced a frustrating time since D-Day. The US 82nd and 101st Airborne Divisions remained in the line until 18 July, when they had been moved back to Britain to re-equip. The British 6th Airborne Division had no such respite and was continuing to hold the Allied eastern flank. Back in Britain itself were the British 1st Airborne Division and the Polish Parachute Brigade, which had been alerted for a number of possible operations which had then been cancelled, either because the weather was unsuitable or they had been overtaken by events. On 2 August, with the two US divisions now back in Britain and ready for further combat, the First Allied Airborne Army was formed under the command of General Lewis H. Brereton, who had been in charge of the US Ninth Air Force. Planning for the Chartres operation began, but like those that had preceded it, the air assault never took place.

On 12 August, Patton's men, in the form of the 2nd French Armoured Division, entered Alençon. The division had landed in France a fortnight earlier and was commanded by General Philippe Leclerc (a pseudonym adopted by Viscount Philippe de Hautecloque to protect his family in Occupied France) who had joined de Gaulle in summer 1940. He had begun by rallying French Equatorial Africa to the Free French cause and

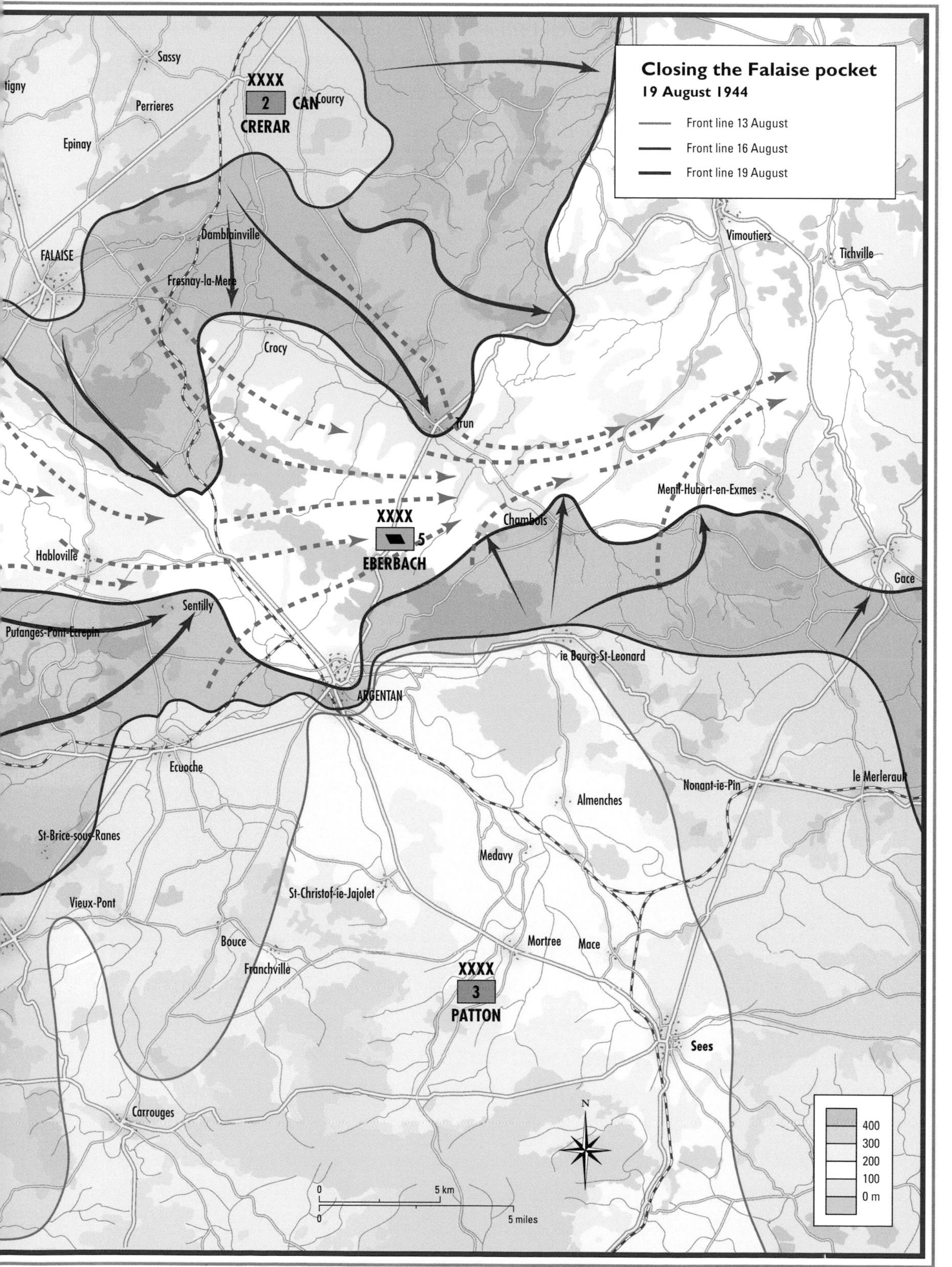

With Model having superseded von Kluge as CinC West, Hausser was finally given leave to extricate the German Seventh Army as best he could. It became a race against time as the neck of the pocket shrank. It was finally sealed by the end of 19 August, although II SS Panzer Corps did launch a counter-attack early the following day, temporarily opening an escape route.

The Falaise pocket at the end of the battle.

then had led a small force from Chad across the Libyan desert to join the British Eighth Army for the campaign in Tunisia. Simultaneously, the 5th Armored Division captured Sées. General Wade Hampton Haislip, the XV Corps commander, now ordered both divisions to make for Argentan. By this time Eberbach had been given permission to switch his Panzer forces from Mortain, and managed to deploy elements of 116th Panzer Division to Argentan just before Haislip's tanks arrived. The latter now took up position on both sides of the town. Patton himself wanted Haislip to press on to Falaise, but this order was countermanded by Bradley, who feared a clash with the Canadians. He was also aware that Eberbach was moving more armour from the Mortain area, threatening the left flank of XV Corps. To guard against this, Patton ordered his XX Corps to move up from the Mayenne–Le Mans area to Carrouges. Even so, he was furious over the halt order, believing that Haislip could have advanced quickly to Falaise and sealed the pocket. Though the decision had been Bradley's alone, Patton was convinced that the order came from Montgomery 'either due to jealousy of the Americans or utter ignorance of the situation or to a combination of the two', as he noted in his diary.

The Canadians renewed their offensive on 14 August. This time they planned to attack by day, using smoke to cover the assault. RAF Bomber Command despatched 411 Lancasters and 352 Halifaxes to attack the German positions astride the River Laison. The bombing was generally accurate, but one Canadian artillery battalion did suffer casualties, when some bombers mis-

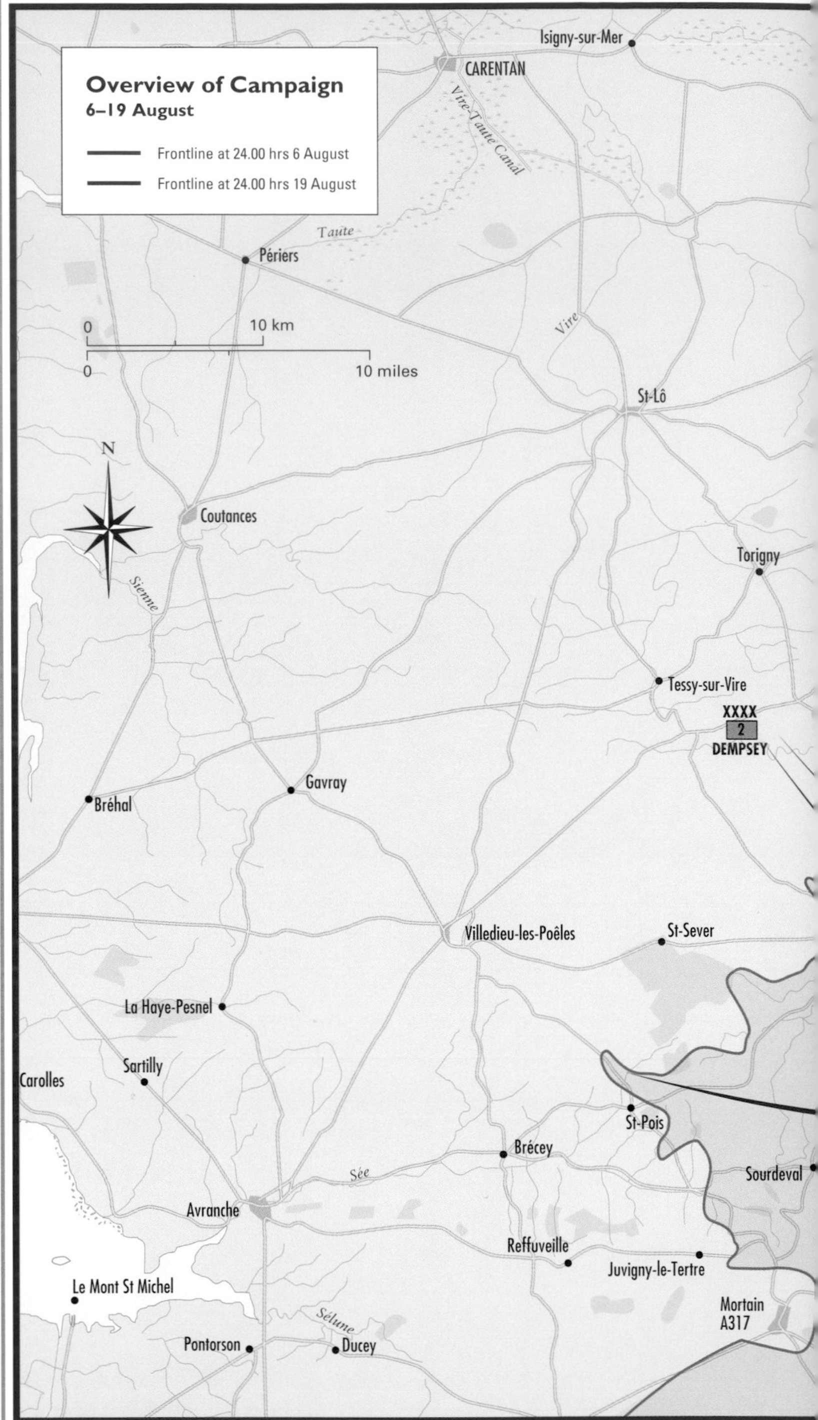

took the yellow flares its men were firing for those used for marking the targets. The Canadian 3rd Division, many of its men mounted on US-made Priest 105mm self-propelled guns, with armament removed and known as Kangaroos or Unfrocked Priests, and 4th Armoured Division, together with the 2nd Armoured Brigade, advanced through the smoke in blocks, rather than columns, using the sun to guide them. They closed quickly to the river and crossed it in the afternoon. By nightfall they were just three miles from Falaise. Unfortunately, that night

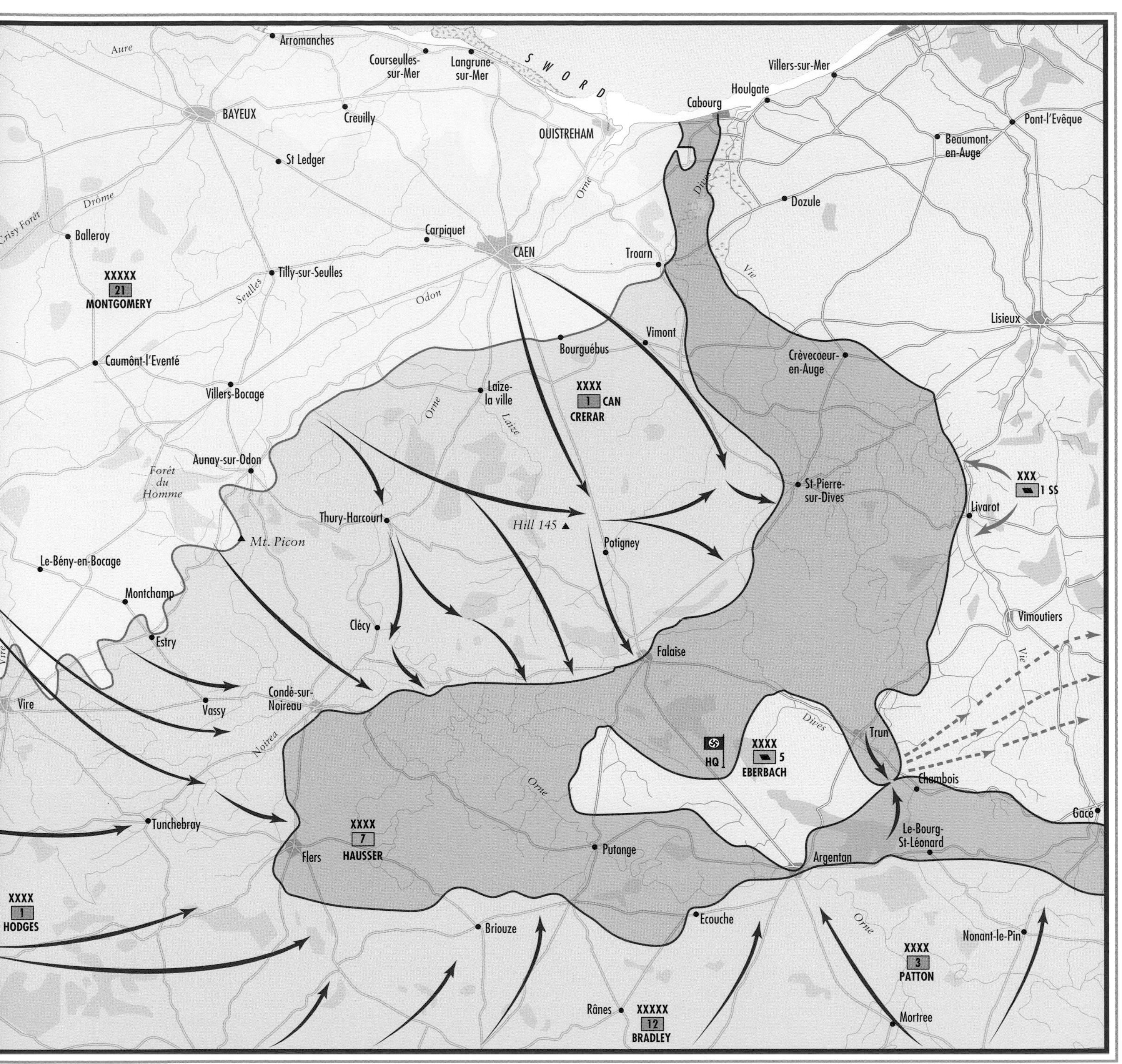

Falaise marked the final phase of the Normandy campaign. Hitler's refusal to countenance an earlier withdrawal condemned much of Army Group B to death or captivity.

the Germans captured an officer who was carrying the attack plan. Consequently, next morning the Canadians once more found themselves up against the 12th SS Panzer Division, which had quickly taken up position on the last ridge before Falaise. Throughout 15 August, although now reduced to some 500 men and fifteen tanks, with a few 88mm guns in support, it resisted all efforts to dislodge it. Only when the 2nd Canadian Division was sent round and threatened Falaise from the west on the following day did the 12th SS relinquish its hold on the ridge. By the end of the 17th, almost the whole of the town was in Canadian hands and the gap between them and Patton's men around Argentan was reduced to a mere twelve miles.

As late as 16 August, when the Canadians began to enter Falaise, von Kluge had still issued no order for Hausser's Seventh Army to withdraw from the pocket that had now been

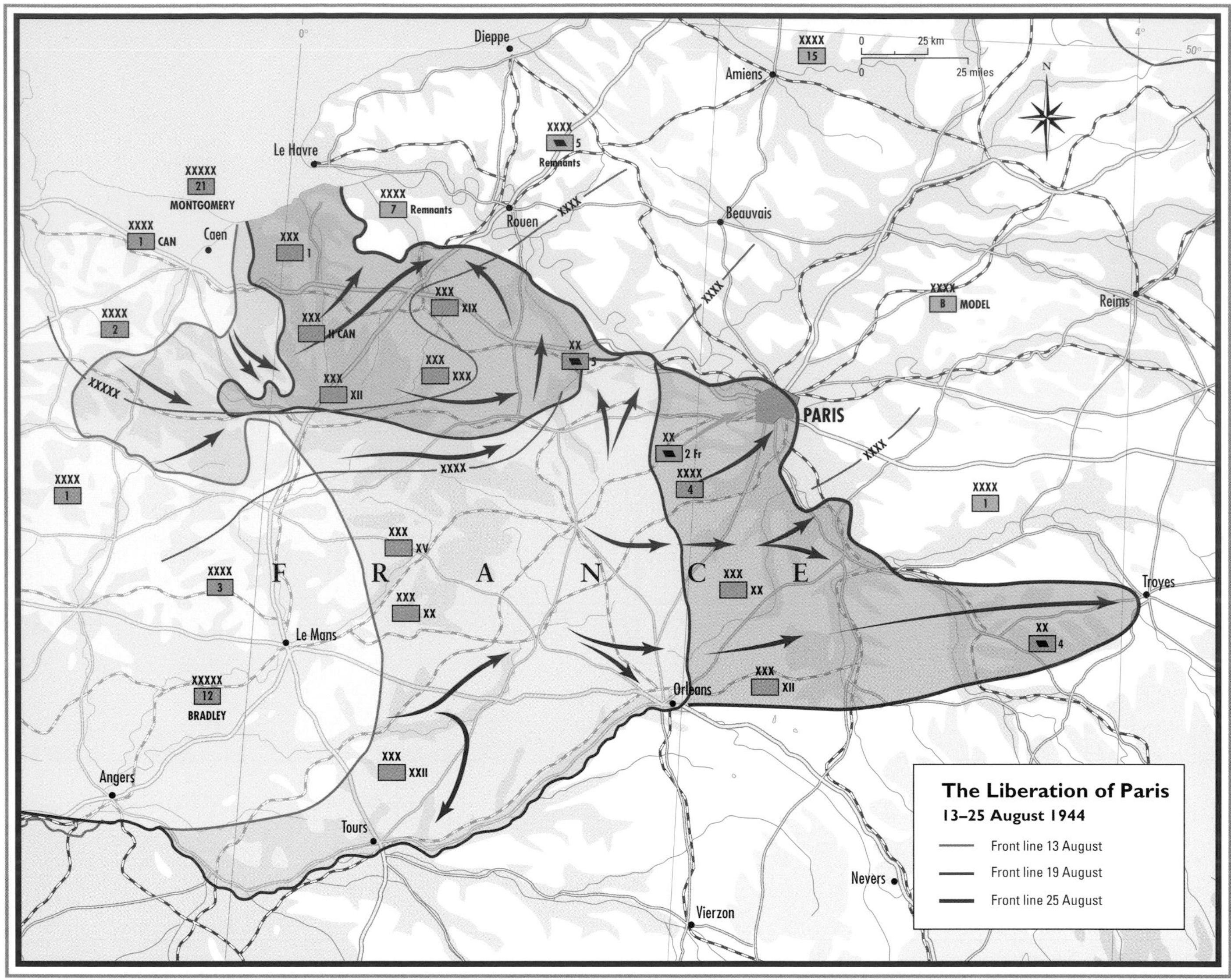

An advance direct on Paris was not part of Eisenhower's plan, but developments within the city caused a change of heart. For diplomatic reasons, it was important that the French be seen to liberate their own city. Meanwhile, Bradley's 12th US Army Group had secured crossings over the Seine to the west and south-east and the German First Army, withdrawing from southern France, was beginning to come into play.

created, apart from logistic elements. He had been hesitant to do this while Hitler continued to demand further counter attacks south of Mortain. The situation was aggravated by what happened to the C-in-C West himself on 15 August. He had set out from HQ Army Group B to visit the pocket, when he came under an artillery bombardment and fighter-bomber attack. His radio car was knocked out and he himself spent much of the day in a ditch, totally out of communications with anyone. Hitler quickly became aware of this and was convinced that von Kluge was in negotiation with the Allies through an unnamed captured German general. He decided there and then that he must be replaced. He immediately summoned Walther Model from the Eastern Front, where he had succeeded in saving the muchbattered Army Group Centre through a vigorous counter-attack, which helped to bring the Russian offensive to a halt. When von Kluge was finally in radio contact once more that night, he was instructed to leave the pocket and place himself at HQ Fifth Panzer Army. From here he telephoned Jodl at OKW and asked permission to withdraw Seventh Army. Hitler's eventual reply was that it should merely withdraw to the east bank of the River Orne and establish a new defence line there. But that was totally unrealistic, since it would mean that it would have the Canadians at its back.

Model arrived in France on 17 August. The wretched von Kluge was ordered back to Germany. Certain that he would be arrested, he committed suicide while en route. Model realized that the situation was desperate, with Allied air-power remorselessly pounding the troops within the pocket. Without seeking Hitler's permission, he ordered Hausser to extract what he could from the now shrinking pocket and establish a new front based on the River Dives. But even this was likely to be very difficult. On that same day, the First Canadian Army launched another attack, this time across the River Dives itself. By the evening of the 18th, Polish tanks were overlooking Chambois. Simultaneously, the Americans had closed up to Le Bourg St-Leonard. Between these two places there was a void of some six miles through which the remnants of Fifth Panzer and Seventh Armies were pouring. Hausser sent II SS Panzer Corps to dislodge the Poles so that the gap could be widened, but to no avail. Twenty-four hours later, the US 90th Division and Leclerc's tanks linked up with the Poles at Chambois and the Falaise pocket was finally sealed. In desperation Hausser's remaining armour launched an attack against the Canadians on the River Dives at dawn on 20 August. It managed to open a narrow corridor north of the village of St-Lambert, which itself was subjected to repeated attacks. Although under constant artillery fire, more men managed to escape the cauldron that the pocket had now become, but by evening the pocket was once more sealed. The following day, II SS Panzer Corps made another attempt against the Poles, but again in vain. It, too, now joined the other remnants streaming back towards the River Seine. They left behind 10,000 dead and 50,000 prisoners in the pocket. The battle for Normandy was finally over.

Model now had to try to re-form his shattered armies and establish a new defence line. But he was also faced by another threat. On 15 August 1944, General Alexander Patch's US Seventh Army landed on the French Riviera. The original intention had been to mount Anvil, as it was originally codenamed, simultaneously with the Normandy landings, but there was insufficient amphibious shipping to make this possible. The British had never liked the concept and, with the Allies finally entering Rome in early June and advancing into northern Italy, they continued to argue for its cancellation, especially since the troops earmarked for Anvil were to come from Italy. They believed that a much more effective strategy was to threaten the Third Reich from the South, as well as the West and East. Eisenhower was insistent that the landings went ahead, since he wanted to open up Marseilles as a supply port. He was supported by the US Joint Chiefs of Staff, who had never attached much importance to Italy, and by President Roosevelt. Consequently, the British were forced to

An American 75mm howitzer in action.

relent and Dragoon, as it was renamed, went ahead.

The southern part of France was the responsibility of General Johannes Blaskowitz and his Army Group G, which consisted of ten divisions, but only three of them were near the beaches. This fact, combined with overwhelming Allied air supremacy and a powerful naval bombardment force, made Dragoon a more straightforward operation than Overlord and the landing force quickly began to press inland and westwards along the coast towards Marseilles. Behind the Seventh Army came Jean-Marie de Lattre de Tassigny's Armée B, soon to become the First French Army. Marseilles would fall on 28 August, while the two armies began to advance rapidly northwards up the Rhône valley, much assisted by the FFI, which was at its strongest and most organized in this region. Model recognized that sooner or later this new thrust would reach the Franco-German border, but, given the ever more desperate situation in northern France, there was little that he could do about it.

Any hopes that Model had of forming a defence line on the River Seine had already been dashed by the time the Falaise pocket was finally sealed. Patton may have been deeply frustrated by Bradley's refusal to allow him to close the pocket more quickly than he did, but he was compensated by Bradley allowing him to use the bulk of his army to advance rapidly eastwards. It was not quite what Montgomery had in mind, since he

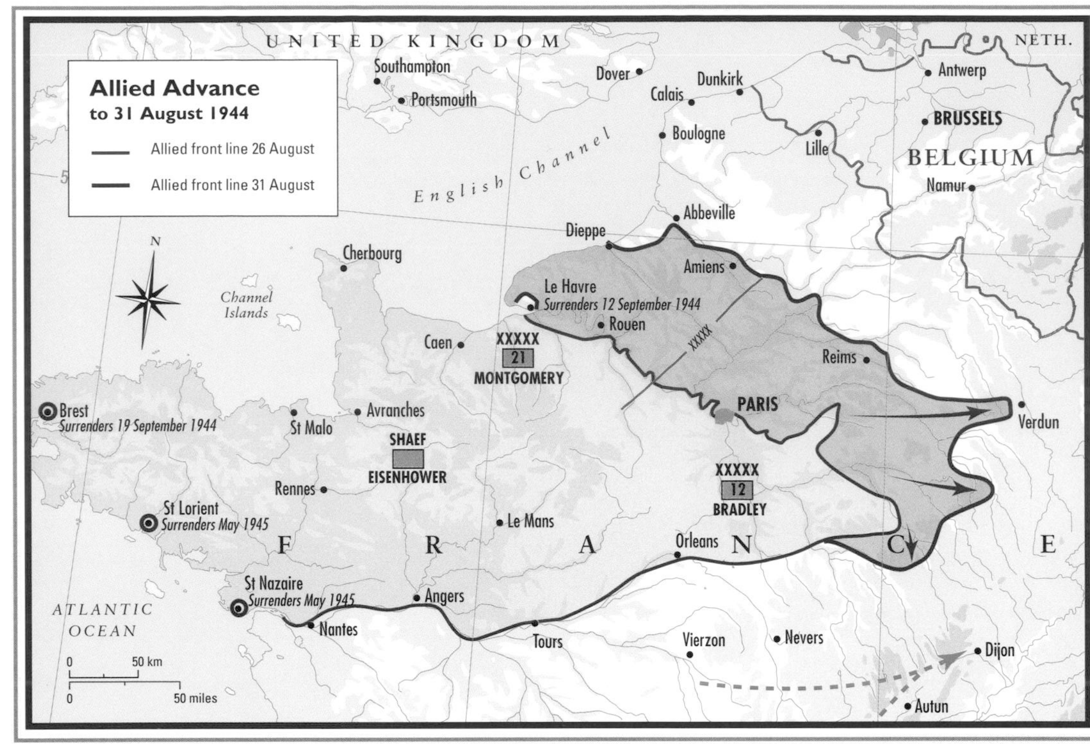

Events were now beginning to move increasingly rapidly as the German forces in northern France struggled desperately to extricate themselves. On the Allied side, however, the supply lines, still largely reliant on the port of Cherbourg, were becoming stretched.

wanted Patton to close to Dreux and then swing north towards Le Havre to act as a backstop for the envelopment of Fifth Panzer and Seventh Armies. Patton had removed the bulk of XV Corps from the Argentan area and duly sent it to Dreux, which it reached on 16 August. Simultaneously, his other two corps had advanced to Chartres, thus negating the airborne assault in this area, and Orléans. Bradley now halted Third Army for two days, fearing that it would become over-extended, but allowed it to resume its advance on the 18th. Next day, General Ira T. Wyche's 79th Division found an intact foot bridge over the Seine at Mantes-Gassicourt, to the west of Paris. Patton hesitated, flying back to consult with Bradley, who gave the green light, and at dawn on the following day two of Wyche's battalions crossed. By that evening he had established a firm bridgehead. Encouraged by this, Bradley ordered Patton to secure another bridgehead, this time at Melun to the south-east of the French capital. This was achieved on 23 August. It meant that the River Seine was no longer a position from which the Germans could draw breath and reorganize.

As for Paris itself, the original Allied intention had been to encircle the city through double envelopment and then hope that the German garrison would surrender without a fight. They feared that, if they entered it directly, there could be heavy fighting, which would cause civilian casualties and damage to its historic buildings and monuments. But events within the capital itself forced a change of plan. Sensing that liberation was close, a series of strikes by public-service workers had begun on 10 August. There was, however, a split in the Resistance movement. The Gaullist elements wanted to adopt a 'wait-and-see' strategy, especially since an envoy had informed them that the Allies were not planning to liberate it until mid-September. The Communists, who had majorities on most of the local committees, were for an immediate uprising. The Gaullists feared that if this happened, the Communists might well seize the machinery of government. Consequently, on 19 August, their leader, who was de Gaulle's delegate-general, initiated an insurrection, just as the Communists were about to launch their own. The Germans in and around the city numbered some 20,000 men under General von Choltitz, the former LXXXIV Corps com-

The break-out over the Seine. A British truck crosses the river on a pontoon bridge.

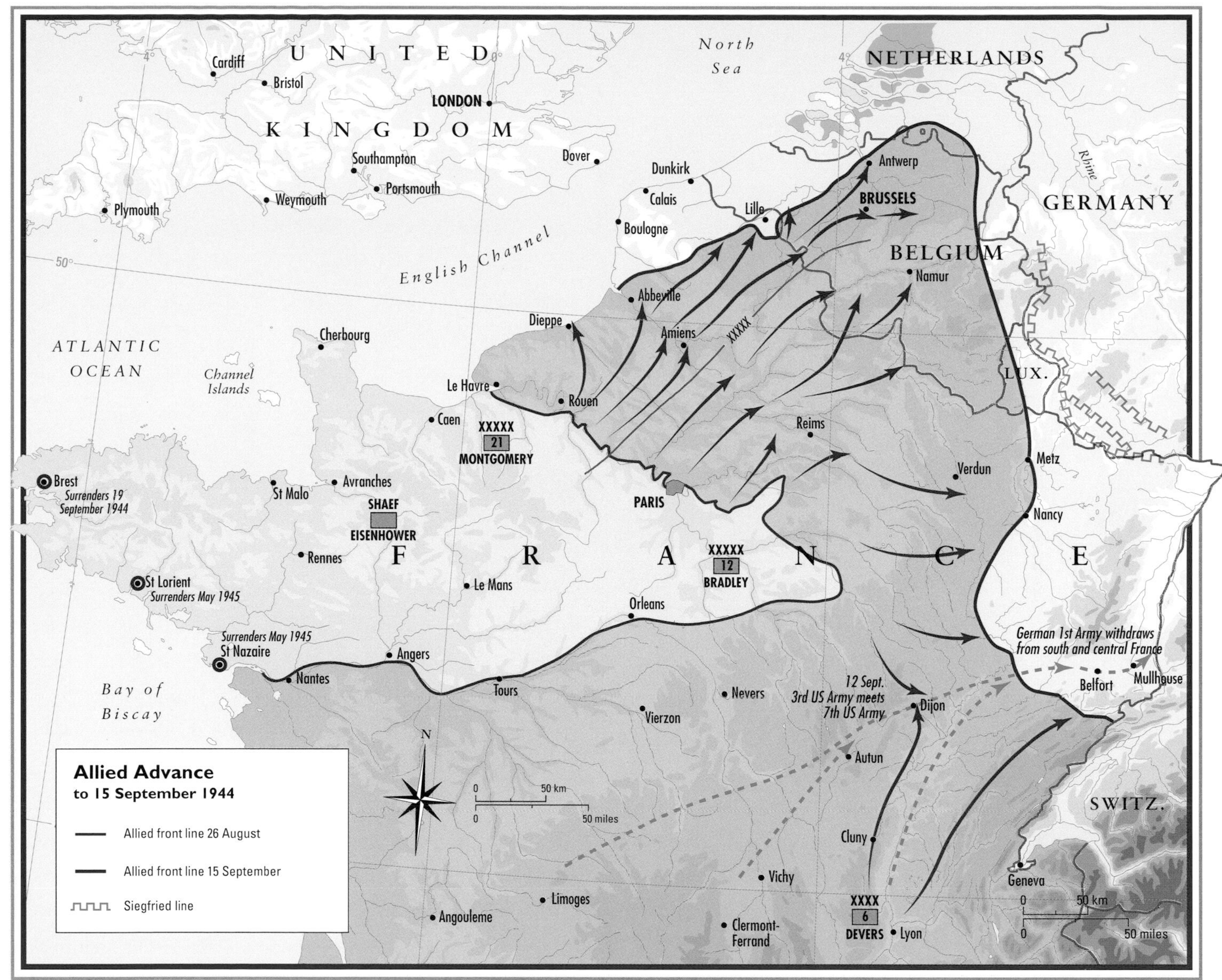

The Allied advance had now come to almost a complete halt. Almost the whole of France, apart from the easternmost region and much of Belgium had been liberated, but prospects for ending the war before 1945 had faded.

mander and who had been involved in the destruction of Rotterdam in May 1940 and Sevastopol, the Russian Black Sea port, in 1942. There were fears that he would use the same methods to crush the poorly armed Resistance groups. There was also awareness that the Poles had risen in Warsaw in expectation of being liberated by the Red Army, which had halted on the other side of the River Vistula at the conclusion of its Bagration offensive against Army Group Centre, and that the Germans were destroying much of the Polish capital.

Thanks to the Swedish Consul-General in Paris, von Choltitz was persuaded not to adopt the same brutal methods and a temporary truce was even arranged, although it was soon broken. This was in spite of an order from Hitler for him to defend Paris to the last round. The skirmishing continued, with more and more Parisians taking part. It was not, however, until 23 August that Eisenhower relented and Leclerc's 2nd Armoured Division was detached from the US Third Army to make a dash for the capital. Leclerc initially made slow progress and the US 4th Infantry Division was deployed to give him support. It then became almost a race between the French and Americans as to who would get to the centre first. Leclerc won, sending an armoured combat group through back streets and side roads on the evening of the 24th. This prompted von Choltitz to order his troops to withdraw east of the Seine. Next day, he himself surrendered to Leclerc, but small groups of German soldiers continued to fight on. That evening, Charles de Gaulle entered Paris and on the following day made a triumphal walk up the Champs Elysées, with snipers still active. This ensured that he, and not the Communists, would now control France.

To the Allied high command, Paris was merely a diversion. With the Germans withdrawing rapidly eastwards in disarray, firm decisions were now needed to develop operations to take best advantage of this. On 21 August, Eisenhower had held a meeting at his Advanced HQ in Normandy. He stated that, with effect from 1 September, he would take personal charge of 12th and 21st Army Groups and that the former was to advance to the Franco-German border. Montgomery objected to this, arguing that the Allies should remain concentrated and advance to the Ruhr via Antwerp. This was the beginning of the Broad-versus Narrow-Front debate, which dogged the high command for much of the remaining part of the war. While Eisenhower agreed that 21st Army Group should clear the Pas-de-Calais and secure Antwerp, he was not prepared to switch Bradley's forces to the north, except to help Montgomery if he got into trouble. The two men met face-to-face on 23 August, the same day that Eisenhower had relented over Paris. Montgomery pressed the single- thrust strategy once more, proposing that, while he seized Antwerp, Bradley should advance on his right flank on an axis Brussels-Aachen-Cologne. He also told Eisenhower that he could not combine the jobs of supreme commander and ground force commander. The latter should either be Montgomery or Bradley. Convinced that US public opinion would not stand for a British general to be formally in command of US troops for any longer, Eisenhower resisted Montgomery's demands. The most that he would concede was that 21st Army Group's advance to Antwerp would be given priority. He also accepted it was not strong enough on its own to advance to the Ruhr. Montgomery would therefore be allowed to co-ordinate US divisions operating on his right flank, although they would not be placed under his command.

The high price of liberation. French inhabitants return to their shattered town after the fighting has passed on.

By 29 August the Allies had closed up to the River Seine. Simultaneously, Model was desperately trying to organize another defence line on the Rivers Somme and Marne. This proved impossible. After the withdrawal across the Seine he had been left with a mere 120 tanks and many of his divisions had been reduced to virtual skeletons, with only the infantry divisions of Fifteenth Army, which had not been fighting in Normandy, still reasonably intact. In addition, Patton, never one to stand inactivity, had already launched Third Army across the Seine and reached the Marne, brushing aside what German resistance there was. The van of his army was now approaching Reims. His rapid advance was, however, bringing into focus a growing problem, that of resupply. While Cherbourg was now functioning to full capacity, the further east the Allies advanced, the more stretched their supply lines became. Patton himself had already outrun his forward depots and was reliant on air resupply, as well as captured German fuel stocks. On 28 August, however, the aircraft bringing him fuel had to be diverted in preparation for an airborne operation in the Pas-de-Calais, which, like so many others before it, did not actually take place. For this reason, Bradley wanted Patton to halt until the advance of First Army on his left was well underway. Only with difficulty did Patton persuade his superior to allow him to push on to the River Meuse.

Model's reaction to Patton's lightning advance was to order what mobile elements he had to concentrate in the area Châlons-Reims-Soissons in order to block Third Army. As for the defence of the Somme, this was quickly compromised by Lawton Collins's US VII Corps, which had passed through the bridgehead across the Seine at Melun and was advancing to Soissons, thus outflanking the Somme.

In the 21st Army Group sector, Montgomery ordered First Canadian Army to advance up the coast and secure the Channel ports. The British Second Army was to advance out of the bridge-

(Right) While stalemate appeared to be developing in the West, elsewhere the pressure on German forces was being maintained by a series of ongoing offensives, especially on the Eastern Front, where the German hold on the Balkans was about to crumble.

Europe
Allied advance to September 1944
Allied or Allied controlled 6 June 1944
Liberated between 6 June and 16 September 1944
Germany
Occupied territories or Allied to Germany
Ongoing Allied offensive
Borders as November 1942
200 km
200 miles
North Cape
Narvik
Luleå
Arctic Circle
ICELAND
Norwegian Sea
NORWAY
SWEDEN
FINLAND
HELSINKI
Leningrad
SOVIET UNION
OSLO
STOCKHOLM
Baltic Sea
DENMARK
Copenhagen
North Sea
Edinburgh
REICHKOMMISSARIAT OSTLAND
Königberg
East Prussia
DUBLIN
IRELAND
UNITED KINGDOM
Hamburg
AMSTERDAM
Neth.
BERLIN
Warsaw
Poland
REICHKOMMISSARIAT UKRAINE
Kiev
LONDON
BRUSSELS
Belgium
GERMANY
Frankfurt
PRAGUE
Bohemia
SLOVAKIA
PARIS
Munich
VIENNA
ATLANTIC OCEAN
BUDAPEST
HUNGARY
BERN
SWITZ.
Geneva
FRANCE
Austria
ROMANIA
Banat
BUCHAREST
Milan
Venice
Genoa
CROATIA
BELGRADE
Danube
SERBIA
SOFIA
BULGARIA
Mont.
Marseille
ITALY
Adriatic Sea
ISTANBUL
Corsica
ROME
ALBANIA
SPAIN
PORTUGAL
LISBON
MADRID
Taranto
TURKEY
GREECE
Aegean Sea
Sardinia
Balearic Is.
ATHENS
Mediterranean Sea
Sicily
to Italy
Algiers
Bone
Tunis
Malta to Britain
Crete
French North Africa
Libya to Italy
Tripoli
Benghazi
Libya to Italy

head that it had established at Vernon and make a 'swift and relentless' advance northwards. It was to be spearheaded by XXX Corps, now commanded by Brian Horrocks, who had proved an able corps commander in North Africa until being badly wounded in a German air attack in Tunisia. He unleashed the now veteran 11th Armoured Division. By midday on 30 August, Roberts's tanks were some forty miles from Amiens, having encountered only light opposition. Horrocks ordered to him drive on through the night to secure the city and its bridges over the Somme. Roberts achieved this before dawn on the following day. This finally put paid to Model's plans for holding the Somme. He also suffered another blow. Sepp Dietrich, who had been commanding Seventh Army for the past two weeks, was in the process of handing over command to Heinrich Eberbach. The headquarters was, however, very close to 11th Armoured Division's axis of advance. Dietrich left in time, but Eberbach and most of his staff were captured while eating breakfast. The US XIX and VII Corps were coming up on Horrocks's flank and by 2 September all three corps had crossed the Belgian frontier. With Patton still rampaging towards the Franco-German border, it seemed as though the German forces in the West were facing imminent collapse.

The Allied fuel crisis was growing, however, by the day. The extensive damage done to the French railways meant that they could not be used, and air resupply could only carry a very limited amount, especially since part of it had to be diverted to bring foodstuffs to the population of Paris and many of the transport aircraft remained tied to the Allied Airborne Army, now preparing for a projected drop to seize crossings over the River Scheldt in Belgium. The bulk therefore had to be transported by road. On 25 August, every available truck was pressed into service to bring the fuel to forward depots south-west of Paris and by the 29th they were delivering over 12,000 tons per day. But the Red Ball Express, from the US railroad slang for fast freight, was itself consuming a daily 300,000 gallons of precious fuel. The rapidity of the advance further aggravated matters. Hopes that Channel ports might be speedily opened were also dashed. As he had done with the Atlantic ports, Hitler declared them Festungen, which were to be defended to the last. Thus, the Canadians quickly closed on Le Havre, but they had to place it under siege and it would not fall until 12 September, too late to affect the outcome. They did quickly capture Dieppe, thus revenging in part the disaster than had befallen them in August 1942, but it took a week to open the port and its capacity was limited. While 21st Army Group was beginning to feel the shortage and was only maintaining its advance by reducing the Canadian allocation so as to maintain the advance into Belgium, 12th Army Group was in serious trouble because of its very much longer supply lines.

On 1 September, Eisenhower duly assumed direct command of the Allied ground forces and considered the fuel crisis, especially that pertaining to 12th Army Group. His priority was still on capturing Antwerp and so he allocated 5,000 tons per day to Courtney Hodges' First Army, the bulk of which was advancing on Montgomery's left flank, and a mere 2,000 tons to Third Army, which was now halted on the Meuse for want of fuel, although its forward elements had got as far as Métz and the River Moselle. This inevitably was not to Patton's liking, especially since he now had his sights set on the main German defence belt covering its western border with France, the Siegfried Line.

He managed to persuade Eisenhower to allow him to press on, once the ports in the Pas de Calais had been secured, and in the meantime was allowed to secure crossings over the Moselle. This decision meant that the Allied forces

British Sappers heaving a section of a Bailey bridge into position.

were diverging north and east still further. Worse, Model was succeeding in gathering troops to bar Patton's way.

In the meantime, the advance of the British XXX Corps continued. On the late afternoon of 3 September, the Guards Armoured Division entered Brussels. At the same time, 11th Armoured made a dash for Antwerp, reaching it on the following day and catching the German garrison by surprise, so much so that its massive docks were still almost completely intact. Furthermore, the German Fifteenth Army, which was facing the Canadians advancing up the French coast, could now be trapped. With the Seventh Army virtually destroyed, the route to the Ruhr now lay open. To Montgomery and Churchill it seemed as though the war could be ended well before the end of the year, that is if the Allied effort was concentrated in this direction. Montgomery tried to persuade the Americans once more to adopt this plan, but Bradley was more interested in Patton's advance to the Saar, and so was Eisenhower. Montgomery was therefore left to do what he could on his own, but his fixation on the Ruhr caused him to ignore the situation around Antwerp. For, unless the estuary of the Scheldt was secured, Antwerp could not be used as a port and Fifteenth Army had an escape route across into Holland. The Canadians, too, had not been able to move quickly. They had been hampered by problems over bridging the numerous rivers which they had to cross and much of their strength was tied up in besieging and opening the Channel ports. In consequence, the fuel problem remained and Fifteenth Army stayed in being and continued to block the seaward approaches to Antwerp.

On the German side, Hitler once more recalled Gerd von Rundstedt to active duty as C-in-C West. Model had been finding it increasingly difficult to combine the task of rescuing Army Group B with that of C-in-C West. Indeed, by the beginning of September the two headquarters were sixty miles apart and he had to leave Günther Blumentritt, his chief of staff, to look after HQ C-in-C West. He was therefore relieved when Hitler proposed bringing back von Rundstedt, who arrived at the HQ, now near Koblenz, on 5 September. Hitler had instructed him to prevent the Allies from opening up Antwerp, which Fifteenth Army was already beginning to do, create a strong base in Holland, and protect the Ruhr and Saar. He was fortunate that the Allied fuel problem had now reached crisis proportions. Thus, the British Second Army's progress began to slow after the capture of Brussels. Worse, it began to meet opposition of the German First Parachute Army, which was forming in Holland, and contained fresh troops of better quality than had been met for some time. The terrain around the canals north of Brussels also favoured the defence. Hodges' US First Army was also suffering, with some of its armoured formations immobilized through lack of fuel. True, patrols did cross the German border close to Luxembourg on 11 September, but there was no fuel available to exploit this. Likewise, Patton had resumed his offensive towards the Saar on 5 September, but could do no more than establish bridgeheads across the Moselle in the face of the force that Model had built up here and the lack of the necessary fuel and ammunition to punch a hole in the defences.

The bizarre resting place of this PzKwIV is likely to have been the result of an Allied air attack.

Thus, by mid-September 1944, the Allied advance, which had held out so much promise just two weeks earlier, had ground to almost a complete halt, enabling the Germans to restore some cohesion to their defence. The odds on ending the war in autumn 1944 had lengthened considerably and the spectre of a grim winter campaign grew ever larger.

EPILOGUE

The Allies did have one more opportunity to break the deadlock on the Western Front. On 10 September 1944, Eisenhower approved a plan drawn up by Montgomery for an operation to outflank Germany's main natural defence barrier in the west, the River Rhine. This would be done from the air, with US and British paratroops seizing a series of bridges over waterways in southern Holland, the furthest of which and the key to the whole operation was that over the lower Rhine at Arnhem. Operation Market-Garden was mounted a week later. The US 82nd and 101st Airborne Divisions succeeded in securing their bridges and the ground force, the British XXX Corps, did eventually link up with them. That at Arnhem, which was the objective of the British 1st Airborne Division and Polish Parachute Brigade, proved a bridge too far. There were numerous reasons for this. One was poor intelligence, which failed to recognize the significance of II SS Panzer Corps refitting in the Arnhem area after the battle for Normandy. Another was that the XXX Corps axis of advance was too narrow, in some places restricted to a single road, which made it very vulnerable to attack from the flanks.

With the failure of Market-Garden, the Allies were committed to a winter campaign, one which saw the Germans recover to such an extent that they were able to mount a major counter-offensive in the Ardennes in mid-December. The port of Antwerp was eventually opened at the end of November, after amphibious landings on the island of Walcheren, which guards the mouth of the Scheldt, and the clearance of both sides of the river. Once the Ardennes counter-offensive had been beaten back, Eisenhower's Broad-Front strategy remained in force, as the Allies closed up to the Rhine, crossed it in late March 1945 and then began to advance into Germany. The Narrow-Front option then surfaced again, with Montgomery's advocacy of a single thrust to Berlin, but Eisenhower rejected it. The German capital would be left to the Russians, while the Western Allies advanced to the Rivers Elbe and Mulde, as well as entering Austria. By then, the D-Day landings and subsequent campaign in the Normandy bocage appeared a distant memory.

American and Russian troops meet at Torgau on the River Elbe, 25 April 1945.

Overlord was a long time in preparation, its origins stretching back to the evacuation from Dunkirk, when it was realized that the Third Reich was unlikely to be defeated unless Allied ground forces returned to the Continent of Europe. Some have since argued that it should have been mounted in 1943, rather than pursuing the Mediterranean strategy agreed at the Casablanca conference of January of that year. Certainly, this is what the Americans wanted. Yet, the landings had to succeed the first time. If the Allies were thrown back into the sea it would be months or even years before they could try again. In 1943, they still had much to learn about amphibious operations and the shipping available was limited. COSSAC's plan of that summer envisaged an initial landing by only three divisions, because of the limited shipping likely to be available, and the smaller the landing area, the easier it would have been for the Germans to concentrate against it, a point that Eisenhower and Montgomery were well aware of when they reviewed the COSSAC plan and expanded the landing beaches. Another factor is that because the Tunisian campaign lasted much longer than the Allies had expected, there would have been little time to bring back the now-combat-experienced formations, essential to the success of Overlord, from the Mediterranean and prepare them for an invasion which had to take place before the uncertainties of the autumn weather in the English Channel intervened.

While the German forces deployed to the Atlantic Wall were comparatively weak until the end of 1943, there is no doubt that Hitler would have strengthened them in time, since it was impossible to conceal the preparations for the landings. Furthermore, the numerical strength of the German Armed Forces peaked in 1943. True, there had been the disaster at Stalingrad at the beginning of the year, but threatened with a cross-Channel invasion in summer 1943, it is unlikely that Hitler would have mounted the subsequently failed counter-offensive at Kursk that July, which incurred some 200,000 casualties, as well as significant losses in armour and aircraft. In addition, the German forces that were allocated to Italy, as a result of the Allied Mediterranean strategy, would also have been available. It is therefore arguable that the Allies might well have encountered significantly stronger German forces if they had come ashore in summer 1943 and would have been operating from a much narrower beachhead than was ultimately the case.

As it was, the planning and preparation for Overlord were meticulous in their detail. No factor was left unconsidered in ensuring the success of the initial landings. In particular, tribute must be paid to those who conceived and executed Operation Bodyguard, the elaborate deception plan. While parts of it were unsuccessful, the two critical aspects of it – the threats to Norway and the Pas-de-Calais – were very effective. Hitler did not remove a single man from Norway and the retention of sizeable German forces north of the Seine until long after D-Day bear this out. The planners also took to heart the many lessons learned from previous and on-going landing operations. Examples of this were the development of specialized armour and the Mulberry harbours. These measures also called for a high degree of technical innovation. That Overlord did succeed is due in no small part to the legions of often faceless scientists, engineers, and others in and out of uniform, the 'boffins' or 'backroom boys', as they were called at the time.

No one on the Allied side ever believed that the actual

Another liberation and a stark contrast to the grim fighting that these American troops had recently experienced.

mounting of Overlord would be easy. Indeed, some of the decisions that had to be made were knife-edge. The most critical of all was Eisenhower's decision to postpone D-Day by twenty-four hours, because of the weather, and then to confirm it for 6 June. Only he could take that decision and, if wrong, he knew that the responsibility for failure was his alone. It was a perfect example of the loneliness of high command. As it turned out, the weather did create some problems during the landings, notably at Omaha, but the Allies got ashore with significantly fewer casualties than they feared. Part of the reason for this was that the adverse weather had convinced the Germans that the landings were not imminent, thus creating additional surprise. Another was the thorough training that the assaulting troops had received, enabling them to quickly overcome the shock of landing under fire and get on with tackling their various tasks for getting off the beaches. It was, however, congestion on these that was the main reason why the D-Day objectives were seldom reached, although some might say that they were unduly optimistic.

Once ashore, it was a matter of who could reinforce the quickest, the Allies or the Germans. The latter suffered from grave disadvantages. First was the deployment of the armour, with Hitler retaining control of part, and other Panzer divisions kept north of the Seine in the belief that the Normandy landings were a diversion. The Allied air campaign against transportation, ably aided by the efforts of the French Resistance, created physical difficulties in moving formations to Normandy, as did the overwhelming Allied air supremacy over the battlefield and beyond. The Germans had one Panzer and six infantry divisions in Normandy on the eve of D-Day and by D+24 this had risen to eight Panzer, seventeen infantry and one airborne division. By this date the Allies had built up their forces from nothing to five armoured, eighteen infantry, and three airborne divisions, reflecting a higher rate of reinforcement. This continued until by the time of Cobra the Allies enjoyed a significant superiority in strength. The rate of replacement of casualties was considerably higher. During the period 6–30 June the Allies suffered some 61,700 casualties, but received 79,000 individual reinforcements to replace them. In contrast, the Germans received only a tenth of the number killed, wounded or captured.

Montgomery's overall strategy for the Normandy campaign, to use the British and Canadians to tie down and wear down the German armour so that the Americans could break out, was realistic and sound. It was assisted by the fact that most of the Panzer divisions found themselves committed to line-holding and could not be concentrated into a powerful enough force to mount a really effective counter-attack. True, in terms of duration, the campaign did not proceed as quickly as Montgomery had envisaged. Cherbourg should have fallen on D+8, but did not do so until D+22, Caen, a D-Day objective, was not secured until D+33, while Falaise should have been seized on D+17, but was not reached until D+71. Part of the reason for this was the tenacity with which the Germans fought, in spite of their disadvantages. The Allies, too, took some time to adjust to the claustrophobic nature of the bocage and it was a major omission in their training that they were not prepared for it.

The break-out itself developed very much more quickly than planned, with the Allies liberating the area between Normandy and the Seine in a mere thirty days, when it was expected to take seventy. Much of this can be put down to Patton's drive and initiative, and operations might have progressed at an even faster rate if he had not been ordered to send one of his corps into Brittany. This was part of the original plan, designed to secure more ports, but Hitler's order that these had to be defended to the end meant that two of Patton's armoured divisions found themselves conducting sieges, when they would have been better employed elsewhere.

Hitler's Festungen policy was the one strategy that he got right. It did deny the Allies ports for a considerable time, with some, like Dunkirk, holding out until the end of the war. It was this, and the unexpectedly rapid advance to the Seine and beyond, which stretched the Allied supply lines to such an extent that they eventually snapped. Otherwise, Hitler's refusal to allow voluntary withdrawals played into the hands of the Allies, enabling them to maintain their attritional strategy. Hitler's insistence on mounting counterstrokes into the flank of the break-out when it was too late to affect the outcome, also proved disastrous, leading as it did to the Falaise pocket. In summary, his refusal to allow his commanders on the ground any freedom of action proved fatal to the defence of Normandy and, indeed, the whole of France.

On the other side is Eisenhower's insistence that he would be both Allied supreme commander and ground force commander. By the time that he formally took over command of the latter on 1 September 1944, the Americans were providing the largest proportion of ground troops and it was therefore logical that an American should be in charge. Furthermore, although there were good arguments for Montgomery to be properly appointed to the post, which he had to all intents and purposes held until then, there were two negative factors. First, many of the American commanders found his cocksure manner abrasive. In addition, it was clear that US public opinion would not stand for a Briton occupying this position. To give him his due, Montgomery did tell Eisenhower that he would be happy to serve under Bradley when he was urging him to appoint a separate ground force commander. Eisenhower did not accept this and perhaps he was right to retain command in his own hands, for, once the Allies were ashore in Normandy, it was what was happening on the ground which largely dictated their strategy. Even if Montgomery or Bradley had been placed in charge, Eisenhower's Broad-Front approach would still have prevailed, because he was the supreme commander. As such, he had a much wider understanding of the political issues involved than did his subordinates and it was these issues which ultimately drove the military strategy. If Montgomery's Narrow-Front concept had been politically acceptable, it is still questionable whether it would have worked and that the Allies would have reached the Ruhr before winter set in. The German powers of recovery should not be underestimated and, with Antwerp still closed as a port, there would still have been a supply problem.

Yet, in spite of the controversies surrounding the Normandy campaign, once the Allies were safely ashore the fate of the Third Reich was ultimately sealed. But the significance of their achievement cannot be regarded in isolation. It has to be remembered that ever since June 1941 the bulk of the German war effort had concentrated against the Soviet Union. It was the Russians who bore the brunt for so long and, when the tide began to turn at Stalingrad, inflicted the greatest damage to the German Armed Forces. They also played their part, albeit indirectly, in the success of the liberation of France. Their massive summer offensive against Army Group Centre meant that the supply of German reinforcements to France was always going to be limited. This, however, cannot take away from the fact that Overlord represents the largest amphibious operation in history. Launched against a defender who knew that it was coming, it was remarkably successful. That it was so is thanks to the efforts of many men and women on both sides of the Atlantic, and in German-Occupied Europe. They were all working towards one end, the defeat of a malevolent dictatorship which was bent on creating a new Dark Age.

Rest in Peace.

CODEWORDS
CONNECTED WITH D-DAY

ABC-1 American-British-Canadian talks held in early 1941 to agree strategy in the event of the USA entering the war.

AJAX British autumn 1941 plan for an attack on Trondheim, Norway.

ANVIL Allied landings in the south of France (later DRAGOON).

ARABIAN 1942 British study on capturing Brittany (later LETHAL)

ARCADIA Anglo-US strategic conference held in Washington DC, December 1941–January 1942.

ARGONAUT Anglo-US strategic conference held in Washington DC, June 1942.

AVALANCHE Allied landings at Salerno, Italy, September 1943.

BIGOT Highest security classification relating to the planning of OVERLORD.

BLACK 1941 US plan for securing French North-West Africa by landing at Dakar.

BODYGUARD Overall Allied plan for deception to support operations in Europe in 1944.

BOLERO Build-up of US forces in Britain.

BOMBARDON Floating breakwater used to protect the MULBERRY harbours.

BUTTRESS Allied landings on toe of Italy, September 1943.

CALIPH Proposal by Churchill to land 5,000 Commandos at Bordeaux during D+20 to D+30 to support French Resistance.

CHASTITY Establishment of a port in Quiberon Bay on the French Atlantic coast.

COCKADE Deception scheme aimed at keeping the German forces tied down in the West during 1943 by making them believe that the Allies were preparing a large-scale assault. It had three elements – STARKEY, TINDALL, WADHAM.

CORNCOB MULBERRY blockship.

CORNELIUS Naval concentration phase of NEPTUNE.

CROSSBOW Allied countermeasures against V-weapons.

CRUIKSHANK Plan to gain a lodgement in the Low Countries prior to advancing to the Ruhr.

DRAGOON Allied landings in southern France, August 1944. Originally ANVIL.

ECLIPSE Allied operations in Europe after a German surrender, largely involving the occupation of the country.

EUREKA Allied strategic conference held at Tehran, Persia, November–December 1943.

FABIUS Final amphibious exercises prior to D-Day.

FERDINAND See ZEPPELIN.

FESTIVAL 1942 landing of troops direct from USA at French North-West African ports after they had been seized by Allied forces sailing from Britain.

FORETOP 1942 plan for large-scale raid on French Atlantic coast U-boat bases.

FORFAR Series of small-scale Commando raids on French Channel coast in 1943.

FORTITUDE NORTH Deception plan to convince the Germans that the Allies were preparing to invade Norway. Part of BODYGUARD.

FORTITUDE SOUTH Deception plan to convince the Germans that invasion the main Allied landings would be in the Pas-de -Calais and that those in Normandy were a diversion. Part of BODYGUARD.

FOYNES Deception plan designed to conceal the transfer of Allied divisions from Italy to Britain for OVERLORD.

GABRIEL 1942 plan for a major raid on the Cotentin Peninsula.

GAMBIT Operations by X-craft (midget submarines) to guide the Normandy fleet to the correct beaches.

GLIMMER Airborne deception operation mounted on night of 5/6 June 1944 to simulate an invasion fleet off Boulogne.

GOOSEBERRY MULBERRY breakwater created from CORNCOBs.

GRAFFHAM Parallel deception plan to FORTITUDE NORTH proposing an approach to Sweden for active co-operation in Anglo-Soviet operations in northern Norway.

GREENBACK Used in 1942 to denote 1943 invasion of the Continent should German morale appear to be cracking. Later RANKIN.

GYMNAST British plan for the invasion of French North-West Africa in 1942. Became SUPER GYMNAST once the Americans became involved. Later TORCH.

HADRIAN Plan to seize and hold the Cotentin Peninsula in 1943.

HALCYON Y-Day, when all naval preparations for OVERLORD were to be complete.

HARDBOILED 1941 deception plan for a notional attack on the Norwegian coast.

HARLEQUIN Sepember 1943 loading exercise, which was part of COCKADE.

HUSKY Invasion of Sicily, July 1943.

IMPERATOR Plan for a large-scale raid on the Continent in 1942.

IRONSIDE Adjunct to FORTITUDE SOUTH designed to create an Allied threat to the French Biscay coast.

JANTZEN Summer 1943 exercise to practise concentration and marshalling of troops for a cross-Channel invasion.

JAEL Overall deception plan for Allied operations in Europe.

JEDBURGH Allied 3-man teams dropped into France from D-Day onwards to co-ordinate French Resistance operations.

JUBILEE See RUTTER.

JUPITER Plan to invade Norway should conditions for OVERLORD not be realized.

LETHAL See ARABIAN.

LINNET Possible airborne operation in northern France post-D-Day.

MAGNET Deployment of US troops to Northern Ireland in early 1942.

MAPLE Allied minelaying operations during NEPTUNE.

MENACE Attempted Anglo-Free French landing at Dakar in September 1940.

MESPOT Original codename for FORTITUDE.

MODICUM US Presidential mission to Britain in April 1942 to present ROUND-UP and SLEDGEHAMMER plans.

MOHICAN Original codename for TORCH.

MULBERRY Artificial harbours deployed to support the Allied forces in Normandy. MULBERRY A supported the Americans and MULBERRY B the British.

NEPTUNE The amphibious landing element within OVERLORD.

OVERLORD The overall Allied cross-Channel invasion of France and subsequent operations.

OVERTHROW Deception plan designed to tie down the maximum German Forces in the west during TORCH. It simulated the seizing of a notional beachhead in Pas-de-Calais.

PHOENIX Reinforced concrete caisson which acted as a sunken breakwater for the MULBERRY harbours.

PLUTO Pipeline under the Ocean.

POINTBLANK Allied strategic air offensive against Germany, 1943-44.

PREMIUM Adjunct to FORTITUDE designed to reinforce the Allied threat to the Pas-de-Calais, Low Countries and Norway.

QUADRANT Allied strategic conference held at Quebec, Canada, August 1943.

QUICKSILVER Deception operation simulating large forces in Southeast England threatening the Pas-de-Calais.

RANKIN Formerly GREENBACK. RANKIN covered a weakening of German forces and morale in the West so as to make invasion possible. RANKIN B reflected a German withdrawal from Occupied Western Europe and RANKIN C an unconditional German surrender.

ROUNDHAMMER Codename for 1944 cross-Channel invasion used at the TRIDENT conference. Changed to OVERLORD at the end of the conference.

ROUND-UP Large-scale Allied assault on the Continent in 1943.

ROYAL FLUSH Deception operations in Sweden and Spain designed to tie down German troops in Norway and southern France.

RUTTER 1942 raid on Dieppe. Later changed to JUBILEE.

SESAME (1) Major raid somewhere on the coasts of Occupied Europe planned for spring 1942.

SESAME (2) Secret D-Day orders not to be opened until at sea.

SEXTANT Allied strategic conference held at Cairo, Egypt, November, December 1942.

SHARPENER See TUXEDO.

SHINGLE January 1944 landings at Anzio, Italy.

SICKLE Move of US air forces to Britain as part of BOLERO.

SKYSCRAPER Cross-Channel attack plan developed by the Combined Commanders in spring 1943.

SKYE Creation of fictitious British Fourth Army in Scotland as part of FORTITUDE NORTH.

SLEDGEHAMMER Allied landing on the Continent in 1942.

SOLO ONE Deception plan for TORCH directed at Norway.

SOLO TWO Deception plan for troops taking part in TORCH designed to make them believe that they were bound for the Middle East and would be landing at Dakar en route.

TARBRUSH Commando reconnaissances of French beaches in May 1944.

TAXABLE Airborne deception operation to simulate an invasion fleet approaching Calais on the night of 5/6 June 1944.

TIGER Force U landing exercise.

TINDALL Part of COCKADE and designed to keep German forces tied down in Norway.

TINDER Plan for a hasty Allied return to the Continent in the event of a sudden German collapse in 1942.

TITANIC Use of dummy parachutists on the night of 5/6 June 1944 to support the Allied airborne landings.

TOMBOLA Supply of fuel from tankers off Normandy to the shore.

TORCH Anglo-US landings in French North-West Africa in November 1942. Formerly GYMNAST.

TORRENT Plan for using Special Forces and French Resistance as part of the OVERLORD deception measures.

TUXEDO SHAEF Advanced Command Post at Portsmouth for D-Day. Changed to SHARPENER.

TRIDENT Allied strategic conference at Washington DC, May 1943.

VENDETTA Creation of a threat to the south of France as part of BODYGUARD.

WADHAM Threat to the Bay of Biscay. Part of COCKADE.

WETBOB Plan to secure a lodgement in the Contentin peninsula in autumn 1942.

WHALE Floating pier forming part of MULBERRY.

WIDEWING Main HQ SHAEF at Bushey Park, near Kingston-upon-Thames.

ZEPPELIN Mediterranean portion of BODYGUARD. Created threats against Bulgaria, Albania and Istria. Changed to FERDINAND in July 1944.

ALLIED

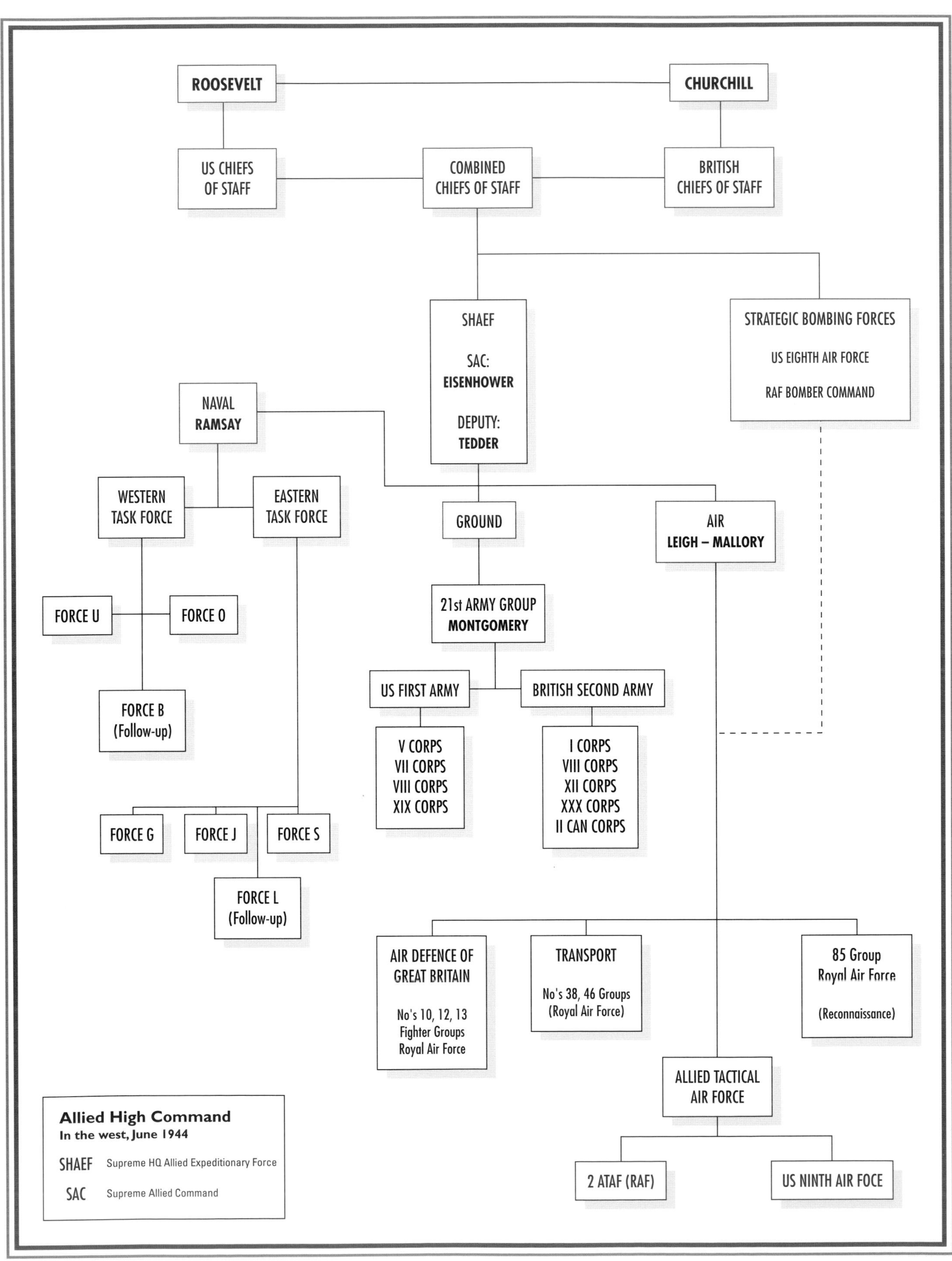
ROOSEVELT
CHURCHILL
US CHIEFS OF STAFF
COMBINED CHIEFS OF STAFF
BRITISH CHIEFS OF STAFF
SHAEF
SAC: EISENHOWER
DEPUTY: TEDDER
STRATEGIC BOMBING FORCES
US EIGHTH AIR FORCE
RAF BOMBER COMMAND
NAVAL RAMSAY
WESTERN TASK FORCE
EASTERN TASK FORCE
GROUND
AIR LEIGH – MALLORY
FORCE U
FORCE O
21st ARMY GROUP MONTGOMERY
FORCE B (Follow-up)
US FIRST ARMY
BRITISH SECOND ARMY
V CORPS
VII CORPS
VIII CORPS
XIX CORPS
I CORPS
VIII CORPS
XII CORPS
XXX CORPS
II CAN CORPS
FORCE G
FORCE J
FORCE S
FORCE L (Follow-up)
AIR DEFENCE OF GREAT BRITAIN
No's 10, 12, 13 Fighter Groups Royal Air Force
TRANSPORT
No's 38, 46 Groups (Royal Air Force)
85 Group Royal Air Force
(Reconnaissance)
ALLIED TACTICAL AIR FORCE
2 ATAF (RAF)
US NINTH AIR FOCE
Allied High Command
In the west, June 1944
SHAEF Supreme HQ Allied Expeditionary Force
SAC Supreme Allied Command

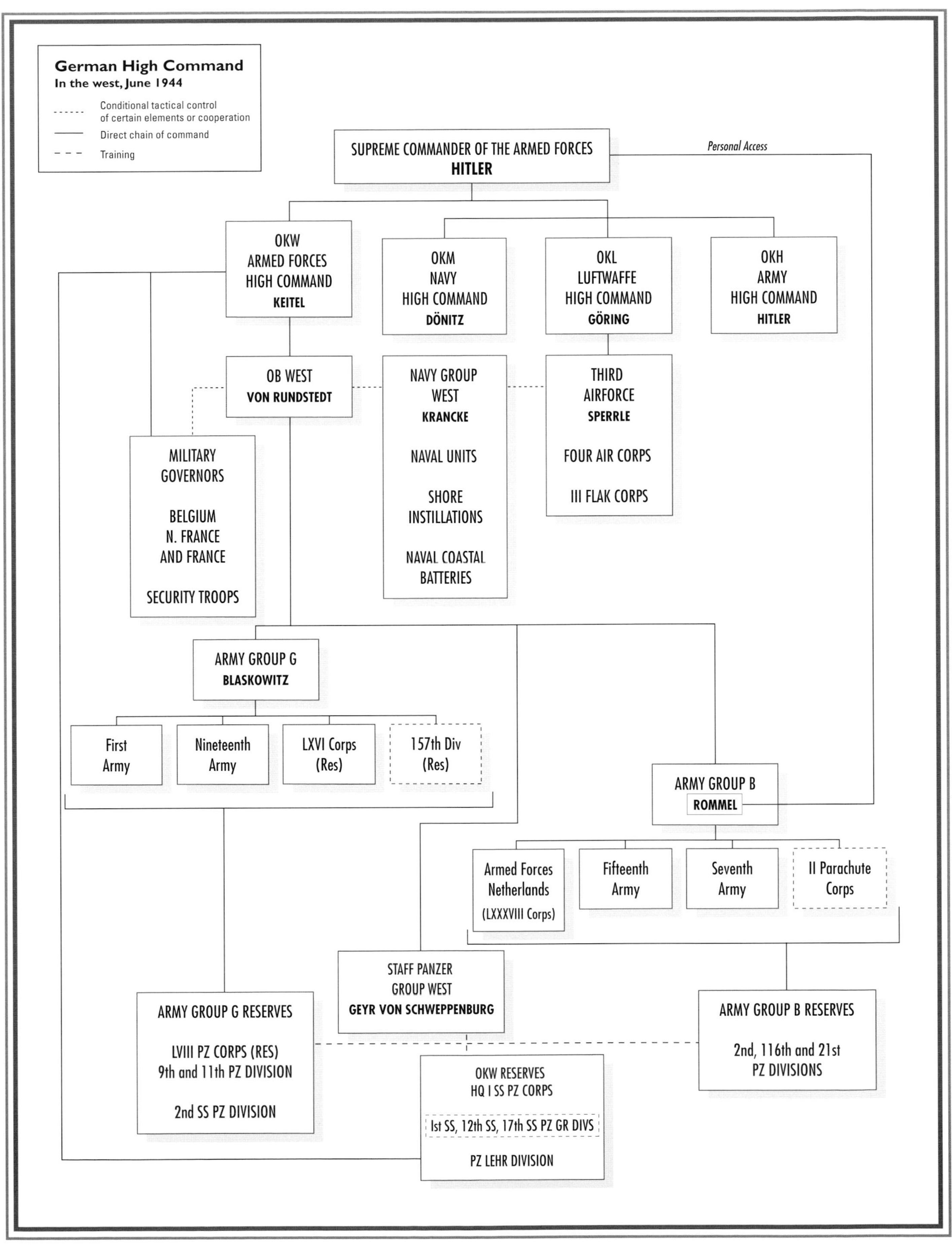
German High Command
In the west, June 1944
Conditional tactical control of certain elements or cooperation
Direct chain of command
Training
SUPREME COMMANDER OF THE ARMED FORCES
HITLER
Personal Access
OKW
ARMED FORCES
HIGH COMMAND
KEITEL
OKM
NAVY
HIGH COMMAND
DÖNITZ
OKL
LUFTWAFFE
HIGH COMMAND
GÖRING
OKH
ARMY
HIGH COMMAND
HITLER
OB WEST
VON RUNDSTEDT
NAVY GROUP
WEST
KRANCKE
NAVAL UNITS
SHORE
INSTILLATIONS
NAVAL COASTAL
BATTERIES
THIRD
AIRFORCE
SPERRLE
FOUR AIR CORPS
III FLAK CORPS
MILITARY
GOVERNORS
BELGIUM
N. FRANCE
AND FRANCE
SECURITY TROOPS
ARMY GROUP G
BLASKOWITZ
First
Army
Nineteenth
Army
LXVI Corps
(Res)
157th Div
(Res)
ARMY GROUP B
ROMMEL
Armed Forces
Netherlands
(LXXXVIII Corps)
Fifteenth
Army
Seventh
Army
II Parachute
Corps
STAFF PANZER
GROUP WEST
GEYR VON SCHWEPPENBURG
ARMY GROUP G RESERVES
LVIII PZ CORPS (RES)
9th and 11th PZ DIVISION
2nd SS PZ DIVISION
ARMY GROUP B RESERVES
2nd, 116th and 21st
PZ DIVISIONS
OKW RESERVES
HQ I SS PZ CORPS
Ist SS, 12th SS, 17th SS PZ GR DIVS
PZ LEHR DIVISION

DIVISIONS
WHICH FOUGHT IN NORMANDY

AMERICAN

1st Infantry 'The Big Red One' was a Regular division which arrived in Britain in August 1942. It landed at Oran during Torch and then went on to fight in Tunisia and Sicily. It returned to Britain in October 1943 and landed on Omaha on D-Day. It formed part of V Corps.

2nd Armored 'Hell on Wheels' was activated in July 1940. Elements of it landed at Casablanca during Torch and fought in Tunisia, but the division as a whole did not come together until the Sicily landings. It went to Britain in autumn 1943 and landed on Omaha on D+3, becoming part of V Corps.

2nd Infantry A Regular division, which arrived in Britain in October 1943. It landed on Omaha during D+1 to D+3 and joined V Corps.

3rd Armored Activated in July 1940 and crossed to Britain in September 1943. It landed in Normandy on 24 June and served in XIX and then VII Corps.

4th Armored Activated in April 1941 and crossed to Britain in December 1943. It landed in Normandy on 11 July and joined VIII Corps.

4th Infantry Activated in June 1940 and crossed to Britain in January 1944. It landed on Utah Beach on D-Day as part of VII Corps, with which it served for the whole campaign, apart from a brief spell with VIII Corps.

5th Armored Activated in October 1941 and crossed to Britain in February 1944. Arrived in Normandy on 24 July and served in XV Corps.

5th Infantry Activated in October 1939 and went to Britain in April 1942. It landed in Normandy on 9 July and joined V Corps.

6th Armored Activated in February 1942 and crossed to Britain in February 1944. It landed in Normandy on 18 July and joined VIII Corps.

7th Armored Activated in March 1942 and arrived in Britain in January 1944. It landed in Normandy on 13–14 August and joined XX Corps.

8th Infantry Activated in July 1940 and went to Britain in December 1943. It landed in Normandy on 4 July and joined VIII Corps.

9th Infantry Activated in August 1940, it took part in Torch, landing at Algiers before going on to fight in Tunisia and Sicily. It sailed to Britain in November 1943 and landed at Utah on D+4, joining VII Corps.

28th Infantry A National Guard division activated in February 1941, it arrived in Britain in October 1943. The Division landed in Normandy on 22 July and joined XIX Corps.

29th Infantry A National Guard division, which was called up for active duty in February 1941 and was known as the 'Blue and Gray' because its components had fought on both sides in the US Civil War. It arrived in Britain in October 1942 and landed at Omaha on D-Day as part of V Corps, but then joined XIX Corps.

30th Infantry A National Guard division, which was activated in September 1940. It crossed to Britain in February 1944, landing on Omaha on D+9. Apart from a very brief spell with VII Corps, it served in XIX Corps.

35th Infantry A National Guard division activated in September 1940, it did not arrive in Britain until May 1944. It landed in Normandy during 5–7 July and served in XIX and then V Corps.

79th Infantry Activated in June 1942, it crossed to Britain in April 1944. It landed on Utah during D+6–D+8, joining VII Corps and then VIII Corps.

80th Infantry Activated in July 1942, it crossed to Europe in July 1944 and landed in Normandy on 3 August, joining XV and then XX Corps.

82nd Airborne Activated in March 1942, it became an Airborne division that August. It arrived in Morocco in May 1943 and then dropped into Sicily. Elements also dropped at Salerno in September 1943. The Division left Italy for Britain in November 1943. It dropped on D-Day and served under VII and then VIII Corps before returning to Britain in mid-July.

83rd Infantry Activated in August 1942 and arrived in Britain in April 1944, it landed at Omaha on D+12 and served successively with VII, VIII, and XV Corps.

90th Infantry Activated in March 1942, crossing to Britain in April 1944. Elements landed at Utah on D-Day and the Division was complete in Normandy by D+4. It served successively in VII, VIII and XV Corps.

101st Airborne Activated in August 1943, it arrived in Britain in December 1943. It dropped on D-Day and served under VII and VIII Corps before returning to Britain in mid-July.

BRITISH

Guards Armoured Formed in June 1941 from Foot Guards battalions, it arrived in Normandy at the end of June 1944 and fought under VIII Corps.

3rd Infantry Known as the Iron Division, a name given to it by Wellington, it was a pre-war Regular division, which was commanded by Montgomery in France in 1940 and landed on Sword Beach on D-Day. Thereafter it served mainly under I Corps.

6th Airborne Formed in May 1943, it landed in Normandy on D-Day and held the eastern flank of the Allied lodgement throughout the campaign.

7th Armoured Formed in 1938 as the Mobile Division, Egypt, it became 7th Armoured in April 1940. It fought throughout the Desert Campaign, gaining its nickname the Desert Rats, and thereafter in Tunisia. It took part in the early months of the Italian campaign and returned to Britain at the end of 1943. It landed on D+1 and served mainly in VIII and XXX Corps.

11th Armoured Formed in Britain in March 1941, it landed on D+7–D+8 and fought mainly under VIII Corps.

15th (Scottish) A second-line Territorial Army division, which was reformed in May 1939. It landed in Normandy on D+8 and served under XXX and VIII Corps.

43rd (Wessex) A pre-war first-line Territorial division, which was complete in Normandy on 24 June and fought under XII Corps.

49th (West Riding) A pre-war first-line Territorial division, it took part in the April 1940 Norwegian campaign. It was then sent to garrison Iceland, returning to Britain in 1943. It was complete in Normandy by D+7 and fought mainly under XXX Corps.

50th (Northumbrian) A pre-war first-line Territorial division, which took part in the 1940 French campaign. It was subsequently sent to the Middle East, fighting from late 1941 onwards in North Africa and Tunisia. It participated in the landings on Sicily and returned to Britain in late 1943. It landed on Gold Beach on D-Day and fought mainly under XXX Corps.

51st (Highland) A pre-war first-line Territorial division, the bulk of it was forced to surrender in France in June 1940. The division was reconstituted and sent to the Middle East in 1942, taking part in the fighting from el Alamein to the end of the Tunisian campaign. It also fought in Sicily and Italy, before returning to Britain, and landed in Normandy on D+2. It served under the Canadians and I Corps.

53rd (Welsh) A pre-war first-line Territorial division, which spent 1940–42 in Northern Ireland before returning to the mainland. It landed in Normandy on 27 June, serving under XII Corps.

59th (Staffordshire) A second-line Territorial division, which landed in Normandy at the end of June and served in XII Corps.

79th Armoured Formed as an ordinary Armoured division in September 1942, its role changed in spring 1943, when it became responsible for the development and operational control of specialized armour ('the funnies'). Although its units spearheaded the landings on 6 June, it never fought as a division.

CANADIAN

2nd Infantry Re-formed at the outbreak of war, the division crossed to Britain in late August 1940, apart from one brigade, which spent the autumn in Iceland before rejoining at the end of the year. It took part in the disastrous Dieppe Raid in August 1942. The division arrived in Normandy on 7 July.

3rd Infantry Mobilized in May 1940, the division crossed to Britain in July 1941. It landed on Juno Beach on D-Day.

4th Armoured Created in Britain in January 1942 from the 4th Canadian Infantry Division, it arrived in Normandy at the end of July 1944.

FRENCH

2nd Armoured Formed in May 1943 from General Leclerc's Free French L Force, which had crossed the Libyan Desert and fought in Tunisia, it was originally called 2nd Free French Division, but was converted to an armoured division in July 1943. It then moved from North Africa to Britain and arrived in Normandy at the end of July, serving in Third US Army.

POLISH

1st Armoured Raised in February 1942 from Free Polish forces which had escaped from France in 1940. It arrived in Normandy at the end of July 1944 and fought under First Canadian Army.

GERMAN

Panzer Lehr Formed in November 1943 from Panzer demonstration units at training schools, it deployed to eastern France in February 1944. It was sent to Hungary that April, returning to France in May and deploying to the Le Mans area. It began to move to Normandy on D-Day and was complete on D+3, serving under I SS Panzer Corps.

1st SS Panzer Leibstandarte Adolf Hitler Originally formed in 1934 as Hitler's personal bodyguard, it fought in Poland as a motorized regiment and in France 1940 as a division. It served on the Eastern Front from 1941, but was transferred to northern Italy in summer 1943, where it was converted to a Panzer division. It returned to the Eastern Front winter 1943–44 and was then sent to Belgium to be reconstituted. It was finally complete in Normandy on 6 July, having begun its move from Belgium on 17 June. Served in I SS Panzer Corps.

2nd Division Formed in 1935, it took part in the Polish and French campaigns, followed by that in the Balkans in April 1941. It took part in the invasion of Russia and remained on the Eastern Front until January 1944 when it deployed to Amiens, France to refit. It arrived in Normandy in late June and was part of XLVII Panzer Corps.

2nd Parachute Formed in spring 1943 from the nucleus of 2nd Parachute Brigade, which fought in North Africa. It was posted to Brittany, but then transferred, in August 1943, to Italy. From here it went to the Eastern Front, where it fought until May 1944, when it returned to Germany to refit. It then deployed to Brittany and remained there.

2nd SS Panzer Das Reich Formed during winter 1940–1 and first saw action in the April 1941 Balkans campaign. It served on the Eastern Front 1941–42, but was sent to refit in France in summer 1942, taking part in the occupation of Vichy France that November. It then returned to the Eastern Front, but was withdrawn again to France to refit in February 1944, being sent to the Toulouse area. It began its move to Normandy on D+1, but was not complete until about D+14.

3rd Parachute Formed in the Reims area of France in late 1943, it was posted to Brittany in January 1944. On D+1 it was ordered to the Avranches area and then to St-Lô, but was not complete until D+12. It came under II Parachute Corps.

5th Parachute Formed in March 1944 at Reims, it was deployed to Rennes in May as Seventh Army reserve. On D-Day it was still not combat-ready, but one regiment was attached to 17th Panzer Grenadier Division. The remainder of the division came under LXXXIV Corps and then II Parachute Corps.

9th Panzer Formed as 4th Light Division in 1938, it fought in Poland and was then converted to a Panzer division. It took part in the May 1940 invasion of the West and the Balkans campaign the following spring. It served in Russia from the outset until January 1944, when it moved to southern France to refit. In June 1944 it was north-west of Marseilles. It was rushed to Normandy in early August, joining II SS Panzer Corps.

9th SS Panzer Hohenstaufen Organized in France in early 1943, it was sent to the Eastern Front in March 1944. It was hastily sent back to France, together with 10th SS Panzer, after D-Day and arrived in Normandy on 25 June. It was part of II SS Panzer Corps.

10th SS Panzer Frundsberg Its history was identical to 9th SS Panzer Division.

12th SS Panzer Hitlerjugend Recruited primarily from members of the Hitler Youth, it was activated as a Panzer Grenadier division in June 1943, carrying out its training in Belgium. It was converted to a Panzer division that October and moved to the Normandy area in April 1944. It formed part of I SS Panzer Corps.

16th Luftwaffe Field Formed in winter 1942–43 and sent to Holland. In late June 1944 it was sent to Normandy, joining LXXXIV Corps.

17th Luftwaffe Field Formed in 1943 as a Static division, it was initially deployed to the French Atlantic coast. In spring 1944 it was deployed east of Le Havre and joined Fifth Panzer Army in mid-August.

17th SS Panzer Grenadier Götz von Berlichingen Named after a German Middle Ages robber baron, it formed in western France in October 1943 and included not just Germans, but Belgian and Roumanian Nationalist elements as well. In June 1944 it was in the Tours area and arrived in Normandy on D+4. It served successively in II Parachute and LXXXIV Corps.

21st Division This bore no relation to its predecessor which had fought under Rommel in North Africa, although it did include some Afrika Korps veterans. It was formed in France in mid-1943 and was the only mobile division deployed close to the beaches on D-Day. It served in I SS Panzer Corps.

48th Infantry Formed in February 1944 in Belgium from 171st Reserve Division, it joined XLVII Panzer Corps in mid-August.

77th Infantry Formed in Poland in winter 1943–44 from the remnants of other formations, it moved to France in early 1944 and was stationed between the Cotentin and Brittany peninsulas as part of LXXXIV Corps.

84th Infantry Formed in Poland in February 1944 from the remains of other divisions, it was sent to the Rouen area of France in May. It joined LXXXIV Corps in early August.

85th Infantry Formed in the rear area of Fifteenth Army in France from various disbanded and newly formed units in February 1944, it joined LXXXI Corps (Fifth Panzer Army) in early August.

89th Infantry Formed in Norway in February 1944, it was posted to Le Havre on the French Channel coast in June. It moved to Normandy at the end of July, joining II Parachute Corps.

91st Airlanding Raised in early 1944 from Reserve Army personnel, it was trained in the anti-airborne role and was deployed to the base of the Cotentin peninsula in May 1944. It was part of LXXXIV Corps.

116th Panzer Formed as 16th Motorized (later Panzer Grenadier) Division in late summer 1940, it fought in the Balkans in April 1941 and then served on the Eastern Front. In early 1944 the remnants were withdrawn to France and, absorbing 173rd Reserve Panzer Division, became 116th Panzer Division. It was deployed to the Pas- de-Calais and was sent to Normandy on 20 July, joining XLVII Panzer Corps.

243rd Infantry Formed in August 1943, using remnants of 387th Infantry Division, it was originally designated a Static division. It was sent to Normandy that October and was given a degree of mobility. It defended the Carentan-Montebourg-Bricquebec-Lessay sector and was part of LXXXIV Corps.

265th Infantry Formed in July 1943 and was a Static division, which was sent to Brittany the following month, where it joined XXV Corps. Apart from one battle group, which joined LXXXIV Corps in July, it remained in Brittany.

266th Infantry Also formed in July 1943 as a Static division and, like 265th Infantry Division, sent to Brittany that August. It included a sizeable number of Russians and other Ostlander and remained in the peninsula, although one battle group at St-Malo came under II Parachute Corps in July 1944.

271st Infantry Initially formed in France in summer 1940 as a Static division, it was disbanded that autumn. It reformed in December 1943, drawing from the disbanded 137th Division, and deployed to Holland. It moved to Montpellier in southern France in March 1944 and joined II SS Panzer Corps in Normandy that July. It subsequently served in LXXIV Corps.

272nd Infantry Like the 271st, it had a brief pre-existence in 1940 and was re-formed in December 1943 in Belgium. In April 1944 it was sent to the Franco-Spanish border and arrived in Normandy on 13 July, joining I SS Panzer Corps. It subsequently transferred to LXXXIV Corps.

275th Infantry Formed as a cadre in western France in January 1944, it deployed to Brittany the following month, where it received Reserve units from Poland and southern France. It was partially motorized in spring 1944 and organized as battle groups. One of these was deployed to Normandy on D-Day, but was not complete under the command of 17th Panzer Grenadier Division until D+7. The remainder moved to Normandy during the middle part of July, coming under LXXXIV Corps.

276th Infantry Briefly in existence in 1940, it was re-formed in December 1943 and sent to Dax, south-western France, the following month to complete its training. It was sent to Normandy in mid-June, joining XLVII Panzer Corps and, later, II Parachute Corps.

277th Infantry It had a brief pre-existence in summer 1940 and was reformed as a cadre in 1942. Having been brought up to strength, it went to Croatia in December 1943 and to Narbonne in southern France in February 1944. It arrived in Normandy in mid-June, joining II SS Panzer Corps. Later it served under II Parachute Corps.

326th Infantry Formed at Narbonne, France, in December 1942, it became part of Fifteenth Army reserve in Febuary 1944. It joined II Parachute Corps in Normandy on 21 July.

331st Infantry Formed in Austria in late 1941, it was sent to the Eastern Front in February 1942. It returned to Germany to refit in February 1944 and was posted to the Pas-de-Calais that May. It joined LXXIV Corps (Fifth Panzer Army) in August 1944.

343rd Infantry Formed as a Static division in October 1942, it went to France the following spring. It was located in the Brest area, where it remained.

344th Infantry Formed as a Static division in the Bordeaux area of France in October 1942, and guarded a sector in the Bay of Biscay. It joined LXXIV Corps (Fifth Panzer Army) in August 1944.

346th Infantry Formed in France in October 1942, it was stationed in Brittany until February 1944, when it was transferred to the Le Havre sector. It joined LXXXIV Corps in early July.

352nd Infantry Formed from elements of 268th and 321st Infantry Divisions in October 1943, it was posted to the eastern part of the Cotentin peninsula in January 1944. It covered the Omaha-Gold sector and came under II Parachute Corps.

353rd Infantry Formed from cadres of 328th Division in October 1943, it was sent to Brittany the following month. It was ordered to Normandy on D+4, arriving by D+12 and joining II Parachute Corps.

363rd Infantry Formed from elements of 339th Division in Poland in October 1943, it deployed to Denmark in April 1944. That June it transferred to Belgium and then joined LXXXIV Corps in Normandy in July.

708th Infantry Formed in May 1941, it was sent to the Bordeaux area of France the following month. It joined II Parachute Corps in Normandy at the end of July 1944.

709th Infantry Formed in May 1941 as a Static division and sent to Brittany the following month. In December 1942 it was moved to Cherbourg and on D-Day covered the east coast of the Cotentin peninsula down to Carentan as part of LXXXIV Corps.

711th Infantry Formed as a Static division in April 1941, it was sent to north-eastern France that August. In December 1941 it moved to Rouen and then, in spring 1944, to the Deauville sector. It joined LXXXVI in Normandy in early July.

716th Infantry Formed in May 1941 as a Static division, it was sent to Normandy the following month. In February 1942 it was transferred to Belgium, but returned to Normandy that June, deploying to the Caen area under LXXXIV Corps. It was still there on D-Day and came under command of I SS Panzer Corps.

Further Reading

There have been literally millions of words written on D-Day and the subsequent campaign. The works cited below represent some of the more worthwhile studies.

Ambrose, Stephen E. *The Supreme Commander: The War Years of General Dwight D. Eisenhower.* Doubleday, New York, 1969

Barnett, Correlli. *Engage the Enemy More Closely: The Royal Navy in the Second World War,* Hodder & Stoughton, London, and Norton, New York, 1991

Bennett, Ralph. *Ultra in the West: The Normandy Campaign 1944-1945,* Hutchinson, London, 1979 and Scribner, New York, 1980

Blumenson, Martin. *The Patton Papers 1940-1945,* Houghton Mifflin, Boston, 1974

Blumenson, Martin. *Breakout and Pursuit* Office of the Chief of Military History, US Army, Government Printing Office, Washington DC, 1961

Buffetaut, Yves. *D-Day Ships: The Allied Invasion Fleet, June 1944,* Conway Maritime Press, London, 1994

Chandler, David G. & Collins, James Lawton Jr. *The D-Day Encyclopedia,* Helicon, Oxford, and Simon & Schuster, New York, 1994

D'Este, Carlo *Decision in Normandy* Collins, London and Dutton, New York, 1983

Ellis, L. F. *Victory in the West: The Battle of Normandy,* HMSO, London, 1962

Fraser, David. *Knight's Cross: A Life of Field Marshal Erwin Rommel* HarperCollins, London and New York, 1993

Hamilton, Nigel. *Monty: Master of the Battlefield 1942-1944* Hamish Hamilton, London, and McGraw Hill, New York, 1983

Harrison, Gordon A. *Cross-Channel Attack* Office of the Chief of Military History, US Army, Government Printing Office, Washington DC, 1951

Hastings, Max. *Overlord: D-Day and the Battle for Normandy,* Michael Joseph, London, and Simon & Schuster, New York, 1984

Keegan, John. *Six Armies in Normandy,* Jonathan Cape, London, and Viking, New York, 1982

Lacey-Johnson, Lionel. *Pointblank and Beyond,* Airlife, Shrewsbury, 1991

Messenger, Charles. *The Last Prussian: A Biography of Field Marshal Gerd von Rundstedt 1875-1953,* Brassey's (UK), London, 1991

Morgan, Frederick E. *Overture to Overlord,* Doubleday, London and New York, 1950

Morison, Samuel Eliot. *History of United States Naval Operations in World War II: The Invasion of France and Germany, 1944-January 1945* Vol 11, Oxford University Press and Little, Brown, Boston, 1957

Reynolds, Michael. *Steel Inferno: I SS Panzer Corps in Normandy,* Spellmount, Staplehurst, Kent, 1997

Stacey, C. P. *Official History of the Canadian Army in World War II: The Victory Campaign: The Operations in North-West Europe, 1944-1945* Vol 3, Queen's Printer, Ottawa, 1960

Weigley, Russell F. *Eisenhower's Lieutenants: The Campaigns of France and Germany, 1944-1945,* Sidgwick & Jackson, London, and Indiana University Press, Bloomington, 1981

Wilmot, Chester. *The Struggle for Europe,* Collins, London, 1953 and Harper, New York, 1952

Wynn, Humphrey & Young, Susan. *Prelude to Overlord,* Airlife, London, 1983

Index

ACKNOWLEDGMENTS

Pictures are repoduced by permission of, or have been provided by the following:

Bundesarchive: p. 6, 48, 121, 138, 141

Charles Messenger: p. 21, 69, 94, 152

Corbis: p. 40, 73, 106

Hulton Getty: p. 2, 6, 8, 10, 22, 24, 29, 34, 35, 43, 44, 50, 53, 54, 74, 77, 78, 79, 87, 98, 100, 103, 104, 105, 108, 114, 118, 122, 124, 126, 128, 129, 132, 134, 145, 155, 156, 158, 160, 161, 162, 163, 165

Popperphoto: p. 6, 42, 67, 108, 112

Private sources: p. 13, 16, 18, 39, 46, 65, 75, 91, 116, 142

Nederlands Instituut voor Oorlogsdocumentatie: p. 85, 111, 134

Illustrations: Peter A. B. Smith

Design: Malcolm Swanston

Typesetting: Francesca Bridges, Jeanne Radford

Cartography: Peter Gamble, Isabelle Lewis, Jeanne Radford, Malcolm Swanston, Jonathan Young

Picture research: Peter Phillips, Michèle Sabèse

Editor: Christine Harris

The Furniture of GUSTAV STICKLEY

History* Techniques* Projects

Joseph J. Bavaro

Thomas L. Mossman

New York London Toronto Sydney Tokyo Singapore

PRENTICE HALL PRESS
15 Columbus Circle
New York, NY 10023

Library of Congress Cataloging-in-Publication Data

Bavaro, Joseph J.
The furniture of Gustav Stickley.

Bibliography: p. 171
Includes index.
1. Stickley, Gustav, 1858–1942. 2. Furniture-making. 3. Furniture industry and trade—United States—Biography. I. Mossman, Thomas L. II. Title.
TS805.S74B38 684.1′042 81-13082
ISBN 0-13-345190-9 AACR2

Designed by Loudan Enterprises

Manufactured in the United States of America

10 9 8 7 6 5 4 3 2 1

First Prentice Hall Press Edition

Quotations from *The Craftsman* appear on the following pages:
page 6: Volume 7, p. 53
page 6: Volume 7, p. 720
page 20: Volume 1, November 1901, Foreword
page 21: Volume 1, October 1901, Foreword
page 34: Volume 29, p. 53
pages 34–35: Volume 7, p. 54 and p. 60
page 37: Volume 4, p. 59
pages 60–62: Volume 8, pp. 524–529, 533–534
pages 84–85: Volume 9, pp. 123–125
page 88: Volume 17, p. 336 and pp. 338–339
page 89: Volume 8, p. 85

Quotations from *Chips From The Craftsman Workshops* appear on the following pages:
page 17: Volume 1, pp. 2–3
page 18: Volume 1, pp. 8–9

Quotations from *Craftsman Homes* appear on the following pages:
pages 87–88: 1909, p. 162
page 88: 1909, p. 164

Contents

Acknowledgments

We would like to express our sincere appreciation to those who were especially helpful to us in the preparation of this book. Their contributions of time, effort, and understanding are greatly appreciated, and without them, this book would not have been possible: a special thanks to Susan Lagler Mossman, whose skill and patience were invaluable, and to Mr. and Mrs. James Marrin for their generosity, support, and the loan of many Arts and Crafts items. We would also like to thank Mrs. Ben Wiles, Sr., Mrs. Louise Stickley, Mr. and Mrs. Alfred J. Audi, Eve MacCloskey (word processer), Kathy Slinkard, and Randell Makinson for their contributions to our effort.

Introduction

This book is intended as a tribute to Gustav Stickley, a pioneer in contemporary design and creator of the first truly American furniture, known throughout the world as Craftsman. A hardworking, dedicated man, Stickley achieved success in the early 1900s as the leader of the Arts and Crafts movement in America.

Were Stickley alive today, he would be immensely pleased with the increasing recognition accorded his furniture in the history of American design. But he might also be dismayed that Craftsman furniture is now so scarce and highly prized for its antique value that it exists largely in private and museum collections rather than in the homes of the working people for whom he intended it. Single pieces have commanded prices in the thousands at recent auctions; yet they were originally created for

> . . . the real Americans . . . the great middle class, possessed of moderate culture and moderate material resources. For them, art should not be allowed to remain as a subject of consideration for critics. It should be brought to their homes and become for them a part and parcel of their daily lives.

In this book, we have included an overview of developments in the arts to which Stickley fell heir, his personal story, and his philosophy to provide an understanding of the man, his accomplishments, and the times in which he lived and worked. Also included are instructions for building nine pieces of Craftsman furniture, presented with as much attention, authenticity, and detail as Stickley himself devoted to their original creation. In offering these projects, we trust that others will find, as we did, the truth of Stickley's words:

> When we come to make things ourselves and because they are needed, instead of depending upon the department store to furnish them, we shall not only find more pleasure in making them, but we shall also take more pleasure in possessing them.

1. The Arts in America

At the Philadelphia Exhibition of 1876, the world gathered to help the United States celebrate one hundred years of independence. But those who attended the centennial festivities found independence of an industrial and political nature only, with cultural dependency apparent in the numerous poorly crafted reproductions of European taste. These ranged from copies of Greek and Roman art to Byzantine, Italian Renaissance, baroque and Louis XV reproductions. The popularity of objects based upon historical style resulted in part from an American need to identify with long-established wealth, status, and "culture."

Beaux arts furniture, with its stately, majestic style that stressed objectivity and the pursuit of formal perfection, had centuries of aristocratic and aesthetic precedence in Europe. In America, however, beaux arts pieces became objects taken out of context to satisfy a culturally dependent society. Manufacturers made little, if any, attempt to break this dependency. Inferior reproduction of furniture with which most Americans had little direct contact and, therefore, no basis of comparison, was much too profitable for them. American buyers could not know that these

1–1. Furniture display of Gardner and Company, Philadelphia Exhibition of 1876. (The Free Library of Philadelphia)

reproductions were mere shadows of the originals in terms of craftsmanship.

Two styles vied with beaux arts classicism for domination of America in the late nineteenth century: art nouveau, a European style adopted by artists seeking new forms as well as different ways to employ traditional ideas; and the Arts and Crafts movement, with British roots linked to the ideas of John Ruskin and William Morris.

Art nouveau saw nature as a source of inspiration rather than as a catalog of forms to be reproduced. Flowers and vines caught in the movement of opening and growing, insects in their immense complexity, and the tender grace and sensuousness of the female figure formed the vital and diverse base from which art nouveau flourished. The movement was adopted by a few architects and designers in America. Its popularity in the United States, though minimal and scattered, can be traced to the work of Louis C. Tiffany and Louis Sullivan, both of whom had studied in France.

1–2. Lamp, glass-and-bronze picture frame, and glassware from Tiffany Studios, 1900–1910. (Private collection)

The efforts of Tiffany and Sullivan and the few other art nouveau proponents in America posed no real threat to the supremacy of the beaux arts tradition. Their work, though familiar to many Americans, was limited in its popularity by its prohibitive cost and its connection to the work of European designers who used erotic imagery freely. The American public was still deeply immersed in puritanism and rarely discussed such controversial topics, let alone displayed objects in their homes with design motifs giving pictorial reality to them.

Art nouveau did receive acceptance in advertising and other graphic media, however. People could enjoy these public images without taking responsibility for their existence. Posters and advertisements that employed the flowing exoticism of art nouveau abounded. In fact, the highest paid commercial artist of his day, Will H. Bradley, was often referred to as the "American Beardsley." One of Bradley's greatest contributions to American design was a unique synthesis of the decorative art nouveau and the more functional Arts and Crafts. He developed a modular type system for the creation of border designs for title pages and advertisements. With this system, decorative borders, a hallmark of art nouveau, could be created by any skilled printer who, rather than hiring an illustrator, could assemble the modules of border type into the correct size and shape.

Bradley, an accomplished designer in the art nouveau style, became a convert to the American Arts and Crafts movement, exemplifying the relative strength of Arts and Crafts in America and its real challenge to the beaux arts tradition. In contrast to art nouveau, the Arts and Crafts move-

ment presented reality instead of fantasy, simplicity instead of complexity, economy instead of extravagance, and distinctly native design instead of European idealism. These differences were well suited to existing middle-class values in America. The Arts and Crafts movement transformed the middle class into a desirable appellation rather than a position to escape by false identification with the upper class.

The American Arts and Crafts movement was inspired by the British movement of the same name, particularly by the writings and work of John Ruskin and William Morris. John Ruskin (1819–1900) advocated a renaissance of medieval arts. An Oxford education and an inherited fortune provided him with the freedom to travel throughout Europe promoting his ideas. The squalid working and living conditions of industrialized England's working class fed the revolutionary fire of Ruskin's words. Eventually he founded the Guild of St. George, an organization of artisans who lived and worked in a cooperative effort. Printing presses and workshops in various trades were reminiscent of the medieval cottage industries idealized by Ruskin. These ventures had a widespread effect upon English taste and became an integral part of changing intellectual movements.

A disciple of Ruskin, William Morris (1834–1896) was also influenced by a group of painters known as the Pre-Raphaelite brotherhood. Beginning as a group of talented young intellectuals who found inspiration in medieval models (those created before Raphael's time), the brotherhood included such artistic geniuses as Edward Burne-Jones, John E. Millais, William Holman Hunt, Dante Gabriel Rossetti, and Ford Madox Brown. William Morris's goal, inherited from Ruskin, was a golden age where artists would replace industrialists and hand labor would bring workers the pleasure lacking in mass mechanical production as well as material reward for their work. In turn, the joy of labor would be evident in the item made by hand.

1–4. John Ruskin (1819–1900). (The Free Library of Philadelphia)

1–5. William Morris (1834–1896). (*The Craftsman*, vol. VII, p. 413)

1–3. Interior and furniture design by Will H. Bradley, 1896, shows use of both art nouveau and Arts and Crafts styles. Designed for the *Ladies' Home Journal*.

Morris, trained in architecture, was drawn to other artistic pursuits through his friendship with Burne-Jones and Rossetti. Eventually he merged his talent and philosophy into the creation of Red House, his home outside London, where every element was designed to meet a functional necessity instead of simply a historic tradition. The house was constructed by hand, of handmade material, and furnished with Morris-designed furniture and other articles. Soon after, Morris opened a shop in London where furniture, decorative glass, pottery, textiles, paintings, and sculpture were displayed and sold. All objects shared a utilitarian and aesthetic purpose, and all were designed by Morris or his associates, Rossetti and Burne-Jones. As the popularity of the items grew, Morris's crusade for prestige for the handmade object expanded. Workshops were established for the production of wallpaper and hand-loomed fabric.

1–6. *St. George's Cabinet*, Morris and Company, 1861. Decorated by William Morris. (The Victoria and Albert Museum, London)

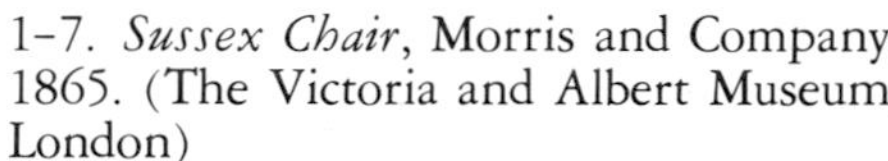

1–7. *Sussex Chair*, Morris and Company, 1865. (The Victoria and Albert Museum, London)

1–8. *The Backgammon Players*, Morris and Company, 1862. Decorated by Edward Burne-Jones. (The Metropolitan Museum of Art, Rogers Fund, 1926)

Morris became increasingly socialistic in his teachings, and turned much energy to the Kelmscott Press, which produced fine, handcrafted books.

The American Arts and Crafts movement borrowed much from the English movement. Some American designers totally embraced the ideals of their British predecessors. Establishing themselves in the medieval guild philosophy, they accepted only those objects conceived and executed by the same individual, without assistance from machinery. Other designers felt this strict adherence to the philosophy of Morris and Ruskin limited the availability of their products, which could not be made at a price affordable to the average middle-class consumer. These designers rejected the implicit elitism of Morris and Ruskin and sought a solution to bring their work back into the grasp of the average working American.

The answer was the recognition of technology as an ally instead of an enemy. Designs were analyzed. Those parts that could best be made by hand were executed by hand, and those that could be made by machine without sacrificing quality of craftsmanship were executed by machine. This approach meant more pieces could be produced daily by artisans and, therefore, a larger portion of society could be served.

Simple, honest, and functional products of the Arts and Crafts movement found their way into the daily lives of many Americans by the early 1900s. Exhibitions were held to display the work of designers all over the country.

1-9. *The Woodpecker Tapestry*, William Morris, 1885. (William Morris Gallery, Walthamstow, England)

Magazines ran pictorial articles showing the work of selected craftsmen, bringing the philosophy of the movement into the homes of the people it was meant to reach.

Functional objects of everyday life—lamps, candlesticks, bookends, fireplace tools and screens, cooking utensils, pottery, textiles, windows, and furniture—were constructed of various materials. Many designers limited their production to specific household items, using only the materials to which they had apprenticed themselves in the classic medieval tradition. Also in line with this tradition, craftsmen would affix their signature to an object in the form of a mark, signifying their personal attention to its design and craftsmanship.

One such craftsman/designer was Dirk Van Erp, a Dutch coppersmith who settled in the San Francisco area in 1886. He supported himself by working in the shipyards as a metalsmith and in his leisure time, formed objects from discarded brass shell-casings. In time, these became popular among visitors to the docks and led to his opening a copper shop in Oakland, California. Because he adhered to his traditional appren-

1–12. Signature of Roycraft Enterprises, East Aurora, NY.

xxx] HOUSE BEAUTIFU

R. R. Jarvie
DESIGNS AND MAKES
Candlesticks & Lanterns
and other good things in Metal for interior decoration............

LANTERN
Like Cut
Iron and Horn
$20.00. Others
$7.50 and up....
CANDLESTICKS
Brass, Copper
Bronze, $5.00

Permanent Green Finish, $5.00 & $6.00

Mr. Jarvie's works are NOT for sale in Department Stores

Catalog had for the asking

608 W. Congress Street, CHICAGO

1–10. Magazine advertisement for R.R. Jarvie, *The House Beautiful*, 1902. Advertisements and magazine articles brought the work and philosophy of the Arts and Crafts movement to the attention of those for whom it was primarily intended: the working middle class.

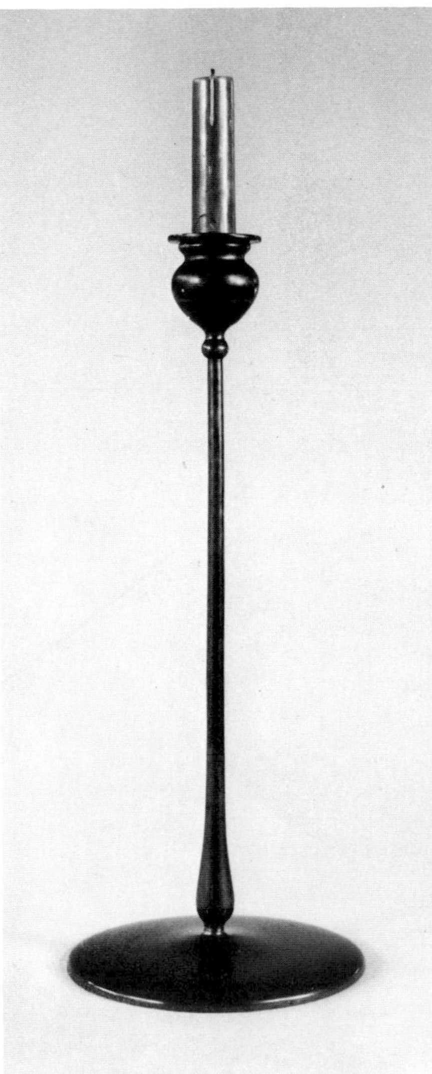

1–11. Candlestick, R.R. Jarvie, c. 1904. The Jarvie shop was a well-known Chicago manufacturer of candlesticks and lanterns, examples of the typical functional objects created by Arts and Crafts designers. (Private collection)

1–13. Signature of Van Briggle Pottery Company, Colorado Springs, CO.

1–14. Signature of Dirk Van Erp, Oakland, CA.

ticeship training, Van Erp maintained that every object produced by his shop should be made solely by hand. Although he had a very limited formal design education, he was gifted with a natural sensitivity for metal and created forms perfectly suited to that material. Lamps, bowls, vases, plates, bookends, desk sets, and other hand-wrought pieces were the products of his professional activity, which spanned approximately twenty years.

1-15. Copper lamps with mica shades, Dirk Van Erp, c. 1915. (Private collection)

1-16. Copper bowl, book cover, and candlestick, Dirk Van Erp, c. 1913. (Private collection)

Elbert Hubbard was another individual who achieved tremendous success in the Arts and Crafts era, largely by virtue of his flamboyant nature and talent in salesmanship. In fact, his fame was such that his name continues to be synonymous with American Arts and Crafts.

Having made his fortune as a soap salesman, Hubbard became enamoured of socialism and the revival of the guilds. In 1893 he visited William Morris's Kelmscott Press in England and returned home to establish a guild known as the Roycrofters, which engaged in the art of bookmaking. Stock in the corporation was owned by the workers, making this a true cooperative. The culmination of Hubbard's efforts several years later included the construction of a medieval manor in East Aurora, New York, complete with a workers' community. Roycroft workshops were a great success, producing a variety of Arts and Crafts items, including books, metalwork, decorative items, and a line of Roycroft furniture. Although Hubbard and his wife died with the sinking of the *Lusitania* in 1915, the Roycroft establishment continued successfully for a number of years thereafter.

Many potteries and tile companies were in operation during this period, producing what was called art pottery. Rookwood Pottery of Cincinnati, Ohio; Grueby Faience and Tile Company of Boston, Massachusetts; Fulper Pottery Company of Flemington, New Jersey; Paul Revere Pottery of Boston, Massachusetts; S. A. Weller of Zanesville, Ohio; Marblehead Pottery of Marblehead,

Massachusetts; and Van Briggle Pottery Company of Colorado Springs, Colorado; were some of the most notable examples. For the most part, these companies were started by craftspeople with an interest in ceramics and glazes in the French and oriental tradition. They filtered these interests through the British craft guild philosophy of William Morris and added highlights of their native American culture. The synthesis of these influences gave American art pottery its characteristic and unique aesthetic elements—simple, incised, hand-decorated images of plant and animal forms emerging from the body of the object, which was usually one color (though sometimes detailed in contrasting colors) covered with a heavy layer of matte glaze that softened the contours of the carved or built-up surface.

All the objects produced during the Arts and Crafts movement were designed for the enhancement of man's environment. This living space, whether home or office, was conceived and executed with the same concerns of honesty to material, simplicity of form, and practicality of function characteristic of pottery, furniture, and metalcraft of the period. In architecture, this philosophy was most successfully applied by Charles and Henry Greene, two brothers whose work epitomizes Arts and Crafts ideals at their highest level.

The mature Greene and Greene style developed gradually through periods influenced by exposure to the interiors of William Morris, adaptations of the Swiss mountain chalet, and the motifs and structure of Japanese architecture. Their love of oriental architecture, with its emphasis on horizontal lines and simple floor plans, combined with the local Californian, shingled bungalow style, produced a series of homes that reflected the Arts and Crafts philosophy carried to its most uncompromised state.

The Greenes believed in creating a totally designed environment. They determined the needs of their client and then formulated a design concept that encom-

1–17. Hammered copper bookends, Roycroft, c. 1910. (Private collection)

1–18. Art pottery. Left to right: Rookwood, Marblehead, Paul Revere, Fulper, and Grueby; 1902–1915. (Private collection)

1–19. Robert R. Blacker house, designed by Charles and Henry Greene, 1907–1909.

passed the home, site, and furnishings. The structure of the house, its joints and motifs, were repeated in appropriate scale in each piece of furniture, rug, light fixture, and accessory for the house. Craftsmen were hired to work in various media under the close scrutiny of the Greenes, each contributing to the project their special skills and reflecting the Greenes' uncompromising philosophy.

Furniture design was an important part of the Arts and Crafts revolution in America, and its true leader was Gustav Stickley, creator of the Craftsman style. Simply designed, functional, "democratic" pieces in native woods (especially oak), remarkable for their excellent craftsmanship and natural finish, were painstakingly designed by Stickley. In his magazine, *The Craftsman*, begun in 1901, Stickley expounded his personal philosophy and brought to the public his revolutionary furniture designs as well as the work of his contemporaries in what he termed the "Craftsman Movement."

By 1904, the Arts and Crafts movement had spread across most of America. Its popularity can be attributed to many factors, foremost among them the public exposure provided by its self-appointed leader and spokesman, Gustav Stickley.

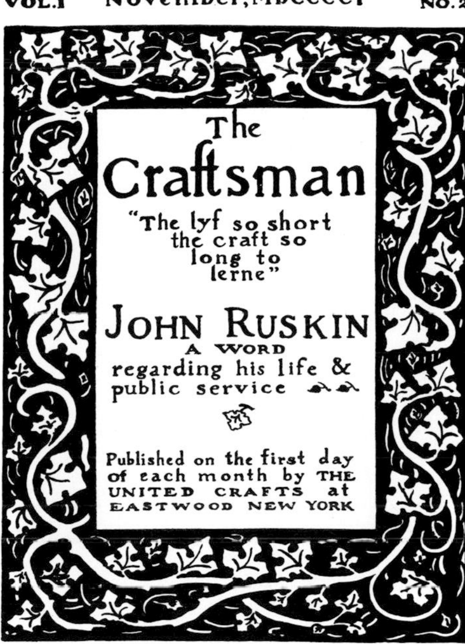

VOL.I November, MDCCCCI NO.2

The Craftsman

"The lyf so short the craft so long to lerne"

JOHN RUSKIN

A WORD regarding his life & public service

Published on the first day of each month by THE UNITED CRAFTS at EASTWOOD NEW YORK

Price 20 cents the copy

1–20. Cover of *The Craftsman*, November, 1901. This issue was devoted to John Ruskin. (Private collection)

2. Gustav Stickley—The Craftsman

In the small town of Osceola, Wisconsin, on March 9, 1857, a son was born to Leopold and Barbara Stoeckel; Gustav (originally spelled with a final *e*) was the first of eleven children. Leopold Stickley (the family name was later Americanized) was a farmer and stonemason, providing for his large family by hard labor in the fields and the building trade. His eldest son had to start working at age twelve to help support the family. Apprenticed as a stonemason, Gustav recalled that he

> had worked as a stone mason from the stage of mixing and carrying mortar up to that of cutting and laying the stone. It was heavy and tedious labor, much too hard for a boy of my age, and being put to it so early gave me an intense dislike for it. . . . I have always felt that it is to this I owe my immediate and lasting delight in working in the comparatively soft and yielding wood, and my quick appreciation of its qualities—an appreciation that has made possible all that I have been able to do.

Within a few years, Gustav's father abandoned the family, and Gustav took on the responsibility of looking after his mother and ten young brothers and sisters. Leaving school in the eighth grade was a bitter disappointment to him, but he worked hard, cutting and hauling wood to market, looking after the farm, and working as a mason. His early experience working with his hands, making farm implements and household items for the family, laid the foundation for his lifelong dedication to the recognition of handcrafts as noble and worthy pursuits.

When Gustav was sixteen, his mother accepted the offer of her brother, Schuyler C. Brandt, to join him in Pennsylvania. The family moved in 1874 to the town of Brandt, where Schuyler owned a furniture factory. Gustav was employed by his uncle and accompanied him on peddling jaunts around the countryside, selling brooms and ironing boards. He also worked in the factory, where plain wooden and cane-seated chairs were manufactured.

To work with wood in this modest plant was undoubtedly a great relief to a boy who had spent so much of his childhood in heavy labor under the shadow of tremendous responsibility. He described these years with his uncle as the time from which "I can date my love for working in wood and my appreciation of the beauty and interest to be found in its natural color, texture, and grain . . . ."

Stickley also resumed his education by reading in his uncle's library. The works of John Ruskin and Thomas Carlyle were well represented, and he became especially interested in Ruskin, and later, logically, in William Morris.

By the age of twenty-one, Stickley was manager and foreman of the Brandt Chair Company. He was experienced in woodworking, steeped in Ruskin's philosophy, and full of youth and vigor; he was ready to combine these influences into independent action. On September 12, 1883, Gustav married Eda Simmons of Susquehanna, and the next year he and two younger brothers, Charles and Albert, opened a wholesale and retail furniture business in Binghamton, New York. Stickley Brothers sold Brandt chairs and period reproduction furniture made in Grand Rapids, the furniture-manufacturing capital in Michigan.

2-1. Gustav Stickley, the Craftsman (1857–1942).

Business was poor at first, and though the brothers employed a uniquely humorous advertising campaign, they were struggling.

An offer of financial support came if Stickley Brothers would manufacture in Binghamton and, according to Stickley:

> . . . the story of how we did this is really the story of how I came to undertake handmade furniture. Before any capital would be put into the concern, it was necessary to show that we were actually manufacturing, and we had no money to buy machinery. I went to a maker of broom-handles who had a good turning-lathe which he used only a part of the time. I hired the use of this, and with it blocked out the plainer parts of some very simple chairs made after the "Shaker" model. The rest of them I made by hand, with the aid of a few simple and inexpensive machines which were placed in the loft of the store. . . . The wood in shape was dried in the sun on the tin roof of the building. The very primitiveness of this equipment, made necessary by lack of means, furnished what was really a golden opportunity to break away from the monotony of commercial forms, and I turned my attention to reproducing by hand some of the simplest and best models of the old Colonial, Windsor and other plain chairs and to a study of this period as a foundation for original work along the same lines.

Stickley had visited Shaker communities, and Shaker furniture was known in the area since it had been exhibited at the Philadelphia Exhibition of 1876. These simple chairs produced by Stickley Brothers were a refreshing change from the heavy, overly ornamented parlor suites of the preceding decade, and soon became quite popular. Other manufacturers began to produce similar products but with a greater use of machinery and little attention to detail, an aspect which Stickley felt so important to the integrity of the pieces. Imitators added novelties and ornamentation to make their chairs distinctive, but these were so poorly done and so out of keeping with the original simplicity of the designs that Stickley was disgusted with the results of the trend he had started. This experience was to repeat itself throughout Stickley's career.

2-2. Mrs. Eda Simmons Stickley (18??–1919)

In 1888 Stickley left Stickley Brothers, though it continued as a sales operation in Binghamton under his brothers, Charles, Albert, and George, who had joined the firm. Always independent in nature, Gustav struck out in several directions. He became the vice-president of the Binghamton Street Railway, a pioneer in electrically equipped trolley transportation. He also supervised the workshops of the Auburn Prison, and he and his family moved to Auburn. But the furniture business was thoroughly ingrained in the man, and while working at Auburn, he began setting up a business in Syracuse to sell and manufacture furniture.

In 1893, leaving his family in Auburn, he took a room at the new Yates Hotel in Syracuse to finish plans for the new business, to be located on Clinton Street. He and his partner called themselves the Stickley-Simonds Company. This brief stay at the Yates marked the introduction of one of the most influential friends in Stickley's life, for Dr. Irene Sar-

2-3. Shaker furniture grouping (The Shaker Museum, Old Chatham, New York; Photo by Louis H. Frohman)

gent also roomed at the hotel. A professor of Romance languages at Syracuse University and a critic of art and architecture, Dr. Sargent taught Stickley French and helped to further his interest in European artistic developments, which were to have a great influence upon him.

Within the year Stickley moved his family to Syracuse. Work was progressing on the downtown shop and on the workshops, which occupied twenty-eight acres of land in nearby Eastwood, a suburb of Syracuse. Two brothers, Leopold and J. George, came to work with Gustav at Stickley-Simonds; after a few years, they quit and started their own company in Fayetteville, outside of Syracuse.

The first furniture produced by Stickley-Simonds was reproduction Windsor, Chippendale, and other simple chairs, much as Stickley had manufactured in Binghamton. In 1898 Simonds left the partnership and Stickley visited Europe. With his newly learned French, childhood German, and background from reading and discussions of trends in European arts with Dr. Sargent, he planned to witness firsthand the art nouveau and Arts and Crafts styles. In France he met Samuel Bing, Lalique, and other leaders of the art nouveau movement at Bing's Maison l'art nouveau and purchased samples of metalwork, glass, ceramics, textiles, and furniture. He also visited the masters of the Arts and Crafts movement in England—Ashbee, Voysee, and Lethaby—and collected examples of Arts and Crafts work as well.

Upon his return to the United States, Stickley changed the name of his company to the Gustav Stickley Company and began designing a new line of furniture. He tried some art nouveau pieces but was never happy with the results, and they were commercially produced only on a limited basis. The Arts and Crafts style was more in keeping with Stickley's love of simplicity and his desire to provide furniture appropriate to the common man's way of life and economic reach.

2-4. Stickley furniture display at Pan-American Exposition of 1901 in Buffalo, NY. (Buffalo and Erie County Historical Society)

A very basic, almost primitive, style emerged from Stickley's hand, which he called "structural." It was extremely simple, with a medieval flavor, and featured little ornamentation except for the structural elements of the construction—the joints and dowels that held the piece together.

Structural furniture was exhibited at the Grand Rapids Furniture Market in 1900, and though it did not receive raves from the retailers, the noted magazine *The House Beautiful* praised Stickley's line, calling it "sensible furniture." In 1901 Stickley showed room settings at the Pan-American Exposition in Buffalo, New York, in a joint exhibit with the Grueby Faience Company of Boston.

The Grueby Faience Company was founded by William H. Grueby in 1894. Grueby was one of the first manufacturers of ceramics to use matte glaze. At first his work was based on historical models, but by 1899 the Grueby form was established and continued throughout the firm's existence.

His pottery was characterized by dense matte glazes, generally dark green, but sometimes yellow, brown, blue, or red. The body surfaces were often decorated with plant forms in low relief. Tiles manufactured by Grueby also used botanical forms, and some featured scenic decoration.

Grueby pottery and tiles were a perfect complement to Stickley's furniture. Stickley was quite fond of Grueby's work, and Craftsman furniture and Grueby tiles and

pottery were seen together in many places. Grueby pieces sitting on Craftsman tables and bookcases and Grueby tile fireplaces were frequently illustrated in *The Craftsman* magazine. Stickley even inlaid the tops of several models of small tables with Grueby tiles. (Though Grueby's work met with popular acclaim, the firm struggled financially and finally declared bankruptcy in 1908.)

The Syracuse business took several years to become established. Stickley continually refined his thinking and applied his philosophy to the design of the furniture he planned to produce and to the organization of the workshops. He called the production shop The United Crafts, reflecting the medieval influences of the guild system so enthusiastically espoused by Ruskin and Morris.

2-5. Advertisement for Grueby pottery, which frequently appeared with Stickley's furniture. *The Craftsman*

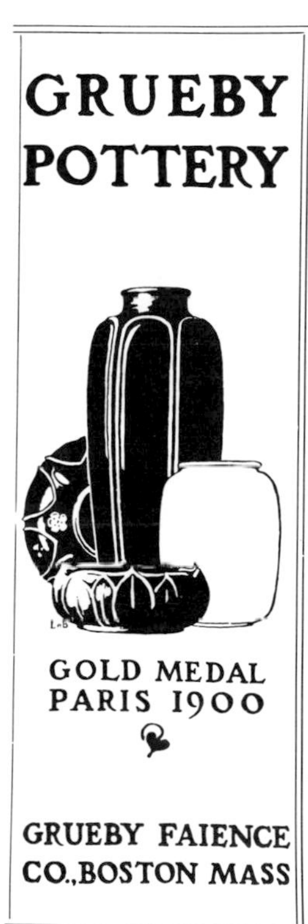

2-6. Early signature, c. 1901, with Stickley's initials, G. S., in the center of the compass.

2-7. Signature variations from 1902–1912.

Stickley set up a profit-sharing plan and considered himself more master craftsman than employer. Furthermore, Stickley felt that all the furniture he designed should be built under one roof so that the quality, color, and feel of the pieces would be harmonious. In keeping with the guild theory, a mark was chosen to act as the official signature of the organization. Stickley chose the motto *Als ik kan*, "if I can," which he adopted from William Morris. As Stickley later described it, the mark represented many things:

> In the Middle Ages, that golden period of the arts and crafts, each master-workman adopted some device or legend which, displayed upon every object of his creation, came finally to represent his individuality as completely as did his face, or his voice; making him known beyond the burgher circle in which he passed his life. . . . Among the legends so employed, the one assumed by Ian van Eyck, the early Flemish painter, has retained its force and point down to our own day. "Als ich kanne" (if I can) appears written across the canvases of this fourteenth century chef d'ecole, placed there, without doubt, as an inspiration toward excellence in that art wherein van Eyck became an epoch maker. . . .
>
> . . . when William Morris, in his early manhood, visited the Low Countries, and there grew fired with enthusiasm for the decorative arts, he found this legend and made it his own. He used it, in French translation . . . Si je puis. . . .
>
> This legend in its modern Flemish form, Als ik kan, has been adopted by the Master of the United Crafts. It here forms an interesting device with a joiner's compass, which is the most primitive and distinctive tool of the worker in wood. The legend is further accompanied by the signature of the Master of the Crafts, Gustav Stickley, which, together with the proper date, appears branded upon every object produced in the workshop of the Guild.

The rapid changes in the early years of Stickley's career can be traced by the changes in his mark.

Several different versions were used until 1912, when a mark was established that remained the Stickley symbol.

Stickley also founded *The Craftsman* magazine in 1901, which sold for twenty cents a copy. The foreword of the first issue of the magazine outlined the ideals and goals of the United Crafts:

> The United Crafts endeavor to promote and to extend the principles established by Morris, in both the artistic and the socialistic sense. In the interests of art, they seek to substitute the luxury of taste for the luxury of costliness; to teach that beauty does not imply elaboration or ornament; to employ only those forms and materials which make for simplicity, individuality and dignity of effect.
>
> . . ."It is right and necessary that all men should have work to do which shall be worth doing, and be pleasant to do; and which should be done under such conditions as would make it neither over-wearisome, nor over-anxious" [William Morris].
>
> With this example before them, The United Crafts will labor to produce in their workshops only those articles which shall justify their own creation; which shall serve some actual and important end in the household. . . . Thus, it is hoped to co-operate with those many and earnest minds who are seeking to create a national, or rather a universal art, adjusted to the needs of the century: an art developed by the people, as a reciprocal joy for the artist and the layman.

The magazine's first issues were dedicated to Ruskin and Morris and followed Morris's Kelmscott Press tradition with a small format, rough paper, and woodcut vignettes. Irene Sargent wrote five articles on William Morris for the first issue and continued to be a major contributor to the magazine for many years. Stickley himself

VOL. I October, MDCCCCI NO. 1

The Craftsman

"The lyf so short the craft so long to lerne"

WILLIAM MORRIS
Some thoughts upon His life: work & influence

Published on the first day of each month by THE UNITED CRAFTS at EASTWOOD, NEW YORK

Price 20 cents the copy

Copyright, 1901, by Gustave Stickley

2–8. Cover design of the first issue of *The Craftsman*

2–9. Joiners at work, Eastwood factory. (*The Craftsman*)

2–10. Rush-seat workers, Eastwood factory. (*The Craftsman*)

2–11. Interior of the Butterick Publishing Company, New York, 1904, contains early Stickley office furniture and windows by Louis C. Tiffany and Company. (Museum of the City of New York)

wrote on the evolution of his structural style and the relation between its form and his views on the value of simplicity in life and his love for wood.

The first Stickley furniture, like the first issues of *The Craftsman*, demonstrated Stickley's immersion in the medieval. The furniture was massive, and the hardware was chemically treated to give it the appearance of age. Still, the basic elements of his style were present, and as they were refined, a new purity of form from function emerged.

By 1902 Stickley needed a larger headquarters. The magazine was doing well, and the furniture business was growing. Stickley purchased an unusual four-story stone building, the Crouse Stables, and remodeled it to accommodate his growing concerns. The building was designed by Archimedes Russel for Edgar Crouse, son of the Crouse College benefactor. Angry that his father had spent so much money on a girl's school, the son commissioned a stable for his horses by the same architect and spent an incredible amount of money to make it as lavish as his father's donation to the school. (The original Crouse Hall still stands on the Syracuse University campus.)

2–12. The first Craftsman Building, Syracuse; formerly the Crouse Stables. (*The Craftsman*)

The first Craftsman Building included a bindery, library, furniture showrooms, drafting, design and editorial offices, and a public lecture hall. It opened its doors to the public on December 1, 1902, with a lecture in French by a member of the prestigious Alliance Française, the first of many public lectures and events to be held in United Crafts Hall. Later speakers included Frank Lloyd Wright, Louis Sullivan, and Louis C. Tiffany. It became quite a popular meeting place, and Stickley enjoyed using it as a gathering spot for those in sympathy with his ideas.

1902 was a landmark year in another respect: house designs first appeared in *The Craftsman* indicating Stickley's increasing interest in the total environment as an extension of his furniture designs. Dr. Sargent continued to be a mainstay of the magazine, but Stickley was taking an increasing interest in expressing his own thoughts and those of his contemporaries in the arts, both at home and abroad.

The magazine soon took on a new format, larger in size and scope. By its second year, it ran over a hundred pages per issue and included articles on social reform and industrial education, architecture, ceramics, and Japanese art. (Stickley was a collector of Japanese prints, and many Arts and Crafts devotees were influenced by the Orient.)

In March, 1903, the Arts and Crafts Exhibition opened in the United Crafts Hall and included the work of more than one hundred American craftsmen and groups. American Indian crafts were represented, as were examples of European Arts and Crafts workmanship and even some art

nouveau pieces from Bing's shop in Paris. Stickley had traveled to Europe early that year to collect items for the show and others to market in the United States under the Craftsman label. The exhibition was a success and "commanded respectful attention from the seaboard cities, and drew many professional visitors from distant Universities."

By this time, Stickley's success was clearly evident. His Craftsman furniture was prospering, and his magazine had become the voice of the Arts and Crafts movement. A variety of textiles, lamps, linens, and other furnishings had been added to the Craftsman line. Stickley turned more energy to convincing people of the merits of Craftsman furniture through his writings and people listened. A significant article appeared in *The House Beautiful:* "The Structural Style in Cabinet-Making" defined Stickley's furniture and his aesthetic eloquently and clearly.

In 1903 Stickley was first identified as an architect in the Syracuse city directory, and the Craftsman building added a textile division. These developments indicated Stickley's growing interest in the total environment. House plans continued to appear in *The Craftsman*, and Harvey Ellis's illustrations brought to them a special quality. Ellis shared Stickley's love of natural materials, and Oriental influences can be seen in his work.

2–13. Lecture hall, the Craftsman Building, Syracuse. Many notable speakers lectured in this popular meeting place. (*The Craftsman*)

2–14. A Craftsman interior. (*The Craftsman*)

2–15. Hammered copper articles produced by the United Crafts.

Ellis had been designing everything from homes to textiles for some years by the time he became associated with Stickley. Many of his designs were used in Stickley textiles. He also created some unusually beautiful and sensitive inlaid furniture for the Craftsman line. He was a rather tragic romantic figure and worked for Stickley only six months before his death. Stickley eulogized him in *The Craftsman* as "a man of unusual gifts; possessing an accurate and exquisite sense of color, a great facility in design and a sound

judgment of effect. . . . Altogether, he is to be regretted as one who possessed the sacred fire of genius."

Stickley was forty-seven in 1904, the father of five girls and a boy. A strict disciplinarian, Stickley apparently ruled his household in accordance with his German background and belief in the work ethic. The family did not accompany Stickley on his trips abroad: Mrs. Stickley minded the children, never leaving them to the care of strangers, while her husband searched out his contemporaries, exchanged ideas, and purchased goods.

In 1904 Stickley began the Craftsman Homebuilders' Club in *The Craftsman*. In this column he offered advice to homebuilders on materials and techniques, and even included complete house plans in each issue. In Stickley's words:

> I saw that the way a man's house was planned and built had as much influence upon his family's health and happiness as had the furniture they lived with. Besides, such unassuming furnishings as mine were out of place in elaborate over-ornamented interiors. They needed the sort of rooms and woodwork and exterior that would be in keeping with their own more homelike qualities. They suggested, by their sturdy build and friendly finish, an equally sturdy and friendly type of architecture. This being the case, why not build the kind of homes that would be in sympathy with the Craftsman ideal? Thus was evolved what has since come to be known as Craftsman architecture.

DINING-ROOM FROM A CRAFTSMAN HOUSE—*The Craftsman, July, 1903.*

The Craftsman Homebuilders' Club

Every Member Receives FREE

COMPLETE PLANS AND SPECIFICATIONS FOR A CRAFTSMAN HOUSE

THE CRAFTSMAN is a magazine devoted to the New Domestic Art. Each issue for the year 1904 will present a design for a house in the simple, structural style in which every architectural detail serves a well-defined constructive use. These houses are provided with Furniture in which the same purpose is strictly followed; the decorative features largely resulting from the introduction of proper color in woods, leather, and textiles. These designs include a wide range of dwellings: City and Country Houses, Farm Houses, Seashore Cottages, and Forest Lodges; the building costs ranging between $2,000 and $15,000. Two numbers of The Craftsman, November, 1903, describing the organization of the Homebuilders' Club, and January, 1904, containing the design of the first Homebuilder's House, will be mailed to any address upon the receipt of 25 cents. Also, any further information will be supplied upon request made to

GUSTAV STICKLEY

No. 14 THE CRAFTSMAN BUILDING - SYRACUSE, N. Y.

2–16. Advertisement for the Craftsman Homebuilders' Club. (*The Craftsman*)

Craftsman houses contained open, large rooms with simple floor plans, exposed beams, a generous use of wood and a fireplace in a comfortable living room to encourage family togetherness. Bungalow-style and shingle-style houses were among the first to be featured in *The Craftsman* and the houses Stickley designed followed this pattern.

In the following year, 1905, Stickley felt it was time to move to the center of activity in the East. The offices of *The Craftsman* as well as the design and drafting departments were moved from Syracuse to New York City.

With the move to New York, Irene Sargent's long and influential association with the publication came to an end. But by this time, the magazine was attracting many contributors, including

2–17. A Craftsman interior. (*The Craftsman*)

noted architects Irving Gill, Charles and Henry Greene, and Grosvenor Atterbury.

The March, 1905, issue of *The Craftsman* carried another new feature, "Home Training in Cabinet-Work," which encouraged readers to build their own furniture. Stickley shared many specific details of construction and finishing from methods used in his workshops. (Some of these projects appear later in this book.) By 1905 United Crafts had become the Craftsman Workshops.

As is the case with most successful trends, many followed in the path so laboriously cut by Stickley and other leaders in modern furniture design. Many imitators sprang up in the early 1900s, manufacturing what had been dubbed "mission furniture." The term *mission* was a misnomer from the first, invented by a salesman who thought the primitive quality of furniture reminiscent of Californian missions. The name stuck, and Craftsman furniture and imitations of it have been known collectively as mission style ever since.

Among Stickley's competitors were his brothers. Trained largely in his employ, they all went into business independently and reaped success in imitating Gustav's line. Many other manufacturers also produced furniture similar to Stickley's and marketed it under

2–18. Furniture catalog, L. and J. G. Stickley. (Private collection)

names reminiscent of Craftsman: Mission, Hand-Craft, Arts and Crafts, Crafts-Style, Quaint, Cloister Style Life-Time Furniture, and Limbert's Holland Dutch Arts and Crafts were among the prominent names. In Stickley's view, the problem was not that he should have inspired others to like accomplishments, but that his competitors generally produced inferior-quality products and then confused the public by marketing them under names so similar to Craftsman.

That Stickley was being imitated indicates, however, just how successful he had become in only a few years. Stickley's name appeared in *Who's Who* in 1906; among his affiliations were the New York Athletic Club, the Engineer's Club, the National Arts Club, and the Society of Craftsmen. Obviously, the leader of the Arts and Crafts movement was well ensconced in a variety of social as well as professional activities, but Stickley's heart must have been turning elsewhere.

Six hundred acres in Morris Plains, New Jersey, became the site of the next Stickley enterprise—Craftsman Farms. In 1908, partly because of his love of natural environments and manual training, perhaps in reaction to city life and the increasing urbanization of the nation in general, Stickley decided to return to the land. He planned to build the most American of homes—a log cabin. But this log house was to be more than a country cottage; it was Stickley's plan that it be a clubhouse and meeting place for his friends and followers. The main house was built along these lines, and the Stickley family lived there. A number of homes were planned for the site; some guest cottages were built, but the family continued to live in the main house. The farm took shape with the planting of crops and raising of livestock. Stickley had returned to the farm, though certainly in a style much different from that of his boyhood.

Around this time a new publication, to be called *The Yeoman*, was considered, but it never reached publication. Instead, *The Craftsman* took on a less aesthetic and cosmopolitan tone and became more practical, with an increasing number of articles de-

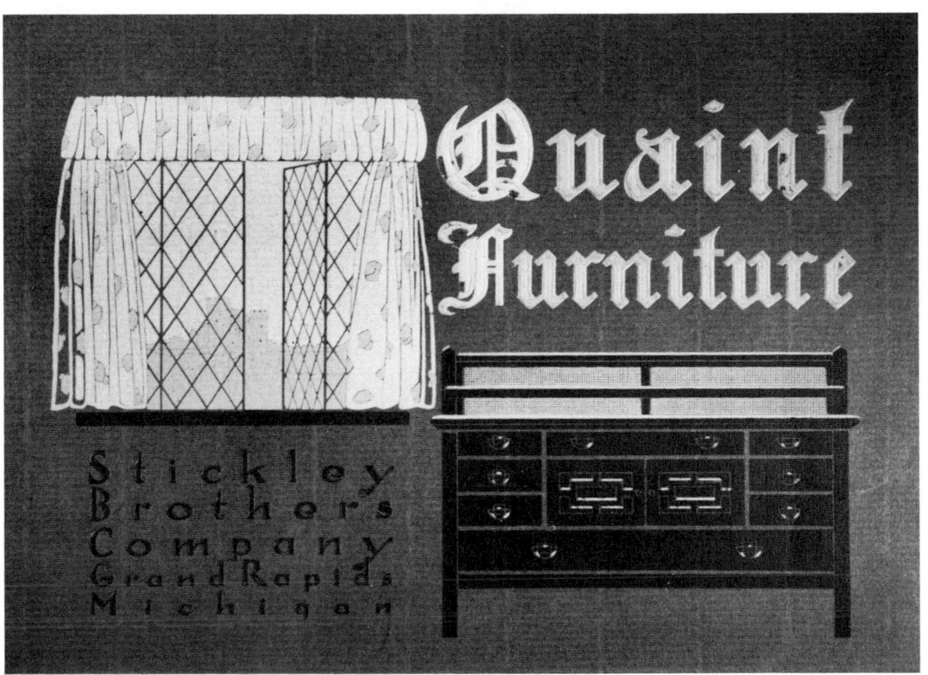

2–19. Quaint furniture catalog, Stickley Brothers, 1914. (Private collection)

2–20. Charles P. Limbert advertisement, *The Craftsman*, 1910.

2–21. The main house at Craftsman Farms. (*The Craftsman*)

2–22. Guest cottages at Craftsman Farms. (*The Craftsman*)

2-23. Dining room, Craftsman Farms. (*The Craftsman*)

2-24. Living room, Craftsman Farms. (*The Craftsman*)

2-25. Fireplace detail, Craftsman Farms. The inscription hammered into the copper fireplace hood reads, "The lyf so short, the craft so long to lerne." (*The Craftsman*)

voted to gardening and home care. Stickley's Homebuilders' Club had grown, and his furniture was being sold throughout the country from more than fifty franchised outlets. Craftsman houses were built in almost every community, and three years later the Craftsman Contracting Company was organized to build Stickley-designed homes. Stickley's holdings were obviously vast: he even owned sawmills in the Adirondacks, where the wood for Craftsman furniture was milled.

Having expressed himself for some years on the subject of education, Stickley put his theories into practice by opening a school for boys at Craftsman Farms. Here he offered "a practical education," believing that farm work would teach the values so difficult to instill in strictly academic programs. The joy of working with one's hands and the satisfactions to be found in the manual arts were favorite subjects in *The Craftsman*; Stickley also suggested that such training could provide a needed sense of worth and accomplishment in the rehabilitation of criminals.

Meanwhile, in New York, Stickley was at work on the crowning touch of his multitude of ventures. Having united all his enterprises under the name of The Craftsman, Inc., he combined them all, except for the farm and workshops,

United Crafts Furniture for Gifts

This large, comfortable Rocker, finished in Baronial Oak, with brown roan leather seat, wide arms. :: :: Price, $9.00.

Arm Chair to match, $9.00

This is only one of the many artistic pieces of the celebrated United Crafts Furniture now shown on our 6th floor.

We are sole Chicago agents and associates

MARSHALL FIELD & COMPANY
CHICAGO

See article in November issue of The House Beautiful

GRUEBY POTTERY

Celebrated for its individuality, imposing strength and simple beauty :: A most appropriate accompaniment for Stickney Furniture :: :: :: ::

RECOMMENDED FOR GIFTS

MARSHALL FIELD & COMPANY

2-26. Craftsman furniture advertisement appearing above a Grueby pottery advertisement. (*House Beautiful*)

under one roof. On October 20, 1913, the new Craftsman Building opened to the public. The twelve-story structure at 6 East Thirty-ninth Street was the culmination of all of Stickley's efforts—an incarnation of the Craftsman ideal.

The four lower floors were devoted to showrooms for Craftsman furniture, rugs, draperies, textiles, and accessories. The top floors housed editorial and business offices, Craftsman clubrooms, a lecture hall, and library. The middle floors were known as the Permanent Home Builders' Exposition. Every manner of product, from wood to paint and plaster, roofing and plumbing materials, flooring, tools, and hardware, was displayed. Indoor gardens and grassy lawns with plantings and working fountains were found in the fifth floor's "Gardens and Grounds" department. The top of the building housed the Craftsman Restaurant, which offered a varied menu of delicious dishes to guests comfortably seated on Craftsman

2–28. First floor showroom for furniture and fittings in the new Craftsman Building. (*The Craftsman*)

2–27. The new Craftsman Building, 6 East 39th Street, New York. (*The Craftsman*)

2–29. Craftsman room display on the first floor of the new Craftsman Building. (*The Craftsman*)

2–30. The Craftsman Restaurant on the top floor of the new Craftsman Building. (*The Craftsman*)

furniture. All foods served at the restaurant were grown at Craftsman Farms.

Stickley enjoyed his prominence from his lofty offices atop The Craftsman Building. He had come a long way from his humble beginnings, and yet he had never really left them behind. For all his success, his sincere motives had been to improve the lot of the common man, to educate him, to make his life more pleasant, more comfortable, and more beautiful.

On March 24, 1915, two years after the opening of the Craftsman Building, Gustav Stickley was declared bankrupt. The great entrepreneurial effort of the building and the incorporation of all the Craftsman enterprises had contributed to this fate; moreover, the Arts and Crafts movement had peaked and waned; Colonial Revival was on the rise.

Typically, Stickley was in the process of developing a line of furniture called Chromewald, which had a new finish whereby color was impregnated in the wood. Shown at the Grand Rapids furniture exhibition of 1916, it did not meet with favorable response. He also designed some Chinese Chippendale furniture, but it was never produced for market on a large scale. By the end of 1916, Stickley's holdings were slipping quickly away.

The last issue of *The Craftsman* appeared in December, 1916. Hired as a consultant by the Simmonds Mattress Company of Kenosha, Wisconsin, Stickley returned to his native state, but the arrangement proved shortlived. In 1918 Craftsman Farms was sold to the Farney family (of the Wurlitzer Company), and Gustav's brother Leopold, of L. & J. G. Stickley, Fayetteville, bought the Eastwood factory where Craftsman furniture had been born. The May 16, 1918, issue of *Furniture World* magazine carried a notice for a new Stickley company, listing Leopold as president, Gustav as vice-president, and J. George as treasurer. A year later, however, Gustav's name was no longer associated with this enterprise. Craftsman-like furniture was produced at Eastwood until 1927, when the Colonial reproduction Cherry Valley line began.

The following year, Stickley's wife, Eda, had a fatal stroke, and he moved to the home of his daughter Barbara. Though he

2–31. Gustav with grandaughter Barbara, c. 1916.

never again worked as he had in the Craftsman years, Stickley was never idle. He tutored Barbara's children and continued to design. He planned the Village Waterworks in Skaneateles, New York, and built a log cabin for his daughter's family on Lake Skaneateles. And for the next twenty-five years he continually worked with wood finishes, one of the interests that led to the creation of his Craftsman furniture. His daughter recalled, "We would sometimes come home and find my father with several drawers pulled out, testing a new penetrating finish formula on the bottoms."

Gustav Stickley died on April 20, 1942, at the age of eighty-five. The workmen from Eastwood took the day off to attend his funeral. Though they had been denied permission to do so, they came to say good-by to the Master Craftsman.

The most lasting and fitting tribute to Gustav Stickley is his furniture. It has stood the test of time, and many fine examples remain. Attesting to the fact that excellent craftsmanship, carefully chosen oak, and patient finishing would produce a thing of enduring beauty, a Craftsman table, chair, desk, or bookcase remains a classic—a complement to any surrounding as honest as it is—a strong, solid, whole, beautifully simple example of the Craftsman ideal.

2–32. Gustav in later years.

3. A Democratic Art

Gustav Stickley's deep-rooted nationalistic fervor was a key factor in the formulation of his aesthetic philosophy. Stickley reasoned that America had been forced to mature too quickly, sacrificing leisure, art, and poetry for the tasks of national growth. We were too busy taking this land from its native inhabitants and then defending it against other nations to establish American culture; our seeds for originality lay ungerminated. We turned to Europe, with its centuries of creative history, for our art. What resulted were reproductions, weak cuttings for transplanting in an environment unsuited for their nourishment or understanding.

This dependence upon other countries for artistic achievement and the resulting reproductions were of great concern to Stickley. "We are surrounded with the concrete expression of almost every phase of European frivolity, rather than with the effort to set forth what we *are* in America by what we do." His recognition of the inappropriateness of European art in American culture was a major impetus for his philosophical attitudes.

Stickley's trip to the 1900 Paris Exhibition confirmed his bias against reproductions. He saw for the first time European styles as integral parts of their environment with proper historical sequence, thus serving as true reflections of their period.

3–1. Victorian sitting room, New York, 1898. (Museum of the City of New York)

For example, European beds had decorative elements such as enclosing draperies and raised platforms, which both protected the occupant from the cold and dampness and isolated the bed from its surroundings, thus defining an area for rest and comfort. This idea of isolation was present in all classes of European society and can be seen in the cupboard beds of Brittany peasants as well as in the great couches of the French monarchs. This treatment of the bed was, in Stickley's view, a proper style for its period, but when these same elements were applied to contemporary American environments, they became relics of the past, without any relevance to the current mode of life. "The modern bed, on the contrary, should be constructed with a recognition of the necessity of pure air and of the curative power of sunlight."

Upon his return from Europe, Stickley vowed never to be obedient to the public demand for reproduction furniture. Instead, he would strive for faithful production. His early reading of Ruskin

and Emerson helped him to form the theories he later termed collectively a "democratic art": ". . . art that holds the mirror up to life and catches its perfect reflection."

In contrast with the reproductions that filled every shop in the early 1900s, Stickley set out to design furniture that would reflect the needs of the American people, not the historic whims of European aristocracy. Stickley believed these needs arose from the democratic form of government and the practical, working-class identity of most Americans. Stickley's new furniture would be created for ". . . the real Americans, deserving the dignity of this name, since they must always provide the brawn and sinew of the nation . . . the great mass of American people hav[ing] moderate incomes with an unusual degree of mental cultivation. . . ."

Stickley felt that art should be of and by the people, stemming from their everyday lives; thus it would be original because of its natural sincerity. He wrote:

> When people know that I am making a new kind of furniture now they say to me, "What period will this be?" It perplexes them when I answer, "No period." I have never sought any period in my work. I am satisfied if it expresses what I believe to be progress in furniture making in America. I believe that there are many people . . . who desire in their homes a certain sturdy elegance, good construction, good craftsmanship, beautiful lines, rich and durable furniture. That is what I am seeking in my new work.

Stickley strove to understand the principles of all art and then to apply them to designing furniture that met the needs of the American people. His first step was to reduce the pieces to their simplest form using vertical and horizontal members in a post-and-lintel system. Aware of the obvious primitiveness of this furniture, he then sought some method of enhancement without sacrificing the structural integrity.

Examination of the early Gothic cathedral provided Stickley with the concept of ornament used as structural necessity. Ornamental features such as the flying buttress were also functional, giving strength and support to the architecture. In later Gothic cathedrals, these features exceeded their function as structural supports and became mere applied surface decoration, a characteristic he despised in period furniture: "Applied ornament is a parasite and never fails to absorb the strength of the organism upon which it feeds." Recognizing the danger in decorativeness for its own sake, Stickley turned his efforts to finding a method of revealing existing structural elements as ornament.

One method he employed was the extension of the mortise-and-tenon joint, previously hidden, through the surface of the furniture. The configuration of the joint was thus ornamental, yet structurally functional. Joinery shown and used both ornamentally and functionally established what Stickley called "structural style."

This structural style embodied Stickley's democratic art. Furniture in the structural style gave the people objects that presented qualities of order, simplicity, harmony, and honesty. When these qualities appear in objects, they have the same positive effect on people as they do when they are possessed by individuals.

> Non-structural objects, those whose forms present a chaos of lines which the

3–2. Craftsman sideboard with hammered copper tray and chafing dish, demonstrating Stickley's use of the extended mortise-and-tenon joint as an ornamental feature. (*The Craftsman*)

eye can follow only lazily or hopelessly, should be swept out from the dwelling of the people, since, in the mental world they are the same as volcanoes and earthquakes in the world of matter. They are the creators of disorder and destruction.

From this belief in the influence of material form over mental mood, Stickley synthesized his fundamental aesthetic: ". . . for the single word 'beauty,' there should be substituted 'the beauty of simplicity.' "

Stickley called furniture in the structural style Craftsman furniture because of the close relation of maker to object. This relation apparently stems from the British Arts and Crafts movement's philosophy at first glance. When Stickley defined this relation, however, he emphasized the motive behind the act, the need for the object, as determining the joy of its construction. "It is what we do ourselves, of our own impelling, that is of value to us. . . . Never do a thing unless something definite justifies it. . . . Let your design grow out of necessity."

The British Arts and Crafts movement advocated singular conception and execution; democratic needs were irrelevant. Stickley viewed the design and construction of objects one at a time and totally by hand as costly. This practice thereby catered to an elite group and fostered an eclectic taste, in direct opposition to a democratic art. In his view this fragmented approach to design could only lead to a halt in the growth of aesthetic identity in society. His desire to see well-designed and crafted furniture available to and within the means of most of his countrymen dictated the necessity for its production in some quantity.

"It is written, 'In the sweat of thy brow . . .' but it was never written, 'In the breaking of thine heart shalt thou eat bread.' " Stickley used this quote from Ruskin to illustrate his own feeling that joy in labor is a necessity without which the product of one's labor is an empty reward. Without it the worker passes the hours trading physical effort for monetary gain, looking to the future for a time when prosperity will release him from this bondage.

Stickley felt trading labor for material gain led to products of an impermanent nature, both physically and asthetically. Inherent in his democratic art is the fulfillment of the needs of the people. The basic needs of the people in a working society are timeless; therefore Craftsman furniture, designed to meet those needs, is also timeless. Manufacturers were well aware of this idea; to ensure their prosperity, they continually fought against it by introducing "up-to-date" styles. This struggle for the new look made the impermanent object a poor standard of excellence. In contrast, Stickley's Craftsman furniture was designed not only for his contemporaries but also for future generations to live with and adapt to their needs; "pieces that would be first of all practical and comfortable, that would last a man's lifetime without being much the worse for wear; the kind of things one could take pride in handing down to one's grandchildren."

3–3. An example of what Stickley referred to as nonstructural furniture. (*The Craftsman*)

Moreover, Craftsman furniture recognized the marriage of hand and machine in its manufacture, while the Arts and Crafts products were based on the celibacy of the hand. In Stickley's words, "The modern trouble lies not with the use of machinery, but with the abuse of it." The structural style and angular lines of Craftsman furniture were Stickley's way of enabling the machine to be both efficient and a vehicle for the expression of beauty. Rather than allowing technology to deprive the workman of the chance to interact with materials, Stickley felt machines in the hand of a skilled craftsman could be used with sensitivity to liberate the worker from purely mechanical hand labor.

. . . Given the real need for production and the fundamental desire for honest self-expression, the machine can be put to all its legitimate uses as an aid to, and a preparation for, the work of the hand, and the result be quite as vital and satisfying as the best work of the hand alone.

This proper use of the machine gives the worker time for careful material selection and surface finishing that the hand alone can give.

Stickley chose oak as the primary material for his furniture. Oak was abundant in American forests (and thus served as an expression of the natural environment of the people), and it had historic use as a strong structural building material (a direct applica-

3–4. Craftsman furniture room setting in use today.

3–5. Another Craftsman interior in the same home.

3–6. Craftsman rocker with rush seat. The structural style and angular lines of Stickley's furniture enabled craftsmen to combine hand and machine labor. (*The Craftsman*)

tion of the theory of structural style). Having chosen his raw material, Stickley developed methods of using it to its full advantage. "Wood is designed to be cut, and metal to be molded; therefore, when the craftsman fails to recognize these separate and distinct methods of treatment he violates the intuitions of taste and the laws of logic."

Stickley's respect for wood dictated that it should never be abused or forced into unnatural states. The simple form of his Craftsman furniture provided the perfect backdrop for displaying the grain pattern with all its inherent beauty. In contrast, highly ornamented furniture would compete with the grain at every turn. By preserving the beauty of the grain and using proper surface finishing, Stickley intended to prevent the overemphasis of structural primitiveness, which he believed was a direct and necessary result of the reformative nature of his structural style.

In reverting to the primitive ideas of articles of household furniture we find simple and even crude lines. These, in accordance with sound, artistic principles, we have preserved; since in architecture—the first of the building arts—the constructive features must be plainly visible and declare the purpose and use of the work.

Surface finishing was another area where Stickley demanded respect for natural materials. Only those finishes that enhanced the natural color, grain, and texture of the wood and did not hide or attempt to imitate qualities of other, more costly woods, were used. In this way the hand and eye would not be isolated or misled in their experience.

Throughout the process of conceiving his Craftsman furniture, Stickley's intellectual endeavors expanded in directions far beyond his primary concern with furniture design. His theory of democratic art applied to many facets of American life, and he saw its potential power to transform the total environment of the working people. In order to bring art to the people and make it applicable to their everyday lives, he published *The Craftsman*. In it he expounded his philosophy with remarkable skill and sought to inspire the public to incorporate the principles of art into their daily lives. He presented not only his own ideas but those of his contemporaries, bringing the words of philosophical and artistic giants of the day including Auguste Rodin, Irving Gill, Myron Hunt, Leopold Stokowski, Louis Sullivan, and Theodore Roosevelt, to his general readership.

He wrote that schools should provide a balance of theory and manual training inspired by nature, the greatest teacher. He referred to this collective approach as "putting the whole child to school." He felt if the child observed nature's unbiased treatment of the environment (no plant or animal ill-prepared to survive, purely functional yet beautiful), then character would be molded in nature's image; no idea or product would be formed that would not fit the precepts of democratic art. Schools were establishing programs of manual training, prompted by the public's interest in the practicality of their children's education. This interest was more than just the desire that children learn a skill; it also encompassed the moral and mental development of self-discipline, thus assuring strong character and joy in labor.

Stickley clearly saw that when men lacked joy in their labor, their frustrations could lead to crime and violence: ". . . the average adult criminal is not uneducated

3–7. Furniture pieces from a manual training class, Los Angeles, CA. (*The Craftsman*)

3–8. California bungalow built in keeping with Craftsman ideals of architecture.

but unskilled." He suggested that rehabilitation of the criminal could be achieved through meaningful work.

From the structural style of his Craftsman furniture, Stickley developed his ideas for Craftsman architecture. He used the same criteria of natural materials, structural style, and evident joinery to build pleasing homes for working people.

Early in the development of industrial, mechanized society, Stickley saw the destructiveness of depersonalization and the need to restore a source of pride and an outlet for originality to the working man. He had great respect for the American public as intelligent, enterprising people and wanted them to practice self-reliance, to seize their unique opportunity to create their own history and art unshackled by class distinction and inappropriate tradition. He provided inspiration to the average person to realize his or her potential and create an environment stripped of artificial trappings—a pure and beautifully simple place to live and work in harmony with nature and mankind.

I did not realize at the time that in making those few pieces of strong, simple furniture, I had started a new movement. Others saw it and prophesied a far-reaching development. To me it was only furniture; to them it was religion. And eventually, it became religion with me as well.

A Selection of Craftsman Furniture

Arm Rocker

No. 311. Arm rocker, rush seat. Height of back from floor, 34 in. (86.36 cm); height of seat from floor, 15 in. (38.10 cm); size of seat, 20 in. (50.80 cm) wide, 19 in. (48.26 cm) deep.

Rocker

No. 305½. Rocker, hard leather seat. Height of back from floor, 31 in. (78.74 cm); height of seat from floor, 14 in. (35.56 cm); size of seat, 16 in. (40.64 cm) wide, 16 in. (40.64 cm) deep.

Side Chair

No. 338. Small chair, with pewter and copper inlays by Harvey Ellis. Height from floor of back, 40 in. (101.60 cm); height of seat from floor, 18 in. (45.72 cm); size of seat, 15 in. (38.10 cm) wide, 14 in. (35.56 cm) deep.

Arm Chair

No. 340. Arm chair, rush seat. Height of back from floor, 41 in. (104.14 cm); height of seat from floor, 18 in. (45.72 cm); size of seat, 18 in. (45.72 cm) wide, 16 in. (40.64 cm) deep.

Reclining Chair

No. 369. Reclining chair, adjustable back, spring cushion seat. Height of back from floor, 40 in. (101.6 cm); height of seat from floor, 15 in. (38.10 cm); size of seat, 23 in. (58.42 cm) wide, 27 in. (68.58 cm) deep.

Settle

No. 209. Settle, spring cushion cloth seat. Height of back from floor, 31 in. (78.74 cm); height of seat from floor, 18 in. (45.72 cm); size of seat, 50 in. (127.00 cm) long, 28 in. (71.12 cm) deep.

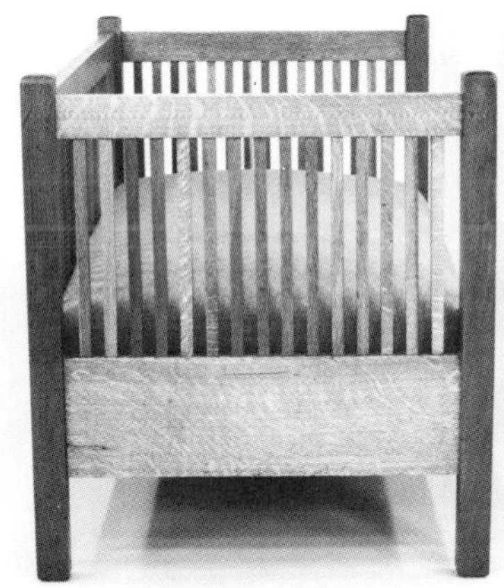

Seat or Footrest

No. 301. Seat or footrest, rush seat. Height of seat from floor, 17 in. (43.18 cm); size of seat, 20 in. (50.80 cm) wide, 16 in. (40.64 cm) deep.

Seat or Footrest

No. 300. Seat or footrest, Craftsman leather. Height of seat from floor, 15 in. (38.10 cm); size of seat, 20 in. (50.80 cm) wide, 16 in. (40.64 cm) deep.

Table

Table with Grueby tile top. Height, 26 in. (66.04 cm); width, 20 in. (50.80 cm); length, 24 in. (60.96 cm).

Taboret

No. 603. Taboret. Height, 20 in. (50.80 cm); diameter, 18 in. (45.72 cm).

Table

No. 607. Table. Height, 29 in. (73.66 cm); diameter, 24 in. (60.96 cm).

Library Table

No. 636. Library table. Height, 29 in. (73.66 cm); diameter, 48 in. (121.92 cm).

Child's Table

No. 628. Child's table. Height, 22½ in. (57.15 cm); length, 36 in. (91.44 cm); width, 22 in. (55.88 cm).

Lunch Table

No. 647. Lunch table. Height, 30 in. (76.20 cm); length, 40 in. (101.60 cm); width, 28 in. (71.12 cm).

Magazine Cabinet

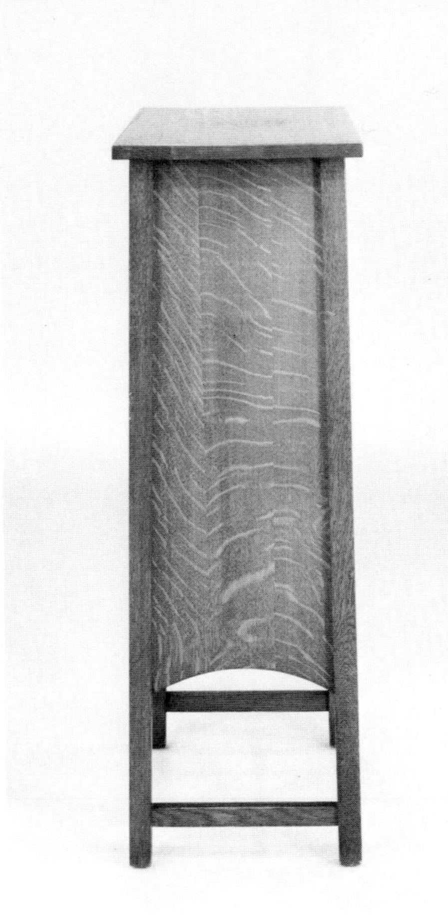

No. 72. Magazine cabinet. Height, 42 in. (106.68 cm); width, 22 in. (55.88 cm); depth, 13 in. (33.02 cm).

China Cabinet

No. 815. China cabinet. Height, 65 in. (165.10 cm); width, 42 in. (106.68 cm); depth, 15 in. (38.10 cm).

Serving Table

No. 818. Serving table. Height, 39 in. (99.06 cm); width, 48 in. (121.92 cm); depth, 20 in. (50.80 cm).

Serving Table

No. 809. Serving table. Height, 40 in. (101.60 cm); width, 54 in. (137.16 cm); depth, 18 in. (45.72 cm).

Library Table and Table Cabinet

No. 615. Library table. Height, 30 in. (76.20 cm); length, 48 in. (121.92 cm), depth, 30 in. (76.20 cm). Table cabinet is 9 in. (22.86 cm) high, 24 in. (60.96 cm) long, and 9 in. (22.86 cm) deep.

Writing Table

No. 720. Writing table. Height, 38 in. (96.52 cm); width, 38 in. (96.52 cm); depth, 21 in. (53.34 cm).

Desk

No. 729. Desk. Height, 43 in. (109.22 cm); width, 36 in. (91.44 cm); depth 14 in. (35.56 cm).

Desk

Desk with reed and raffia basket. Height, 46 in. (116.84 cm); width, 20 in. (50.80 cm); depth, 16 in. (40.64 cm).

Piano Lamp

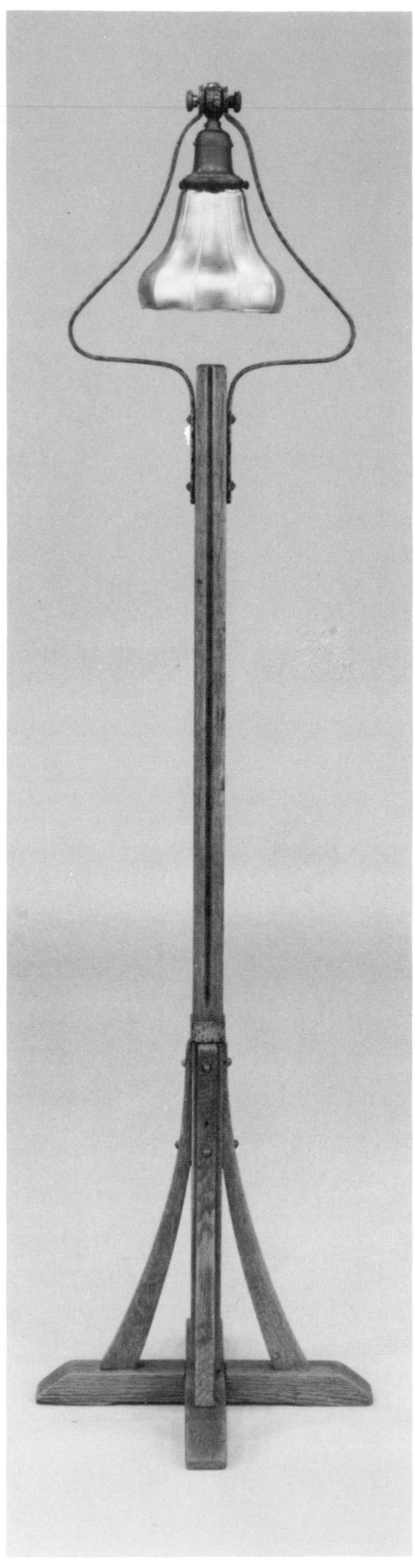

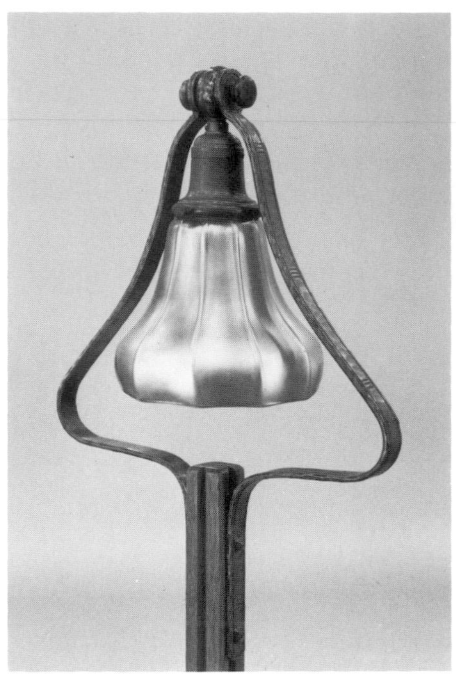

No. 500. Piano lamp, oak standard with hand-wrought copper frame supporting the shade. Height, 60 in. (152.40 cm).

Desk Lamp

No. 501. One-light electric desk lamp. Height, 16 in. (40.64 cm); width, 8½ in. (21.59 cm).

Hall Mirror

No. 67. Hall mirror. Height, 28 in. (71.12 cm); length, 42 in. (106.68 cm).

Costumer

No. 53. Costumer. Height, 72 in. (182.88 cm); width, 14 in. (35.56 cm); 6 iron hooks.

Three-Fold Screen

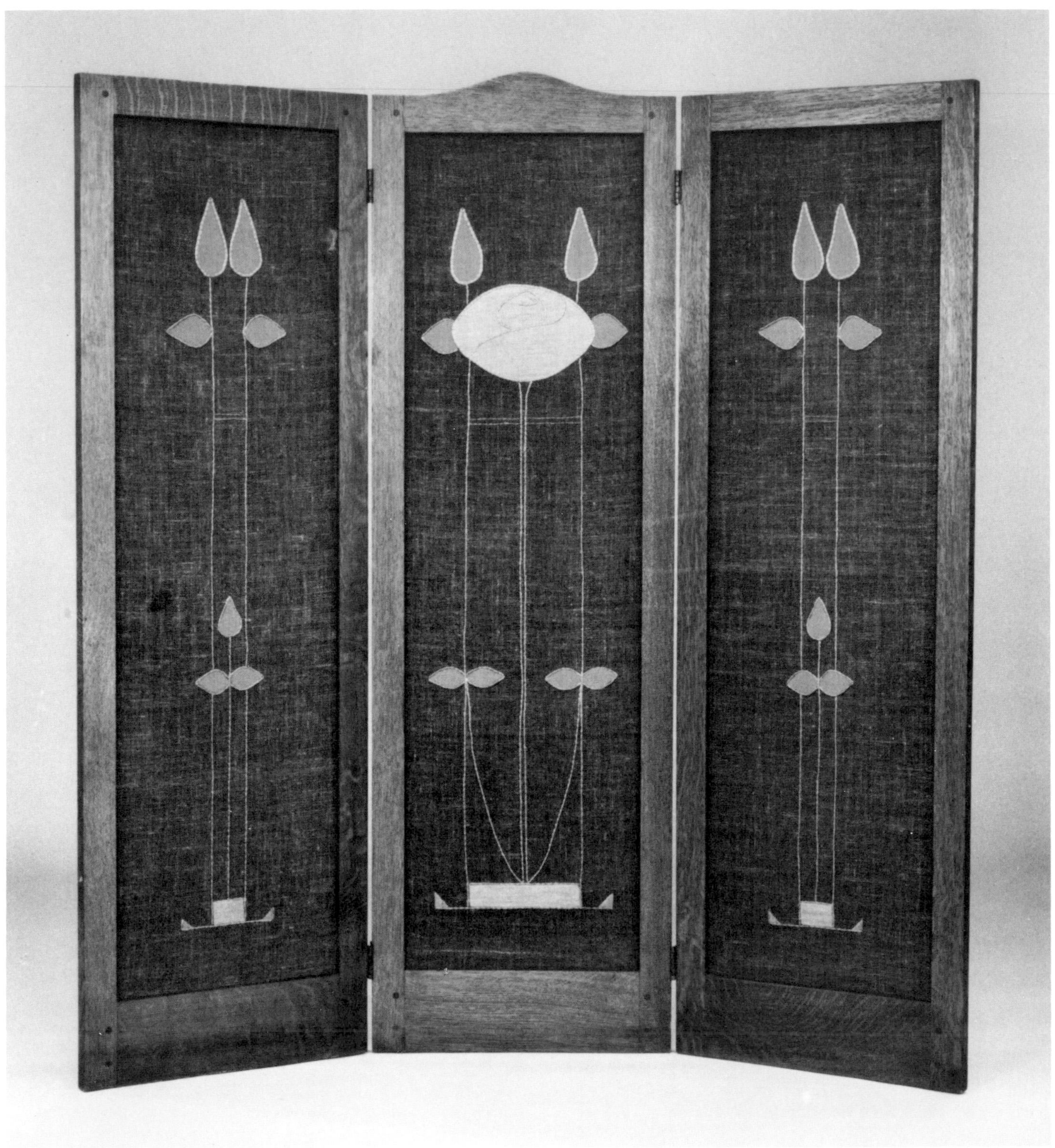

No. 81. Three-fold screen, Craftsman canvas appliquéd with flower motifs in panels. Height, 58 in. (147.32 cm); width, 54 in. (137.16 cm).

4. Materials and Methods

WOOD AND ITS SELECTION

Stickley's Notes on Wood

The world has never found any substitute for wood in its many utilities and its natural beauty. Time and the forces of Nature have wrought out the many wonderful fibers and textures, and the almost endless variety of beautiful traceries in the grains and the interesting age-mark rings which keep the record of the birthdays of the forest trees.

Writers innumerable have expatiated, and justly too, upon the beauty of the trees—the trunk, the branches, the leaves, the shadows they cast and the shelter the branches and leaves afford to the birds. The mystery of the vast forests; even the cutting down of trees, the rafting of them down the streams to the mill, and, eventually, the singing of the saws that divide them into lumber, have been subjects for writings and poems that move and stir the soul. In this article I wish with all earnestness to comment upon the beauty of the trees when cut up into lumber. There is a charm as individualistic and as marked in the wood itself as is that of the trees in the forest. This beauty lies in the grain, or markings; the texture, or surface appearance; the natural shades, or colors; the marvelous varieties in grain and texture; the readiness with which they yield themselves to color treatment, and the results so attained. Many a worker in wood loses much of the joy he might have in his work by not making a study of these beautiful details. Is it not evident that he who loves to look at the wood upon which he is engaged will enjoy his work far more than one who sees no beauty in it? It is to help arouse this joy—that is one of the essential conditions of artistic work—that I wish briefly to comment upon the special beauties certain woods possess, and how best in the finishing processes to bring these into prominence and retain them.

And, in addition, there exists in wood a quality so satisfying that the proper use of it in the structural features of a house produces an effect of completeness which does away with the need of elaborate furnishings or decoration. I believe that one reason why so many people pile unnecessary furniture, pictures and bric-a-brac into their houses is because the *necessary* furniture, the woodwork (or other treatment) of the walls, and the color scheme as a whole are not interesting enough. This is a point that can hardly be too strongly emphasized in its bearing upon the creation of beautiful and restful surroundings in the home.

If the woodwork of your house is finished so that the natural beauty of the woods is enhanced; if the same thing were done in the furniture; and you then see that the color scheme of woodwork, furniture and hangings harmonize, you cannot fail to secure in each room a charm and beauty that is a great step accomplished towards the simplicity and restfulness that it is so desirable to gain. For let it never be forgotten that if a room is pleasing and restful, one of the highest and best of results has been attained.

In the American Museum of Natural History in New York is one of the largest and finest collections of woods in America, possibly in the world. A variety of trees from all parts of the world is shown, and each specimen, as a rule, consists of a portion of the trunk, just as it grew, a sawed section unpolished, and a section polished. For decades, and in some instances for centuries, these trees have been absorbing from the soil and atmosphere the elements necessary to their life. Slowly, so slowly that the eye alone could not record it, ring by ring has been added to their growth, the proper coloring matter absorbed, and the particles of which they are composed deposited in never-failing arrangement. Year after year, century after century, the same plan of structure was followed, until now, when a tree is cut down and its texture and color revealed, we find it harmonious with its species, yet individual in its possession of distinctive and personal qualities. It is this personal quality that gives such delight to the observant woodworker. There is absolutely as much difference between the personality of woods as there is in human beings.

This peculiar charm of grain and texture in woods is owing to the way the tree builds up its cell structure. Each tree does this after its own fashion, and wood is called hard, soft, light, heavy, tough, porous, elastic or otherwise according to these cells. All are more or less familiar with the circular rings that appear when the tree is cut down, or as a log is sawed across. These rings or layers are deposited, one each year, on the outside. So it is apparent the oldest portion of the tree is on the inside. This old portion is what is known as the heartwood, and is tougher, heavier, and stronger than the younger wood or sap wood. Growths materially differ in spring and summer, and these differences are marked in the rings. In the Southern pines, for instance, the spring and summer growths are shown by solid bands.

As a rule these cell structures and their corresponding markings are vertical, but there is a lesser system of cells equally inportant to the life of the tree, which extend horizontally. These are the cells that form the peculiar wavy lines seen in quarter-sawn oak, which cross the vertical rays, and are called medullary rays. These transverse rays are what bind the tree together. When one thinks of the hundreds of tons of weight the trunk of a tree is compelled to bear he cannot help

wondering at its strength. It is these medullary rays that bind the perpendicular fibers together and give this amazing strength. Were it not for them the tree would "telescope," as we sometimes see in the case of a tree of which the lower part of the trunk has decayed.

All these matters, which at first sight may seem unimportant, have a practical bearing upon the art of cabinet-making. The young worker should know that, owing to the difference in density in the old and new rings, and also in the growth of spring and summer, some woods when cut have a strong tendency to split or "check." Others incline to warp badly, and still others, of softer fiber, if placed where there is much wear will "sliver" and soon present an uneven and unpleasing surface. To avoid this checking, warping and slivering some logs, when cut into boards, instead of being cut the whole width of the trunk are quartered and then sawn, as shown by the lines in the accompanying diagram [see figure 4-1]. This is called quarter sawing. There are woods that, in their very nature, do not warp easily, such as chestnut, pine, and mahogany, etc. These, for general purposes, therefore, are usually plain sawn.

Let us now, for a few moments, consider the question of wood sawing; why the different methods are followed on certain woods, and the objects that are attained.

The quarter-sawing method of cutting oak,—that is, the making of the cut parallel with the medullary rays and thus largely preserving them, instead of cutting across them and thus destroying their binding properties, renders quarter-sawn oak structurally stronger, also finer in grain, and, as before shown, less liable to check and warp than when sawn in any other way.* Its cost, however, is largely increased on account of the greater waste in sawing.

On the other hand plain sawn oak is an entirely different wood. It presents a marked coarseness of texture that relegates its use to purposes that do not demand finer and more pleasing qualities.

The long wide markings that are discernible in the accompanying illustrations [figure 4-2] are called "flakes." These are caused by the saw's cutting through the more solid portions of the yearly rings which extend the whole length of the trunk from bottom to top. To make clearer what I mean: If one holds in his hands a piece of wood of any of the kinds named, he can observe by looking at the ends, that these long flakes are portions of the yearly rings exposed by the cut of the saw. To distinguish these perpendicular flakes (that band the whole tree trunk) from the horizontal medullary "ray flakes," I shall call them "ring flakes"—from the yearly rings that cause them. So that in future when I speak of "ring flakes" and "ray flakes," the qualifying adjective will denote the kind of flakes meant.

When wood is sawn in the ordinary way, that is, with the "lay" of the yearly rings, the wood is called "plain sawn." The ring flake is produced only by plain sawing, while the ray flake is produced only by quarter sawing.

The drying of woods is not a thing to

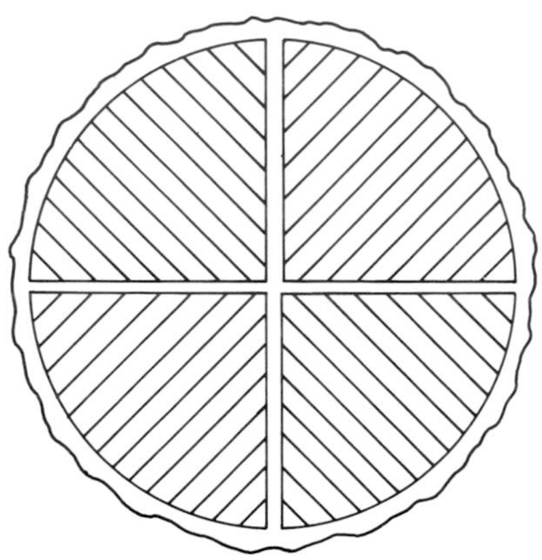

4-1. Quarter-sawing method of cutting boards.

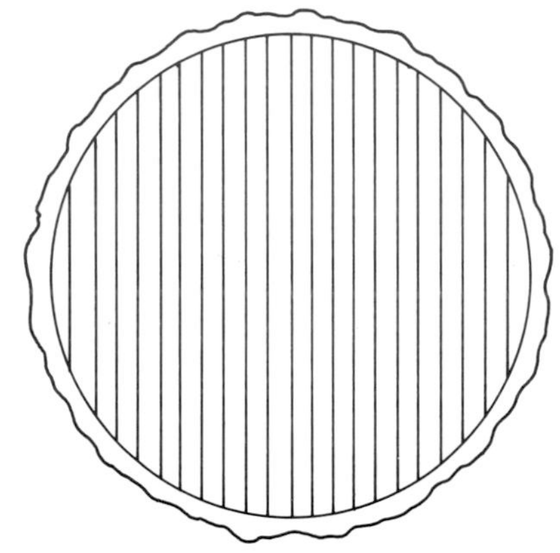

4-3. Plain-sawing method of cutting boards.

4-2. Quarter-sawn white oak.

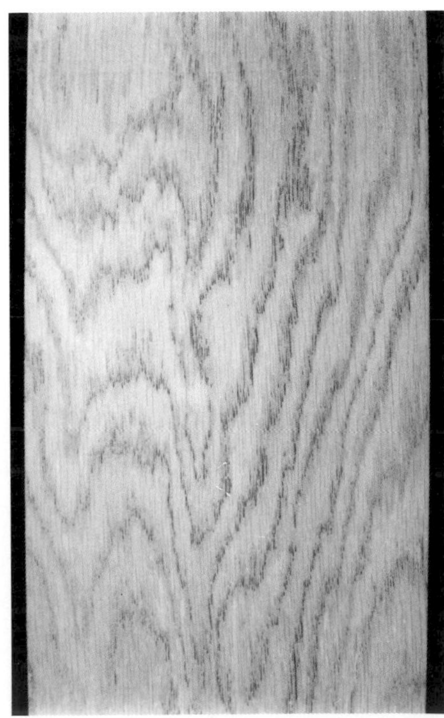

4-4. Plain-sawn white oak.

*This of course, makes a difference when it comes to making large panels, table tops, or anything else that shows a large plain surface, and for these uses quarter-sawn oak is preferable merely because it "stands" better [Stickley's note].

be attempted unadvisedly or indiscreetly. It demands knowledge, care, experience and constant watching. If the outside of lumber is dried too rapidly it produces what is known as "case-hardening." This is the solidification of the outside so that moisture of the inside is confined. This causes the checking (splitting at the ends) and warping of the wood.

Experience demonstrates that in the first stages of drying, the air should not be too dry. To prevent this in the "dry-kiln" a small jet of steam is injected into the room so as to keep the air slightly moist. If this is properly done and the heat not too great at first the lumber will dry from the inside outwards, instead of on the outside first. This is the whole—or, at least, the chief—secret of the proper drying of woods.

It must not be overlooked, however, that science as yet has discovered no way of overcoming the prior necessity of "air-drying" all lumber before it goes into the kiln. By this is meant the piling of lumber out-of-doors so that the sun-warmed air may get to it and first "season" it before any further artificial drying is attempted. Experimentalists have tried again and again to dispense with this process, on account of the time it consumes, but every attempt to subject "green" wood (wood not yet air-dried) to artificial drying processes has proven a failure, thus demonstrating that in some things, at least, Nature insists upon the observance of her own methods.

Quarter sawn oak is the hardest of all woods to dry, and requires the longest time. The reason for this is that the flat surfaces of the ray flakes being almost as impenetrable as glass prevent the moisture from escaping through them, and therefore it has to come out at the ends and sides. It is obvious how carefully and thoroughly this must be done, and that only men of large experience and trustworthiness can be placed in charge of such responsible work.

To ensure thoroughness all quarter sawn oak is carefully inspected again, after it leaves the dry-kiln, not only to see that it is ready for use, but also for the purpose of selecting the pieces best adapted to certain work, and that match well in color and grain. Woods with beautiful or special markings are set aside for extra fine work, and more ordinary pieces are used for the more ordinary work.

Then saw, chisel, planer and other tools do their work, and, in due time, after the scraper and smoother has done his part, the chair, table or other article is ready for the final coloring process, which heightens, beautifies and renders permanent the texture and traceries bestowed by Nature.

Determining Board Feet

Hardwood is sold in units identified as board feet. A board foot is 12 inches (30.48 cm) wide, 12 inches (30.48 cm) long and 1 inch (2.54 cm) thick, or 144 cubic inches (365.76 cm³). Hardwood is normally milled in random widths and lengths to maximize the use of each hardwood log. Each board is sawed as wide and long as the log allows and then trimmed just enough to square the ends and edges.

In order to determine the number of board feet in any given piece of furniture, you must convert the dimensions for its parts to cubic inches and then to board feet. When computing the board feet in a selected piece of wood, you measure the piece's length, width, and thickness in inches and, using the following formula, convert the measurements to board feet:

$$\frac{\text{length} \times \text{width} \times \text{thickness}}{\text{144 cubic inches}} = \text{number of board feet}$$

For example, a board 48 inches long, 6 inches wide, and 2 inches thick would be figured as follows:

$$\frac{\text{48 inches} \times \text{6 inches} \times \text{2 inches}}{\text{144 cubic inches}} = \frac{\text{576 cubic inches}}{\text{144 cubic inches}} = \text{4 board feet}$$

Grading

Hardwood is graded according to the percentage of clear face cuttings, those that are unblemished by knots or other defects, that can be obtained from any selected piece. Hardwood has four grades: FAS (firsts and seconds), Select, #1 Common, and #2 Common.

FAS (firsts and seconds): clear face on both surfaces, yielding approximately 91 percent clear face cuttings. Minimum board widths, 6 inches (15.24 cm); lengths, 8 to 16 feet (2.44 to 4.88 m). FAS is actually a combination of firsts (premium quality boards) and seconds (slightly less perfect boards). These are almost always grouped together under the grade FAS, and one cannot specify only firsts when ordering. FAS lumber is used almost exclusively for furniture construction.

Select: clear face on one surface only, yielding a minimum of 91 percent clear face cuttings. Minimum board widths, 4 inches (10.16 cm); lengths, 6 to 16 feet (1.83 to 4.88 m).

#1 Common: some defects on both surfaces, yielding a minimum of 66 to 75 percent clear face cuttings. Minimum board widths, 3 inches (7.62 cm); lengths, 4 to 16 feet (1.22 to 4.88 m).

#2 Common: many defects on both surfaces, yielding a minimum of 50 to 66 percent clear face cuttings. Minimum board widths, 3 inches (7.62 cm); lengths, 4 to 16 feet (1.22 to 4.88 m).

In choosing a grade of wood for furniture construction, clear face cuttings are essential for visual continuity. When encountering defects such as knots, you should not immediately rule out the use of that section unless the defect makes the board structurally un-

sound. If the defect is visual in nature, it can sometimes be positioned so as not to detract from the lines of the piece of furniture. This careful selection allows latitude in mixing wood grades.

Ordering

The thickness of hardwood is expressed in quarters of an inch, with the minimum thickness being 4/4 (1 inch [2.54 cm]) for all hardwoods. 8/4 (2 inch [5.08 cm]) and 12/4 (3 inch [7.62 cm]), are also standard thicknesses for hardwood. When ordering wood in the aforementioned quarters, you are expressing a measurement of the board's thickness in its first cut from the log. It still has large saw marks and may contain pieces of bark, making further surface cleaning necessary. The finished piece of lumber will therefore actually be slightly less than the 4/4, or one inch, of its original measurement.

Buying wood in the rough (before final cleaning) and having it surfaced at the lumberyard is less costly than buying surfaced wood at a hardwood specialty shop. On the other hand, buying at a specialty shop allows you to look at the grain pattern of each available board and select those you want. In unsurfaced wood the grain pattern is obscured by the extremely rough surface, and you get a chance selection. Whether you should buy surfaced or unsurfaced wood is a choice that must be made on an individual basis. When ordering unsurfaced stock, it never hurts to request highly figured wood, since the lumberyard will usually try to accommodate you.

Defects

Lumber defects occur in all grades and are categorized according to the following descriptions:

Cupped: a board that is hollow across its width, forming a rounding on its underside. Cupping usually results from incorrect stacking.

Bowed: a board curved along its length so that it rocks on one of its faces. Bowing is usually caused by uneven or too widely placed spacers in stacks.

Sprung or Edge-bent: a board that retains its flatness but bends along its edge plane.

Warped: a board twisted along its length.

Checked: a board that has separated or split along its length. Checking occurs when wood is dried too rapidly or improperly.

Stained: irregular markings that can be caused by wood-rotting fungi, soil conditions, frost factors, chemical contamination, or natural oxidation or weathering.

Methods of dealing with various defects in construction will be discussed in the following sections.

4-5. Lumber defects. Top to bottom: warped, sprung, bowed, cupped.

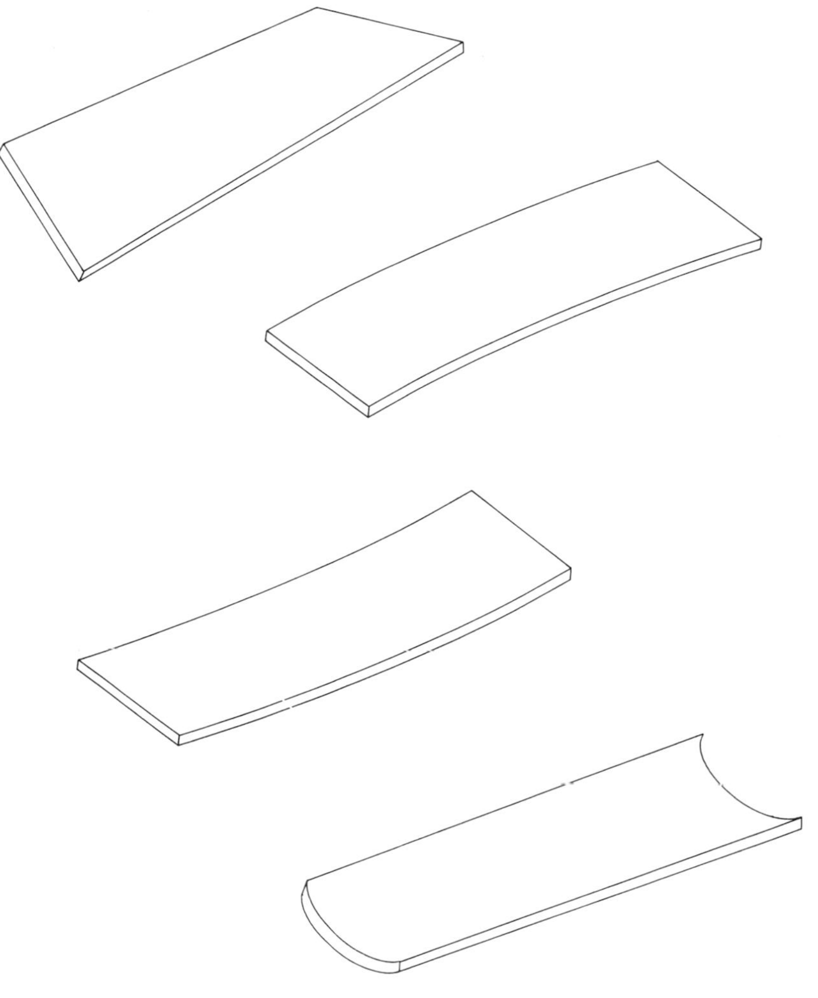

Layout

You should always spread out the boards you have purchased for a project and take note of their size, grain patterns, and defects before cutting. You can then match grain patterns with the proper size and use of each part of the project, and you will use your wood as economically as possible.

To lay out the project, consult the drawing of the project and the materials list and make a series of rough paper patterns of the parts. These rough paper patterns should be ¼ inch (.64 cm) to ½ inch (1.27 cm) wider than finished width and 1 inch (2.54 cm) longer than finished length. Label these patterns with the part name and location (e.g., right front leg) and place these patterns on the boards, keeping in mind any defects in the wood as well as design considerations.

Defects can be grouped into two categories, wood distortions and physical breaks. Cups, bows, springs, and warps are wood distortions and will affect the cutting and fitting of a joint. Physical breaks such as checks and loose knots may affect the structural strength of a board.

A distorted piece of wood can be used if certain procedures are followed. A bowed board can be used when cut into short sections. A cupped board can be used when cut into long, narrow sections. A warped board is difficult to use and must be cut into both short and narrow pieces. Physical breaks, such as severe checks and loose knots, must be cut away. Small checks or secure knots should not affect the soundness of the wood and can be cosmetically filled and carefully positioned.

When placing patterns on the boards, remember that similar parts should have some grain pattern and color in common. Small parts should have small grain markings so as not to have their shape altered visually, while larger parts will accommodate most grain patterns well. Matching grain patterns may lead to a good deal of waste, but the most economical cut may not be visually satisfying. Therefore, each craftsman must strike his own balance between economics and aesthetics. If you chose the wood carefully for each part, you will have a series of parts that form a piece of furniture well balanced in color and grain when finally assembled.

Once the patterns have been positioned, draw around each with a piece of chalk, remove the pattern, and mark each piece of wood with the information from the pattern. Add marks to indicate outside and inside surfaces.

PREPARATION

Once the wood has been marked with rough patterns and labels, you are ready to begin cutting. Before you make any cuts, look at the materials list provided with each project and plan cutting sequences so that pieces of the same length and width can be cut at the same time. This saves time and ensures greater consistency of measurements.

Using a handsaw, a circular saw, or a radial arm saw, rough-cut each board into workable lengths. Now each workable length can be jointed, planed, and cut to width according to the dimensions given in the materials list. To cut pieces to length, square one end and mark it so it is easily identified as the squared end. Then measure from the squared end to the appropriate length for the piece, mark, and cut. To accurately cut several pieces the same length, use a jig: square one end of all matching pieces, and then use the jig to make the final cut to length for each one.

Safety Reminders

The following list contains general safety reminders to protect you and others near you when working with and around tools in the shop.

1. Do not use any tool until you thoroughly understand how it works.
2. Use guards on power equipment. Some operations may require removal of the guard, but additional safety precautions should be used to take the place of the guard (such as using a push stick or jigs, or devising alternative guards as aids to specialized cutting).
3. Always keep loose clothing tucked in, shirt sleeves rolled up, and long hair tied back. Remove all jewelry from hands, wrists, and neck.
4. Wear approved eye protection.
5. Carefully check stock for loose knots, splits, metal objects, and other defects before milling.
6. Keep the floor around work areas clean to prevent slipping and falling. Keep all power tool surfaces clean.
7. Never talk to or interrupt anyone who is working on a machine or turn your attention away from the machine while you are working on it. Keep your eyes focused on the cutting action at all times.
8. Make all adjustments and blade or cutter changes with the power off or disconnected and the machine at a dead stop.

JOINERY

I thus clearly recognized the dangers of applied ornament and advanced a step from which I have never retrograded. I endeavored to turn such structural devices as the mortise and tenon to ornamental use; to employ them in such a way as to force them to give accent and variety to the outlines of the object in which they occurred . . . structural devices such as the mortise and tenon, which, while strengthening the framework and so heightening the serviceability of the object, also emphasize, at the proper points, the outlines presented to the eye.

The mortise-and-tenon joint became to Stickley furniture what the claw foot was to Victorian furniture: a decorative signature. The mortise and tenon is one of the best joints for building furniture because of its superior strength. Its primary function in Craftsman furniture is to join the major frame of each piece (legs to rails, slats to rails, and stretchers to rails). A variety of mortise-and-tenon joints exist in Stickley furniture, including keyed, doweled blind, and doweled through. Each variation uses the basic mortise-and-tenon form explained in the sections that follow.

Tenon Layout and Cutting

Determine the length of the tenon and measure in the appropriate distance from the end of the stock. Using a square, draw a line all the way around the stock. This line defines the shoulders of the tenon. Do this on both ends of the stock. Then check the length of the stock from shoulder to shoulder to make sure the measurement is exactly the same on all faces. This is an important dimension since it will determine the finished size and alignment of the piece of furniture.

Draw lines from the shoulders towards the ends on each face and edge showing the material to be removed. A marking gauge can be used to transfer measurements. Connect these lines to the opposite face or edge across the ends of the stock, forming a square or rectangle on the end surface. If not otherwise specified, the tenon should be about one-half the thickness of the stock.

Use a wide dado blade on a table saw and a miter guide to cut away wood from each face and edge, following these steps:

Using the drawing on the end of the stock as a guide, adjust the blade height to remove material from the lower face. Position the stock with its edge against the miter guide, aligning the shoulder line with the edge of the blade. Cut away material on the down face. Turn the stock over and repeat (figure 4-6).

Slide the shoulder of the stock away from the blade and remove any remaining material on both faces with additional passes (figure 4-7).

Using the drawing on the end of the stock again, adjust the blade height to remove material from the lower edge. Place the stock with its face against the miter guide (clamped if over 24 inches [60.96 cm] long), aligning the previous cut on the face with the blade. Cut away material on the down edge. Turn the stock over and repeat (figure 4-8).

4-6. Align the shoulder line with the edge of the blade and cut material from each face.

4-7. Remove remaining material on both faces.

4-8. Place the face against the miter guide, align the shoulder-line cut with the edge of the blade, and cut material from each edge.

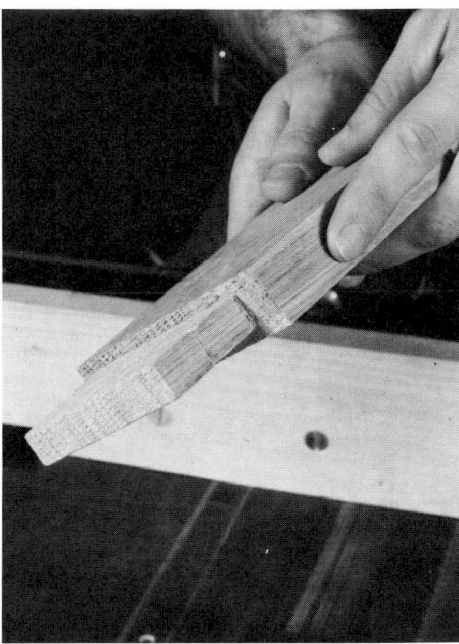

4-9. Finished tenon.

Slide the shoulder of the stock away from the blade and remove any remaining material on both edges with additional passes (figure 4-9).

Cutting Tenons on Bent Stock

In some cases a tenon must be cut on the end of a piece that has been bent. Begin by laying out the angle of the tenon shoulder. Place the bent slat, convex side up, so that it curves over and rests on the two members it will enter. These two members should be lying on a flat surface, spaced as they will be in the finished piece. Draw a pencil line on both edges of the bent slat, using a straightedge as an extension of the inside face of each member the slat rests upon. Remove the bent slat and draw lines across both faces of it to connect the edge marks.

Draw the tenon on the edges of the slat, perpendicular to the shoulder line using dimensions given for the specific project. Using a backsaw, cut on the shoulder line into the top and bottom faces to the tenon drawn on the edge.

4-11. Cutting a dado to the desired depth and width.

Then, using a bandsaw, cut in from the end along the top and bottom of the tenon until you meet the shoulder cuts you made in each face.

Measure and mark the width of the tenon on the tenon faces and on the end according to the dimensions given for the specific project (figure 4-10). Cut into both edges of the tenon 1/16 inch (.15 cm) away from the shoulder line on the tenon side, using a backsaw. Continue this cut until you reach your tenon width line. Using the backsaw, cut in from the end on both tenon width lines until you reach your previous cut.

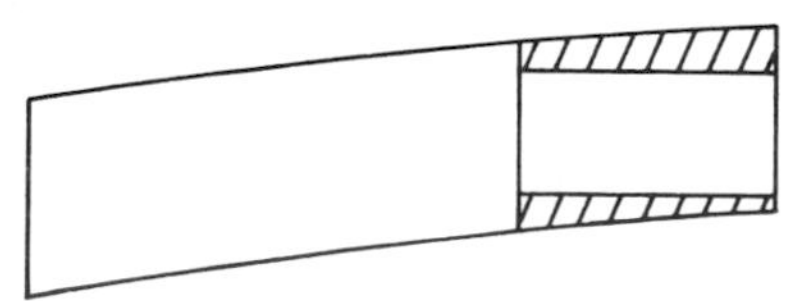

4-10. Blind tenon for bent back slats. Shaded area indicates waste material.

Remove the 1/16 inch (.15 cm) of material to the shoulder lines on the edge of the stock. Use a flat chisel, removing a little material at a time, until you have a smooth, even shoulder.

Barefaced Tenons

Set the dado blade of a table saw to cut to the appropriate depth, and clamp a stop on the miter guide to remove the required material from the end of the stock. Cut with the face of the stock resting on the table (figures 4-11 and 4-12). Reset the dado blade of the table saw to cut the opposite face to the appropriate depth, and reclamp the stop on the miter guide to remove the required material from the same end. This time, cut with the back

4-12. Finished dado in end of stock.

of the rail resting on the table (figure 4-13). With the blade and miter guide stop in the same positions, place the face against the miter guide and make the final tenon cut (figures 4-14, 4-15, and 4-16).

4-13. Cutting a barefaced tenon onto the stock.

4-15. Outside view of the finished barefaced tenon.

4-14. Cutting the shoulder of the barefaced tenon.

4-16. Inside view of the finished barefaced tenon.

Mortise Layout and Cutting

Determine whether the tenon that fits into the mortise is blind or through, and find the proper face or edge of entry and exit (exit for through tenons only). Mark the dimensions of the tenon on the stock at the entry and exit points. You should now have a square or rectangular drawing showing where the mortise will be cut. Proceed with cutting, following the instructions below. (The mortise shown is for a key in a tenon. The cutting procedure is the same for any mortise in any part.)

Mark the center points of the mortise as guides for drilling (figure 4-17).

To remove excess material in the center of the mortise, use a drill bit that is not larger than the width of the mortise. Drill a series of holes to the desired depth (figure 4-18). When drilling through mortises, place a piece of wood under the stock to prevent splintering when the drill exits, and drill completely through the stock.

Using a sharp, flat chisel with the bevel facing in, gently incise the mortise perimeter until you have a cleanly defined opening. Remove remaining material, working out to the previously marked lines on all sides (figure 4-19).

When both mortise and tenon have been cut, some additional adjustments are usually required for proper fitting of the joint. A well-fitted joint is one that can be assembled with hand pressure but is not so loose that it falls apart by itself. If a joint must be trimmed, always remove material from the piece that fits into the second member. Trim the tenon, for example, not the mortise.

Chalk can be used to locate areas on the tenon that need trimming. Rub the chalk over the interior surface of the mortise, and slide the tenon with hand pressure into the mortise until it stops. Remove the tenon and check its surface for chalk marks, which indicate areas to be trimmed. Remove excess wood gradually with a flat chisel. Check the fit by inserting the tenon into the mortise again. Continue to refine the joint by repeating the above procedure until a perfect fit is achieved and the shoulder of the tenon cleanly meets the surface of the opposing piece.

When the fitting of the mortise and tenon is complete, mark each piece of the joint with a pencil using the same number or letter. This allows quick and accurate identification during assembly.

4-17. Mark the center points on the mortise.

4-18. Drill holes into the mortise to remove center material. Use the center points as drilling guides.

4-19. Remove remaining material with a sharp, flat chisel.

4-20. Cutting a beveled edge by hand, using an angled block of wood as a guide.

4-21. Cutting a beveled edge with a disc sander.

Beveling

Through tenon ends should be beveled to prevent splitting and to cut down the visual harshness of the tenon's projection. Two methods can be used for beveling.

1. Using a block of wood that has been cut at the desired bevel angle (indicated for each project), align and clamp the block to the end of the tenon as shown in figure 4-20. Using the block as a guide, plane the tenon end with a hand plane so that its bevel is the same as the angle cut on the guide block. Move the block and reclamp on the opposite face, then plane that face as well. The edges of the tenon can be beveled without using the guide block by working toward the end. Never plane across the grain.

2. Clamp a straight , clean piece of wood to the table of a disc sander at the desired bevel angle, forming a jig. Slide the tenon end into the disc, keeping it flush to the jig and table surface and cut until the desired depth is reached (figure 4-21). Repeat this procedure on all sides of the tenon end. *Note:* Be sure that you are sanding on the down stroke of the disc sander to prevent the stock from lifting off the table.

Dowels

Many types of joints are strengthened by the insertion of dowels. Stickley used the dowel to strengthen the mortise-and-tenon joint and to butt-join larger pieces edge-to-edge. In the mortise-and-tenon joint, the dowel passes through both the mortise and the tenon, preventing the tenon from backing out of its mortise. The end of the dowel is left exposed on the mortise stock and operates like the exposed tenon as a decorative signature. The use of dowels

to pin mortise-and-tenon joints is one of the final steps in construction and is discussed in detail in the assembly section.

Dowel rods are made from many woods, the most common being birch. For the Stickley furniture described in this book, oak doweling has been chosen to complement the wood used in construction. Doweling can be purchased in diameters from ⅛ to 1 inch (.32 to 2.54 cm) in 3-foot (.91-m) lengths.

Butt Joints

To butt-join two pieces edge-to-edge, as for tabletops, wide shelves, and sides, locate the positions of the dowel holes on the two edges that are to be joined. To do this, lay the two rough-cut pieces of stock edge-to-edge as they will be in the finished piece and mark the location of the dowels on both faces. After marking the faces, separate the two pieces, and with a square, transfer the lines to the edge of each piece. With a marking gauge set at one-half the thickness of the stock, mark a line along the length of the edge, intersecting the other lines. This line indicates the centers of each dowel hole. (This step is unnecessary when using a doweling jig.)

4-22. Drilling dowel holes with a self-centering doweling jig.

In selecting a dowel size for butt joints, a general rule to follow is that the diameter of the dowel should be not more than one-half the thickness of the stock. The length of the dowel should always be about ¼ inch (.64 cm) shorter than the total depth of the two holes into which it will fit. The ends of the dowels should be beveled, to ease the movement into the hole, and grooved, to allow glue retention and eliminate air pockets that prevent complete insertion of the dowel. Pregrooved and beveled dowels can be purchased in various lengths and diameters for this purpose.

A self-centering doweling jig can be used for locating the position of the holes and guiding the drill bit accurately for boring. This jig has several guide holes for bits of different diameters. It is clamped over the edge of the stock and aligned with the cross line (figure 4-22). Follow instructions provided with the jig to ensure its accuracy.

A piece of masking tape wrapped around the drill bit can serve as a depth indicator. After drilling the holes, try the dowel for fit. It should fit snugly but should be removable by hand. You can sand the dowel for a snug fit.

4-23. Dowels can be spaced at 6-, 8-, or 10-in. (15.24-, 20.32-, or 25.40-cm) intervals.

VENEER

Stickley did not use veneer extensively. He used it to cover visible seam lines in small surfaces, such as table legs, caused by the lamination of several pieces of wood. He also veneered laminated cores in expansive door fronts in drop-front desks and large sideboards needing stability from warping and splitting. He found it necessary to cover these seams and core constructions because they disrupted the visual proportion of that face and thereby detracted from the unity of the piece.

Three of the projects in this book require leg veneers; the following instructions can be used in cutting veneer for each.

First, select a straight piece of 4/4 stock with a definite flake pattern. Cut the stock to width, ½ inch (1.27 cm) larger than the face of the leg to which it will be glued. Mark the face of the stock that is to be the outside of the veneer with an *X*. Set the fence ⅛ inch (.32 cm) away from the fence side of the blade. Set the blade depth to cut no more than ¾ inch (1.91 cm) with each pass, to prevent burning and binding.

Place the *X* face against the fence, and pass the stock through the saw. Put the opposite edge down with the *X* face against the fence, and pass the stock over the blade. Raise the blade (no more than ¾ inch [1.91 cm]) and repeat on both edges. Continue turning,

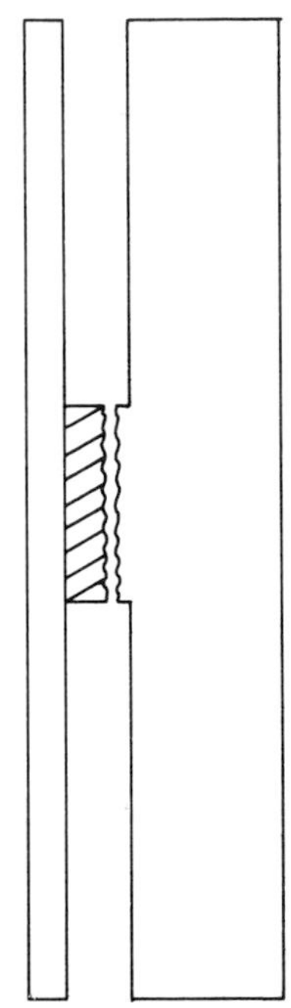

4–24. Veneer cut. Shaded area is planed away.

4–25. Apply glue to veneer strips and leg sides with a small paint roller.

4-27. Place softwood pads between veneer and clamps to prevent denting. Apply clamps alternately, beginning from the center and moving out in both directions.

4-26. Tack each end of the veneer strips with a small brad to prevent slipping when clamp pressure is applied.

cutting and raising the blade until you have ½ inch (1.27 cm) of wood connecting the veneer to the original stock. You do not want to cut the veneer completely away from the stock on the table saw, because the veneer or the stock may fall into the blade.

To separate the veneer, use a handsaw or a band saw and cut down the center of the connecting strip. Then, using either a small hand plane or a planer, remove the remains of the connection from the back face of the veneer (figure 4-24). The veneer is now ready for gluing to the face of the leg.

Apply glue to the veneer strips and leg sides with a small paint roller (figure 4-25). Place the veneer strips on each side to cover the seams, and tack each end of the veneer strips with a small brad to prevent slipping when clamp pressure is applied (figure 4-26). Before clamping, place pine pads between the veneer and clamps to prevent denting. Apply clamps alternately, beginning from the center and moving out in both directions (figure 4-27).

THE ROUTER

The portable router is a versatile tool used for small, accurate milling operations. It consists of an electric motor with a vertical shaft. On the end of the shaft is a collet-type chuck that is designed to hold various-shaped cutting bits, the most durable being carbide. Many people use the router to do decorative molding or edge trimming. Since Stickley furniture has no decorative edgework, we have limited the use of the router to cutting small mortises, beveling panel edges, cutting dados, trimming tabletops, and doing specialized joint work. The router can be used freehand, against a guide or fence, or mounted upside down in a table.

When laminating several boards edge-to-edge for making tabletops or wide shelves, the uneven ends must be trimmed after assembly. This unevenness results when the grains of the different boards are matched. End-trimming after lamination assures an exact end cut for the entire piece. (The trim material has been allowed for in the initial rough length cut of each piece.)

Because the cut necessary to trim such large pieces is so long, table saws, circular saws, and jigsaws give unsatisfactory results. We found the best solution to this problem was to use a router for trimming.

Draw a cutoff line, perpendicular to the edge, at one end. Measure the desired distance from this

4–28. Trimming the end with a router. The router base plate moves along the fence (hidden by right arm), aligning the bit with the pencil cutoff line.

4–29. End after one trimming pass with the router, showing fence clamped in place.

line toward the other end. Draw a second cutoff line perpendicular to the edge at this point.

Clamp a fence or guide parallel to the cutoff line so that when the base plate of the router moves against the fence, the bit edge closest to the fence aligns with the cutoff line. Cut to gradually increasing depths to ensure accurate results. Use a ½- to ¾-inch (1.27- to 1.91-cm) straight bit. Depending upon the type of router you have, you may have to repeat the trim procedure from the opposite face to trim thick stock.

The Router Table

By mounting the router in a table, you can perform some of the operations of a more expensive piece of machinery, the shaper. The construction of a router table is explained here for those who would like to take advantage of its capabilities.

Construct a box with two open sides. The top should be a piece of ½- to ¾-inch-thick (1.27- to 1.91-cm) particle board or birch plywood. Laminate a piece of dull-surface plastic laminant material such as Formica or ⅛-inch (.32-cm) tempered masonite (roughed gently with #220 sandpaper) to the particle board or plywood. Mount the router upside down underneath the top with its base plate countersunk into the underside of the table top (figure 4-30). The chuck extends through a 1-inch (2.54-cm) hole drilled in the tabletop. Countersinking the base plate allows maximum bit extension through the tabletop. The router is held in position under the table by machine screws with heads countersunk into the upper side of the tabletop to give a smooth working surface.

4–30. Router mounted to the underside of a router table. Note countersunk base plate.

4–31. Router table should be secured to a work surface with a clamp. The fence or guide should also be clamped in position.

4-32. Stock is ready to have mortise cut into it. *X* areas indicate where cuts will be made. Left bit guideline on router table aligns with left mortise end line.

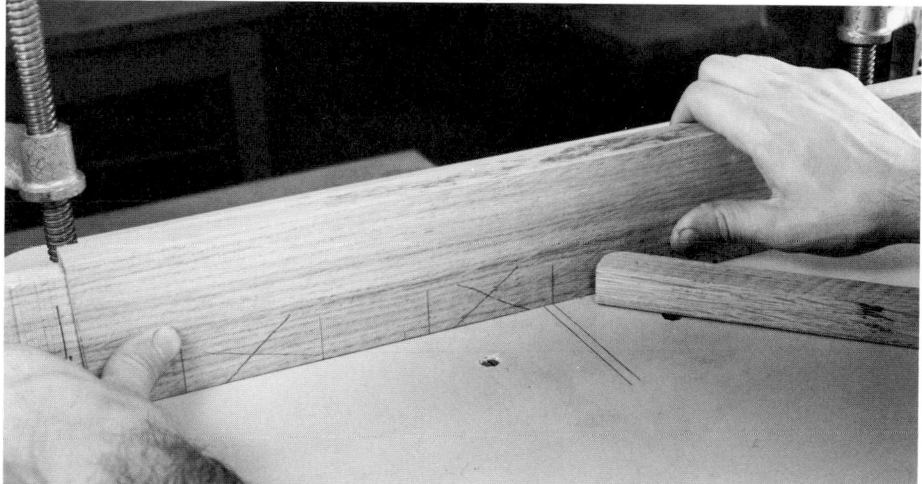

4-33. To cut, slowly slide stock to the left until right bit guideline aligns with right mortise end line.

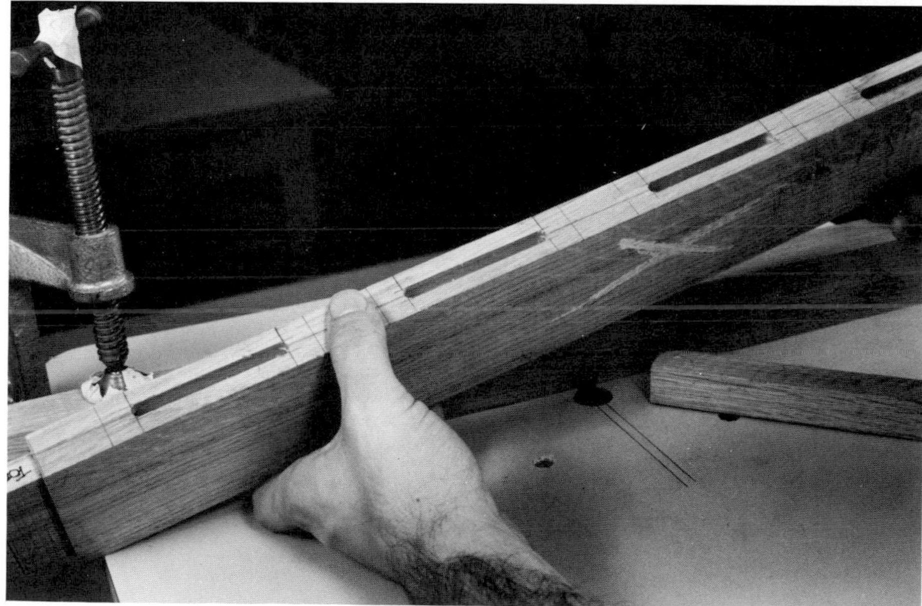

4-34. Finished mortise.

When using the router table, a fence or guide is necessary to maintain control and consistency in cutting. The fence should be made of clean, straight stock and clamped to the table as shown in figure 4-31.

When cutting, feed against the rotation of the bit. Your judgment on how fast to feed will have to be a factor of material and experience. The router operates at high speed when not under a load and depends on this speed for accurate cutting. The motor will slow down during cutting. This is normal, but feeding too fast will slow the motor down too much, causing a poor cut. Feeding too slowly overheats the bit, possibly drawing temper from the cutting edge and/or burning the wood.

One application for the router with table is cutting mortises.

1. Mark the face of stock to be mortised with lines indicating length and position of the mortise.
2. With a square, transfer the marks to the edge to be mortised. If several mortises are to be cut in a single piece of stock, it helps to mark an *X* on the face between the end-point lines of each mortise for easy identification of the areas to be cut (figure 4-32).
3. Set up a fence or guide at the proper distance behind the bit so that when the face of the stock is placed against the fence and brought down slowly on the bit, it will cut a mortise in the *center* of the edge.
4. Draw two parallel lines on the table perpendicular to the fence to indicate the width of the cut the bit will make.

These lines are used to stop and start your cut at the desired points.

5. Clamp a small piece of stock with one rounded corner to the table as shown. This piece keeps the stock firmly positioned against the fence, and its rounded end prevents binding.
6. To prevent inaccurate or burned and chipped cuts, the mortise should be cut in several passes of increasing bit depth. Use a straight bit the width of the mortise. To begin your cut, place the stock against the fence, gradually lower it, watching your guidelines on the face of the wood and the top of the table. Align the left mortise end line with the left bit-width line on the table.
7. Slowly slide the stock to the left, stopping when the right mortise end line is aligned with the right bit-width line (figure 4-33).
8. Slowly slide the stock to your right until the two bit-width lines are centered between the mortise end lines.
9. Slowly lift the stock, pivoting on one end, until it clears the bit.
10. Inspect the mortise for proper length, depth, and cleanness of cut. Refine as necessary (figure 4-34).

The router table can also be used for more specialized cuts. These cutting procedures will be discussed in connection with the projects where they are used.

BENDING

In Stickley furniture, bending is used primarily for chair backs and rockers.

All the rockers now used on Craftsman rocking chairs are cut straight with the grain of the wood and then bent with steam pressure by bending machines. This precaution makes the rocker as strong as any other part of the chair and entirely does away with the danger of breaking that exists when the rocker is cut on a curve that partly crosses the grain.

You can use either of two methods to bend wood: steam bending or immersing the wood in boiling water. Both methods introduce moisture to the wood, partially returning the elasticity that the wood had prior to kiln- or air-drying. In this moisture-laden state, the wood can be bent to a desired curve and, if allowed to dry in that position, will permanently retain the arc. The best method to use depends upon your requirements. Steam bending requires less steaming time (approximately one hour of time for each inch of thickness), but you must build a steaming chamber, which could be impractical for just a few pieces. Immersion in boiling water requires an extended soaking period of five to seven hours (depending on thickness), but the equipment needed is minimal and economical for several pieces.

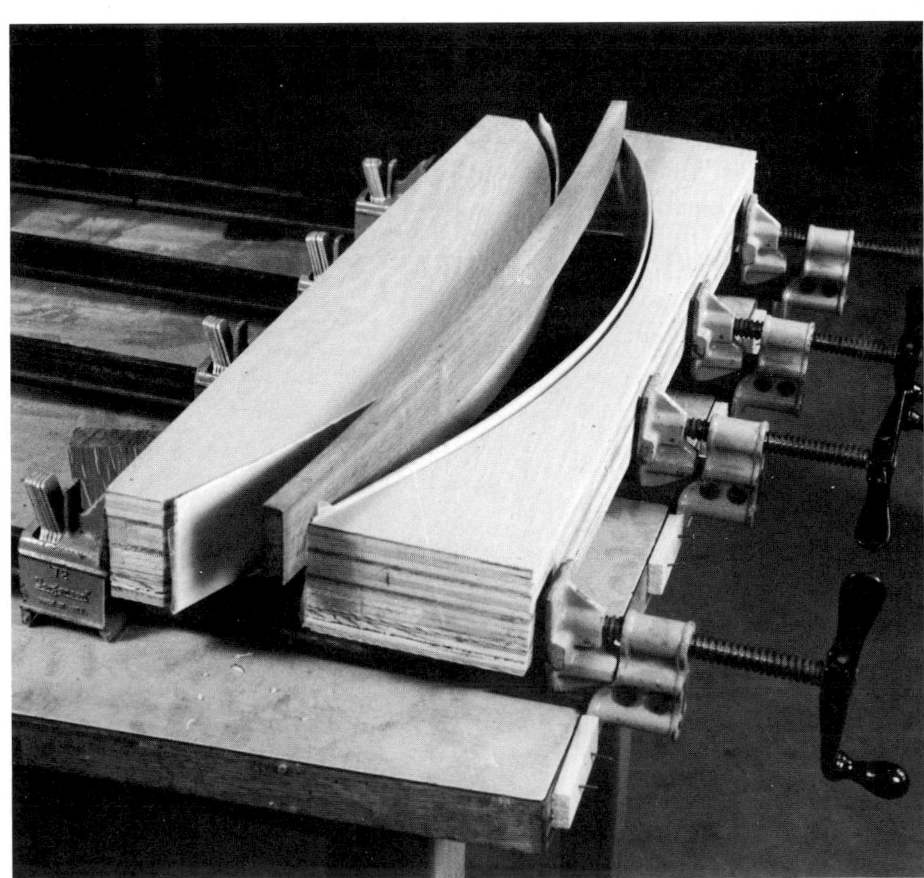

4-35. Mold shown in clamps, with piece to be bent in position. Remember to place clamps spanning the top of the mold once the piece to be bent is in position.

The actual bending process for both steaming and immersion is the same. A mold is used to form the wood when it becomes elastic. To make a mold, glue and nail enough pieces of plywood together to form a stack that is at least 1 inch (2.54 cm) wider than the piece to be bent. Draw an arc, using the radius measurement given in the materials list, across the center of the top face of the mold. The radius given for each project part will be less than the finished radius. This allows for partial recovery of the bent part during drying. Cut along this line as accurately as possible with a band saw. Line the curves of both halves of the mold with poster board to keep saw marks from embossing the face of the stock being bent.

To begin bending, place the mold on a set of evenly spaced clamps (see figure 4-35) and insert the soaked or steamed stock. Tighten the clamps alternately so that even pressure is applied on all surfaces. After the bottom clamps are partially tightened, place additional clamps over the top of the mold in between the bottom clamps. Tighten these alternately to completely close the two halves of the mold. *If, at any time during the tightening, you hear any cracking sound, loosen the clamps alternately to evenly reduce tension, and continue steaming or immersion.* Allow the wood to remain in the mold for twenty-four hours. *When removing the clamps, remember to release the tension gradually, alternating clamps for even release.*

SURFACE PREPARATION

After all pieces are cut and their joints are properly fitted, you are ready to prepare surfaces for finishing. The first step is to check each piece, noting any surface irregularities such as dents, minor checks, small open knots, or wormholes.

Small dents can be removed with a household steam iron and a piece of white cotton cloth. Dampen the cloth and place it over the dent. Rub the hot iron lightly over the cloth, forcing the steam to penetrate the cells of the dented area. As the cloth dries, it will need to be redampened. Through repeated applications of steam, the cells will regain their suppleness; the trapped steam will expand them to remove the dent. This process will probably raise the dent above the surrounding wood. Sand the surface level when it is completely dry.

Minor surface checks, small open knots, and wormholes should be filled. Many filling materials are available, but most of them do not match the color and texture of surrounding wood. We obtain the best results with lacquer or shellac sticks or fine sawdust and quick-drying epoxy resin glue.

Lacquer and shellac sticks are available in many tints, enabling close color matches. The stick material is applied to the area to be filled with a small electric soldering iron or a small spatula heated by an alcohol lamp. The heated filler is forced into or glazed over the imperfection and allowed to harden for later sanding.

Epoxy resin glue and sawdust produce a surface quite similar in appearance to that produced by a lacquer or shellac stick. With the epoxy and sawdust method, the color variations result from mixing the epoxy with sawdust from different pieces of wood. (Always use sawdust gathered from sanding with #220 or #320 sandpaper.) Mix epoxy glue according to package instructions; then slowly add sawdust until a sticky, pastelike mixture is obtained. With a small spatula, force this mixture into deep holes and checks. When the surface is dry, it must be sanded level.

Sanding removes any remaining marks on the wood. Four types of sandpaper are used in woodworking.

Flint paper: a grayish material made of soft sandstone, flint paper is good only for simple hand sanding. It has a short sanding life.

Garnet paper: coated with garnet, a reddish brown, hard, natural mineral, garnet paper is excellent for hand sanding and for some power sanding.

Aluminum oxide paper: electrically coated with synthetic abrasive that is either reddish brown or white, aluminum oxide paper is used almost exclusively in commercial furniture making. It is excellent for both hand and power sanding.

Silicon carbide paper: electrically coated with a black, synthetic abrasive, silicon carbide paper is harder and sharper than aluminum oxide but not as tough. It is best therefore to work with light pressure. In the woodworking field, this abrasive is most often used for finish coat sanding.

We chose to use aluminum oxide paper for the projects in this book because of its durability and fast cutting qualities. Though it is more expensive than some other

types, it lasts longer under hard use and therefore is just as economical.

All types of sandpaper are graded according to the coarseness of their surface. Two numerical methods grade abrasives; a third method grades papers using descriptive terms such as coarse, medium, or fine. The most precise of these three methods is called the grit number system. In this system each grade is given a number according to the smallest opening through which the abrasive particles will pass. For instance, abrasive particles that will pass through a screen with 100 openings per linear inch (but not through the next smallest screen) are given a grit number of 100. This system ranges from grades of 12 to 600. The second numerical system, called the zero grade system, also uses numbers to indicate abrasive sizes, but it is not as commonly used. For the purposes of this book, references to sandpaper will therefore use the grit number system.

Sanding should be done with a combination of a hand sanding block and an electric orbital sander. Always remember to sand in the direction of the grain. Burn marks, tool marks, and natural grain roughness should be removed by starting with #50 grit paper and progressing in order through the following grades: #80, #100, #120 and #220. Brush the surface to remove all residue before moving to the next finest grade of paper.

When sanding, secure the piece you are working on with a clamp and a softwood pad to prevent damage from the jaw of the clamp. When you are finished sanding with #220 paper, use a short natural bristle brush to buff the surface clean. This final brushing burnishes the wood surface to a smooth, soft luster, eliminating the need for finer finish sanding.

All corners and edges should be softened by sanding with #220 paper until the sharp edge disappears. This treatment of corners and edges is typical of all Stickley furniture and is but another indication of Stickley's attention to the comfort and longevity of his Craftsman furniture.

When all surfaces, edges, and corners have been sanded and the final brushing has been completed, the furniture is ready for assembly.

ASSEMBLY

Clamps

Clamps are used to apply pressure to joints during assembly. Enough clamps must be used along a seamline to give uniform pressure. Clamps should be tightened evenly and to a point where they exert about 150 pounds of pressure per square inch (68.04 kg per square cm). Usually, tightening with one hand will apply the proper pressure. Overtightening will squeeze too much glue from the joint, thus weakening it, or can cause bowing or twisting, thus misaligning the pieces.

Many kinds of clamps are available. We have listed those we feel work satisfactorily for the projects in this book (figure 4-36).

Sliding head bar clamp: widely used in place of C-clamps because of instant adjustment to working size. A multiple-disc clutch allows for quick adjustments.

Fixed head bar clamp: also called cabinet or furniture clamp. Available in lengths from 12 to 76 inches (30.48 to 193.04 cm). A multiple-disc clutch for adjustment is on the tail instead of the head.

Pipe clamp: similar to a fixed head bar clamp, but uses ½- or ¾-inch (1.27- or 1.91-cm) steel pipe in place of the bar. Head and tail fixtures are purchased separately and installed on standard ½- or ¾-inch (1.27- or 1.91-cm) steel pipe. A disadvantage of the pipe clamp is that the pipe flexes more easily than the bar in the bar clamp.

C-Clamp: the name C-clamp is derived from the C shape of the clamp. It is a fixed head-and-tail clamp; therefore, adjustment is slower and its use is limited to small clamping operations. The depth of the throat limits use of the C-clamp to edge clamping.

Adjustable hand screws: made of maple, these are good for clamping irregular shapes that result from two handscrew adjustments. They have broad wooden jaws, reducing the tendency to mar work and cause twisting and slipping.

Band or strap clamp; a nylon band clamps irregular shapes and simultaneously draws together several joints, as when gluing chair stretchers and rails. These clamps are available in several lengths. The band is wrapped around the work and tightened by means of a ratchet. The amount of pressure that can be exerted is limited.

When using any of the above clamps, pads placed between the clamp and your work are necessary to prevent damage. You can use small softwood blocks or attach heavy leather pieces to the clamp with contact cement to form permanent pads.

Dry-Clamping

After selecting the proper size and type of clamp, the next step in assembly is called dry-clamping. This involves putting together all parts or subassemblies without glue. Clamps are positioned and tightened as if each piece were actually being glued. Each joint's fit and proper relationship to surrounding parts is checked at this point. If there are problems with joint fit or alignment, moving the position of the clamp will sometimes cause the joint to shift to its proper alignment. If clamp movements do not remedy the situation, disassembly and some surface cutting or sanding may be necessary to align the joint. After adjustment, dry-clamp the joint again and check alignment. Repeat this procedure until proper fit is achieved. When all joints fit properly when dry-clamped, mark the position of each clamp on the wood with a small piece of masking tape.

Disassemble, removing the clamps so that each can be easily matched with its particular location on the wood again. This will eliminate any major clamp size adjustments when gluing. You are now ready for the final assembly and gluing.

For some projects, gluing and final assembly must be done in a series of steps or subassemblies. Determine which parts require subassembly, and glue and clamp these first. The final assembly steps will be to glue and clamp the subassembled units together.

When assembling or laminating pieces edge-to-edge, dry-clamp by alternating bar clamps under and over the surface to equalize pressure as illustrated in figure 4-37. Use a straightedge laid across both boards (perpendicular to the seam) to check for bowing because of unequal clamp pressure. Adjust clamps until the boards are level and the straightedge lies flush across both boards. If bowing cannot be corrected by clamp adjustment, it may be caused by poor dowel fit or alignment or by a cup in one of the boards. Correct as necessary by sanding, jointing, or planing. Dry-clamp again until a satisfactory fit and level surface are achieved.

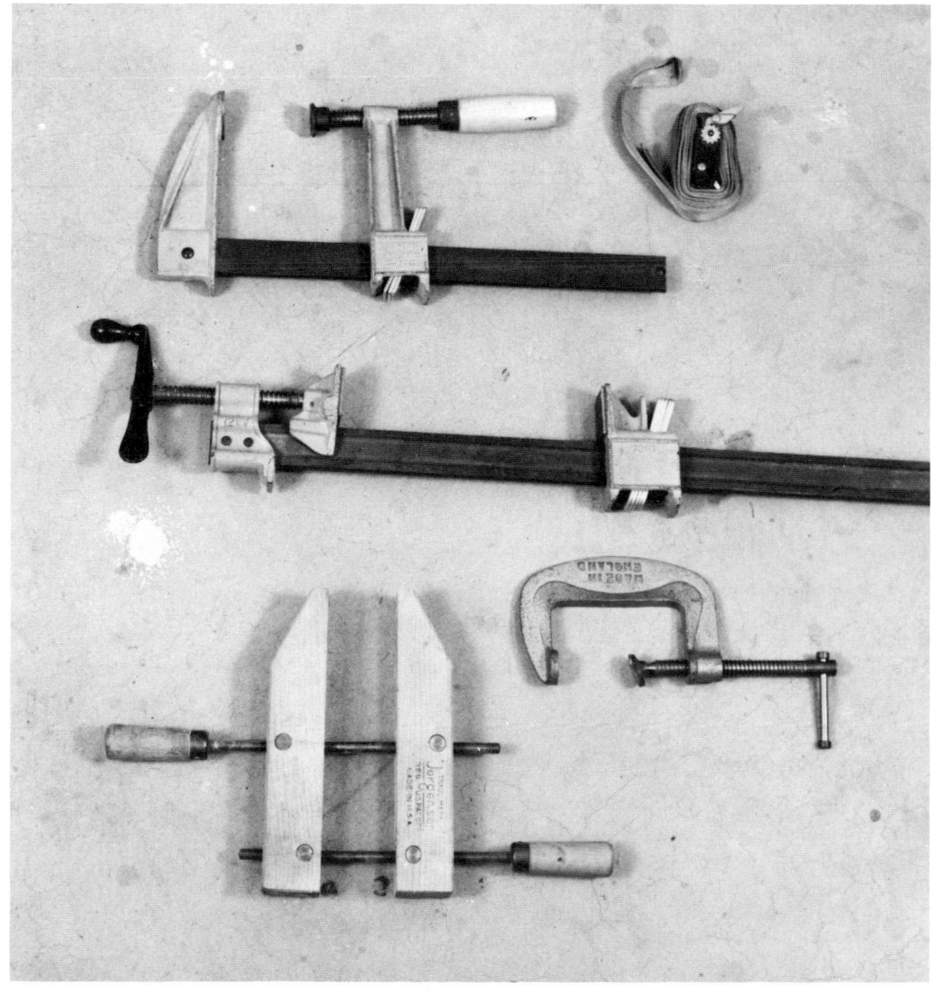

4-36. Clamps. Top to bottom: sliding head bar, strap, fixed head bar, hand screw, and C-clamp.

Glue Selection and Procedure

Selecting a glue for furniture involves considerations of strength, elasticity, working time, and sanding characteristics. The glue should be strong enough to bear stress loads applicable to the piece (a chair, for example, must bear more stress than a screen or mirror). The glue must have elasticity to accommodate the expansion and contraction of the wood. Working time must be long enough to allow for minor adjustments during final clamping, and the glue, when dry, must be able to be sanded without breaking down.

Stickley used a hide glue in the assembly of Craftsman furniture, since it offered strength and elasticity and was commonly used during his time. Technology has since developed new adhesives that are

4–37. Bar clamps alternated to equalize pressure on laminated boards.

more practical for the woodworker today. We have chosen to use aliphatic resin glue because it meets all the above requirements and additionally requires short clamping time, dries clear, and cleans up with warm water. This glue should not be confused with polyvinyl acetate (white or Elmer's glue), which is a wood glue with different properties. The aliphatic resin glue is harder and more elastic when dry and therefore superior for the purposes of the projects herein.

Before applying glue to any of the parts, collect the following items: a container of warm water; some clean, white, cotton rags; a variety of sizes of brushes; and an old, flat chisel or metal scraper. These will be used to apply and clean off excess glue that is squeezed out from joints as they close. You will also need a rubber or rawhide mallet and some scrap pieces of pine.

Apply glue with a brush of an appropriate size to all surfaces of both parts of each joint. Assemble all pieces with hand pressure. Bring the clamps back to their positions and begin to tighten. If any joint should slip out of position, the mallet and a block of pine can be used to tap it back into alignment. Finish tightening clamps, using an alternating pattern to equalize pressure.

For edge-to-edge joining, position the bottom row of clamps and lay several strips of wood (all the same thickness) across the clamps to cushion the stock and prevent staining. (Stains can result when the glue comes in contact with the wood and the steel clamps.) With the bottom clamps ready, apply glue to the dowels, dowel holes, and both edges of the stock. Insert the dowels into one of the boards. Set the board on edge, dowels extending upward, and lower the second board onto the upright dowels until it meets the first board. Carefully set the two joined pieces onto the clamps; tighten them just to bring the pads into position. Add the top clamps and tighten alternately to equalize pressure.

Cleaning Up

Some excess glue will squeeze from the joint and need to be removed. Using an old chisel or scraper, gently remove the excess glue. Wipe the seam with a damp rag, making sure to remove all

glue residue. If any glue is left around the seam, it will seal the surface and cause spots when the finish is applied.

After the appropriate drying time (check manufacturer's instructions on the glue container), remove the clamps in reverse order of their application. Remember to release pressure evenly from clamp to clamp.

The water used to clean around the joints will probably raise or roughen the grain slightly. These areas will need spot sanding, starting with #120 paper and progressing to #220, and brush burnishing. When all joints have been glued, assembly is complete and the piece is ready for finishing.

Glides

Before the final finishing steps, you may wish to add glides to protect the legs of your project from chipping. We suggest the use of Teflon glides with self-contained nails. They can be purchased at most hardware stores and should be attached at this point in the finishing process.

Dowel-Pinning Mortise and Tenon

To pin a mortise-and-tenon joint with a dowel, locate a center point on the surface of the mortised member. This center point will vary with each application of the joint, and more specific location information will be given for each project. After the center point is located, choose the proper bit size and mark the bit with tape to indicate depth.

1. Clamp a block of wood perpendicular to the face where the dowel will enter. Draw lines on this block to serve as vertical alignment guides in one plane (figure 4-38). Pressure against the block itself will provide vertical alignment in the opposite plane.
2. Drill a hole, maintaining vertical alignment with the block and its lines, through one face of the mortised piece, through the tenon, and halfway through the remaining stock toward the opposite face (figure 4-39).

4-38. Guidelines on block of wood clamped to mortised member will maintain vertical alignment when drilling dowel hole.

3. Cut a dowel at least ½ inch (1.27 cm) longer than the depth of the hole and fit it. Apply glue to the inside of the hole and to the dowel. Using a rawhide mallet or a soft pine block and hammer, drive the dowel into place. Wipe the excess glue off with a damp rag.
4. Soak the dowel with water by squeezing a few drops of water on the exposed end; the dowel will swell into its hole for a tighter fit. After a few minutes, wipe off the excess water with a rag and let the surfaces dry.
5. Pad the area around the dowel, as shown in figure 4-40, using three or four layers of masking tape. This pad will prevent the saw from marking the surface when cutting off the dowel. With a coping saw or backsaw, cut off the dowel, leaving a 1/16-inch (.15-cm) projection. Remove the masking tape in one piece (this tape can be used for two or three more dowel trimmings if handled carefully).
6. Sand the dowel flush.

4-39. Drill dowel hole through upper mortised face, tenon, and halfway to lower mortised face.

4-40. With masking tape in place to protect the surface, saw off the dowel.

FINISHING

Finishing was of such importance to Stickley that he was still experimenting with new formulas and methods of application during the later years of his life. In building the projects for this book, we have tried to follow as closely as possible the methods he used in order to maintain the integrity of his designs. In accordance with this, we believe the best expression of Stickley's finishing theory can be found in his own words.

Stickley's Notes on Finishing

. . . it should be understood that our methods of finishing are for the purpose of getting the best possible results from the wood itself as well as the most pleasing effect in completing the color scheme of a room, and never for the purpose of imitating a more costly wood in the finish of a cheaper one. The beauty of each wood is peculiarly its own, and the sole aim of our finishing is to show that beauty to the best advantage.

That a clearer understanding may be given of the effects we try to obtain with the finishes to be described later, it seems best first to explain the method in ordinary use of furniture and other woodworking establishments, where naturally the effort is made to get the most showy and commercially finished results from the least possible expenditure of time and material. In such cases the wood is first "filled" with prepared wood filler made from a very finely ground silex. When this preparation is carefully rubbed into the pores, the surface of the wood becomes as smooth and even as glass. After the filler has become thoroughly dry, the wood is varnished and rubbed, and either polished to a mirror-like brilliancy or left "in the dull." This destroys the texture by covering it with an enamel that completely alters its character. Whether dull or polished, the woodiness of texture that is so interesting has given place to an artificial smoothness of surface that passes for fineness of finish and that makes all wood alike to the touch.

It is easy to finish wood in this way and yet leave it natural in color, if desired, for the filler made from silex is colorless. If a darker or different color is required, the pigment is usually mixed with the filler. This gives a finish in which the figure of the wood is made very prominent, for the reason that, when the color is carried on in that way, the pigment does not penetrate the glassy surface of the pith ray or figure, and is rubbed off by the same operation that rubs it into the softer parts of the wood. This effect is much sought after in showy furniture, where a highly emphasized figure is considered very desirable, but it is just what we seek most earnestly to avoid, as the figure in the woods mentioned above is already so strong that it needs to be subdued by an even tone rather than heightened by a marked contrast.

Of the woods in the class we are discussing now, oak and chestnut are the only ones affected by the fumes of ammonia. As was discovered some years ago by the use of oaken beams and panelling in the woodwork of fine stables, the effect of ammonia on this wood is to produce quickly the mellow darkness of hue that formerly was supposed to come from age alone. Careful experiment showed that this effect resulted from a certain affinity between the tannic acid in the wood and the ammonia with which the air was heavily charged, and that the same result could be artificially produced by subjecting to the fumes of strong ammonia any wood which contained a sufficient percentage of tannin. This process is the only one known that acts upon the glassy pith rays as well as the softer parts of the wood, coloring all together in an even tone so that the figure is marked only by its difference in texture. This result can not be accomplished by stains, and for this reason we always subject these woods to more or less fuming before applying a stain.

In fuming woods the best results are obtained by shutting the piece into an air-tight box or closet, on the floor of which has been placed a shallow dish containing liquor ammonia (26 per cent). The length of time required to fume to a good color depends largely upon the tightness of the compartment, but as a rule forty-eight hours is enough. Where fuming is not practicable, as in the case of a piece too large for any available compartment, or of the trim of a room, a satisfactory result can be obtained by applying liquor ammonia (26 per cent) direct to the wood with a sponge or brush. In either case, the wood must be in its natural condition when treated, as any previous application of oil or stain would prevent the ammonia from taking effect.

After the wood is thoroughly dry from the first application, sandpaper it carefully with fine sandpaper, then apply another coat of ammonia and sandpaper as before.

Some pieces fume much darker than others, according to the amount of tannin left free to attract the ammonia after the wood has been kiln-dried. Where any sapwood had been left on, that part will be found unaffected by the fumes. To meet these conditions, it is necessary to make a "touch-up" to even up the color. This is done by mixing Vandyke brown, ground in Japan, with German lacquer [clear lacquer], commonly known as "banana liquid," and adding a very little lampblack, also ground in Japan. The mixture may be thinned with wood alcohol to the right consistency for use, and the color of the piece to be touched up will decide the proportion of black to be added to the brown. In touching up the lighter portions of the wood, the stain may be smoothly blended with the dark tint of the perfectly fumed parts by rubbing along the line where they join with a piece of soft, dry cheesecloth, closely following the brush. If the stain should dry too fast and the color is left uneven, dampen the cloth slightly with alcohol.

After fuming, sandpapering and touching up a piece of furniture, apply a coat of lacquer made of one-third white shellac and two-thirds German lacquer. If the fuming process has resulted in a shade dark enough to be satisfactory, this lacquer may be applied clear, if not, it may be darkened by the addititon of a small quantity of the stain used in touching up. Care must be taken, however, not to add enough color to show laps and brushmarks. The danger of this makes it often more advisable to apply two coats of lacquer, each containing a very little color. If this is done, sandpaper each coat with very fine sandpaper after it is thoroughly dry, and then apply one or more coats of prepared floor wax. These directions, if carefully followed, should give the same effects that characterize the Craftsman furniture.

Sometimes it is not deemed practicable or desirable to fume oak or chestnut. In such a case a finish may be used for

which directions will be given, and which applies to all woods in this class. For these woods a water stain should never be used, as it raises the grain to such an extent that in sandpapering to make it smooth again the color is sanded off with the grain, leaving an unevenly stained and very unpleasant surface. The most satisfactory method we know, especially for workers who have had but little experience, is to use quick-drying colors (colors ground in Japan) mixed with German lacquer. Both can be obtained at almost any paint shop. After getting the desired shade of the color chosen, apply as quickly as possible, as it dries very rapidly. It is best to cover a small portion of the surface at a time, and then go over it with a soft, dry cloth, to "even it up" before it dries. When it is ready for the final finish, apply a coat of white shellac, sandpaper carefully and apply one or more coats of wax.

Fuming Tent

We have based our fuming tent on those used at the Craftsman workshops. Instead of tarred canvas, however, we substituted heavy (4 mil), clear plastic stapled to a collapsible pine frame. The tent frame is built of five panels, each panel reinforced at the corners with a nailed and glued plywood triangular corner plate (figure 4-41).

The panels are assembled to form the tent by using carriage bolts and wing nuts through holes drilled at the corners of the frame. When ready to fume, assemble three sides and the top of the tent, leaving one end open for access. The final panel is secured into place after the furniture and ammonia have been placed inside the tent.

Testing for Color

It is advisable to run a test with small scraps of wood from the furniture, since pieces of wood may darken at different rates when exposed to the ammonia fumes. A test will give you some idea of what to expect when you put your furniture into the tent for full-scale fuming. In order for the test to be most helpful, you should make notes of relative times and color changes for each sample.

To conduct a test, you will need a cardboard box large enough to hold the scraps of wood you are testing, a large plastic trash bag (big enough so the box can be placed inside and the bag securely fastened around it), a small glass container, and a small amount of 26 percent aqua ammonia, available from chemical or blueprint supply houses.

First, cut each scrap in half and mark both halves with the same letter. Place the cardboard box inside the plastic bag, and place one-half of each scrap into the box so that no two pieces are touching. The remaining halves should be set aside for comparison with the fumed pieces.

Important: Every precaution must be taken when working with the ammonia during the test and the actual fuming! The fumes are extremely dangerous and harmful if inhaled or in contact with skin. Always work outside. Hold open containers away from you when handling and avoid breathing the fumes or getting the solution on your skin. Read and follow manufacturer's instructions carefully at all times.

Pour ¼ cup (.06 l) of ammonia into the glass container, and place

4-41. Fuming tent, showing plywood corner braces and plastic walls.

it into the box with the wood pieces. Close the box and secure the bag around it with a tie.

Check the samples after two hours for color change. Again, open the bag and box carefully because of the accumulated fumes. Remove the fumed scraps and compare them to their matching halves. Note the degree of color change that has taken place (figure 4-42). If a deeper tone is desired, return the pieces to the box and continue fuming. Check the samples every two to three hours until the desired color is reached. When testing is complete, return any remaining ammonia to its container *immediately.*

The length of fuming time will probably vary for each sample piece. Color choice is a matter of personal taste; however, care should be taken not to overfume, thereby changing the character of the oak by making it unnaturally dark.

The results of this test will help you determine what to look for as you fume your finished furniture in the tent. The length of time required for desired color is not necessarily predictable, since the concentration of fumes in the box may be greater than in the larger tent. By matching the samples to the furniture parts from which they came, however, you will be able to determine which pieces or areas will take a longer or shorter fuming time. Note the location of any wood which has darkened especially fast. Be sure to check that part of the piece of furniture when assessing progress in the tent. Other areas of the furniture can be darkened slightly with stain to even out the color, but if one area of the furniture piece reacts more quickly than other areas, it will be too dark when the rest of the piece has reached its optimum color.

4-42. Both blocks in each pair are from the same board. The left blocks are unfumed; those on the right were fumed for eight hours.

Fuming

When you load the tent, allow space around each piece for the fumes to act on all surfaces. Parts that must come in contact with another surface should be elevated from that surface with small wooden blocks to allow fumes to circulate underneath. Place several shallow dishes on the floor of the tent (figure 4-43). Starting from the rear of the tent, pour ammonia into each dish; back your way out of the tent, filling the dishes as you go. Work as quickly as possible. Close the end of the tent and fasten in place with wing nuts.

Because the tent sides are made of clear plastic, you can check the progress of the fuming without opening the tent. When the desired color is reached, carefully remove the end panel and allow the tent to air out. Cut some cardboard squares large enough to cover the ammonia dishes. When some of the fumes have dissipated, quickly cover the dishes with the cardboard, leave the tent, and allow time for the remaining fumes to dissipate. Remove the dishes, keeping the covers intact, and pour any remaining ammonia back into the original container. You can then safely remove the furniture pieces from the tent.

With fuming complete, you may continue with the finishing process as described by Stickley above. This will give you the exact method by which his Craftsman furniture was finished and results in a warm, even, rich finish that will withstand the test of time.

Alternate Finishing Method

The following alternate method is offered for those who wish a simpler procedure than the one given by Stickley. Its results are quite satisfactory.

To touch up areas after fuming that are either uneven in color or contain unfumed sapwood, use a mixture of clear penetrating resin oil and enough oil stain of an appropriate tint or mixture of tints to even the surface color. Use the fumed test samples to match colors. When you have achieved the proper color, apply it locally to the desired areas with a brush and allow it to penetrate for approximately fifteen to twenty minutes. Wipe off the excess with a clean cotton cloth and allow to dry for approximately twenty-four hours. This touch-up process may not be necessary. If not, you may proceed as follows after fuming.

A mixture of one part penetrating resin oil and one part clear satin-finish polyurethane varnish, with tint added if desired, forms the final finish. Mixing should be done in a clean metal can. Heat the finish on an electric hot plate set at medium (do *not* use open flame). This heating provides greater penetration of the finish into the wood. Brush the finish over the surface, making sure to soak the entire piece generously. Allow the finish to penetrate for a few minutes, then apply more to any dull areas. Continue this procedure until the entire surface remains wet for about forty-five minutes. Using clean cotton rags, wipe the surface *with the grain*, removing any surface finish which has not penetrated. Allow the piece to dry for twenty-four hours, checking intermittently and wiping dry any spots of finish that bleed from the wood. This bleeding indicates maximum penetration of the finish.

Repeat this procedure two or three more times, allowing the furniture to sit for at least twenty-four hours between each application. This process will give you a finish comparable to Stickley's original method.

4-43. Elevate pieces to be fumed and space shallow dishes on the floor of the tent.

HARDWARE

Some of the projects in this book require metal hardware such as hinges, door-pulls, and table irons. Hinges and table irons can be purchased, but door-pulls like Stickley's must be made. A drawing of the door-pulls for the book case is provided in the project section. Having these pulls made (or making them yourself) will give the finished piece an authenticity and integrity well worth the effort or expense.

To Stickely hardware was just as important to each piece of furniture as its design, wood selection, and finishing.

We found out very soon after we began to make the plain oak furniture that even

the best of the usual machine-made and highly polished metal trim was absurdly out of place, and that in order to get the right thing it was necessary to establish a metal-work department in the Craftsman Workshops where articles of wrought metal in plain rugged designs and possessing the same structural and simple quality as the furniture could be made.

Solid brass or bronze hinges are recommended for those projects requiring them. Solid copper hinges are too soft and are not easily obtainable. Stickley used either brass or copper-plated steel. We suggest that you copper-plate brass or steel hinges in keeping with his procedures. This should be done by a local plating shop. Newly plated hinges are too bright for the character of the furniture and will need further surface treatment.

To give the copper the deep mellow brownish glow that brings it into such perfect harmony with the fumed oak, the finished piece should be rubbed thoroughly with a soft cloth dipped in powdered pumice stone, and then left to age naturally. If a darker tone is desired, it should be held over a fire or torch and heated until the right color appears. Care should be taken that it is not heated too long, as copper under too great heat is apt to turn black. We use no lacquer on either copper or brass, age and exposure being the only agents required to produce beauty and variety of tone. All our brass work is made of the natural unfinished metal, which has a beautiful greenish tone and a soft dull surface that harmonizes admirably with the natural wood. Like copper, it darkens and mellows with age.

The authentic treatment of hardware will add immeasurably to the aesthetic quality of these projects, and knowing the time and care given to each detail by Stickley himself, we feel it is essential to follow his recommendations as completely as possible.

All hardware is put on after finishing is completed. Hinges should be mortised flush to all edges. To do this, measure and mark the position of the hinges on the edges where they will be mounted. Trace around the hinge leaf, using it as a pattern for the mortise. Score the hinge outline with a chisel inside the pencil mark. Cut the mortise to a depth equal to the thickness of the hinge leaf with a flat chisel, working first the length of the mortise and then across it with feathered cuts.

Place the hinge in the mortise and trace around the screw holes with a pencil. Make a punch mark in the center of each circle with a center punch and then drill a pilot hole, using a bit approximately half the diameter of the screw, to a depth equal to that of the screw. The pilot hole must be enlarged to accommodate the shank of the screw to avoid splitting the wood or breaking the screw when it is driven in. Use a drill bit the same diameter as the screw shank and drill into the pilot hole to a depth equal to the length of the shank. When all holes have been prepared, screw the hinge into place.

SEAT FRAMES AND UPHOLSTERY

The following description of seat frame and upholstery construction is taken from an article written by Stickley in *The Craftsman*. This article pertains to a recliner, but the same procedures can be followed for the settle with heavier frame pieces and the number of springs increased proportionately. It offers authentic information invaluable to those who want to construct their seat to his specifications.

. . . the inner seat frame for this chair is made with what is called a slip seat, or a seat that is made and upholstered separately and then slipped inside of the frame of the chair. The seat frame may be made of 1½ inch x ¾ inch hardwood, with the corners mortised and firmly glued. Care should be taken to make it small enough to allow it to slip into the frame of the chair after the leather has been drawn over it, but it should fit tightly into the chair when it is finished.

The seat itself is made by tacking a strip of strong webbing, about 3½ inches wide, over the top of this inner frame. These strips are interlaced like basket work so closely that it is almost solid, and when stretched tightly over the frame and tacked firmly to the wood it forms a strong support. Then twelve springs are sewed to the webbing, care being taken to place them where the strands cross and to stitch them firmly, so that the support afforded will be as strong as possible. Then a strong cord is stretched over the tops of the springs to hold them in place. This should be drawn down tightly both ways and tied to each spring as it passes over it, making all firm and secure so that no amount of wear will make the springs slip out of place. It is important that care should be exercised in this matter, as it would be very difficult to adjust a spring after the leather is on. After the springs are securely fastened to the webbing a layer of burlap should be stretched over them and tacked to the edge of the frame. This also should be drawn very tightly and sewed to each spring. Then a layer of tow, about 1 inch in depth should be laid evenly over the burlap and sewn firmly down to it. Upon the top of this some loose tow should be spread, taking care to leave no lumps or hollows, and this again should be covered with a smoothly-packed layer of curled hair about 2 inches in depth, special care being taken to build up the edges firmly and evenly. Another layer of burlap is then placed over the hair, and the edges are stitched so that the hair is kept in place and the edges well filled. Lastly the leather is stretched over the frame and tacked to it as already de scribed. The seat is now ready to slip into the frame of the chair, where it is held firmly by two cleats screwed to the front and back rails to afford support for the inner seat frame. The back itself is not upholstered, but is made comfortable by a large, loose cushion covered with soft leather or sheepskin and filled with cotton floss.

5. Projects

The instinct of doing things is a common one, and can be made a source of pleasure, healthy discipline and usefulness, even when the work is taken up as a recreation, and it is this purpose mainly that this series of Home Training in Cabinet-Work is intended to serve.

When one has made with his own hands any object of use or ornament there is a sense of personal pride and satisfaction in the result, that no expenditure of money can buy, and this very fact serves to dignify the task and to stamp it with individuality.

This quote comes from a series of articles entitled "Home Training in Cabinet Work: Practical Talks on Structural Woodworking," written by Stickley and first appearing in the March, 1905, issue of *The Craftsman*.

We have chosen nine pieces of furniture designed by Stickley as projects for this book. Five pieces: the screen, combination bookcase and table, recliner, bookcase, and clock case, come from the Home Training in Cabinet-Work series; four projects: the mirror, rocker, settle, and dining table, are based upon pieces produced at the Eastwood factory.

Our selections were based upon the fundamental furnishing needs of most homes. We were also concerned about project complexity and have provided projects requiring varying skill levels. Specific information about each project such as measurements and special joinery are found under the title for that project. General construction information pertaining to all (or at least several) projects is given in chapter 4 and will be referenced as needed.

The materials list for each project contains only those items specific to that project. General woodworking tools and materials, described in chapter 4, are not included on these lists, although they will be needed to complete the projects.

All measurements not given in the project instructions can be found in the working drawings that accompany each project.

Mirror

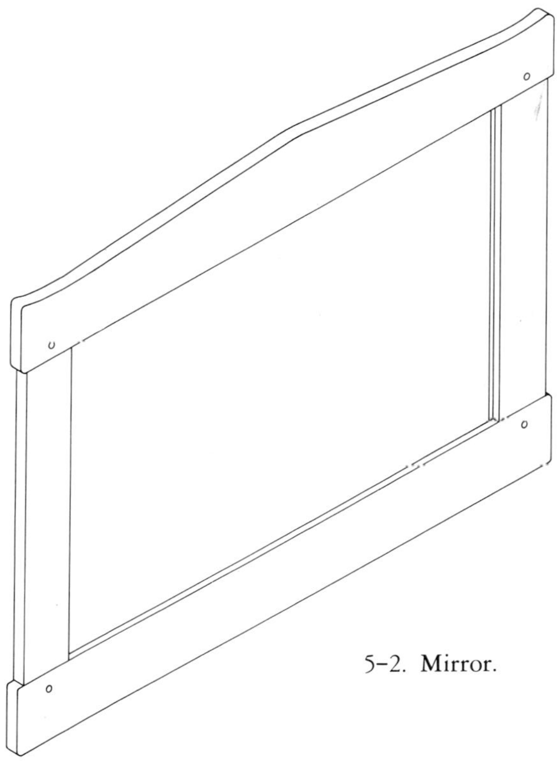

5–2. Mirror.

A mirror is a simple but very functional piece of furniture that can enhance any room. The graceful curve of this Craftsman design, with its slight lift at the ends, and the extension of both horizontal members past their vertical intersections soften an otherwise harsh rectangular shape. Instead of a sharply punctuated hole, this mirror forms a soft silhouette.

The mirror is an easy piece to construct, consisting of five pieces. Four pieces comprise the frame; the fifth piece is the back panel, which holds the mirror in place. Cut your stock to the dimensions given in the materials list. The top of the mirror is cut on a band saw using a pattern made from dimensions given in figure 5-3.

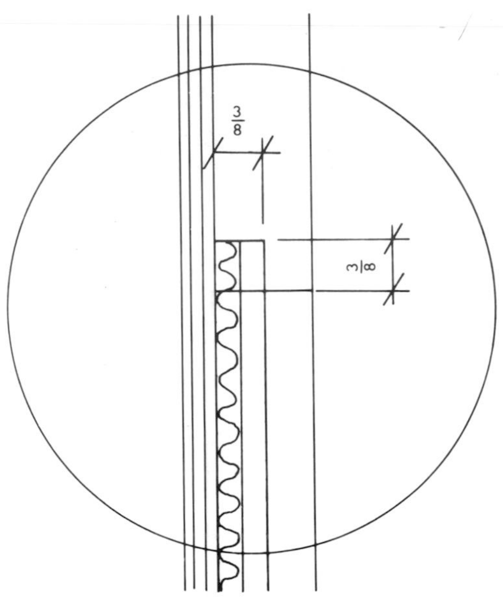

in.	cm
⅜	.95
¾	1.91
3	7.62
4	10.16
4¾	12.08
19	48.26
27¾	70.50
36	91.44

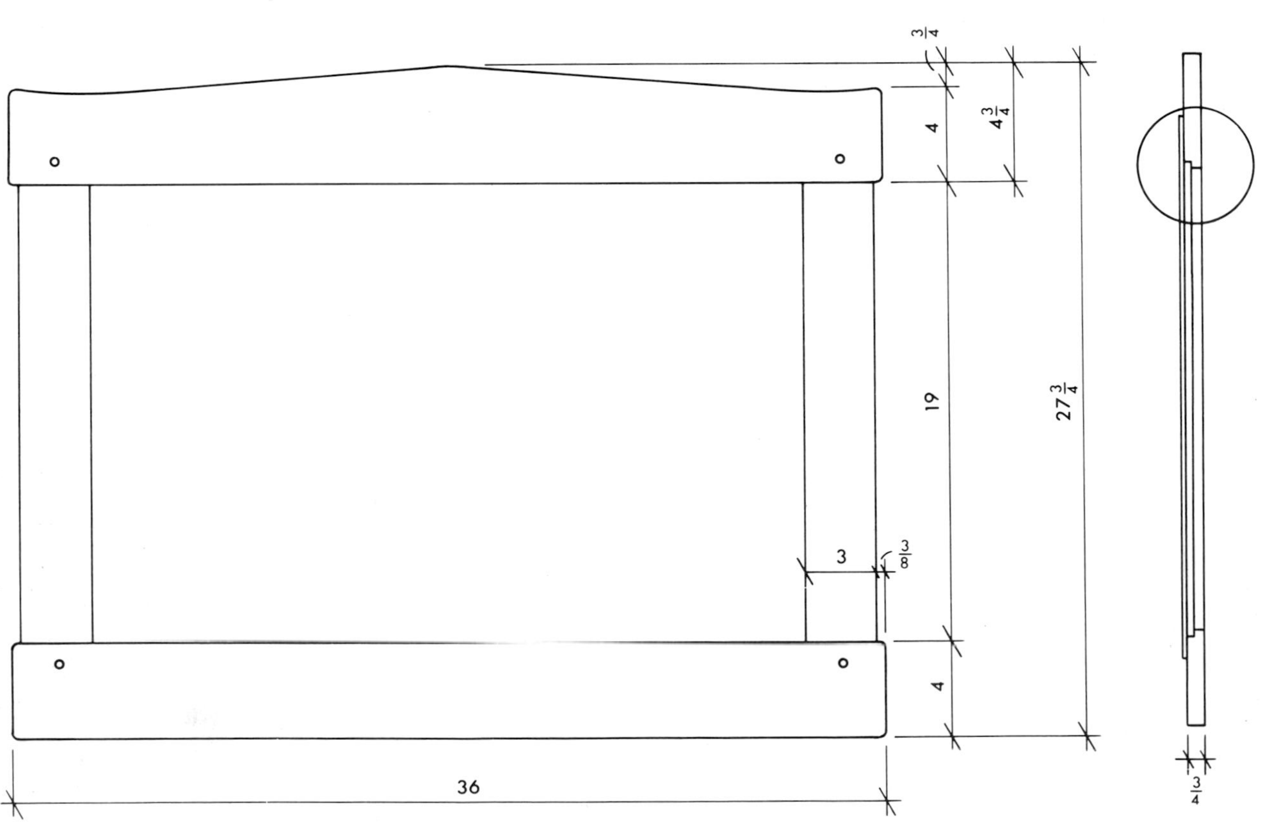

5-3. Working drawings for mirror. Front view, side view, cross section, and cross section detail.

MATERIALS

	Number of Pieces	Length in.	Length cm	Width in.	Width cm	Thickness in.	Thickness cm
Top	1	36	91.44	4¾	12.06	¾	1.91
				(pattern-cut)			
Bottom	1	36	91.44	4	10.16	¾	1.91
Side	2	21½	54.61	3	7.62	¾	1.91
Back Panel	1	33	83.82	23	58.42	⅜	.95

⅜-inch (.95-cm) dowels
1 piece cardboard, 29¼ × 19¾ × ¼ (74.30 × 50.17 × .64 cm)
1 mirror, 29¼ × 19¾ × ⅛ inches (74.30 × 50.17 × .32 cm)
14 brass flathead wood screws

PROCEDURE

In addition to the instructions given below, you may need to refer to the general instructions in chapter 4 for the following procedures:

Cutting tenons, pages 65–66
Cutting mortises with drill and chisel, page 69
Dowel-pinning, pages 82–83
Assembly, pages 79–83
Finishing, pages 84–87

Frame

Join the frame at the corners with blind mortise-and-tenon joints. Cut the tenons on the vertical members to fit into mortises cut into the horizontal members. Each tenon is 2 inches (5.08 cm) wide by 1¼ inches (3.17 cm) long by ⅜-inches (.95 cm) thick.

After assembling the frame, pin the tenons in place with ⅜ inch (.95 cm) dowels. Locate the center of each dowel ¾ inch (1.91 cm) from the seam line, centered on the tenon.

Assembly

Following subassembly of the frame, cut a ⅜-inch-deep (.95-cm) rabbet into the back side of the frame with a 1⅜-inch (.95-cm) rabbeting bit (see circle detail drawing, figure 5-3).

Apply a finish to the piece, using the procedure described in chapter 4.

Insert the mirror, with the cardboard behind it, into the rabbet that was cut into the frame. The cardboard prevents the silvering from being scratched off the back of the mirror. The mirror and cardboard are held in place by the back panel, a piece of oak plywood. Attach this panel to the back of the frame with brass flathead wood screws. Sand the edges and corners of the plywood backing until they are soft.

Screen

A folding screen is a very versatile item. It can be used to shade an area from light, divide a large room into smaller spaces, accent a corner, or provide privacy. The screen shown here is made in three sections. The lower part of each section has panels connected with butterfly joints, and the upper area of each section is covered with a curtain held in place by a brass rod.

5–5. Exploded view of screen; butterfly joints not shown.

MATERIALS

	Number of Pieces	Length in.	Length cm	Width in.	Width cm	Thickness in.	Thickness cm
Frame							
Sides	6	60	152.40	2¼	5.71	⅞	2.22
Top Rail	3	17½	44.45	4¼ (pattern-cut)	10.80	⅞	2.22
Center Rail	3	17½	44.45	2¼	5.71	⅞	2.22
Bottom Rail	3	17½	44.45	4	10.16	⅞	2.22
Panels							
Outer Panel	6	16	40.64	5	12.70	½	1.27
Center Panel	3	16	40.64	6½	16.51	½	1.27
Spline	6	16	40.64	1½	3.81	⅛	.32
Butterfly Joints							
Butterfly	12	2¾	6.98	1⁹⁄₁₆ (pattern-cut)	3.97	⅝	1.58

⅜-inch (.95-cm) dowels
6 brass rods, ¼-inch (.64-cm) diameter, 16½ inches (41.91 cm) long
4 1¾-inch (4.44 cm) double-acting brass or steel hinges
3¼ yards (2.97 m) curtain fabric

Each section of the screen is made from ten pieces plus butterfly joints. Five pieces (two sides and three rails) make up each frame, and five pieces (two outer panels, one center panel, and two splines), plus butterflies, comprise the paneling. Cut your stock to the dimensions given in the materials list. The curved top of each section is cut on a band saw following a pattern made according to the dimensions given in figure 5-8 (see figure 5-6).

5–6. Use a drum sanding attachment on a drill press to sand the pattern cut in the top rails.

5–7. Screen.

in.	cm	in.	cm	in.	cm
⅞	2.22	4	10.16	15	38.10
1¾	4.46	4⅛	10.48	15½	39.37
2	5.08	4¼	10.80	20	50.80
2¼	5.72	4½	11.43	32½	82.55
2½	6.35	6½	16.51	60	152.40

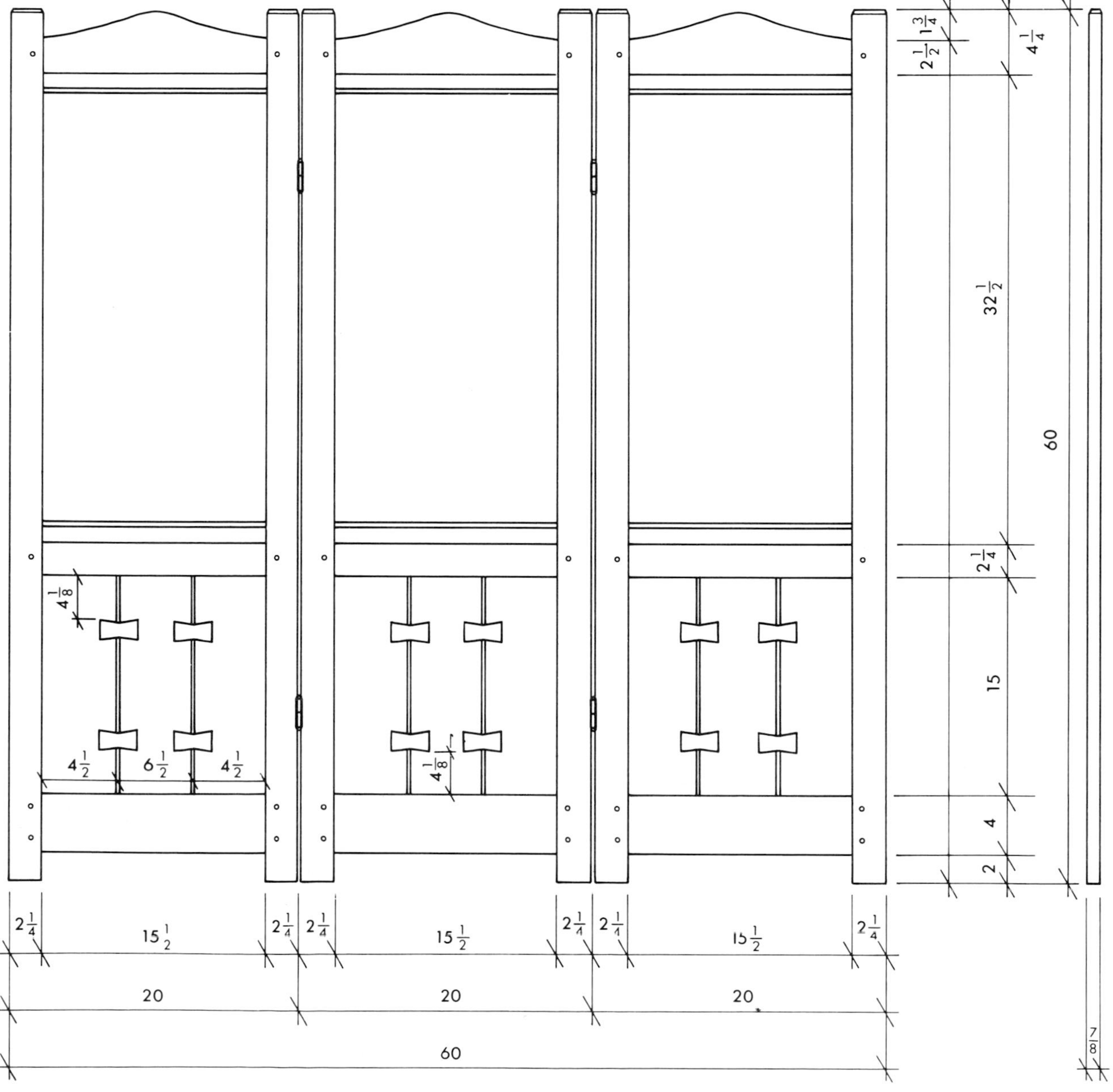

5–8. Working drawings for screen. Top, front, and side views.

PROCEDURE

In addition to the instructions given below, you may need to refer to the general instructions in chapter 4 for the following procedures:

Cutting tenons, pages 65–66
Cutting mortises with router table, pages 76–77
Dowel-pinning, pages 82–83
Beveling, page 70
Attaching hinges, page 88
Assembly, pages 79–83
Finishing, pages 84–87

Frame

Join the frame with blind mortise-and-tenon joints. The tenons on the top and center rails are 1½ inches (3.81 cm) wide by 1 inch (2.54 cm) long by ½ inch (1.27 cm) thick. Use a router table to cut the mortises in the side.

Cut a ½-inch-deep (1.27-cm) dado in the top of the bottom rail, the bottom of the center rail, and the sides, on center, with a ½ inch (1.27-cm) dado blade (figures 5-9 and 5-10). These will accommodate the panels.

Using a ¼-inch (.64-cm) bit, drill holes for the curtain rods on the inside edges of each side of the frames. Locate these holes 1 inch (2.54 cm), on center, below the mortises for the top rails to hold the top rods and above the mortises for the center rails to hold the bottom rods. Drill the two holes on the left side of each frame 1 inch (2.54 cm) deep and the two holes on the right side of each frame ½ inch (1.27 cm) deep. The extra depth on the left sides allows for easy insertion and removal of the brass rods when installing the curtains.

5–9. Two panels resting in the dado cut in the bottom rail.

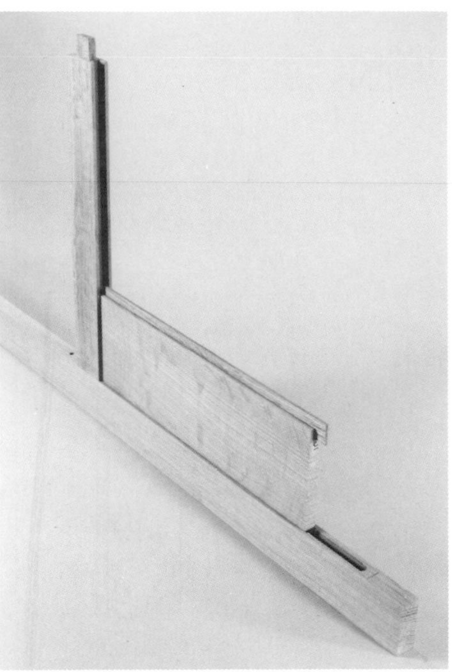

5–10. One panel resting in dado cut in the side and the center rails. Note spline in edge of panel.

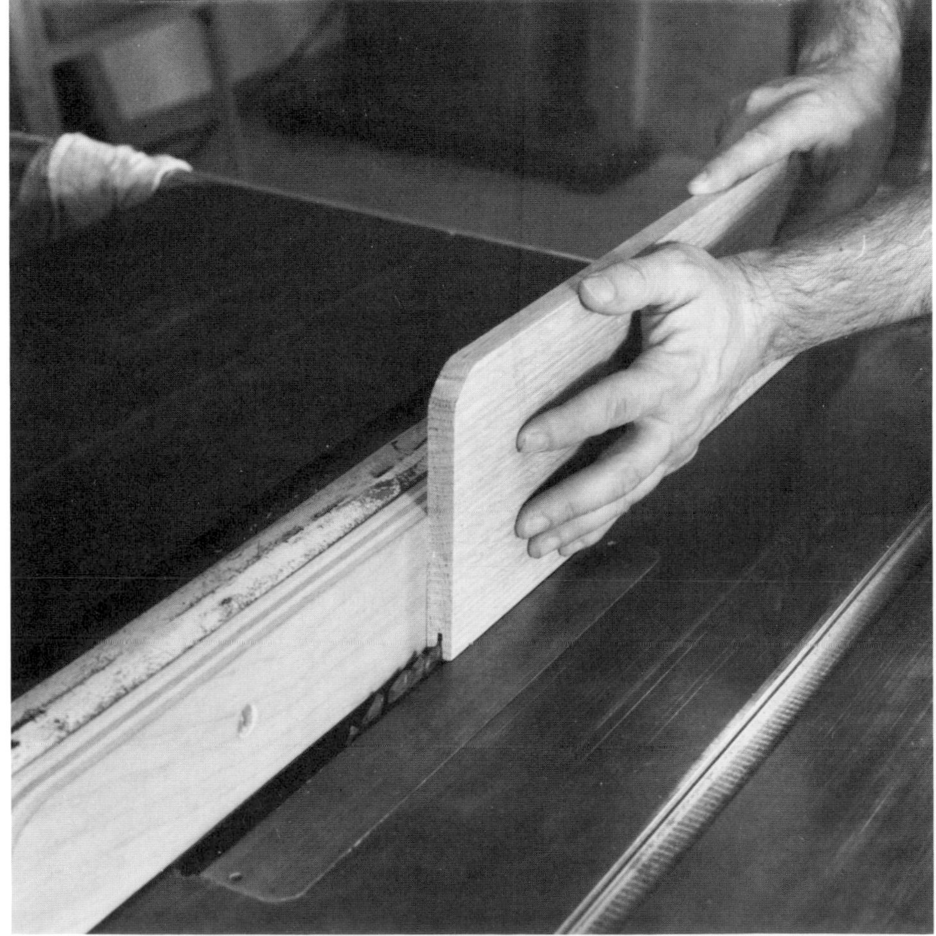

5–11. Cutting the spline dado in the edge of a panel.

Panels

Make cuts ¾ inch (1.91 cm) deep and ⅛ inch (.32 cm) wide, on center, into the panels' edges to accommodate the splines (figure 5-11). Using the router table and a beading bit, slightly bevel the splined edge of each face of all panels, as shown in figure 5-12.

Round the two outside corners of each outer panel as shown, to allow for movement and ease in assembly.

Subassembly

Assemble each frame by applying glue to only the mortise-and-tenon joints (figure 5-13); allow the whole panel section free movement. This movement is necessary to prevent the panels from splitting or putting undue pressure on the frame if they expand.

Pin each tenon in place with a ⅜-inch (.95-cm) dowel that penetrates the full thickness of the frame and shows on both sides. Use one dowel on each of the tenons for the top and center rails. Locate the center of each dowel ½ inch (1.27 cm) from the seam line, centered on the tenon. Pin the bottom rail in place with two dowels on each end. Place the dowels' centers ½ inch (1.27 cm) from the seam line and 2 inches (5.08 cm) apart, on center.

Bevel the top of each side of the sections with a block and sandpaper. Cut the bevel using guidelines placed ⅛ inch (.32 cm) down from the top edge on each side and ⅛ inch (.32 cm) in from all edges.

Butterfly Joints

The butterfly joints are the last pieces to be made and fitted. They prevent the loose panels from separating along their seams and add a decorative motif to the panels.

To prepare the panels, make a cardboard template of the butterfly, using the dimensions given

5–12. Beveling the splined edge of a panel on the router table with a beading bit.

5–13. Frame clamped with bar clamps. Check the frame for alignment using a combination or framing square.

in figure 5-14. With this template, draw the location of each butterfly on the panels. Drill ½-inch (1.27-cm) holes in each of the butterfly "wings." Draw guidelines from each hole to the corners of the wing, as shown in figure 5-15. With a keyhole saw, cut along the guidelines. To finish each butterfly hole, remove the last piece of material with a flat chisel, bevel facing in (figure 5-16).

Using the same template, draw outlines of the butterflies on ⅝-inch-thick (1.58-cm) stock, making sure the template is placed so that its length is parallel to the grain of the wood. Cut the butterflies slightly oversize and file each to fit its hole. Then mark each butterfly and its hole with the same letter or number. When all butterflies are fitted, glue each in place, allowing a 1/16-inch (.15-cm) projection from the panel faces on both sides.

Final Touches

Apply a finish to the piece, using the procedure described in chapter 4.

Because of the special movements required by a folding screen, double-acting hinges should be used. Two hinges join each section pair, one placed 10½ inches (26.67 cm) down from the top and the other 10½ inches (26.67 cm) up from the bottom.

Curtains for the screen should be made of plain, neutral-colored fabric of medium weight, such as linen. Each fabric panel is gathered on the solid brass rods at top and bottom.

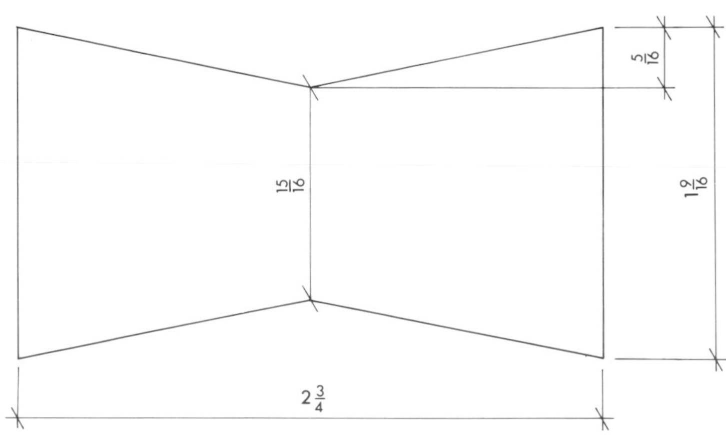

5-14. Working drawing for butterfly.

in.	cm
5/16	.79
15/16	2.38
1 9/16	3.96
2 3/4	6.98

5-15. Cutting butterfly joint with a keyhole saw.

5-16. Removing remaining material with a flat chisel, bevel of chisel facing in.

Combination Bookcase and Table

This piece of furniture was originally designed by Stickley for students who found it necessary to have their books as close at hand as their writing pad. The table surface is high enough to be used as a writing surface when the user is seated on most side chairs. The shelf area is divided into quarters to take advantage of the full shelf as storage space; books can be stored on all four sides. This Craftsman piece is designed to bear heavy loads.

5-18. Exploded view of combination bookcase and table.

The combination bookcase and table is composed of fifty-four pieces. Twelve pieces: four legs, four top rails, and four bottom rails, comprise the frame. The bottom shelf, composed of several boards laminated edge-to-edge, contains thirty-six slats, which form the book holders. Four cleats support the tabletop, which is also made from several boards laminated edge-to-edge. Cut your stock to the dimensions given in the materials list.

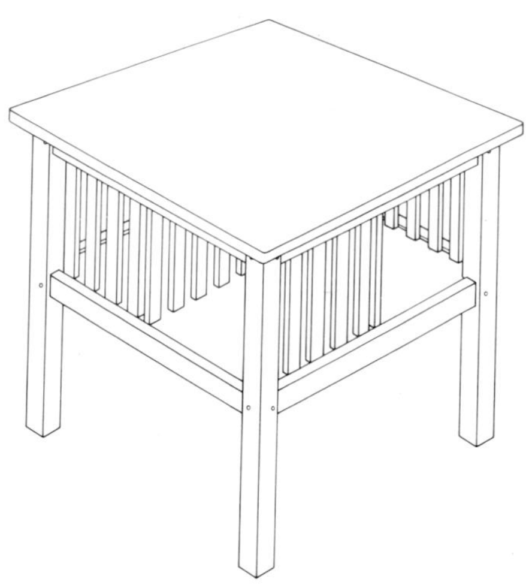

5-19. Combination bookcase and table.

MATERIALS

	Number of Pieces	Length		Width		Thickness	
		in.	cm	in.	cm	in.	cm
Frame							
Leg	4	31	78.74	1¾	4.44	1¾	4.44
Rail	8	23	58.42	2	5.08	⅞	2.22
Bottom Shelf and Slats							
Shelf	1	21¾	55.26	21¾	55.26	¾	1.91
Slat	36	15¼	38.74	1	2.54	½	1.27
Cleats							
Cleat	4	23¼	59.06	1	2.54	⅝	1.58
Tabletop							
Top	1	28	71.12	28	71.12	⅞	2.22

⅜-inch (.95-cm) dowels
8 table irons
16 steel flathead wood screws

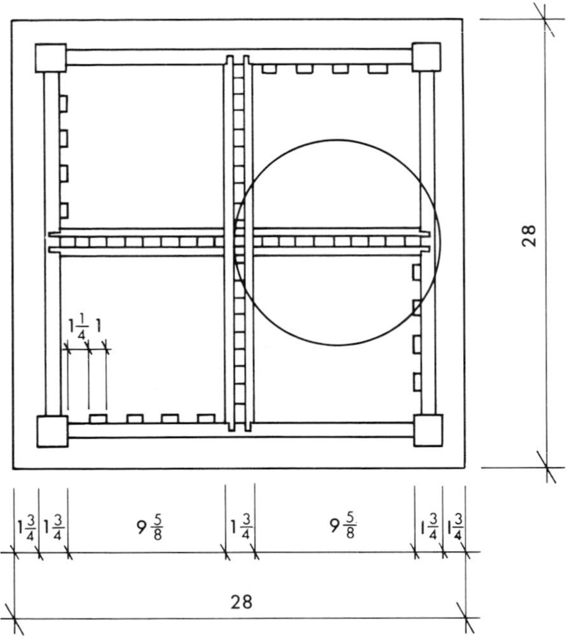

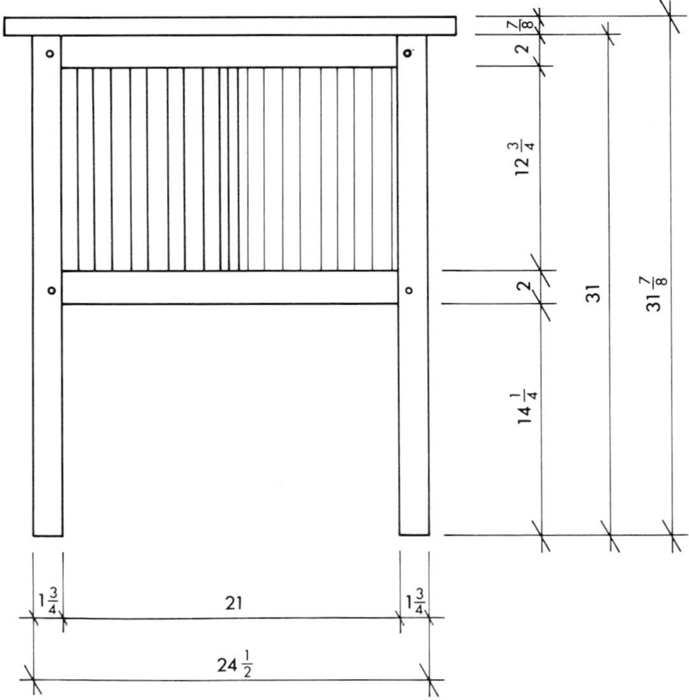

5–20. Working drawings for combination bookcase and table. Top and side view. (For circled detail, see figure 5-25.)

PROCEDURE

In addition to the instructions given below, you may need to refer to the general instructions in chapter 4 for the following procedures:

Cutting tenons, pages 65–66
Cutting mortises with router table, pages 76–77
Butt-joining, page 71
Cutting mortises with drill and chisel, page 69
Dowel-pining, pages 82–83
Squaring laminated boards, pages 74–75
Assembly, pages 79–83
Finishing, pages 84–87

Frame

The mortise-and-tenon joint is the main joint used for the construction of this piece. Connect the rails and legs with blind mortise-and-tenon joints (figure 5-21).

in.	cm
⅞	2.22
1	2.54
1¼	3.17
1¾	4.44
2	5.08
9⅝	24.44
12¾	32.38
14¼	36.19
21	53.34
24½	62.23
28	71.12
31	78.74
31⅞	80.96

5-21. Blind mortise-and-tenon joints connect top rails with legs.

The rail tenons measure 1 inch (2.54 cm) wide by 1 inch (2.54 cm) long by ½ inch (1.27 cm) thick. Measure in 11/16 inch (1.75 cm) from the two outside faces of each leg to locate the center line for each mortise. Locate the center of each mortise for the bottom rails 15½ inches (39.37 cm) up from the bottom of each leg; those for the top rails, 1 inch (2.54 cm) down from the top of each leg. Cut the mortises with the router table.

Dado the four bottom rails along their inside faces to hold the edge of the shelf. Cut these dados ⅛ inch (.32 cm) down from the top edge, ¾ inch (1.91 cm) wide, to a depth of ⅜ inch (.95 cm) (figure 5-22).

5-22. Dados cut in bottom rails hold shelf edges.

Bottom Shelf and Slats

Laminate three or four boards (depending on width) edge-to-edge with 3/8-inch (.95-cm) dowels to form the 21¾- by 21¾-inch (55.25- by 55.25-cm) bottom shelf. Notch a 3/8-inch (.95-cm) square on each corner to accommodate the legs.

Cut tenons onto only the bottom ends of the slats. These tenons measure ½ inch (1.27 cm) wide by 3/8 inch (.95 cm) long by ¼ inch (.64 cm) thick. Locate the position of each slat on the shelf (see figures 5-20 and 5-24) and mark the shelf for cutting the mortises. Using a fence or guide clamped to the shelf, cut the mortises with a router and a ¼-inch (.64-cm) straight bit (figure 5-23).

5-23. Cut mortises for slats into shelf with a router and fence.

5-24. Insert slats into their mortises and check for proper fit.

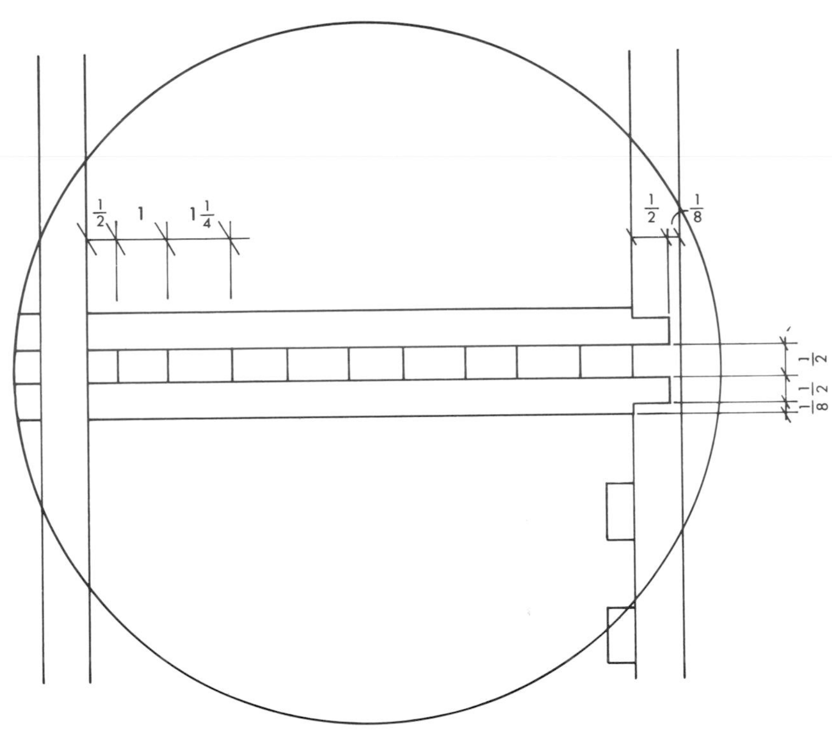

5-25. Detail of cleat joint and slat position.

in.	cm
⅛	.32
½	1.27
1	2.54
1¼	3.17

Cleats

Cut barefaced tenons measuring ¾ inch (1.91 cm) wide by ½ inch (1.27 cm) long by ½ inch (1.27 cm) thick onto both ends of each cleat. Join the four cleats at their centers using an edge cross-lap joint. To make this joint, set a ⅝-inch-wide (1.58-cm) dado blade on the table saw to a depth of ½ inch (1.27 cm). Locate center lines for lap joint cuts 10 9⁄16 inches (26.83 cm) from the end of each cleat. Cut joints using the miter guide as a support. Remember, one pair of cleats should be cut on the top edge and the other pair on the bottom edge (figure 5-26).

Cut mortises, measuring ½ inch (1.27 cm) wide by ¾ inch (1.91 cm) deep by ½ inch (1.27 cm) long, for the barefaced tenons into the top edge and inside face of each top rail (figure 5-27). Locate these mortises 10 inches (25.40 cm), on center, from the inside edge of each post. Cut mortises using the drill and chisel cleanout method.

5-26. Four cleats joined at their centers with an edge cross-lap joint.

5-27. Barefaced tenons on cleat ends fit into mortises on inside of top rails.

Subassembly

Assemble frame and bottom shelf as shown in figure 5-28. Pin each rail tenon into the leg with a ⅜-inch (.95-cm) dowel placed ⅝ inch (1.58 cm) from the seam, centered on the tenon. When this assembly is dry, glue the cleats into place and clamp as shown in figure 5-29. Then glue the slats into position, clamping their top ends to the cleats and top rails (figure 5-30).

Tabletop

The tabletop is constructed of three or four pieces of stock (depending on width) laminated edge-to-edge with ⅜-inch (.95-cm) dowels. Lay out the top, being careful to alternate the end grain direction to minimize warping. Using a router, trim one end square, then measure to length and trim the other end.

Final Touches

Apply a finish to the piece, using the procedure described in chapter 4.

The top is held in position on the base with eight table irons. Countersink the irons into the top edge of the top rails above the open area in each side, as shown in figure 5-31. Place the first iron 5 inches (12.70 cm) from the outside corner of each leg and the second iron 9 inches (22.86 cm) from the outside corner of each leg.

5–28. Assembly of frame: legs, rails, and shelf.

5–29. Cleats glued and clamped into top rails.

5–30. Slats assembled and clamped with a C-clamp.

5–31. Table irons in position on top rail.

Rocker

The rocking chair has traditionally been a favorite in American homes. Its rhythmic back-and-forth motion produces a mesmerizing serenity, soothing people of all ages. This Craftsman chair is from a line of rockers produced at Stickley's Eastwood factory.

Of all pieces of furniture, chairs are the most difficult to build because of the critical alignment of their many parts and the large number of surfaces to finish. In the rocking chair, these factors are compounded by bent horizontal back slats and rockers. We recommend that you begin this project by drawing full-size drawings of the side and top cross section views of the chair (see figures 5-35 and 5-36). The side view will give you the correct angle to cut the shoulders of the front and back stretchers.

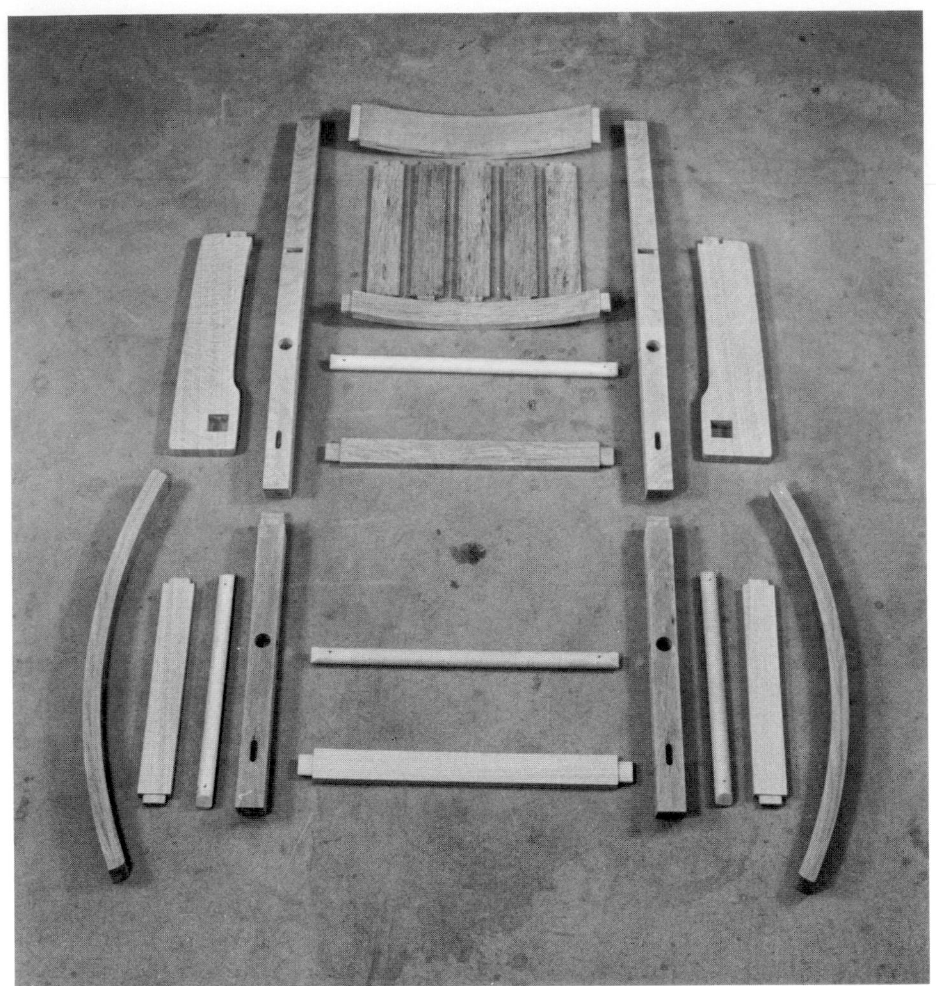

5–33. Exploded view of rocker.

The rocker consists of twenty-five pieces. Its frame has four legs connected near their bottoms by four stretchers, one in front, one in back, and one on each side. Four dowels connected to the legs comprise the seat frame. The back consists of two bent, horizontal slats attached to the back legs. Five vertical slats that provide support are connected to these two horizontal slats. The two arms are supported by arm supports on the front legs. Two bent, laminated boards form each rocker, which is attached on either side to the front and back legs. Cut your stock according to the dimensions given in the materials list. Use paper patterns to accurately cut the front and back legs, top horizontal back slat, arms, and arm supports.

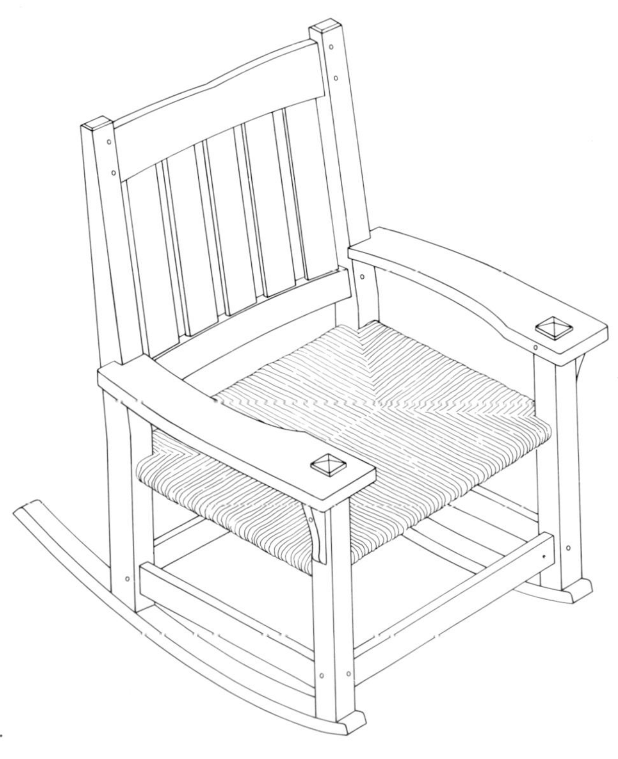

5–34. Rocker.

MATERIALS

	Number of Pieces	Length in.	Length cm	Width in.	Width cm	Thickness in.	Thickness cm
Frame							
Front Leg	2	21	53.34	1¾	4.44	1¾	4.44
Back Leg	2	33⅝	85.40	(pattern-cut)		1¾	4.44
Front Stretcher	1	20¼	51.44	2	5.08	⅝	1.58
Back Stretcher	1	19	48.26	2	5.08	⅝	1.58
Side Stretcher	2	16¾	42.55	2	5.08	⅝	1.58
Seat Frame							
Front Dowel	1	20¼	51.44			1 (diam.)	2.54
Back Dowel	1	19	48.26			1 (diam.)	2.54
Side Dowel	2	16¾	42.55			1 (diam.)	2.54
Rockers							
Rocker	2	29 32 (radius)	73.66 81.28	1¾	4.44	1⅛	2.86
Back							
Bottom Horizontal Back Slat	1	19¼ 23 (radius)	48.90 58.42	2	5.08	⅝	1.58
Top Horizontal Back Slat	1	19¼ 23 (radius)	48.90 58.42	4 (pattern-cut)	10.16	⅝	1.58
Vertical Back Slat	5	14¼	36.20	2 5/16	5.87	⅜	.95
Arms							
Arm	2	19¼	48.90	4½ (pattern-cut)	11.43	⅞	2.22
Arm Support	2	5⅞	14.92	1¾ (pattern-cut)	4.44	1	2.54 .

⅜-inch (.95-cm) dowels
¾-inch (1.91-cm) dowels
rush seat

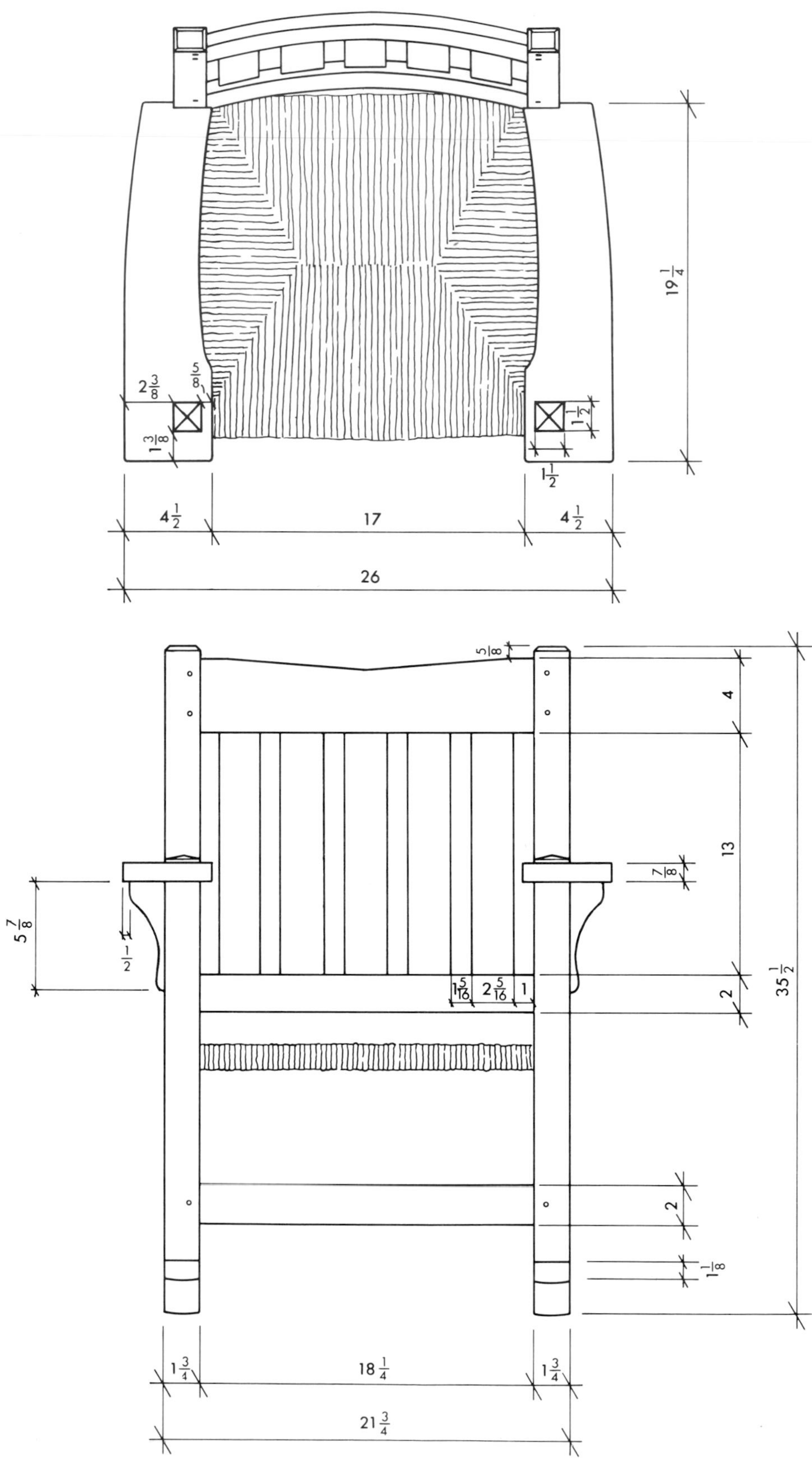

in.	cm
1/2	1.28
5/8	1.58
7/8	2.22
1	2.54
1 1/8	2.86
1 5/16	3.33
1 3/8	3.49
1 1/2	3.81
1 3/4	4.44
2	5.08
2 1/4	5.71
2 5/16	5.87
2 3/8	6.03
4	10.16
4 1/2	11.43
5 7/8	14.92
13	33.02
17	43.18
18 1/4	46.35
19 1/4	48.89
21 3/4	55.24
26	66.04
35 1/2	90.17

5–35. Working drawings for rocker. Top and front views.

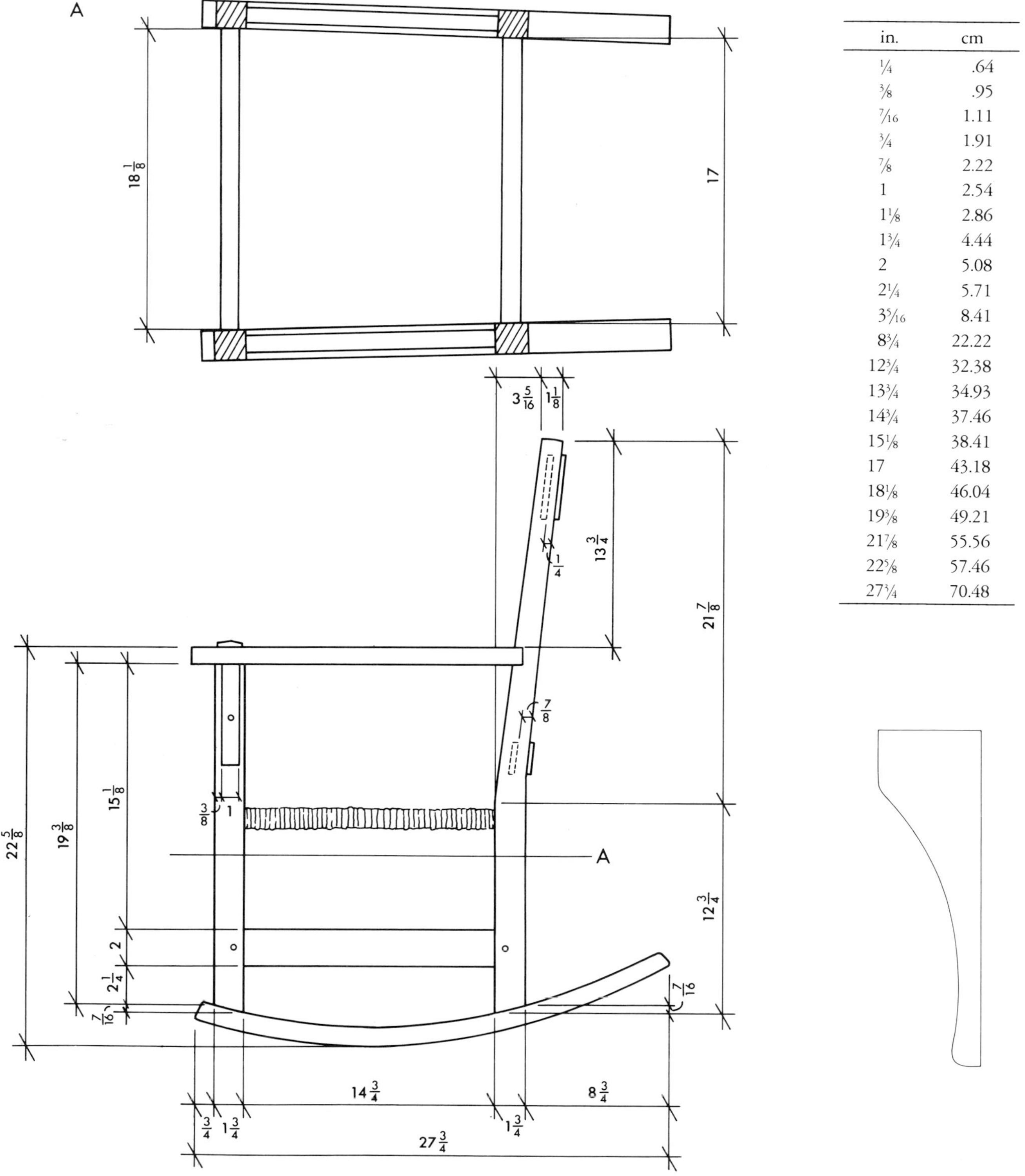

in.	cm
1/4	.64
3/8	.95
7/16	1.11
3/4	1.91
7/8	2.22
1	2.54
1 1/8	2.86
1 3/4	4.44
2	5.08
2 1/4	5.71
3 5/16	8.41
8 3/4	22.22
12 3/4	32.38
13 3/4	34.93
14 3/4	37.46
15 1/8	38.41
17	43.18
18 1/8	46.04
19 3/8	49.21
21 7/8	55.56
22 5/8	57.46
27 3/4	70.48

5-36. Working drawings for rocker. Top view cross section at A, side view, and rocker arm support.

PROCEDURE

In addition to the instructions given below, you may need to refer to the general instructions in chapter 4 for the following procedures:

Cutting tenons, pages 65–66
Cutting mortises with router table, pages 76–77
Bending, pages 77–78
Cutting tenon on bent stock, pages 66–67
Cutting mortises with drill and chisel, page 69
Beveling, page 70
Dowel-pinning, pages 82–83
Assembly, pages 79–83
Finishing, pages 84–87

Frame

Cut blind tenons measuring 1¼ inches (3.17 cm) wide by 1 inch (2.54 cm) long by ⅜ inch (.95 cm) thick on the ends of the four stretchers. Note that the front and back stretchers should have angled shoulders. Locate and cut mortises in the legs to accommodate the stretcher tenons, using the router table.

Seat Frame

The rush seat frame construction requires 1-inch (2.54-cm) diameter birch dowels. Drill 1-inch (2.54-cm) diameter holes into the same faces on the legs, where the stretcher mortises were cut 7⁹⁄₁₆ inches (19.20 cm) up from the center of each stretcher mortise. Because the holes will meet inside each leg, you must cut the ends of each dowel at a 45-degree angle so they can make full penetration. Mark each dowel and hole for later matching.

Rockers

Bend the rockers and horizontal back slats to the radii given in the

5–37. After rocker halves are bent, apply glue to both pieces.

5–38. Tape both halves together to maintain alignment when clamp pressure is applied.

5-39. Rocker halves in mold, with alternating clamps in position.

5-40. With block plane, level one side of each rocker.

5-41. Using a jig to keep rocker from riding up on the blade, trim to width, remembering to put planed side against the fence.

materials list. Because the rockers are so thick, you should construct each from two pieces of stock laminated together.

To laminate a rocker, apply glue to both pieces after the halves are bent (figure 5-37). Tape both halves together to maintain alignment when clamp pressure is applied (figure 5-38). Place the taped halves into the mold and clamp, alternating clamp positions to equalize pressure (figure 5-39). After the glue has dried, remove the rocker from the mold and level one side using a block plane (figure 5-40). Use a table saw, with a jig to keep the rocker from riding up on the blade of the table saw, to level the opposite side. Remember to place the block-planed side against the fence (figure 5-41) when leveling the opposite side with the table saw.

Back

Cut blind tenons measuring 1⁵⁄₁₆ inches (3.33 cm) wide by ¾ inch (1.91 cm) long by ¼ inch (.64 cm) thick in both ends of the five vertical back slats. Locate mortise positions for these tenons on the two bent horizontal back stats (see figure 5-35 for measurements). Cut these mortises using the drill and chisel cleanout method.

Cut blind tenons onto the ends of both horizontal back slats. The top horizontal tenons measure 3 inches (7.62 cm) wide by 1 inch (2.54 cm) long by ⅜ inch (.95 cm) thick; the bottom horizontal tenons measure 1 inch (2.54 cm) wide by 1 inch (2.54 cm) long by ⅜ inch (.95 cm) thick. Cut these bent tenons using the method described in chapter 4. Locate the mortises for these tenons on the legs (see figures 5-35 and 5-36), and cut with the drill and chisel cleanout method.

Cut the curved edge on the top horizontal back slat. At its narrowest point (in the middle of the slat), the slat should be 2¼ inches (5.72 cm) wide.

Arms

Cut each arm with a band saw, using a pattern made from the drawings (figure 5-42). Connect the arm to the front leg with a through mortise-and-tenon joint. Cut through tenons that measure 1½ inches (3.81 cm) wide by 1⅛ inches (2.86 cm) long by 1½ inches (3.81 cm) thick onto the tops of the front legs. Bevel the tenons on the ends, beginning 15/16 inch (2.38 cm) from the shoulder and meeting in the center to form a peak. Locate the mortises on the arms (see figure 5-35) and cut, using the drill and chisel cleanout method.

Connect the arms to the back leg with blind haunched mortise-and-tenon joints (figure 5-43). Cut a blind haunched tenon in the back of the arm measuring 1 inch (2.54 cm) wide by 1 inch (2.54 cm) long by ½ inch (1.27 cm) thick with a ¼ inch (.64 cm) by ½ inch (1.27 cm) haunch. Begin the tenon cuts ½ inch (1.27 cm) from the inside of each arm, 3/16 inch (.47 cm) down from the top. In order for the shoulders of these tenons to fit flush against the back leg, they must be cut at an angle. The angle can be taken from your full-size side view drawing. Cut these bent tenons using the method described in chapter 4. Locate mortises using the full-size side view drawing, and cut with the drill and chisel cleanout method.

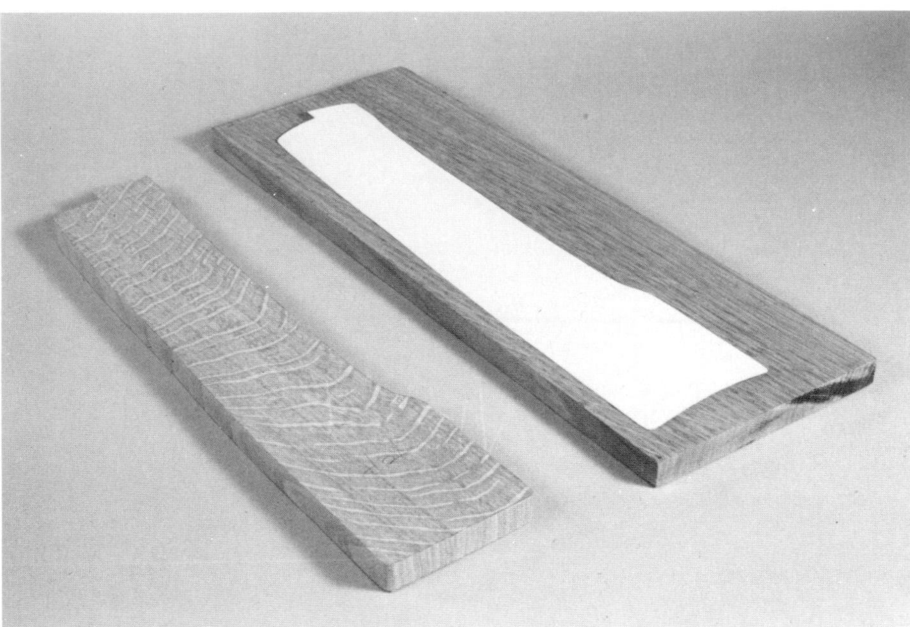

5-42. Place pattern in position and trace onto stock. The same pattern can be used for the other arm. Remember to flip the pattern over before tracing the second arm.

5-43. Shaded area shows material to be removed to make blind haunched tenons.

Assembly

Glue together all of the chair's parts except the rockers.

Pin the tenons of the four stretchers with ⅜-inch (.95-cm) dowels placed ⅜ inch (.95 cm) from the inside leg edge, centered on the tenons.

Pin the tenons of the bottom horizontal back slat with a ⅜-inch (.95-cm) dowel placed ⅜ inch (.95 cm) from the inside back leg edge, centered on the tenon. Pin the top horizontal back slat with two ⅜-inch (.95-cm) dowels at each end, placed ⅜ inch (.95 cm) from the inside back leg edge. Locate the top dowel 1¼ inches (3.17 cm) down from the top of the post; center the bottom dowel 2½ inches (6.35 cm) below the top one.

Pin the through tenon of the front leg to the arm with a ⅜-inch (.95-cm) dowel, centered on the tenon, on the inside edge of the arm.

Cut two arm supports with a band saw, using a pattern made from figure 5-36. Sand each curve, using a drum sanding attachment on a drill press. Glue into place, and pin to the legs with ⅜-inch (.95-cm) dowels placed 2¾ inches (6.98 cm) up from the bottom of the support, on center.

The rockers are now fitted and glued into place. Mark each rocker with a penciled outline of where it meets each leg. Chalk the areas within the lines. Place the rocker in its proper position on the legs and rub back and forth, moving the rocker toward and away from the opposite legs. This will deposit chalk on the leg bottoms; those areas on the leg bottoms showing chalk need adjustment. Remove excess stock by filing or block sanding. Repeat until the bottom of each leg is covered with chalk.

To ensure a precise fit, tape #80-grit sandpaper to the curve of the rocker, and trim it to the exact width of the rocker. Draw a series of pencil lines diagonally across the bottom of each leg. Sand by moving the rocker with the same motion described above until the pencil marks are gone. Glue the rockers to the legs, as shown in figure 5-44.

To reinforce this joint, use a 2-inch-long (5.08-cm), ¾-inch (1.91-cm) dowel. Drill a ¾-inch (1.91-cm) diameter hole to a depth of 1⅞ inches (4.76 cm), on center on each leg, through the rocker. Cut a ¾-inch-deep (1.91-cm) slot into both ends of each dowel; the slots on one end should be perpendicular to those on the other (figure 5-45). Insert ½-inch-long (1.27-cm) wedges into the slots; when the dowel is glued and driven into place, these wedges expand and lock the dowel in position.

Final Touches

With a file or hand plane, remove protruding dowels and slightly round the bottom surface of each rocker. Bevel the top of each back leg with a block and sandpaper. Cut these bevels according to guidelines placed ⅛ inch (.32 cm) down from the top edge on each side and ⅛ inch (.32 cm) in from all edges on the top.

Apply a finish to the piece using the procedure described in chapter 4.

The rush seat should be completed after the chair has been fumed and finished. The rush seat could be woven by the builder with the help of a text on the subject or done by a professional.

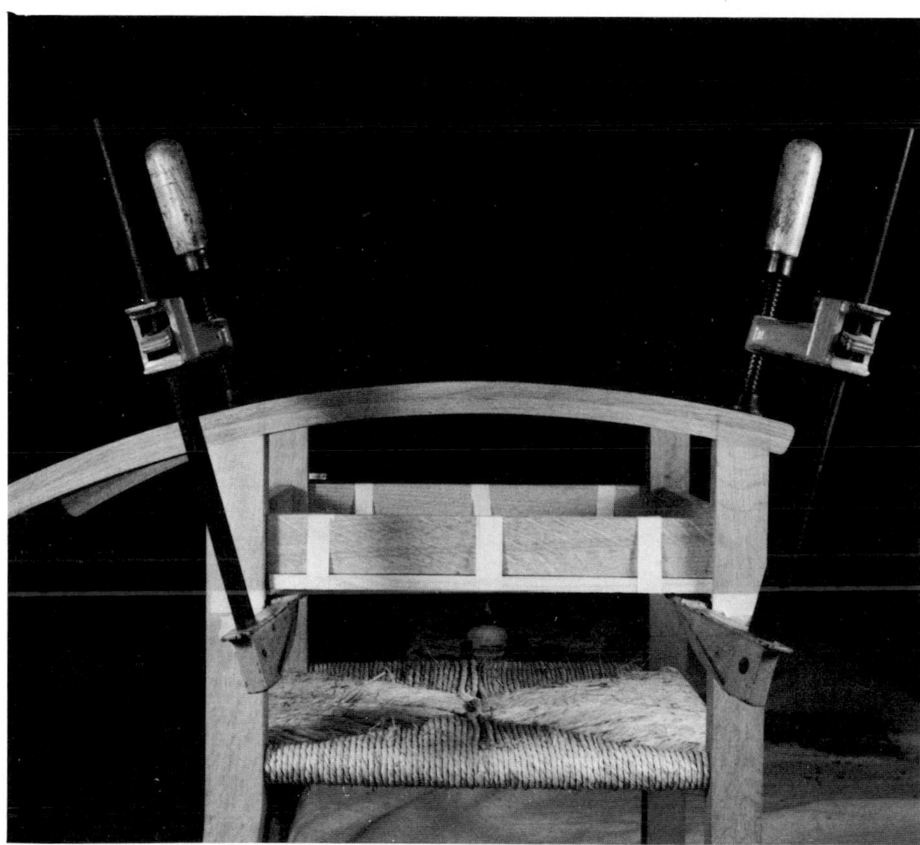

5-44. Before clamps are put in position, tape a piece of pine to the top edge of the side stretcher to prevent damage from clamps.

5-45. Dowel in position, with opposing slots. Perpendicular slots prevent the dowel from splitting when driven into place. Wedges are cut ½ inch (1.27 cm) in length to assure full penetration.

Recliner

The mechanics of this chair are based upon a design that has been adapted by many furniture designers. The original mechanical concept is attributed to the British Arts and Crafts designer William Morris, and often these chairs, no matter what they look like, are called Morris chairs.

This recliner is one of several designed by Stickley. It is constructed of heavy members and meant to remain in a more or less fixed position in a room, unlike a rocker or side chair. The back of the recliner is fastened to the inside of the legs with pins, upon which it pivots. The back can be adjusted to four positions: the posts of the back rest on adjusting pins that can be inserted in any of the four pairs of holes drilled in the back inside edges of the arms. The many through mortise-and-tenon joints in this chair demonstrate Stickley's philosophy of structural ornament.

Begin this project by making a full-size drawing of the side view of the recliner (see figure 5-50). This will give you patterns for the angle cuts on the top and bottom side rails, the tops and bottoms of the side slats, the profiles of the arms, and the angles of the shoulders at the tops of the back legs.

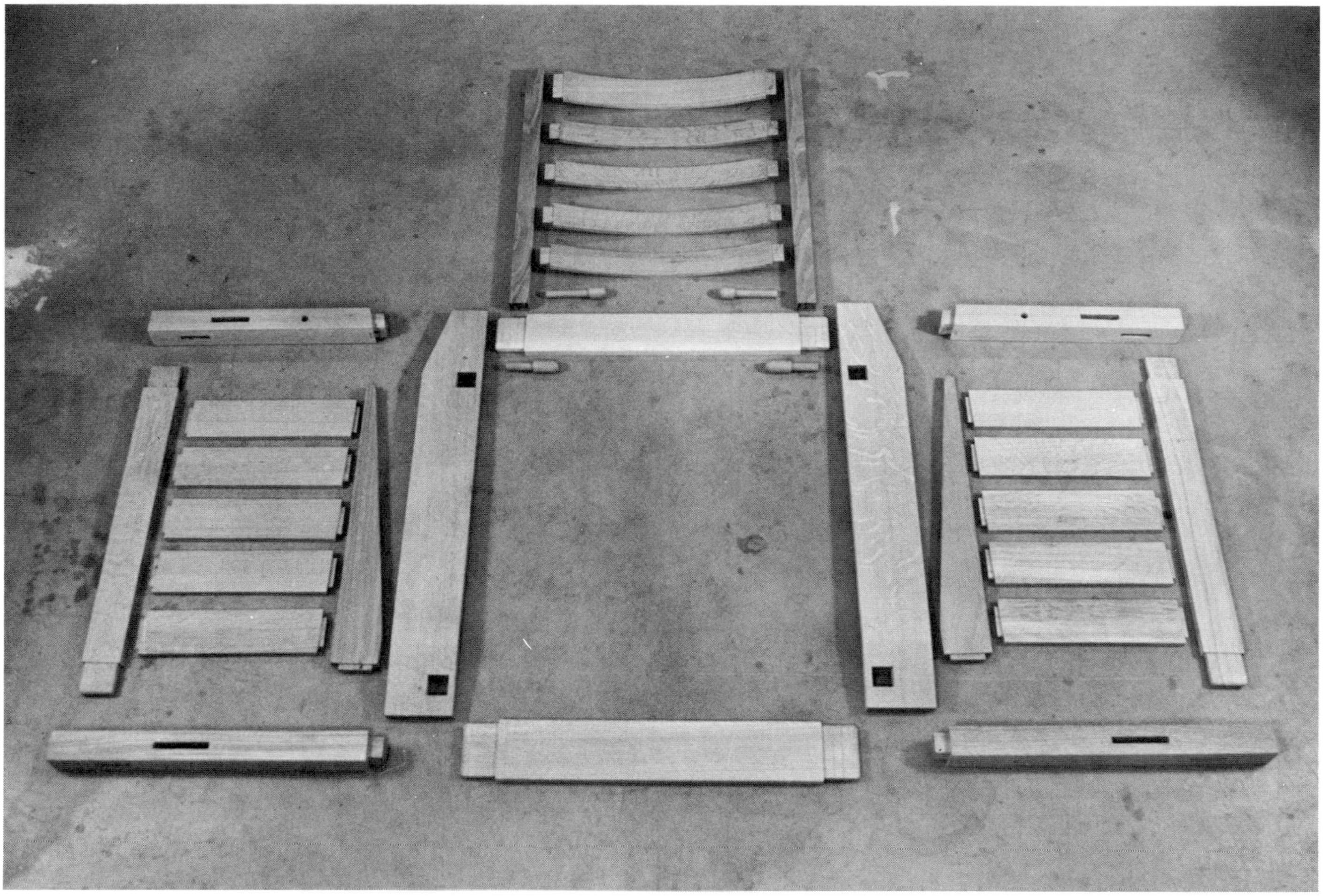

5–47. Exploded view of recliner.

5–48. Recliner.

Three subassemblies are required to build this chair: two sides, each assembled independently, and the back. Each side is made up of twelve pieces: two legs, two rails, five slats, one arm, and two arm supports. The back consists of seven pieces: two posts, a top horizontal slat, and four bottom horizontal slats. Once the sides are assembled, they are connected by a front and back rail, forming the base of the chair. The back is then attached with four removable pins. Cut your stock according to the dimensions given in the materials list.

Welcome to Dalton-Whitfield Library !
You have the following items:

---

1. Live wire
   Barcode: 31685002484542 Due:
   05/28/2013 11:59 PM
2. Hell's corner
   Barcode: 31685002465970 Due:
   05/28/2013 11:59 PM

NGRL-DW 2013-05-14 12:24
You were helped by Deborah

Welcome to Dalton-Whitfield Library !
You checked out the following items:

---

1. The furniture of Gustav Stickley :
   history, techniques, and projects
   Barcode: 31057902144081 Due:
   05/28/2013 11:59 PM

NGRL-DW 2013-05-14 12:24
706-876-1360

Cost of buying these items: $18.95
Cost of using the library: Priceless!

MATERIALS

	Number of Pieces	Length		Width		Thickness	
		in.	cm	in.	cm	in.	cm
Base							
Front Leg	2	24⅛	61.28	2¼	5.71	2¼	5.71
Front Leg Halves	4	24⅛	61.28	2	5.08	1⅛	2.86
Front Leg Veneer	4	25⅛	63.36	3¼	8.26	⅛	.32
Back Leg	2	20¼	51.44	2¼	5.71	2¼	5.71
Back Leg Halves	4	20¼	51.44	2	5.08	1⅛	2.86
Back Leg Veneer	4	21¼	53.98	3¼	8.26	⅛	.32
Bottom Side Rail	2	29⅞	75.88	3	7.62	¾	1.91
Top Side Rail	2	26⅞	68.26	3¾	9.54	¾	1.91
Side Slat	10	14½	36.83	3⅝	9.20	½	1.27
Arm							
Arm	2	37	93.98	5	12.70	1	2.54
Arm Support	4	9⅞	25.08	1¾	4.44	1¼	3.17
Rails							
Front Rail	1	28¼	71.76	4½	11.43	¾	1.91
Back Rail	1	28¼	71.76	4	10.16	¾	1.91
Back							
Top Horizontal Back Slat	1	21½ 23 (radius)	54.61 58.42	3⅞	9.84	⅜	.95
Bottom Horizontal Back Slat	4	21½ 23 (radius)	54.61 58 42	2½	6.35	⅜	.95
Post	2	29¼	74.30	1⅝	4.12	1⅛	2.86
Pivot Pin	2	4¾	12.08	1	2.54	1	2.54
Adjustment Pin	2	4¼	12.08	1	2.54	1	2.54
Cleats	2	23¼	59.06	⅝	1.58	1	2.54

⅝-inch (1.58-cm) dowels
⅜-inch (.95-cm) dowels
2 wooden washers
8 steel flathead wood screws

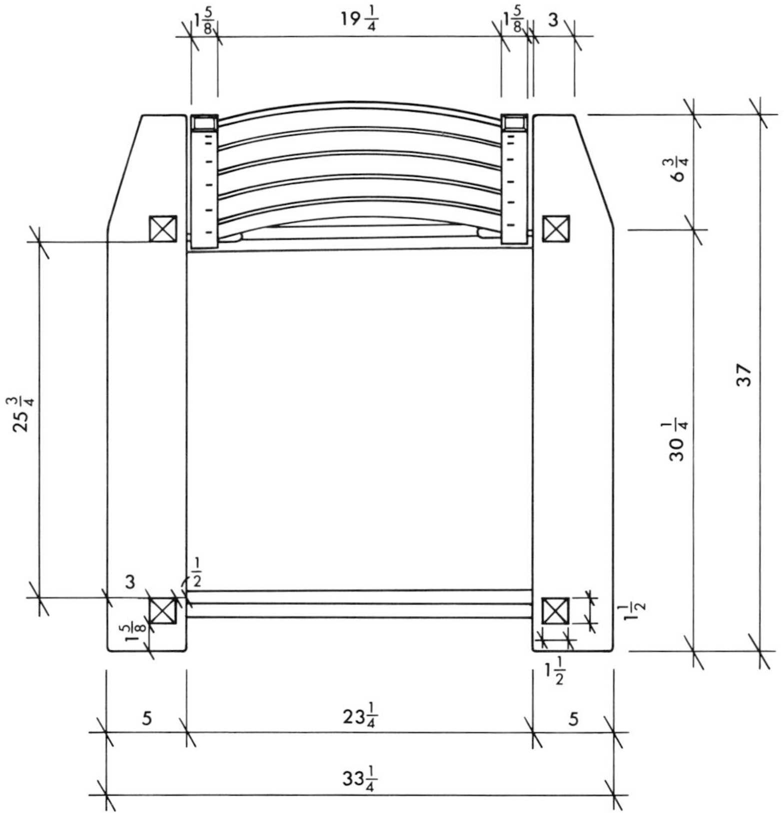

in.	cm
½	1.27
¾	1.91
1½	3.81
1⅝	4.12
2¼	5.71
3	7.62
4	10.16
4½	11.43
5	12.70
6¾	17.14
7¼	18.41
7½	19.05
9⅞	25.08
11⅛	28.25
19¼	48.89
23¼	59.05
23⅞	60.64
25¾	65.40
27¾	70.48
30¼	76.83
33¼	84.45
37	93.98

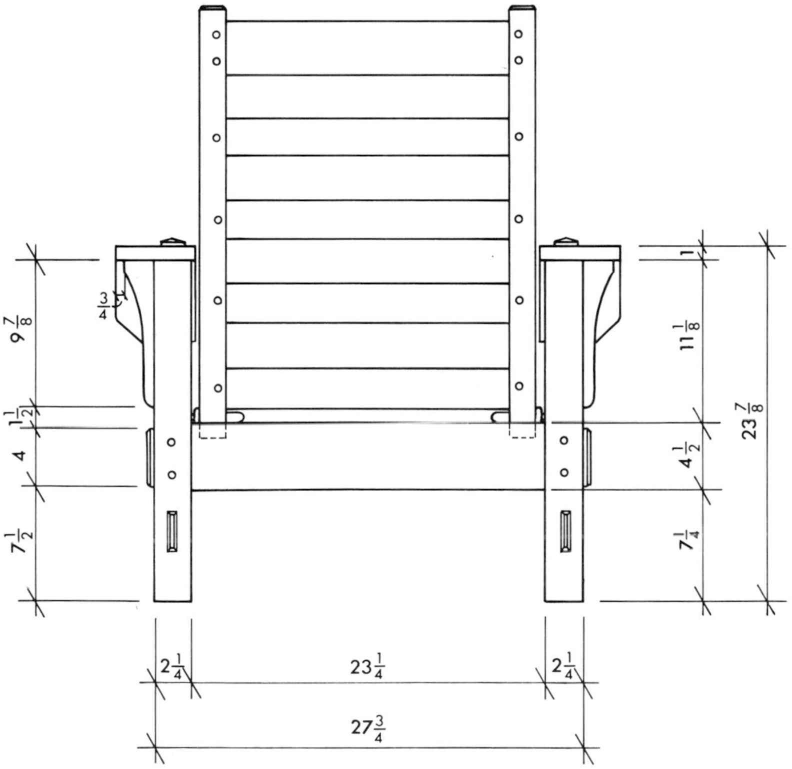

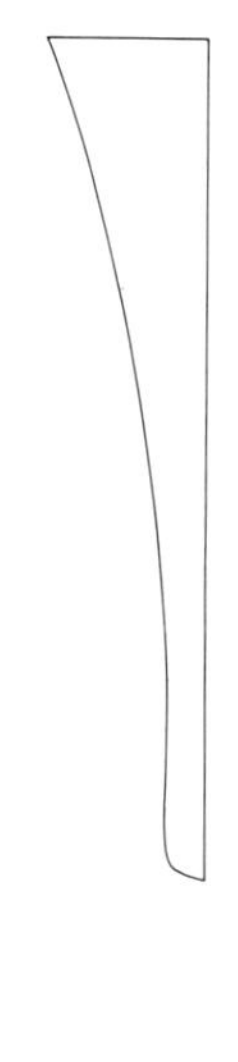

5–49. Working drawing for recliner. Top and front views and arm support.

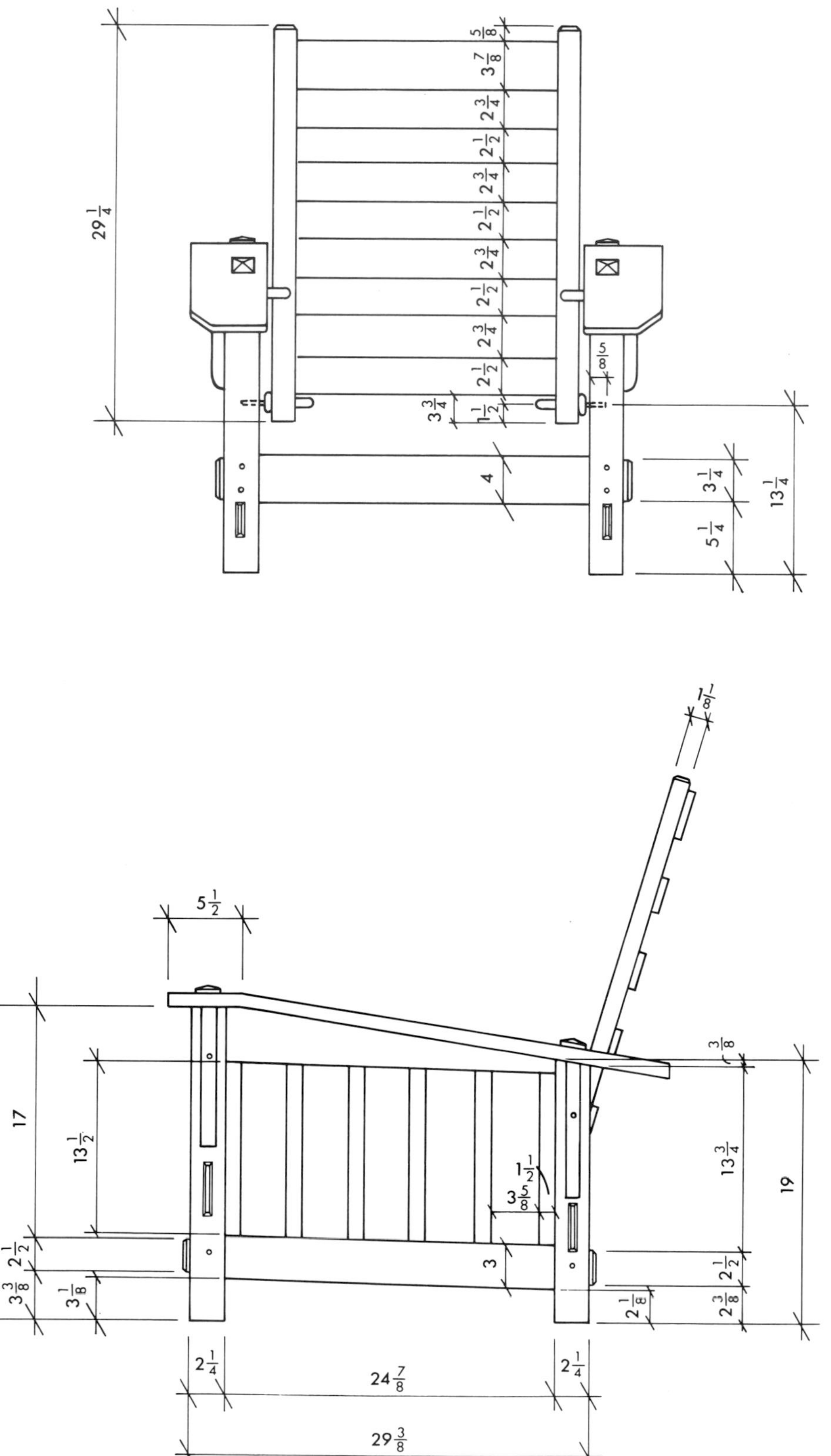

in.	cm
⅜	.95
⅝	1.58
1½	3.81
2⅛	5.39
2¼	5.71
2⅜	6.03
2½	6.35
2¾	6.98
3	7.62
3⅛	7.93
3¼	8.25
3⅜	8.57
3⅝	9.20
3¾	9.52
3⅞	9.84
4	10.16
5¼	13.33
5½	13.97
13¼	33.65
13½	34.29
13¾	34.92
17	43.18
19	48.26
22⅞	58.10
24⅞	63.18
29⅜	74.61
29¼	74.29

5–50. Working drawing for recliner. Back and side views.

PROCEDURE

In addition to the instructions given below, you may need to refer to the general instructions in chapter 4 for the following procedures:

Butt-joining, page 71
Cutting and applying veneer, pages 72–73
Cutting tenons, pages 65–66
Cutting mortises with drill and chisel, page 69
Cutting mortises with router table, pages 76–77
Beveling, page 70
Bending stock, pages 77–78
Cutting tenons on bent stock, pages 66–67
Dowel-pinning, pages 82–83
Constructing seat frame and upholstering, page 88
Finishing, pages 84–87
Assembly, pages 79–83

Side

Base

Each leg is made up of four pieces: two leg halves and two veneer strips. Laminate the leg halves with a butt joint and ⅝-inch (1.58-cm) dowels. The two resulting seams are each covered with a veneer strip. Once the legs are assembled, cut each leg to rough length: the front legs to 24½ inches (62.23 cm) and the back legs to 21 inches (53.34 cm).

Cut a through tenon measuring 1⅝ inches (4.12 cm) long by 1½ inches (3.81 cm) wide by 1½ inches (3.81 cm) thick onto the top of the front leg. Then cut a through tenon measuring 2 inches (5.08 cm) long by 1½ inches (3.81 cm) wide by 1½ inches (3.81) thick onto the top of the back leg. Note that its shoulder must follow the slope of the underside of the arm.

5–51. Blind mortise and tenon joints connect bottom side rails and slats.

Using the full-size drawing, determine the shoulder angles on the top and bottom side rails and mark.

Cut through tenons on the bottom side rails measuring 2½ inches (6.35 cm) wide by 2¾ inches (6.98 cm) long by ½ inch (1.27 cm) thick. Locate the mortises on both the front and back of each leg, noting the angle of incline shown in the full-size drawing. Cut these mortises using the drill and chisel cleanout method.

Cut blind tenons on the top side rail measuring 2¾ inches (6.98 cm) wide by 1 inch (2.54 cm) long by ½ inch (1.27 cm) thick.

Cut the top edge of the top side rail with a pattern made from the full-size side view drawing using the underside of the arm to determine the angle of the top edge of the top side rail. Allow for a ½ inch (1.27 cm) insertion of the upper edge of the top side rail into a dado to be cut in the underside of the arm.

Locate mortises for the topside rails in the legs and cut them using the drill and chisel cleanout method. Cut blind tenons measuring 2⅝ inches (6.66 cm) wide by ½ inch (1.27 cm) long by ¼ inch (.64 cm) thick on the five side slats. (Note the angle of their shoulders from the full-size side view drawing.) Locate mortise positions for these tenons on the edges of the two bottom side rails and cut using the router table and a ¼-inch (.64-cm) straight bit (figure 5-51).

Arm

From the extra length of the arm provided by the oversize dimension given in the materials list, cut a piece 5½ inches (13.97 cm) in length. Place this piece on the bottom side of the arm at the end from which it was cut. This added thickness allows for the change in angle of the front of the arm. Make a pattern of the edge of the arm from the full-size side view drawing. Place this pattern on the edge of the arm and draw its profile. Shade areas to be removed (figure 5-52). Remove the shaded area from the small block with a band saw, holding the wood in a screw clamp. Cut halfway into the block, keeping the blade on the outside edge of the pattern line (figure 5-53).

With the block still in the clamp, cut in from the side until you meet your first cut (figure 5-54). Place

5-53. Using a screw clamp to hold stock, make a cut with a band saw halfway down the stock, cutting on the outside of the pattern line.

5-52. Block placed on bottom side of arm, shaded areas indicate material to be cut away.

5-54. With stock still in clamp, cut in from the side until you meet your first cut.

5–55. Place cut end in clamp and finish removing material by cutting from the opposite end.

5–56. Cut the waste material from the top side of the arm.

the end from which material has been cut into the clamp and finish removing shaded area from the opposite end (figure 5-55). Cut the shaded area from the top of the arm (figure 5-56). Laminate the block to the arm, using four C-clamps (figure 5-57). After the arm lamination is dry, remove any saw marks from the top and underside with a sanding block (figure 5-58).

Locate the mortises in the arm that will receive the through tenons already cut on the top of each leg (figure 5-49). (Note in figure 5-59 that the mortises for the back legs' tenons are cut at an angle.) Cut these using the drill and chisel cleanout method.

Dado the underside of the arm ¾ inch (1.91 cm) from the inside edge to a depth of ½ inch (1.27 cm) using a router with a ¾-inch (1.91-cm) straight bit and then a drill with a ¾ inch (1.91 cm) forstner or boring bit. Use the router, with the aid of a fence, to cut the dado from the back mortise to just behind the bend in the arm. Then use the drill to make a series of holes from that point to the front mortise. Chisel clean to form the complete dado, as shown in figure 5-60.

Drill four ⅝-inch (1.58-cm) holes 2¼ inches (5.71 cm) deep in the back inside edge of each arm to hold adjusting pins. Locate the first hole 1½ inches (3.81 cm), on center, from the end of the arm; space the remaining holes 1¼ inches (3.17 cm) away, on center, from the preceding hole.

Cut the back edge of the arm to the profile shown in the top view drawing (figure 5-49).

5–57. Using four C-clamps, laminate the two sections together.

5–58. Finished arm.

5–59. Using a drill press with its table adjusted to the angle needed, drill out excess material to create mortise in arm for back leg tenon.

5–60. Dado cut in the bottom side of the arm holds the top side rail.

Rails

Cut the through tenons on the front and back rails that will join the two side assemblies. The tenons on the front rail should measure 4 inches (10.16 cm) wide by 2½ inches (6.35 cm) long by ½ inch (1.27 cm) thick. The tenons on the back rail should measure 3¼ inches (8.26 cm) wide by 2½ inches (6.35 cm) long by ½ inch (1.27 cm) thick. Locate the mortises for these tenons on the legs (see figures 5-49 and 5-50) and cut, using the drill and chisel clean-out method.

Subassembly

Final preparation of all through tenon ends is necessary prior to assembly. All through tenon ends project ¼ inch (.64 cm) beyond their exit point. Bevel the ends of all through *rail* tenons with a disc sander or block plane according to guidelines placed 3/16 inch (.47 cm) down from the end along each side and ⅛ inch (.32 cm) in from each edge on the end. Bevel the ends of all through *leg* tenons beginning 1 1/16 inches (2.69 cm) from the shoulder and meeting in the center to form a peak.

Assemble each side independently. When both sides are dry after gluing, join them together with the front and back rails.

Cut arm supports on a band saw or jigsaw, using a pattern adapted from figure 5-49. Sand and shape supports on the drill press with a drum sanding attachment. Sand and fit the bevel on the rear arm supports to contour to the slope of the rear portion of the arm. Glue each arm support in place so that they touch the underside of the arm and are centered on the leg.

5-61. Back assembly, clamped. Notched wood pads hold the bar and C-clamps in place. Assemble the back on two boards, bridging tables, or stools to aid in positioning bar and C-clamps.

Back

Bend the horizontal slats using the procedure described in chapter 4.

Cut blind tenons on the bent slats with either a band saw or backsaw. The top back slat tenons should measure 2⅞ inches (7.30 cm) wide by 1 inch (2.54 cm) long by ¼ inch (.64 cm) thick. The four remaining slats should have tenons measuring 1½ inches (3.81 cm) wide by 1 inch (2.54 cm) long by ¼ inch (.64 cm) thick.

Locate the mortises, on center, on the inside edge of each post (see figure 5-50). Cut each mortise using the drill and chisel cleanout method.

Drill a ⅝-inch (1.58-cm) hole, on center, 1½ inches (3.81 cm) from the bottom of each post. Drill from the inside edge of each post completely through the post. Drill the same size hole on the inside surface of each leg, 13¼ inches (33.66 cm) on center from the bottom of the leg, to a depth of 2 inches (5.08 cm). These holes will accommodate the pivot pins for the back.

Assembly

Assemble the back as indicated in figure 5-61. Because the back slats will flex during clamping, use additional clamps to counteract this and to ensure a proper seam line between the shoulder of each back slat and the post. Attach these clamps with wooden pads notched to fit over the bar clamps holding the posts and slats together.

All tenons can now be pinned with ⅜-inch (.95-cm) dowels. Insert the lower side rail dowels in the centers of the legs, centered on the tenons. Pin the front rail tenons with two dowels on each leg. Locate the lower dowel 8¼ inches (21.5 cm), on center, from the bottom of the leg, and the upper dowel 10¾ inches (27.32 cm), on center, from the bottom of the leg. Pin the back rail tenons in the same manner as those for the front rail, with the lower dowel 6 inches (15.24 cm), on center, from the bottom of the leg and the upper dowel 8¼ inches (21.5 cm) on center, from the bottom of the leg.

To pin the through tenons on the top of each leg, center the dowel on the inside edge of the arm, centered on the tenon. Pin the arm supports 5½ inches (13.97 cm), on center, from the bottom of the support. Pin the top back slat with two dowels on each tenon, ¾ inch (1.9 cm) from the inside edge of each post. Locate the upper dowel 1⅝ inches (4.12 cm), on center from the top of the post and the lower dowel 3⅜ inches (8.5 cm), on center, from the top of the post. Pin the four lower back slats with one dowel in each tenon, ⅜ inch (.95 cm) from the inside edge of the post, centered on each tenon.

Use a lathe to turn the pivot and adjustment pins according to the dimensions in figure 5-62.

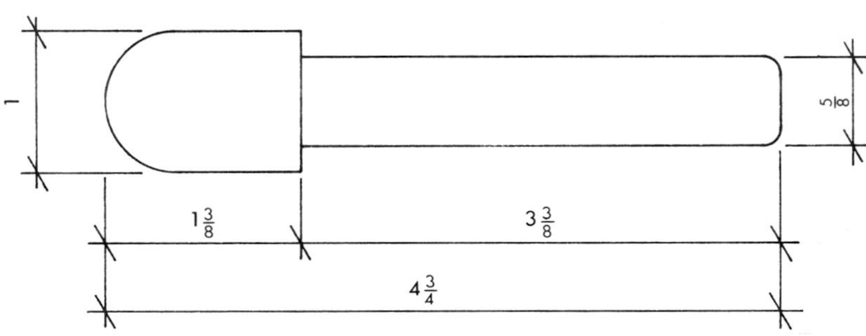

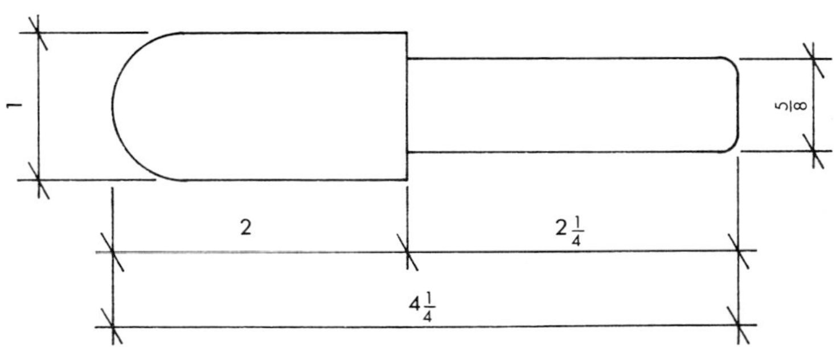

in.	cm
⅝	1.58
1	2.54
1⅜	3.49
2	5.08
2¼	5.71
3⅜	8.57
4¼	10.80

5-62. Working drawings for pivot and adjustment pins. The top is the pivot pin; the bottom is the adjustment pin.

5-63. Pivot and adjustment pins in position.

Make wooden washers for the pivot pins by first laminating two pieces of ⅛-inch-thick (.32-cm) stock with their grains perpendicular. Cut two 1-inch (2.54-cm) squares from this laminated stock. Find the center of each square and, with a compass, draw two concentric circles with diameters of ⅝ inch (1.58 cm) and 1 inch (2.54 cm). Drill a ⅝-inch (1.58-cm) hole in the center of the square. With a disc sander or file, round the outside corners to the 1-inch circle line. Round the outside edges with a file and sandpaper.

Braces called cleats are used to support the seat frame. These cleats measure ⅝ inch (1.58 cm) thick by 23¼ inches (59.06 cm) long by 1 inch (2.54 cm) wide. Place the 1-inch (2.54-cm) dimensions of the cleats against the inside surfaces of the front and back rails, 1½ inches (3.81 cm) down from the top edge. Glue each cleat to its rail. Strengthen them with four wood screws in each cleat.

Apply a finish to the piece using the procedure described in chapter 4.

You have now completed construction of the recliner. Information for construction of the seat frame and upholstery is given in chapter 4.

Settle

Stickley designed the settle or couch for lounging. Quite unlike the Victorian sofa, the settle encouraged one to relax, while the Victorian piece had an air of formality that almost demanded a prim, upright posture. Each settle was designed to be used with throw pillows instead of an upholstered back, thereby offering versatile seating to accommodate anyone.

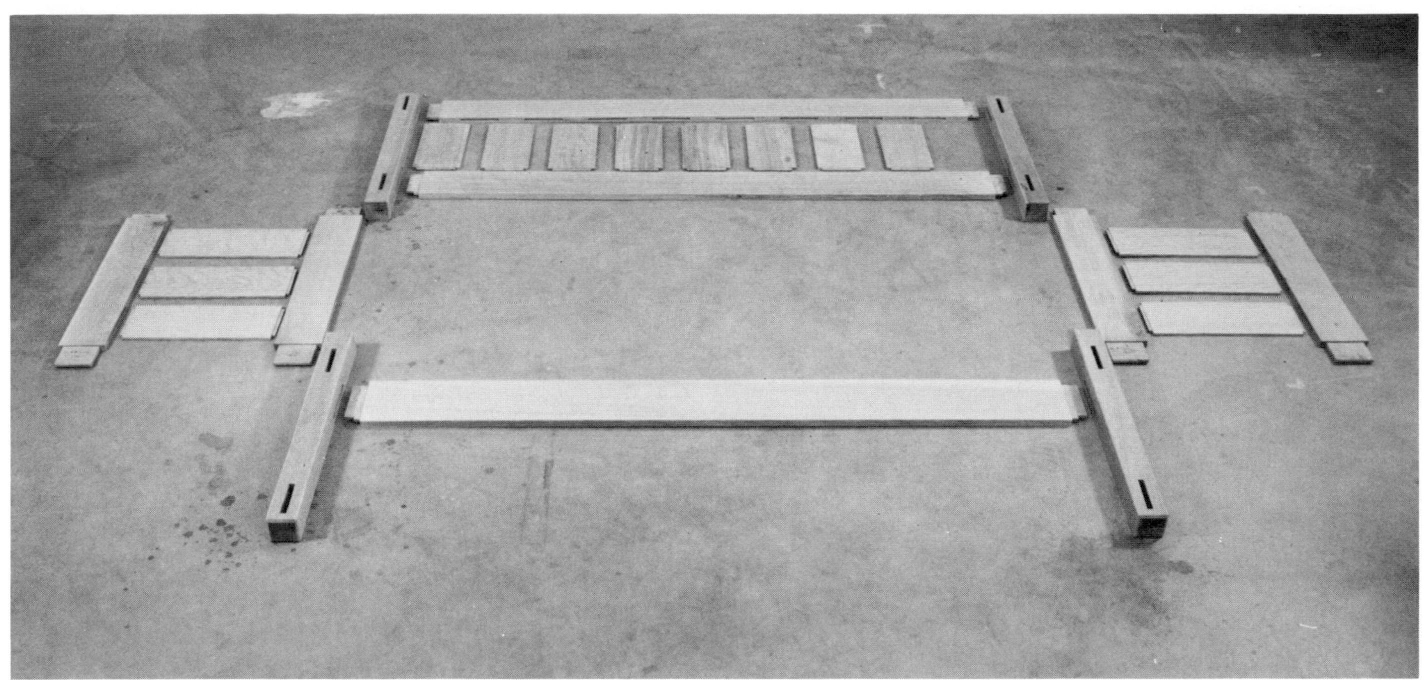

5–66. Exploded view of settle.

MATERIALS

	Number of Pieces	Length		Width		Thickness	
		in.	cm	in.	cm	in.	cm
Legs							
Leg	4	29	73.66	2¾	6.98	2¾	6.98
Leg Halves	8	29	73.66	2½	6.35	1⅜	3.49
Leg Veneer	8	30	76.20	3¼	8.26	⅛	.32
Rails							
Bottom Side Rail	2	32	81.28	5	12.70	⅞	2.22
Top Side Rail	2	30½	77.47	5	12.70	⅞	2.22
Front Rail	1	76½	194.31	6½	16.51	⅞	2.22
Bottom Back Rail	1	76½	194.31	6½	16.51	⅞	2.22
Top Back Rail	1	73½	186.69	5	12.70	⅞	2.22
Slats							
Side Slat	6	17¼	43.82	6	15.24	⅜	.95
Back Slat	8	12	30.48	6	15.24	⅜	.95
Cleats							
Cleat	2	70½	179.07	1¾	4.44	1	2.54

⅜-inch (.95-cm) dowels
⅝-inch (1.58-cm)dowels
16 steel flathead wood screws

The settle is a relatively easy piece to construct because it contains only mortise-and-tenon joinery. Two subassemblies are required to build the settle: each side is assembled independently. The sides are then connected by three rails, one in the front and two at the back. The sides are identical; each consists of two legs, two side rails, and three vertical side slats. Eight vertical slats connect the top and bottom back rails. Cut your stock according to the dimensions given in the materials list.

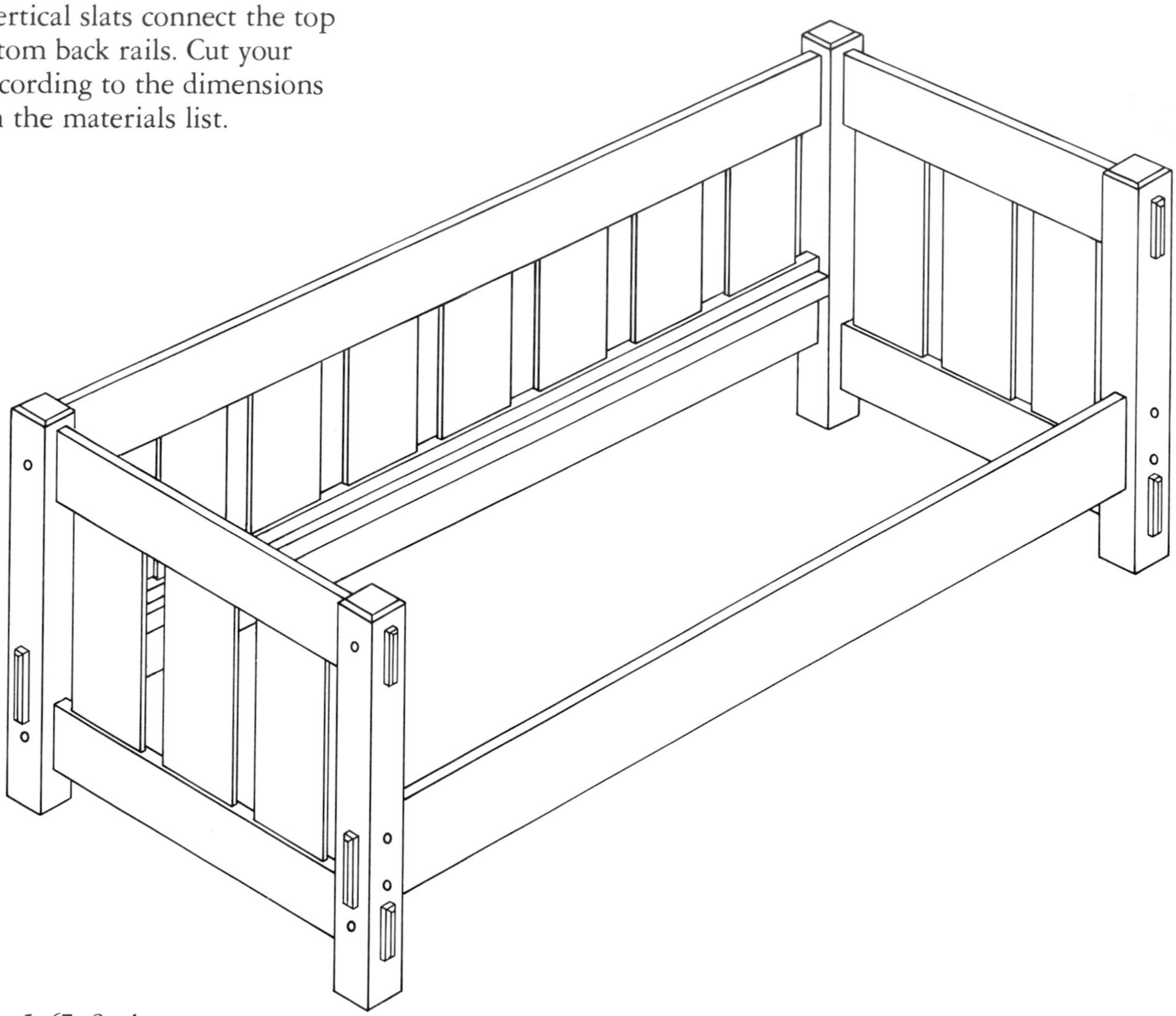

5-67. Settle.

in.	cm	in.	cm
½	1.27	6¼	15.87
2½	6.35	6½	16.51
2¾	6.98	6¾	17.14
5	12.70	10¾	52.70
5½	13.97	70½	179.07
6	15.24	76	193.04

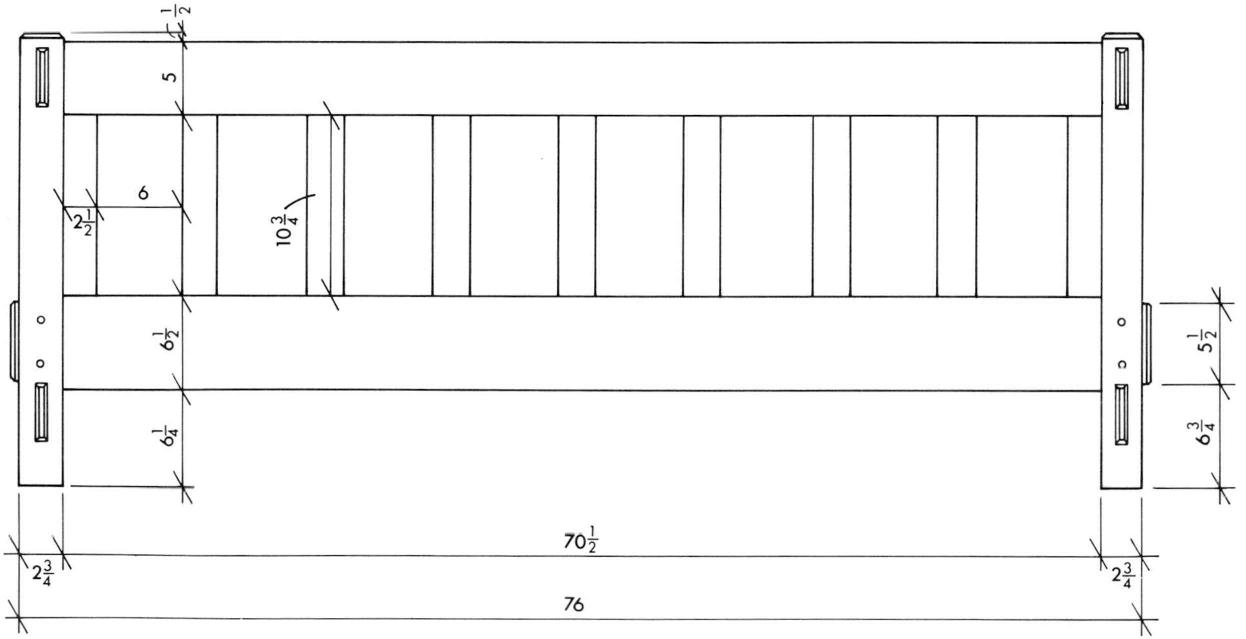

5–68. Working drawing for settle. Top and back views. (See figure 5–70 for detail of circled area.)

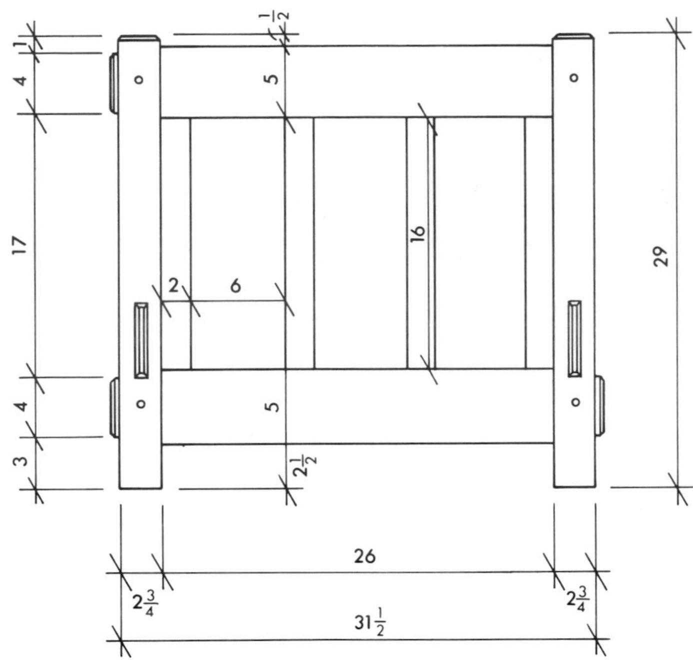

in.	cm
½	1.27
1	2.54
2	5.08
2½	6.35
2¾	6.93
3	7.62
4	10.16
5	12.70
6	15.24
16	40.64
17	43.18
26	66.04
29	73.66
31½	80.01

5-69. Working drawing for settle. Side view.

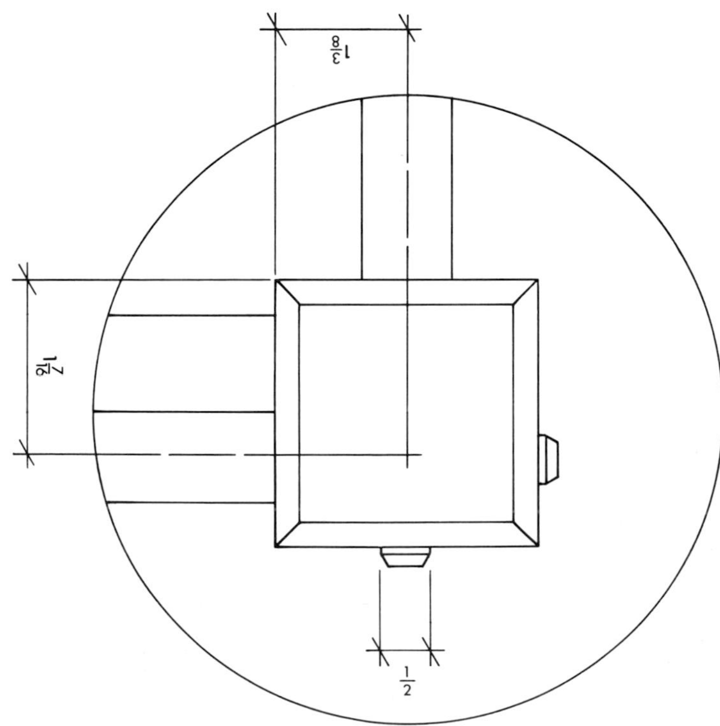

in.	cm
½	1.27
1⅜	3.49
1 7/16	3.65

5-70. Detail showing location of side, front, and back rails on legs.

PROCEDURE

In addition to the instructions given below, you may need to refer to the general instructions in chapter 4 for the following procedures:

Butt-joining, page 71
Cutting and applying veneer, pages 72–73
Beveling, page 70
Cutting tenons, pages 65–66
Cutting mortises with drill and chisel, page 69
Cutting mortises with router, pages 76–77
Dowel-pinning, pages 82–83
Assembly, pages 79–83
Constructing seat frame and upholstering, page 88
Finishing, pages 84–87

Legs

Each leg is made up of four pieces: two leg halves and two veneer strips. Laminate the leg halves with a butt joint, using ⅝-inch (1.58-cm) dowels. Cover the two resulting seams on each leg with veneer strips. Cut each leg to length.

Bevel the top of each leg with a disc sander or a block and sandpaper. Cut this bevel according to guidelines drawn ¼ inch (.64 cm) down from the top edge on each side and ¼ (.64 cm) in from all edges on the top.

Rails

Cut through tenons measuring 4 inches (10.16 cm) wide by 3 inches (7.62 cm) long by ½ inch (1.27 cm) thick on both ends of the bottom side rails. Cut a through tenon measuring 4 inches (10.16 cm) wide by 3 inches (7.62 cm) long by ½ inch (1.27 cm) thick on the *front* ends of the top side rails. Cut a blind tenon measuring 4 inches (10.16 cm) wide by 1½ inches (3.81 cm) long by ½ inch (1.27 cm) thick on the *back* ends of the top side rails.

Locate the mortises for these tenons (see figure 5-68); center the mortises on each leg (figure 5-70). Cut them using the drill and chisel cleanout method.

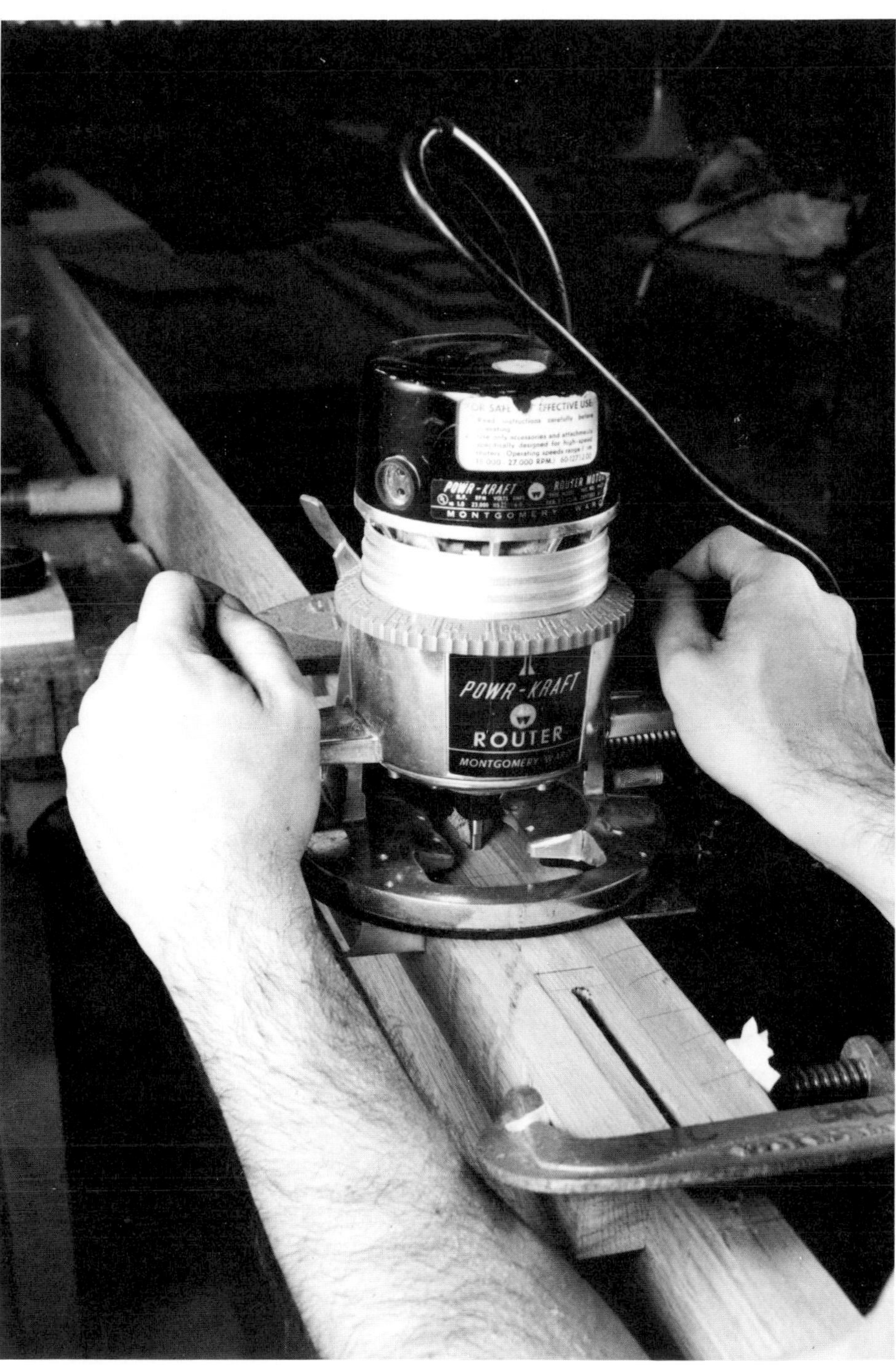

5–71. Cut mortises in rail using router. Clamp boards to each side of the rail to support the router base plate.

Cut the front and bottom back rail through tenons to measure 5½ inches (13.97 cm) wide by 3 inches (7.62 cm) long by ½ inch (1.27 cm) thick. Cut the back top rail blind tenons measuring 4 inches (10.16 cm) wide by 1½ inches (3.81 cm) long by ½ inch (1.27 cm) thick.

Locate mortise centers for the front and both back rails 1 7/16 inches (3.65 cm) from the inside leg corner (see figures 5-69 and 5-70). The top back rail mortise begins 1 inch (2.54 cm) down from the top of the leg. Cut these mortises using the drill and chisel cleanout method.

Slats

Cut blind tenons measuring 5 inches (12.70 cm) wide by ⅝ inches (1.58 cm) long by ¼ inch (.64 cm) thick on the six vertical side slats. Locate the mortises (see figure 5-69) and center them on the top edge of the bottom side rail and the bottom edge of the top side rail. Cut the mortises with a router and a ¼-inch (.64-cm) straight bit, using a support jig, as shown in figure 5-71.

Cut blind tenons measuring 5 inches (12.70 cm) wide by ⅝ inch (1.58 cm) long by ¼ inch (.64 cm) thick on the eight vertical back slats. Locate and cut the mortises on the back rails using the same measurements and procedure as on the side rails.

Assembly

Bevel all through tenons with a disc sander or block plane. Bevel according to guidelines drawn 3/16 inch (.47 cm) down from the end along each side and ⅛ inch (.32 cm) in from each edge on the end.

Glue each side subassembly together. When both sides are dry, connect them with the front and back rails. Remember, the back slats must be glued in place at the same time that the front and back rails are assembled with the sides.

Pin all rail tenons with ⅜-inch (.95-cm) dowels. Locate the dowels for the top and bottom side rails and the top back rail in the center of the leg, centered on the tenon. Pin the front and bottom back rail tenons with two dowels each. Locate both dowels in the center of the leg, the lower dowel, 8 ¼ inches (20.96 cm), on center, from the bottom of the leg, and the upper dowel, 10 ¾ inches (27.31 cm), on center, from the bottom of the leg.

Braces called cleats are used to support the seat frame. Place their 1¾-inch (4.44-cm) dimension against the inside surfaces of the front and bottom back rails, 1¾ inches (4.44 cm) down from the top edge of each rail. Glue each cleat to its rail. Strengthen them with eight wood screws in each cleat.

Apply a finish to the piece using the procedure described in chapter 4.

You have now completed the settle. Information for construction of the seat frame and upholstery is given in chapter 4.

Dining Table

The dining table is one piece of furniture designed to be used simultaneously by the entire family. In most families it functions as more than just a dining surface: it also provides a forum for discussing the events of the day. Of the dining tables designed and built by Stickley, this table most typifies his belief in traditional structural systems. That most basic of structural systems, the post and lintel, forms the support for the massive top. The construction of the table is simple; because of its massiveness, however, you will require assistance during some construction procedures.

5–73. Exploded view of dining table.

This dining table requires three subassemblies: two identical leg units that consist of two legs, a bottom rail, and a top horizontal support, which are connected after subassembly by a stretcher; and a laminated top.

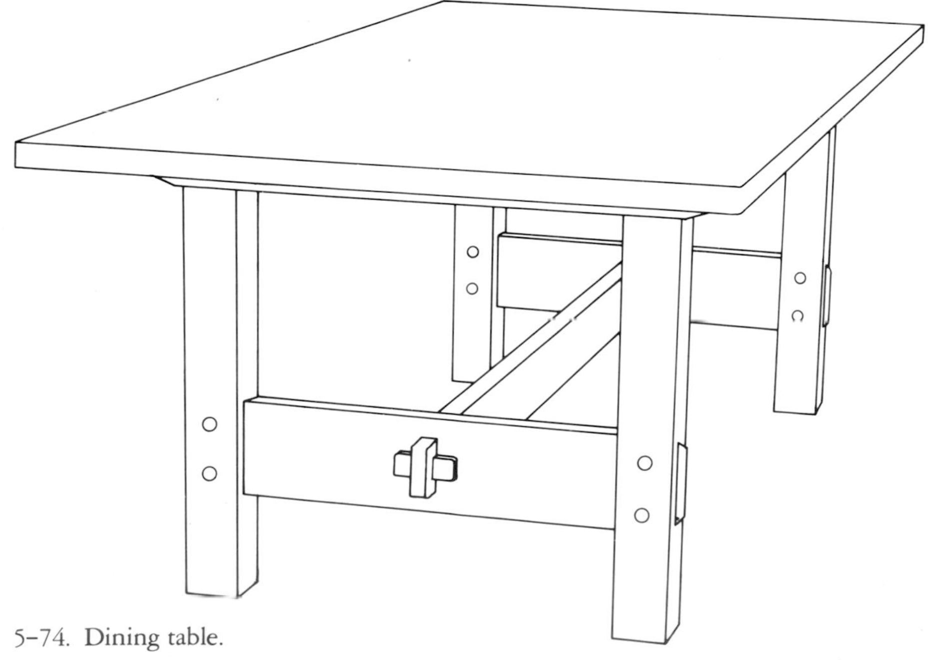

5–74. Dining table.

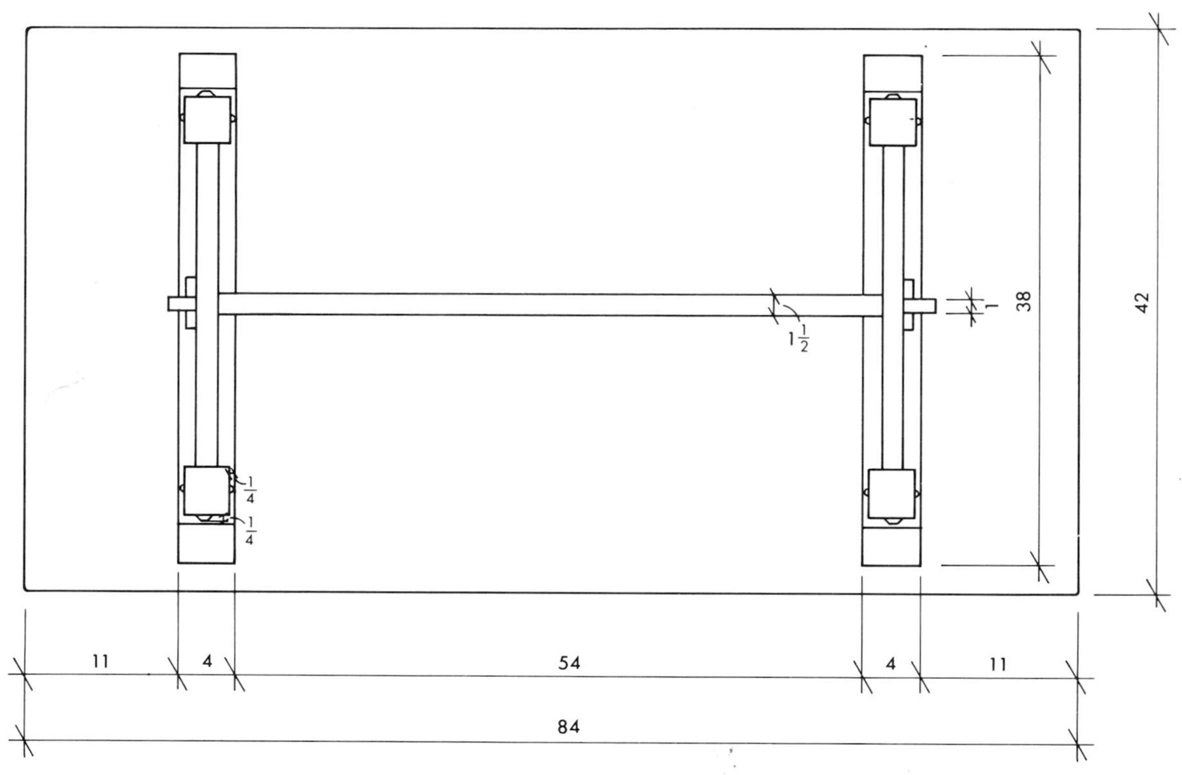

in.	cm	in.	cm	in.	cm
¼	.64	3⅜	8.57	38	96.52
¾	1.91	3½	8.89	42	106.68
1	2.54	4	10.16	54	137.16
1½	3.81	4½	11.43	54½	138.43
2½	6.35	6½	16.51	84	213.36

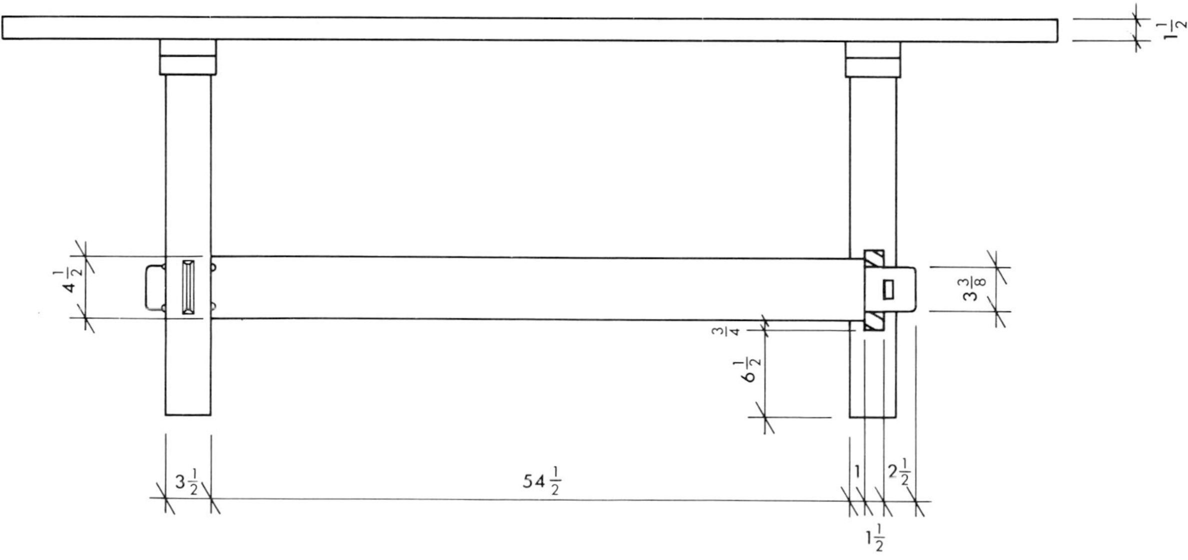

5–75. Working drawing for dining table. Bottom and side views.

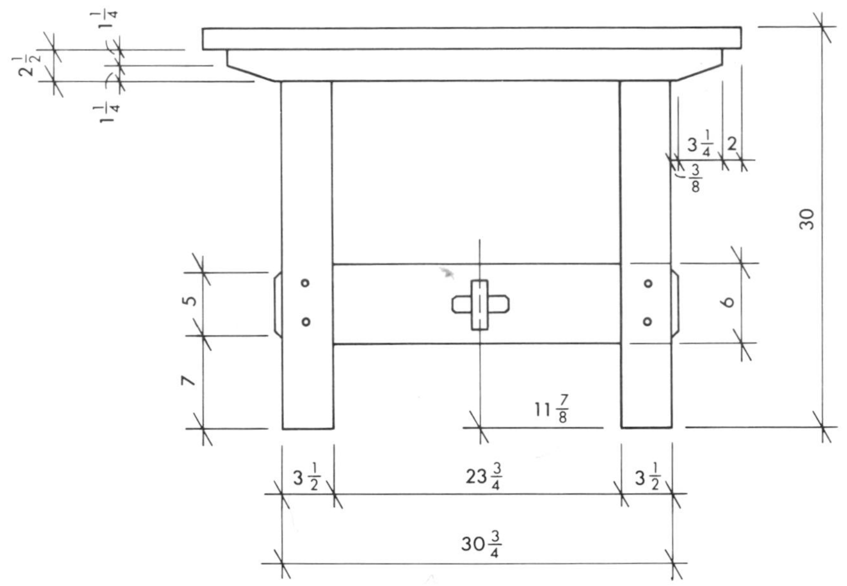

in.	cm
¼	.64
⅜	.95
1¼	3.17
2	5.08
2½	6.35
3¼	8.25
3½	8.89
5	12.70
6	15.24
7	17.78
11⅞	30.16
23¾	60.32
30	76.20
30¾	78.10

5-76. Working drawing for dining table. End view.

MATERIALS

	Number of Pieces	Length		Width		Thickness	
		in.	cm	in.	cm	in.	cm
Leg Units							
Leg	4	28	71.12	3½	8.89	3½	8.89
Leg Halves	8	28	71.12	3¼	8.26	1¾	4.44
Leg Veneer	8	29	73.66	4½	11.43	⅛	.32
Horizontal Top Support	2	38	96.52	4	10.16	2½	6.35
Bottom Rail	2	31¼	79.38	6	15.24	1½	3.81
Stretcher	1	64½	163.83	4½	11.43	1½	3.81
Key	2	3⅞	9.84	1⅜	3.49	¾	1.91
Table Top							
Top	1	84	213.36	42	106.68	1½	3.81
Caps	16	1	2.54			¾	1.91 (diam.)

⅝-inch (1.58-cm) dowels
14 1¼-inch (3.17-cm) table irons
28 flathead wood screws

PROCEDURE

In addition to the instructions given below, you may need to refer to the general instructions in chapter 4 for the following procedures:

Butt-joining, page 71
Cutting and applying veneer, pages 72–73
Cutting tenons, pages 65–66
Beveling, page 70
Cutting mortises with drill and chisel, page 69
Dowel-pinning, pages 82–83
Squaring laminated boards, pages 74–75
Assembly, pages 79–83
Finishing, pages 84–87

Leg Units

Legs

Each leg is composed of two halves and two veneer strips. Laminate the leg halves with butt joints, using ⅝-inch (1.58-cm) dowels. Cover the resulting seams with the veneer strips. After veneering, cut the legs to length, allowing for a 2-inch-long (5.08-cm) blind tenon on the top of each.

Cut blind tenons measuring 1½ inches (3.81 cm) wide by 2 inches (5.08 cm) long by 1½ inches (3.81 cm) thick on the top of each leg (figure 5-77).

Horizontal Top Supports

Laminate the horizontal supports with ⅝-inch (1.58-cm) dowels. Bevel their bottom corners as shown in figure 5-76. Locate mortises for the blind tenons on the legs (see figure 5-76). Cut mortises in the underside of the top horizontal supports using the drill and chisel cleanout method (figure 5-77).

5–77. Blind mortise-and-tenon joint connects leg and horizontal top support.

5–78. Mortise and tenon join rail and leg.

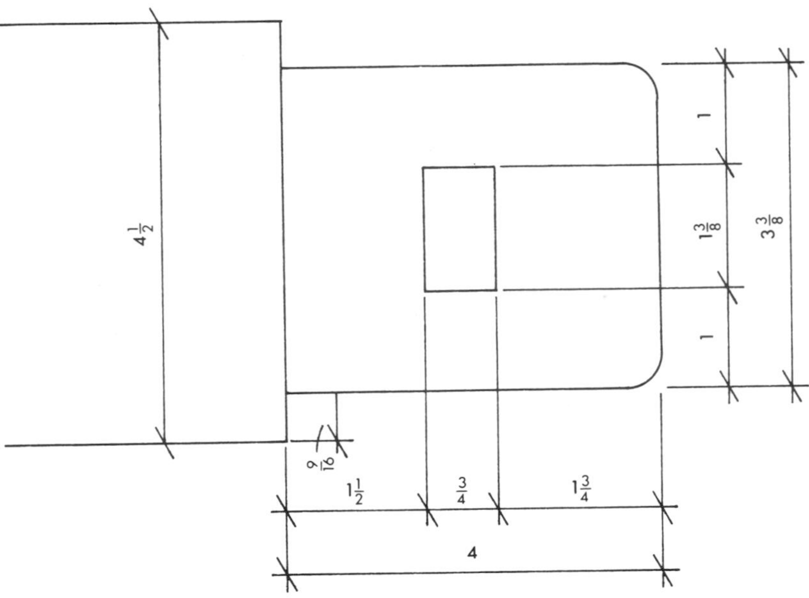

5-79. Working drawing for stretcher tenon and its mortise.

in.	cm
9/16	1.43
3/4	1.91
1	2.54
1 3/8	3.49
1 1/2	3.81
1 3/4	4.44
3 3/8	8.57
4	10.16
4 1/2	11.43

Rails

Cut through tenons measuring 5 inches (12.70 cm) wide by 3 1/4 inches (8.26 cm) long by 1 inch (2.54 cm) thick on both ends of each rail. Locate mortises in the center of each leg (see figure 5-76), and cut, using the drill and chisel cleanout method (figure 5-78)

Final preparation of the rail tenon ends is necessary prior to subassembly. Bevel the tenon ends, which project 5/16 inch (.79 cm) beyond their exit points, with a disc sander or block plane. Use guidelines placed 1/4 inch (.64 cm) down from the end along each side and 1/4 inch (.64 cm) in from each edge on the end of the tenon.

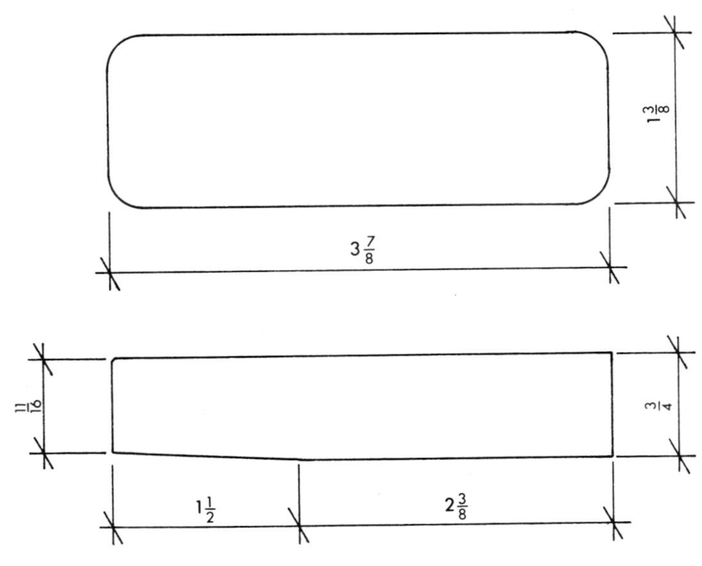

5-80. Working drawing for key.

in.	cm
11/16	1.75
3/4	1.91
1 3/8	3.49
1 1/2	3.81
2 3/8	6.03
3 7/8	9.84

Stretcher

Cut through tenons measuring 3 3/8 inches (8.57 cm) wide by 4 inches (10.16 cm) long by 1 inch (2.54 cm) thick on each end of the stretcher. Round the tenon ends as shown in figure 5-79, and lightly bevel the shaded area with a medium crosscut file. Locate mortises for the tenons in the center of each rail. Cut using the drill and chisel cleanout method.

The stretcher tenons will be locked in place with keys inserted through mortises cut in the end of

each tenon. To locate the mortises for the keys, insert the stretcher tenons into their mortises in the rails. Draw a pencil line around each tenon at the point where it exits the rail. Remove the tenons from the rails. The pencil lines indicate the edge of the key mortises closest to the rail.

Locate the other three sides of each mortise (figure 5-79), and cut with the drill and chisel clean-out method. Cut the keys on a band saw or jigsaw (figure 5-80) and shape with a file, block plane, or sanding block. Care should be taken in fitting each key exactly to its mortise.

Subassembly

Set the horizontal top support in place (not glued) to maintain leg alignment while gluing the rails. Glue the rails into the legs. When the glue is dry, assemble the horizontal top support with glue and clamp.

After the leg units are assembled, pin the rail tenons with two ⅝-inch (1.58-cm) dowels on each, as shown in figure 5-81. The dowels are recessed to accommodate caps, which can be turned to the size indicated on a lathe or shaped from ¾-inch (1.91-cm) diameter oak dowel using a flat, medium crosscut file.

Tabletop

The table is laminated from five to seven pieces of stock, depending upon the stock widths available. Lay out the top, being careful to alternate end grain direction or pattern so as to minimize the warping so characteristic of large, solid tabletops. Butt-join the boards edge-to-edge with ⅝-inch (1.58-cm) dowels. Assemble the boards in pairs first, because of the massiveness of the top.

After tabletop assembly is complete, use a router to trim one end square. Measure the top to length and trim the other end. Round the corners with a medium crosscut file using a ½ inch radius template as a guide.

Assembly

Attach the two leg units to the stretcher. Glue the keys into place. Seven evenly spaced table irons are used on each horizontal top support, four on one side, three on the other. With a 1-inch (2.54-cm) forstner or boring bit, countersink each table iron flush with the top of the horizontal support. Secure the irons with flathead wood screws.

Apply a finish to the piece. Place the tabletop in position. Secure it with steel flathead screws driven through the table iron into the underside of the top.

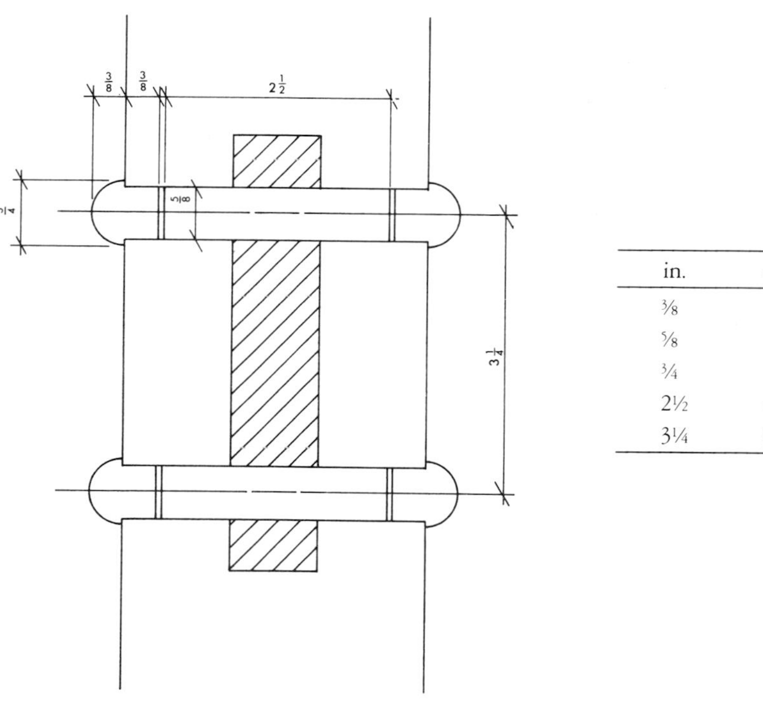

in.	cm
⅜	.95
⅝	1.58
¾	1.91
2½	6.35
3¼	8.25

5-81. Working drawing showing location of ⅝-inch (1.58-cm) dowels and their caps.

Bookcase

Although this bookcase is one of the projects from the Home Training in Cabinet-Work series in *The Craftsman*, it is not a simple piece to build. The bookcase is not technically difficult, but because of the number of pieces, extensive joinery, and critical alignment requirements involved, it requires much time and patience.

5-83. Exploded view of bookcase showing sides, doors, shelves, and front bottom rail.

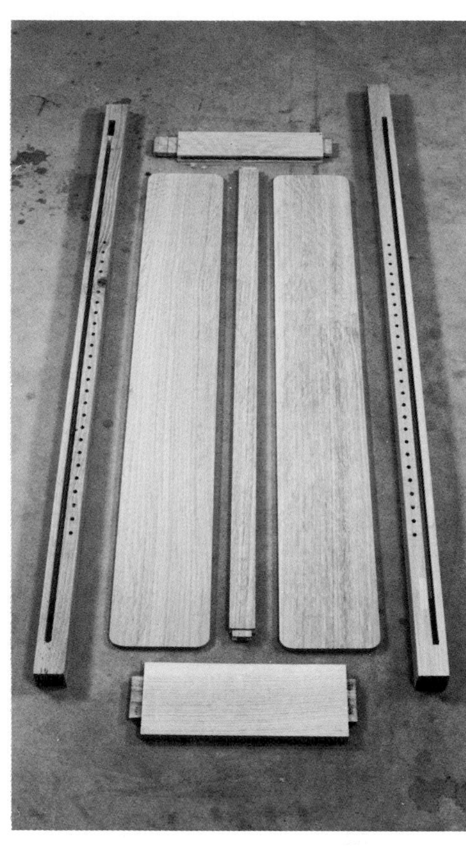

5-85. Exploded view of bookcase side.

5-84. Exploded view of bookcase showing sides, back rails, and back panels.

5-86. Exploded view of bookcase door.

The bookcase has four subassemblies: two identical side units and two identical doors. Each side unit consits of seven pieces: two posts, a top and a bottom side rail, a center vertical side rail, and two panels. The accurate milling of the two posts is essential to proper alignment of the parts they join. The two side units are connected by the back and by a front bottom rail to form the bookcase's frame. The frame contains three permanent shelves, at the top, middle, and bottom. The second subassemblies, the two doors, each consist of eight pieces: two stiles, a top and a bottom door rail, one horizontal mullion, and three vertical mullions. Each door is connected to the frame with hinges. Cut your stock according to the dimensions given in the materials list.

5–87. Bookcase.

MATERIALS

	Number of Pieces	Length in.	Length cm	Width in.	Width cm	Thickness in.	Thickness cm
Side Units							
Bottom Side Rail	2	12¾	32.40	4½	11.43	¾	1.91
Front Post	2	51	161.94	1¾	4.44	1¾	4.44
Back Post	2	54	137.16	1¾	4.44	1¾	4.44
Top Side Rail	2	14¾	37.48	3½	8.89	¾	1.91
Center Vertical Side Rail	2	41¾	106.06	1½	3.81	¾	1.91
Side Panel	4	41¼	104.78	6	15.24	½	1.27
Shelves							
Top Shelf	1	46¾	118.76	14⅛	35.88	¾	1.91
Middle Shelf	1	44	111.76	12	30.48	¾	1.91
Bottom Shelf	1	44	111.76	14⅛	35.88	¾	1.91
Front Bottom Rail							
Front Bottom Rail	1	46¼	117.48	4½	11.43	¾	1.91
Back							
Back Bottom Rail	1	46¼	117.48	3	7.62	¾	1.91
Top Back Rail	1	44¾	113.68	2½	6.35	¾	1.91
Back Panel	5	46¼	117.48	9	22.86	½	1.27
Spline	4	46¼	117.48	1	2.54	⅛	.32
Doors							
Door Stile	4	42⅜	107.63	1½	3.81	¾	1.91
Door Rail	4	20	50.80	1½	3.81	¾	1.91
Horizontal Mullion	2	20	50.80	1	2.54	¾	1.91
Center Vertical Mullion	2	41⅜	105.09	1	2.54	¾	1.91
Side Vertical Mullion	4	8¾	22.23	1	2.54	¾	1.91
Stops							
Top and Bottom Door Stops	2	2	5.08	½	1.27	½	1.27
Hinge Supports	2	42⅜	107.63	½	1.27	1	2.54
Glass							
Outside Panes	4	8¹¹⁄₁₆	22.07	4⁷⁄₁₆	11.27	⅛	.32
Inside Panes	4	8¹¹⁄₁₆	22.07	4³⁄₁₆	10.63	⅛	.32
Lower Panes	4	31¹⁄₁₆	78.89	9³⁄₁₆	23.33	⅛	.32

⅜-inch (.95-cm) dowels
4 loose-pin brass or steel box hinges
2 door pulls
1 spring-action cupboard latch
1 small cupboard lock
2 molding strips, 25 feet (7.62 m) by ¼ inch (.64 cm) by ⅜ inch (.95 cm)
brads

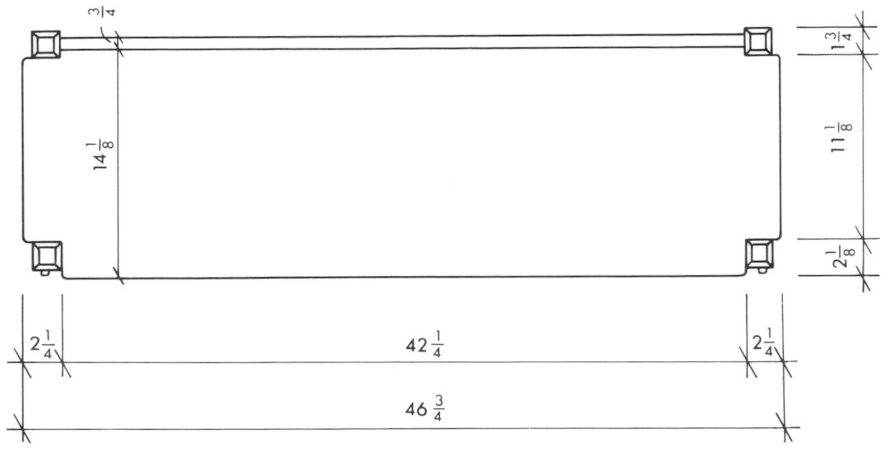

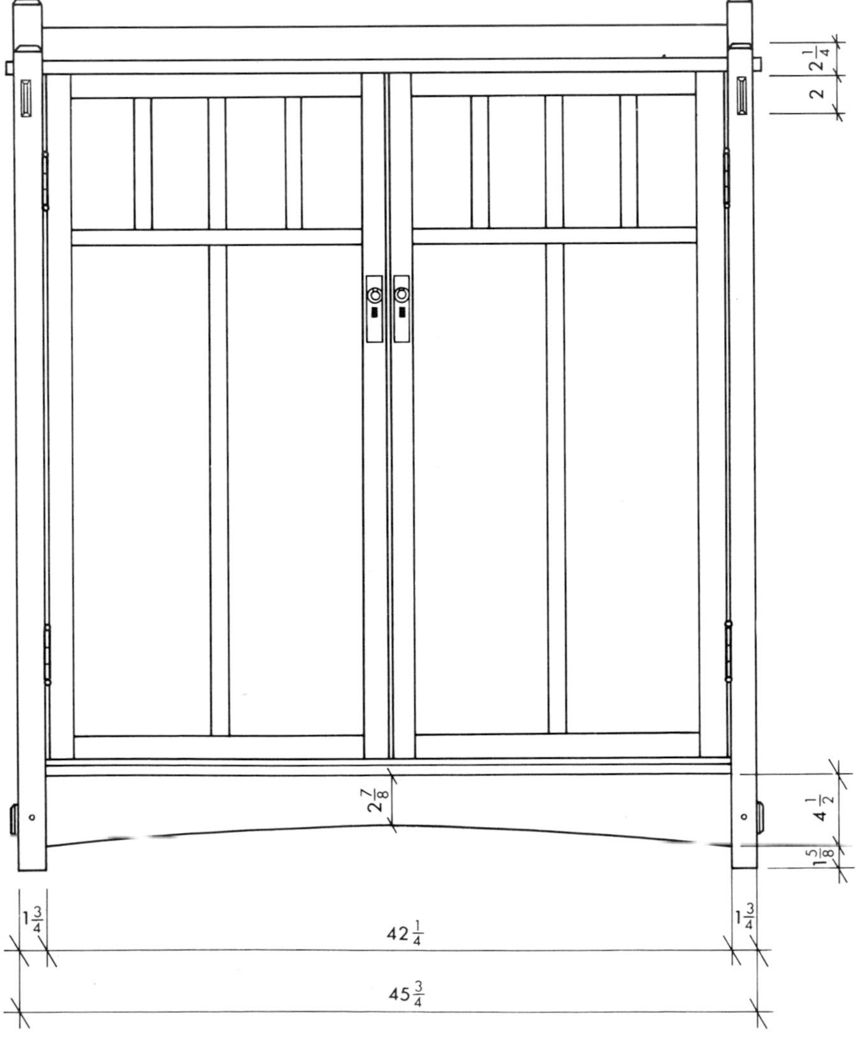

5–88. Working drawing for bookcase. Top and front views.

in.	cm
¾	1.91
1⅝	4.12
1¾	4.44
2	5.08
2⅛	5.39
2¼	5.71
2⅞	7.30
4½	11.43
11⅛	28.25
14⅛	35.87
42¼	107.31
45¾	116.20
46¾	118.74

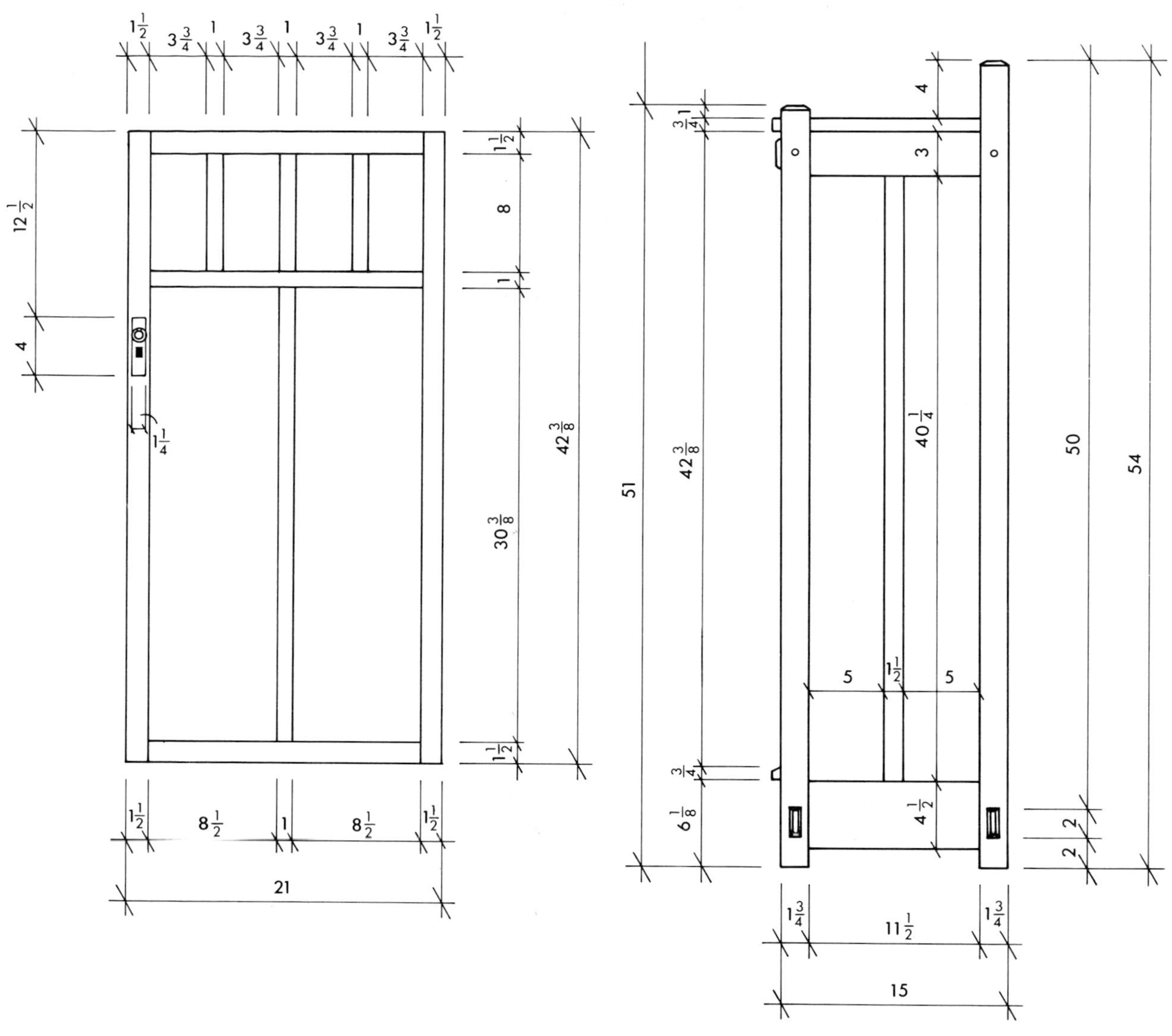

5–89. Working drawing for bookcase. Door and side view.

in.	cm	in.	cm
¾	1.91	8	20.32
1	2.54	8½	21.59
1¼	3.17	11½	29.21
1½	3.81	12½	31.75
1¾	4.44	15	38.10
2	5.08	21	53.34
3	7.62	30⅜	77.15
3¾	9.52	40¼	102.23
4	10.16	42⅜	107.63
4½	11.43	50	127.00
5	12.70	51	129.54
6⅛	15.55	54	137.16

PROCEDURE

In addition to the instructions given below, you may need to refer to the general instructions in chapter 4 for the following procedures:

Cutting tenons, pages 65–66
Cutting mortises with drill and chisel, page 69
Constructing and using a router table, pages 75–76
Butt-joining, page 71
Squaring laminated boards, pages 74–75
Beveling, page 70
Dowel-pinning, pages 82–83
Cutting barefaced tenons, pages 67–68
Treating hinges, page 88
Attaching hinges, page 88
Assembly, pages 79–83
Finishing, pages 84–87

Frame

Side Units

Cut blind tenons measuring 3½ inches (8.89 cm) wide by ⅝ inch (1.58 cm) long by ½ inch (1.27 cm) thick on each end of the bottom side rail. Locate the mortises on the posts; draw the mortises' center lines ⅜ inch (.95 cm) in from the outside edges of the posts and the bottom of the mortise 2 inches (5.08 cm) from the bottom of the post. Cut the mortises using the drill and chisel cleanout method.

The top side rails each have a blind tenon at the back and a through tenon at the front. Tenons begin 1 inch (2.54 cm) from the top edge of each rail. Cut the blind tenon to measure 2 inches (5.08 cm) wide by 1¼ inches (3.17 cm) long by ½ inch (1.27 cm) thick. Then cut the through tenon to measure 2 inches (5.08 cm) wide by 2 inches (5.08 cm) long by ½ inch (1.27 cm) thick. Locate the mortises ⅜ inch (.95 cm), on center, from the outside post edge on the front and back posts. The front post mortise begins 2¼ inches (5.71 cm) from the top of the front post. The back post mortise begins 5¼ inches (13.33 cm) from the top of the back post. Cut the mortises using the drill and chisel cleanout method.

Cut blind tenons measuring 1 inch (2.54 cm) wide by ¾ inch (1.91 cm) long by ⅝ inch (1.58 cm) thick on each end of the center vertical rail. Locate and cut mortises for this rail in the center of the top edge of the bottom side rail and the bottom edge of the top side rail, using the drill and chisel cleanout method (see figures 5-85 and 5-89).

Round the corners of each side panel to aid in assembly.

Using the router table and a ½-inch (1.27-cm) straight bit, cut a ½-inch-wide (1.27-cm) dado ½ inch (1.27 cm) into the posts, aligning with and connecting the mortises for the top and bottom side rails (see figure 5-85). Cut the same size dado —½ inch (1.27 cm) wide by ½ inch (1.27 cm) deep—centered, on the top edge of the bottom side rail and the bottom edge of the top side rail. Cut the same dado, on center, on both edges of the center vertical side rail. These dados extend the full length of each rail and will accommodate the side panels.

Front Bottom Rail

Cut through tenons measuring 2 inches (5.08 cm) wide by 2 inches (5.08 cm) long by ½ inch (1.27 cm) thick on each end of the front bottom rail. These tenons are *not* centered on the front bottom rail, but begin ½ inch (1.27 cm) up from the bottom edge.

Cut the pattern or arc in the bottom edge of the front rail using a band saw. Remember that the center measurement given in figure 5-88 is from the underside of the shelf, not from the top edge of the rail. Because the front bottom rail will be inserted into a ½-inch-deep (1.27-cm) dado to be cut in the bottom shelf, the center measurement from the top to bottom edge of the rail should be 3⅜ inches (8.57 cm) and the measurement at each end should be 5 inches (12.7 cm). Sand clean on a drill press using a drum sanding attachment.

Locate and cut mortises centered on the front posts using the drill and chisel cleanout method.

Back

Cut through tenons measuring 2 inches (5.08 cm) wide by 2 inches (5.08 cm) long by ½ inch (1.27 cm) thick on both ends of the back bottom rail. Locate and cut mortises into the back posts in the same position as those mortises for the front bottom rail that were cut on the front posts, using the drill and chisel cleanout method.

Cut blind tenons measuring 1½ inches (3.81 cm) wide by 1 inch (2.54 cm) long by ½ inch (1.27 cm) thick on both ends of the top back rail. Cut mortises, on center, on the inside of the back post, beginning 2½ inches (6.35 cm) down from the top the posts; use the drill and chisel cleanout method.

The body of the back is constructed of five oak plywood panels joined along their edges with splines. Using the table saw, cut a ⅛-inch-wide (.32-cm) dado, ½ inch (1.27 cm) deep, into the inside edge of the two end panels

and into both edges of the three remaining panels. After the dados have been cut, slightly bevel the edges of each panel on both sides with a sanding block. You may need to remove a triangular sliver from the top and bottom corners of the end panels to provide a proper fit into the posts (see figure 5-84).

Using the router table and a ½-inch (1.27-cm) straight bit, cut a ½-inch-wide (1.27-cm) dado ½ inch (1.27 cm) deep, on center, into each back post for insertion of the end panels of the back. This dado should connect the mortises of the top and bottom back rails. Cut a ½-inch-wide (1.27-cm) dado ½ inch (1.27 cm) deep into the center of the bottom edge of the top back rail and the center of the top edge of the back bottom rail. These dados extend the full length of each rail.

Shelves

If you plan to add additional shelves to the bookcase, drill ¼-inch (.64-cm) holes for adjustable peg shelf supports parallel to the side panel dados on the front and back posts. Locate the bottom hole 8 inches (20.32 cm), on center, from the bottom of the post. Drill the remaining twenty-five holes at 1-inch (2.54-cm) intervals. Drill all holes to a depth of ¾ inch (1.91 cm).

Laminate the bottom, center, and top shelves by butt-joining two or three pieces (depending on stock width) of stock edge-to-edge with ⅜-inch (.95-cm) diameter dowels. Lay out the shelves, being careful to alternate the end grain direction of the boards to minimize warping.

Trim the laminated shelf ends with a router. First trim one end square, measure to length, and then trim the other end.

Notch the top shelf to fit around the four posts using the dimensions given in figure 5-88, top view. Round the corners indicated in the drawing with a ¼-inch (.64-cm) radius template as a guide.

Locate and cut ¾-inch wide, (1.91-cm) ½-inch deep (1.27-cm) dados, beginning ¾ inch (1.91 cm) from each side end of the bottom surface of the top shelf, using a router and fence and a ¾-inch (1.91-cm) straight bit. This dado fits over the top edge of the top side rails, locking the shelf in place.

Cut ¾-inch-long (1.91-cm) notches into the inside corners of each post to hold the middle shelf in place. Locate the notches in the back post ⅞ inch (2.22 cm) in from the inside surface and ¼ inch (.64 cm) in from the front surface of the back post. Locate the notches in the front posts ⅞ inch (2.22 cm) in from the inside surface and ¼ inch (.64) in from the back surface of the front post. The back post notches begin 14¼ inches (36.20 cm) down from the top of each post, and front post notches begin 11¼ inches (28.58 cm) down from the top of each post.

Cut ¾-inch-long (1.91-cm) notches into the inside corners of each back post to hold the bottom shelf in place. These notches have the same dimensions as those for the middle shelf. Begin each notch 6⅛ inches (15.56 cm) up from the bottom of each post. Cut a ¾-inch-wide (1.91-cm), ½-inch-deep (1.27-cm) dado into the underside of the shelf, ⅞ inch (2.22 cm) from the front of the shelf. The dado should extend the full length of the shelf. This dado will receive the top edge of the front bottom rail. The front corners of the bottom shelf are cut to fit around each of the posts.

Bevel the top front edge of the bottom shelf according to guidelines drawn ¼ inch (.64 cm) down from the top along the front edge and ¾ inch (1.91 cm) back from the front edge along the top. Cut the bevel with a block plane. Round the front two corners of the bottom shelf with a ¼-inch (.64-cm) radius template as a guide.

Subassembly

Bevel all through tenons with a disc sander or block plane. Use guidelines drawn 3/16 inch (.47 cm) down from the end along each side and ⅛ inch (.32 cm) in from each edge on the end.

Also bevel the top of each post according to guidelines drawn ¼ inch (.64 cm) down from the top edge on each side and ¼ inch (.64 cm) in from all edges on the top.

Glue together each side unit, applying glue only to the mortise-and-tenon joints while allowing the panels free movement. This movement is necessary to prevent the panels from splitting or putting undue pressure on the frame if they expand.

When each side unit is dry, connect the two sides with the shelves, rails, and back panels to form the frame. Like the side panels, the back panels are left free.

Pin the tenons in the front bottom, the back, and the top side rails with ⅜-inch (.95-cm) dowels, centered on the post and tenon.

Door

Door Frame

Cut a ½-inch-wide (1.27-cm) by ½-inch-deep (1.27-cm) rabbet into

5–90. Cut a rabbet in the stile using a table saw. A support clamped to the table holds the stile against the fence as it passes over the blade.

the inside edges of the stiles and rails with a table saw. Use a support clamped to the table to hold the stock in place while you cut (figure 5-90). Cut a 1/4-inch-wide (.64-cm) by 1/2-inch-deep (1.27-cm) rabbet in both edges of all mullions (figure 5-91).

5–91. Finished rabbet cut in the stile.

Cut barefaced tenons measuring 13/16 inch (2.06 cm) wide by 5/16 inch (.79 cm) thick onto the ends of the top and bottom rails (figure 5-92). Set the dado blade of the table saw to cut 1/4 inch (.64 cm) in depth. Clamp a stop on the miter guide to remove 1 inch (2.54 cm) of material from the end. Cut with the face of the rail resting on the table. Reset the dado blade of the table saw to cut 3/16 inch (.47 cm) in depth and clamp a stop on the miter guide to remove 1/2 inch (1.27 cm) of material from the end. Cut with the back of the rail resting on the table. With the blade and miter guide stop in the same positions, place the face against the miter guide and make the final tenon cut.

Locate mortises on the inside edge of the stiles; draw the mortise 3/16 inch (.47 cm) in from the end and 3/16 inch (.47 cm) in from the back of the stile. Cut the mortise using the drill and chisel clean-out method (figure 5-93).

Mullions

Measure and mark the position of each lap joint on the horizontal mullions (figure 5-95). Cut a dado 1/2 inch (1.27 cm) wide and 1/4 inch (.64 cm) deep into the body of the rabbet. Clamp a jig with a round bottom into position to prevent the stock from chattering on the saw.

Measure and mark the position of each lap joint on the vertical mullions (figure 5-95). First cut the wider, 1-inch (2.54-cm) dado into the face of the vertical mullions. Cut to a depth of 1/4 inch

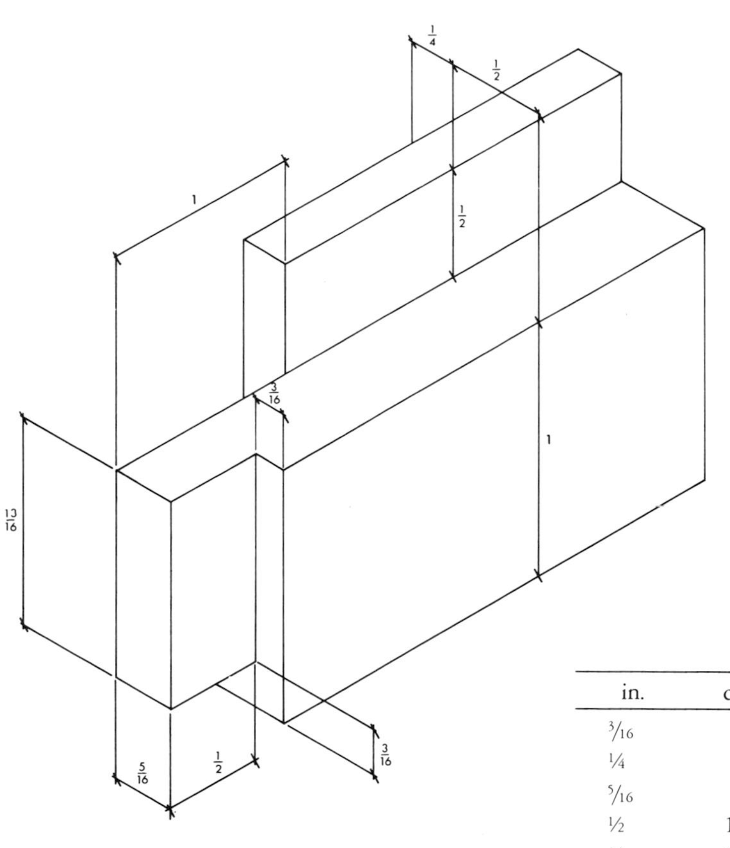

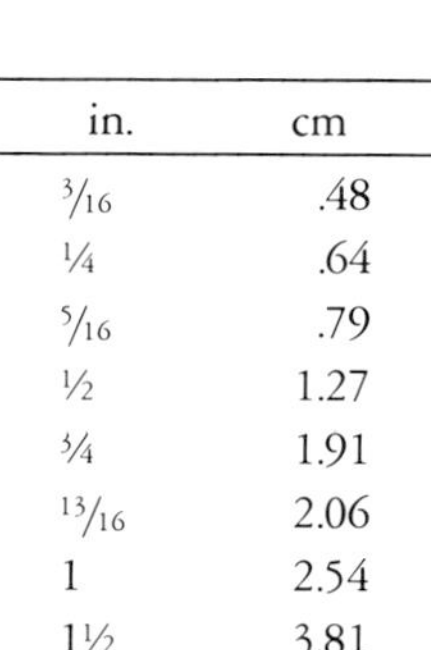

in.	cm
3/16	.48
1/4	.64
5/16	.79
1/2	1.27
3/4	1.91
13/16	2.06
1	2.54
1 1/2	3.81

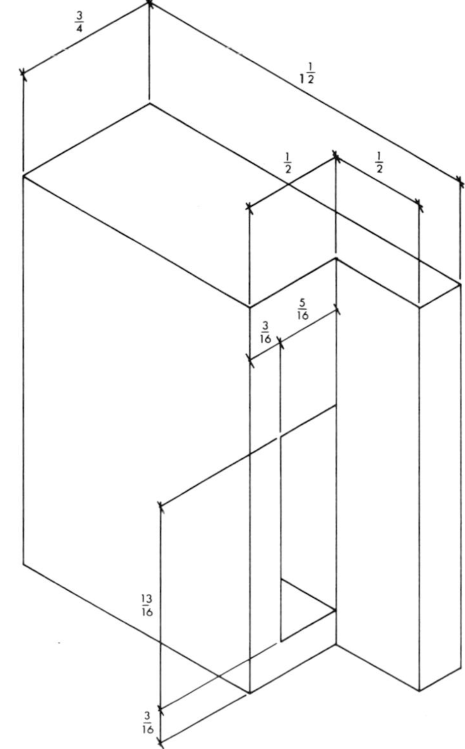

5–92. Working drawing for barefaced tenon.

5–93. Cut a mortise in the stiles using drill and chisel cleanout method.

5–94. Finished barefaced mortise-and-tenon joint for door stile and rail.

in.	cm
¼	.64
½	1.27
¾	1.91
1	2.54

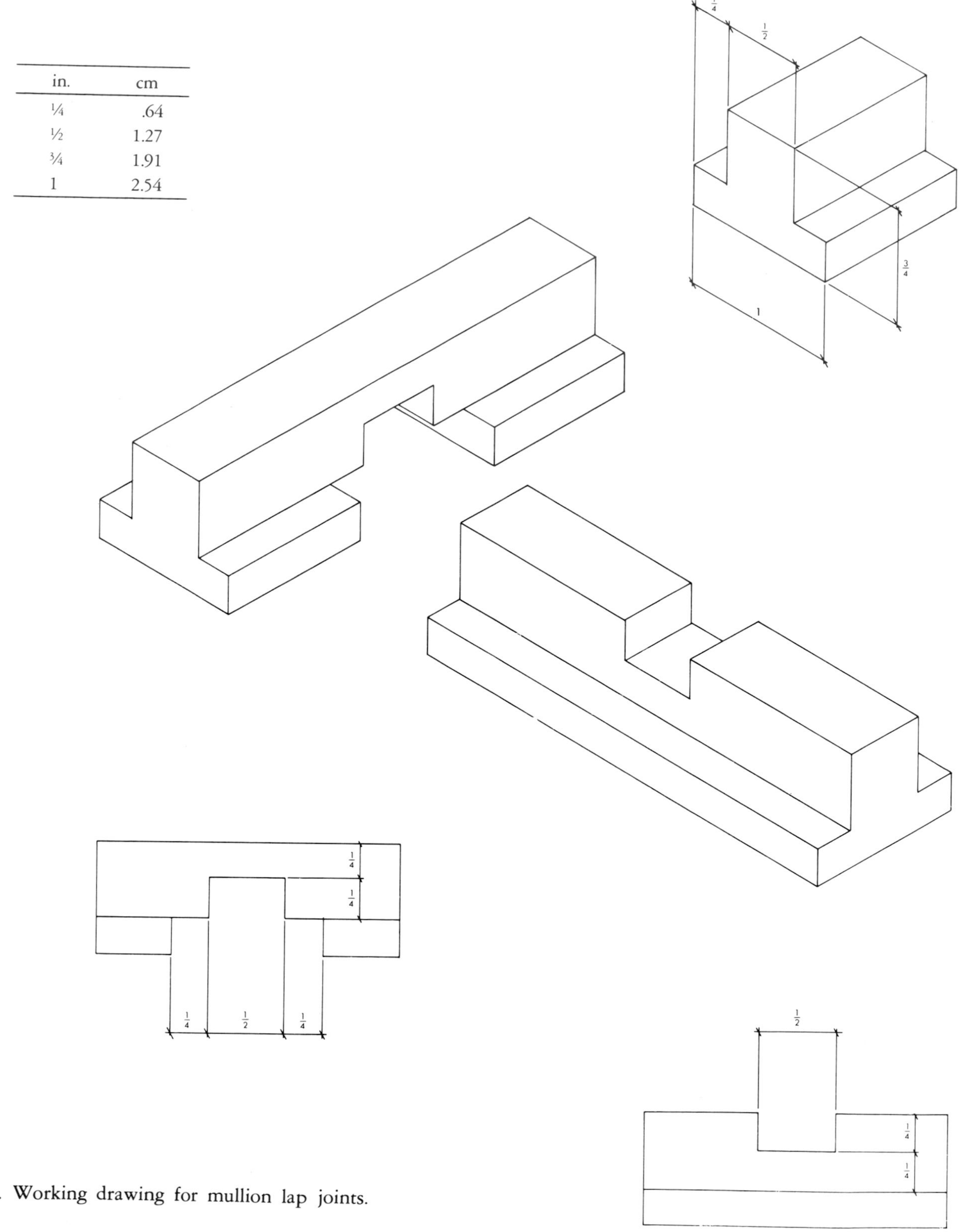

5–95. Working drawing for mullion lap joints.

(.64 cm), which should be exactly through the shoulders of the rabbet. You will have to make two passes to obtain the required width for the dado. Again, use a jig to prevent the stock from lifting. A second lap cut must be made to accommodate the rabbet bodies of the horizontal mullions. Set the table saw to cut to a depth of ½ inch (1.27 cm). Center this cut on the 1-inch (2.54-cm) dado.

Cut combination rabbet and mortise-and-tenon joints on the ends of the center vertical mullion and the horizontal mullion (figure 5-97). Set the dado blade of the table saw to cut ¼ inch (.64 cm) depth and clamp a stop on the miter guide to remove 1 inch (2.54 cm) of material from the end. Cut with the face of the mullion resting on the table. With the blade of the table saw at the same depth and a stop on the miter guide set to remove ½ inch (1.27 cm) of material from the end, make a final cut with the back of the mullion resting on the table (figure 5-98). See chapter 4 for general instructions on cutting barefaced tenons.

Locate mortises on the inside edge of the stiles; draw the mortises' center lines ⅜ inch (.95 cm) from the backs of the stiles, and the tops of the mortises 9⅞ inches (25.08 cm) from the tops of the stiles. Locate the mortises on the inside edge of the rails; draw the mortises' center lines ⅜ inch (.95 cm) from the back of the rail and the ends of the mortises 9⅞ inches (25.08 cm) from the end of the rail. Cut mortises using the drill and chisel cleanout method.

Cut a rabbet into the ends of the side vertical mullions where they will join the frame. Set the dado blade of the table saw to cut to a ¼-inch (.64-cm) depth, and clamp a stop on the miter guide to remove ½ inch (1.27 cm) of material from the top of each mullion. Cut with the face of the mullion resting on the table. Move the stop on the miter guide to remove ¼ inch (.64 cm) of material from the bottom of each mullion. Cut with the face of the mullion on the table.

Glue and clamp together the stiles, the top and bottom rails, and the center vertical and horizontal mullions. When this assembly is dry, glue and clamp the two side vertical mullions in place.

5-96. Lap joint in center vertical and horizontal mullions.

Assembly

Two pairs of stops are needed to properly align the doors. One pair, square in cross section, measures ½ inch (1.27 cm) wide by ½ inch (1.27 cm) thick by 2 inches (5.08 cm) long. The other pair, L-shaped in cross section, measures ½ inch (1.27 cm) wide by 1 inch (2.54 cm) thick by 42⅜ inches (107.63 cm) long (figure 5-99).

The L-shaped stops, also called hinge supports, are used to aid in mounting the box hinges for the doors to the case. They keep the hinge pin and its casing from rub-

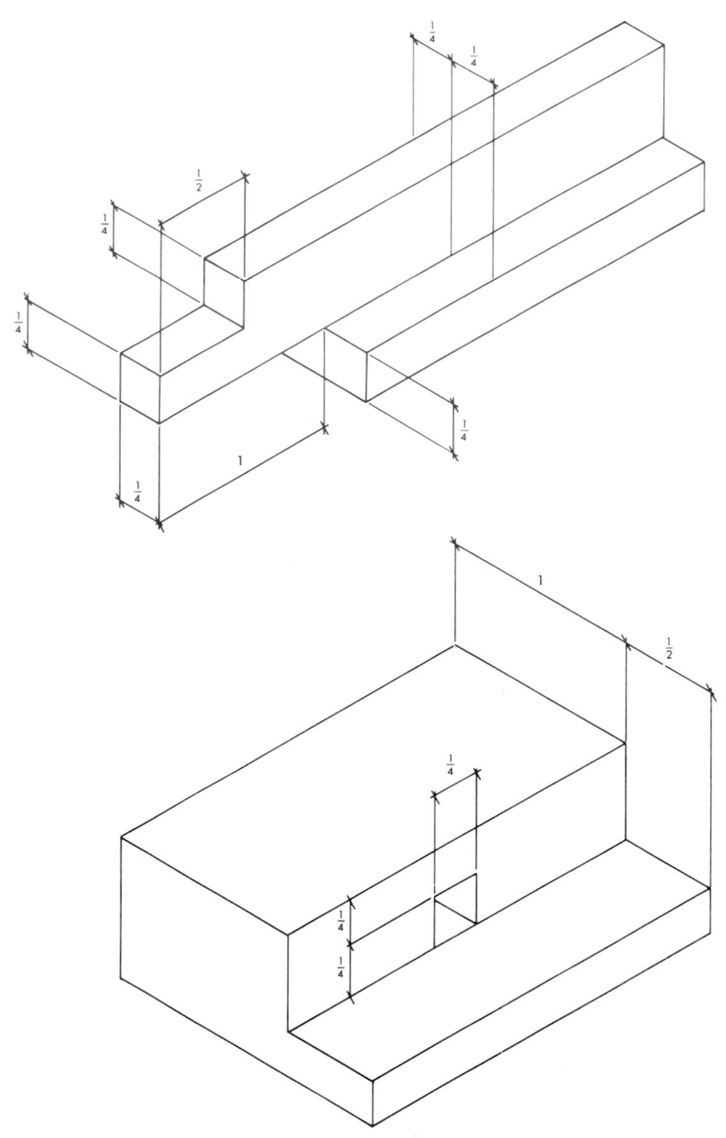

in.	cm
¼	.64
½	1.27
1	2.54

5–97. Working drawing for combination rabbet/mortise-and-tenon joint.

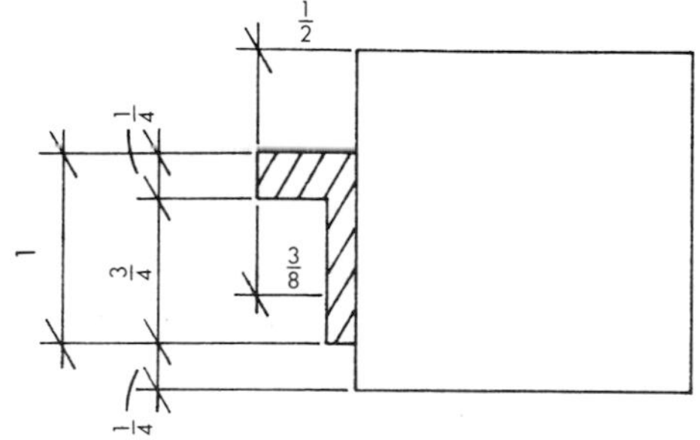

in.	cm
¼	.64
⅜	.95
½	1.27
¾	1.91
1	2.54

5–99. Working drawing for L-shaped stop.

5–98. Combination rabbet/mortise-and-tenon joint connecting mullions to stiles and rails.

in.	cm
¼	.64
⅜	.95
⅝	1.58
1	2.54
1⅛	2.86
1¼	3.17
4	10.16

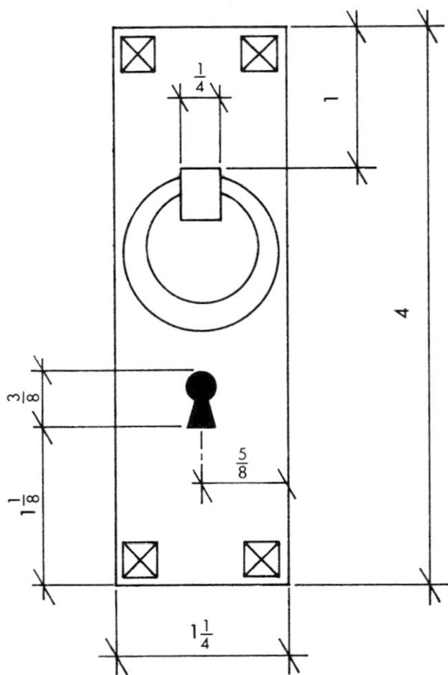

5–100. Working drawing for door-pull, front view.

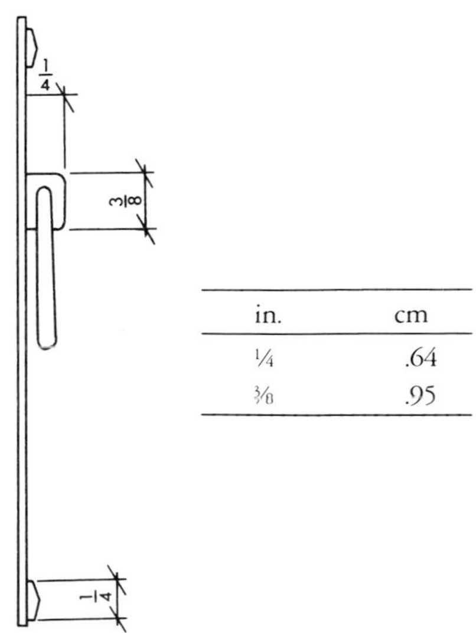

in.	cm
¼	.64
⅜	.95

5–101. Working drawing for door-pull, side view.

bing against the inside surface of the post. This is necessary because the door fronts are recessed from the front face of the posts. Glue the L-shaped stops with their 1 inch (2.54 cm) dimension against the post and their front edges ¼ inch (.64 cm) back from the front face of the post along the inside edge of the post between the top and bottom shelves.

Apply a finish to the piece using the procedure described in chapter 4.

Use four 3-inch (7.62-cm) loose pin brass box hinges to attach the doors to the case. Treat the surfaces of the hinges according to the instructions given in chapter 4. Position the top hinge on each door so that the top of the hinge is 4 inches (10.16 cm) down from the underside of the top shelf. Position the bottom of the lower hinge 4 inches (10.16 cm) up from the top surface of the bottom shelf.

Cut hinge-plate mortises using the instructions given in chapter 4. Then connect hinges and doors to the case.

The square stops will prevent the doors from closing too far into the case. Close both doors and hold a long, steel straightedge horizontally against their front faces, making sure it makes contact along its full length with the door faces. Mark the bottom and top shelves by running a pencil along the inside of both doors where they meet. This line gives you the position of the forwardmost edge of the square stops. Glue both stops in place with their front edges along this line, centered on each shelf.

Drawings of the door-pull (figures 5-100 and 5-101) have been included so that you can make the pull or have it made by a metalsmith. The pulls are made of solid copper; the plate, from 14-gauge (.625-inch [.16-cm]) sheet stock; the drop ring, from ¼-inch (.64-cm) rod stock; the pyramid shaped caps (which are soldered to the heads of brass wood screws) from 8-gauge (.128-inch [.32-cm]) sheet stock; and the drop ring pivot block from ¼-inch (.64-cm) by ⅜-inch (.95-cm) bar stock. The plate is planished, and forging marks are left in the drop ring. See figure 5-89 for location of pulls on the doors.

The left door is held closed by a spring-action elbow latch attached to the inside of the door and the underside of the center shelf. This latch should be installed according to the instructions provided by the manufacturer. The right door is held closed with a small mortise cupboard lock. The bolt of this lock enters a mortise in the edge of the left door. Position the lock so that its keyhole is in line with the keyhole cut in the door pull. This lock mechanism can be purchased at most hardware stores and should be installed according to the manufacturer's instructions.

To install the glass, remove the pins from the hinges and take off the doors. Measure each opening in the back side of the door for glass size. Cut or have the glass cut so that it fits each opening with 1/16 inch (.15 cm) of play. To hold the glass in position, nail ¼ inch (.64 cm) wide by ⅜ inch (.95 cm) thick molding strips in place with small brads.

Additional shelves can be made as desired for the areas above and below the middle shelf. These adjustable shelves can be supported by dowel pins inserted in the holes or by shelf brackets, which can be purchased in most hardware stores.

Clock Case

This hall clock case, as Stickley named it, exemplifies the structural style applied to a traditional furniture piece. The clock case retains the formality of a grandfather clock, but Stickley redefined the usual ornamentation in terms of the functional mullions on the door. A rather detailed design for a Craftsman piece, the elements nonetheless remain functional.

MATERIALS

	Number of Pieces	Length in.	Length cm	Width in.	Width cm	Thickness in.	Thickness cm
Frame							
Side	2	71¼	180.98	10	25.40	1¼	3.17
Top Shelf	1	20½	52.07	10¾	27.31	1¼	3.17
Bottom Shelf	1	16¾	42.55	8¼	20.96	⅞	2.22
Front and Back Bottom Rail	2	19	48.26	4	10.16	⅞	2.22
Top Back Rail	1	17	43.18	5⅞	14.92	⅞	2.22
Back Panel	1	47⅛	119.70	17	43.18	½	1.27
Movement Shelf	1	17	43.18	5	12.70	⅞	2.22
Back Door							
Top and Bottom Back-Door Rail	2	16	40.64	2½	6.35	⅞	2.22
Side Back-Door Rail	2	9	22.86	2½	6.35	⅞	2.22
Back-Door Panel	1	12	30.48	10	25.40	½	1.27
Front Door							
Door Stile	2	66	167.64	1⅞	4.76	¾	1.91
Top and Middle Door Rail	2	13⅞	35.24	2	5.08	¾	1.91
Bottom Door Rail	1	13⅞	35.24	3	7.62	¾	1.91
Vertical Door Mullion	3	48⅞	124.14	1	2.54	¾	1.91
Horizontal Door Mullion	11	13⅞	35.24	1	2.54	¾	1.91
Stops							
Front Stop	1	66	167.64	½	1.27	½	1.27
Front Hinge Support	1	66	167.64	1⅛	2.86	⅝	1.58
Back Stop	1	14	35.56	½	1.27	½	1.27
Back Hinge Support	1	14	35.56	1⅛	2.86	⅝	1.58
Glass							
Corner Panes	4	3 11/16	9.37	2 15/16	7.46	⅛	.32
Side Panes	20	3 7/16	8.73	2 15/16	7.46	⅛	.32
Center Top and Bottom Panes	4	3 11/16	9.37	2 11/16	6.83	⅛	.32
Center Panes	20	3 7/16	8.73	2 11/16	6.83	⅛	.32
Clock-Face Pane	1	12 15/16	32.86	12 15/16	32.86	⅛	.32

⅜-inch (.95-cm) dowels
⅝-inch (1.58-cm) dowels
3 loose-pin brass or steel box hinges, 3 inches (7.62 cm) long
2 loose-pin brass or steel box hinges, 1½ inches (3.81 cm) long
1 small mortise cupboard lock
molding strips: for lower door, 1 strip, 52 feet (15.86 m) by ¼ inch (.64 cm) by ⅜ inch (.95 cm); for clock face, 1 strip, 5 feet (1.52 m) by ½ inch (1.27 cm) by ⅜ inch (.95 cm)
brads

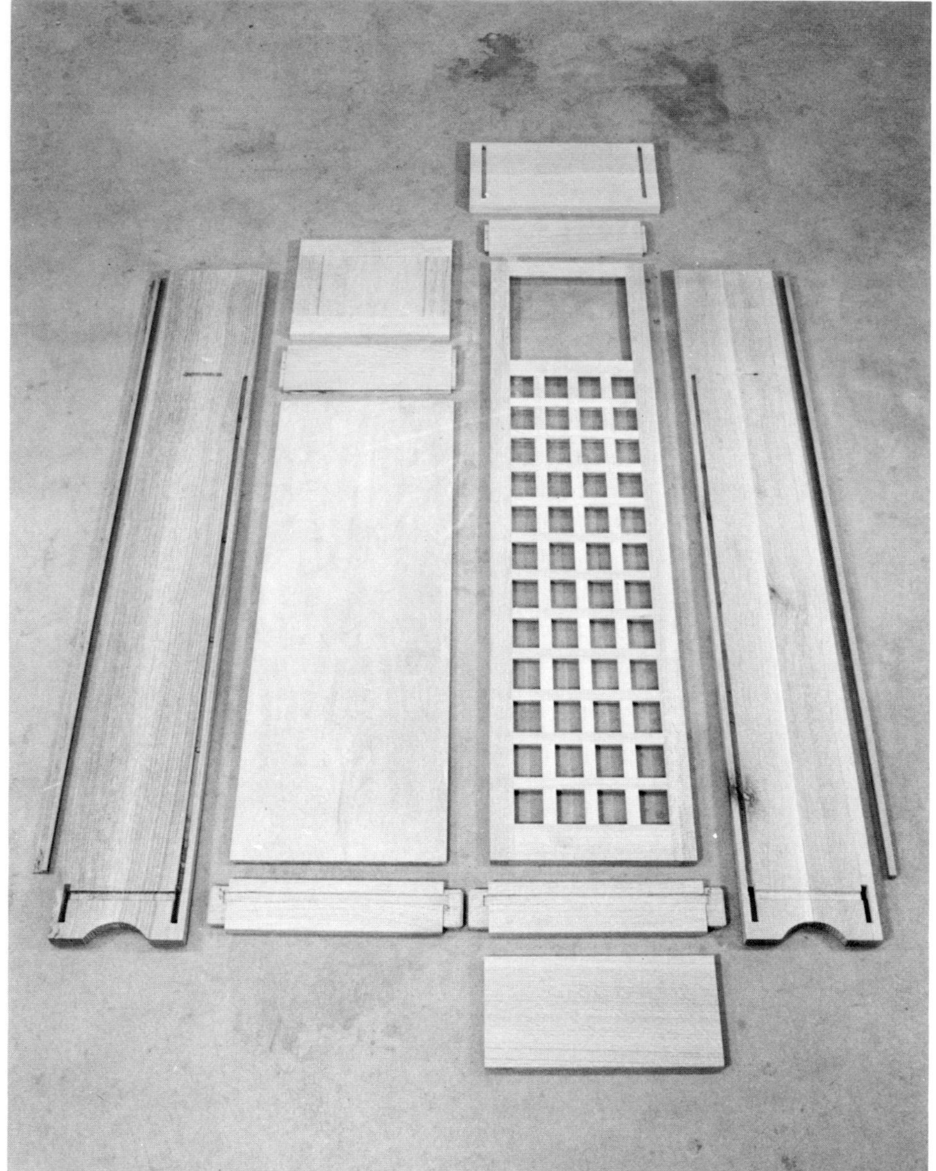

5–103. Exploded view of the clock case.

5–104. Clock case.

This clock case has three subassemblies: the frame, the back door, and the front door. The frame, which is constructed first, consists of two sides, a top and bottom shelf, a front and back bottom rail, a top back rail, a back panel, and a movement shelf that will hold the clock. The back door, a simple frame construction, is made from a top and bottom rail, two side rails, and a back-door panel. The most difficult of the subassemblies, the front door is built with two stiles, a top, middle, and bottom rail, three vertical mullions, and eleven horizontal mullions. Cut your stock according to the dimensions given in the materials list.

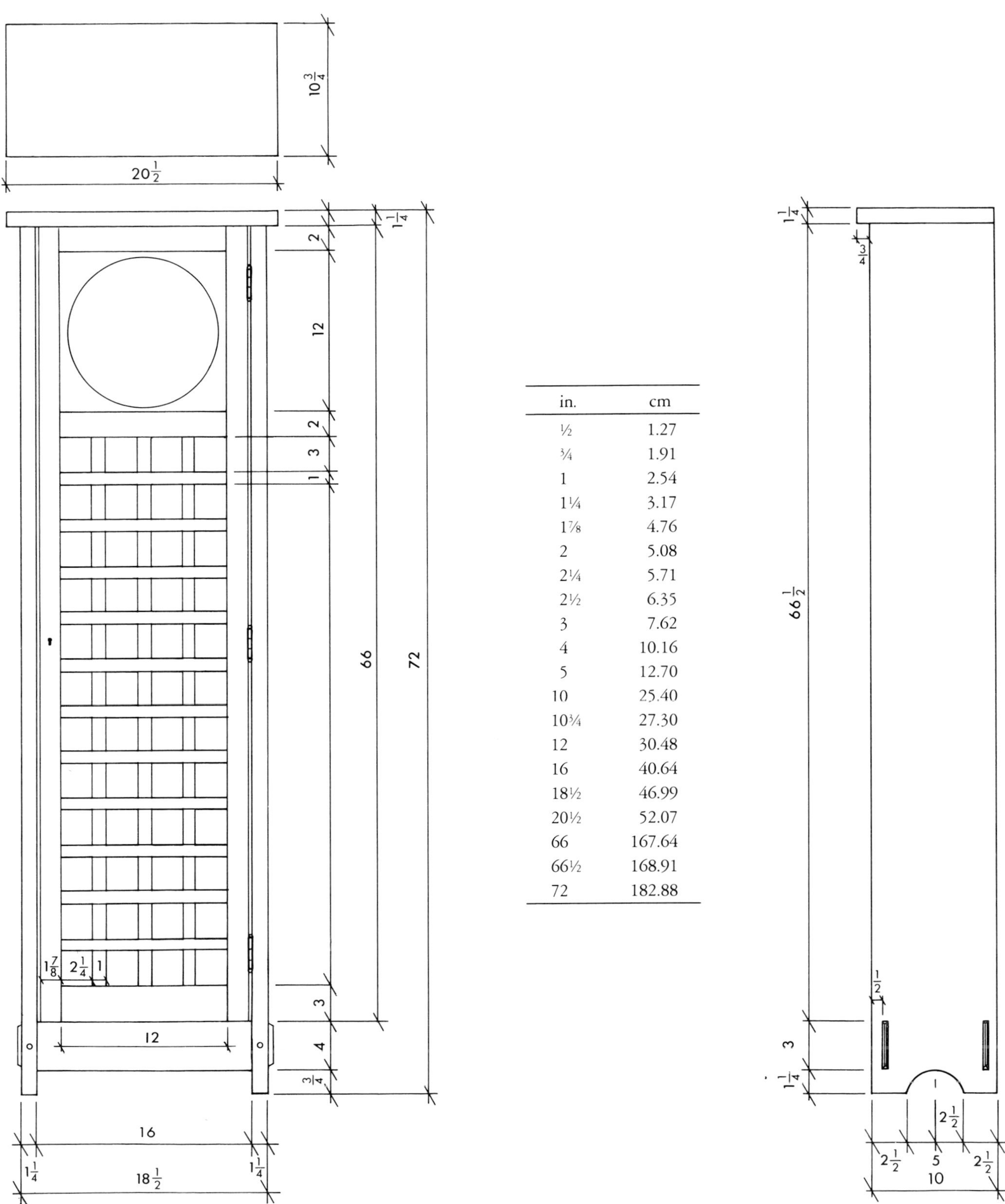

in.	cm
½	1.27
¾	1.91
1	2.54
1¼	3.17
1⅞	4.76
2	5.08
2¼	5.71
2½	6.35
3	7.62
4	10.16
5	12.70
10	25.40
10¾	27.30
12	30.48
16	40.64
18½	46.99
20½	52.07
66	167.64
66½	168.91
72	182.88

5–105. Working drawing for clock case. Front and side views.

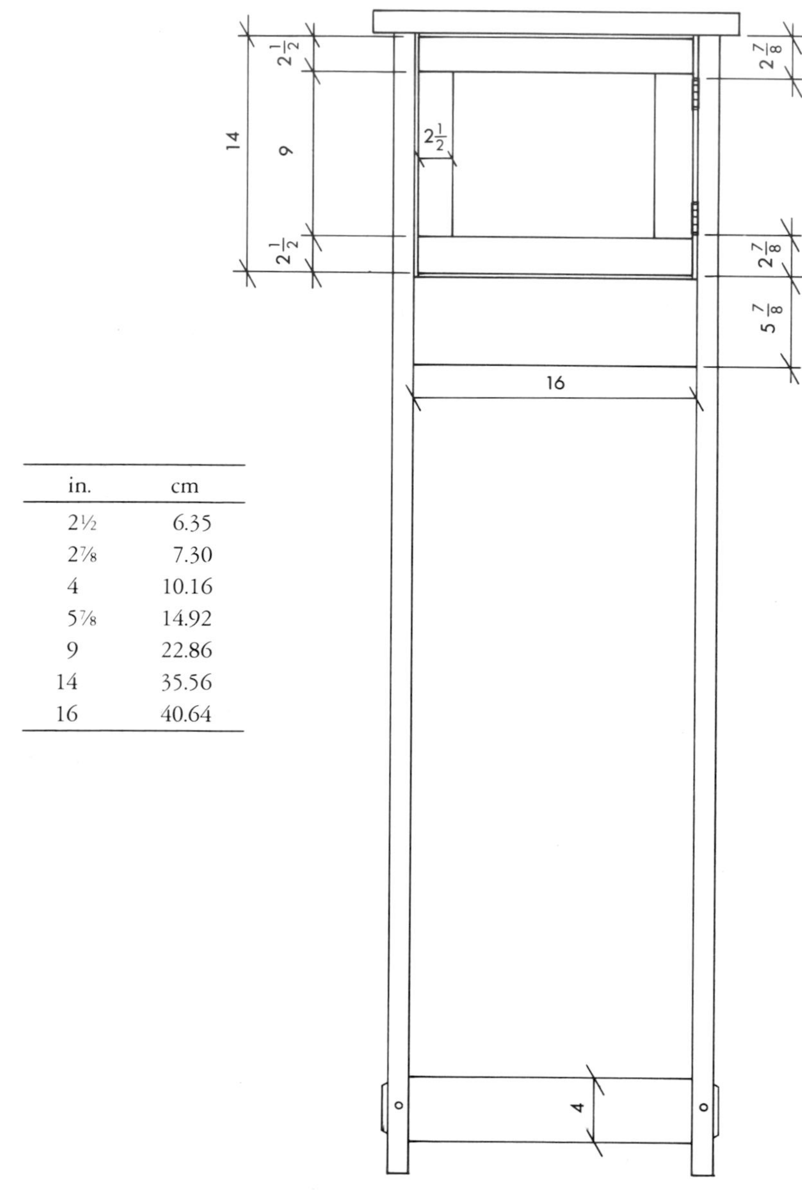

in.	cm
2½	6.35
2⅞	7.30
4	10.16
5⅞	14.92
9	22.86
14	35.56
16	40.64

5-106. Working drawing for clock case. Back view.

PROCEDURE

In addition to the instructions given below, you may need to refer to the general instructions in chapter 4 for the following procedures:

Butt-joining, page 71
Squaring laminated stock, pages 74–75
Cutting tenons, pages 65–66
Cutting mortises with router, pages 76–77
Cutting mortises with drill and chisel, page 69
Beveling, page 70
Assembly, pages 79–83
Treating hinges, page 88
Cutting hinge mortises, page 88
Finishing, pages 84–87

Frame

Laminate the sides, the top shelf, and the bottom shelf by joining two boards edge-to-edge with ⅝-inch (1.58-cm) dowels. Lay out each part carefully, alternating the end grain direction of the boards to minimize warping.

Trim one end of each laminated piece square with a router. Measure the pieces to length and trim the other end.

Cut a blind tenon measuring 9 inches (22.86 cm) wide by ½ inch (1.27 cm) long by ⅝-inch (1.58-cm) thick on the top end of each side (figure 5-107). Using a router and a ⅝-inch (1.58-cm) straight bit with a fence or guide, make a cut 5/16 inch (.79 cm) in depth from each face. This will give you the ⅝-inch (1.58-cm) thickness and ½-inch (1.27-cm) length of the tenon. (Make your router cut in several passes.) To establish the width, cut in from each edge ½ inch (1.27 cm) in depth with a backsaw. To finish the tenon,

slowly chip away material with a flat chisel, on the end grain and moving toward the saw mark. Make several cuts, each taking off more material, until you approach the end of the saw cut. Make your last cut at a ninety-degree angle to the saw cut.

Cut mortises for these tenons in the underside of the top shelf with a router and a ⅝-inch (1.58-cm) straight bit. Locate the center of each mortise 1¼ inches (3.17 cm) in from the side edge, beginning ½ inch (1.27 cm) from the back edge (figure 5-107).

Cut through tenons measuring 3 inches (7.62 cm) wide by 1½ inches (3.81 cm) long by ½ inch (1.27 cm) thick on both ends of the front and back bottom rails. Locate their mortises in the sides (figure 5-105) and cut, using the drill and chisel cleanout method.

Bevel the ends of the through tenons with a disc sander or block plane. Cut the bevel according to guidelines drawn 3/16 inches (.47 cm) down from the end along each side and ⅛ inch (.32 cm) in from each edge on the end.

Using a table saw with a ⅞-inch (2.22-cm) dado blade, cut a dado ⅞ inch (2.22 cm) wide by ⅜ inch (.95 cm) deep into the inside faces of the front and back bottom rails. The top edge of each dado should begin 1 inch (2.54 cm) down from the top edge of each rail. Cut only shoulder to shoulder on each rail; chisel out the remainder of the dado so that the full bottom shelf seats properly (figure 5-108).

Dry-clamp both bottom rails into their mortises. With a pencil, locate where each dado intersects the sides of the clock case. Remove the rails and connect the intersection marks mortise to mortise. This gives you the position of the bottom shelf dado. Cut a dado ⅞ inch (2.22 cm) wide by ⅜ inch (.95 cm) deep on each side, using a router with a ⅝-inch (1.58-cm)

5–107. Mortise and tenon join side and top shelf of clock case.

straight bit along a fence or guide. Two passes with the ⅝-inch (1.58-cm) bit, moving the fence or guide between passes, are necessary to cut a ⅞-inch-wide (2.22-cm) dado.

Cut blind tenons, measuring 4⅞ inches (12.38 cm) wide by ½ inch (1.27 cm) long by ½ inch (1.27 cm) thick on both ends of the top back rail. Locate and cut mortises on inner clock sides using the router with a ½-inch (1.27-cm) straight bit and a fence or guide. Cut these mortises the same distance from the back edge of the sides as the mortises for the back bottom rail.

Cut ½-inch-wide (1.27-cm) by ½-inch-deep (1.27-cm) dados, on center into the top edge of the back bottom rail and the bottom edge of the top back rail, using the

5–108. Dados cut in bottom rails hold bottom shelf.

5-109. Back-door frame, showing panel in place and doweled butt joint in corners.

router and a ½-inch (1.27-cm) straight bit. These dados will accommodate the back panel.

Using the router with a ½-inch (1.27-cm) straight bit and a fence or guide, cut a ½-inch-deep (1.27-cm) dado into each side for insertion of the back panel. This dado should connect the mortises of the top and bottom back rails.

Cut blind tenons measuring 4½ inches (11.43 cm) wide by ½ inch (1.27 cm) long by ½ inch (1.27 cm) thick in the ends of the movement shelf. Locate its mortises 14 ⅜ inches (36.51 cm) on center, from the underside of the top shelf. Cut the mortises with a router and a ½-inch (1.27-cm) straight bit.

Using a saber saw, cut the arc in the bottom of each side to the dimensions given in figure 5-108. Finish the arc with a file and sandpaper.

The frame of the clock case is now ready for subassembly. Apply glue only to the mortise-and-tenon joints; leave the back panel free to prevent it from splitting or putting undue pressure on the frame if it expands.

Back Door

The back door is a simple frame construction held together with butt joints and ⅜-inch (.95-cm) dowels (figure 5-109). After making the butt joints, cut a ½-inch-wide (1.27-cm) dado ½ inch (1.27 cm) deep, on center, into the inside edges of all four door rails with the router table and a ½-inch (1.27-cm) straight bit. Round the corners of the back-door panel for ease in assembly. To assemble the back door, apply glue only to the butt joints, leaving the back-door panel free.

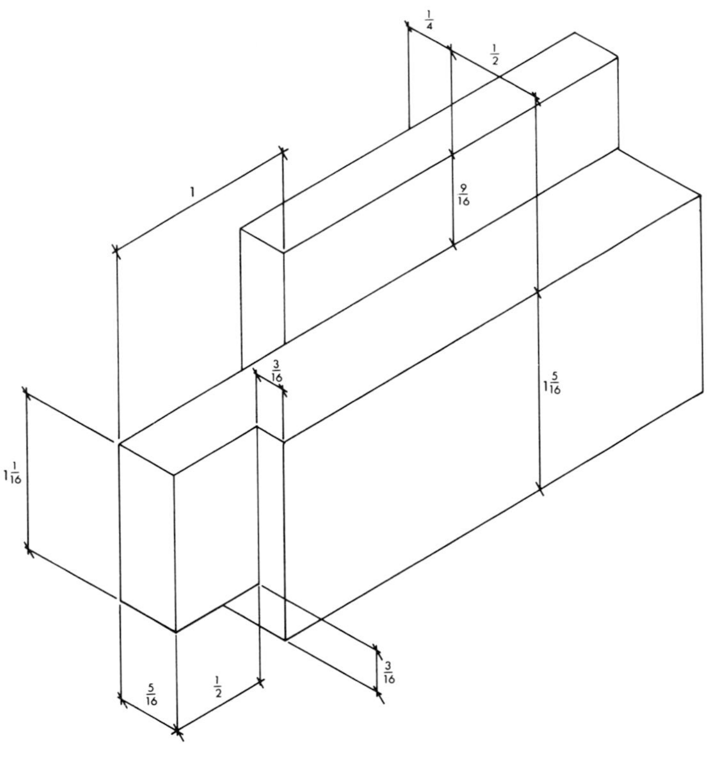

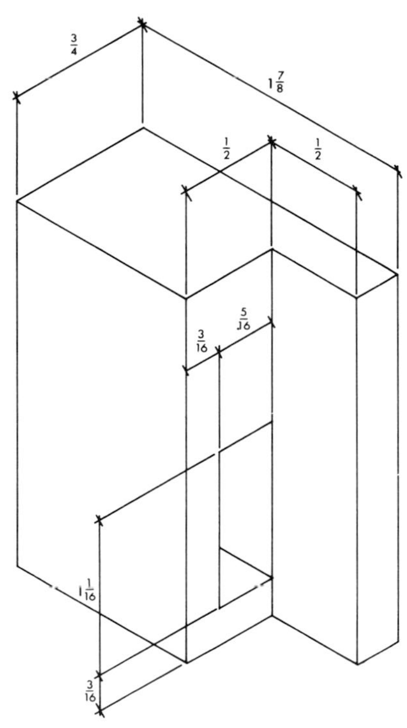

5-110. Working drawing of barefaced tenon.

Front Door

Door Frame

Cut a rabbet ½ inch (1.27 cm) deep by ½ inch (1.27 cm) wide into the inside edge of each stile and rail (both edges of the middle rail).

Cut barefaced tenons measuring 1 1/16 inch (2.7 cm) wide by 5/16 inch (.79 cm) thick onto both ends of the top and bottom rails (figure 5-110). Set the dado blade of a table saw to cut ¼ inch (.64 cm) in depth. Clamp a stop on the miter guide to remove 1 inch (2.54 cm) of material from the end. Cut with the face of the rail resting on the table. Reset the dado blade of the table saw to cut 3/16 inch (.47 cm) in depth and clamp a stop on the miter guide to remove ½ inch (1.27 cm) of material from the end. Cut with the back of the rail resting on the table. With the blade and miter guide stop in the same positions, place the face against the miter guide and make the final tenon cut.

in.	cm
3/16	.48
¼	.64
5/16	.79
½	1.27
9/16	1.43
¾	1.91
1	2.54
1 1/16	2.70
1 5/16	3.33
1 7/8	4.76

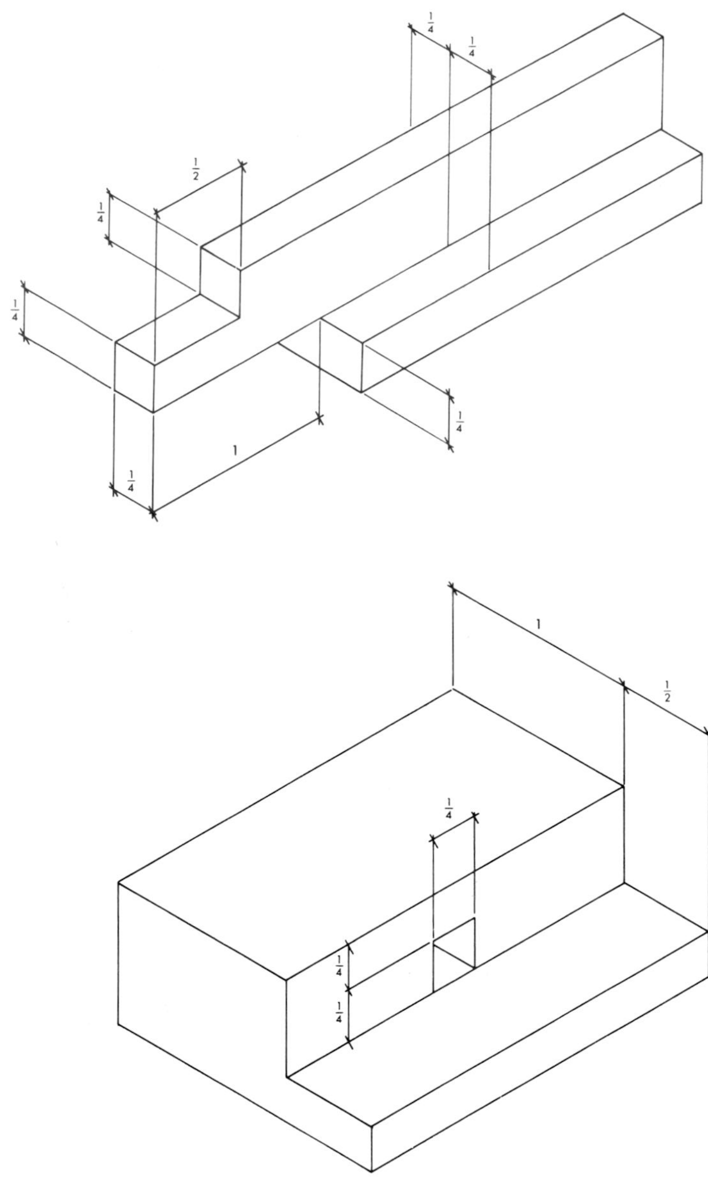

5-111. Working drawing for combination rabbet/mortise-and-tenon joint.

Cut the mortises in the stiles using the drill and chisel cleanout method (see figure 5-105 for location).

Cut a rabbet joint and then a tenon on the middle rail (figure 5-111). Set the dado blade of the table saw to cut ¼ inch (.64 cm) in depth. Clamp a stop on the miter guide to remove 1 inch (2.54 cm) of material from the end. Cut with the face of the rail resting on the table. With the blade of the table saw at the same depth and a stop on the miter guide to remove ½ inch (1.27 cm) of material from the end, make the final cut with the back of the rail resting on the table.

Locate the position of the rail mortises on the stiles and cut, using the same procedure as for the top and bottom rails.

Glue and assemble the door frame.

in.	cm
¼	.64
½	1.27
1	2.54

Mullions

Cut a rabbet on two sides of each mullion ½ inch (1.27 cm) deep by ¼ inch (.64 cm) wide (figures 5-112 and 5-113). Measure and mark the position of each lap joint on the horizontal mullions (see figures 5-105 and 5-114) To cut the lap joints in the horizontal mullions, cut a dado ½ inch (1.27 cm) wide and ¼ inch (.64 cm) deep into the body of the rabbet (figure 5-115). Clamp a jig with a round bottom into position to prevent the stock from chattering on the saw. Use a stop on the end of the stock to aid in positioning the cuts equidistant from each end. Cut all lap joints on horizontal mullions this way.

With the jig in place, line the stock up with the dado blade to cut the center lap. Reposition the stop at the end of the stock and cut all center laps on all horizontal mullions.

Measure and mark the position of each lap joint on the three vertical mullions (figure 5-114). First cut the wider, 1-inch (2.54-cm) dado into the face of the vertical mullions. Cut to a depth of ¼ inch (.64 cm), which should be exactly through the shoulders of the rabbet. You will have to make two passes to obtain the required width for the dado. Again, use a jig to prevent the stock from lifting. After cutting the first dado in each mullion, insert a stop into the shoulder of the first cut and clamp it at the appropriate distance from the blade to align the second cut. This will serve as a guide for the remaining cuts as the stock is moved along (figure 5-116).

5-112. Cut a rabbet in a mullion with a table saw. A support clamped to the table holds the mullion against the fence as it passes over the blade.

5-113. Finished mullion, showing rabbet cut in both edges.

in.	cm
¼	.64
½	1.27
¾	1.91
1	2.54

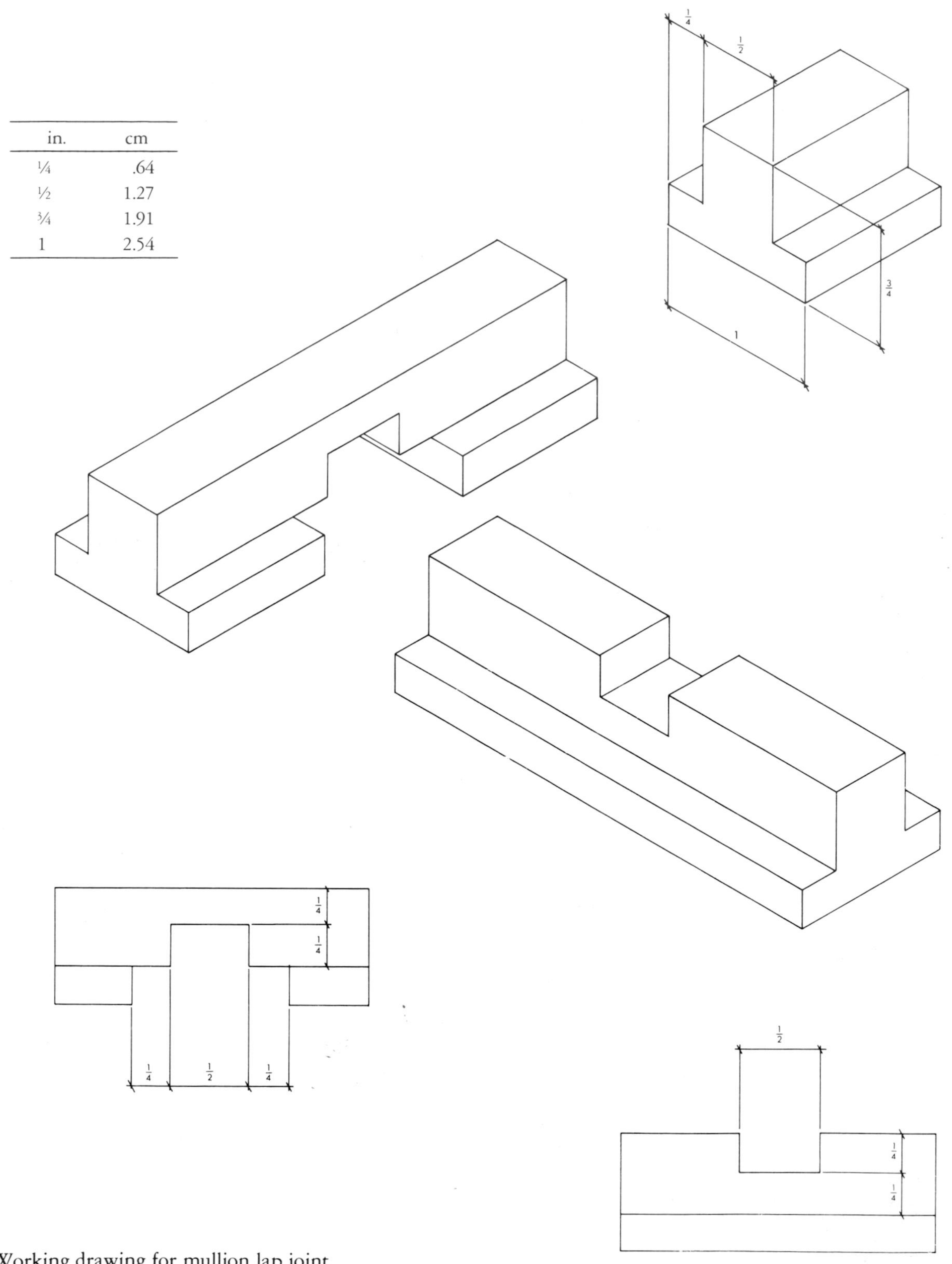

5–114. Working drawing for mullion lap joint.

5–115. Cutting lap joints in the horizontal mullions. A radiused jig and a stop are clamped to the miter guide.

5–116. Cutting the second lap joint on a vertical mullion, radiused jig and stop in place.

When all of the 1-inch-wide (2.54-cm) dados have been cut in the vertical mullions, a second lap cut must be made to accommodate the rabbet bodies of the horizontal mullions. Center these cuts on the 1-inch (2.54-cm) dados. Using the same stop, make your first lap cut. Move the stock into position for the second cut and clamp the stop into position, touching the inside shoulder of the first dado cut. Proceed to make all lap cuts on each vertical mullion.

Cut a rabbet into the face of each end of all mullions where they will join the frame. Make these rabbets ¼ inch (.64 cm) deep and ½ inch (1.27 cm) back from the end.

Assembly

Because so many joints must be assembled, you should glue the horizontal mullions to the vertical mullions three at a time. Tape unglued mullions in place to maintain proper alignment as you proceed. When all mullions have been glued, try the resulting mullion assembly in the door frame and make any adjustments to assure a perfect fit. With adjustments completed, glue the mullion subassembly into the door frame.

The front and back stops will prevent the front and back doors from closing too far into the case. A second pair of stops, one for each door, also serves as a hinge support. These stops will require a rabbet cut, as illustrated in figure 5-117.

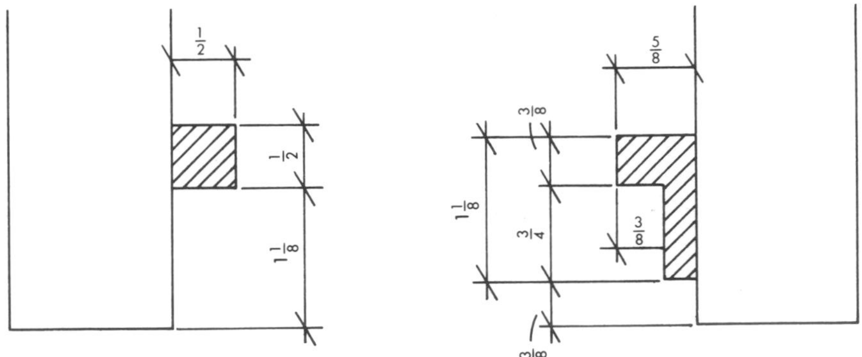

5–117. Working drawing for hinge supports and stops.

in.	cm
⅜	.95
½	1.27
⅝	1.58
¾	1.91
1⅛	2.86

5–118. Door stop clamped in position with the aid of pine alignment blocks. Alignment block should be dry-clamped to the clock side before door stop is glued and clamped in place.

Glue the front stop to the left front side of the clock case, with its front face set back 1⅛ inch (2.86 cm) from the front edge of the side of the frame (figure 5-118). Glue the front hinge support to the right front side, its front face set back ⅜ inch (.95 cm) from the front edge of the side of the frame.

Glue the back stop to the left backside of the frame, with its front face 1¼ inches (3.17 cm) from the back edge of the frame. Glue the back hinge support to the right back side of the frame, set back ½ inch (1.27 cm) from the back edge of the frame. Apply a finish to the piece.

Next, locate the position of the hinges for the doors. The back door uses two 1½-inch (3.81-cm) brass loose-pin hinges. Locate the top of the upper hinge 2 ⅞ inches (7.30 cm) down from the underside of the top shelf. Position the bottom of the lower hinge 2⅞ inches (7.30 cm) up from the top edge of the top back rail (figure 5-119).

The front door uses three 3-inch (7.62-cm) brass loose-pin hinges. Locate the top of the upper hinge 4 ½ inches (11.43 cm) from the underside of the top shelf. Position the bottom of the lower hinge 4½ inches (11.43 cm) up from the top edge of the bottom rail. Locate the top of the center hinge 31½ inches (80.01 cm) down from the underside of the top shelf.

Treat the hinge surfaces according to the instructions given in chapter 4. Then connect the hinges and doors to the clock.

5–119. Finished back door of the clock.

The final step is to install the locking mechanism opposite the center hinge, centered on the left door stile. The lock is a small mortise cupboard lock, the bolt of which enters a mortise in the left clock side. This lock mechanism can be purchased at most hardware stores and should be installed according to the manufacturers instructions.

To install the glass, remove the pins from the hinges and take off the door. Measure each opening in the back side of the door for glass size. Cut or have the glass cut to fit each opening, allowing 1/16-inch (.15-cm) of play. To hold the glass in position in the lower door, nail ½-inch-wide (.64-cm) by ⅜-inch-thick (.95-cm) molding strips in place with small brads. Do the same for the clock-face glass, but instead use ½-inch (1.27-cm) by ½-inch (1.27-cm) molding strips.

The clock itself can be chosen from any supplier but should meet several requirements. It should be a pendulum movement driven by weights. The maximum pendulum swing should be less than 16 inches (40.64 cm).

The face of the clock can be made of wood or metal. If you choose wood, it should be a fine-grained species, such as holly or orange, with numbers burned in or inlaid with pewter. If you decide on a metal face, it should be made of copper with pewter numbers. We also suggest that the numbers chosen for any face be from an old-style typeface.

Bibliography

BOOKS

Andrews, Edward and Faith. *Shaker Furniture*: The Craftsmanship of an American Communal Sect. 1937. Reprint. New York: Dover Publications, 1964.

Bossaglia, Rossana. *Revolution in Interior Design*. London: Orbis Connoisseurs, 1973.

Champigneulle, Bernard. *Art Noveau*. Woodbury, New York: Barrons Educational Series, 1976.

Charlish, Anne, ed. *The History of Furniture*. New York: William Morrow and Company, 1976.

Clark, Robert Judson, ed. *The Arts and Crafts Movement in America*. Princeton, New Jersey: Princeton University Press, 1972.

Cobden-Sanderson, T. J. *The Arts and Crafts Movement*. Hammersmith Publishing Society, 1905.

Feirer, John L., and Hutchings, Gilbert R. *Advanced Woodwork and Furniture-Making*. 4th ed. Peoria, Illinois: Chas. A. Bennett Company, 1972.

Franco, Borsi, and Egio, Goduli. *Paris 1900*. New York: Rizzoli, 1977.

Freeman, John Crosby. *The Forgotten Rebel*. Watkins Glen, New York: Century House Publishing, 1966.

Handlin, Oscar, ed. *Readings in American History*. New York: Alfred A. Knopf, 1957.

Hayes, Carlton J. H. *Contemporary Europe Since 1870*. New York: The Macmillan Company, 1958.

Joyce, Ernest. *Encyclopedia of Furniture Making*. New York: Sterling Publishing Company, 1979.

Kane, Patricia E. *Three Hundred Years of American Seating Furniture*. Toronto, Canada: Little, Brown and Company, New York Graphic Society Books, 1976.

Leonard, John W., ed. "Stickley, Gustav." In *Who's Who in America, 1906–07*. Chicago: A.N. Marquis Company, 1907.

Rheims, Maurice. *The Flowering of Art Nouveau*. New York: Harry N. Abrams, 1966.

Schmutzler, Robert. *Art Nouveau*. New York: Harry N. Abrams, 1978.

Smelser, Marshall. *American History at a Glance*. New York: Harper and Row Publishers, Barnes and Noble Books, 1971.

Stickley, Gustav. *Craftsman Homes*: Architecture and Furnishings of the American Arts and Crafts Movement. New York: Dover Publications, Reprint. 1979.

Stickley, Gustav. *More Craftsman Homes*. New York: Craftsman Publishing Company, 1913.

Talmon, J. R. *Romanticism and Revolt: Europe 1815–1848*. New York: W. W. Norton and Company, 1979.

Thompson, Paul. *The Work of William Morris*. New York: Quartet Books, 1977.

PERIODICALS

Gilbert, Charles B. "Manual Training in Public Schools." *Manual Training Magazine*, April, 1902, p. 129.

Koch, Robert. "Will Bradley." *Art in America*, Fall, 1962, pps. 78–83.

Priestman, Mabel Tuke. "History of the Arts and Crafts Movement in America." *The House Beautiful*, September, 1904, pps. 15–16.

Stickley, Gustav. *Chips from the Workshops of Gustav Stickley*. (2 issues.) New York, 1907.

Stickley, Gustav. *The Craftsman*. October, 1901–December, 1916.

Stickley, Gustav. "The Structural Style in Cabinet Making." *The House Beautiful*, December, 1903, pps. 20–25.

Index